ALSO BY DENISE A. SPELLBERG

Politics, Gender, and the Islamic Past:
The Legacy of 'A'isha bint Abi Bakr

THOMAS JEFFERSON'S
Qur'an

THOMAS JEFFERSON'S

Qur'an

Islam and the Founders

DENISE A. SPELLBERG

ALFRED A. KNOPF NEW YORK 2013

www.aaknopf.com

Grateful acknowledgment is made to The Johns Hopkins University Press for permission to reprint an excerpt from *The Cheese and the Worms: The Cosmos of a Sixteenth-Century Miller* by Carlo Ginzburg, translated by John and Anne C. Tedeschi. Copyright © 1980 by The Johns Hopkins University Press and Routledge Kegan Paul Ltd. Reprinted by permission of The Johns Hopkins University Press.

Library of Congress Cataloging-in-Publication Data
Spellberg, D. A. (Denise A.)
  Thomas Jefferson's Qur'an : Islam and the founders / Denise A. Spellberg. — First Edition.
     pages cm
  Includes bibliographical references and index.
ISBN 978-0-307-26822-8 (hardcover) 1. Jefferson, Thomas, 1743–1826—Political and social views. 2. Jefferson, Thomas, 1743–1826—Religion. 3. Muslims—Civil rights—United States—History—18th century. 4. Islam and politics—United States. 5. Freedom of religion—United States—History—18th century. 6. Constitutional history—United States. I. Title.
  E332.2.S65 2013
  973.4'6092—dc23   2013010153

Jacket images: (top) *Thomas Jefferson* by James Sharples (detail) © Bristol City Museum and Art Gallery, UK/The Bridgeman Art Library; (bottom) Jefferson's copy of the Qur'an, George Sales, trans. (detail), Rare Book and Special Collections Division, Library of Congress.
Jacket design by Joe Montgomery

In memory of those who arrived first:
Sebastiana Campochiaro Pavone and Antonio Pavone
&
Dvira Goldman Spellberg and Zvi Hersch Spellberg
And for all my students, with hope

Contents

Preface and Acknowledgments   ix

INTRODUCTION Imagining the Muslim as Citizen   3
at the Founding of the United States

1. The European Christian Origins of Negative but   13
   Sometimes Accurate American Ideas About Islam and
   Muslims, 1529–1797

2. Positive European Christian Precedents for the Toleration   41
   of Muslims, and Their Presence in Colonial America,
   1554–1706

3. What Jefferson Learned—and Didn't—from His Qur'an: 81
   His Negative Views of Islam, and Their Political Uses,
   Contrasted with His Support for Muslim Civil Rights,
   1765–86

4. Jefferson Versus John Adams: The Problem of North   124
   African Piracy and Their Negotiations with a Muslim
   Ambassador in London, 1784–88

5. Could a Muslim Be President? Muslim Rights and the   158
   Ratification of the Constitution, 1788

6. Jefferson Wages War Against an Islamic Power;   197
   Entertains the First Muslim Ambassador; Decides
   Where to Place the Qur'an in His Library; and Affirms
   His Support for Muslim Rights, 1790–1823

7. Beyond Toleration: John Leland, Baptist Advocate for   240
   the Rights of Muslims, 1776–1841

   AFTERWORD Why Can't a Muslim Be President?   270
   Eighteenth-Century Ideals of the Muslim Citizen and
   Their Significance in the Twenty-First Century

   Notes   303
   Index   377

Preface and Acknowledgments

When a stranger resides with you in your land, you shall not wrong him. The stranger who resides with you shall be to you as one of your citizens; you shall love him as yourself, for you were strangers in the land of Egypt.

—Leviticus 19:33–34 (New JPS Translation)

ONE RAINY APRIL MORNING in 2011, I requested Thomas Jefferson's Qur'an from the Rare Book Room in the Library of Congress. Outside, tulips blazed in bright patches of red around the Capitol building. The flowers reminded me of their origins in the Ottoman Empire. The sultan had first sent them as diplomatic gifts to European rulers in the sixteenth century, and by the mid-seventeenth, the trade in the bulbs of these plants had reached a frenzied pitch in the Netherlands.[1] Jefferson would add them to his garden at Monticello in 1806.[2] And so it was that, through contact with Muslims long ago, this stunning flower had eventually reached North America, where it now reigns as a sign of spring.

Summoned with nothing more than the requisite library card and the relevant call number, the two volumes of Jefferson's Qur'an arrived unceremoniously at my desk in less than ten minutes. I sat amazed. A national treasure was mine to peruse. As a historian and a citizen, I'd thought for years about what Jefferson's Qur'an might have meant. Now, suddenly, I could touch the brown leather bindings, and hear the slight crackle of the yellowing pages as I turned them. The volumes were far too delicate, I thought, to be touched by *anyone*. I could not help but recall that eight months earlier in Florida an addled pastor of a nearly nonexistent congregation had held press conferences promising to burn multiple Qur'ans in protest against a proposed mosque in New York City. (He had made his threat good days before in March 2011, with disastrous consequences in Afghanistan.)[3] The Florida minister believed he was exercising his First Amendment right to express how execrable he thought Islam was. Inadvertently, he revealed how little he knew about the historical importance of the Qur'an to Protestants in both Europe and America. For them, it had been more common since the seventeenth century to translate the sacred text for Christian readers than to consign it to the flames.

For me, the pages of Jefferson's Qur'an represented sacred historical evidence, not of the truth of Islam, but of the capacity and eagerness of some early Americans to learn about that faith. As a professor of Islamic history, I wanted to know what early Americans knew about Islam and how they'd learned about the religion and its history. To my surprise, I found that many Americans in the founding era, despite the tenacious legacy of misinformation from Europe, refused to yield to contemporary fears promoting the persecution of Muslims. They preferred to be heirs to a less prominent but important strain of European tolerance toward Muslims, one whose influence had thus far been overlooked in early American history.

Jefferson's two-volume English translation of the Qur'an had grabbed the national spotlight in January 2007, when Keith Ellison, the country's first Muslim congressman, chose to swear his private oath of office on the Founder's sacred text. At the time, I thought that the outrage expressed by some toward Congressman Ellison's election and private swearing-in on the Qur'an might have been averted if only more Americans had known their own founding history better, a past that had prepared an eventual place for Congressman Ellison, not in spite of his religion, but because of it.

The idea of the Muslim as citizen and federal officeholder is not new to the United States. It was first considered in the eighteenth century. Yet today some claim that even the concept of a Muslim citizen in elected office is threatening to the nation's identity. I argue the opposite in this book: The concept of the American Muslim as citizen is quintessentially evocative of our national ideals. Indeed, the inclusion of Muslims as future citizens in early national political debates demonstrates a decided resistance to the idea of what some would still imagine America to be: a Christian nation.

This book about the American past began accidentally for me as a specialist in Islamic history. Initially, I'd wondered why a French play, ostensibly about the Prophet Muhammad, had been performed in Baltimore during the Revolutionary War. To make sense of this more than a decade ago, I had the privilege of attending the ideal summer school: Professor Bernard Bailyn's International Seminar on the History of the Atlantic World at Harvard University. I took to paddling in this new Atlantic pond and found that the experience had prompted a sea change in my academic research, which I incorrectly assumed would be temporary.

By 2005, at the Atlantic Seminar's tenth-anniversary conference, I had found a new document about Muslims in early American political debates. Again, I was fortunate to be invited to present this research to fellow students of Atlantic history. Professor Bailyn's thoughtful, enthusiastic response to my ideas about Thomas Jefferson and his views of Muslim rights was rooted in his deeper knowledge of these constitutional sources. His interest in these ideas convinced me that what people thought about Muslims as citizens in 1788 should be included in the study of the Constitution. Did more data about Muslims as potential citizens in the founding era exist? Over the next seven years, I learned the breadth of that affirmative answer.

By the time Congressman Ellison was elected and swore his private oath of office on Jefferson's Qur'an in 2007, I thought as a historian that I might have something to contribute, beyond the fact of Jefferson's mere ownership of the Islamic sacred text. I wanted to know why Jefferson and others had included Muslims in the nation's nascent ideals. At this juncture, Professor Bailyn introduced me to Jane Garrett, his kindly, patient editor at Knopf. *Thomas Jefferson's Qur'an* was born as a book project—with the blessing of an editor who was actually keen on the project. My deep gratitude to Jane endures, despite the sad fact that I failed to finish the final draft before her retirement. My profound thanks go to George Andreou for his insightful editing of the final stage of this manuscript and to Juhea Kim, his assistant.

Many eyes, hands, and brains more agile than my own supported this book's evolution and improvement. I remain humbled that Professor Bailyn, ever busy, took the time over the last few years to read two long, early, and rambling draft chapters about Jefferson and, finally, what I believed to be the last draft of the manuscript. His comments I treasure. Many saved me from obvious idiocies. If any remain, they are my own fault, not his or those of the many colleagues and friends who also sought to help me.

Over the years, I have been blessed by the insight of many scholars and friends. First among these is Robert M. Haddad, the professor who first inspired my interest in Islamic history as an undergraduate. Since those days long ago, his wisdom and kindness have endured, for which I remain eternally grateful. Anver Emon, always enthusiastic and energetic, believed in this project from the first. He commented on almost every word of this text, pointing out errors in logic, gaps in argument, and problems with my representation of the Islamic past. Once my gifted graduate student, he took time from his duties as an eminent professor of Islamic law to support his former instructor.

At the University of Texas at Austin, my colleague Neil Kamil, expert in the Atlantic history of religion and violence, introduced me to a pivotal source, a catalog that revealed how Jefferson had ordered the books in his vast library. More than that, Neil's own important work, *Fortress of the Soul: Violence, Metaphysics, and Material Life in the Huguenots' New World, 1517–1751,* underscored the significance of a sixteenth-century Italian miller named Menocchio. Beyond his own key reading of this figure, Neil's deft analysis of an unusually tolerant group of Dutch protestors in seventeenth-century Long Island also opened new possibilities for thinking about early modern religious pluralism. In addition to suggesting these research directions, Neil kindly also read all the chapters of the book.

Linda Ferreira-Buckley, a specialist in rhetoric and patience, carefully untangled arguments throughout, particularly in the introduction and conclusion. Janet Davis, expert in American studies and transnational histories, read most of the book's chapters, despite her exhausting schedule. My colleague Syed Akbar Hyder, ever generous, also contributed a valued critique of the conclusion. I am also grateful to the historian A. Azfar Moin for his acuity and humor in smoothing out many rough spots.

The expertise of other colleagues also deserves my thanks. Despite being on leave, Laurie Green critiqued a chapter and provided valuable comments. Mervat Hatem, who supported the project from its inception, offered key suggestions and timely encouragement that improved the structure of the book. Carel Bertram doggedly rescued the introduction and the first two chapters from their twisted incarnations as first drafts, devoting much time to untangling organizational snafus. Kim Alidio and Elizabeth Englehardt also provided helpful suggestions at early stages of the book's evolution. Expert advice about the Reformation Susan Boettcher generously provided, although especially in this era all errors remain mine alone.

I am grateful to Margaret Larkin, an extraordinary Arabist, for a memorable evening during which she shared her insights into the Arabic grammatical nuances in an American Muslim slave narrative. Cutting through eighteenth-century North African Arabic calligraphy, Linda Boxberger and Abraham Marcus helped me to finally see and check the original Arabic language in key American treaties. Over the years, helpful students Tommy Buckley, Reem Elghonimi, Zaid Hassan, Elizabeth Nutting, and Sharon Silzell undertook varied research tasks with care.

The College of Liberal Arts at the University of Texas at Austin generously provided me with both supported leave and leave without pay to write this book. Evan Carton, director of the UT Humanities Institute in 2007, and other members of the institute offered valuable encouragement at an early stage. In 2009, the Carnegie Foundation intervened with the generous award of their Carnegie Scholarship, without which I could not possibly have finished this project. The timely intercession of Gail Davis, then History Department administrator extraordinaire, prompted me to submit the initial Carnegie Scholarship application at my university when I might otherwise have missed the deadline.

My thanks go to Columbia University Press for allowing me to draw upon an early part of chapter 1 that first appeared in my wonderful dissertation advisor Richard W. Bulliet's *festschrift* as "Islam on the Eighteenth-Century Stage: Voltaire's *Mahomet* Crosses the Atlantic," in *Views from the Edge: Essays in Honor of Richard W. Bulliet,* ed. Neguin Yavari, Lawrence G. Potter, and Jean-Marc Ran Oppenheim (New York: Columbia University Press for the Middle East Institute, 2004), 245–60. Thanks also go to the editor Julia Simon for allowing me to use portions of an early version of chapter 5, previously published as "Could a Muslim Be President? An Eighteenth-Century Constitutional Debate," *Eighteenth-Century Studies* 39 (2006): 485–506. (The final paragraph of that article I now utterly disavow.) My thanks to the editor Gregory Starrett for allowing me to use parts of "Islam in America: Adventures in Neo-Orientalism," *Review of Middle Eastern Studies* 43 (2009): 25–35.

———

This has been a long, unforgiving first decade of the twenty-first century for many close friends and my immediate family. At the University of Texas, I lost two powerful female mentors. The first, Elizabeth W. Fernea, a pioneer in the study of Middle Eastern Muslim women, I remember as a rare colleague. Unfailingly thoughtful, she read a very early draft of what became one of this book's chapters, insisting that she had faith in the project when few others did. In the History Department, Janet Meisel, a spectacular teacher and loyal friend, listened to my ideas with customary generosity. Despite years of ill health, her integrity and sense of fairness never ebbed. Both women were giants in their own way, and both I deeply miss. Their exemplary courage in the face of adversity still inspires.

I could not have completed this project, or kept my job, without the extraordinary intervention of Paula Malkey, who helped care for both of my ailing and elderly parents over a period of eight difficult years. It is no exaggeration to add that Paula, a great soul and an utterly generous Texan, saved my family and my sanity. Without her professional expertise in elder matters, energy, and sagacity, dosed always with her unfailing sense of humor, I would have been unable to teach or write during multiple periods of parental illness. After she had ministered to so many with such kindness, Paula's sudden death in 2012 shocked me. I lost in her friendship a protean strength, a person rare and irreplaceable. She could laugh at anything except bigotry. I feel her absence profoundly because she is no longer here to be thanked for all her years of strength and support.

Near the beginning of this past decade, after years of suffering, my mother died. Two years before the end of this project, my father abruptly joined her. I mourn their loss, but know that this is a book they would have understood. My father, Israel Abraham, known to his friends in the South End of Boston as Larry, and my mother, Angelina Rita, who preferred Ann, were two people who wanted to fit into their country desperately at a time when they believed that meant choosing less obvious religiously and ethnically identified monikers. Both believed in God and found one another in spite of theological differences. In the face of prejudice, they proved always true to themselves and each other.

When I asked my mother what she thought was an individual's most important quality, she replied instantly, "Fairness." My father's favorite song, "You've Got to Be Taught," from the 1949 musical *South Pacific,* lyrically proclaimed that "hate and fear" were lessons learned early about "people whose skin was a different shade and people whose eyes are oddly made." But my father refused to "hate all the people your relatives hate." Neither parent ever lectured, but they were both powerful teachers.

Their integrity, as much as their refusal to make religion a barrier to respect or love, shaped my world, as did their shared insistence that all people deserve to be treated equally—without exception. When I began to notice that the idea of the Muslim as citizen at the founding of the United States was as contentious a subject as the citizenship of Jews and Catholics, I felt as if my study of the Islamic world had led me to appreciate an aspect of the American past that specialists had overlooked. Thus all history is autobiography, however unintended.

As Americans, the vast majority of us might recall that our ancestors began here as outsiders, immigrants and strangers, not citizens; an even more compelling reason to remember the Golden Rule. Jefferson would do so at the end of his life, following a pronounced pattern in those who had fought before him against the persecution of Muslims.

THOMAS JEFFERSON'S
Qur'an

Imagining the Muslim as Citizen at the Founding of the United States

[He] sais "neither Pagan nor Mahamedan [Muslim] nor Jew ought to be excluded from the civil rights of the Commonwealth because of his religion."

—Thomas Jefferson, quoting John Locke, 1776

AT A TIME when most Americans were uninformed, misinformed, or simply afraid of Islam, Thomas Jefferson imagined Muslims as future citizens of his new nation.[1] His engagement with the faith began with the purchase of a Qur'an eleven years before he wrote the Declaration of Independence. Jefferson's Qur'an survives still in the Library of Congress, serving as a symbol of his and early America's complex relationship with Islam and its adherents. That relationship remains of signal importance to this day.

That he owned a Qur'an reveals Jefferson's interest in the Islamic religion, but it does not explain his support for the rights of Muslims. Jefferson first read about Muslim "civil rights" in the work of one of his intellectual heroes: the seventeenth-century English philosopher John Locke.[2] Locke had advocated the toleration of Muslims—and Jews—following in the footsteps of a few others in Europe who had considered the matter for more than a century before him. Jefferson's ideas about Muslim rights must be understood within this older context, a complex set of transatlantic ideas that would continue to evolve most markedly from the sixteenth through the nineteenth centuries.

Amid the interdenominational Christian violence in Europe, some

Christians, beginning in the sixteenth century, chose Muslims as the test case for the demarcation of the theoretical boundaries of their toleration for *all* believers. Because of these European precedents, Muslims also became a part of American debates about religion and the limits of citizenship. As they set about creating a new government in the United States, the American Founders, Protestants all, frequently referred to the adherents of Islam as they contemplated the proper scope of religious freedom and individual rights among the nation's present and potential inhabitants. The founding generation debated whether the United States should be exclusively Protestant or a religiously plural polity. And if the latter, whether political equality—the full rights of citizenship, including access to the highest office—should extend to non-Protestants. The mention, then, of Muslims as potential citizens of the United States forced the Protestant majority to imagine the parameters of their new society beyond toleration. It obliged them to interrogate the nature of religious freedom: the issue of a "religious test" in the Constitution, like the ones that would exist at the state level into the nineteenth century; the question of "an establishment of religion," potentially of Protestant Christianity; and the meaning and extent of a separation of religion from government.

Resistance to the idea of Muslim citizenship was predictable in the eighteenth century. Americans had inherited from Europe almost a millennium of negative distortions of the faith's theological and political character. Given the dominance and popularity of these anti-Islamic representations, it was startling that a few notable Americans not only refused to exclude Muslims, but even imagined a day when they would be citizens of the United States, with full and equal rights. This surprising, uniquely American egalitarian defense of Muslim rights was the logical extension of European precedents already mentioned. Still, on both sides of the Atlantic, such ideas were marginal at best. How, then, did the idea of the Muslim as a citizen with rights survive despite powerful opposition from the outset? And what is the fate of that ideal in the twenty-first century?

This book provides a new history of the founding era, one that explains how and why Thomas Jefferson and a handful of others adopted and then moved beyond European ideas about the toleration of Muslims. It should be said at the outset that these exceptional men were not motivated by any inherent appreciation for Islam as a religion. Muslims, for most American Protestants, remained beyond the outer limit of those possessing acceptable beliefs, but they nevertheless became emblems of two competing conceptions of the nation's identity: one essentially preserving the Protestant status quo, and the other fully realizing the pluralism implied in the Revolutionary rhetoric of inalienable *and* universal rights. Thus while some fought to exclude a group whose inclusion they feared would ultimately portend the undoing of the nation's Protestant character, a pivotal minority, also Protestant, perceiving the ultimate benefit and justice of a religiously plural America, set about defending the rights of future Muslim citizens. *

They did so, however, not for the sake of actual Muslims, because none were known at the time to live in America. Instead, Jefferson and others defended Muslim rights for the sake of "imagined Muslims," the promotion of whose theoretical citizenship would prove the true universality of American rights. Indeed, this defense of imagined Muslims would also create political room to consider the rights of other despised minorities whose numbers in America, though small, were quite real, namely Jews and Catholics. Although it was Muslims who embodied the ideal of inclusion, Jews and Catholics were often linked to them in early American debates, as Jefferson and others fought for the rights of all non-Protestants.[3]

In 1783, the year of the nation's official independence from Great Britain, George Washington wrote to recent Irish Catholic immigrants in New York City.[4] The American Catholic minority of roughly twenty-five thousand then had few legal protections in any state and, because of their faith, no right to hold political office in New York.[5] Washington insisted that "the bosom of America" was "open to receive . . . the oppressed and the persecuted of all Nations and Religions; whom we shall welcome to a participation of all our rights and privileges."[6] He would also write similar missives to Jewish communities, whose total population numbered only about two thousand at this time.[7]

One year later, in 1784, Washington theoretically enfolded Muslims into his private world at Mount Vernon. In a letter to a friend seeking a carpenter and bricklayer to help at his Virginia home, he explained that the workers' beliefs—or lack thereof—mattered not at all: "If they are good workmen, they may be of Asia, Africa, or Europe. They may be Mahometans [Muslims], Jews or Christian of an[y] Sect, or they may be Atheists."[8] Clearly, Muslims were part of Washington's understanding of religious pluralism—at least in theory. But he would not have actually expected any Muslim applicants.

* their issue is Authority, as revealed in religion, not an understanding of spiritual awareness.

Although we have since learned that there were in fact Muslims resident in eighteenth-century America, this book demonstrates that the Founders and their generational peers never knew it. Thus their Muslim constituency remained an imagined, future one. But the fact that both Washington and Jefferson attached to it such symbolic significance is not accidental. Both men were heir to the same pair of opposing European traditions.

The first, which predominated, depicted Islam as the antithesis of the "true faith" of Protestant Christianity, as well as the source of tyrannical governments abroad. To tolerate Muslims—to accept them as part of a majority Protestant Christian society—was to welcome people who professed a faith most eighteenth-century Europeans and Americans believed false, foreign, and threatening.[9] Catholics would be similarly characterized in American Protestant founding discourse.[10] Indeed, their faith, like Islam, would be deemed a source of tyranny and thus antithetical to American ideas of liberty.

In order to counter such fears, Jefferson and other supporters of non-Protestant citizenship drew upon a second, less popular but crucial stream of European thought, one that posited the toleration of Muslims as well as Jews and Catholics. Those few Europeans, both Catholic and Protestant, who first espoused such ideas in the sixteenth century often died for them.[11] In the seventeenth century, those who advocated universal religious toleration frequently suffered death or imprisonment, banishment or exile, the elites and common folk alike. The ranks of these so-called heretics in Europe included Catholic and Protestant peasants, Protestant scholars of religion and political theory, and fervid Protestant dissenters, such as the first English Baptists—but no people of political power or prominence. Despite not being organized, this minority consistently opposed their coreligionists by defending theoretical Muslims from persecution in Christian-majority states.

As a member of the eighteenth-century Anglican establishment and a prominent political leader in Virginia, Jefferson represented a different sort of proponent for ideas that had long been the hallmark of dissident victims of persecution and exile. Because of his elite status, his own endorsement of Muslim citizenship demanded serious consideration in Virginia—and the new nation. Together with a handful of like-minded American Protestants, he advanced a new, previously unthinkable national blueprint. Thus did ideas long on the fringe of

European thought flow into the mainstream of American political discourse at its inception.

Not that these ideas found universal welcome. Even a man of Jefferson's national reputation would be attacked by his political opponents for his insistence that the rights of all believers should be protected from government interference and persecution. But he drew support from a broad range of constituencies, including Anglicans (or Episcopalians), as well as dissenting Presbyterians and Baptists, who suffered persecution perpetrated by fellow Protestants. No denomination had a unanimously positive view of non-Protestants as full American citizens, yet support for Muslim rights was expressed by some members of each.

What the supporters of Muslim rights were proposing was extraordinary even at a purely theoretical level in the eighteenth century. American citizenship—which had embraced only free, white, male Protestants—was in effect to be abstracted from religion. Race and gender would continue as barriers, but not so faith. Legislation in Virginia would be just the beginning, the First Amendment far from the end of the story; in fact, Jefferson, Washington, and James Madison would work toward this ideal of separation throughout their entire political lives, ultimately leaving it to others to carry on and finish the job. This book documents, for the first time, how Jefferson and others, despite their negative, often incorrect understandings of Islam, pursued that ideal by advocating the rights of Muslims and all non-Protestants.

A decade before George Washington signaled openness to Muslim laborers in 1784 he had listed two slave women from West Africa among his taxable property. "Fatimer" and "Little Fatimer" were a mother and daughter—both indubitably named after the Prophet Muhammad's daughter Fatima (d. 632).[12] Washington advocated Muslim rights, never realizing that as a slaveholder he was denying Muslims in his own midst any rights at all, including the right to practice their faith. This tragic irony may well have also recurred on the plantations of Jefferson and Madison, although proof of their slaves' religion remains less than definitive. Nevertheless, having been seized and transported from West Africa, the first American Muslims may have numbered in the tens of thousands, a population certainly greater than the resident Jews and possibly even the Catholics.[13] Although some have speculated that a few former Muslim slaves may have served in the Continental Army, there is little direct evidence any practiced Islam and none that these individ-

uals were known to the Founders.[14] In any case, they had no influence
on later political debates about Muslim citizenship.

The insuperable facts of race and slavery rendered invisible the very
believers whose freedoms men like Jefferson, Washington, and Madison defended, and whose ancestors had resided in America since the
seventeenth century, as long as Protestants had.[15] Indeed, when the
Founders imagined future Muslim citizens, they presumably imagined
them as white, because by the 1790s "full American citizenship could
be claimed by any free, white immigrant, regardless of ethnicity or
religious beliefs."[16]

The two actual Muslims Jefferson would wittingly meet during his
lifetime were not black West African slaves but North African ambassadors of Turkish descent. They may have appeared to him to have more
melanin than he did, but he never commented on their complexions
or race. (Other observers either failed to mention it or simply affirmed
that the ambassador in question was not black.)[17] But then Jefferson was
interested in neither diplomat for reasons of religion or race; he engaged
them because of their political power. (They were, of course, also free.)

But even earlier in his political life—as an ambassador, secretary
of state, and vice president—Jefferson had never perceived a predominantly religious dimension to the conflict with North African Muslim
powers, whose pirates threatened American shipping in the Mediterranean and eastern Atlantic.[18] As this book demonstrates, Jefferson
as president would insist to the rulers of Tripoli and Tunis that his
nation harbored no anti-Islamic bias, even going so far as to express the
extraordinary claim of believing in the same God as those men.

The equality of believers that Jefferson sought at home was the same
one he professed abroad, in both contexts attempting to divorce religion
from politics, or so it seemed. In fact, Jefferson's limited but unique
appreciation for Islam appears as a minor but active element in his presidential foreign policy with North Africa—and his most personal Deist
and Unitarian beliefs. The two were quite possibly entwined, with
their source Jefferson's unsophisticated yet effective understanding of
the Qur'an he owned.

Still, as a man of his time, Jefferson was not immune to negative
feelings about Islam. He would even use some of the most popular anti-
Islamic images inherited from Europe to drive his early political arguments about the separation of religion from government in Virginia.
Yet ultimately Jefferson and others not as well known were still able to

divorce the idea of Muslim citizenship from their dislike of Islam, as they forged an "imagined political community," inclusive beyond all precedent.[19]

The clash between principle and prejudice that Jefferson himself overcame in the eighteenth and nineteenth centuries remains a test for the nation in the twenty-first. Since the late nineteenth century, the United States has in fact become home to a diverse and dynamic American Muslim citizenry, but this population has never been fully welcomed. Whereas in Jefferson's time organized prejudice against Muslims was exercised against an exclusively foreign and imaginary nonresident population, today political attacks target real, resident American Muslim citizens. Particularly in the wake of 9/11 and the so-called War on Terror, a public discourse of anti-Muslim bigotry has arisen to justify depriving American Muslim citizens of the full and equal exercise of their civil rights.

For example, recent anti-Islamic slurs used to deny the legitimacy of a presidential candidacy contained eerie echoes of founding precedents. The legal possibility of a Muslim president was first discussed with vitriol during debates involving America's Founders. Thomas Jefferson would be the first in the history of American politics to suffer the false charge of being a Muslim, an accusation considered the ultimate Protestant slur in the eighteenth century. That a presidential candidate in the twenty-first century should have been subject to much the same false attack, still presumed as politically damning to any real American Muslim candidate's potential for elected office, demonstrates the importance of examining how the multiple images of Islam and Muslims first entered American consciousness and how the rights of Muslims first came to be accepted as national ideals. Ultimately, the status of Muslim citizenship in America today cannot be properly appreciated without establishing the historical context of its eighteenth-century origins.

Muslim American rights became a theoretical reality early on, but as a practical one they have been much slower to evolve. In fact, they are being tested daily. Recently, John Esposito, a distinguished historian of Islam in contemporary America, observed, "Muslims are led to wonder: What are the limits of this Western pluralism?"[20] *Thomas Jefferson's Qur'an* documents the origins of such pluralism in the United States in order to illuminate where, when, and how Muslims were first included in American ideals.[21]

Until now, most historians have proposed that Muslims represented nothing more than the incarnated antithesis of American values.[22] These same voices also insist that Protestant Americans always and uniformly defined both the religion of Islam and its practitioners as inherently un-American. Indeed, most historians posit that the emergence of the United States as an ideological and political phenomenon occurred in opposition to eighteenth-century concepts about Islam as a false religion and source of despotic government.[23] There is certainly evidence for these assumptions in early American religious polemic, domestic politics, foreign policy, and literary sources.[24] There are, however, also considerable observations about Islam and Muslims that cast both in a more affirmative light, including key references to Muslims as future American citizens in important founding debates about rights. These sources show that American Protestants did not monolithically view Islam as "a thoroughly foreign religion."[25]

This book documents the counterassertion that Muslims, far from being definitively un-American, were deeply embedded in the concept of citizenship in the United States since the country's inception, even if these inclusive ideas were not then accepted by the majority of Americans.[26] While focusing on Jefferson's views of Islam, Muslims, and the Islamic world, it also analyzes the perspectives of John Adams and James Madison. Nor is it limited to these key Founders. The cast of those who took part in the contest concerning the rights of Muslims, imagined and real, is not confined to famous political elites but includes Presbyterian and Baptist protestors against Virginia's religious establishment; the Anglican lawyers James Iredell and Samuel Johnston in North Carolina, who argued for the rights of Muslims in their state's constitutional ratifying convention; and John Leland, an evangelical Baptist preacher and ally of Jefferson and Madison in Virginia, who agitated in Connecticut and Massachusetts in support of Muslim equality, the Constitution, the First Amendment, and the end of established religion at the state level.

The lives of two American Muslim slaves of West African origin, Ibrahima Abd al-Rahman and Omar ibn Said, also intersect this narrative. Both were literate in Arabic, the latter writing his autobiography in that language. They remind us of the presence of tens of thousands of Muslim slaves who had no rights, no voice, and no hope of American citizenship in the midst of these early discussions about religious and political equality for future, free practitioners of Islam.

Imagined Muslims, along with real Jews and Catholics, were the consummate outsiders in much of America's political discourse at the founding.[27] Jews and Catholics would struggle into the twentieth century to gain in practice the equal rights assured them in theory, although even this process would not entirely eradicate prejudice against either group.[28] Nevertheless, from among the original triad of religious outsiders in the United States, only Muslims remain the objects of a substantial civic discourse of derision and marginalization, still being perceived in many quarters as not fully American.[29] This book writes Muslims back into our founding narrative in the hope of clarifying the importance of critical historical precedents at a time when the idea of the Muslim as citizen is, once more, hotly contested.[30]

The European Christian Origins of Negative but Sometimes Accurate American Ideas About Islam and Muslims, 1529–1797

Now, in comparing the Turk with the pope, if a question be asked, whether of them is the truer or greater Antichrist, it were easy to see and judge, that the Turk is the more open and manifest enemy against Christ and his church.

—John Foxe, English compiler of
Protestant martyr accounts, 1570

The sword and the Alcoran in my bloody hands,
Will impose silence on the rest of humanity.
—from Voltaire's play
Fanaticism, or Mahomet the Prophet, 1742

I would not bring the sacred volume of our faith in any comparative view with the Alcoran of Mahomet; but I cannot help noticing it as extraordinary, that the Mahometan should abominate the Christian on account of his faith, and the Christian detest the Mussulman for his creed; when the Koran of the former acknowledges the divinity of the Christian Messias [*sic*], and the Bible of the latter commands us to love our enemies. If either would follow the obvious dictates of his own scripture, he would cease to hate, abominate, and destroy the other.

—Royall Tyler, American novelist and member
of the Vermont Supreme Court,
from his novel *The Algerine Captive,* 1797

BY THE TIME John Leland reached the age of twelve in 1766, this future ally of Thomas Jefferson reckoned that he'd heard about "Mahomedan imposture" every Sunday from his Congregational minister in Massachusetts.[1] Indeed, by 1776 most American Protestants believed Islam to be the invention of Muhammad, a false prophet and an impostor. No matter their denomination, they had generally been primed not only from the pulpit but by books and theater to think the worst about Islam and Muslims. Such a view, however, was not an American innovation, but a legacy of European precedents.[2] In the absence of much contrary evidence, American Protestants had little reason to think differently about Islam than their coreligionists across the Atlantic.[3] This bias would find its way into the evolution of political polemic in both Britain and the United States. In the developing discourse about individual freedom and the role of government, Muslim rule would come to be identified with tyranny, the antithesis of Anglo-American political ideals.[4]

American Protestant prejudice toward Islam, though directly inherited from European precedents, already existed among Catholics on the Continent. These negative views first emerged among Eastern Christians when Islam spread from Arabia throughout the Middle East in the seventh century. Eastern Christians suddenly found themselves subordinate to a new religious minority. Their immediate response to this subjugation was to repudiate Islam as both a religion and a political system.[5] In later polemic, no matter what their denomination, Christians continued to assert the superiority of their own faith as the true faith over all others. Unlike Muslims, who accepted that Jews and Christians as People of the Book had received revelation from the same God, Christian theologians rejected any overlap with Islamic tradition. Christians also rejected the Islamic doctrine that the Qur'an was God's final, perfect revelation to all humankind, which superseded human distortions that arose in Judaism and Christianity. Instead, Christian theologians denounced Muslim belief as a corruption of their own faith invented by Muhammad or borrowed from, according to various accounts, a heretical monk, the Jews, or the devil.[6]

This chapter examines how a millennium after the advent of Islam, Christian prejudice against Muslims crossed the Atlantic with profound impact on American religious and political beliefs at their foundation.

It also traces how Christians of all denominations repeatedly employed anti-Islamic rhetoric against one another for doctrinal, political, and personal reasons. Protestant debates about Islam shaped American views of government in ways seldom acknowledged today.

ISLAM AND THE ANTICHRIST: PROTESTANT THEOLOGY AND THE ROOTS OF ANTI-ISLAMIC THOUGHT IN EUROPE

American Protestants inherited their hostility to Islam directly from sixteenth-century Protestant reformers in Europe, who defined the Antichrist in terms of Islam. They supported this based on scriptures, including the book of Daniel and the book of Revelation, both of which had, of course, been revealed to address entirely different religious and political concerns long before the rise of Islam. With creative interpretation, however, the Antichrist could be defined variously as the Prophet, or the sultan of the Ottoman Empire, then the most powerful Muslim military force in Asia and Europe.[7] In other references, the Ottoman army as a whole was invoked as the manifestation of the Antichrist.

The German Protestant reformer Martin Luther (1483–1546) envisioned the Antichrist incarnated as a dual enemy, both Catholic and Islamic, writing, "The person of the Antichrist is at the same time the pope and the Turk." Later he would refine his earlier statement, claiming that the spirit of the Antichrist is the pope, but his "flesh" is that of "the Turk."[8] By "Turk," Luther referred to the Ottoman sultan, whom he incorrectly deemed the supreme spiritual and political leader of Islam, analogous to the pope for Catholicism. German Protestant woodcuts from the sixteenth century depict Luther's vision of the Antichrist as a beast with two heads—one a mitered pope and the other a turbaned Ottoman sultan.[9] Luther, however, was not the first Christian to envision the Antichrist in terms of Islam. As early as the twelfth century, Catholic theologians had asserted that Muhammad was the precursor of the Antichrist.[10] Although Luther denounced Catholicism as inimical to his true version of Christianity, he nevertheless found aspects of Rome's anti-Islamic polemic useful enough to appropriate for his own needs.

By Luther's time, Ottoman expansion threatened Western Europe, having already begun to engulf Christians in Eastern Europe in the fourteenth century. In 1453, Constantinople, the last bastion of the

Christian Byzantine Empire, fell to the Ottoman Turks. In the six-teenth century, the Ottomans continued to advance on Europe, defeat-ing the Hungarian army in 1526 and besieging Vienna for the first time in 1529. Although that first siege failed, European fears of Muslim mil-itary might would persist throughout the seventeenth century, until 1683, when the Ottomans would attempt to seize the Austrian capital a second and final time. Though this attack would also fail, and by 1700 the Ottoman menace would recede, the memory of the Turkish mili-tary conquests remained a potent symbol in Christian thought into the eighteenth century.[11]

Luther believed that God allowed the Ottomans to triumph over the Catholics as punishment for their sinful beliefs, also asserting that "true" Christian prayers might defeat the Turks. For his part, the Otto-man sultan reputedly saw Luther and other Protestants as potential allies against the Catholic Hapsburg enemies of the Turks, a charge Luther quickly denied even though he and other Protestants knew that con-quering Ottomans in Eastern Europe treated their denomination better than persecuting Catholics did.[12] Still, Luther's Catholic opponents would question his opposition to the Ottomans. He did in the end support the war against the Muslims, urging Christians not to worry about killing Turks; according to Luther's interpretation of the book of Daniel, Muslim souls were already forfeit, condemned to hell for all eternity.[13] Luther also considered their most sacred text, the Qur'an, "a foul book of blasphemy."[14] He supported the 1542 publication in Basel, Switzerland, of a Latin translation of the Qur'an so that Chris-tians would learn firsthand of its "lies and fables."[15] To further edu-cate his followers, Luther also translated one thirteenth-century Latin anti–Islamic polemic and wrote two anti–Ottoman tracts.[16] His literary production was part of a larger trend in writing about Islam and the Ottomans, and by 1600, aided by the advent of the printing press, Euro-pean authors had generated roughly six thousand titles on the feared but fascinating subject of the Ottoman Turks.[17]

John Calvin (1509–1564), the sixteenth-century French Protestant reformer, was another theologian whose views on Islam directly influ-enced American Protestants. Like Luther, he identified the Antichrist in Islamic terms, but he envisioned the Prophet Muhammad rather than the sultan as the pope's twin in the "two horns of the Antichrist."[18] Cal-vinist theology was by far the most influential on Protestants in North

America. And so the majority of early Americans, regardless of their Protestant denomination, would adopt Calvin's idea about Islam and the Antichrist as theological truth.

Just as Martin Luther and John Calvin denigrated the Catholic Church and the pope by comparing them to Islam, their Catholic opponents employed similar insults against both Protestant reformers. Catholic authorities asserted:

> The Turk tears down churches and destroys monasteries—so does Luther, the Turks turn convents into horse stables and make cannon out of church bells—so does Luther. The Turk abuses and treats lasciviously all female persons, both secular and spiritual. Luther is just as bad for he entices monks and nuns out of their monasteries into false marriages.[19]

One sixteenth-century Catholic tract claimed, "Both seek to destroy the Christian faith, both deny the divinity of Christ, not only is the pseudo-Gospel of Calvin no better than the Qur'an of Muhammad, but in many respects it is wickeder and more repulsive."[20] Islam was thus for Christians of all denominations a weapon with which to vilify fellow believers, and it would prove effective, eventually to be appropriated for additional political and personal attacks on both sides of the Atlantic.[21]

The perception of Islam as a theological and military threat was not limited to the European continent. In England, John Foxe (1516–1587), a Protestant who chronicled in eight illustrated volumes the suffering of his coreligionists as martyrs of Catholic zealotry, added in 1566 a two-hundred-page section that briefly mentions the origins of Islam but mostly focuses on Ottoman military history.[22] Foxe described the "unspeakable cruelty and slaughter" of "Turkish tyrants upon poor Christian men's bodies, within the compass of these latter three hundred years." To stir his readers' sympathies, he exaggerated Turkish atrocities and the enslavement of conquered Christians, even comparing new Christian "martyrs" of the Ottoman conquests to the early Christians who suffered "the first persecutions of the Romans."[23] In reality, the Ottomans adhered to the Qur'anic command, "There is no compulsion in religion" (Qur'an 2:256).[24] Indeed, Islamic law allowed both Christians and Jews to retain their faith as tolerated believers, as long as they paid an annual tax and accepted key disabilities that reinforced their subordinate political and religious status (Qur'an 9:29).[25]

But Foxe did accurately refer to an Ottoman innovation that ran counter to the Qur'anic command of religious tolerance: their practice of seizing Christian boys and youths in the Balkans and forcing them to convert to Islam. The captives were then trained as crack musket-bearing soldiers or administrators loyal only to the sultan. These troops known originally in Turkish as the "new troops" became famous in English as the janissaries.[26] Foxe decried this institution as "of all bondage and servitude that the Christians suffer under the Turks" the "most intolerable." He lamented for the Christian families who suffered their children to be "pulled from the faith of Christ" and to become "professed enemies of Christ, and his church, to make war against Heaven, and to perish everlastingly."[27]

Foxe concluded his addendum on the Ottomans with "A Prayer against the Turks," which attempted to rally the faithful against "the malicious fury of these Turks, Saracens, Tartarians, against Gog and Magog, and all the malignant rabble of Antichrist, enemies to thy Son Jesus, our Lord and Saviour." By invoking the last battle between Gog and Magog in the book of Revelation, Foxe drew a now familiar comparison between the pope and the Ottoman sultan, judging that "the Turk is the more open and manifest enemy against Christ and his church." But he could not in the end decide whether the Ottoman sultan or the pope "hath consumed and spilt more Christian blood."[28] Aided by illustrations, Foxe's work would become "the most influential" of Protestant martyrologies in America's British colonies.[29]

Islam as the Antithesis of True Christianity: Humphrey Prideaux's Attacks on Deism and Socinianism in England, 1697

Foxe's book was followed by an equally popular anti-Islamic polemic by another Englishman, which would prove extremely influential in the American colonies. In 1697, an Anglican clergyman named Humphrey Prideaux (1648–1724) wrote *The True Nature of Imposture Fully Display'd in the Life of Mahomet. With a Discourse Annex'd for the Vindicating of Christianity from this Charge, Offered to the Consideration of the Deists of the Present Age,* to attack both Deists and Socinians. Charging that these sects believed "the Gospel of Jesus Christ is an Imposture," Prideaux thus likened them to the followers of the ultimate impostor, the Prophet Muhammad.[30] Mahomet, Prideaux argued, had "pretended to receive all his Revelations from the Angel Gabriel," and had "forged" chapters of the Qur'an based on Jewish and Christian sources.[31]

Prideaux drew other similarities between Islam and the two new Protestant sects. The Deists in England were never "an organized religious group"; nevertheless, they were deemed dangerous because they emphasized that God could be understood by human reason.[32] Even more alarming was their rejection of miracles and the divine authority of the Bible.[33] The Deists also opposed religious intolerance and the clergy's imposition of Christian orthodoxy.[34] Most important, Deists, like Socinians, rejected both the divinity of Jesus and the Trinity; both, like Muslims, believed in a unitary God.[35] Indeed, some Deists and Socinians looked favorably upon Islam's uncompromising monotheism, much to the consternation of their critics.[36]

Prideaux claimed to know Arabic, which would have been taught at both his secondary school of Westminster in London and his college of Christ Church, Oxford; but his published works demonstrate little interest in the original sources of the faith.[37] Instead, *The True Nature of Imposture Fully Display'd in the Life of Mahomet* merely echoes earlier English texts in its depiction of the Prophet as an impostor. Already in 1678, nineteen years before Prideaux, Lancelot Addison had anonymously published a book titled *First State of Muhametism, or an Account of the Author and Doctrine of that Imposture.*[38] Drawing from such contemporary English publications, flawed Latin translations of Arabic texts, and medieval Christian polemic, Prideaux would make numerous erroneous assertions about Islam.[39]

Prideaux's book may have been written as a response to a treatise authored by Henry Stubbe in 1671.[40] Stubbe denied the charge that Islam was spread by the sword, and portrayed the Prophet in a uniquely positive light.[41] The pro-Islamic argument of Stubbe's work had prevented it from being published; nevertheless, it had circulated widely in manuscript form.[42] In contrast, Prideaux's rebuttal would become enormously popular in England, with three editions the first year and multiple later ones on both sides of the Atlantic.[43] British editions of Prideaux appeared in Philadelphia in 1758 and in Connecticut in 1784; an American edition was published in Vermont in 1798.[44] Through Prideaux's book, the Prophet in American political discourse evolved to become not just a religious impostor, but also a militant zealot who held the "sword in one hand, and the Qur'an in the other."[45]

EARLY AMERICAN USES OF ISLAM: THE ANTICHRIST
AND SLURS AGAINST FELLOW PROTESTANTS

After crossing the Atlantic, anti-Islamic polemic found a ready audience
in Protestant congregations throughout the American colonies. Following their European predecessors, American preachers across denominations demonized Islam (or the Prophet or the Ottoman sultan) as one
of the twin-headed manifestations of the Antichrist.[46] In the colony
of Massachusetts Bay, the Puritan leader Cotton Mather (1663–1728)
and the banished Anne Hutchinson (d. 1643) would both condemn
Islam, invoking the familiar image of the Ottoman Antichrist's head
merged with that of the pope.[47] In New York, the Lutheran pastor Erick
Tobias Bjorck identified the Antichrist with Martin Luther's grotesque
conflation of the pope and "Mahomet."[48]

But such vilification of Islam did not preclude selective appropriation
of its ideas and precedents. In his 1721 book *The Christian Philosopher*,
Mather directs his Christian readers to excel Muslims in their piety and
intellectual pursuits: *"May our Devotion exceed the Mahometan as much as
our Philosophy!"*[49] And although Mather denigrated Islam as a religion,
he found in it a useful example for the reconciliation of natural science
and philosophy. He had read a 1686 English translation of the medieval Muslim philosopher Ibn Tufayl (d. 1185), who had demonstrated
that human reason led ineluctably to belief in the existence of God.[50]
Mather found this idea so compelling that despite his general disdain
for Islam, he would urge, "Reader, even a *Mahometan* will shew thee
one, without any *Teacher*, but *Reason* in a serious View of *Nature*, led
on to the Acknowledgement of a Glorious GOD." Mather even proclaimed that *"God has thus far taught* a Mahometan!"—thus acknowledging Islam's solution to a philosophical problem he himself also wished
to solve.[51] The first Latin translation of Ibn Tufayl's Islamic treatise that
Mather thus praised had earlier influenced the English philosopher John
Locke to develop one of the key ideas of the Enlightenment.

But for the most part the example of Islam was put to disparaging use, and American Protestants of all denominations also learned to
deploy it against fellow Christians when they deviated theologically.[52]
In 1676, Roger Williams, the Puritan whose heterodox ideas led to
his banishment from Massachusetts Bay, summoned anti-Islamic imagery to condemn the Quakers at his new colony in Providence, Rhode
Island. Williams reiterated that the Qur'an was an invention of the

Prophet Muhammad's when he charged that George Fox, the founder of the Religious Society of Friends, or Quakers, likewise laid false claims to divine inspiration.[53] According to medieval Catholic lore that was later adopted by Protestants, the Prophet had trained a dove, the Christian symbol of the Holy Spirit, to trick his followers into believing his revelation divine.[54] Yet Williams also correctly identified the core Islamic tenet that Muhammad, the seal of the prophets and God's final messenger, superseded the revelations of both Moses and Jesus, earlier prophets sent by the same divine source. Williams thus concluded that both Muslims and Quakers were deceived by false revelations.[55]

In spite of his vehement condemnation of George Fox, however, Williams admitted and tolerated Quakers in his new colony when they would have been executed in Massachusetts Bay. Similarly, his defamation of Islam's founder belied his very different views about the proper treatment of individual Muslims, as will be detailed in the next chapter.

Even the dramatic, compelling sermons of the Great Awakening, a revival of evangelical Protestant religious fervor throughout the American colonies in the 1730s and 1740s, featured preachers who applied such anti-Islamic rhetoric to new circumstances both theological and personal. The American Congregational pastor Jonathan Edwards (1703–1758), a key figure in the movement, preached and wrote against Islam, contending that the destruction of both the Catholic Church and Islam would usher in the Judgment Day foretold in the book of Revelation.[56]

Around this time, the itinerant British evangelical preacher George Whitefield (1714–1770) made several trips across the Atlantic to great acclaim. Whitefield was popular, but he also harshly condemned an Anglican bishop, stating that he was "no more a true Christian than Muhammad, or an infidel."[57] But such insults were so commonly used that even Whitefield himself was not spared similar attacks: his own former printer in London showered him with anti-Islamic slurs, calling him "a Mahomet, a Caesar, an impostor, a Don Quixote, a devil, the beast, a man of sin, the Antichrist."[58]

In 1739, multitudes flocked to hear Whitefield's sermons in Philadelphia. Benjamin Franklin observed that the local clergy refused to let him preach from their pulpits, and so "he was obliged to preach in the fields." To remedy the "inclemencies" attendant on these outdoor meetings, a new building was commissioned by the city's trustees "expressly for the use of any preacher of any religious persuasion who

might desire to say something to the people of Philadelphia." Franklin
added that "the building's design" would not cater to any particular
sect, "so that even if the Mufti of Constantinople were to send a missionary to preach Mahometanism to us, he would find a pulpit in his
service."[59] Franklin's apparently universal religious toleration and inclusion of Islam in planning this new Philadelphia religious gathering site
ignored the reality that even if a Muslim cleric were to be dispatched
from the hated regime of the Ottoman Turks, Whitefield and other
Protestants would certainly have monopolized the building to demon-
ize Islam.[60] Franklin's inclusion of Islam as a potential American faith
was a decidedly unusual point of view, one that the majority of Protestant Americans would have abhorred and rejected.

DESPOTISM AND TYRANNY:
BRITISH AND AMERICAN POLITICAL DEPICTIONS
OF THE OTTOMAN EMPIRE, 1720–76

The view of the Prophet as a militant zealot laid the foundation of the
idea that the Ottoman Empire, ruled by the sultan and his standing
army of janissaries, was the epitome of tyranny. In this political defamation, the pope and the Catholic powers, such as France and Spain,
were again linked to the Ottomans, just as Islam and Catholicism were
conflated to represent the Antichrist in apocryphal imagery.[61] As colonists, rebels, and citizens of a new nation, Americans, long fed Protestant eschatological dogma, rapidly adopted these political fears of Islam
and Catholicism. Later these suspicions would also influence prejudices
about Muslims and Catholics as citizens of the new country.

Eighteenth-century American hatred of the Ottoman Empire was
further fueled by anti-government tracts evoking the Whig ideology
then emerging in England. These treatises emphasized the importance
of individual rights, including the natural right to form a government
by compact, exercise freedom of speech and the press, and worship
freely without government control.[62] Inherent in these uniquely British
liberties was the belief that a government that infringed on these rights
could be legitimately overthrown. The Whigs proposed the Ottoman
regime as an antithesis of these ideals, commonly calling the sultan's
subjects his "slaves." Beginning in the late seventeenth century, Ottomans depicted as the symbol of despotism allowed Englishmen to make
veiled criticisms of their own government.[63] The Whig characterization

of the Ottomans would eventually cross the Atlantic and become the antithesis of American political ideals. Americans thus sought to assert their rights as British subjects, in opposition to Ottoman and all other Islamic governments—a pattern that would prevail through the Revolution and during the framing and ratification of the Constitution.[64]

Among the Whig texts, those of John Trenchard (1662–1723) and Thomas Gordon (d. 1750) especially influenced the American revolutionaries. The two first united to produce a London weekly called the *Independent Whig*, as a vehicle to attack the establishment of religion. From 1720 to 1723, Trenchard and Gordon together adopted the pen name Cato the Younger (95–46 BCE), after the Roman critic of political corruption, authoring a series of tracts known as *Cato's Letters, or Essays on Liberty, Civil and Religious, and Other Important Subjects*, first issued in the *London Journal* and later produced as a book.[65] In these essays, they would repeatedly vilify the Ottoman Empire and North African states as symbols of Islamic religious and political tyranny in order to advance their Whig agenda.[66]

In one essay on absolute monarchy, Trenchard and Gordon depicted the Ottoman sultan's "power" as "absolutely despotick: His will, that is to say, his lust, his maggots, or his rage, is his only law, and the only bounds to the authority of the vice-regent of God."[67] Likewise, Sultan Ismail of Morocco (r. 1672–1727) was called a despot, "an armed tyrant" who waged "unrelenting war . . . upon his unarmed subjects."[68] This Whig example referred to North African naval forces' attacks on English ships by Morocco, Algeria, Tunisia, and Libya beginning in the sixteenth century. The British navy would quell the threat by 1750, but when Trenchard and Gordon were writing *Cato's Letters*, North African pirates still dominated the seas.[69]

Taking a page from Protestant polemic, *Cato's Letters* tied tyranny to Islam in asserting that the problem with all Islamic governments was the faith they shared: "the Mahometan religion, which enjoins a blind submission to all [the sultan's] commands, on a pain of damnation," leaving the sultan's subjects in "abject postures of crouching slaves." Yet the authors of *Cato's Letters* were also aware that this extreme characterization of the Ottomans, though useful political rhetoric, was not fully accurate. Even the janissaries, those most feared, musket-bearing Ottoman troops, the authors of *Cato's Letters* admitted, sometimes "killed the tyrants."[70] Throughout the sixteenth century, in fact, local uprisings in Damascus, Macedonia, and Baghdad plagued the Ottoman Empire.

In 1622 Osman II (r. 1618–22) became the first sultan to be assassinated by janissary revolt, setting an unfortunate precedent. After him, others would also be deposed, including Mehmed IV in 1687, in the aftermath of the second failed siege of Vienna. Trenchard and Gordon would also have known that in 1703 a janissary rebellion forced the abdication of the sultan Mustafa II (r. 1695–1703).[71] But the authors of *Cato's Letters* may not have known—and certainly never acknowledged—that in this last uprising the military elite in Istanbul were also joined by members of the *ulama,* or religious authorities, and tradesmen. So much for the British belief that Islam fostered mindless political passivity.

In a tract entitled "Arbitrary Government proved incompatible with true Religion, whether Natural or Revealed," Trenchard and Gordon argued that "true" religion could not "subsist under tyrannical governments." They claimed that the Islamic faith of the Ottoman Empire was "founded on imposture, blended with outrageous and avowed violence; and by their religion, the imperial executioner is, next to their Alcoran, the most sacred thing amongst them,"[72] views that echoed those of Prideaux, whose work on matters theological and historical was well known to both authors.[73] The blend of imposture and violence linked to the Qur'an found a ready audience among Protestants in Britain and the American colonies.

Predictably, the Ottoman Turkish sultan (termed "the Turk") and the pope as the two heads of the Antichrist appeared again in one of *Cato's Letters,* reiterating the Protestant idea promoted since the sixteenth century. Thus an originally theological symbol was transformed in these tracts into a political vision of individual oppression:

> [W]hen people are taught to reverence, butchers, robbers, and tyrants, under the reverend name of rulers, to adore the names and persons of men, though their actions be the actions of devils: Then here is confirmed and accomplished servitude, the servitude of the body, secured by the servitude of the mind, oppression fortified by delusion. This is the height of human slavery. By this the Turk and Pope reign. They hold their horrid and sanguinary authority by false reverence, as much as the sword.[74]

The dichotomies were clear and intractable on both sides of the Atlantic: Islamic imposture versus Protestant Christian truth and Ottoman tyranny versus English liberty.

These anti-Islamic tracts continued to inspire American revolutionaries, who might have read reprints of *Cato's Letters* in newspapers from
New England to the southern colonies.[75] And so when they began to
apply the Whig political theory of *Cato's Letters* in defense of their rights,
the American rebels defamed British tyranny in anti-Islamic terms.

Samuel West, a Congregational minister in Massachusetts, wrote
in 1776 "On the Right to Rebel against Governors." As he argued,
for American rebels, the British were now the new "merciless tyrants"
whose "barbarity" surpassed even that of the Ottomans—the ultimate
political insult.[76] West's tactic had been pioneered by Protestants of all
denominations, who had long impugned their theological foes in the
same way. By the American Revolution, the slur best understood on
both sides of the Atlantic, whether theological or political, remained an
unfavorable comparison to Islam.[77]

PROBLEMATIC TERMS FOR MUSLIMS AND THE QUR'AN INHERITED BY AMERICANS FROM EUROPE

Embedded within "Turk" and "Mahometan," the two most popular
European terms for Muslims, were older, more pejorative connotations.
The term "Turk" was often used as a synonym for "Muslim," even
though Turks were a small portion of an enormous variety of ethnic and
linguistic identities in the Islamic world, and it was not a neutral designation. Reflecting fears of Ottoman conquests, a "Turk" in English-
language usage since the sixteenth century signified "a cruel, rigorous,
or tyrannical man" capable of barbaric behavior.[78] Even when the Ottoman military threat subsided in Europe, their continued aggression
from the North African coast (as ethnic rulers of all pirate states except
Morocco) kept the term in use on both sides of the Atlantic. These multiple negative connotations survived in American religious and political
discourse through the seventeenth and eighteenth centuries.

Another sixteenth-century English word, "Mahometan," incorrectly
identified a Muslim as a worshipper of "Mahomet," or Muhammad,
rather than as a worshipper of God alone.[79] This misrepresentation of a
basic Islamic tenet became popular in America, as indicated by a variety of spellings: "Mahomedan," "Mahommedan," and "Musselman."[80]
(Thomas Jefferson had his own orthographic variation of the word:
"Mahamedan.") American reference to the faith as "Mahometanism"
rather than Islam, as both Catholics and Protestants had historically

done in Europe, thus compounded inherited European misconceptions of Islamic beliefs.[81]

Englishmen and Americans in the seventeenth and eighteenth centuries also referred to Muslims with more ethnically accurate designations. By 1785, various American newspapers used the terms "Arab," "Moroccan," "Tunisian," and "Tripolitan." The term "Moor" was more problematic in origin and application.[82] This English word derived from the Latin *Maurus,* meaning someone from Mauretania, the name for the northwestern region of North Africa since Roman times. Ethnically, a Moor could be a Berber or an Arab, who had conquered and ruled the Iberian Peninsula until the Reconquista, while some still remained as a subject population until 1614. As late as the seventeenth century, the term also referred to a person of black or dark skin, in which case it was also rendered as "blackamoor."[83] A tertiary meaning of "Moor" was Muslim, although Muslims did not use this term for themselves.

If words for Muslim were fraught with complexities, so was the word for the Islamic sacred text. The Arabic meaning of the word is "Recitation," a reference to the oral revelation of what, after the Prophet's death, became a book. The exact transliteration of the Arabic characters into English should be rendered *Qur'an,* but this spelling was never used in Europe during the medieval or early modern period. More prevalent in both French and English in the seventeenth and eighteenth centuries was the term "Alcoran," which wrongly fused the Arabic definite article, *al,* with the French spelling "Coran." So when Europeans called it "the Alcoran," they were effectively terming it "the the Coran," a convention that Voltaire recognized as an idiocy, even while maintaining it.[84] "Koran," another common spelling in the eighteenth century, was what George Sale would use for the title of his 1734 English translation, which Thomas Jefferson would eventually acquire for his library. But Americans preferred Alcoran, or "the Alcoran of Mahomet," wrongly intimating that the Prophet was the sacred text's author.

With such distortions of Islam and its adherents prevalent, fictional representations could only worsen popular misunderstandings. The following analysis of two eighteenth-century works reminds us of the choice that European and American authors faced in representing Islam: to reprise and elaborate standard misconceptions, or to depict the faith and its adherents more accurately. The latter approach would ultimately prove too extreme for eighteenth-century American Protestant audiences.

The American Reception of European Ideas About Islam and an American Fictional Account of the Religion, 1742–97

The first play about Islam performed in America was written by François-Marie Arouet, better known as Voltaire (1694–1778). *Le Fanatisme, ou Mahomet le Prophète,* ostensibly about Islam's founding era, was first staged in Paris in 1742, two years before an English-language production in London. By 1776, a revival of the play had become a hit on the London stage. During the Revolutionary War, *Mahomet* would be performed on both sides, first by the British troops in 1780, and for American and French allied forces two years later.[85] In France, Britain, and America, this play was appropriated as a template for religious and political attacks against various enemies, foreign and domestic, all of them Christians. Voltaire had chosen to depict only the Prophet's aggressive pursuit of his political ends, a caricature who was both a religious impostor and a political fanatic. Through the filter of a distorted Islamic past, Voltaire intended French audiences to receive a more general message about the evils of religious persecution and intolerance. At a time when Catholic violence against Protestants was a national policy, Voltaire used an imagined Islamic context to avoid direct censure from the clergy and the government. But his ploy failed to fool Catholic censors. The play would find a more receptive audience when reinterpreted in British and American contexts. In the former, with the addition of new prologues, newspaper advertisements, and reviews, this play ostensibly about Muhammad became freighted with concerns about religion and political liberty.[86] Americans at war with Britain would follow suit in adapting the play's Muslim villains to serve their ideological ends.

In contrast to Voltaire's distorted representation of Islam, the American Royall Tyler's 1797 novel *The Algerine Captive* advanced a more accurate depiction of the faith. Tyler claimed his protagonist's captivity in Algiers was based on facts culled from real American experiences, in line with an older British genre of North African captivity narratives with which Americans were familiar.[87] Unlike Voltaire, Tyler allowed his Muslim characters to speak forcefully and often accurately about their beliefs, and in doing so, he criticized European authors for their bigotry against Islam. Along the way, the author condemned Christian religious intolerance and castigated the practice of slavery in both America (by white Americans) and North Africa (by Muslims).[88]

Like Voltaire's play, *The Algerine Captive* provided an opportunity for Americans to reflect upon their own most pressing religious and political issues through the prism of an Islamic context.[89] But both literary efforts revealed more about their authors and audiences than about their ostensible subjects.[90]

LE FANATISME, OU MAHOMET LE PROPHÈTE BY VOLTAIRE: ISLAM AS A VEHICLE FOR THE CRITIQUE OF CATHOLIC RELIGIOUS INTOLERANCE IN PARIS, 1742

In *Mahomet*, Voltaire recounted the founding of Islam as a polemical tale of a licentious villain, whose relentless lust and pursuit of power victimize all who stand in his way. Since the eighth century, Christians had charged that the Prophet's multiple marriages could only be the evidence of unbridled desire, emphasizing a notable contrast with the celibacy of Jesus.[91] Criticism of the Prophet's marriages had become a cornerstone of his polemical biography in medieval Catholic sources, and would be reiterated in seventeenth- and eighteenth-century Protestant texts.[92]

The majority of the characters in *Mahomet* were Voltaire's creations, with no relation to historical reality.[93] His plot reimagined how the intransigent Meccan pagans of the seventh century were forced through violence to yield their faith and sovereignty to the duplicitous false prophet Mahomet. In fact, the final capitulation of pagan Mecca to the Prophet's monotheist forces in 630 had been negotiated by a treaty two years before. When the city surrendered, only four inhabitants were actually killed.[94] But Voltaire's point about religious fanaticism would not be served by retelling this basically peaceful resolution. By imagining the murder of pagans, Voltaire condemns rather than celebrates the triumph of Islam as a new monotheistic religion. To further stimulate outrage against the Muslim "oppressors," he depicts the Meccan pagans as true, honest, heroic martyrs.

In contrast, Voltaire portrays his Mahomet as a lascivious predator, who lusts after a beautiful young woman called Palmira, a name drawn not from Arabic but a pre-Islamic site in Palmyra, Syria. Captured by Mahomet as a child, Palmira grows up not knowing that her father, Zopire, is the leader of the Meccan pagan opposition. Although Palmira reveres Mahomet as a father figure, a ruler, and a prophet, she does not return his affections. Instead she loves Seide, who had also been taken captive as a child, but whom she does not know is her brother.

Mahomet commands Seide to assassinate Zopire, his own father. Out of loyalty to Mahomet, Seide carries out the order, but duplicitous Mahomet then poisons his rival. In the last scene, Palmira realizes too late that both her father and brother have died at the fanatic's direction. Maddened with grief, she commits suicide, exposing Mahomet's true nature with her final breath:

> You blood-smeared impostor . . . Executioner of all my loved ones . . .
> The holy prophet, the king I served, the god I worshipped! Monster!
> whose madness and treacherous plots have made two murderers out of
> two innocent hearts![95]

While the audience identifies with this suffering, Voltaire makes clear his vision of Mahomet, who alone on stage admits that he is a violent impostor: "The sword and the Alcoran in my bloody hands, / Will impose silence on the rest of humanity."[96] When his first choice to play Mahomet bowed out, Voltaire found another actor he said was even better than his original choice because of "his simian appearance."[97] On stage, the character of Mahomet was conceived by the playwright as both subhuman and inhumane.

But Voltaire's caricature belies his knowledge of actual Islamic history and religious doctrine. By 1738, he too owned George Sale's English translation of the Qur'an, which included a long expository section on history and religion.[98] By ignoring this relatively accurate information available to him, Voltaire betrays a deliberate decision to distort Islamic history as a means of warning against religious persecution and despotism.

Although Voltaire's condemnation of the Catholic persecution of Protestants was indirect, church authorities recognized the analogy and quickly banned the play after its Paris premiere in 1742. They correctly charged that Voltaire's intent was to attack Christianity rather than Islam; some even contended that he was promoting Deism.[99] Voltaire resented the Catholic censorship of his play, but he agreed that Ottoman ambassadors in Paris would have had legitimate reason to object.[100] In this case, he admitted, "It would not be decent to blacken the Prophet while entertaining the envoy."[101] But the calumny against Islam had proved too useful to abjure. In 1745, attempting to have the ban lifted, Voltaire wrote directly to Pope Benedict XIV, paying homage to him in Italian as "the head of the true religion" and casting the Prophet, unsurprisingly, as "the founder of that false and barbarous sect."[102] But his papal strategy failed, and the play would not be performed again in Paris until 1751.

MAHOMET THE IMPOSTOR IN BRITAIN AS PROPAGANDA AGAINST FRANCE AND CATHOLICISM, 1744

When Voltaire's play opened in London in 1744, under the new English title Mahomet the Impostor, it had undergone a few changes. Palmira's father, named Alcanor instead of Zopire, was now styled not as an Arab leader, but as the head of an unhistorical "senate," and Zaphna, rather than Seide, was Palmira's love interest and brother. The changes had been made by two Protestant British authors, who translated and reworked Voltaire's Fanatisme for the London production.[103] The first, James Miller (d. 1744), an Anglican minister, took charge of the first four acts. In his hands, the play became an attack on the oppressive Catholic regime in France, which stood in contrast to the "unique" tolerance of Protestant British freedoms. The idea that Islam and Catholicism were both violent faiths, spread by the sword, had already been a common Protestant claim, and was even used in a newspaper advertisement, which proclaimed, "The original was by Authority forbid to be played in France on account of the free and noble Sentiments with regard to Bigotry and Enthusiasm, which shine through it; and that Nation found as applicable to itself, as to the bloody propagators of Mahomet's Religion."[104] The play thus served to characterize the freedom of religion and thought as innately British. This Whig view of individual rights would go on to inspire American revolutionaries twenty years later.

It was not a coincidence that the advertisement for Mahomet the Impostor echoed key concepts of Cato's Letters. Both were the products of Whig thought. John Hoadly (d. 1776), who stepped in to rework the play's fifth and final act when James Miller died in 1744, probably also wrote the advertisements and the new prologue for the piece. Hoadly has been described as a "libertarian pamphleteer," but he was also the son of the famed Whig and Anglican bishop Benjamin Hoadly (d. 1761),[105] who'd been defended in 1717 by one of the authors of Cato's Letters when he had preached about the king that "the Gospels provided no textual support for any visible church authority."[106] When controversy ensued, support for Bishop Hoadly's views became a public affirmation of one's Whig affiliation.[107]

Truly his father's son, the younger Hoadly probably wrote a rhymed prologue for *Mahomet the Impostor* that praised British freedoms absent in repressive Catholic France. He also stressed his father's Whig ideals of anticlericalism and toleration:

> *No clergy here usurp the free-born mind,*
> *Ordained to teach, and not enslave mankind;*
> *Religion here bids persecution cease,*
> *Without, all order, and within, all Peace*
> *Religion to be Sacred must be free;*
> *Men will suspect—where bigots keep the key.*[108]

After some of the play's extensive verses in the last act were excised in 1765, *Mahomet the Impostor* finally became a hit both as a stage production and a book. In the print editions from 1776 and 1777, the engravings of an actor named Bensley dressed in an approximation of Ottoman garb, with "the Alcoran" in one hand and a scimitar in the other, embodied in a single image the themes of religious fraud and violence.[109] Frequently republished, the play would be widely disseminated in writing on both sides of the Atlantic.[110] And it was immensely popular as a London stage staple from 1776 and beyond.

Mahomet the Impostor as a British Vehicle for the Critique of the American Revolution in New York City, 1780

In 1780, British officers besieged by American rebels performed *Mahomet the Impostor* in New York City.[111] They penned a new rhymed prologue, which was recited by a member of the Royal Navy, dressed as a Native American chief, who condemned the American traitors as heretics:

> *Make false apostate Subjects blush to own,*
> *That Indians are more Loyal to the Crown,*
> *Than those the Parent Country bred and bore,*
> *Clasp'd to her Breast, and nourish'd on this Shore.*[112]

The Indian chief goes on to predict Britain's victory in America, her commercial domination of the world, and the defeat of her Catholic enemies Spain and France:

The sword shall sheath when stern rebellion's dead
And Cities rise, where gallant Soldiers bled.
Then shall the produce of this Land be bore,
To foreign Marts, and every distant shore
Receive our Commerce, and acknowledge too
That while we are to Parent England true,
To France and Spain defiance shall be hurl'd,
And leagued with her, we'll conquer all the World.[113]

The British officers identified the American revolutionaries with the forces of Mahomet, an anti-Islamic condemnation of the enemy.[114]

MAHOMET THE IMPOSTOR AS A POSSIBLE AMERICAN CRITIQUE OF BRITISH TYRANNY, 1782

Two years later in Baltimore, the American revolutionaries presented their own production of *Mahomet the Impostor*. The Americans certainly did not identify with Mahomet, viewing the play as a parable of the dangers of tyranny.[115] Instead, they likened King George III to "the Impostor." Advertisements in the local paper praised the French troops, still stationed in town since helping the Americans defeat the British at Yorktown the previous year, for their "great politeness," and saw the play as an "Opportunity to declare, that the prejudices against the French Nation which the English so pertinaciously attributed to the Americans" were false.[116] Voltaire, a supporter of the American Revolution, might at last have been pleased with the reception of his play.

No special prologue exists from this first Baltimore performance of *Mahomet,* but one dedicated to George Washington for another contemporary production by the same theater company reflects the sentiments of the American audience in the wake of their recent victory over the British. The actress who declaimed the prologue celebrated the virile Revolutionary virtues of courage, liberty, freedom, and independence possessed by her imagined future husband:

To be a patient wife, I grant's a curse;
But then, old Maid! O Lud! that's surely worse,
But hold, what kind of men will suit us best?
A Fool—no, no—there we can't agree—

The Man of Courage is the man for me.
Who fights for glorious Liberty, will find
His empire rooted in the female mind.
'Tis base Slave that stains the name of Man,
Who bleeds for Freedom will extend his plan;
Will keep the generous principle in view,
And with the Ladies Independent too.[117]

Extant broadsides announce the Baltimore performances of *Mahomet* on October 1 and October 15, 1782.[118] The last American performance would be in 1796, when it may have served to criticize the violence of the French Revolution.[119]

Broadside announcing the performance of
Voltaire's *Mahomet* in Baltimore.

THE ALGERINE CAPTIVE AND THE MULLAH:
AN AMERICAN LESSON IN COMPARATIVE RELIGION
AND TOLERATION, 1797

In 1797, the American lawyer and playwright Royall Tyler (1757–1826) published *The Algerine Captive; or The Life and Adventures of Doctor Updike Underhill, Six Years a Prisoner among the Algerines.* By this time, the United States had suffered the captivity of its sailors for more than a decade, because independence from Britain had left the new country without naval protection or sufficient funds to establish treaties with North African pirate states. By 1793, more than one hundred Americans had been captured and imprisoned in Algiers, but negotiations to free them stalled for lack of ransom.[120] The earliest group of twenty-one Americans seized in 1785 was thus held for eleven years in Algiers. Two of them were rescued by private donations; almost half would die of disease waiting for their freedom.[121] In 1797, six months before the publication of Tyler's novel, survivors of the earliest group along with more recently imprisoned Americans were released as the result of a treaty.[122] By 1800, the United States had established peace treaties with all four North African powers: Morocco (1787), Algiers (1796), Tripoli (1797), and Tunis (1799).[123] But the problem of piracy remained so serious that Thomas Jefferson chose military action as a response during his first term as president, from 1801 to 1805. With the exception of Jefferson's attack against Tripoli and a final assault against Algiers in 1815, the so-called Barbary Wars consisted, in effect, of North African fleets' raids of American ships.

Unlike Voltaire's imagined account of the distant past, *The Algerine Captive* dealt with an urgent contemporary issue through the experience of a fictive New Hampshire native taken captive by Algerian pirates.[124] The main character, Dr. Updike Underhill, though appalled by his exposure to slavery in the southern United States, nevertheless participates in the African slave trade, as did many seafaring New Englanders: "I execrated myself for even the involuntary part I bore in this execrable traffic: I thought of my native land, and blushed."[125]

One day, the unfortunate Yankee is captured at sea by Algerian pirates. The pirate commander is impractically decked out for a corsair: "the captain, glittering in silks, pearl, and gold, sat cross-legged upon a velvet cushion to receive me."[126] As Underhill suffers from vermin, thirst, and hunger, he is befriended by a West African slave who, in a display of profound humanity, feeds the man who had helped enslave him.[127] The former American slaver, ashamed, and now himself a slave, vows that if he were "once more to taste the freedom of my native country," then "every moment of my life shall be dedicated to preaching against this detestable commerce" of the American slave trade.[128] Neither Tyler nor his readers were aware of the double irony of American slavery: Muslims were among those West Africans seized and sold to Americans as slaves.

In 1788, the year of Underhill's capture, the Constitution of the United States had just been ratified after heated debate. Underhill declares yearningly, "Let those of our fellow citizens, who set at nought the rich blessings of our federal union, go like me to a land of slavery, and they will then learn how to appreciate the value of our free government."[129] By contrast, he depicts the dey of Algiers as an Islamic despot, with "a diamond crescent" upon his turban, surrounded by prisoners literally "licking the dust as a token of reverence and submission."[130] In this regard, Tyler's novel echoes earlier political theory distinguishing British and American liberty from Islamic tyranny.[131]

Stripped of everything, Underhill remains captive in Algiers for six years, unable to pay his own ransom or obtain help from his government, like so many real-life American captives. Eventually, he becomes the private property of a former Turkish military officer, who has only one wife, as was common, despite the allowance for four, akin to "the patriarchal manners described in Holy Writ."[132] In other words, the author here refuses the stereotype of supposedly unbridled sexuality among Muslim males while also reminding readers of the similar behavior of the Old Testament prophets. This was to challenge the general consensus in Europe and the United States that polygamy was a decadent, uniquely Islamic practice.

After defending himself against an overseer, Underhill is sent to work in a stone quarry, often the lot of real Christian captives. Debilitated by harsh treatment, he is urged by a British Muslim convert to forsake Christianity and join Islam to gain his freedom.[133] In fact, many Europeans and a few American captives in North Africa were thus converted to Islam.[134] To aid in Underhill's conversion, his friend arranges a meeting for him with "the mollah," a term for a Muslim cleric more common in Turkey, Iran, and India than in North Africa. With the promise of rest from hard labor during this proselytizing attempt, Underhill agrees to listen to arguments in support of Islam. The author assures the reader that his American hero will resist any attempt at conversion to a faith long held in contempt on both sides of the Atlantic. He wonders "what could be said in favour of so detestably ridiculous a system as the Mahometan imposture."[135] But as Underhill listens to a series of persuasive arguments about the positive aspects of Islam and Christianity's history of religious intolerance toward fellow Christians and Muslims, his reaction surprises.

The Muslim cleric is a former Greek Christian from Antioch, also captured by Algerian pirates, who assures Underhill that conversion to Islam will involve only persuasion through discussion. This the cleric presents in contrast to "the church of Rome and its merciless inquisitors," who in contrast employ "all the honour and profit of conversion by faggots, dungeons, and racks." Tyler's predictable anti-Catholicism is thus expressed by his Muslim character who favors "rational argument" over torture.[136]

In his compelling speeches, the Muslim asserts that religious affiliation is a geographical and cultural accident rather than a choice: "Born in New England, my friend, you are a Christian purified by Calvin. Born in the Campania of Rome, you had been a papist."[137] Having mapped out the possibilities that Underhill might have wound up as a Hindu, a follower of the Dalai Lama, Confucius, or Zoroaster, the cleric continues, "A wise man adheres not to his religion because it was that of his ancestors. He will examine the creeds of other nations, compare them to his own, and hold fast that which is right." When Underhill remains quietly skeptical, the cleric urges him to "Speak out boldly" and without fear, acknowledging that Christians have understood Islam as "the Mahometan imposture." The cleric then goes on to compare the relative merits of Christianity and Islam by posing four questions:

> First, which of them has the highest proof of its divine origin? and which inculcates the purist morals? that is, of which have we the greatest certainty that it came from God? and which is calculated to do the most good to mankind?[138]

The cleric then argues that the "Alcoran" was "written by the finger of the Deity himself," but the Bible was "written by men." When Underhill weakly protests that he has "good evidence" of the "truth" in the Bible, the cleric also asserts the same for Islam, declaring that the Prophet "received the sacred volume from the hand of Gabriel."[139]

Although this does not accurately represent the Muslim belief that the Angel Gabriel conveyed divine directives orally over time, Tyler's intent here is clear: to depict Islam's revelation as a direct communication from God, rather than from a human "impostor," a position that supports Islamic tradition rather than Christian polemic.

Underhill goes on to argue that the truth of Christianity is proved "from its small beginnings and wonderful increase." The Muslim counters that Mahomet was an "illiterate," and adds, "Could he, who could not read or write, have published a book, which for its excellence has astonished the world?"[140] Underhill the Christian recoils, fuming: "My blood boiled to hear this infidel vaunt himself thus triumphantly against my faith."[141] The Yankee then insists that the spread of the faith was not accomplished by coercion, in contrast to Islam: "Our religion was disseminated in peace; yours was promulgated by the sword." The cleric retorts, "The history of the Christian church is a detail of bloody massacre," citing the persecutions of the first Christian Roman emperor Constantine, the expulsion of the Muslims from Catholic Spain, and "the dragooning of the Huguenots" from Catholic France.[142]

The violence within Christianity is confirmed by the protagonist's own past; Underhill's ancestor had been banished from Puritan Massachusetts in the seventeenth century because "his ideas of religious toleration" were "more liberal than those around him"; Underhill also notes sympathetically that "the celebrated Anne Hutchinson" and "good Roger Williams" suffered the same fate.[143] And so the protagonist comes around to Tyler's own view that Christian religious history is one of violent persecution of fellow Christians and Muslims.

The Muslim cleric offers a final argument reflecting on the worldwide diffusion of Islam and the practice of allowing Christians and Jews to retain their faith in Islamic lands. The Muslim emphasizes the Qur'anic principle that there is to be no coercion in religion (Qur'an 2:256). In addition, he invokes the Qur'anic command to deal gently with slaves and, on their conversion, to manumit them (Qur'an 5:89). According to this tenet, even a slave would be received "as a brother" once he "pronounces the ineffable creed" of Islam.[144]

To this Muslim tolerance, the cleric contrasts "the Christians of your southern plantations" who "baptize the unfortunate African into your faith, and then use your brother Christians as brutes of the desert." And Underhill is unable to defend his compatriots' inhumane practice of slavery.[145] The cleric judiciously admits, "Your Scriptures contain many excellent rules of life," but he regrets that it does not forbid "gaming" and "the use of wine," both prohibited in Islam.[146]

Underhill listens to a final entreaty to convert and "learn the unity of God," which Tyler rightly identifies as the "fundamental doctrine" of the Qur'an.[147] He would not be required to "renounce" his "prophet," Jesus, whom Muslims "respect as a great apostle of God, but only to acknowledge that Mahomet is the seal of the prophets." In the end, the American refuses to convert, though he offers no brilliant retort to the powerful arguments of the "artful priest."[148]

Outwardly silent, the protagonist reveals his confusion in an inner monologue, admitting that he was "disgusted with [the cleric's] fables, abashed by his assurance, and almost confounded by his sophistry."[149] Underhill also concedes that the Muslim cleric spoke Latin with "fluency and elegance," but without the "proper" pronunciation used at Harvard.[150] (Here the author, a graduate of Harvard, class of 1776, cannot resist a bit of chauvinism.)[151] Still, in the face of the overwhelming polemic against Islam circulating in America, the dominance of the Muslim cleric in this religious exchange is not only unexpected but curious.

When Underhill becomes ill, the same Muslim cleric visits him in the infirmary. The captive resists renewed attempts to convert him, saying, "The religion of my country is all that I had left of the many blessings I once enjoyed in common with my fellow citizens." This is a ringing endorsement of the nation, but not an effective argument for Christianity's superiority. Underhill admits that the mullah had impressed him: "I was charmed with the man, though I abominated his faith."[152] Underhill thus acknowledges having found a Muslim worthy of respect in spite of his religion, though he concludes with a standard Christian polemic about the Prophet's "ambition" and his invention of a "new religion."[153]

The novel's apparent sympathy for Islam does not extend to either Catholicism or Judaism. Jews are described as a "cunning race" that "solace themselves with a Messiah whose glory is enshrined in their coffers" and "wallow in secret wealth."[154] Underhill describes the Jewish quarter of Algiers and accurately portrays the importance of the Jews as intermediaries in North African rulers' banking and diplomacy.[155] He is befriended by an elderly Jew, who kindly (but against type) helps raise money for him to buy his freedom when his countrymen fail to do so; but his chance of release is dashed when the old man suddenly dies and

the benevolent Jew's son pretends not to know about his father's benefi-
cence.[156] Underhill, who'd been a doctor, saves the younger Jew's life,
but the ingrate sells him into slavery a second time.[157] Now he is put
aboard a ship, and only a serendipitous intervention by the Portuguese
navy returns the captive of Algiers to freedom.[158]

The most striking display of Tyler's universalism occurs as Underhill derides the "bigoted aversion" of both George Sale, the translator
of the Qur'an, and the anti-Islamic polemicist Humphrey Prideaux.[159]
Underhill declares that he will "endeavour to steer the middle course of
impartiality," and though he was not always objective, his mere attempt
proved controversial.[160]

A reviewer for a Boston magazine would object to the Muslim cleric's
argument for Islam's superiority, in contrast to Underhill's inability to
make a compelling case for Christianity.[161] The novelist was forced
to rebut the charge of "infidelity." In his defense, Tyler admitted that
he had intended "to do away the vulgar prejudices against Islamism,"
and that, contrary to what his protagonist had said about Sale's "bigoted aversion," he himself had deliberately adopted "the liberality of
the good Sale." Despite these intentions, Tyler was forced to publicly
traduce Islam again in favor of the "truths of Christianity," writing
apologetically:

> [F]or the Author considered then, and now considers, that, after exhibit-
> ing Islamism in its best light, the Mahometan imposture will be obvious
> to those who compare the language, the dogmatic fables, the monstrous
> absurdities of the Koran, with the sublime doctrines, morals and lan-
> guage of the Gospel dispensation.[162]

Tyler should not have been surprised at the public outrage in eighteenth-
century America at a failure to espouse Christianity's absolute superiority over Islam. The charge of "infidelity" implies that Tyler was seen as
not just an unbeliever but a Muslim, for that had been a significant part
of the Christian definition of the word "infidel" in English since the
fifteenth century.[163]

Tyler was not the first American to attempt to introduce a more
positive view of Islam. Six years earlier, in 1791, *New York Magazine* had
included a story entitled "Mahomet: A Dream."[164] In it, the Prophet
is first called "an impostor," but then upheld as "a great man," and
Islam is defined as a faith promising salvation and morality.[165] Later, in

1801, a few years after the publication of *The Algerine Captive*, another novel entitled *Humanity in Algiers* would depict a Muslim who frees an American captive and leaves a bequest to do this annually.[166] But these three works were exceptions among contemporary texts that remained overwhelmingly hostile to Islam.

At the end of the eighteenth century, it was still theologically and politically dangerous to suggest that Islam retained some merit even for Muslims. In fact, Tyler had, in certain paragraphs in his novel, done just that. He had chastised the mutual enmity of Muslims and Christians and held each group to account for their violence as a perversion of their own creeds:

> Neither their Alcoran nor their priests excite them to plunder, enslave, or torment. The former expressly recommends charity, justice, and mercy, towards their fellow men. I would not bring the sacred volume of our faith in any comparative view with the Alcoran of Mahomet; but I cannot help noticing it as extraordinary, that the Mahometan should abominate the Christian on account of his faith, and the Christian detest the Mussulman for his creed; when the Koran of the former acknowledges the divinity of the Christian Messias [*sic*], and the Bible of the latter commands us to love our enemies. If either would follow the obvious dictates of his own scripture, he would cease to hate, abominate, and destroy the other.[167]

The only factual flaw in this compelling passage was Tyler's misunderstanding of the Islamic stance on Jesus: The Qur'an accepts Jesus only as a prophet, and does not acknowledge his "divinity." But otherwise it was a cogent call for mutual tolerance.

There were, however, earlier European precedents for religious tolerance. A handful of scattered Christians spoke bravely against religious violence while it raged around them in the sixteenth and seventeenth centuries. Many were accused of heresy. Even fewer opposed systematic persecution by the state in the name of doctrinal difference. Among these, a subset of Catholics and Protestants also defended Muslims from coerced conversion, state persecution, and violence. Their ideas were never considered acceptable while they lived. But these ideas evolved over centuries, eventually to be espoused by Jefferson and other Founders as religious freedom, political equality, and citizenship.

2

Positive European Christian Precedents for the Toleration of Muslims, and Their Presence in Colonial America, 1554–1706

Let them be heretikes, Turcks, Jewes, or whatsoever it apperteynes not to the earthly power to punish them in the least measure.
—Thomas Helwys,
English Baptist, 1612

And I aske whether or no such as may hold forth other *Worships* or *Religions*, (*Jewes, Turkes,* or *Antichristians*) may not be peaceable and quiet *Subjects,* loving and helpfull *neighbours,* faire and just *dealers,* true and loyall to the *civill government?* It is cleare they may from all *Reason* and *Experience* in many flourishing *Cities* and *Kingdomes* of the World, and so offend not against the *civill State* and *Peace;* nor incurre the punishment of the *civill Sword* . . .

—Roger Williams, English Puritan
exiled to Rhode Island, 1644

Besides, I think you are under a mistake, which shews your pretence against admitting Jews, Mahometans, and Pagans, to the civil rights of the commonwealth is ill-grounded; for what law I pray is there in England, that they who turn to any of those religions, forfeit the civil rights of the commonwealth by doing it?

—John Locke,
English philosopher, 1692

ON APRIL 28, 1584, a garrulous miller from a town near Venice, Italy, told the Inquisition that Jesus commanded all to "Love God and your neighbor," an application of the Golden Rule he interpreted to include Muslims: "the majesty of God has given the Holy Spirit to all, to Christians, to heretics, to Turks, and to Jews; and he considers them all dear, and they are all saved in the same manner."[1] Domenico Scandella, known by the nickname Menocchio (d. 1601), advocated the equality of Islam, Judaism, and Christianity, a shocking and heretical idea for the Catholic inquisitors who believed there was no salvation outside of the Catholic Church.[2] But God, in this miller's estimation, did not play favorites based on religion or Christian denomination. This meant that the church held no exclusive claim on the only or true faith—an intolerable heresy for the Inquisition.

Since the Italian miller believed God loved and saved everyone equally, he had argued for universal religious tolerance, although "tolerance" was a word he never used. In so doing, Menocchio had unwittingly professed the heresy of Origen of Alexandria (d. 254), and of that he was accused at his first Inquisition trial in 1584: "You brought again to light Origen's heresy that all peoples would be saved, Jews, Turks, pagans, Christians, and all infidels, since the Holy Spirit has been given equally to them all."[3] For these and other heretical beliefs, Menocchio would be imprisoned for two years, in squalid conditions. His health broken, he was released, but required by Inquisition order to wear a smock with a cross as a penitential sign, and enjoined never to speak of his beliefs or leave his village.[4]

In his monumental inquiry into Menocchio's cosmology and persecution, *The Cheese and the Worms,* Carlo Ginzburg first tried to make sense of these beliefs in the context of the Reformation, a time of religious violence throughout Europe that set Catholics against Protestants and various denominations of Protestants against one another.

The miller's heretical ideas about tolerance toward Muslims were predicated upon his assumption of their ultimate capacity for salvation, an unusual position among both Catholics and Protestants. More commonly, the Christians who argued for the toleration of Muslims did so with an eye toward the eventual conversion of the adherents of Islam to Christianity, presumed to be the only Muslim path to heaven. Few indeed were those Christians in the sixteenth and seventeenth centuries who would have argued for the toleration of Muslims as Muslims, and they never much disrupted the consensus of anti-Islamic sentiment among the Christian majority. Nevertheless, these ideas about universal tolerance evolved into policies that often explicitly included Muslim toleration in a variety of Christian societies on both sides of the Atlantic from the sixteenth through the seventeenth centuries.[5] Eventually these marginalized views laid the groundwork for eighteenth-century ideas about Muslims as future citizens of the United States.

Menocchio's defense of Muslims as saved and equal in God's eyes extended also to Jews, who would be linked with Muslims in other European arguments about tolerance during this period. Unlike Muslims, who were a powerful external political force and for the most part lived outside of European society, Jews were a scattered, resident minority who were never considered a military danger to their Christian neighbors.[6] But, like Muslims, Jews were deemed "quintessential religious outsiders," whose refusal to convert and acknowledge Jesus as messiah provoked resentment and sporadic violence.[7] The term "infidel," synonymous with Muslims, would also be applied somewhat less frequently to Jews.[8] Uniquely, Jews were also implicated as deicides, complicit in perpetuity for the death of Jesus.[9] In Catholic and most Protestant theologies, both Muslims and Jews remained "in different ways, an immanent presence and perceived threat to Christian society."[10] Whether described as objects of Christian persecution, forced conversion, salvation, or tolerance, Muslims *and* Jews continued to be conjoined in these disputes.[11]

Some of Menocchio's ideas of tolerance seem to echo earlier medieval European peasant lore about Muslims in Catholic France, Italy, and Spain. They remind us that these perspectives existed even among some common folk in Europe.[12] Twenty years before Menocchio's first Inquisition trial, an Italian poem by an anonymous peasant expressed ideas similar to his. In verses never published yet part of a rich peasant oral culture, the poet declaimed that Muslims, Jews, and Christians all had a "law" based on the Ten Commandments dictated to them by the same God. Describing Muhammad as "a prophet and a great warrior of God," the poem commanded Turks and Christians to end their strife:

> *You Turk and you Christian by my decree*
> *Do not go on as you have in the past:*

Turk take a step forward
And you Christian take a step backward[13]

There is no proof that Menocchio heard these verses recited. Nor do we know whether the words circulated in nearby villages. However, the equality of the three monotheisms and the divine command for Christians and Turks to cease military strife (even if this meant Christian retreat and Muslim advance to a stalemate) were consistent with the miller's own worldview. Such pacifist sentiments are remarkable in light of the ongoing Ottoman military threat to Western Europe. Only thirty-five years before, in 1529, the Ottomans had attempted their first unsuccessful siege of Vienna. By 1537, Sultan Suleyman's fleet had attacked the coasts of Italy, with the Ottoman military remaining a significant threat to Western Europe until the end of the seventeenth century.[14]

Menocchio paraphrased a second popular European source, known as *The Legend of the Three Rings,* an allegorical tale identifying the God of Muslims as the one of Christians and Jews.[15] In this medieval tale, all three religions were literally a family, with God as their father. As Menocchio boldly told his inquisitors in a second trial in 1599, God was merciful to all his children:

> Likewise, God the Father has various children whom he loves, such as Christians, Turks, and Jews and to each of them he has given the will to live by his own law, and we do not know which is the right one. That is why I said that since I was born a Christian I want to remain a Christian, and if I had been born a Turk I would want to live like a Turk.[16]

If Christianity, Islam, and Judaism were all religions of the same God, then no religion could claim superiority. Menocchio's implication that Christianity was not *the* religion, but merely *one* religion among the three divinely inspired, was a dangerous departure from the vast majority of his contemporaries.

The inquisitors seized upon the miller's heretical words, and immediately asked him which religion represented the "right law."[17] The only doctrinally correct answer—Christianity—was obvious, but Menocchio refused to provide it. Instead, he offered a sociological reason for the existence of religious differences. The miller affirmed, "Yes sir, I do believe that every person considers his faith to be right, and we do not know which is the right one: but because my grandfather, my father, and my people have been Christians, I want to remain a Christian, and believe that this is the right one."[18] The correct answer but for the wrong reasons. This failure to assert the summary superiority of Christianity confirmed Menocchio as a heretic.[19]

Menocchio was not the first Catholic in Italy to have come under scrutiny for his strange ideas about the salvation of Muslims and Jews. More than a decade before him and hundreds of miles away, another miller whom Menocchio never met asserted that "the Hebrew, the Turkish," and all other believers should retain their faiths.[20] Similar utterances are to be found in Spanish Inquisition records beginning in the fifteenth century, even while mid-fourteenth-century Castilian legal codes forbade the forced conversion of Jews and Muslims in Christian territory.[21] In 1488, a Catholic peasant woman named Juana Pérez declared that "the good Jew would be saved and the good Moor, in his law, and why else had God made them?"[22] It wasn't until four years later, in 1492, that their Catholic majesties Ferdinand and Isabella conquered the last Islamic dynasty in Spain and expelled the Jews for their beliefs. Beginning in the early sixteenth century, Muslims in Spain would be forcibly converted to Catholicism.

Stuart Schwartz has documented numerous other instances in Inquisition records of religious universalism in Spanish and Portuguese dominions on both sides of the Catholic Atlantic in the sixteenth century.[23] In Spain in 1535, for instance, there was a public disputation between a Catholic clergyman and Joseph Arabigo, who spoke for the Moriscos, Muslims who often secretly maintained Islam after forced conversion. Arabigo, whose own name would seem to indicate a Morisco identity, asserted, "Some of the learned men among the Moors say that each can be saved in his own law," including "the Jew in his, the Christian in his," and "each will find happiness in his law and believe it is the truth." His Catholic opponent declared such ideas "false, mad, and stupid."[24] In 1582, two years before Menocchio's first trial by the Inquisition, a pastry chef in Mexico named Tomé de Medina, suggested that the individual's salvation was God's will, regardless of one's faith. He was denounced by Catholic Spanish authorities, as Menocchio would be two years later, for what the church termed the heresy of Pelagius (d. c. 418–20). The English monk had first proposed the idea that all people were essentially good and could be saved on merit.[25]

Menocchio's views of Muslims were not drawn entirely from popular oral peasant tales. Unlike most peasants, the miller was literate. He had access to an Italian translation of the Bible, and he was accused of possessing almost a dozen other works. Among his treasured tomes inventoried by the Inquisition was an Italian translation of the *Travels* of Sir John Mandeville, written originally in fourteenth-century France.[26] The book contained both real and imaginary geographies of the Holy Land and points as far east as China.

Islamic beliefs were also described in this work. The miller may have found his own doubts about the divinity of Jesus confirmed by the Qur'an's definition of him as a human prophet, who had never been crucified but ascended into heaven while another died in his place (Qur'an 4:157–58).[27] Indeed, Menocchio would assert that "it seemed a strange thing to me that a lord would allow himself to be taken in this way, and so I suspected that since he was crucified he was not God, but some prophet."[28] The medieval work of Mandeville nevertheless maintained the supremacy of Christianity over Islam and Judaism, which Menocchio did not. The miller would be denounced by a local innkeeper as "worse than a Turk."[29]

There is tantalizing but not definitive evidence that Menocchio may have read the Qur'an, which had been translated into Italian in 1547, forty years before his first trial. The record of his second trial in 1599 mentions "an unidentified book" that may or may not have been the Qur'an.[30] A mysterious figure named Simon, a Jewish convert to Catholicism Menocchio met in Venice, testified that the miller described a "most beautiful book"—one he lost. And though Menocchio never confirmed the assertion, Simon "judged [this] was the Koran."[31] Geographically and linguistically the text was within the miller's reach, if not his grasp. Menocchio might have even met with real Ottoman Turkish merchants in Venice. Indeed, despite a war between Venice and the Ottomans in 1570, more Turkish Muslim traders resided there in the late sixteenth and early seventeenth centuries than any other European city.[32]

At his second and final trial that began in 1599, the miller Menocchio stood accused of sliding back into his original heretical beliefs. When pressed to implicate others who might share his views, he refused and suffered torture.[33] Menocchio had his arms tied behind his back. He was then hoisted in the air by his wrists, an Inquisition technique designed to dislocate the shoulders. When the miller, hanging by his bound wrists in midair, would not answer the inquisitors, they jerked the rope again. Still, Menocchio would not implicate anyone else. After a half hour, the torture ceased.[34]

Two years later, in 1601, Menocchio received a death sentence from the Inquisition. Branded a heretic, he would die for his unorthodox tolerant beliefs, claiming to the last that they were no one's but his own.[35] Although it is impossible to prove, the miller's ideas about the toleration and salvation of Muslims may have been influenced by so-called heretical Protestant sects such as the Anabaptists, who took up covert residence in northern Italy.[36] Thomas Muntzer (d. 1525), an Anabaptist leader, insisted that "even if someone were born a Turk he still has the beginning of the same faith, that is, the movement of the holy spirit."[37] Meeting in Venice in 1550, the Anabaptists of northern Italy also promoted the idea Menocchio espoused that Jesus was not divine but human.[38] But whatever their origin, Menocchio's ideas about Muslims, Jews, and heretics would remain buried in the records of the Inquisition until they were unearthed by a historian in the twentieth century. They changed no one's mind in the sixteenth century.

By contrast, almost fifty years before the death of the obscure Italian miller, reaction to the immolation of the Protestant heretic Michael Servetus would prompt the first systematic written challenge to the state-sponsored killing of Christian heretics. Toward this end, the text also contained a sampling of the first Protestant attempts to promote an attitude of religious tolerance toward Muslims and Jews in Europe.[39] There were strong precedents for including Muslims in these debates on heretics, because by the twelfth century Islam was often described in Catholic teaching as the "summit of all heresy."[40] Outside of Catholic Spain, where the final expulsion of Muslims would occur between 1609 and 1614, discussions in Western Europe about the treatment of Islamic inhabitants, though still largely theoretical, were increasingly important.

The Death of Michael Servetus, and Sebastian Castellio's First Compendium of Arguments Against the Killing of Heretics, Muslims, and Jews in 1554

Michael Servetus burned at the stake in 1553 before the gates of Geneva, aged approximately forty-two.[41] His 1531 treatise on *The Errors of the Trinity* was condemned by both Protestants and Catholics.[42] Caught earlier by the Catholic Inquisition in France, Servetus fled to the Swiss city of Geneva, where the Protestant reformer Calvin ultimately accused him of two heresies: rejection of the Trinity and infant baptism.[43] It was common at the time for European religious authorities and the state to collaborate in exacting the death penalty for heresies against Christian doctrine. Most Christians in Europe, whatever their denomination, agreed with these theocratic proceedings. But a few did not.

Servetus had been denounced for his ideas by Calvin, but was ultimately condemned by the canton of Geneva, which imposed the capital sentence "in the name of the Father, Son, and Holy Ghost."[44] In his offending treatise, Servetus had argued that the concept of the Trinity could not be found in the New Testament. He did not deny the Trinity doctrine, only the validity of the extrascriptural scholarship on the subject. His work also emphasized the humanity of Jesus.[45] But even to question the derivation of a doctrine accepted by both Catholics and Protestants was enough to condemn Servetus in either Christian sphere.

As a Spaniard, Servetus knew that hundreds of thousands of Jews who refused to convert to Catholicism and accept the Trinity had been expelled from his country in 1492.[46] In addition, thousands of former Muslims and Jews who had nominally adopted Catholicism, often under duress, had been burned at the stake by the Spanish Inquisition in the fifteenth and sixteenth centuries for covertly retaining their own brand of monotheism.[47] Based on logic alone, Servetus asked why Muslims and Jews should be so persecuted for refusing a concept not found in Christian scripture, and whose abstruse nature remained a barrier to the ultimate Christian aim of the conversion of both Muslims and Jews.[48]

Those who attacked Servetus's religious views also impugned his character by inventing tales of his associations with Muslims. They falsely charged that he had visited North Africa to learn Arabic among the local Muslims, a claim based only on the references Servetus made to the Qur'an in his book.[49] According to another accusation made by both Catholics and Protestants, Servetus was the secret ally of the Ottoman sultan.[50] Thus for his doctrinal questioning Servetus was branded a secret Muslim and a political traitor, a supporter of the final Islamic conquest of Europe.

A year after the public immolation of Servetus, Sebastian Castellio composed a treatise entitled *Concerning Heretics: Whether They Are to Be Persecuted and How They Are to Be Treated: A Collection of the Opinions of Learned Men Both Ancient and Modern.* A French Protestant biblical scholar whose work had been condemned by Calvin, Castellio was also known as Sébastien Châteillon, but it was under the pseudonym Martin Bellius that he published his work against the persecution of heretics and Muslims in Basel, Switzerland, in 1554.[51] He argued that the violent behavior of Christians toward those individuals was, ultimately, unchristian and ineffective. "Therefore, to kill a man," he wrote, "is not to defend a doctrine. It is simply to kill a man."[52] Although Castellio admitted that he felt "hate" for heretics, he also worried that those who had been killed did not deserve their fate:[53]

> Although [different religious] opinions are almost as numerous as men, nevertheless there is hardly any sect which does not condemn all others and desire to reign alone. Hence arise the banishments, chains, imprisonments, stakes, and gallows of this miserable rage to visit daily penalties upon those who differ from the mighty about matters hitherto unknown, for so many centuries disputed, and not yet cleared up.[54]

Ultimately, Castellio believed heresy was in the eye of the flawed human accuser. He admitted that divergent religious opinions abounded, but violence toward heretics had not produced the desired end of Christian theological unity. To prove his point, he collected attitudes of religious tolerance among Christian thinkers, from ancient times to those of his own era.

Castellio's knowledge of Islam is notable because most of it was accurate. He identified a commonality of Muslim, Jewish, and Christian belief in the idea that there was "but one God." He noted that "the Turks share with the Christians a higher regard for Christ than that of the Jews." The scholar also knew that "the Turks disagree with the Christians as to the person of Christ, and the Jews with both the Turks and Christians, and the one condemns the other and holds him for a heretic."[55] (Muslims actually did not consider either group as heretics, but rather People of the Book. According to Islamic tradition, Jews and Christians each possessed a divinely revealed scripture—the Torah and Gospels, respectively, but humans had corrupted the true message over time.)

Like Menocchio, Castellio endorsed an attitude of Christian tolerance toward Muslims, but unlike the Italian miller, he believed in the superiority of Christianity over all other, false religions. Muslims, for him, were neither equal as believers nor worthy of salvation. Yet strife among religions did nothing to further the salvation of non-Christians through their conversion to Christianity: "Let not the Jews or Turks condemn the Christians, nor let the Christians condemn the Jews or Turks, but rather teach and win them by true religion and justice."[56]

Castellio implored his fellow believers to lead by noncoercive example: "let us, who are Christians, not condemn one another, but, if we are wiser than they [Muslims and Jews] let us also be better and more merciful." Paramount in his argument was what appeared to be the Golden Rule, an ideal of mutual respect found in both the Hebrew Bible and the Gospels.[57]

When violence happened between Christians, Castellio argued, "[w]e degenerate into Turks and Jews" and cannot convert them.[58] Yet here was the inversion of Menocchio's egalitarian view of the Golden Rule. For Castellio, not only were Muslims and Jews subordinate and degenerate in their beliefs relative to Christians, but their nonviolent treatment was a matter of Christian sufferance, a view that assumed a perpetual Christian majority in power. In fact, missionary efforts, as opposed to martial conflict with Islam, had been debated for centuries in Europe by Christian theologians, with advocates of the peaceful conversion of Muslims dating from the twelfth century.[59]

In the previous chapter we observed both Luther and Calvin's abhorrence of Islam, but in pleading for an end to the state's death penalty for differences in religious doctrine, Castellio's method was to draw upon the scattering of antiviolent, nonpersecutory statements of these men and many others. In Luther, for instance, he found this experience of lenience with regard to non-Christians: "If all the Jews and Turks were killed or tormented none thereby would be overcome and converted to Christ."[60] (Luther would later abandon such practical pacifism, endorsing the death penalty for heretics and others in 1530.[61] Three years before his death, he declared the conversion of the Jews impossible and urged rulers to destroy synagogues as well as Jewish houses and books.)[62]

Words supporting tolerance were even harder to find in Calvin, because he consistently considered heresy treason, worthy of the death penalty.[63] But Castellio managed to find one example of a more tolerant attitude. In 1536, Calvin declared an apparent limit to his motivation to kill unorthodox believers as well as nonbelievers: "we should try by every means, whether by exhortation and teaching, clemency and mildness, or by our prayers to God, to bring them to a better mind that they may return to society and unity of the Church."[64] This approach, argued Calvin, should be applied to "even the Turks and Saracens and other enemies of the true religion."[65] How, Castellio argued, could the Calvin who wrote of such restraint and nonviolence toward non-Christians, then put a fellow Christian like Servetus to death as a heretic?[66] Like Luther's, however, Calvin's support for tolerance toward Muslims and Jews was ephemeral, appearing only in the first edition of his most important work, *Institutes of the Christian Religion.*[67] There is some debate over whether his later removal of this statement signaled a return to a less tolerant and more violent feeling about Muslims and Jews, or instead reflected his view of their collective irrelevance to what had become his more pointed discussion of Christian theology.[68]

Sebastian Franck, Protestant Champion of Muslim Religious Equality

Unlike Luther and Calvin, the Protestant Sebastian Franck (1499–1542 or 1543) expressed ideas about Muslims that the miller Menocchio seemed to share almost fifty years later. Franck, too, argued that God did not play favorites among religions.[69]

Castellio included in his compendium many of Franck's ideas about tolerance toward Muslims. A former Catholic priest, and Lutheran convert, Franck finally cut his ties with any organized religion, endorsing ideas in print that included religious tolerance and freedom of speech, for which he would be imprisoned, then banished from Strassburg in 1529. Despite the popularity of his writings, they were ultimately banned.[70] Banished from other cities for his views, which included sympathy for the heretical Anabaptists, he was forced to move frequently, taking on the manual labor of soap making, while continuing to write theological works.[71] He died in Basel, in his early forties.[72]

Refusing to accept the labeling of fellow Christians as heretics by either the Catholic Church or Protestant authorities, he proclaimed that all those killed as unbelievers were actually "all true Christians."[73] He reviled persecution as a dark human trait.[74] For Franck, individual free will and religious belief were gifts of God, not to be coerced by violence: "Where the Spirit of God is, there is freedom—no constraint, tyranny, partisanship, or compulsion, that He should drag anyone to heaven by the hair or push anyone into hell and deprive him of the grace which is extended to all men. Man alone deprives himself of it."[75]

Franck had much to say about the Turks, but without the malice of most of his contemporaries.[76] He was not unfamiliar with Muslim beliefs and practices, having translated a fifteenth-century Christian account of the Turks in 1529.[77] Far from condemning Muslims, he proposed that "one of the marks of their superiority was their refusal to force anyone to the faith," accurately referring to the Qur'an and Ottoman imperial practice.[78] The Ottoman practice of toleration was also cited by a French Catholic clergyman in a 1554 treatise.[79] In both Protestant and Catholic sixteenth-century contexts, then, the Islamic precedent for religious tolerance was used to critique more immediate denominational differences between Christians.[80]

Franck's tolerance for Christians as well as non-Christians amounted to a form of "universal theism."[81] Most of his contemporaries must have been astonished by his claim, "The Turk and the heathen are made in the image of God as much as the German, and the nonpartisan God has written His law and word in their hearts."[82] Franck insisted:

> Wherefore my heart is alien to none. I have my brothers among the Turks, Papists [Catholics], Jews and all peoples. Not that they are Turks, Jews, Papists, and Sectaries [heretics] or will remain so; in the evening they will be called into the vineyard and given the same wage as we. From the East and from the West children of Abraham will be raised up out of the stones and will sit down with him at God's table.[83]

And so, believing that all the "children of Abraham" could be saved, regardless of their religion, Franck became another perpetrator of the heresy of Origen.

Finding their way into Castellio's treatise, Franck's ideas circulated in print in Latin, French, and German translations. Harsh criticism was immediate. A colleague of Calvin's in Switzerland quickly issued a refutation, blasting the book. Disputes about Castellio's work arose in France, Germany, and Italy.[84] It is possible that through Castellio's publication, Franck's ideas influenced Menocchio's later views of Muslim tolerance and salvation, which were so similar, but this remains unproven.[85]

It was in Holland, where religious diversity and freedom flourished, that Castellio's work gained the widest acceptance.[86] And it was to Holland that the first English Baptists fled in 1608, after suffering persecution in their own country.[87] When one of these early refugees eventually returned to his native land, he would endorse a state policy of toleration toward Muslims. And so though Castellio's work had no

direct influence in seventeenth-century English thought about toleration toward Muslims, it made itself felt indirectly. This English thought
in turn would become the most direct influence on similar American
ideas in the seventeenth and eighteenth centuries.

Thomas Helwys: An Early Baptist Advocates the Toleration of Muslims and Jews in London, 1612

Thomas Helwys (c. 1575–c. 1614), one of the first English Baptists,
was forced to leave home in 1608 because of his religious beliefs. In
Amsterdam in 1612, he published a treatise, *The Mistery of Iniquity,* a
protest against the injustice of English religious persecution.[88] His was
the earliest English-language defense of universal religious toleration to
include Christian heretics along with Muslims and Jews, and although
this combination was not new, the degree of toleration he proposed
as government policy surpassed anything discussed on the Continent.
Helwys declared, "Let them be heretikes, Turcks, Jewes, or whatsoever it apperteynes not to the earthly power to punish them in the
least measure."[89] He returned to England with his book shortly after its
publication.

As a Baptist, Helwys had already been branded a heretic by his
sovereign and the majority of his fellow English Protestants. He had
sacrificed a comfortable life for his religious beliefs. The son of a leading country gentleman, he'd studied the law, married, and sired seven
children. But it was his association with John Smyth (d. 1612), the first
English leader of the Baptist movement, that led him to break from the
Church of England and espouse the idea of the baptism of adult believers, which resulted in the imprisonment of early Baptists in England.
When Helwys left for Holland, his wife, Joan, remained behind and
suffered imprisonment for her beliefs.[90]

Helwys believed Christianity to be the best religion, while all
others were full of grievous errors, a position like Castellio's. But like
Castellio again, he also rejected government coercion regarding faith.
Both wished non-Christians to be converted, but by peaceful means.[91]
The state, Helwys declared, had no right to use violence to persuade,
whether Christian dissenters or non-Christians.

His defense of the religious freedom of Muslims involved two inter-
locking new principles: the separation of the state from control over
religious practice, and the individual's complete liberty of conscience.

He knew that without the first established as government policy, there would be no guarantee of the second. On his return to England in 1612, Helwys would find out quickly how untenable his proposals were.

Helwys addressed his plea directly to King James I (r. 1603–25), reminding the sovereign that he had only civil, not spiritual, authority over his subjects:

> Our lord the King is but an earthly King, and he Hath no aucthority as a King but in the earthly causes, and if the Kings people be obedient and true subjects, obeying all humane laws made by the King, our lord the King can require no more: for mens religion to God is betwixt God and themselves; the King shall not answere for it, neither may the King be jugd betweene God and man.[92]

To the end of this bold statement, Helwys added his judgment that so long as his subjects remained law-abiding, the sovereign had no right to interfere in their spiritual lives, even if they professed Islam or Judaism.

At the time, Muslims from the Ottoman Empire and North African powers visited London on diplomatic and trade missions, but none were counted as inhabitants of the realm.[93] There had been fewer than four thousand Jews when they were officially and completely expelled from England in 1290. Although a few had fled to London from the Spanish Inquisition in the mid-sixteenth century, by the time Helwys wrote his treatise that small group had disappeared.[94] To mention these hypothetical populations, then, was more a symbolic gesture in the larger attempt at truly universal religious toleration. Indeed, after making his case for the protection of heretics, Turks, and Jews, the Baptist added, "or whatsoever," to demand toleration for everyone of every faith without exception, including even the most feared and detested non-Christians.

Helwys's proposal of universal religious toleration as official policy was certain to offend James I, who as king was also supreme head of the Church of England. Helwys's words thus made him not just a heretic but a traitor. Even more subversive than his idea of the toleration of Muslims, Jews, and Christian heretics was this Baptist's call for an end to the persecution of English Catholics.[95] On November 5, 1605, during the reign of the Protestant King James, Catholics disgruntled at the exile of their priests plotted unsuccessfully to blow up Parliament. The conspirators were executed. Helwys would have condemned such lawlessness from anyone of any faith, but Catholics at this time were nevertheless not only numerous in England but universally suspect, and as such did not enjoy full civil rights.

Also on his return to England, Helwys founded the country's first Baptist church in London,[96] in full awareness of "the cost and danger" his beliefs still held for him.[97] Though he probably was never able to present his work to King James personally as intended,[98] he evidently understood the royal wrath, writing that "our lord the king is but dust and ashes as well as we. . . . Yet though he should kill us we will speak the truth to him."[99] Indeed, shortly after his return, Helwys was thrown into Newgate prison, never to regain his freedom. He died there sometime between 1614 and 1616.[100]

Nevertheless, Helwys's insistent call for the separation of government from religious affairs made a unique and resonant contribution to the scope of an idea that would not die with him in England.[101] Following John Smyth, Helwys had defined the proper sphere of government influence as purely civil, based on the division of the two tablets of the Ten Commandments. The first tablet, observed Smyth, concerned commands about the worship of God. They pertained to "matters of conscience," as Smyth defined them. He claimed that the second tablet contained five injunctions that were strictly for civil enforcement:

> That the magistrate is not by virtue of his office to meddle with religion or matters of conscience, to force or compel men to this or that form of religion or doctrine, but to leave Christian religion free to every-man's conscience, and to handle only civil transgressions (Rom. xiii), injuries, and wrongs of man against man in murder, adultery, theft, etc., for Christ only is the king and lawgiver of the church and conscience (James iv.12).[102]

Smyth had limited the king's (or magistrate's) interference into religious matters to Christians. Helwys expanded the scope into a form of universal toleration, which included not just Christian heretics but also Muslims and Jews.[103]

This momentous inclusion of Muslims in defense of religious freedom would not go unnoticed by Roger Williams, an Englishman who would challenge the Puritan theocracy in Massachusetts. He objected to the idea that "Christian liberty" entitled the colony to persecute, jail, or kill Christian dissenters, including Baptists, Quakers, Anglicans, and Catholics, as well as all non-Christians.[104] In devising an alternative for his Rhode Island colony, Williams, briefly a Baptist, would attempt the first experiment in "soul liberty." His settlement would be a refuge where the rights of conscience and religious freedom would be safe from government control for the first time in seventeenth-century America. He would welcome to his colony any who had been persecuted for their religious beliefs, including Muslims.[105]

ROGER WILLIAMS AND MUSLIMS: "SOUL LIBERTY" AND THE SEPARATION OF RELIGION AND STATE IN NORTH AMERICA, 1644

Roger Williams (c. 1606–1683), who had forsaken the Anglican Church for Puritanism while at Cambridge University, had become a minister before leaving England for the Massachusetts Bay Colony in 1631. But four years later he would be banished, having run afoul of the Puritan establishment there. He'd demanded that all Puritan ties to the Anglican Church in England be severed, and he also rejected Puritan claims to land he believed rightfully belonged to Native Americans.[106] More provocative still, he insisted that the Puritan theocracy of Massachusetts Bay did not have the right to enforce their will over individuals in religious matters.[107] Like Helwys and the early Baptists, he believed only the second, civil tablet of the Ten Commandments to be the proper purview of the state.[108]

Williams's exile in 1635 occurred during a bitter New England winter, and he sought refuge among the Native American Narragansett tribe to the south.[109] In 1636, he purchased land from them, founding a town he called Providence in thanks for his deliverance.[110] In 1644, just over thirty years after the Baptist Helwys's bold proposal, Williams wrote a treatise of his own. No doubt influenced by the early Baptists, Williams condemned the role of Calvin in the martyrdom of Servetus in Geneva. He may well have read Castellio's work too.[111] Like Menocchio, Castellio, and Franck before him, Williams had much to say about the rights of Muslims and Jews, but unlike Menocchio and Franck, he believed Christianity to be superior, as had Castellio and Helwys.[112]

As noted in the previous chapter, Williams was aware of Islam's basic premise regarding the Prophet as final messenger in a continuum that included the Hebrew prophets and Jesus. But he rejected this understanding utterly, condemning the Prophet to hell as an impostor who had misled his followers.[113] Contrary to Menocchio and Franck, there would be no salvation for Muslims in Williams's theology. However, he did not deny the right of Muslims to believe, even in what he defined as their "false" faith.[114] Instead, he defended their liberty of conscience, along with all other believers, from state interference. Williams's banishment of government from spiritual matters thus extended even the individual's right to profess a creed that he personally vilified, his own prejudices trumped by the innate rights of any person to adhere to their faith. Needless to say, this was an unpopular idea in Protestant America, and in Providence its feasibility would be put to the test.

A man of deep faith who distrusted organized religion, Williams recognized the moral sensitivity of all individuals as an aspect of their universal humanity.[115] He had disavowed attempts at forced conversion, and now he offered protection to those suffering sometimes violent persecution at the hands of fellow Christians. Although essentially elaborating views that Baptists like Helwys had already expressed, he became the first to put such theories of "toleration," a word he used frequently but apparently disliked, and what he termed "soul liberty" into practice, eventually to be regarded as the nation's "first great defender of natural and religious liberty."[116] And within his espousal of universal toleration, he included numerous explicit references to Muslims and Jews.[117]

Williams's protest against his treatment in Massachusetts, *The Bloudy Tenent, of Persecution for Cause of Conscience,* was published in London in 1644, when Williams returned there to claim a parliamentary charter for territory in what is today the state of Rhode Island. Taking the opportunity to become friendly with the Lord Protector, Oliver Cromwell, and the poet John Milton, he hoped to press his case for freedom from state interference in all spiritual matters on both sides of the Atlantic by addressing his treatise to Parliament.[118]

Cast as a dialogue between Truth and Peace, Williams's *Bloudy Tenent* is rambling and repetitive, yet full of unique insights. It so horrified readers in England that it was publicly burned a month after its publication, but Williams returned to his Rhode Island colony with many copies, intending that it not be ignored, especially in the Massachusetts colony from which he had been expelled.[119] The word "bloudy" in the title meant "intractable," but also alluded to Williams's painful recollection of violent religious persecution in Europe: "the blood of so many hundred thousand soules of Protestants and Papists, spilt in the Wars of present and former Ages, for their respective Consciences, is not required nor accepted by Jesus the Prince of Peace."[120]

Bloudy Tenent focused on Christian political and religious fanaticism, but there are also numerous strategic references scattered throughout the treatise—thirteen in all—to the toleration of Muslims. Most notably, in his introduction, when he enumerated the first twelve theses, Williams ranked as sixth the prohibition of violence against non-Christians, including Turks or Muslims:

> It is the will and command of *God,* that (since the Coming of his Sonne, the *Lord Jesus*) a *permission* of the most *Paganish, Jewish, Turkish,* or *Antichristian consciences* and *worships,* bee granted to *all* men in all *Nations* and *Countries*: and they are onely to bee *fought* against with that *Sword* which is only (in *Soule matters*) *able* to *conquer,* to wit, the *Sword of Gods Spirit,* the *Word* of God.[121]

Like Castellio, Williams here appeared to retain hope for the peaceful conversion of non-Christians, yet his eighth and ninth theses propose that in matters of the soul or conscience the individual should not suffer violent coercion by the state, an early plea for religious freedom from civil control. Later, however, Williams appeared to reject even persuasion in the conversion of Jews and Muslims. Instead, he pled for an end to "our desires and hopes of the Jewes conversion to Christ," in terms that implicitly included such "hopes" for Muslims as well.[122]

Williams's linkage of Turks, Jews, and pagans (by which he meant Native Americans) became a consistent triad in his work "against the bloody *Doctrine of Persecution for cause of conscience*." More than one historian has argued that Williams's repeated enumeration of Jews with Turks and pagans betrayed only an intention to place the former among "the stereotypical alien outside the pale of Christianity."[123] But Williams's main message makes clear that no one is to be excluded from the universal rights he proposed: liberty of conscience and freedom from persecution. Muslims and Jews, he argued, both deserved what all Christians enjoyed, and the onus for this social change rested upon the Christian majority:

> Two *mountaines* of crying *guilt* lye heavie upon the backes of All that name the name of *Christ* in the eyes of *Jewes, Turkes,* and *Pagans.*

First, The blasphemies of their *Idolatrous inventions, superstitions,* and most *unchristian conversations.*

Secondly, The bloody irreligious and inhumane *oppressions* and *destructions* under the maske or vaile of the Name of *Christ,* &c.[124]

In Williams's view, religious error did not prevent non-Christians, including Muslims and Jews, from being loyal subjects, and hence represented no basis for state coercion, whose proper purview was civil order and peace:[125]

And I aske whether or no such as may hold forth other *Worships* or *Religions* (*Jews, Turkes,* or *Antichristians*) may not be peaceable and quiet *Subjects,* loving and helpfull *neighbours,* faire and just *dealers,* true and loyall to the *civill government?* It is cleare they may from all *Reason* and *Experience* in many flourishing *Cities* and *Kingdomes* of the World, and so offend not against the *civill State* and *Peace;* nor incurre the punishment of the *civill Sword* . . .[126]

In Williams's words may be heard references to tolerant precedents. Calling non-Christian neighbors "peaceable" but also "loving and helpful" echoes the Golden Rule, while "reason and experience in many other flourishing cities and kingdoms" may allude to Holland, where religious toleration for all Christians, including Jews, had been noted in England as a directly positive contribution to their national success in trade and commerce.[127]

Williams's treatise challenged the very basis of the Massachusetts Bay theocracy that had expelled him, in particular the minister John Cotton (d. 1652), whose religious authority helped enforce Williams's political exile and to whose refutation Williams dedicated his effort.[128] Five years earlier, in *A Discourse about Civil Government,* Cotton warned of the dangers of allowing "heretics" and Muslims to interfere with the established Puritan religious and political order.[129] Insisting that only those in complete spiritual accord with the Commonwealth's Puritan faith should be allowed to govern, Cotton asserted that this same principle undergirded Muslim rule in the Ottoman Empire: "Yea, in Turkey itself, they are careful that none but a man devoted to Mahomet bear publick Office." What Cotton believed essential in his Christian Commonwealth (and all others) was a "form of Government as best serveth to Establish their Religion," as the only one "Established in the

Civil State."[130] Williams by contrast saw no necessity, only harm from this fusion of the spiritual and the civil function of government.

Citing the Gospel of Matthew, Williams argued that it was not for humans to decide upon uprooting the "tares," or weeds, from the garden. He argued that Christ himself condemned the destruction of Christian heretics and non-Christians as tares among the Christian wheat, and that the only legitimate judgment would be made at the Second Coming, which he believed to be imminent: "Christ commandeth to let alone the *Tares* and *Wheat* to grow together unto the *Harvest* Mat 13.30.38."[131] Williams does not subscribe to the heresy that all can be saved, regardless of their faith, believing the prospect of non-Christian salvation grim, but he insists that the fate of Christian and non-Christian alike will be decided on the Day of Judgment. And meanwhile, Jesus's example would remain the best argument against religious persecution on earth: "Christ calleth for *Toleration*, not for *penall prosecution*."[132] Williams, unlike his predecessors, frequently used the word "toleration," though he emphasized the sanctity of conscience, as had the early Baptist Smyth.

In 1647, John Cotton responded to what he deemed outlandish ideas with another tract entitled *The Bloudy Tenent, Washed and Made White in the Bloud of the Lamb.* After asserting that he had not personally persecuted Williams, Cotton refused Williams's analogy of toleration and leaving judgment to God as described in Matthew; to do so was to allow the spread of "dangerous" and "damnable infection."[133] Williams had the final word in 1652, the last year of Cotton's life, when he published another attack against him in *The Bloody Tenent Yet More Bloody.* Addressed to the English Parliament, Williams's new tract cited the example of Holland, which he said had "paid so dearly for the purchase of their freedoms," but had finally learned "that one poor lesson of setting absolutely the consciences of all men free."[134]

Williams had been, at least for a few months in 1638 or 1639, a Baptist.[135] Indeed, he helped found America's first Baptist church in Providence, but he began to regret his decision to join after a few months.[136] Ultimately, though Williams realized that no earthly organized church could fulfill his needs, he would continue to welcome Baptists fleeing persecution in Massachusetts for Rhode Island, and also the Quakers, a sect persecuted in both England and North America. Such was his principled tolerance that the refuge he gave Quakers came despite having disputed Quaker leaders in Newport for three days in 1672 and writing a tract attacking their beliefs in 1676.[137]

In 1655, while serving as the elected president of the Providence Plantations, Williams described his vision of the ideal government, one that made room for Muslims, Jews, and Catholics, as long as they obeyed civil authority in earthly matters.[138] Almost a decade after he had first imagined universal toleration, Williams adopted a new metaphor to define his ideal society:[139]

There goes many a ship to sea, with many hundred souls in one ship, whose weal and woe is common, and is a true picture of a commonwealth, or a human combination or society. It hath fallen out sometimes, that both papists and protestants, Jews and Turks, may be embarked on one ship; upon which supposal I affirm, that all the liberty of conscience, that ever I pleaded for, turns upon these two hinges— that none of the papists, protestants, Jews or Turks, be forced to come to the ship's prayers or worship, if they practice any. I further add, that I never denied, that notwithstanding this liberty, the commander of the ship ought to command the ship's course, yea, and also command that justice, peace and sobriety, be kept and practiced, both among the seamen and all the passengers.[140]

In Williams's ideal, religiously plural society, passengers might even refuse to come to prayers.[141] In a swipe at Puritan Massachusetts, he described his model as "the true picture of a commonwealth," a society whose "weal and woe" is common to all.

In reality, no Muslims, Jews, or Catholics applied to join Williams's experiment in religious liberty and pluralism. In 1656 or 1658, a few Jews from Spain and Portugal arrived in Newport, only to leave before a second group arrived in 1678.[142] But they lived outside of Williams's Providence jurisdiction. There is thus no way to know whether the political equality for those non-Christians who figured so consistently in his writings ever would have worked in practice.[143] Still, it seems likely that at the very least he would have offered the adherents of Islam safe harbor in Providence. He had despised, debated, and vilified the beliefs of the Quakers by comparing them to Muslims, and yet in practice, Williams had continued to offer Quakers a protected place in his colony.

TOLERATION IN AMERICAN PRACTICE:
THE FLUSHING REMONSTRANCE, 1657

Two years after Williams framed his vision of a multireligious ship of state, thirty-one residents of the Dutch territory of Flushing, in New Amsterdam (now Long Island, New York), would advocate a similar tolerated protection for both Christians and non-Christians. They had never read Roger Williams, but as Williams himself was well aware, the Dutch had their own history of religious toleration. Freedom of conscience had been guaranteed by Article 13 of the Dutch Union of Utrecht in 1579.[144] Yet how applicable was this precedent across the Atlantic? That would become clear when the principle of freedom of conscience was threatened in 1657.

Like the Puritans of Massachusetts, Dutch authorities feared the spread of Protestant sects outside their tradition, most particularly Baptists and Quakers.[145] Peter Stuyvesant, the Dutch director-general of the territory, "commanded" that "no conventicles or meetings shall be kept in this Province" other than those of the Dutch Reformed Church.[146] By Dutch law, a "conventicle" was defined as a public gathering for worship that included many families, and it was a legal practice for the state's Dutch Reformed Church, but not for other religions in Holland.[147] While not abrogating the guarantee of liberty of conscience, Stuyvesant did threaten to curtail freedom of public worship for those outside the state church. But this distinction between individual religious belief and public practice was not acceptable to some in Stuyvesant's colony.[148]

Thirty-one residents of Flushing and Jamaica signed what would later be known as the Flushing Remonstrance, astutely characterized by Neil Kamil as "seventeenth-century 'multiculturalism' . . . extending even to the Jews and Islam."[149] The signatories charged Stuyvesant with interfering in matters of conscience and refused to participate in what they deemed the persecution of Quakers and Baptists. As an alternative, they promoted a form of "Christian *inclusiveness*," which now had precedents in Rhode Island, England, and the European continent:[150]

> [W]ee desire therefore in this case not to judge lest wee be judged neither to Condemn lest wee bee Condemned but rather let every man stand and fall to his own. Maister wee are bounde by the Law to doe good unto all men, especially to those of the Household of faith.[151]

In addition to proclaiming the individuality of faith, the signatories made the point that the state was without power to mediate for human salvation: "who shall pleade for us in the case of Conscience betwixt god and our owne soules the power of this world can neither attack us neither excuse us for if god justifye who can Condemn and if god Condemn there is none can justifye."[152]

Referring to the standard in their native Holland for a freedom of conscience that included Muslims (termed "Turkes and Egiptians") and Jews, they asserted:

> The law of love peace and libertie in the states extending to *Jewes Turkes* and *Egiptians* as they are Considered the sonnes of Adam which is the glory of the outward State of *Holland,* soe love peace and libertie extending to all in Christ Jesus Condemns hatred, warre and bondage . . . desireing to doe unto all men as wee desire all men shoulde doe unto us which is the true law both of Church and State.[153]

Such protestations, however, did not stop Director-General Stuyvesant from arresting a notable Quaker named John Bowne, imprisoning him, and, ultimately, banishing him from Dutch territory, just as he would arrest and banish Tobias Feake, the first to sign the Remonstrance.[154]

The Immediate Failure of Williams's Ideas and Their Possible Later Impact, 1663

In 1663, Roger Williams was forced by competing claims to apply for a new charter for his Providence colony, finally receiving one from Charles II (r. 1660–85). In it the king confirmed the individual's right to freedom of religious practice:

> Our royal will and pleasure is that no person within the said colony, at any time hereafter, shall be in any wise molested, punished, disquieted, or called into question, for difference in opinion in matters of religion, [that] do not actually disturb the civil peace of our said colony; but that all and every persons may, from time to time, and at all times hereafter, freely and fully have and enjoy his and their own judgments and consciences in matters of religious concernment.[155]

Williams joyfully declared, "Our Charter excels all in New England or the world as to the souls of men."[156] An exact echo of this promise of freedom of conscience "in matters of religious concernment" would appear in 1664 in New Jersey's charter and again in 1665 in the charter for the two Carolinas.[157] But Williams rejoiced too soon. His treatises on religious persecution failed to persuade the English Parliament to extend his vision of toleration to Muslims or Jews.[158] Failing to become a legal precedent, his precocious idea about extending liberty of conscience to Muslims would have no direct influence on Thomas Jefferson or other pivotal figures of the American Revolutionary era more than one hundred years later.[159] Even his books, which remained rare in Massachusetts, would not be accessible to most Americans. Not until the nineteenth century would any work of his be republished in the United States.[160]

Nevertheless, many of Williams's key ideas appear to resurface in John Locke's pivotal *A Letter Concerning Toleration* (1689), though a direct connection is difficult to prove.[161] Locke (1632–1704) was only twelve when Roger Williams's *Bloudy Tenent, of Persecution for Cause of Conscience* was published in London, but forty-five years later he would reach remarkably similar conclusions concerning the toleration of Muslims.[162] Locke, a great borrower, never credited Roger Williams as a source, possibly because he had other, closer sources of inspiration.[163] And while both men supported the religious liberty of Muslims and their civil toleration in a Christian polity, they approached the issue differently.[164]

In his letter, Locke emphasized a new theory of inalienable natural rights, derived from reason, in contrast to Williams's exclusively theological claim.[165] Locke's ideas about toleration evolved over time; indeed, they reversed direction from intolerance early in his career toward toleration as a state policy in his later thought. His references to Muslims, however, remained constant, despite his change of mind on the broader, more pressing issue of the toleration of Christian heretics, or dissenters, from the Anglican Church. As with Williams, his views would force him to write about religious toleration in exile. Ultimately, Locke would first promote "civil rights" for Muslims, moving beyond Williams, but he would not divorce this idea completely from the precedents of the Gospels. He maintained that it was a Christian duty to tolerate most others in a predominantly Anglican Protestant state.[166]

John Locke in the "Age of Arabick": His Interest in Islam and Toleration, 1646–71

In England, "the Age of Arabick," to use G. A. Russell's evocative phrase, began during John Locke's lifetime as a thinker and writer, and Locke's education included exposure to Arabic and Islam as well as scholars of Islamic history.[167] A chair in Arabic was established at Oxford University in 1636, when Locke was four years old.[168] Underlying this new interest in the language was a combination of theological, diplomatic, and commercial developments. Protestants who wished to study the Hebrew Bible found Arabic, also a Semitic language, philologically helpful. In 1580 Elizabeth I had licensed the Turkey Company, which a decade later became the Levant Company, to do business in the Ottoman Empire.[169] More immediate contacts resulted from the rise of North African pirates in the Atlantic and Mediterranean from Elizabethan times to the mid-eighteenth century. The threat to English shipping necessitated constant attempts at negotiating treaties and ransoming English captives, for which Arabic was needed.[170]

Locke probably first studied Arabic in 1647 at Westminster, his secondary school, where his headmaster emphasized the language, having become convinced at Oxford of its importance.[171] At Christ Church College, Oxford, in 1652, while he also studied history, astronomy, and mathematics, Locke probably attended twice-weekly Hebrew and Arabic instruction,[172] delivered by Dr. Edward Pococke, who held the chair in both languages.[173] While there is no evidence that he ever used the language in his research, it is known that Locke developed close friendships with those who taught and translated Arabic, and by 1660 Dr. Pococke was one of them, a professor "he most revered."[174] Locke would later also tutor Pococke's son, also named Edward.

Under his father's supervision, the younger Pococke translated *Hayy ibn Yaqzan*, a medieval Arabic philosophical text by Ibn Tufayl, a native of Granada, who served at the court of a North African dynasty.[175] The work, known as *Philosophus Autodidactus* in Latin, was an allegorical tale whose hero, alone on an island from infancy, demonstrates that his innate powers of observation and reason are sufficient to master all knowledge.[176] The Arabic title in English stresses instead the relationship of the protagonist, Hayy ("Alive"), to his mind and soul's realization of God.

Pococke's Latin translation created a sensation in Europe, where it was repeatedly reprinted, influencing many European thinkers, including the English Quaker George Keith.[177] Translated later into English, the text inspired Daniel Defoe's 1719 novel *Robinson Crusoe*.[178] By 1721, the impact of the Islamic text would be noted across the Atlantic in Massachusetts, where the Puritan Cotton Mather took time off from his vilification of the Prophet as Antichrist to praise this medieval Muslim philosopher's idea that reason and revelation could be reconciled in natural philosophy.[179]

Locke may also have drawn inspiration for empirical philosophy in his *Essay on Human Understanding* from Pococke's translation first published in 1671, the very year in which Locke began his *Essay,* which was published in 1690.[180] Indeed, Locke's concept of the human mind as a blank slate, capable of acquiring all knowledge though empirical observation, is tantalizingly similar to ideas expressed in the medieval Islamic philosopher's allegory, even if Locke left no direct evidence of the influence of this work on his thought.[181] As to Locke's ideas on religious toleration, those exemplified by Hayy, who refuses to use coercion to rescue others from religious error and accepts the existence of other faiths, also bear comparison.[182] But Locke had begun to read about toleration directly more than a decade earlier in the work of the English author Henry Stubbe.[183]

HENRY STUBBE: TOLERATION AND A DEFENSE OF ISLAM, 1659–71

Locke's first documented interest in religious toleration was prompted by a 1659 treatise by Henry Stubbe (1632–1676), a fellow student of Arabic at Westminster and Christ Church, Oxford.[184] Stubbe's *An Essay in Defence of the Good Old Cause, or a Discourse concerning the Rise and Extent of the Power of the Civil Magistrate in reference to Spiritual Affairs* sought to define the proper limit of political authority regarding religion and outlined a history of religious toleration. After reading the book, Locke wrote the author full of praise for the "strength and vigor" of his style, suggesting that Stubbe expand his history of toleration to include Holland, France, and Poland.[185] As to Stubbe's belief that government authorities should not meddle in religion, and that individual faith was a matter better left between the believer and God, Locke, while not explicitly disagreeing, did not share these ideas at the time.[186]

He did, however, warn Stubbe that toleration for Catholics was a mistake, believing their loyalty to the pope made their civil allegiance suspect. The disagreement did not prevent him from signing his letter to Stubbe, "your Admirer."[187]

In 1671, the same year that Locke read Pococke's Latin translation, Stubbe attempted the first sustained English defense of Islam and its Prophet. Presenting Islam as a more tolerant faith than Christianity, Stubbe contrasted it with his own Christian society's intolerance, but his rigorous defense of Islam and critique of English religious persecution proved too inflammatory for publication, and his work circulated only in manuscript form.[188]

An Account of the Rise and Progress of Mahometanism: with the Life of Mahomet and a Vindication of him and his Religion from the Calumnies of the Christians drew heavily upon Dr. Pococke's Latin translations of early Islamic history, suggesting that the author of the first English treatise defending Islam was, like Locke, unable or unwilling to use Arabic, or else found it unnecessary.[189] Stubbe's intention was to assault the "great untruths" and "little integrity" in Christian histories of Islam,[190] single-handedly challenging a millennium of anti-Islamic Christian polemic. Unlike all of his predecessors, he characterized the seventh-century Islamic conquests of the Middle East as "that Stupendous Revolution." He postulated that the triumph of Islam could be explained in part by Christianity's being weak, rife with "irreligion, impiety, & division into Sects,"[191] in what was clearly also a comment on circumstances in seventeenth-century England.

But while aiming to correct certain prevailing distortions, Stubbe made several glaring mistakes of his own. He claimed, for instance, that the Prophet traveled to North Africa and Spain during his lifetime, and served in Christian armies under a powerful early convert named Abu Bakr (d. 634), whom Stubbe claimed to be his uncle, but was actually his father-in-law.[192] Finally, following one of the more common Christian misrepresentations of Islamic tradition, Stubbe insisted that the Prophet "wrote" the Qur'an.[193]

Stubbe praised the Prophet as a political leader, contradicting what he described as "the Calumnies charged upon him by the Christians." His Muhammad was an "extraordinary person," of "ready Wit," "penetrating Judgment," and "undaunted courage," who was "equally qualified for Actions of Warr, or the Arts of Peace and civil Government."[194] At the same time, Stubbe expressed admiration for Islam's emphasis on the oneness of God and its rejection of the Trinity, which he attributed to the influence of Arianism, a Christian heresy.[195] By implication, then, the Prophet Muhammad's religion was not new; he had revived an early, truer form of Christianity, in which the Trinity and Jesus's divinity were later corruptions.[196] Clearly, Stubbe's support for these unorthodox and unpopular ideas made him a Christian heretic.

Polygamy and warfare, two aspects of Islam historically denigrated by Christian authors, also found a champion in Stubbe. Stubbe reminded readers that King David had been a polygamist. Rather than institutionalizing licentiousness, Stubbe argued, the Prophet had solved a social problem because, as he asserted strangely, "East and South" "there are far more Women than Men." In the chapter devoted to "the justice of the Mahometan Warrs," Stubbe refuted as "a falsehood" the notion that Islam was spread by the sword.[197] At the same time, he noted that many Christian theologians had addressed spreading their own faith by force, a premise the author rejected.[198]

Stubbe emphasized that the Islamic precedent for the toleration of Christians and Jews came from the Qur'an, was practiced by the successors of the Prophet during the conquest of the Middle East, and continued to protect the Christians of the Ottoman Empire.[199] The lesson for his readers? Toleration for fellow Christians would promote peaceful coexistence and prevent the sort of civil strife witnessed repeatedly in seventeenth-century England.[200]

Noting that "Christians and other Religions might peaceably subsist under their Protection, if they payed the Tribute demanded," meaning the annual poll tax called the *jizya,* Stubbe implied that Christians defined as heretics in England might in fact be better treated in the Islamic world: "As Mahomet persecuted none for Religion, who believed one God & the day of Judgment, so lest of all the Christians, who, as we have seen before, enjoyed more of his Favours than any of the other Religions."[201] That he "did not see fit to publish" his manuscript may well suggest he knew that King Charles II would have answered such criticism with prison or worse.[202]

Stubbe's treatise would remain unpublished during Locke's lifetime, but as a friend and correspondent, Locke may have had access to the widely circulated manuscript.[203] In his later work on toleration, Locke also notes the Ottoman Turkish toleration of Christians, but this does not appear to be the origin of his support for the "civil rights" of Muslims.[204] Still, plagiarized parts of Stubbe's manuscript would find their

way into the English Deist Charles Blount's *Oracles of Reason* (1693), four
years after Locke's first letter on toleration was published, as part of the
connection between Deism's remote but unitary God and the God of
Islam that was first established in late-seventeenth-century England.[205]
A form of this heretical association with Islam would be linked to Locke
at the end of his life.[206]

The partial appearance of Stubbe's treatise in the Deist Blount's work
may have in turn provoked Humphrey Prideaux's 1697 attack on the
Prophet Muhammad, which was also intended as an indictment of the
ideas of English Deists.[207] By the end of the seventeenth century, not
only Deists but Unitarians (as the Socinians, who rejected the Trinity,
came to be known) and Muslims were "linked in the public mind,"
according to James Jacob.[208] More recently, John Marshall has asserted
that "Islam was thus central to tolerationist debates in late seventeenth-
century England because of the similarities alleged between Islam and
anti-Trinitarianism," including both Deism and Unitarian thought.[209]
Both were heresies in need of extirpation in the eyes of Anglican Protestants like Humphrey Prideaux, who compared them to Islam.[210] By
contrast, the English minority who embraced Deist or Unitarian viewpoints often represented Islam in a positive light, presenting it as one
of three similar "pristine" monotheisms, its revelations equal to but not
surpassing those of the Old and New Testaments.[211] But such relatively
positive views of Islam were limited to the extent that the faith mir-
rored their own heterodox Deist and Unitarian Christian-based theologies. In 1682, English Unitarians attempted to meet with the Moroccan
ambassador in London to discuss their theological unity.[212] Locke knew
about this meeting and wrote an acquaintance for a description of the
Muslim ambassador.[213] He would eventually in his work on toleration
defend both Unitarians and Muslims from persecution. In other ways,
the same English Protestants also simultaneously denigrated Islam in
order to critique repressive Anglican Christianity, the established faith
of the English government. And so Islam, understood on its own terms,
remained selectively overwritten and frequently distorted.[214]

Views like Prideaux's anti-Islamic, anti-Deist, and anti-Unitarian
arguments would prevail among Protestants into the eighteenth century.[215] Prideaux eventually rose through the Anglican clerical ranks to
become dean of Norwich.[216] In contrast, Stubbe's surreptitiously circulated manuscript in defense of Islam would not be published in England
until 1911, thanks to a subscription by a group of Muslims residing in

London.[217] Although Humberto Garcia has emphasized the importance and scope of Stubbe's underground circulation in England, his views in praise of Islamic toleration did not contribute directly to debates about Muslim rights or citizenship in the Anglo-Atlantic world, having been limited to the reform of English religious and political liberties.[218]

Locke's long association with the seditious Lord Shaftesbury, a founder of the opposition Whig party and advocate of religious and civil toleration for dissenters but not Catholics, resulted in suspicion falling on Locke too. (Locke never knew that Prideaux, a copy of whose anti-Islamic polemic Locke owned, had spied on him at Oxford in 1681, reporting directly to Charles II's undersecretary of state.)[219] Locke wrote a pamphlet to aid Shaftesbury's defense, which only exacerbated suspicions about the author. After his exoneration at trial, Shaftesbury fled to Holland in 1682, where he died the next year. In 1683, Shaftesbury's radical Whig associates plotted to assassinate the king and his brother. Although Locke's involvement in this conspiracy is also debated by scholars, his acquaintance with the conspirators put him at risk.[220] He too fled to Holland in 1683, where he remained active in opposition to the government. By 1685, all associates of the Whig movement in England had been removed from office, imprisoned, or fled the country amid renewed persecution of religious dissenters. Locke's support for the failed insurrection forced him to live in hiding in Holland beginning in 1685, when the rule of the Catholic James II (r. 1685–88) began.[221] It was then that he began to write his first letter on toleration.

Locke would travel throughout the Netherlands during his exile, but his idea of religious toleration for Muslims had already been formed in England a quarter century before. He had acquired it from someone with whom he disagreed, initially, about the toleration of Christian dissenters.

LOCKE'S PRECEDENT FOR THE TOLERATION OF MUSLIMS, DRAWN FROM EDWARD BAGSHAW IN 1660

Unlike Stubbe, Locke never found in Islam a theology or a prophet worthy of praise.[222] Yet Locke chose to use the example of Muslims in England to advance the toleration of Christian dissenters there, building initially on a conceptual connection that had originated in Europe in the sixteenth century. Both the Baptist Helwys and Roger Williams had already advocated complete religious liberty for Muslims (in

1612 and 1644 respectively), together with the separation of church and state, based on purely Christian references to Jesus and the New Testament. Locke took the same cause but argued for it as an individual right grounded in "immutable principles of reason." His *A Letter Concerning Toleration* (1689) would be far more influential than either of these earlier works.[223]

Locke may have been aware of both Helwys and Williams, but his most direct influence was Edward Bagshaw's work *The Great Question concerning Things Indifferent in Religious Worship*, published in 1660.[224] Bagshaw (1629 or 1630–1671) was a fellow graduate of Westminster and Christ Church, Oxford, but unlike the Anglican Locke, he was a Christian dissenter for whom the matter of religious freedom for non-Anglicans was of more personal urgency.

As shown by Nabil Matar, Bagshaw was the first to make the case for greater toleration of Christian dissenters in England, based on an analogy to the protections already extended to Muslims and Jews by Cromwell's government (1649–60) for the purpose of increasing trade.[225] In 1656 Jews were allowed to return to England, for the first time since the Edict of Expulsion forced them out in 1290.[226] Muslim diplomats, traders, and possibly a very few English converts to Islam seem also to have practiced their faith privately without government interference.[227]

Locke would cite Bagshaw in his own unpublished *Two Tracts on Government* (1660–61):[228] "'tis agreed that a Christian magistrate cannot force his religion on a Jew or a Mahomedan, therefore much less can he abridge his fellow-Christian in things of lesser moment."[229] But while Bagshaw supported complete religious toleration for all Christians, arguing that they should enjoy whatever protections Muslims and Jews already did, Locke rejected toleration for Christian dissenters. In 1660, he still believed the magistrate or king had power over religious issues where Christians were concerned. It made sense to him, since at the time he was interested in promoting civil order, not toleration per se.[230]

What is most interesting, however, is that Locke, again according to Nabil Matar, "rejected neither the presence nor the toleration of Muslims and Jews" while accepting the "political logic" behind royal religious authority over non-Anglican dissenters and Catholics. Locke rejected any English ruler's interference with Muslim or Jewish practice because it would "give Christian legitimacy to a non-Christian belief."[231]

By 1667, Locke had reversed his views about the king's right to interfere with Christian dissenters, while his support for the toleration of Muslims and Jews endured unchanged.[232] In his *An Essay Concerning Toleration,* he presented two pragmatic reasons for the toleration of dissenting Christians: The individual's relationship to God could pose no danger to society, and the ruler was not infallible in matters spiritual.[233] By this time, Locke had also rejected religious coercion for both political and moral reasons, charging that such tactics did not change belief and only provoked opposition to the government. What accounts for this shift is unclear, but his arguments moved closer toward depriving the state of control over religion.[234]

In 1685, as Locke began *A Letter Concerning Toleration,* the issue of religious toleration continued as a pressing public concern.[235] He became close friends with men of various Christian denominations deemed heretical, and listened to their arguments in favor of toleration.[236] The same year, Locke watched as French Protestants, or Huguenots, fled their country for Holland after King Louis XIV revoked the Edict of Nantes, which had previously provided them some protection from Catholic persecution.[237] Important works on toleration by Huguenot refugees, such as Pierre Bayle (d. 1706), with whom Locke met in 1687 or 1688, also came to his attention.[238] While preserving Bagshaw's 1660 justification for the toleration of Muslims and Jews, Locke also noted Bayle's assertion that "Pagans, Jews and Turks have a right to it," meaning religious toleration, a statement that predated that of Locke, who developed his own more expansive plea to include Christian dissenters and non-Christians.[239]

LOCKE'S EMPHASIS ON MUSLIM CIVIL RIGHTS IN HIS FIRST LETTER ON TOLERATION, 1689

Accepting that a handful of Muslims were probably already lodged in London for diplomatic or trade purposes, Locke did not consider the practice of Islam a barrier to residence or rights in his country.[240] Under English law, "aliens" including Muslims were divided into "friends" and "enemies,"[241] but a mid-seventeenth-century ruling designated resident Muslims as friends, thus obviating any "enmity" toward "Turks" or "Infidels."[242] But while religious persecution of Muslims was forbidden, as aliens they were still denied full citizenship.[243] Locke's advocacy of equal "civil rights" for Muslims rejected their designation as "denizens," a subcategory for non-English and non-Christian alien residents.[244] With one key qualification, Locke proposed that Muslims be granted the same legal rights to religious toleration and, presumably, citizenship that he also insisted upon for Christian dissenters.

Locke's proposal carefully disqualified all those who would hold primary allegiance to "another Prince," a foreign Muslim ruler, and would thus be deemed enemy aliens in England.[245] In particular, Locke worried about adherence to Islamic law as a sign of allegiance to the Ottoman sultan, though as John Marshall suggests in his magisterial study of Locke, his concerns would have included only a "small" number of Muslims.[246] Locke wrote:

> It is ridiculous for any one to profess himself to be a *Mahumetan* in his Religion, but in every thing else a faithful Subject to a Christian Magistrate, whilst at the same time he acknowledges himself bound to yield blind obedience to the *Mufti of Constantinople;* who himself is intirely obedient to the Ottoman Emperor, and frames the feigned Oracles of that Religion according to his pleasure. But this Mahumetan living among Christians, would yet more apparently renounce their Government, if he acknowledged the same Person to be Head of his Church who is the Supreme Magistrate in the State.[247]

Locke revealed some basic misconceptions by referring to the mufti of Constantinople. He probably meant instead the position of *shaykh al-Islam,* also known as the chief mufti of Istanbul, whose role in the Ottoman Empire had evolved by the seventeenth century to allow him to render verdicts in consultation with the sultan on policy issues, such as war and peace.[248] But far from being subject to the sultan, this legal expert often was consulted about the ruler's depositions. In any case, the function of the chief mufti was not to demand religious and political allegiance from Muslims outside the Ottoman sphere.[249] Nor would all Muslims with dealings in England in the seventeenth century owe allegiance to the Ottoman Empire. Moroccans, for example, had first established trade relations with England under Ahmad al-Mansur (d. 1603), who was never subject to the Ottomans; neither were those Moroccan rulers who founded the Alawi dynasty in 1664.[250] As for rulers in Algiers, Tunis, and Tripoli, while they had acknowledged Ottoman rule in the sixteenth century, during the seventeenth century as they became more autonomous, that allegiance became increasingly nominal.

Whether Muslims could properly reside outside Muslim lands had been vigorously debated by Islamic legal scholars, beginning in the eighth century. Although theoretically the world might be divided between the land of Islam (where the Sharia, or Islamic law, prevailed) and the land of war or unbelief, in practice Muslim minorities continued to live in non-Muslim territory for a variety of historical reasons. Among the four schools of Sunni law, no consensus on the issue was reached between the twelfth and seventeenth centuries.[251] The exception to this diversity of legal opinion was the Maliki school, which predominated in North Africa, where memories of warfare with Catholic Spain and Portugal and the expulsion of Muslims in the sixteenth and seventeenth centuries remained fresh, resulting in doctrinaire insistence on residence only in Islamic lands, though exceptions were made for specific contexts of war or peace, and living in a non-Muslim country for the purpose of trade, for example, was allowed.[252]

The Islamic judgment about residing outside of Islamic dominion often hinged on whether Muslims could safely practice their faith, something that Locke would guarantee later in his treatise.[253] The question divided Sunni and Shi'i Muslim jurists.[254] Locke might have been interested to know, although he probably did not, that Sunni scholars presumed that non-Muslim authorities would offer an *aman,* or "safe conduct" guarantee, to a Muslim resident.[255] As part of what would have been deemed reciprocity for tolerance of Christians in Islamic realms, it was generally accepted that a Muslim living outside of the Islamic world "may not commit acts of treachery, betrayal, deceit or fraud, and may not violate the honor or property of non-Muslims."[256] By this arrangement, Muslims could abide by the local Christian ruler's authority in civil if not religious matters. Here in essence is exactly what Locke would demand as a precondition for Muslim citizenship and elevation from resident alien status: "But those whose Doctrine is peaceable, and whose Manners are pure and blameless, ought to be on equal Terms with their Fellow-Subjects."[257]

Locke's concern about the divided allegiance of Muslims in England is perhaps a reflection of his more immediate anxieties about Catholics, whom he distrusted for their allegiance to the pope.[258] By contrast, these concerns were based on history as well as paranoia. (Accusations in 1678 of a "Popish Plot" to assassinate the king and institute Catholicism, though spurious, were not forgotten.) There was no real parallel between a Catholic's obedience to the pope and the individual Muslim's relationship to the Ottoman sultan. Locke would eventually determine that Catholics who disavowed allegiance to the pope should also qualify for full civil rights, but he would remain wary of them.[259] Catholics would continue to represent an imminent rather than a theoretical threat to Anglican Protestant government.

In Locke's 1689 *A Letter Concerning Toleration* his pivotal statement about Muslim civil rights followed immediately after his defense of Christian dissenters of various sects. Among them, Socinians (later Unitarians) were included in his original Latin text published in Holland, but not the English translation of the same year.[260] Socinians were of course also present in England, and their views were well known to Locke. He certainly would have approved the first, anonymous edition of the English translation. Locke's first English translator, William Popple, a supporter of religious toleration, was an avowed Socinian. Popple may have omitted Socinians knowing that they (and he) would continue to be denied religious and political rights because of their rejection of the Trinity, even after the 1689 Act of Toleration granting protection to all Protestants who embraced the triune divinity.[261] Popple doubtless appreciated how dangerous the mention of his own outlawed beliefs remained. Also excluded in the act were Roman Catholics, atheists, and, implicitly, Muslims and Jews. The English Socinian's translation of Locke was destined for enormous popularity and longevity on both sides of the Atlantic:

> But those whose Doctrine is peaceable, and whose Manners are pure and blameless, ought to be upon equal Terms with their Fellow-Subjects. Thus if Solemn Assemblies, Observations of Festivals, publick Worship, be permitted to any one sort of Professors; all these things ought to be permitted to the *Presbyterians, Independents, Anabaptists, Arminians, Quakers*, and others, with the same liberty.[262]

It was at this critical juncture in his defense of Christian dissenters in England, that Locke now demanded the same civil equality for Muslims and Jews:[263]

> Nay, if we may openly speak the Truth, and as becomes one Man to another, neither *Pagan*, nor *Mahumetan*, nor *Jew*, ought to be excluded from the Civil Rights of the Commonwealth, because of his Religion.[264]

Inverting the logic of Bagshaw's 1660 precedent, which argued for extending Muslim and Jewish prerogatives to Christian dissenters, Locke now argued that if all Christians deserved civil rights, so too did non-Christians, a case he made only *after* his earlier qualification about the potential for Muslim foreign loyalties. There is a further emendation of Locke's original Latin text: Popple's addition of the phrase "Civil Rights." A more literal translation of Locke's Latin would read "neither Pagan nor Mahometan nor Jew should be excluded from the commonwealth because of his religion."[265] But Locke approved this change and went on to defend the concept of "civil rights" for Muslims and Jews in three subsequent English letters.[266]

Locke's was not "the first favorable pronouncement about the status of Muslims in Christian England"—Helwys and Williams had preceded him in that—but it was the earliest, most resonant attempt to make the case as part of a political rather than purely religious argument.[267] Nevertheless, Locke's ultimate argument that Muslims ought not to be excluded from "the civil rights of the commonwealth" still rested on his assertion, "The Gospel commands no such thing." And so Locke promoted a reasoned, Christian argument for the toleration of non-Christians in "a Christian Commonwealth."[268] Locke's toleration, after all, was also motivated by a desire to spread Protestant Christianity, his toleration being a form of mission, one that reached out not only to Jews and Muslims but also to "pagan" Native Americans and African slaves throughout the colonial Americas, specifically in seventeenth-century Virginia and the Carolinas.[269] (He could not have known that some of those African slaves were not actually pagans, meaning polytheists, but Muslims from West Africa.)

In 1689, Locke also made a break with European precedents that linked Christian heretics to Muslims and Jews. He declared both Islam and Judaism to be unique religions, not heresies. This critical distinction would save Muslims and Jews from persecution in England by Anglican authorities as heretics, as well as safeguarding former Christians, including the few English seafarers who, captured by North African pirates, had converted to Islam in order to gain their freedom:[270]

[I]f any man fall off from the Christian Faith to *Mahumetism*, he does not thereby become a Heretick or Schismatick, but an Apostate and an Infidel. This no body doubts of. And by this it appears that men of different Religions cannot be Hereticks or Schismaticks to one another.[271]

Despite this seeming equanimity, the distinction makes clear enough that Locke held no high opinion of Islam and indeed his understanding of the faith was significantly errant.[272]

In 1690, a year after the appearance of *A Letter Concerning Toleration* in London, Locke was attacked in print by Jonas Proast, an Anglican clergyman of All Souls College, Oxford.[273] (Locke's authorship, while officially anonymous, quickly became known.) Proast argued that although extreme violence should be avoided, the use of "moderate" force and other penalties were acceptable in the treatment of Muslims, Jews, and Christian dissenters.[274] Locke responded quickly in his *Second Letter on Toleration,* attempting to refute Proast's rejection of the inclusion of Muslims and Jews as citizens. In defense of Muslim and Jewish civil rights, Locke would never waver, answering with "the largeness of the toleration" he proposed.[275]

While allowing that "we pray every day for their conversion," he reaffirmed that this end would not be achieved by their exclusion, either by "driving them" away or "persecuting them when they are among us." For the first time, Locke defined toleration as the opposite of religious persecution: "Force, you allow, is improper to convert men to any religion. Toleration is but the removing of that force."[276]

Locke continued this line of argument on legal grounds in his *Third Letter* in 1692:[277]

> Besides, I think you are under a mistake, which shews your pretence against admitting Jews, Mahometans, Pagans, to the civil rights of the commonwealth is ill-grounded; for what law I pray is there in England, that they who turn to any of those religions, forfeit the civil rights of the commonwealth by doing it?[278]

Locke also sarcastically reminded his opponent that Christians in the Ottoman Empire faced no force at all, compared with the "moderate" or "sufficient force" Proast proposed to use against non-Christians in England:

> I think a conscientious and sober Dissenter might expect fairer dealing from one of my Pagans or Mahometans, as you please to call them, than from one who professes moderation, that what degrees of force, what kind of punishments will satisfy him, he either knows not, or will not declare.[279]

He also expressed a new religious relativism when he suggested that Turks, like Christians, also "sincerely seek the truth," however misguided he knew them to be.[280] In fact, he allowed that Muslims believed as adamantly in their salvation through the Qur'an as Christians did through their own scripture. Both groups, he understood, were fixed on the rewards of the next life:[281]

> Do not think all the world, who are not of your church, abandon themselves to an utter carelessness of their future state. You cannot but allow there are many Turks who sincerely seek the truth to whom you could never bring evidence sufficient to convince them of the truth of the Christian religion, whilst they looked on it as a principle not to be questioned, that the Koran was of Divine revelation.[282]

Pressing the point even further, Locke sounds almost like Menocchio, the heretical Italian miller, when he allows that Turks believed in their "way," just as Christians did. Yet the philosopher held out as the only possibility for the salvation of Muslims their conversion to Christianity:[283]

> And why then may you not allow it to a Turk, not as a good way, or as having led him to the truth; but as a way, as fit for him, as for one of your church to acquiesce in; and as fit to exempt him from your force, as to exempt any one of your church from it?[284]

Irrespective of their rightness or wrongness, Locke believed that doctrinal differences, whether among Christians or between Christians and non-Christians, should not be subject to state coercion.

In a fourth, posthumous letter, published in 1706, Locke would reaffirm the futility of religious polemic. These matters were not to be resolved on earth, particularly not by the magistrate or ruler:

> Try when you please with a Brahmin, a Mahometan, a Papist, Lutheran, Quaker, Anabaptist, Presbyterian, etc., you will find if you argue with them, as you do here with me, that the matter will rest here between you, and that you are no more a judge for any of them than they are for you. Men in all religions have equally strong persuasions, and every one must judge for himself; nor can anyone judge for another, and you last of all for the magistrate.[285]

The ultimate form of Locke's near universal religious toleration resulted, then, from a kind of disapproving empathy, a reasoned if saddened understanding of why Muslims and Jews continued to defend their beliefs, even unto death. What others had defined previously as heresy or fanaticism, Locke finally describes as natural and common to all believers:

> Nor is there among the many absurd religions of the world, almost any one that does not find votaries to lay down their lives for it: and if that be not firm persuasion and full assurance that is stronger than the love of life, and has force enough to make a man throw himself into the arms of death, it is hard to know what is firm persuasion and full assurance. Jews and Mahometans have frequently given instances of this highest degree of persuasion.[286]

Violence over matters of religion, Locke understood, produced only more violence and death. These were the unjust if predictable wages of state coercion.[287] Even in the aftermath of the second Ottoman siege of Vienna in 1683, the year Locke fled to Holland, when most other European Christians viewed all Muslims as agents of religious error and a foreign threat, Locke chose to defend the civil rights of Muslims.[288] In this context, particularly, it was a remarkable choice. From 1660 until his death in 1704, the adherents of Islam would remain part of Locke's principled, reasoned, and ultimately Christian ideal of state-supported universal toleration. He would not live to see it become a political reality in his lifetime, but his words would survive him, granting him his most notable afterlife in eighteenth-century America.

Locke, Defender of Muslims and Socinians or Unitarians, Attacked as Both, 1696

After repeatedly defending the religious and political rights of Muslims, in 1696 Locke would be accused in print of being one as well as a Socinian and a Deist.[289] John Edwards (d. 1716), an Anglican clergyman and friend of Proast's, attacked the theological views Locke expressed in *The Reasonableness of Christianity* in 1695.[290] Impugning Locke's apparent lack of support for the Trinity, Edwards defamed him as a heretic Christian and, by extension, a supporter of Islamic monotheism.[291] The connection in England between Islam and the Socinian or Unitarian

heresy was an insidious attempt to place Locke beyond any legally tolerated status in his own country.

In all, Edwards would write three tracts attacking Locke's religious
views as heretical: *Some Thoughts Concerning the Several Causes of Atheism*
(1695), *Socinianism Unmask'd* (1696), and *The Socinian Creed* (1697).[292] It
is likely that Locke did indeed embrace Socinian or Unitarian theology
by the late 1690s, for he read extensively on the subject and knew many
Socinians, but he prudently never professed the position publicly, and
would be counted an Anglican during his lifetime.[293]

Nonetheless, Locke's presumed rejection of the Trinity cleared a
path for the accusation of his being a Muslim. Edwards wrote that "it is
likely I shall further exasperate this author when I desire the reader to
observe that this lank faith of his is in a manner no other than the faith
of a Turk."[294] A subsidiary charge was that he "seems to have consulted
the Mahometan bible," a damning accusation.[295] Indeed, Locke had in
his library a copy of the 1647 French translation of the Qur'an by André
du Ryer.[296]

The assumption that Locke was both a Christian heretic *and* a
Muslim, perhaps, was also the result of his repeated pleas for the rights
of both groups in his work on toleration. As we have seen, accusing
a Christian theological or political adversary of being a Muslim (or a
Turk) was by now a time-honored feature of Christian polemic. Menocchio, Servetus, and the Italian translator of Servetus's questioning
of the Trinity had all been termed Turks or Muslims in the sixteenth
century. Thomas Jefferson, almost two centuries later, would suffer the
same fate for his own defense of Muslim rights, only to find in John
Locke's thoughts about toleration his most powerful precedent.

3

What Jefferson Learned—and Didn't— from His Qur'an

His Negative Views of Islam, and Their Political Uses, Contrasted with His Support for Muslim Civil Rights, 1765–86

To be acquainted with the various laws and constitutions of civilized nations, especially those who flourish in our own time, is, perhaps, the most useful part of knowledge.

> —George Sale, from the "Preliminary Discourse"
> to his English translation of the Qur'an, 1734

[T]hat our civil rights have no dependance on our religious opinions . . . that therefore the proscribing any citizen as unworthy the public confidence by laying upon him an incapacity of being called to offices of trust and emolument, unless he profess or renounce this or that religious opinion, is depriving him injuriously of those privileges and advantages to which, in common with his fellow citizens, he has a natural right.

> —Jefferson's Bill for Establishing Religious Freedom,
> drafted in 1777; proposed in Virginia, 1779;
> made state law, 1786

IN 1765, the *Virginia Gazette,* the local newspaper in Williamsburg, which also served as the only bookseller in the colony, recorded a purchase by Thomas Jefferson.[1] The item at the bottom of page 2, under the heading "Williamsburg October 1765," indicates Jefferson acquired

"Sale's Koran," in "2 Vols," for sixteen shillings.[2] The books had been shipped from London, where in 1734 George Sale had first published his translation of what in English was commonly called "the Alcoran of Mohammed."[3] Jefferson would have bought the third edition, printed in 1764.[4]

Jefferson was not the only one to possess Sale's Qur'an in eighteenth-century Virginia. In 1781, Dr. James Bryden of Goochland County would claim that British troops during the Revolutionary War had seized not just his many medical books but also what he listed as "Al Coran of Mahomet" in two volumes, whose value he estimated at one pound, more than Jefferson had paid sixteen years before. Dr. Bryden did not mention Sale as translator, but that the book was in two volumes with the title "the Alcoran of Mohammed" makes the identification certain.[5] Whether Bryden was ever reimbursed for his loss is unknown, but the more important question remains: What happened to Jefferson's Qur'an of 1765?

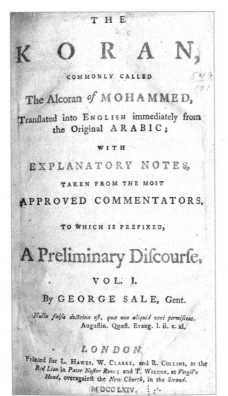

Above: Jefferson's purchase of "Sale's Koran, 2 Vols." recorded in the *Virginia Gazette Daybooks*.

Left: The title page of Jefferson's Qur'an, now in the Library of Congress.

ONE QUR'AN—OR TWO? 1770

In February 1770, five years after his purchase of the Qur'an, Thomas Jefferson wrote his friend John Page with calamitous news: "My late loss may perhaps have reached you by this time, I mean the loss of my mother's house by fire, and in it, of every paper I had in the world, and almost every book."[6] (The *Virginia Gazette* would also confirm that Jefferson "lost all his furniture, a valuable collection of books, and what is perhaps worse, his papers.")[7] A true bibliophile, Jefferson lamented, "Would to God it had been the money; then had it never cost me a sigh!"[8] What was worse, the loss "fell principally" on his "books of Common Law, of which [he had] but one left, at that time lent out."[9] The answers to the questions of how many and which books were lost remain elusive, but for the lawyer-in-training, the books were all critical.[10] There would have been additional losses too, as recorded purchases from the accounts of the *Virginia Gazette* attest, including the Acts of Parliament and British Common and Chancery law, and the works of Machiavelli and Milton.[11] All these were purchased around the same time he acquired the Qur'an.

When he bought the Qur'an in 1765, Jefferson was an impassioned law student engaged in criticizing the recently passed British Stamp Act.[12] The most immediate reason for wishing to study the Qur'an would have been to gain an insight into Islamic law and religion.[13] These may have interested him per se—Jefferson had an immense curiosity and a cosmopolitan outlook—but he may have had a more immediate purpose, for in seeking legal precedents for local Virginia cases, he would often look to other cultures around the world.

After the fire, Jefferson made no mention of the fate of the Qur'an he had purchased five years earlier. Did it perish in the flames, or was it miraculously spared? We will never know. During the mid-1760s, Jefferson had taken detailed notes on the texts he'd read with particular interest; these notes too, however, were lost in the fire at Shadwell, his mother's house. But if Jefferson's Qur'an was destroyed in 1770, then what are we to make of the two volumes of Sale's Qur'an he initialed, now at the Library of Congress in Washington, D.C.?[14]

There are two possibilities: The original Qur'an either survived the fire, or it was later replaced with another copy of the same edition.[15] If Jefferson did indeed buy the Qur'an twice, it would be an extraordinary testament to his desire to understand Islam. But even if he purchased the text only once, Jefferson remains unique among America's Founders in his desire to understand Islam on its own terms, looking directly to its most sacred source. In fact, his purchase of the Qur'an marked only the beginning of his study of Islam. After the 1770 fire, as he immediately began to reconstruct his lost library, Jefferson undertook to acquire numerous volumes about Middle Eastern languages,[16] history, and travel, and he continued doing so for the rest of his life.[17]

This chapter traces how Sale's introduction to the Qur'an may have influenced Jefferson's thoughts on Islam, in particular his notes on English law and Islam in the decade following his acquisition of the Islamic sacred text. In 1776, as a Virginia legislator, he would resort to anti-Islamic rhetoric in his effort to end the establishment of Anglicanism as the state religion. His notes from the same year, however, reveal that Locke's *A Letter Concerning Toleration* prompted his interest in the rights of Muslims.

GEORGE SALE'S QUR'AN AND THE PROBLEM OF TRANSLATION

George Sale (c. 1696–1736), a lawyer and an Anglican, described the Prophet Muhammad on the first page of his translation as "the legislator of the Arabs," words that would have appealed to Jefferson the lawyer.[18] Since the twelfth century, Christian translators of the Qur'an had commonly defined the text not as divine revelation but as a repository of Islamic law. Robert Ketton's first Latin translation in 1143 was entitled *Lex Saracenorum,* or *Law of the Saracens.*[19] The translations from the twelfth to the eighteenth century served primarily Christian polemics rather than scholarly interest in the accurate representation of Islamic beliefs.[20]

Ketton's translation of the Qur'an in the twelfth century resulted from an attempt to convert Muslims, a strategy conceived after the failure of the Crusades.[21] Knowing one's enemy, however, was a tricky business for Christian translators, who now sought to win by superiority of reason rather than force.[22] They thus often willfully distorted key aspects of the Qur'an, with the political aim of representing Islam as a heresy and the Prophet as an impostor.

Sale's translation was commissioned by the Society for Promoting Christian Knowledge, a British Anglican Protestant group dedicated to "missionary and educational goals."[23] As the group also had an anti-Catholic bent,[24] Sale inextricably linked Catholicism with Islam, a connection previously expounded in the Whig treatise *Cato's Letters*.[25] Sale's immediate goal was to remind his Christian readers that Islam was a false religion, but he also intended his work to help convert Muslims to Protestant Christianity, which, like preceding translators of the Qur'an, Sale believed to be their only hope of salvation.[26]

But Sale also seemed determined to present his translation as a rigorously scholarly work, referring to it as "an impartial version."[27] He acknowledged a debt to earlier Christian translations, but did not neglect to criticize their mistakes. Having, for instance, made a careful study of the seventeenth-century Latin translation by the Catholic priest Ludovico Maracci (d. 1700), who worked from several manuscripts in the Vatican,[28] Sale rejected many of what he termed Maracci's "impertinent" interpretations, claiming that "Protestants alone are able to attack the Koran with success."[29]

The first English translation of the Qur'an was published almost a century before Sale's appeared in 1734. Alexander Ross's dubious effort of 1649 was translated not from the original Arabic but from a French edition published two years earlier by the diplomat André du Ryer.[30] And yet Ross's work was deemed explosive: Even before publication, his publisher was imprisoned and all copies were seized. After Ross's testimony at a hearing before the Council of State, the charges were dropped. When the book was finally published on May 7, 1649,[31] a cautionary disclaimer was added. The Qur'an, it declared, may be "dangerous and scandalous" to a few weak Christians, but true believers would not be "swayed from their faith."[32]

Ross's translation was also the first to cross the Atlantic, read by colonists such as Cotton Mather, who branded the Prophet the Antichrist.[33] When Sale's Qur'an appeared in the American colonies, it was deemed the most informative and accurate translation then available, which indeed it was, for Sale had attempted to correct some of the most egregious distortions about Islam, out of a sincere desire for accuracy.[34] Sale also critiqued Ross's translation as "utterly unacquainted with the Arabic, and no great matter of French," filled with "fresh mistakes."[35] (Not that Sale was immune to mistakes, as when he identified the tribe of Khazraj in Medina as Jewish rather than Arab.)[36]

Sale appended footnotes to earlier translations of the Qur'an, which he'd read closely, and referred to Muslim as well as Christian commentaries on the sacred text.[37] He'd studied the prophetic precedents, or *hadith,* compiled by the Sunni scholar al-Bukhari (d. 870), as well as the medieval Qur'anic commentary, or *tafsir,* of al-Zamakhshari (d. 1144). Sale also drew from the Latin translations of Islamic history by Dr. Edward Pococke.[38]

An enormous success throughout Europe, Sale's translation was reprinted four times during the eighteenth century, and was translated into German, French, Russian, and Dutch.[39] It would remain the best available English version of the Qur'an into the nineteenth century.[40]

Voltaire, who owned Sale's Qur'an and praised it as "wise and judicious," would claim that the translator had spent twenty-five years in Arabia to complete the work.[41] In fact, Sale had never left England, and learned Arabic from two Arab Christians in London, Salomon Negri of Damascus and Carolus Dadichi of Aleppo. The two had themselves already produced an Arabic translation of the New Testament, intended for distribution to the Arab Christian communities along the Mediterranean, in the parts of the Ottoman Empire within reach of the British Levant Company—and Anglican attempts at the conversion of indigenous Christians there.[42]

The first volume of Sale's 1764 edition contained a two-hundred-page "Preliminary Discourse" on the history of Islam. What Jefferson may have learned from the "Preliminary Discourse" remains critical because Sale, despite his missionary objectives, had collected a substantial amount of relevant, accurate information on Islamic history, ritual practice, and law. Sale sought to approach the conversion of Muslims in much the same manner as that of the Jews: with well-informed reason. To that end, he proposed four rules for the mission that was presumably to take place in the Middle East rather than in London. First, he argued that one must "avoid compulsion," with a grudging admission that Islamic political dominance made the point moot anyway: "though it [compulsion] be not in our power to employ at present, I hope will not be made use of when it is."[43] Sale did not mention that the Qur'an states categorically that "there is no compulsion in religion" (Qur'an 2:256), substituting the word "violence" in his translation of the verse: "Let there be no violence in religion." In a footnote, however, Sale adds incorrectly that this principle lasted only during the Prophet's lifetime, when he protected Medinan pagans and Jews from forced conversion to Islam.[44]

Secondly, Sale urged would-be missionaries to "avoid arguments against common sense," adding that Muslims particularly resisted "worshipping images," and "the doctrine of transubstantiation," or the mystical transformation of the host into the flesh and blood of Jesus. Thirdly, he urged that "ill words" should be avoided with Muslims.[45] Finally, he directed Christian missionaries "not to quit any article of the Christian faith to gain" the conversion of the Muslims.[46] In this vein he criticized the Unitarians, previously known as Socinians, who had emphasized Islam and Christianity's essential similarity as monotheisms in their heretical denial of Jesus's divinity and the Trinity:[47] "it is absolutely necessary to undeceive those who, from the ignorant or unfair translations which have appeared, have entertained too favorable an opinion of the original, and also to enable us effectually to expose the impostures."[48] Sale, then, was as determined to save the Unitarians from being misled by the "ignorant" translations casting Islam in a positive light as he was to redeem Islam's own followers.[49]

Nevertheless, under the inevitable influence of treatises by Christian dissenters, Deists, and Unitarians, who endorsed Islam as a religion and as a philosophy,[50] Sale's treatment of the Prophet and Islam was ultimately more sympathetic than those of previous European translators, and he himself would eventually suffer from charges of pro-Islamic bias.[51] Even while condemning the heresy of such heterodox sects and their view of Islam as an uncorrupted monotheism, Sale was perhaps softened a bit, at least on the margins, by familiarity with their work. Consider their emphasis on Muhammad's role as a legislator, which had gathered traction among some Anglicans as well as Christian dissenters since the seventeenth century.[52] Sale echoes their speculation as to whether Muhammad "deserves not equal respect, though not with Moses or Jesus Christ, whose laws came really from heaven, yet with Minos or Numa,"[53] who were legislators in ancient Greece and Rome.[54]

Sale, for example, also criticizes Prideaux, the Anglican dean of Norwich and the author of *The True Nature of Imposture* (1697), the anti-Islamic and anti-Deist polemic immensely popular on both sides of the Atlantic.[55] Conceding that Prideaux "has given the most probable account" of the Prophet as an impostor, Sale deftly attacks his sources as "Christian writers, who generally mix such ridiculous fables with what they deliver, that they deserve not much credit."[56] He also allows that Muhammad "gave the Arabs the best religion he could, as well as the best laws."[57] Apart from Henry Stubbe's unpublished vindication of Islam of 1671, Sale's objectivity is unexampled in his time, reflecting his preoccupation with fairness.[58] He also avoids "all reproachful language," a habit he claims as a rule in his personal moral code.[59] Sale explained, "I have not, in speaking of Mohammed or his Koran, allowed myself to use those opprobrious appellations, and unmannerly expressions, which seem to be the strongest arguments of several who have written against them."[60]

And so while offering a standard disclaimer—"for how criminal soever Mohammad may have been in imposing a false religion on mankind"—Sale allows that "the praises due to [Muhammad's] real virtues ought not to be denied him."[61] These the translator enumerates as "piety, veracity, justice, liberality, clemency, humility, and abstinence," and especially charity and selflessness. As to the polygamy for which the Prophet was commonly vilified, Sale asserts that it was not only "frequently practiced in Arabia" in Muhammad's time, but was common even among the Jews of the Old Testament, implying that the Prophet might have thought the custom "the more just and reasonable, as he found [it] practiced or approved by the professors of a religion, which was confessedly of divine origin."[62] Thus Sale underscores the Prophet's belief in God's revelations to the Jews.

As to the standard Christian anti-Islamic polemical claim, that Islam spread by violence, Sale is again a voice of moderation. While he does not explicitly mention any instance of Islamic tolerance,[63] he declares that "they are greatly deceived who imagine it ['the law of Mohammed'] to have been propagated by the sword alone."[64] He does admit, in the sixth chapter of his "Preliminary Discourse," that the Qur'an promised rewards in the next life for those who fought "infidels," but he refuses to portray Islam as the only monotheism that has incited war, reminding his readers that both Jews and Christians have warred in the name of faith, never having "been ignorant of the force of enthusiastic heroism, or omitted to spirit up their respective partisans by the like arguments and promises."[65]

Perhaps finding it easier to condemn Catholics than Christians generally, Sale cites the Crusades in his only usage of the phrase "holy war."[66] And while pointing out that both Judaism and Islam presumed a "divine commission" to "destroy enemies of their religion," he finds it "very strange" that Christians in particular should "teach and practice a doctrine so opposite to the temper and whole tenour of the gospel." In conclusion, Sale allows that Christians have "shewn a more violent spirit of intolerance" than either Jews or Muslims.[67]

SALE'S DISCUSSION OF GOD, JESUS, AND THE TRINITY IN THE QUR'AN

But more than his judicious descriptions of Muhammad, Sale's great accomplishment was his grasp of the most crucial parts of a central Islamic tenet:

> The great doctrine then of the Koran is the unity of God; to restore which point Mohammed pretended was the chief end of his mission. . . . And he taught that whenever this religion became neglected or corrupted in essentials, God had the goodness to reinform and readmonish mankind thereof, by several prophets, of whom Moses and Jesus were the most distinguished, till the appearance of Mohammed, who is their seal, no other being expected after him.[68]

Sale properly identifies Muhammad's role in Islam as the seal of all previous prophets, sent by the God of Abraham to correct and renew what humans had inevitably corrupted. Like Deists and Unitarians before him,[69] he emphasizes the connectedness in Islam of the great prophets, from Adam to Moses to Jesus and, finally, Muhammad.[70] Sale furthermore acknowledges Muhammad's acceptance of the divine authority of the Pentateuch, Psalms, and the Gospels, though wrongly pointing out that parts of the Bible, as well as the Apocrypha, appear in the Qur'an, contrary to Muslim belief in the Qur'an as God's literal words to the Prophet.[71]

Sale takes particular pains to delineate the weaknesses of Christianity in the seventh century, when the Prophet had promulgated Islam, by way of a rationale for the success of the Islamic conquests in the Christian Middle East.[72] As an explanation for Christian defeat, Sale accuses Middle Eastern Christians of various heresies, including worshipping the Virgin Mary, which charge served also to implicate more generally Catholics and Eastern Orthodox Christians, who venerate Mary. The sanctification of Mary, he points out, led to the idea that both she and Christ were coequal with the Father, a view expressed in the fact that seventh-century Christians sometimes called Mary "the complement of the Trinity."[73] It was such error, the Anglican asserts, that enabled Muhammad to attack the Trinity itself:[74] "And say not three" (Qur'an 4:171).[75] Yet Sale does not elaborate upon the Islamic definition of Jesus as merely a prophet and a mortal, albeit one who could perform miracles.[76] Perhaps he did not intend to emphasize what Unitarians had done in England since the seventeenth century, which was to define Islam as a monotheism that rejected both the Trinity and the divinity of Jesus.

Sale does, however, expound the Islamic vision of the afterlife in detail, emphasizing its belief in a final judgment, which would determine rewards in heaven or punishment in hell. In this connection, he challenges the "falsehood of a vulgar imputation . . . that women have no souls, or, if they have, that they will perish, like those of brute beasts, and will not be rewarded in the next life."[77] By contrast, Sale allows that the Prophet "had too great a respect for the fair sex to teach such a doctrine," and he correctly identifies several passages in the Qur'an "which affirm that women, in the next life, will not only be punished for their evil actions, but will also receive the rewards of their good deeds, as well as the men, and that in this case God will make no distinction of sexes."[78]

It is an indication of Sale's deep immersion in early Islamic prophetic precedents that he even appends to his Qur'an's chapter 66, verses 11–12, a note about the two most praised women of the sacred text: Maryam, or Mary the mother of Jesus, and the pharaoh's wife, later called Asiya. Sale does not cite the source, al-Tabari (d. 929), a famed Sunni Qur'anic commentator, but he paraphrases his commentary: "That among men there had been many perfect, but no more than four of the other sex had attained perfection; to wit, Asia [Asiya], the wife of Pharaoh, Mary, the daughter of Imran, Khadijah the daughter of Khowailid (the prophet's first wife,) and Fatema [Fatima] the daughter of Mohammed."[79]

Detailing the five pillars of Muslim belief, Sale begins with the first, known as the *shahada:* "there is no god but the true God; and that Mohammed is his apostle." (He included "the true" in his addition to the original Arabic phrase, and he inserted the word "that" in the second clause, but both changes serve to clarify the intended meaning.) The four remaining pillars are accurately described as well: prayer five times a day (*salat*); the giving of alms annually in support of the needy in the community (*zakat*); fasting during the holy month of Ramadan in commemoration of the beginning of the Qur'an's revelation (*sawm*); and the pilgrimage to Mecca (*hajj*).[80] Sale devotes considerable attention not only to the specifics of the pilgrimage ritual, but also the configuration of the holy city with the help of a map and a diagram of the sacred shrine of the Ka'ba.[81]

In addition to describing Muslim obligations, Sale also details the prohibitions: wine, pork, gambling, theft, murder, and adultery. He also explains more recent Islamic legal debates concerning two new products: tobacco, from North America, and coffee, from Yemen.[82] The latter had first reached the Ottoman Empire and continued westward, with the first coffee house in England appearing around 1652; the English would come to regard the new beverage as a brew of "the Mahometan berry."[83] Sale was informed enough to understand that Muslim legal authorities did not initially agree about the lawfulness of either tobacco or coffee.

Praising the Prophet as "the lawgiver of the Arabians," Sale devotes sections six and eight of his introduction to a brief outline of Islamic legal schools.[84] He describes the four Sunni schools, noting that all were considered orthodox by the majority of Muslims.[85] Of the famed jurist al-Shafi'i (d. 820), Sale tells us that he "is said to have been the first who discoursed of jurisprudence, and reduced that science into a method,"[86] and particularly emphasizes legal precedents concerning marriage, divorce, and inheritance for both men and women.[87] Sale also defines the basic doctrinal differences between Sunni and Shi'i Muslims, chiding the philosopher Spinoza for his ignorance of this division.[88]

The Importance of Sale's Qur'an in Jefferson's Library

Committed as he was to cultivating an awareness of law and culture beyond those of Britain and continental Europe,[89] Jefferson probably would have approved of Sale's introductory statement: "To be acquainted with the various laws and constitutions of civilized nations, especially those who flourish in our own time, is, perhaps, the most useful part of knowledge."[90] In his *Notes on Virginia,* published in 1784 in Paris and 1787 in London, he had a rather similar recommendation for students in America: "History, by apprizing them of the past, will enable them to judge of the future; it will avail them of the experience of other times and other nations."[91]

But is there evidence that Jefferson gleaned anything from Sale's work to enhance his own knowledge and judgment? Jefferson's voluminous writings, including legislation and correspondence from 1765 to 1776, offer virtually none. Although Jefferson owned a Qur'an, there is no indication that he scrutinized the text verse by verse, as he would the New Testament much later, to create two expurgated volumes of

Gospel selections he could accept as true, a version known after his death as the Jefferson Bible.[92]

The phrase "Thomas Jefferson's Qur'an" implies no such interest in creating a version of the Islamic text he could approve, but it symbolizes a pivotal starting point in his lifelong exploration of Islamic belief and history. His direct references to the Qur'an, with one exception, appear neither as numerous, detailed, or systematic as those issuing from his lifelong engagement with Christianity. Indeed, Jefferson has been criticized for his "many unfair, unnuanced, and shallow caricatures" of several faiths, including Calvinism, Catholicism, Judaism, and Islam.[93] Such a sweeping assertion does not reflect the totality of his views about Islam. At this juncture, suffice it to say, Jefferson did subscribe to the anti-Islamic views of most of his contemporaries, and in politics he made effective use of the rhetoric they inspired.

In the absence of any notes of Jefferson's on Sale's translation of the Qur'an, we can only speculate how Sale's views would have struck him. Although both men were lawyers and Anglicans, Jefferson privately rejected the theological doctrines that Sale unquestioningly accepted. But they had in common a rejection of coercion or violence against religious minorities on account of their faith, and this alone puts them both within an alternative strain of European thought endorsing religious toleration; Jefferson would go even further, calling for the guarantee of individual rights regardless of religion.

Sale's attempt to present a relatively unbiased picture of the Prophet and Islam would result in the cooling of relations with his employer, the Anglican Society for Promoting Christian Knowledge.[94] And he would suffer even more illustrious disapproval: Edward Gibbon (d. 1794) condemns Sale in the fifth volume of *The Decline and Fall of the Roman Empire* (1788) as "half a Musulman" for criticizing Prideaux's anti-Islamic invective.[95] But Sale, who had died two years after the completion of the translation that would make him famous, would never read it, nor its echo in the treatment of Royall Tyler, who, just over a decade later, would be condemned for being influenced by the "liberality of the good Sale" in his novel *The Algerine Captive*.[96] Anything less than a complete condemnation of Islam reliably provoked rebuke in eighteenth-century Britain and America.

Jefferson, like Sale, would not be daunted by the certain negative reception for any views sympathetic to Islam. But unlike Sale, Jefferson had no interest in converting Muslims, seeking only their acceptance and enfranchisement, toward which end he applied his study of their faith. His earliest preserved references to Islam, however, relied *not* on Sale's extensive overview, but instead on four European authorities on religion and law.

JEFFERSON'S EARLIEST REFERENCES TO ISLAM: A SEVENTEENTH-CENTURY ENGLISH LEGAL PRECEDENT AND BOLINGBROKE'S VIEWS ON RELIGION AND RATIONAL PROOFS, 1765

In the decade between 1765 and 1775, Jefferson wrote on Muslims and Islamic theology, practice, and history in four separate series of notes in his *Literary and Legal Commonplace Books.*[97] What appears to be his earliest reference to Muslims under British law may also be his most terse—and provocative. In notes on William Salkeld's *Reports of Cases Adjudg'd in the Court of the King's Bench* (1717), Jefferson duly numbered and copied out hundreds of legal decisions, with the original volume and page number, to which he added a single-line description. For case 97, Jefferson wrote, "Turks and Infidels, perpetui inimici," meaning "enemies for life." But to that he added "groundless," a word he preserved from the original English legal ruling, an older precedent dating to the rule of King Charles I (r. 1625–49).[98] Under the text's subheading "Aliens" regarding "Allegiance, Denizen," the legal precedent refuted the idea that Muslims and "Infidels," probably including Jews, are perpetual enemies of the English crown:

> Turks and Infidels are not perpetui inimici, nor is there a particular Enmity between them and us; but this is a common Error founded on a groundless Opinion of Justice Brooke; for tho' there be a difference between our Religion and theirs, that does not oblige us to be Enemies to their Persons; they are the Creatures of God and of the same kind as we are, and it would be a Sin in us to hurt their Persons. Per Littleton (afterwards Lord Keeper to Charles I).[99]

Jefferson was studying British legal precedents in order to apply them to his practice in Virginia. What he learned from this passage established a foundation for his initial conception of the toleration of

Muslims in America, predating his later notes on John Locke's views of Muslims and "civil rights." It may have even spurred him to examine Locke's view of the issue. What is clear is that by the mid-1760s, Jefferson had considered Muslims and Jews as people "of the same kind," who should not be legally proclaimed enemies or persecuted because of their religion, either in Britain or in Virginia.[100] This refusal to cast Muslims as perpetual enemies would later be formalized in his legislation on religious freedom, but his comment on this British precedent marks the dawn of Jefferson's distinctively positive view about the possibility of Muslim citizenship in America.

Jefferson's first reference to Islam (as opposed to the status of individual Muslims) appears in his extensive notes on Henry St. John, Viscount Bolingbroke's (d. 1751) five-volume *Philosophical Works*.[101] In fact, Jefferson transcribed from Bolingbroke more than from any other author.[102] Samuel Johnson once called Bolingbroke "a scoundrel for charging a blunderbuss against religion and morality," but Jefferson was clearly fascinated by this fellow Deist who remained deeply skeptical of religion, including not just Judaism and Christianity but also Islam.[103]

Douglas L. Wilson, editor of Jefferson's *Literary Commonplace Book,* was first to observe the remarkable degree to which Jefferson embraced Bolingbroke's philosophy. The direct effect is notable not only in Jefferson's views on religion, but in his reliance on reason as the only valid path to knowledge, as well as a corresponding distrust of theologians and clergymen. Jefferson would also adopt Bolingbroke's aversion to Plato and his influence on Christian theology, as well as a skepticism about the historicity of biblical accounts.[104]

Jefferson took careful note of Bolingbroke's analysis of the basic tenets of Christianity—the divinity of Jesus, his crucifixion and resurrection—all of which Jefferson too would come to doubt, and of Bolingbroke's criticism of how Christian dogma gave rise to an unfortunate history of schism, persecution, and torture.[105] Paraphrasing Bolingbroke's moral relativism, Jefferson wrote:

> Who are reputed to be good Christians? go to Rome, they are papists.
> go to Geneva, they are Calvinists. go to the north of Germany, they
> are Lutherans. come to London, they are none of these[.] orthodoxy
> is a mode. it is one thing at one time and in one place. it is something
> else at another time, and in another place, or even in the same place: for
> in this religious country of ours, without seeking proofs in any other,

men have been burned under one reign, for the very same doctrines they were obliged to profess in another. you damn all those who differ from you.[106]

Almost twenty years later, and eight years after rejecting the establishment of a state religion in the legislation of 1776, Jefferson would again echo Bolingbroke in his *Notes on Virginia:* "Is uniformity attainable? Millions of innocent men, women, and children, since the introduction of Christianity, have been burnt, tortured, fined, imprisoned; yet we have not advanced one inch towards uniformity."[107]

Jefferson also restated in a nutshell the skeptical premise of Bolingbroke's multivolume treatise concerning all revealed religions, including Islam:

> We must not assume for truth, what can be proved neither à priori, nor à posteriori. a mystery cannot be proved à priori; it would be no mystery if it could: and inspiration is become a mystery, since all we know of it is, that it is an inexplicable action of the divine on the human mind[.] it would be silly, therefore, to assume it to be true, because god can act mysteriously, that is, in ways unknown to us, on his creature man . . . and the proofs that brought à posteriori for Christian inspiration, are not more decisive to Christians, than those, which the Stoicians brought in favor of vaticination [prophecy] and divination, were to them; nor than those which the Mahometans and the worshippers of Foe bring of the same kind, are to them.

Jefferson also recorded Bolingbroke's own more succinct statement of the same: "No hypothesis ought to be maintained if a single phaenomenon stands in direct opposition to it."[108] This premise undermined the acceptance of the miraculous without logical analysis in any belief system, be it Christian, Stoic, or Muslim.

A SCANDALOUS DIVORCE AND ISLAMIC LAW: JEFFERSON REPEATS MISINFORMATION FROM THE LEARNED VON PUFENDORF, 1772

In 1767, two years after his purchase of the Qur'an and his first written reference to Islam, Jefferson was admitted to the bar in Virginia.[109] In 1772, while working on a difficult divorce case, he would have occasion to seek out Islamic legal precedents, but, once again, he apparently did not consult Sale's introduction or his translation of the Qur'an. He might have made his job easier if he had.

Dr. James Blair of Williamsburg was sued for divorce by his wife, Kitty Eustace, who demanded separate maintenance and alimony based on a specific prenuptial agreement.[110] The delicacy of the situation had the potential for a local scandal: Jefferson's notes indicate that the marriage was never consummated, probably due to Dr. Blair's illness.[111] Between November 1772 and Dr. Blair's death at the end of that year, Jefferson made extensive notes on divorce law from Freiherr von Pufendorf's legal treatise *Of the Law of Nature and Nations*. (The work of the eminent jurist Von Pufendorf had been first published in 1692 in Latin, but Jefferson consulted a 1749 English edition.)[112] For Anglicans, divorce was nearly impossible without an act of Parliament, which was the equivalent of an annulment.[113] Such long odds of succeeding would explain why Jefferson's search for precedents eventually led him so far afield, even to non-Western jurisprudence and Sharia law.

Jefferson divided his findings on divorce into "pro" and "con" sections, comparing the permissive and prohibitive cases around the world. Under the heading "Miscellaneous Practices of several Nations," he included references to the Dutch in Japan, ancient Athens, the Maldives, the Amazons, and the Jews.[114] Jefferson then chose only one Islamic precedent, despite the fact that Von Pufendorf cites many others:[115] "Among the Turks is a kind of marriage called Kabin, where parties agree on the fixt time of separation, securing to the woman a sum of money on dismission."[116] The Persian term *kabin* had two distinct Ottoman legal applications, depending on location.[117] Von Pufendorf correctly defines one form, a temporary marriage that was in practice in European Balkan territories of the empire. That variant is generally known by the Arabic legal term *mut'a,* or a marriage "contracted for a fixed period" that remunerates the woman at its end with an "indemnity payable to a divorced wife where no *mahr* or dowry has been stipulated."[118] In Anatolian regions of the Ottoman Empire, however, the same term referred instead to the dowry or "marriage portion contracted to be paid by the husband to his wife if he divorces her without sufficient cause."[119] So, for example, on becoming the legal wife of the Ottoman sultan Suleyman (r. 1520–66), Hürrem (d. 1558), the favorite concubine, known in Western history as Roxelana, received the *kabin* of five thousand ducats as dowry.[120]

Again, Jefferson apparently did not consult Sale's excursus on Islamic law. Had he done so, he would have found the following, a more helpful and accurate description of a Muslim woman's grounds for divorce:

[Y]et the women are not allowed to separate themselves from their husbands, unless it be for ill usage, want of proper maintenance, neglect of conjugal duty, impotency, or some cause of equal import; but then she generally loses her dowry, which she does not, if divorced by her husband.[121]

Indeed, under Islamic law, Kitty Eustace would have had a claim to dissolve her marriage based on her husband's alleged "impotency." Sale had described exactly what Jefferson had been looking for.

Another Burned Library: Jefferson Absorbs Voltaire's Negative Views of the Qur'an and Islam, 1775

Jefferson's notes around 1775 about law and history in his *Legal Commonplace Book* included entries about Islam based on Voltaire's observations.[122] As detailed in chapter 1, Voltaire's mostly ahistorical play demonized the Prophet as a violent and lascivious religious impostor. This harshly negative view of Voltaire's would be unchanged when he later attempted a world history.

Jefferson, who attended the theater in Williamsburg, never bought or saw Voltaire's play, but he encountered a similarly unforgiving vision of Muhammad in the philosophe's 1756 *Essai sur les moeurs et l'esprit des nations*, or, as translated for the 1759 London edition, *An Essay on the Universal History, Manners, and Spirit of Nations*.[123] Jefferson cited volume 14 of the original French edition, his notes beginning briefly in English before switching to French.[124] He took few notes on the disparaging portrait of the Prophet himself.[125]

He likewise ignored Voltaire's footnote praising Sale as "wise and judicious."[126] Instead, Jefferson focused on Voltaire's description of the reign of Umar ibn al-Khattab (r. 634–44), the second caliph and the Prophet's political successor, whose conquests pushed the borders of Islam from the Arabian Peninsula to Egypt in the west and Iran in the east. Jefferson also recorded Voltaire's account of the fall of Iran and the demise of Zoroastrianism, the pre-Islamic faith of the country.[127] Most of the Zoroastrian population, known in the eighteenth century as Parsis, relocated to remote reaches of Iran and India, which prompted Voltaire to group them with the Jews, describing both groups as "ignorant, scorned, and in their poverty close"; he claimed that the Zoroastrians in diaspora, like the Jews, were "so long dispersed without allying themselves with other nations."[128]

A second paragraph Jefferson copied from Voltaire concerned Umar's conquest of Egypt. Here Voltaire falsely claimed that the Muslims "burned the famous library of Alexandria, monument to the understanding and the errors of men, begun by Ptolemy."[129] Probably the library was destroyed much earlier than 642 CE, when the Islamic siege of Alexandria was lifted by truce; the true arsonists, according to scholars versed in Greek, Latin, and Arabic sources, were either Caesar's legions in 48 BCE or Coptic Christians battling Hellenistic pagans in the fourth century CE. The popular myth of the library's destruction by Muslims would nevertheless persist into the twentieth century.[130]

Although he did not refer to the anecdote, Voltaire's supposition was based upon a curious command falsely attributed to the caliph Umar, and cited five hundred years after the fact; he supposedly ordered the library destroyed because its "books of wisdom" concerning philosophy, medicine, mathematics, and law challenged "the Book of God"— the Qur'an.[131] What must Jefferson, the bibliophile, who'd lost his own library to fire in 1770, have thought of a religion that Voltaire presented as demanding the burning of books?

Voltaire's belief in the myth about the destruction of the library inspired a further misrepresentation, which Jefferson also recorded in his notes: "The Saracens wanted no science except the Alcoran."[132] This was a peculiar assertion for Voltaire, who knew better: Only four pages later, he included a partial list of Islamic scientific, medical, and mathematical achievements that had enhanced European understanding in the late medieval period. He admitted that algebra was "one of their inventions"[133] and that "chemistry and medicine were cultivated by the Arabs," adding for good measure that chemistry was initially unknown to Europeans.[134] Voltaire then praised the Muslims' preservation of ancient medical remedies from the schools of Hippocrates and Galen, which survived via Latin translations from Arabic, though he failed to mention significant advances in diagnostics, surgery, and pharmacology transmitted from the Arabs to Christian Europe.

Voltaire might have explained that the works of Aristotle were also directly inherited by the Arabs, who added their own extensive commentaries. This allowed the medieval Spanish Muslim jurist and philosopher Ibn Rushd, known in Western Europe as Averroes (d. 1198), to explore the tension between reason and revelation, the very problem Jefferson would address in his own analysis of Christianity. In fact, Ibn Rushd's detailed annotations of Aristotle, translated in Spain from Arabic into Latin in the thirteenth century, fired the progress of empiricism and rationalism at universities in Paris and Bologna. Medieval Islamic scholarship would thus contribute to European Renaissance debates, without which Jefferson's rationalist philosophy could not have come into being.

By 1788, in a letter written from Paris, Jefferson would acknowledge the importance of Arabic manuscripts as a repository of classical learning, writing with excitement about a discovery in Sicily as a possible source of the historian Livy's lost volumes. Jefferson was determined to procure the texts upon their translation from Arabic into Italian.[135] But in 1775, he would note only one of the major Islamic contributions to European culture cited by Voltaire, where he observes that the numerals in use in Europe were adopted from those of the Arabs, who borrowed them from India.[136] Still, it is Voltaire's depiction of Islam as an enemy of science that made the stronger impression on Jefferson: As late as 1785, commenting on the possibility of the Turks being driven "out of Europe" in support of the Greeks regaining control of "their own country," Jefferson describes the Ottomans as "a set of Barbarians with whom an opposition to all science is an article of religion."[137]

Voltaire's condemnation of Islam contained another element of lasting impact on Jefferson. In his final clause regarding the Qur'an, Voltaire charged Muslims with forced religious conversion after military conquest, claiming that they "already showed that their genius would be to extend [the Qur'an] over all."[138] It was merely a rote assertion of the old anti-Islamic polemic that the faith was spread by the sword alone. Islam did not become the dominant religion of the Middle East overnight, or by sheer force. Most historians now believe that conversion of the mainly Christian and Zoroastrian populations took centuries, spurred by a host of economic, social, and religious factors unique to each denomination and region.[139] But in the Atlantic culture of the eighteenth century, the narrative of violent conquest was accepted as fact.

Jefferson's Attempt at Ending the Anglican Establishment of Religion in Virginia Through Reference to Islam, November 1776

After writing the Declaration of Independence in the summer of 1776, Jefferson returned to Virginia in the autumn to draft new laws for the Commonwealth concerning the separation of religion and government.[140] It was, apart from much else, a critical year for his thinking on Islam. For in attempting to end the establishment of Anglicanism, which discriminated against other religions and Protestant sects, Jefferson would draw upon precedents in Voltaire and various British political tracts depicting Islam as a coercive force inimical to scientific inquiry.

The door to toleration for non-Anglican Protestants had been opened by the last clause of the June 1776 Virginia Declaration of Rights:[141]

> That religion, or the duty which we owe to our Creator, and the manner of discharging it, can be directed only by reason and conviction, not by force or violence, and therefore all men are equally entitled to the free exercise of religion, according to the dictates of their conscience; and that it is the mutual duty of all to practice Christian forbearance, love, and charity, towards each other.[142]

In theory, the clause opened the door to full freedom of religion in Virginia, but it assumed that the state's population remained exclusively Christian, and thus implicitly excluded non-Christians from the sphere of equal rights. Under the establishment of Anglicanism, other Protestants, though lacking religious equality, were obligated to pay for the financial support of Anglican churches and ministers. So were non-Protestants. Jews and Catholics were also denied religious freedom or political equality, but they were present in much smaller numbers. Muslims, if any had been known to exist in Virginia, would have been similarly denied full rights of citizenship.

As a member of the Virginia House of Delegates, Jefferson was appointed to the nineteen-member Committee on Religion on October 11, 1776.[143] Having proposed throwing off the yoke of British political tyranny in the Declaration of Independence in the spring and summer of that year, he was not about to relent in the face of home-grown oppression. Indeed as the Presbyterian petitioners in Virginia put it, Jefferson was "forming independent Governments upon equitable and liberal foundations . . . freed from all the incumbrances which a spirit of Domination, prejudice, or bigotry hath interwoven with most other political systems."[144] For Presbyterians and Baptists particularly, this necessitated a complete separation of the Anglican religion from the state in Virginia, and that is precisely what they demanded. Reflecting on this time in his 1821 autobiography, Jefferson would allow that these petitions "brought on the severest contests in which I have ever been engaged."[145]

One petition addressed to Jefferson's committee was called "Memorial of the Presbytery of Hanover," Virginia. Dated October 24, 1776, it demanded "*free exercise of Religion, according to the dictates of our Consciences.*" The Presbyterians charged that this ideal was infringed by the levy of taxes supporting the construction of Anglican churches and "the established Clergy." Such, they said, represented "so many violations of their natural Rights; and in their consequence a restraint upon freedom of inquiry and private judgment."[146] The Protestant dissenters sought the disestablishment not just of the Anglican Church but also of Christianity, for which they asked no preferment beyond what Islam might claim,[147] "no argument in favour of establishing the Christian Religion, but what may be pleaded with equal propriety for establishing the tenets of Mahommed by those who believed the Al-Coran; or, if this be not true, if it is at least impossible for the Magistrate to adjudge the right of preference among the various Sects that profess the Christian Faith without erecting a Chair of Infallibility which would lead us back to the Church of Rome."[148]

Dissenting Presbyterian petitioners well understood the difference between asking for religious equality among Christians, which would require an official status for Christianity, and a universal religious freedom, which might include the most far-fetched of possible Virginian believers—Muslims. But whatever their distaste for Islam—and it would have been typical of their day—they more passionately feared the establishment of some repressive regime like that of the pope, whom they viewed as the chief, eternal persecutor of Protestants. It was inscribed in the collective memory of these dissenting Protestants to prefer no established religion at all, and an end to all religious inequality, even at the expense of a Christian polity.[149]

These petitioners may not have owned a Qur'an as Jefferson did, but they knew of the text's sacredness to Muslims. It was a commonplace of English culture. As early as 1386, Geoffrey Chaucer referred to the Qur'an's "holy laws," and many English authors would express the same notion in the fifteenth, sixteenth, and seventeenth centuries, most without having read the Muslim holy book. Even later in 1777, the Scottish philosopher David Hume, whose works Jefferson owned, would refer to the Qur'an as "a sacred book."[150]

In 1776, as a response to numerous petitions from Presbyterians as well as Baptists, Jefferson proposed two separate pieces of legislation. The first was a bill for Disestablishing the Church of England and for Repealing Laws Interfering with Freedom of Worship; the second, for Exempting Dissenters from Contributing to the Support of the [Anglican] Church.[151] These groundbreaking efforts were clearly the logical extension of the same beliefs Jefferson had expounded about the new nation's government in the Declaration of Independence. For it must have occurred to Jefferson that he could scarcely declare all (free, white) men "created equal" and "endowed by their creator with certain inalienable rights" if the Virginians among them did not have the right to freely practice their chosen faith.[152] Furthermore, he questioned the legitimacy of compelling payment to support a sect to which the majority of citizens did not belong, proposing that this was but another form of taxation without representation.[153]

In his autobiography, Jefferson would reflect upon the oppressive status quo his bills aimed to reform as "unrighteous compulsion, to maintain teachers of what they deemed religious errors," and he referred to the petitioners as having sought "to abolish this spiritual tyranny."[154] When it came to matters of conscience, whether political or religious, Jefferson advocated complete intellectual freedom.[155] Religion, as he understood it, was after all "a system of opinions," and these were "formed in the mind."[156]

But at this time, how did he define Islam? In 1776, Jefferson's speeches in the Virginia House of Delegates to disestablish the Anglican Church relied on negative comparisons to Islam, which he described as a religion that repressed free inquiry. It was an illegitimate characterization but it served Jefferson's immediate goal: to discredit the coercion of a state religion.[157] Extant Protestant polemics would suffice for his negative representation of Islam, but he would tweak the emphasis. For Jefferson was not aiming to elevate another Protestant denomination, as others in Britain—and America—had before him.[158] Instead, he compared the Anglican Church to Islam, in order that no Protestant denomination could legally oppress another.

"Not a ready debater," in the judgment of some historians, Jefferson made painstaking outlines to bolster his legislative proposals.[159] His notes, comprising a four-page document "written in a long, narrow column," are organized in question-and-answer format; the shorthand abbreviations are sometimes difficult to interpret.[160] Most, however, are straightforward. For example, in support of his resolution for "Religs. Lib.," or religious liberty,[161] he outlined the long history of Christian heresy, dissent, and repression.[162]

Jefferson included two direct negative references to Islam. First, he likened his opponents to Muslims, with a variation of Voltaire's claim that Muslims wished for no form of science other than the Qur'an. Jefferson then asserted more generally that a state religion quashed "free enquiry," by which he meant the spiritual exploration of others whose "uncoerced reason" led them to a different truth.[163] In his shorthand, his point was rendered thus:

ans. *Truth* cnt. suffr. by fre. Enquiry—only w. propag.
[Answer: Truth cannot suffer by free enquiry—only with propagation.][164]

His main theme throughout the argument was the protection of the individual's right to choose, and to question everything, even religion: "Free enquiry enemy only to Error," by which he meant that rational inquiry could threaten only religion that could not reasonably defend itself. By 1784, when he had finally revised his *Notes on Virginia*, he would reproduce this argument:

Reason and free inquiry are the only effectual agents against error. Give a loose to them, they will support the true religion by bringing every false one to their tribunal, to the test of their investigation. They are natural enemies of error, and of error only.[165]

In 1776, however, Jefferson took the Islamic counterexample against an Anglican establishment further, by suggesting that the Prophet Muhammad had denied rational argument, and that this was the mark of repressive religion. As he wrote in his debate notes:

if m. forbd. free Argum'—Mahomsm.
prevnt. Reformn.

[If Mahomet forbade free argument—Mahometanism prevented Reformation.][166]

Jefferson used Voltaire's notion about Islam and free inquiry a second time under the heading, "Is Uniformity [of religion] desirable?"[167] His shorthand provides his answer:

if evr. cd. b. obtd. wd. be b. suffoctg. free enqry.
[If ever [uniformity of religion] could be obtained, it would be by suffocating free enquiry.][168]

Jefferson then provided some historical examples of the dangers attending a single state religion. He included Islam, but only after first expounding the dangers of Catholicism. It was a long-standing Protestant polemical approach to denigrate both Islam and Catholicism together, as also reflected in his reference to the Reformation:

Monksh. Imposns.—ignorce.—darknss. suppd. on
ruins Enqry.
[Monkish impositions—ignorance.—darkness. supported on
ruins [of] enquiry.]
Glorious Reformn. effect of shakg. off Pub. opn.
[Glorious Reformation [had] effect of shaking off public opinion.]
Mahomsm. supportd. by stiflg. *free enqry.*
[Mahometanism supported by stifling free enquiry.][169]

Under this declaration, Jefferson concluded that "Philos. reformd by *free* enq.," or "Philosophy is reformed by free enquiry," to which he appended as proof the names of two towering scientific figures: Galileo and Newton.[170] (Galileo, whose ideas were repressed by the Catholic Inquisition, may seem rather a victim of "monkish impositions" than a proof of "free enquiry," but Jefferson acknowledged as much later in his *Notes on Virginia*.)[171] He argued that suppression of rational thought, whether religious or not, was a sign of the weakness, even error, of whatever system relied on such means to control its adherents. This premise, he believed, held true universally, whether that system of thought was Islam or Christianity.

Why Jefferson Chose Not to Draw Explicitly on Sale's Qur'an, Choosing Instead *Cato's Letters* in His Political Vocabulary on Islam

Why did Jefferson neglect Sale's Qur'an and its more thorough, better-informed views of Islam? In short, he recognized what he needed when he saw it.[172] Though a meticulous reader and note taker, Jefferson was also a politician and knew what his audience would respond to and how to sway them.

Long before taking notes on Voltaire's anti-Islamic essay, Jefferson had probably absorbed similar caricatures from *Cato's Letters,* an even more popular text in the American colonies. He owned the 1748 edition[173] of these Whig political tracts, which were published between 1720 and 1723,[174] and though he recorded no notes regarding Islam, he had certainly read *Cato's Letters* long before his debates on religion in Virginia, as had most of his Revolutionary American cohort.[175] As described in chapter 1, these tracts contained repeated pleas for greater civil and religious liberties, along with a vision of Islam as the foundation of the most religiously and politically repressive regimes on earth.[176]

Attempting to divorce religion from state control, Jefferson found in *Cato's Letter* number 66 an example of the Islamic fusion of these spheres. The tract "Arbitrary Government proved incompatible with true Religion, whether Natural or Revealed," published on February 17, 1721, condemned both the Islamic conquests and Muslim rulers. The conquests in the Middle East were inaccurately attributed to "the *Caliphs* of *Egypt,* who founded the *Saracen* Empire there," and who "were at once Kings and Priests." As to the rulers, Trenchard and Gordon revile them roundly: "there never lived more raging Bigots, or more furious and oppressive Barbarians." But the kernel of the objection here was to the merging of political and religious power in one entity, the caliph, as *khalifat rasul Allah,* or "the successor to the Prophet of God."[177]

Jefferson's debate points in Virginia in 1776 echoed the anti-Islamic precedents that his fellow legislators would have already known and accepted.[178] His point in comparing Islam to the Anglican establishment of state religion in Virginia would have been lost on no one as he suggested that this form of repressive Christianity had become antithetical to individual liberties, a belief his listeners already attributed to Islam. Jefferson did not pioneer this strategy, but he put it to good use in the House of Delegates. But, unlike Voltaire, Jefferson distinguished between Islam, which he freely disparaged, and its adherents, whose civil rights figured in his most important Virginia legislation, A Bill for Establishing Religious Freedom, which sought political and religious equality for all believers. In framing this legislation in 1777, he followed his intellectual hero, John Locke, but would surpass him by aiming for universalism.[179] Unlike Locke, Jefferson would brook no exceptions based on religion in his concept of citizenship in Virginia—and, by extension, the newly founded United States.[180]

While Locke proposed that Muslims and Jews should be officially tolerated as citizens in English Anglican society, Jefferson imagined them as full citizens with equal civil rights in a non-Anglican, and even a non-Christian society.[181] Nor did he share Locke's qualms about including Catholics or atheists in the new country.

JEFFERSON BORROWS IDEAS ABOUT MUSLIM AND JEWISH RIGHTS FROM LOCKE, OCTOBER 1776

In October 1776, a month before his debate to end the Anglican establishment in Virginia, Jefferson considered a more universal question: "Why persecute for diffce. [difference] in religs. [religious] opinion?"[182] Many in Europe had already struggled and suffered in the absence of an answer, leading a critical minority in seventeenth-century England and North America to consider the toleration of Muslims as a basis for ending the scourge of religious persecution of Christians. But no one until Thomas Jefferson had ventured to legally substantiate the idea of Muslims as citizens in the United States.

Jefferson drew his inspiration for Muslim "civil rights" directly from John Locke's 1689 A Letter Concerning Toleration. While Locke had made multiple references to Muslims and Islam, Jefferson preserved only the salient ones in his notes: "[He] sais 'neither Pagan nor Mahamedan nor Jew ought to be excluded from the civil rights of the Commonwealth because of his religion.'"[183] Here in Jefferson's notation is the first attempt in the new nation to consider the "civil rights" of both Muslims and Jews.[184]

As in earlier European thought on tolerance and toleration, the fates of both groups remained entwined. While Locke, as we have seen, would continue a vigorous defense of Muslim civil rights in his second, third, and fourth letters on toleration, Jefferson never cited these, relying entirely on the first letter for his precedent.[185]

Jefferson's paraphrase of Locke included a slight abbreviation of the original, omitting the introductory words: "Nay, if we may openly speak the Truth, and as becomes one man to another." But he does replicate William Popple's 1689 English translation of Locke's groundbreaking idea that "neither Pagan nor Mahumetan, nor Jew, ought to be excluded from the Civil Rights of the Commonwealth because of his Religion."[186]

Jefferson's notes ignore Locke's defense of various Christian heretical sects preceding his mention of Muslims and Jews: "Presbyterians, Independents, Anabaptists, Arminians, Quakers and others." It was perhaps another matter of rhetorical strategy: Locke was using the case of Christian heretics to clear his way to toleration for Muslims and Jews, whereas Jefferson was using the case of Muslims and Jews to extend tolerance not just to dissenting Protestants but to all faiths. Nor did Jefferson choose to repeat Locke's reference to the Christian scriptures—"The Gospel commands no such thing"—which immediately followed his demand not to exclude Muslims and Jews from the civil rights of the Commonwealth on religious grounds. Defending the rights of non-Christians, Jefferson would make no appeal to Christian

Jefferson's notes on Locke: "[He] sais 'neither Pagan nor Mahamedan nor Jew ought to be excluded from the civil rights of the Commonwealth because of his religion.'"

precepts, as Locke, Helwys, and Williams had done in the seventeenth century.[187]

Instead, paraphrasing Locke's defense of the rights of non-Christian groups, Jefferson posed a question grounded in what appeared to be cultural neutrality: "shall we suffer a Pagan to deal with us and not suffer him to pray to *his god*?"[188] Locke had originally put the question in more ecumenical terms, asking, "shall we not suffer him [the pagan] to pray unto and worship God?"[189] It is a subtle distinction: Jefferson's absolute tolerance of other religions as against Locke's qualified plea for tolerance, based on an implicit belief in the superiority of Protestant Christianity. But both men, to be sure, placed commercial and diplomatic considerations above any disapproval they harbored of the idolatrous religious beliefs of "pagans," by which term Locke also encompassed Native Americans and African-born slaves, a measure of inclusiveness that Jefferson, a slave owner, would have likely rejected.[190]

Locke might tolerate Muslims and Jews as residents under an Anglican Protestant government, but he never expected their salvation except through conversion to the state religion.[191] (In this regard, his view was not unlike that of George Sale.) Jefferson, however, believed it was not for the state but the individual to be concerned about his own salvation, be he Christian, Muslim, Jew, or pagan. His ideal society was, from the first, one of religious pluralism and not foundationally Protestant or even Christian, a fact reflected in his legislation of October 1776 on immigration and citizenship.

Non-Protestant Citizenship as Law: Jefferson's Earliest Legislation About Immigration Without Regard to Religion, October 1776

Though Jefferson might accept Locke's thinking about the civil rights of Muslims and Jews, the question remains: Did he intend for them to become citizens of his state? The answer is clarified by one of his earliest pieces of legislation put forth on October 14, 1776: A Bill for the Naturalization of Foreign Protestants.[192] Jefferson crossed out the original title from the first draft by his fellow legislator Edmund Pendleton and replaced it with A Bill for the Naturalization of Foreigners, thus implicitly opening the door to Catholics, as well as Muslims and Jews.[193] He later removed "Foreigners" and made it "Persons."[194]

By November, the bill was debated by the state Committee on Religion, on which Jefferson served. On the back of the bill, he wrote debate notes, most specifically supporting the admission of Jews, and listing some of the "advantages" of universal citizenship, including the economic and demographic considerations of "Consumption, Labor, Procreation." He then defended Jewish character with the words "Honesty" and "Veracity." He added a rhetorical question somewhat later: "Religion—is theirs less moral." Jefferson also enumerated the dangers of religious discrimination, warning that "all who have not *full rights* are secret enem[ies]."[195] This idea might have been inspired by Locke, who wrote in his first letter on toleration:

> Let those Dissenters enjoy the same Privileges in Civils as his other Subjects, and he will quickly find that these Religious Meetings will no longer be dangerous. For if men enter into Seditious Conspiracies, 'tis not Religion that inspires them to it in their Meetings; but their Sufferings and Oppressions that make them willing to ease themselves. Just and moderate Governments are everywhere quiet, every where safe. But Oppression raises Ferments, and makes men struggle to cast off an uneasie and tyrannical Yoke.[196]

Jefferson then wrote that "this Obj.[ect] no nation allows them to realize," referring to the reality that Jews were barred from full citizenship everywhere in the world. Finally, he concluded, "Jews advantageous."[197] Despite Jefferson's best efforts, however, the bill never became law.[198]

Julian Boyd, the editor of Jefferson's voluminous early papers, was first to emphasize that this rejection of Protestant exclusivity in immigration and naturalization in Virginia—and by extension the United States—opened the door to Catholics.[199] Indeed, the bill mentioned no religious qualification in affirming that "all persons born in other countries," after residing for an unspecified number of years in Virginia, "shall be considered as Free Citizens of the same and shall be entitled to the Rights, privileges and immunities civil and religious of this Commonwealth, as those born therein."[200] There was, however, a requirement that an "Oath of Fidelity" to the "Commonwealth" be taken by new residents. Jefferson would draft his own version of this pledge of allegiance to the state in 1779.

Jefferson probably knew no Jews personally during this period.

There were only about two thousand in the country at the time, and a Baptist contemporary noted that there were no synagogues in Virginia.[201] Indeed Jefferson's support of Jewish rights was given without understanding very much about Judaism; what he did know, he found "defective in several respects." He rejected the idea that the Old Testament was divinely revealed, believing that God's existence must be proven only through rational means. Though embracing what he defined as Jewish "Deism," he rejected the religion's vision of God as "cruel, vindictive, capricious, and unjust."[202] Nor did he have much regard for the rabbinate or its politically coercive policies, which he described as "bloodthirsty," "cruel," and "remorseless."[203]

Yet in spite of his reservations about the faith, Jefferson supported Jewish religious and political equality, and would later collaborate and correspond with a few American Jews. One, David S. Franks, a patriot of the Revolutionary War, would serve as his secretary from 1782 to 1783. They also worked together in France, when Jefferson served as minister and Franks as vice-consul in Marseille.[204] In 1820, Jefferson wrote Joseph Marx, also a Jew, of his "regret . . . at seeing a sect, the parent and basis of all those of Christendom, singled out by all of them for persecution and oppression." Six months before his death, the former president would aver that colleges forcing Jewish students to study Christianity were making "a cruel addition to the wrongs which that injured sect have suffered," excluding them "from the instructions in science afforded to others in our public seminaries by imposing on them a course of theological reading which their consciences do not permit them to pursue."[205]

This theological objection to a religion together with support for the rights of its adherents would be replicated in Jefferson's stance on Islam and Muslims. As with Jews at this early point, there was no personal acquaintance with actual Muslims to inspire his advocacy for their religious and political equality. And although he attempted to study Islam, his learning was limited and often faulty, and sometimes entirely negative. Still, his low opinion of Islam as a religion and a political system had no bearing on his support for the rights of a future population of American Muslims. His principles of toleration and inclusion were universal respecting not only religion but immigration and citizenship, and so implicitly Muslims too had a place in the pluralist society he envisioned for Virginia and the United States.

THE LIMITS OF TOLERATION FOR LOCKE
SURPASSED BY JEFFERSON

In his notes on Locke, Jefferson's first reference to Muslims notes that Locke "denies toleration" to those whose opinions are "contrary to those moral rules necessary for the preservation of society," including people whose "obedience is due to some foreign prince," or those "who will not own & teach the duty of tolerating all men in matters of religion, or who deny the existence of a god."[206] As mentioned, Locke had been concerned that some Muslims in England would owe fealty to the chief cleric in Istanbul and, by extension, to the Ottoman sultan. He had also refused toleration to atheists, citing their will to "undermine and destroy all Religion," and considered their oaths untrustworthy, since they recognized no otherworldly consequences for lying.[207] Jefferson harbored no such fears, and included atheists as well as Muslims in his vision for a new society.[208] Likewise, he rejected Locke's belief that Catholics should be considered a threat because of their allegiance to the pope. In a footnote, Jefferson affirmed that it was a civil offense for a citizen to acknowledge "a foreign prince," but refused the idea that any religious devotion would necessarily corrupt civic loyalty.[209] Indeed, unlike Locke, Jefferson never specifically attributed any conflict of loyalties to either Muslims or Catholics.[210]

In 1779, Jefferson drafted A Bill Prescribing the Oath of Fidelity and the Oaths of Certain Public Officers. The legislation required that anyone "migrating hither to become citizens of the commonwealth shall take the following oath of fidelity before some court of record." The would-be citizen had to "relinquish and renounce the character of subject or citizen of any Prince, or other state, whatsoever, and abjure all allegiance, which may be claimed by such Prince, or other state." The oath concluded, "and I do swear to be faithful and true to the said commonwealth of Virginia, so long as I continue a citizen thereof."[211] Most notable in this pledge, which was also to be taken by all would-be holders of government office, is its absence of a religious test. There is nothing to exclude non-Protestants from citizenship, and by implication no religious requirement for any who might seek office. Here then is the first American legislative precedent for the Constitution's explicit proscription of a religious test in Article VI, section 3, which states that an individual should be bound only "by Oath or Affirmation, to support this Constitution." The traditional notion expressed by Locke that the validity of an oath is contingent on one's faith thus fell away.

In his 1784 *Notes on Virginia,* we find Jefferson's only reflections in print about his legislative struggle from 1776 through 1779 over religious freedom in the Commonwealth. Offering "a summary view of that religious slavery under which people have been willing to remain," he concludes, "The rights of conscience we never submitted, we could not submit. We are answerable for them to our God." Despite this evidence of Jefferson's own belief in a divine being, immediately thereafter comes his famous defense of the freedom to believe—or *not* believe—in anything:

> The legitimate powers of government extend to such acts only as are injurious to others. But it does me no injury for my neighbor to say there are twenty gods or no God. It neither picks my pocket nor breaks my leg.[212]

In proposing that government's only rightful purview was over behavior and explicitly not the metaphysical beliefs of its citizens, Jefferson unintentionally invited his political enemies to question his Christian convictions, an attack that would continue throughout his political life.[213]

Jefferson agreed with Locke that toleration should be denied those "who will not own & teach the duty of tolerating all men in matters of religion," but where Locke stipulated other exceptions, Jefferson demanded universal toleration beyond the ranks of the intolerant. "[It was a great thing to go so far (as he himself sais of the parl. [parliament] who framed the act of tolern.) [toleration]," he writes of Locke's effort, "but where he stopped short we may go on.]"[214] (The 1689 Toleration Act had granted freedom of worship and political office to certain non-Anglican Protestants, including Baptists and Congregationalists, but explicitly excluded Catholics and Unitarians, and implicitly Jews and Muslims.) The safeguard Jefferson proposed to make his more expansive vision work was the mandatory oath that would stipulate tolerance as a precondition for like treatment: "Perhaps the single thing which may be required of others before toleration to them would be an oath that they would allow toleration to others."[215]

Jefferson's insistence on this expansive vision was not built on ideal-

ism for its own sake but a practical awareness of the terrible legacy of
European religious violence, which he determined his own state and
country should escape. He had collected several books by Sebastian
Castellio, who in the sixteenth century had proposed an end to religious
persecution in the name of Christianity, advocating for Christian heretics as well as Muslims and Jews, even in his preface to his Latin New
Testament,[216] which Jefferson inscribed with his initials.[217] Though he
did not possess Castellio's most important treatise, *Concerning Heretics,*
written in response to the 1553 immolation of Michael Servetus, Jefferson did note Voltaire's description of Calvin's role in Servetus's fiery
death.[218] Perhaps it inspired his later, private assessment of Calvin as
"an atheist," whose "religion was daemonism." His final word on the
Protestant reformer could apply equally to all intolerance in the name
of faith: "If ever a man worshipped a false God, he did."[219]

JEFFERSON'S CRITIQUE OF COERCION IN RELIGION: MOVING BEYOND LOCKE'S CHRISTIAN STATE AND TOWARD SUPPORT FOR "DIFFERENCE OF OPINION" IN RELIGION

As much as Jefferson despised Calvin, he venerated John Locke, placing him among "my trinity of the three greatest men the world had
ever produced,"[220] the other two being Isaac Newton (d. 1727) and
Francis Bacon (d. 1626).[221] In Locke, Jefferson would find the language
he needed to frame a legal abolition of his state's control over religion.
Borrowing from the philosopher, he writes:

> [Co]mpulsion in religion is distinguished peculiarly from compulsion
> in every other thing. I may grow rich by art I am compelled to follow,
> I may recover health by medicines I am compelled to take agt. [against]
> my own judgmt. [judgment], but I cannot be saved by a *worship* I dis-
> believe & abhor.[222]

A year later, in 1777, Locke's thought would be echoed by Jefferson
in his Bill for Establishing Religious Freedom, which decried not only
religious coercion but its material support through taxation: "that to
compel a man to furnish contributions of money for the propagation
of opinions which he disbelieves *and abhors* is sinful and tyrannical."[223]

The two words taken directly from Locke—"and abhors"—would be deleted from the legislation as finally passed, no doubt out of political necessity, but surely suggest Jefferson's unvarnished opinion.

Jefferson further elaborated his own view later in his *Notes on Virginia,* justifying his universalism by setting American Protestantism in a global perspective. The practical futility of the alternative is clear, even if one allowed for evangelical aspirations:

> What has been the effect of coercion? To make one half the world fools, and the other half hypocrites. To support roguery and error all over the earth. Let us reflect that it is inhabited by a thousand millions of people. That these profess probably a thousand different systems of religion. That ours is but one of that thousand. That if there be but one right, and ours that one, we should wish to see the nine hundred and ninety-nine wandering sects gathered into the fold of truth. But against such a majority we cannot effect this by force. Reason and persuasion are the only practicable instruments. To make way for these, free inquiry must be indulged; and how can we wish others to indulge it while we refuse it ourselves.[224]

In fact, Jefferson was prepared to acknowledge no religion as uniquely "right," but even if such existed and "ours [be] that one," there was still no justification for converting others by "force."[225] On this point, he agrees broadly with Castellio, Locke, and Sale, but goes beyond all of them in envisioning a society in which the rights of non-Christians would not depend on the Christian sentiments of the majority.

Locke, by contrast, maintains an ultimately Christian frame of reference, even as he laments Christianity's loss of prestige owing to an inclination toward "Factions, Tumults, and Civil Wars," a history that fostered in some an impression that "the Christian Religion is the worst of all Religions, and ought neither to be embraced by any particular Person, nor tolerated in any Commonwealth." Locke vehemently rejects this critique, arguing that Christianity is "the most modest and peaceable religion that ever was."[226] He professes a sincere belief in the "genius" of Christianity, even while admitting its presence in "turbulent and destructive" cases of religious intolerance. Indeed, Locke believed that his definition of toleration—rooted in Christian precepts—could itself prevent religious persecution, so long as the majority remained firmly Christian:

We must therefore seek another cause of those evils that are imputed to religion. And if we consider rightly, we shall find it to consist wholly in the subject that I am discussing: It is not the diversity of opinions, which cannot be avoided, but the refusal of toleration to people of diverse opinions, which could have been granted, that has produced most of the disputes and wars that have arisen in the Christian world on account of religion.[227]

Characteristically, Jefferson condenses this sentiment and questions the "genius" of Christianity that Locke so admired:

[Wh]y have Xns. [Christians] been distinguished above all people who have ever lived for persecutions? is it because it is the genius of their religion? No, it's [*sic*] genius is the reverse. It is the refusing toleration to those of a different opn. [opinion] which has produced all the bustles & wars on account of religion.[228]

But not until 1784 would Jefferson explicitly enunciate a radical idea taken from Locke that had motivated his groundbreaking legislation on religious freedom: "Difference of opinion is advantageous in religion."[229] It was a notion that would shock many of his contemporaries in the newly formed United States.

Making Locke's Ideas into Law: Jefferson's Bill for Establishing Religious Freedom, 1777

Between 1776 and 1779, Jefferson drafted over one hundred pieces of legislation for the state of Virginia, but until his dying day he would remain most proud of number eighty-two: A Bill for Establishing Religious Freedom, which would be called "the Statute of Virginia for religious freedom" on his tombstone.[230] It was Jefferson's will that it be so listed among what he deemed his three major achievements, the other two being his authorship of the Declaration of Independence and the founding of the University of Virginia. Jefferson drew several points for the statute directly from Locke, including the aforementioned argument against taxes supporting the "abhorred" state religion.[231] From Locke's first letter on toleration, Jefferson had noted that "the magistrate's jurisdn. [jurisdiction] extends only to civil rights."[232] From Locke's poetical assessment of the limitations of temporal authority—

"the narrow way which leads to Heaven is not better known to the Magistrate than to other private Persons"[233]—Jefferson produced a more lawyerly paraphrase in his notes: "I cannot give up my guidance to the magistrate; because he knows no more the way to heaven than I do & is less concerned to direct me right than I am to go right."[234] But in drafting the bill, he evokes his own powerful voice:

> [T]he impious presumption of legislators and rulers, civil as well as ecclesiastical, who, being themselves but fallible and uninspired men, have assumed dominion over the faith of others, setting up their own opinions and modes of thinking as the only true and infallible, and as such endeavoring to impose them on others, hath established and maintained false religions over the greatest part of the world and through all time.[235]

If government has no business meddling in matters of faith, it follows that every individual's religious freedom should be protected by law. But such protection would require a perfect neutrality toward religion on the part of the state, and in 1777 such did not exist in the United States or in Europe. As Merrill D. Peterson explains:

> Everywhere in the world, church and state were united, and dissenters from the one true faith—the established religion—while they might be tolerated, suffered numerous pains and penalties. Jefferson proposed a revolutionary change based on two principles: first, absolute freedom of religious conscience and opinion; and second, the separation of church and state. Each principle was dependent on the other, in his view. True religious freedom cannot exist as long as the state is a party to or adopts as much as an opinion about religion; and the state cannot be disentangled from religious quarrels and hatreds except under conditions of freedom, wherein no church or sect is dominant.[236]

To achieve a separation of civic and religious authority, upon which true religious freedom depended, Jefferson would appropriate not only Locke's idea about the fallibility of the ruler in spiritual matters, but also another point from Locke's first letter:

> No private Person has any Right, in any manner, to prejudice another Person in his Civil Enjoyments, because he is of another Church or Religion. All Rights and Franchises belong to him as a Man, or as a

Denison, are inviolably to be preserved to him. These are not the business of Religion.[237]

In translating Locke's notion of rights by natural law, Jefferson's statute rejects any denial of rights on the basis of religion, and in particular the denial of the privilege of office:

[T]hat our civil rights have no dependance on our religious opinions ... that therefore the proscribing any citizen as unworthy the public confidence by laying upon him an incapacity of being called to offices of trust and emolument, unless he profess or renounce this or that religious opinion, is depriving him injuriously of those privileges and advantages to which, in common with his fellow citizens, he has a natural right.[238]

It is difficult to reach any conclusion but that Jefferson intended his statute's application to extend beyond Christian denominations to include all faiths. The letter of the law as written went beyond Locke's ideal of a tolerant but still dominant Protestant establishment, prefiguring the no-religious-test clause of Article VI, section 3 of the Constitution as well as the First Amendment.

The Fight over the Final Passage of Jefferson's Bill, 1785–86, and the Inclusion of Muslims as Citizens in Jefferson's Universal Intent, 1821

That Jefferson's universalism was meant to include Muslims as well as Jews is attested by a passage in his 1821 autobiography.[239] However, the lack of explicit references in his legislation did not prevent it from being blocked in 1779, when it was first proposed. But in 1785, while Jefferson was away in France, James Madison undertook to lobby for the bill, winning Jefferson's admiration. Jefferson praised Madison for his "unwearied exertions" in directing his most important bill's passage, a monumental victory achieved on January 16, 1786,[240] only after "warm opposition" in the last days of 1785.[241] Jefferson describes "the endless quibbles, chicaneries, perversions, vexations and delays of lawyers and demi-lawyers" that the bill suffered along the way. Indeed, while "most of the bills were passed by the legislature, with little alteration," Jefferson admitted that his original text did undergo changes.[242]

Jefferson believed that the bill had been "drawn in all the latitude of reason and right," only to encounter resistance over the breadth of its principled reach: "It still met with opposition; but, with some mutilations in the preamble, it was finally passed; and a singular proposition proved that its protection of opinion was meant to be universal." Jefferson laid bare his "universal" intent when describing a last-ditch effort to resist the insertion of the words "Jesus Christ":

> Where the preamble declares, that coercion is a departure from the plan of the holy author of our religion, an amendment was proposed, by inserting the word "Jesus Christ," so that it should read, "a departure from the plan of Jesus Christ, the holy author of our religion."[243]

In his 1776 notes on Locke, the basis of his original conception, Jefferson omitted most of the philosopher's seventeenth-century synonyms for Jesus, including "the Captain of our salvation" and "that Prince of peace," who "not armed with the sword, or with force . . . furnished the Gospel, the message of peace."[244] Jefferson did, however, understand the point of Locke's characterization of a religiously tolerant Jesus, according to his notes of 1776:

> [O]ur Saviour chose not to propagate his religion by temporal punmts [punishments] or civil incapacitation, if he had it was in his almighty power. [B]ut he chose to ["enforce" crossed out] extend it by it's [sic] influence on reason, thereby shewing others how [they] should proceed.[245]

Nevertheless, in 1777 Jefferson's legislative language deliberately departed from Locke's explicit Christian references even while alluding to Jesus's teaching, in which, by Jefferson's novel assertion, reason had taken the place of force:

> [T]hat all attempts to influence by temporal punishments, or burthens, or by civil incapacitations, tend only to beget habits of hypocrisy and meanness, and are a departure from the plan of the holy author of our religion, who being lord both of body and mind, yet chose not to propagate it by coercions on either, as was in his Almighty power to do, *but to extend it by its influence on reason alone.*[246]

The italicized final clause, which appears in Jefferson's original draft, was excised in the final version.

The question remained: Did Jefferson intend "the holy author of our religion" to be synonymous with Jesus Christ as Locke clearly had? Most fellow legislators, all Anglican Christians, would certainly have assumed as much. Not surprisingly, some moved to make the reference explicit, but the bill's author emphatically refused. In his final word on the subject, Jefferson rejoiced in the ultimate rejection of the attempted assertion of those two pivotal words: "Jesus Christ":

> [T]he insertion [of "Jesus Christ"] was rejected by a great majority, in proof that they meant to comprehend, within the mantle of its protection, the Jew and the Gentile, the Christian and Mahometan, the Hindoo, and Infidel of every denomination.[247]

From Jefferson's "Autobiography": At the bottom of the page, he advocates for the protection of "the Jew and the Gentile, the Christian and Mahometan, the Hindoo, and Infidel of every denomination."

Thus one can comfortably infer that since the 1760s and most certainly in 1776, Jefferson's ideal of national religious and political equality included Muslims, as well as Jews and all others "of every denomination," who would never have referred to themselves as "infidels."[248] On account of such convictions, by 1821 Jefferson would know firsthand what it felt like to be an "infidel," but his own use of it indicates none of the venom with which it was attached to him.

Jefferson was not alone in appreciating the impact of omitting the words "Jesus Christ"; Madison agreed that allowing them would have vitiated the universal intent with an implied establishment of Christianity, or as he wrote years after the bill's passage, the mention of Jesus was designed "to imply a restriction of the liberty defined in the Bill, to those professing his [Jesus Christ's] religion only."[249]

By standing fast, Jefferson ended the establishment of Protestant Christianity in Virginia. In the final lines of his bill's text he warned future generations against overturning the law, reminding them that "the rights hereby asserted are of the natural rights of mankind, and that if any act shall be hereafter passed to repeal the present or to narrow its operation, such act will be an infringement of natural right."[250] The right to one's chosen faith was to be understood ever after as a natural endowment, not contingent on even the most beneficent God.

THE FIRST AMERICAN MUSLIMS: RACE, SLAVERY, AND THE LIMITS OF JEFFERSON'S "UNIVERSAL" LEGISLATION

Jefferson believed until the end of his life that his legislation concerning religious freedom had universal scope, protecting all believers, including Muslims. But he was wrong. While his bill would retain enormous importance for future free American Muslim citizens in the nineteenth, twentieth, and twenty-first centuries, his universal vision never included the first American Muslims, who in the seventeenth and eighteenth centuries were West African slaves transported to North America against their will. Considered by Jefferson to be property rather than citizens, a view his hero Locke had also endorsed, these Muslims of African descent enjoyed no freedoms of any kind.[251] They could not practice their faith anywhere, except secretively or at least circumspectly in the proximity of Protestant slaveholders and among an increasing majority of slave converts to Protestant Christianity.[252] Nor could they ever claim political equality. Race and slavery placed them beyond rights and, apparently, beyond Jefferson's vision, despite the distinct possibility that slaves of Muslim heritage might have lived on his own plantations.

There were certainly more Muslim slaves in eighteenth-century America than Jews, and possibly more than the twenty-five thousand Catholics in the United States at its inception.[253] How many Muslim slaves? Their numbers while significant remain difficult to specify exactly. The historian Michael Gomez observed that "53 percent of all those imported to North America" were taken from four areas of West Africa in which "Islam was of varying consequence." Of the estimated 481,000 West Africans "imported into British North America" as a result of the slave trade, "nearly 255,000 came from areas influenced by Islam."[254] It is therefore reasonable to conclude, as Gomez has, that "Muslims arrived in North America by the thousands, if not tens of thousands."[255] Other historians have proposed an unverified estimate that 15 to 20 percent of all those enslaved in the Americas and the Caribbean were Muslim, but their numbers in Jefferson's Virginia would be even more difficult to define with any precision.[256]

The first twenty African slaves arrived in Virginia in 1619, but by 1756, when Jefferson was thirteen years old, there were 120,156.[257] If even 10 percent of those were Muslim, they constituted a scattered but significant minority. By 1774, Jefferson owned 187 slaves, and throughout his life this number would rise and fall with his financial fortunes.[258] Although Jefferson attempted and failed to end "this execrable commerce" of the slave trade in the first draft of the Declaration of Independence, there is no evidence that he ever met a Muslim on his Virginia plantations.[259] In the detailed inventories of slaves he kept in his *Farm Book,* which also kept account of his horses, mules, oxen, and cattle on his multiple plantations from 1774 until his death, no name of any Islamic resonance is obvious.[260]

In contrast, at Mount Vernon plantation, where Jefferson's Virginian neighbor George Washington owned more than three hundred slaves, at least two and possibly four names register a distinct Islamic identity. These include a mother and daughter, named "Fatimer" and "Little Fatimer," after the Prophet's daughter.[261] Other African slaves named Fatima have been documented in Florida, South Carolina, and Georgia in the eighteenth century.[262]

Another woman called "Nila," possibly a variation on the Arabic name Naila, and a man named Sambo, a common but not exclusively

Muslim name, also resided on Washington's plantation.[263] Sambo, which means "second son" in the Hausa and Fulbe West African languages, was also the name of a runaway slave of definitively Islamic ancestry whose return was sought in 1775 in a Savannah, Georgia, newspaper.[264] As for George Washington's Sambo, a skilled carpenter, he fled to Philadelphia during the Revolutionary War, but later was returned forcibly to Mount Vernon. The terms of Washington's will freed Sambo in 1801. As a free man, the former slave volunteered in 1835 to work on his former master's tomb at Mount Vernon.[265] Like Jefferson, Washington supported universal religious freedom for all Americans, but never considered the possible presence of Muslim slaves on his own property.[266] Unlike Jefferson, Washington's will freed all his slaves, while Jefferson, the owner of two hundred souls, manumitted only three during his lifetime and five at his death.[267]

And neither Founder ever spoke even theoretically to the potential contradiction concerning Muslim slaves.[268] But Washington's case allows us to consider the probability that Jefferson, too, owned slaves of Muslim origin, no matter what their names. But until 1786 his knowledge of Muslims and their faith would remain entirely book-bound.

Given Jefferson's now certain intimacy with his slave Sally Hemings, and their resulting seven children (only five of whom survived infancy), it even remains possible (though as yet not provable) that the Founder's children may have had a Muslim great-grandmother of West African origin.[269] Recent scholarship by Annette Gordon-Reed, depicting the Hemingses as "an American family" also opens space for speculating about them as a potential American Muslim family.[270] If this could be documented, then the tragedy of Jefferson's most cherished achievement, which in principle included Muslims, would be its failure in practice to embrace his own children—and their mother.[271]

The founding father of Muslim rights in America, Jefferson had legislated theoretical equality for a population he presumed to be foreign, never recognizing those already present in his country. Although prepared to take an unusual leap on behalf of future free, white Muslims, he could not, as a man of his times, see beyond the race and enslaved status of Americans already present in Virginia, to imagine a day when they might be counted as citizens.

The complications of race and slavery would render Jefferson's theory of rights, in both the Declaration of Independence and A Bill for Establishing Religious Freedom, less than universal in application. He could acknowledge this contradiction in the former founding document, but never in the latter Virginia statute, in part because he never realized that there were slaves who were being denied, among other rights, the freedom of religion. The first American Muslims remained invisible to the new country's most impassioned defender of Muslim rights.

Before he crossed the Atlantic to take up diplomatic duties in Europe, Jefferson had never met a Muslim. This would change when he and his friend John Adams met in London to negotiate a peace treaty with the Muslim ambassador from Tripoli in 1786. The two Founders would try to solve the problem of North African piracy through negotiation, despite diametrically opposed views of effective foreign policy.

4

Jefferson Versus John Adams

The Problem of North African Piracy and Their Negotiations with a Muslim Ambassador in London, 1784–88

Would it not be better to offer them an equal treaty. If they refuse, why not go to war with them? Spain, Portugal, Naples and Venice are now at war with them. Every part of the Mediterranean therefore would offer us friendly ports. We ought to begin a naval power, if we mean to carry on our own commerce. Can we begin it on a more honourable occasion or with a weaker foe?

—Thomas Jefferson supports war against North African pirates, November 1784

The policy of Christendom has made Cowards of all their Sailors before the Standard of Mahomet.

—John Adams to Thomas Jefferson, July 1786

"THERE IS a Tripolitan Ambassador with whom I have had three conferences," wrote John Adams from London on February 21, 1786, inviting Thomas Jefferson, then serving as a diplomat in Paris, to help negotiate a treaty with the Muslim envoy from Tripoli, the North African coastal city in what is today Libya. Jefferson would comply the next month.[1]

In March 1786, three months after the landmark legislation on religious freedom in Virginia was passed in his absence, Jefferson would for the first time encounter a real Muslim, one of only two he ever knowingly met. The month before had been Adams's first time meeting a Muslim too.

In London, Jefferson and John Adams listened as the ambassador from Tripoli referred to the Qur'an to justify naval attacks against American shipping in the Mediterranean, which the two Americans duly noted in their joint communiqué. It is possible that the Muslim ambassador's invocation of specific passages in the sacred text caused Jefferson to consult his own copy, perhaps even presenting the occasion when the Founder saw fit to mark the book with his initials. To judge by Jefferson's single reference to the Qur'an in the context of Adams's three earlier meetings with the Muslim ambassador, as well as the fourth, at which Jefferson was present, it is clear that religion, however convenient a rationale for "Islamic piracy," was not the paramount issue in American negotiations with Tripoli. Still, in this earliest face-to-face cultural encounter, it would be Adams, not Jefferson, who emphasized religion in his perceptions of the enemy.

This chapter traces the evolution of Jefferson's thinking about the piracy problem from 1784 to 1788. His strategy was, from the first, governed not by religious but political and economic considerations. These drove his early, somewhat duplicitous attempt to solve the problem by military means without informing Adams, who believed that payment for peace was the nation's better course. As early as 1784, Jefferson preferred a military response to what he considered piratical extortion, but not until 1801, when he was president, would he act on this impulse. Until then, his diplomatic efforts were doomed to failure, since the United States had neither a navy to protect its ships nor even a central government authorized to collect taxes that might be used to pay tribute for peace or the ransom of American captives held in North Africa.[2] Piracy, as this chapter documents, was not an exclusively Muslim practice in the Mediterranean, but the taking of captives did provoke difficult questions in America about individual liberty and freedom in the face of what was essentially a faith-based form of slavery.[3] Ironically, throughout the effort to end this bondage of their fellow citizens, most Americans, including Jefferson, would never connect it to the contemporaneous American practice of race-based slavery inflicted on captured West Africans.

* God as the authority for violence

PIRACY AND RELIGION

The problem of piracy was at the heart of Jefferson's diplomatic career in Europe, and his effort to fight this mischief perpetrated by the four Islamic powers of Morocco, Algiers, Tunis, and Tripoli (collectively known in Europe and America as the Barbary States) has been well documented elsewhere.[4] But his refusal to construe this threat to American lives and commerce as primarily a conflict between a Christian United States and an Islamic North Africa has not been sufficiently explored.[5] Recent histories of the U.S. encounter with North Africa confirm this point more generally. As the historian Frank Lambert asserts, "Evidence abounds that neither the pirates nor the Americans considered religion central to their conflict."[6] Instead, the motivations on both sides were more mercenary: American merchants were willing to risk their liberty for commercial gain in the Mediterranean, while the pirates of North Africa believed it their right to attack and hold for ransom all those who ventured into waters they controlled.[7] *commercial gain*

nor should they have?

The liberty and equality that were in Jefferson's view the natural rights of white American males were threatened by the North African powers, which also rejected his internationalist notions of universal free trade in other nations' waters.[8] From the North Africans' perspective, these lofty and naive American suppositions only disrupted a business plied profitably in the Mediterranean by both Christians and Muslims since the sixteenth century. Americans, like Europeans before them, had a choice about how to secure access to coveted markets in the eastern Atlantic along the coasts of Spain and Portugal and on the northern Mediterranean littoral. They knew this could be done by purchasing expensive peace settlements with the pirates. But absent this cost of safe passage, they would run the acknowledged risk of the seizure of ships, goods, and civilians, the latter being taken with the express purpose of securing lucrative ransoms for their freedom. This was the customary arrangement, and it took no account of the self-evident rights Americans believed they had secured by breaking from Great Britain.[9]

Adams: Religion.
Jefferson: commercial

Six months after the fruitless negotiations with the ambassador from Tripoli, John Adams, unlike Jefferson, saw the conflict as a religious one. As he wrote Jefferson in July 1786, "The policy of Christendom has made Cowards of all their Sailors before the Standard of Mahomet."[10] Jefferson, who had deliberately disestablished Christianity in Virginia, could see the problem at this first stage in the 1780s and early 1790s

only in political terms. Even in his private letters, he never emphasized the religious differences of the opposing sides. As a consequence,
their respective responses to the crisis differed, amounting to the first
major break in what would later evolve into a tempestuous relationship
between the two men.

AMERICANS AS CAPTIVES: THE POSSIBILITY OF RANSOM

American captives seized by North African pirates defined themselves as
slaves, just as their captors defined them, but the terms of their captivity
differed from those of American slavery, although the differences were
not always obvious. For one thing, Muslims theoretically distinguished
between captivity (*asr*) and slavery (*ubudiyya*),[11] a Qur'anic distinction,
admittedly often lost on captive Americans.[12] Also blurring the difference was that Muslims practiced their own race-based enslavement of
black West and sub–Saharan Africans; these slaves lost freedom for life,
a practice supported by Islam as it was by Judaism and Christianity.

Nevertheless, the captive/slave distinction was ultimately crucial,
and Christians captured by Muslim pirates were not considered as
slaves, perpetually unfree, but as captives. As people "taken in military or naval encounters between armies or privateers," they might be
exchanged for ransom.[13] If their countrymen could raise the money for
their release, their freedom could be restored. There is no question that
most American captives suffered years of privation, harsh forced labor,
intermittent cruelty by their overseers, outbreaks of plague, and death.
The captivity they endured was comparable to slavery, although Christian captives were free to practice their faith.[14] And they had the hope,
at least in principle, of being released, but for many it took years to
be ransomed through negotiation and treaty agreements. Some gained
their freedom another way: through conversion to Islam.

A few American captives, such as James Cathcart, even prospered
as prisoners in North Africa. Beginning in 1785, Cathcart spent eleven
years as a captive in Algiers, where he rose from coffee maker to chief
Christian clerk of the Muslim ruler. He helped negotiate the treaty
that led to his release, arriving back in the United States in a ship he
purchased with the money he earned while a prisoner.[15] (Cathcart was
allowed to run a tavern in prison and retain half the income.)[16] He
later returned to North Africa as the U.S. consul to Tripoli.[17] Richard

O'Brien, a ship's captain also held in Algiers, would later return to that city as the U.S. consul.[18]

WEST AFRICAN AND NORTH AFRICAN SLAVES: TWO TYPES OF SLAVERY SELDOM COMPARED BY AMERICANS

In contrast to the lot of American prisoners, tens of thousands of West Africans remained in permanent slavery in the United States, a condition that would also trap their progeny for generations. American protests against the enslavement of their countrymen abroad naturally prompted some to object to African slavery at home, but these early dissenters remained in the minority.[19] For Jefferson, as for most other Americans, the exclusion of blacks from the rights enumerated in the Declaration of Independence may have been more than an appeasement of colonies economically dependent on slavery; their view of the races as essentially unequal allowed them to conclude that while white, American captives deserved their freedom, black, West African (and Muslim) slaves did not. Indeed, Jefferson's thoughts about racial difference emphasize the inferiority of blacks and, ultimately, his resistance to their emancipation.[20] Some, including Benjamin Franklin, supported the abolition of all slavery. But Jefferson, though he advocated the abolition of the slave trade in 1776, never considered North African and North American slavery as comparable evils.[21] Or as Paul Finkelman observed, Jefferson "willingly went to war to protect whites from enslavement, while retaining his own black slaves."[22] What to us today seems hypocritical did not trouble Jefferson, or indeed most Americans of his day.

Others did try to persuade Jefferson about the evils of slavery everywhere, including his daughter Martha and his friend the Marquis de Lafayette (d. 1834), French hero of the American Revolutionary War. Martha wrote her father, who was traveling in southern France in 1787, the year after his negotiations in London with the ambassador from Tripoli, that a ship from Virginia en route to Spain had nearly been captured by an Algerian "corser." Martha explained that after an exchange of fire, the American vessel had prevailed, whereupon the victorious Americans boarded the Algerian vessel, where they "found chains that had been prepared for them."[23] The Americans "made use of them for the Algerians themselves."[24] Martha wrote in great detail about this incident, but it apparently never happened.[25] Her inspiration appears to have been her horror at the idea that the Algerians might be sold as slaves in the United States, if they could not be exchanged in Algiers for Christian captives. She worried about both the fate of the Muslim slaves from Algeria in Virginia and their West African counterparts long held in the United States:

> Good god have we not enough? I wish with all my soul that the poor negroes were all freed. It greives [sic] my heart when I think that these our fellow creatures should be treated so teribly [sic] as they are by many of our country men.[26]

Jefferson never responded to his daughter's anxieties about the evils of American slavery, or the clever way she broached them by telling a story of alleged American captives.[27] A little more than a month later, Sally Hemings, the slave who would become Jefferson's mistress, accompanied Martha's younger sister to France. Sally joined her brother James, who had served Jefferson in Paris since 1784, where the law would have granted both Sally and James their freedom, if they chose to claim it.[28] They never did.[29]

In February 1786, Lafayette had written John Adams about the issue of slavery while the latter was in London negotiating with the ambassador from Tripoli. America's involvement in the West African slave trade was, he chided Adams, a travesty committed under "the flag of liberty":

> In the case of my black brethren I feel myself warmly interested, and most decidedly side, so far as respects them, against the white part of mankind. Whatever the complexion of the enslaved, it does not, in my opinion, alter the complexion of the crime which the enslaver commits, a crime blacker than any African face. It is to me a matter of great anxiety and concern, to find this trade is sometimes perpetrated under the flag of liberty, our dear and noble stripes, to which virtue and glory have been constant standard-bearers.[30]

Adams responded to Lafayette via another correspondent. The letter was dated a few days before Jefferson's arrival in London in early March. Adams identified slavery as the result of war, part of an African "system" that he believed affected the entire continent: "The idea that captives in war are slaves, is the foundation of the misfortunes of our negroes." He then went on to connect American slavers with those Europeans "who

pay tribute to the states of Barbary."[31] Adams finally referred to a strategic connection between the North African enslavement of Americans
and the American enslavement of West Africans—a connection that in
reality did not exist:

> I expect that one part of Africa will avenge upon my fellow citizens the
> injury they do to another by purchasing their captives. Yet I presume
> we shall be compelled to follow the base example of submission, and pay
> tribute or make presents, like the rest of Christians, to the mussulmen.[32]

In conclusion, he urged Lafayette to consider slavery as a problem: "I
wish you would take up the whole of this African system, and expose it
altogether. Never, never will the slave trade be abolished, while Christian princes abase themselves before the piratical ensigns of Mahomet."[33]
Adams was prepared to acknowledge the injustice of enslaving Africans
in America, but he deflected the blame to the continent where the
Africans had come from and where they were now inflicting a reciprocal injustice on Americans. Underlying the entire ugly business in his
understanding was a religious explanation, the evil attending Christian
submission to the will of Muslims.

British Policy After 1783:
The New Vulnerability of American Shipping

Without British naval protection, Americans learned quickly that their
goods, lives, and national values were newly vulnerable to piracy in the
eastern Atlantic and the Mediterranean. In fact, after 1783, the British
found it in their commercial interest to encourage attacks against their
upstart former colonists.[34] As Lord Sheffield told the House of Commons in 1783, "The Americans cannot pretend to a navy and therefore
the great nations should suffer the Barbary pirates as a check on the
activities of the smaller Italian states and America."[35] The American
diplomat and North African captive Richard O'Brien recognized the
zero-sum situation in 1787, when he observed that "those nations at
peace with the Barbary States do not wish that any other nation should
obtain a peace," nor should they "reap part of those advantageous
branches of commerce in the Mediterranean."[36] And Benjamin Franklin reputedly heard wags about London remark, "If there had been no
Algiers, it would be worth England's while to build one."[37]

As ambassador to Britain, John Adams was acutely aware of London's anti-American predilections. In his first letter to Secretary of State John Jay about the Muslim ambassador from Tripoli, Adams expressed fear of the cooperation between Tripoli with London: "there are not wanting persons in England who will find means to stimulate this African to stir up his countrymen against American vessels." It was clear to Adams that the Muslim ambassador was in London for one of two reasons: "chiefly with a view to the United States, to draw them into a treaty of peace, which implies tribute, or at least presents; or to obtain aids from England to carry on a war against us."[38]

THE ORIGINS OF PIRACY IN NORTH AFRICA: A CHRISTIAN AND MUSLIM PRACTICE

The newly independent United States was not the most lucrative and therefore not the primary target of Islamic piracy. Nor was there a long-standing religious hostility toward American Christians among Muslims in North Africa. With independence, the United States simply became the latest in a long line of countries vulnerable to piracy. Americans now faced a problem that the Europeans first encountered in the sixteenth century, but at that time they too were also engaged in piracy and the enslavement of their captives. As Nabil Matar first asserted, "That the Barbary corsairs captured thousands of Europeans is not in question; but then, the Europeans captured and enslaved more."[39] And if one counts American slavery, Americans also captured and enslaved more Muslims than Muslim pirates seized in North Africa: tens of thousands (at top count) as against roughly seven hundred.[40]

Ironically, North African piracy in the Mediterranean and eastern Atlantic began as a desperate measure to repulse a Spanish invasion of Muslim territory. After Ferdinand and Isabella conquered and expelled the last Islamic dynasty in Spain in 1492, the Spanish went on to capture and enslave nearly one hundred thousand Muslims in their own lands in the sixteenth century.[41] The action was rationalized under the Catholic doctrine of just war, by which they acknowledged an Islamic parallel: "This is according to the custom in taking captives which is done between Muslims and Christians."[42]

Even after the Ottomans seized Tripoli, Tunis, and Algiers in the first three decades of the sixteenth century, these cities, as well as others in Morocco, still suffered Spanish military incursions. With the backing

of the Catholic rulers of Spain, Archbishop Jiménez de Cisneros established numerous *presidios,* or fortifications, along the North African
coast, seizing Oran in 1509 and Tripoli in 1510. The Spanish would hold
the former post until 1791, though they could not retain the latter.[43]

During the Spanish siege of Oran, in present-day Algeria, four thousand Muslims were killed and more than eight thousand taken as slaves.
When Tripoli fell, fifteen thousand Muslims were captured.[44] All of
these Muslims were sold in European slave markets. In 1511, King Ferdinand levied a "50 percent surtax on Algiers's woolen imports" for the
express purpose of funding "Spain's North African expeditions of conquest." Apart from subsidizing Spanish belligerence, the surtax undermined the North African economy, which was traditionally based on
agriculture, commerce, and the export of "black slaves, Barbary horses,
salted fish, leather hides, salt, wax, grain, olive oil, and dates." It was
both to fight back the invaders and to recoup some of these economic
losses that Algiers, along with Tripoli, Tunis, and Morocco, turned to
piracy.[45]

Some historians have underscored that in the seventeenth century
both North African and European "pirates" (or more accurately, "corsairs") were not free agents but employed by their respective governments, to which they returned a percentage of the profit on ships and
captives seized.[46] Indeed, several of the most famous and successful corsair captains did not begin life as Muslims; a number were actually
European, often English renegades.[47] But all North African corsairs, no
matter their ethnic origin, were organized by local rulers into guilds,
which evolved into major state industries at their height. Among the
four Barbary States, Algiers profited most, emerging as the most powerful.[48] Thus, as Frank Lambert has observed, European aggression
"transformed Algiers and other Barbary powers . . . from commercial
to pirate states."[49]

But the Islamic lands were not alone in thriving on state-sponsored
criminality: the Christian dominions did so throughout the sixteenth,
seventeenth, and eighteenth centuries. Among those from Catholic
countries, which seized Muslim slaves in the Mediterranean with the
support of the pope, the Knights of St. John of Malta were particularly
known until their destruction by Napoleon.[50] But there were others
sponsored by the British, French, and small northern and southern Italian principalities, who also engaged in privateering and the enslavement
of Muslim captives.[51] Religion, not race or ethnicity, defined this form

of slavery, with Muslim pirates functioning much like European and American privateers, sailing the Atlantic and Mediterranean in search of enemy ships and their crews to seize as prizes.[52] The English, though not least in profiting from such activity—having enacted the Prize Act in 1708, resulting in "the highest level of privateering activity" in both the Mediterranean and the Atlantic[53]—were vocal about condemning others, reserving the derogatory term "pirate" for "the buccaneers of the Caribbean" and all Muslims.[54] In practice it was a distinction without a difference.

Jefferson and Adams: War or "Tribute"

In October 1784, the American merchant ship *Betsey* was seized by Moroccan pirates on the orders of Sultan Muhammad ibn Abd Allah, who ruled from 1757 to 1790.[55] The sultan was piqued because Morocco had been the first country to recognize American independence in 1778, but the United States had ignored this overture and failed to send an envoy to establish a treaty of peace.[56] Jefferson acknowledged this delay, but would not lay the blame on Congress, citing only "unlucky incidents." He was happy to report in an August 1785 letter that the Moroccan ruler had released all American prisoners as a gesture of goodwill even before a treaty could be arranged. At the time Jefferson could rightly claim that the *Betsey* was "the only vessel ever taken from us by any of the states of Barbary."[57] But she would not be the last. Between 1784 and 1816, thirty-six merchant ships and one American naval vessel would be captured by North African states.[58]

Jefferson and John Adams would finally sign the peace with Morocco in 1787.[59] But two years earlier Jefferson confided in a private letter his bitterness at the prospect. He wrote that the sultan "is ready to receive us into the number of his tributaries," a state of subjection he deemed unworthy of "a free people," and likely to weaken the country's standing not only in the eyes of "pyrates" but also "the nations of Europe."[60] In August 1785, Jefferson cast the problem succinctly, in both pecuniary and principled terms: "You will probably find the tribute to all these powers make such a proportion of the federal taxes as that every man will feel them sensibly when he pays those taxes. The question is whether their peace or war will be cheapest? But it is a question which should be addressed to our Honour as well as our Avarice?"[61] It was more than a patriot's opinion.

In 1784, the same year that the *Betsey* was seized by Morocco, Jefferson took his place in Paris as minister plenipotentiary, faced with the task of establishing terms of peace and commerce with the Ottoman Empire, the North African states of Tripoli, Tunis, Algiers, and Morocco, and sixteen other European countries, negotiations in which, as ambassador to Britain, John Adams would also play a role.[62]

The next year, Jefferson sent John Adams a draft treaty for the Barbary States, based on his own insights and "the notes Dr. Franklin left me." "A Treaty of Amity and Commerce" was intended for "the purpose of establishing, peace, friendship and commerce between the United States . . . and his [foreign Barbary] subjects on the other."[63] It contained twenty-nine articles, more than found in most actual American treaties later in the eighteenth century. The second article, after peace, secured the release of U.S. citizens and property, while the third aimed to ensure that no North African pirates would prey on American shores: "No vessel of his majesty shall make captures or cruise within sight of the coasts of the United States."[64] This provision of Jefferson's would not survive to the final draft, but it reflected a view shared by other Americans of marauding North African pirates nearby.

In 1786, one Massachusetts newspaper reported that Algerian ships had been sighted in the Caribbean, while four others printed false stories about Algerians actually invading the United States in order to capture Americans.[65] The previous year, in the wake of the Algerian seizure of two American ships, three hapless strangers carrying Hebrew documents no one could read were seized in Virginia and summarily deported as possible Algerian spies.[66]

In his treaty template Jefferson had described the adversaries as "Moorish pirates," which usually was intended to imply that some were formerly from Spain, though Jefferson used the term to mean indigenous Muslim North Africans—whether Arab or Berber. The original term *moro* ("dark-skinned") in Spanish yielded the English equivalent "Moor," but it was not a term Muslims used to describe themselves, because the European usage fused the faith of a Muslim from Spain or North Africa with a racial implication.[67] The term "Barbary" developed much the same way, in this case from "barbarian," the Greco-Latin pejorative for those who chattered in a foreign, undecipherable tongue.[68] In Arabic, the verb *barbara* would also come to mean talking noisily and confusedly, becoming synonymous with Berber, another pejorative term used to describe indigenous peoples who did not use it to describe themselves.[69] Like "Barbary" it denoted otherness (at best) and absence of civilization (at worst).[70] As for "barbarian," it too was a common American designation for the pirates of North Africa, appearing, for instance, in Jefferson's 1804 presidential address to Congress, in which he explained that "by the sufferings of war" he hoped to "reduce the barbarians of Tripoli to the desire of peace on proper terms."[71] This, however, seems to be his only application of the term to North Africans, though he also used it to describe the Ottoman Turkish presence in Greece.[72]

Jefferson had drafted his treaty with the intent of establishing peace for "fifty years," an optimistic hope to be sure.[73] As it happened, only Morocco initially accepted this term.[74] Had the other North African states done likewise, the peace would have lasted until 1835, twenty years after the end of official hostilities with other North African powers.

Adams Describes the Pressing Need for a Treaty with North African States, 1786

In his letter of February 21, 1786, to Jefferson, John Adams describes the pirates of North Africa and their depredations as the most pressing foreign policy problem facing the new nation. Only the year before, two American ships and twenty-one prisoners had been seized by Algiers off the coast of Portugal:

> There is nothing to be done in Europe, of half the importance of this, and I dare not communicate to Congress what has passed without your concurrence. What has been already done and expended will be absolutely thrown away and we shall be involved in a universal and horrible war with these Barbary States, which will continue for many years, unless more is done immediately. I am so impressed and distressed with this affair that I will go to New York or to Algiers or first to one and then to the other, if you think it necessary, rather than it should not be brought to a conclusion.[75]

Adams's eagerness to negotiate and pay a tribute for peace with the pirates would be supported by Jefferson in his official capacity, but in private he opposed this expediency. Having worked together to forge a final draft of the Declaration of Independence, the two Founders would be divided over how most wisely and economically to protect American interests from piracy.

Less than three months after negotiating with the ambassador from Tripoli, Adams set about calculating how much it would cost to secure treaties with the Ottoman Turks, Tunis, Tripoli, Algiers, and Morocco. He reckoned that half a million pounds sterling, perhaps even two or three hundred thousand pounds, might suffice for all. But he saw the economic damage to the new nation as ultimately greater "if we do not treat." His reasoning was strictly practical: "Compute six or eight per cent. insurance upon all your exports and imports; compute the total loss of all the Mediterranean and Levant trade; compute the loss of one half your trade to Portugal and Spain." Adams concluded that alternatives to tribute would cost "at least half a million a year, without protecting your trade; and when you leave off fighting, you must pay as much money as it would now cost you for peace. For £30,000 sterling or as little as £10,000, he reckoned "we can have peace, when a war would sink us annually ten times as much." Nevertheless, like Jefferson, Adams well understood that paying for peace would mean the imposition of additional taxes upon Americans.[76] In debt and without a central government mandate for taxation, the new nation could not raise the revenue. The primary obstacle to establishing peace, for Adams, was fiscal.

Jefferson's Desire for a Military Response to Piracy, 1784

By contrast to Adams's analysis, Jefferson's response to the piracy crisis is another example of his contradictory impulses. As the historian Bernard Bailyn first remarked, Jefferson was "a pacifist in principle," but he "argued for a retributive war against the piratical Barbary states" as early as 1784, two years before meeting the ambassador from Tripoli.[77] In a letter to James Monroe, he describes his attempt in Paris to ascertain the amount "the nations of Europe give to the Barbary states to purchase their peace." He reported that he could never uncover more than "glimmerings" of payment that "appears to be very considerable."[78]

That same year, Jefferson rejected the European precedent of paying for peace, proposing instead the prosecution of war and the creation of a navy:

Surely our people will not give this. Would it not be better to offer them an equal treaty. If they refuse, why not go to war with them? Spain, Portugal, Naples and Venice are now at war with them. Every part of the Mediterranean therefore would offer us friendly ports. We ought to begin a naval power, if we mean to carry on our own commerce. Can we begin it on a more honourable occasion or with a weaker foe? I am of the opinion Paul Jones with half a dozen frigates would totally destroy their commerce: not by attempting bombardments as the Mediterranean states used to do, wherein they act against the whole Barbary force brought to a point, but by constant cruising and cutting them to peices [*sic*] by peicemeal [*sic*].[79]

Jefferson's resistance to paying "tribute" and his determination to create a navy represented to him an "honourable" option. (By implication, capitulation to piracy by treaty was dishonorable.) Yet Jefferson also carefully calculated the potential dividends of a military action against a "weaker foe," taking account of multiple "friendly" European ports in the Mediterranean. Nowhere, however, in the course of his considerations, by turns ethical, military, fiscal, and commercial, did he characterize the situation as a conflict between a Christian America and her Muslim adversaries. Affronted by extortion, Jefferson wished to end piracy on principle: He believed in free trade with all nations and, ultimately, peace. And he well understood that the assault on American interests was based on opportunism born of a sense of territorial privilege, not particular animus toward his country.

It was in fact not the first time Jefferson had considered the problem of piracy. As a Virginia legislator, sometime between the years 1776 and 1779 he revised an English legal precedent of 1699, which he entitled A Bill to Prevent Losses by Pirates, Enemies, and Others on the High Seas. Finally enacted in January 1787, Jefferson's legislation set terms of compensation for the widows and orphans of men whose lives and goods were lost at sea, with rewards for those who defended their ships against piracy and penalties for those who capitulated without a fight.[80] Nowhere did it mention a specific North African pirate threat or ransom for captives; indeed, during the Revolutionary War, when Jefferson drew up the legislation, it was the British who harassed American ships and impressed their crews into the Royal Navy. Piracy was piracy, no matter the perpetrators, and throughout his career Jefferson would consistently take a pragmatic view of the problem, and just as consistently he would see military action as the best answer.

ADAMS NEGOTIATES IN LONDON WITH AN AMBASSADOR FROM TRIPOLI, FEBRUARY 1786

Jefferson's first policy disagreement with John Adams did not prevent him from visiting London to negotiate with the ambassador from Tripoli in March 1786. Adams's private letters concerning his three prior meetings with the ambassador reveal a wealth of suggestive detail absent from the official report he and Jefferson ultimately sent to their secretary of state. Adams admitted to being "sometime in doubt, whether any Notice Should be taken of the Tripoline Ambassador [Abdurrahman]." Perhaps this feeling explains why nowhere else in his correspondence did Adams even mention the envoy by name, which today would be rendered Abd al-Rahman. Upon learning that the ambassador "made enquiries about me; and expressed surprise that when other foreign ministers visited him, the American had not," Adams changed his mind about a meeting. Confirmation that the representative was also "a universal and perpetual Ambassador" sealed his decision. Intending only to leave his card on the evening of February 17, 1786, Adams was surprised to find the ambassador at home and immediately "ready to receive me."[81] And so a courtesy call turned into a first attempt at negotiation.

Adams's vivid letter to Jefferson about this first meeting contains his reflections on the diplomatic problems of language, protocol, and American treaty-making with other Islamic powers. In a severely edited official version of the encounter sent to Secretary John Jay the same day, Adams declared, "It would scarcely be reconcilable to the dignity of congress to read a detail of the ceremonies which attended the conference," adding that such would be "more proper" as an "amusement . . . at the New York theatre."[82] But while allowing that the report of the meeting "is to be sure very inconsistent with the Dignity of your Character and mine," Adams was far more forthright and revealing when he wrote Jefferson.[83]

With what was perhaps a mixture of pride and relief, Adams wrote, "I was received in State," a welcome change, no doubt, from the cool reception he'd received at the Court of St. James's.[84] Jefferson would later say of his presentation to the British king and queen that "it was impossible for anything to be more ungracious, than their notice of Mr. Adams and myself."[85] In contrast, "His Excellency," as Adams referred to the ambassador from Tripoli, cordially sat with him in one of two "great chairs before the fire." During the interview, Adams noted, "Two secretaries of legation, men of no small consequence," continued "standing upright in the middle of the room, without daring to sit, during the whole time I was there."[86] Impressed by this feat of endurance, Adams added that they might still be standing there for all he knew.

Lack of a common language proved "the difficulty," because, wrote Adams, "His Excellency speaks scarcely a word of any European language, except Italian and Lingua Franca in which, you know, I have small pretensions."[87] Lingua Franca, according to the Massachusetts seaman John Foss, who spent four years in Algiers as a captive, was "a kind of dialect, which without being the proper language of any country whatever, has a kind of universal currency all over the Mediterranean, as the channel of information for people, who cannot understand each other through any medium but this."[88]

The lack of a common language would be even more troublesome in the eventual process of drafting treaties in both English and Arabic or Ottoman Turkish, the latter being languages only a few U.S. diplomats could speak but not read, let alone write. Treaties with Morocco and Tripoli would be drafted in English and Arabic, sometimes with an Italian version. Those with Algiers and Tunis were drafted in Ottoman Turkish and English. The necessity of relying on foreign diplomats, whether Muslim or Christian, to certify the Arabic or Turkish version as faithful to the English perilously limited what confidence the Americans had in the accuracy of the bilingual treaties they signed.

Adams admitted to Jefferson that he was no linguist, but as he reported to Jefferson, he and the Tripolitan managed "with a pittance of Italian and a few French words."[89] To Secretary Jay, Adams allowed that the meeting was "carried on with much difficulty, but with civility enough on both sides, in a strange mixture of Italian, Lingua Franca, broken French and worse English."[90]

For his part Jefferson, who was a linguist, had shown an interest in Arabic (and Persian and Hebrew) as early as 1778. In that year, he first attempted to buy an eight-volume collection of Arabic and Persian poetry by the British scholar Sir William Jones (d. 1794) from a former philosophy professor at William and Mary, who had left Virginia for

England during the Revolutionary War.[91] But those books would not yet have arrived when he wrote from Paris in March 1785, a year before his negotiations with the ambassador from Tripoli.[92] Still, the volumes were eventually added to Jefferson's library collection on his return from Europe in 1789 and his acquisition of books to further his study of Arabic would continue, his curiosity whetted by access to European book markets—and the continuing problem of piracy.

Tobacco, Coffee, and Tribute: Tripoli's Ambassador Reveals to Adams That Their Two Countries Are at War

The North African emissary opened his first meeting with Adams by venturing some pleasantries about the comparative merits of American and Tripolitan tobacco. He explained to his American guest that his native tobacco was "too strong," but diplomatically conceded, "Your American tobacco is better."[93] On this cue, one of the servants "brought two pipes ready filled and lighted." Adams was given the longer, which he "placed with bowl upon the carpet, for the stem was fit for a walking cane" of "more than two yards in length."[94] By his own admission, "it was long" since he'd smoked a pipe, but Adams matched his host "whiff for whiff" rather than do the "unpardonable" and be thought "wanting in politeness in so ceremonious an interview."[95]

They continued smoking until coffee was brought in. Adams wrote Jefferson that he "alternately sipped at his coffee and whiffed at his tobacco."[96] One of the two standing secretaries, reported the American, "appeared in raptures," over Adams's behavior until "the superior of them who speaks a few words of French cryed out in extacy, 'Monsieur votes etes un Turk,'" or "Mr., you are a Turk!"[97] This was meant as the highest form of praise for the American, but one wonders whether Adams appreciated the attendant irony of what was a common pejorative in early American political rhetoric being turned on its head in his honor. With the serving of tobacco and coffee, products from the New World and the Old, "the necessary civilities" had concluded.[98] It was time to negotiate.

Politely, the ambassador from Tripoli "asked many questions about America: the soil climate heat and cold, etc., and said it was a very great country." He then added, "But Tripoli is at war with it." Adams replied, "Sorry to hear that." He averred that he "had not heard of any war with

Tripoli" and "America had done no injury to Tripoli, committed no hostility; nor had Tripoli done America any injury or committed any hostility against her, that I had heard of." Abd al-Rahman responded, "True," but continued to press his point:

> [B]ut there must be a Treaty of Peace. There could be no peace without a treaty. The Turks and Affricans [*sic*] were the souvereigns [*sic*] of the Mediterranean, and there could be no navigation there nor peace without treaties of peace. America must treat as France and England did, and all other powers. America must treat with Tripoli and then with Constantinople and then with Algiers and Morocco.[99]

These assertions, in brief, summed up the view from Tripoli: The Mediterranean was their lake; to sail it freely required a diplomatic agreement and a financial arrangement such as North African powers had demanded for centuries from European countries. It was simply business as usual. The declaration of war was not merely an invitation to sue for peace, but implicitly to pay for it as well. And there was a specific hierarchy of treaty-making to be concluded: Tripoli first (of course), then the Ottoman Turks, to whom nominal suzerainty was still owed by Tripoli, Tunis, and Algiers.[100]

Presenting the American with a French translation of his authorization to make treaties with all European powers, the ambassador, Adams understood, "was ready to treat and make Peace." Adams reported being asked to return "tomorrow or the next day, or any other day and bring an interpreter. He would hear and propose terms, and write to Tripoli and I might write to America, and each party might accept or refuse them as they should think fit."[101]

The matter was urgent to both sides. "How long would it be before one could write to Congress and have an answer," the ambassador was keen to know. Adams replied that it might take three months, which the ambassador pronounced "too long." From this impatience, Adams concluded that "his Excellency was more ready and eager to treat than I was as he probably expected to gain more by the treaty." At the invitation to return straight away, the American demurred, promising to "think of it." He was convinced that Abd al-Rahman's demands, when known, would be "higher I fear, than we can venture."[102] And these anxieties would prove well founded.

"How can we preserve our dignity in negotiating with such nations?" Adams wrote in his concluding lines to Jefferson,[103] though a few lines earlier he had allowed that the Muslim ambassador was "a sensible man."[104] Writing that same day to Secretary Jay, Adams likewise summed up his host: "The minister appears to be a man of good sense and temper."[105] Unfazed by the hospitality, then, Adams saw an immediate opportunity to accomplish a major national objective. He also saw an experienced, serious diplomat, one he could do business with.

Adams held two more meetings with the ambassador, the details of which he sent only to John Jay. On February 20, Abd al-Rahman sent his interpreter to initiate a noon meeting, whom Adams describes as "a Dr. Benamor, an English Jew most probably, who has formerly resided in Barbary and speaks the Arabic language, as well as the Italian and Lingua Franca."[106] By the second meeting, on the twenty-second, Adams was prepared to call the interpreter "a decent man, and very ready in the English as well as Arabic and Italian." He had since learned that "it is the custom of all the ambassadors from Barbary to be much connected with the Jews, to whom they are commonly recommended."[107]

Jews were a significant group in North Africa, especially after their expulsion from Spain in 1492 and from Portugal in 1496.[108] Estimates suggest that almost two hundred thousand settled in Ottoman territories, encouraged by Muslim sultans. In contrast to their medieval and early modern persecution throughout most of Catholic and Protestant Europe, Jews in Islamic lands were defined as People of the Book according to the Qur'an, and allowed to practice their faith, often rising to positions of influence at Muslim courts, whether in medicine, commerce, or diplomacy. In North Africa, the Jewish banking house of Bacri and Busnah proved essential to brokering financial terms for the United States in treaty negotiations in Algiers and Tunis.[109] But John Adams may not have been favorably impressed, to judge by his opinion of the Jewish financiers of Europe:

> Jews and Judaizing Christians are now Scheeming to buy up all our Continental Notes at two or three shillings in a Pound, in order to oblige us to pay them at twenty shillings in a Pound. This will be richer Plunder than that of Algerines or Lloyd's Coffee House.[110]

As Abd al-Rahman revealed at the first meeting, he had chosen the Jew Benamor over "the interpreter assigned him by the Court." He had refused the suggestion of the British "because he was sorry to see that this nation was not so steady in its friendship to America as the French," a quite accurate diplomatic summation.[111] Adams nevertheless remained wary of the "interested motives" of "the Jews," noting that "their interference cannot be avoided," and concluding that "Benamor soon betrayed proofs enough that he had no aversion to the ambassador's obtaining large terms."[112] Why Adams would have expected a Jew would do less than accurately present the intentions of the Muslim employing him is unclear, but Adams was clearly wary of both.

The ambassador presented his wish for a peace treaty as altruism, suggesting that "the whole pleasure of his life" was "to do good; and he was zealous to embrace an opportunity . . . of doing a great deal." But still, he warned that "time was critical," and if the enterprise were delayed "another year, it would after that, be difficult to make." There were also other Islamic powers and the horrors of slavery for captured Americans to consider:

> If any considerable number of vessels and prisoners should be taken, it would be hard to persuade the Turks, especially the Algerines, to desist. A war between Christian and Christian was mild, and prisoners, on either side, were treated with humanity; but a war between Turk and Christian was horrible, and prisoners were sold into slavery. Although he himself was a musselman, he must still say he thought it a very rigid law; but, as he could not alter it, he was desirous of preventing its operation, or, at least, of softening it as far as his influence extended.[113]

This specter of present and future American captives held in North Africa must surely have filled Adams with dread, as intended.

Abd al-Rahman went on to offer practical advice about how to negotiate with Algiers, the most powerful of the pirate states. He warned that they had the most and the largest ships. They would likely refuse a treaty at first. But they could be won over by first establishing terms with Tripoli, because once "a treaty was made by Tripoli, or any one of the Barbary states, they would follow the example." In just this way, the ambassador allowed, a treaty had been concluded with Spain. Then, calling "God to witness," Abd al-Rahman "swore by his beard, which is a sacred oath to them," insisting "that his motive to this earnestness for peace although it might be of some benefit to himself, was the desire of doing good." In reality, his humanitarianism assured the most profitable outcome for Tripoli. When the North African ambassador learned that America had also sent an agent to negotiate with Morocco, "he rejoiced to hear it."[114]

Adams reported that "no harm could be done by dealing frankly" with the ambassador. Abd al-Rahman "rejoiced" to see the envoy's congressional commission to make treaties with Tripoli as well as Morocco, Algiers, and Tunis, saying he would undertake to negotiate terms for both Tunis and Tripoli. He would "also write in favor of any person who might be sent or go with him in person, to assist in the completion of peace with all the States of Barbary," which Adams added "was more than he had ever before said to any ambassador or minister in Europe."[115]

When Adams asked Abd al-Rahman specifically about "the terms," he was told to come see the ambassador at his house the next evening. Before leaving Adams took the opportunity to remind his visitor that although "America was an extensive country, the inhabitants were few in comparison with France, Spain, and England" and that they "were just emerged from the calamities of war" and had few potential ships that the corsairs could seize as prizes.[116] Abd al-Rahman took the point immediately. "God forbid," he said, "that I should consider America upon a footing at present, in point of wealth, with these nations." He then said that he would rather depart than "stipulate anything precisely."[117]

Adams, impressed but wary, observed of Abd al-Rahman, "This man is either a consummate politician in art and address, or he is a benevolent and wise man. Time will discover whether he disguises an interested character, or is indeed the philosopher he pretends to be. If the latter, Providence seems to have opened to us an opportunity of conducting this thorny business to a happy conclusion."[118]

Despite this guarded optimism, Adams reported that money would be the problem: "If the sum limited by congress should be insufficient, we shall be embarrassed; and indeed, a larger sum could not be commanded, unless a new loan should be opened in Holland."[119]

Of the second meeting, on the twenty-first, Adams reported the next day, "The ambassador, who is known to many of the foreign ministers here, is universally well spoken of."[120] Yet shortly thereafter his worst fears about the price of a peace were confirmed. Terms, Abd al-Rahman explained, differed "according to the duration." There were two types, a "perpetual treaty" being more expensive than one of fixed term. The ambassador recommended the pricier option, counseling that once lapsed, a treaty "might be difficult and expensive to revive." Adams was aghast at the sums he called "vastly beyond expectation," to which the ambassador answered that "they never made a treaty for less." This sum, he explained, had to offset what the ruler of Tripoli and his officers were entitled to by law as their share of spoils of all ships seized.[121] In piracy as in peace, profit was foremost in this diplomat's mind.

Adams's official assessment for the secretary of state was that peace with Tripoli, though dear, would not simply keep pirates at bay, but would favor the prestige and finances of America in the long run. "If a perpetual peace were made with these states, the character of the United States would instantly rise all over the world. Our commerce, navigation, and fisheries would extend into the Mediterranean to Spain and Portugal, France and England. The additional profits would richly repay the interest, and our credit would be adequate to all wants."[122] He also reported that Jefferson had arrived in London on March 11, partly to assist in the effort with Tripoli, but mainly to conclude his own negotiations with Portugal.[123] In Jefferson's presence Abd al-Rahman would invoke the Qur'anic justification for continued conflict and the seizure of American captives, but his preoccupation with the finances would persist.[124]

JEFFERSON AND ADAMS NEGOTIATE WITH ABD AL-RAHMAN, MARCH 1786

Though signed by both Jefferson and Adams, the report of the fourth meeting was clearly written by the latter, who began the page-and-a-half-long missive to John Jay by observing, "Soon after the arrival of Mr. J. in London, we had a conference with the Ambassador of Tripoli, at his House."[125] Perhaps as ambassador to Britain, the country in which they were negotiating, Adams considered it his responsibility to author the report, but Jefferson would certainly have read and approved the contents.

The meeting began and ended with America's financial dilemma; the new country was eager for peace but short on funds. Abd al-Rahman confirmed the price difference between a "perpetual" and a limited-term deal, again advising that "a perpetual peace was in all respects the most advisable, because a temporary treaty would leave room for increasing demands upon every renewal of it, and a stipulation for annual payments would be liable to failures of performance which would renew the war, repeat the negotiations and continually augment the claims of his nation."[126]

The price asked for even one year seemed staggering to the Americans: 12,500 guineas, plus 10 percent for the ambassador. The perpetual peace at over twice as much was a bargain, though further out of reach: 30,000 guineas, plus the ambassador's £3,000, or 10 percent[127] (in present-value terms about $2.6 million).[128] Abd al-Rahman, then, had a considerable personal stake in the outcome of negotiations, one for which he offered no justification, diplomatic or Qur'anic. For the same price, he said, Tunis would also be covered, but the ambassador could not predict what terms Algiers or Morocco would demand.

At this point, Adams and Jefferson attempted a diversion from the subject of money. They reminded Abd al-Rahman that the United States did not consider Tripoli, or any other nation, an enemy. It was an attempt at declaring peace unilaterally, and perhaps solving the problem by means of a technicality. The pair wrote, "We took the liberty to make some inquiries concerning the grounds of their pretensions to make war upon nations who had done them no injury, and observed that we considered all mankind as our friends who had done us no wrong, nor had given us any provocation."[129] It was worth a try.

ABD AL-RAHMAN REFERS TO THE QUR'AN— AND THE DEVIL—IN DEFENSE OF PIRACY

It was now that Abd al-Rahman offered a religious rationale for the state of hostilities, one that conveniently also happened to support his financial objectives, both diplomatic and personal. Tripoli's bellicosity toward the United States, he allowed, "was founded on the Laws of the Prophet, that it was written in their Koran, that all nations who should not have acknowledged their authority were sinners, that it was their right and duty to make war upon them wherever they could be found, and to make slaves of all they could take as prisoners, and that every Musselman who should be slain in battle was sure to go to Paradise."[130] It was, to be sure, a selective presentation of the Qur'an's teaching, but not one meant to invite discussion even if the Americans had been so inclined or prepared.[131]

In fact, all of the ambassador's references to the Qur'an were accurate, including the precedents for preemptive war against People of the

Book, meaning Christians and Jews (Qur'an 9:29); the taking of captives (Qur'an 47:4); and the heavenly rewards for slain Muslim warriors (Qur'an 2:154). Jefferson may have recalled some of them from his reading of Sale's translation eleven years before in Virginia. Might he also have remembered that various verses about warfare had been revealed in the midst of seventh-century Muslim struggles in Arabia against superior, pagan foes whom the good Muslim was obliged to fight to the death, failing an effort to convert them (Qur'an 9:5)? The presumably Christian Europeans and now Americans, as People of the Book, however, could justifiably be fought only until they were dominated. In piratical warfare in the Mediterranean, this did not mean submitting to Islamic rule and paying the *jizya,* or poll tax, but merely accepting Islamic terms of tribute for peace and the ransom of prisoners. To this extent, Abd al-Rahman's quest for peace and a lucrative treaty were acceptable Islamic practices.[132] All Sunni legal schools promoted the idea that peace, when in the interest of the Islamic community, was an acceptable alternative to war, even the variety of war known as *jihad,* or struggle.[133] Variants of the word "jihad" occur in thirty-six verses of the Qur'an, covering various forms of religious exertion, but there are only ten explicitly on warfare.[134]

Traditionally, *jihad* is not considered in references to warfare and killing, the justification of which was limited to righting wrongs or self-defense: "And whoso defendeth himself after he hath suffered wrong—for such, there is no way [of blame] against them" (Qur'an 42:41).[135] But Abd al-Rahman might have based his declaration of war against the United States on continuing European bombardments of Tripoli and other Muslim ports in the eighteenth century. An American captive in Algiers had explained to Jefferson that the locals retained a special hatred against the Spanish "for persecuting the Mahometan religion" and for expelling those Muslims who remained in Catholic Spain in 1609.[136] But the United States, as Adams and Jefferson pointed out, had nothing to do with those assaults. (James Madison would later argue more broadly that the United States did not share this European Christian history of Muslim persecution.) Nonetheless, all the North African pirate states, including Tripoli, believed themselves to be safeguarding the Islamic frontier—on land and sea. How, Abd al-Rahman might have wondered, could the policy of the United States toward Tripoli be shown to differ from that of their European coreligionists? Nevertheless, however sound his scriptural justification for war, the fact was that hostilities, even if presumed, had never been continuous. Thanks to treaties dictated by the North African powers, interludes of peace had frequently occurred from the seventeenth through the early nineteenth centuries.

The ambassador omitted to tell Adams and Jefferson that even the most bellicose pronouncements in the Qur'an included injunctions to limit conflict, establishing terms with the enemy if they were to submit and request a treaty. And this, after all, was what the Americans were attempting to do by refusing the notion of a presumed state of war with Tripoli. If he had been inclined to accept the American protestations, he could have cited very different Qur'anic verses, including one depicting Muslim reluctance to initiate conflict: "Fight in the way of God against those who fight against you, but begin not hostilities. Lo! God loveth not aggressors" (Qur'an 2:190).[137] War is elsewhere described in the Qur'an as something Muslims must engage in, despite the fact that it is "hateful unto you" (Qur'an 2:216).[138] Abd al-Rahman might also have referred to the second chapter of the Qur'an, where there is a marked emphasis on accepting surrender and terms of peace with one's enemies: "But if they desist, then lo! God is forgiving, merciful" (Qur'an 2:192).[139] Elsewhere, the Islamic sacred text states, "And if they incline to peace, incline thou also unto it, and trust in Allah" (Qur'an 8:61).[140] Numerous verses insist that fighting must end when one's enemy wishes to end it: "So, if they hold aloof from you and wage not war against you and offer you peace, Allah alloweth you no way against them" (Qur'an 4:90).[141] Other verses repeat these sentiments, and some invoke the fulfillment and establishment of treaties for peace (Qur'an 2:193, 8:39, 9:4, 9:7). There is no mention of payment for peace in any of these verses.

Nor did the ambassador emphasize that treaties are acceptable in the Qur'an and Muslims are to abide by their terms: "Fulfill the covenant of Allah when ye have covenanted, and break not your oaths after the assertion of them, and after ye have made Allah surety over you. Lo! Allah knoweth what you do" (Qur'an 16:91).[142] Abd al-Rahman's offer of a perpetual peace for the United States, the most costly kind, had little precedent in Islamic history. Sunni jurists disagreed about the proper duration of treaties, and while many allowed for two years at most, others specified that the terms should not exceed a decade.[143] The idea of perpetual peace seems to have been a financially motivated North African invention.

When Abd al-Rahman described the heavenly rewards of piracy to Thomas Jefferson, the latter may have remembered, as George Sale made clear in his first volume, that the religious impetus to fight for heavenly reward was not uniquely Islamic; it had likewise motivated both Jews and Christians.[144] In any case the official copy of the letter to Jay suggests that Jefferson was more focused on the tribute demanded than on any Qur'anic justification offered. His original copy of the report, preserved in his correspondence, reveals a telling orthographical error: "laws of the profit," which in the official version was corrected to read "laws of the prophet."[145] The error suggests Jefferson's skepticism of Abd al-Rahman's rationale, and it conforms neatly with his numerous references to "avarice" and "cupidity" where pirates were concerned. It was perhaps not an uncommon play on words: a couple of months later in a letter from Captain Richard O'Brien, a captive in Algiers, Jefferson would be told, "but money is the God of Algiers & Mahomet their prophet," a variation on the Islamic creedal statement "There is no god but God and Muhammad is His Prophet."[146]

Finally, Abd al-Rahman thought he would seal the deal for the priciest option, perpetual peace, by painting a picture of what American sailors could expect in a pirate assault:

> That it was a law that the first who boarded an enemy's vessel should have one slave, more than his share with the rest, which operated as an incentive to the most desperate valour and enterprise, that it was the practice of their corsairs to bear down upon a ship, for each sailor to take a dagger in each hand and another in his mouth, and leap on board, which so terrified their enemies that very few ever stood against them, that he verily believed the Devil assisted his countrymen, for they were almost always successful.[147]

It was probably a wild overstatement of the pirate's martial zeal as well as his lust for captives—and the ransom they would bring, particularly considering that war for the sake of profit is condemned in the Qur'an as the practice of liars, hypocrites, and unbelievers (Qur'an 48:15). But it was true that the seizure of prisoners, who might be killed, sold into slavery, or ransomed, could be sanctioned by the sacred text (Qur'an 33:26–27, 47:4). Not surprisingly, the ambassador failed to mention that the Qur'an also enjoined Muslims to feed prisoners, out of compassion toward the less fortunate (Qur'an 76:8). And while it was lawful to keep property seized in warfare (Qur'an 48:15, 48:19, 48:20, 8:69), the rules had not always been the same. During the Prophet's lifetime, a revelation called for one-fifth designated for the financial support for his relatives as well as the poor (Qur'an 8:41). Over time, more complex calculations evolved for the divisions of spoils, both property (*ghanima*) and captives (*asra*).[148]

The ambassador's description of the devil's involvement as guarantor of Muslim success was simply wrong. *Al-shaytan,* meaning Satan or the devil, far from aiding Muslims in the Qur'an, is a beguiler, who lies in wait to lead them astray, as he did both Adam and Eve in the garden of heaven (Qur'an 4:76, 4:60, 20:120–23).[149] But even without satanic assistance, the ambassador had the Americans where he wanted them.

The Americans hazarded no response based on Christian belief to this line of reasoning, realizing that their only option was to accede to the demands, which they must have reluctantly understood from the beginning. Adams and Jefferson recorded no comment on Abd al-Rahman's selective reading of the Qur'an. In the same paragraph reporting invocation of the devil, they merely said, "We took time to consider and promised an answer, but we can give him no other, than that the demands exceed our expectations, and that of Congress, so much that we can proceed no further without fresh instructions."[150]

In the penultimate paragraph, Adams and Jefferson suggest why Holland might be the only potential source of the necessary funds, before presenting an update on their agent's negotiations with Algiers and Morocco, commenting grimly, "and we wish it may not be made more disagreeable than this from Tunis and Tripoli."[151] Adams and Jefferson understood the predicament in which they found themselves.[152] Though of divided opinion on the influence of religion in the conflict, they were in perfect agreement as to the ultimate issue. As Frank Lambert observed, "Indeed, in all of the treaty negotiations, tribute, not theology, was the sticking point."[153]

Adams's fifth and final meeting with Abd al-Rahman took place in London in January 1787, after which the Tripolitan ambassador planned to return home. Adams reported that he had no direction from his government with which to continue or conclude negotiations.[154] There would be no treaty for all these protracted negotiations between Tripoli and the United States.

Jefferson Explains His Differences on Piracy Policy to Adams, July 11, 1786

Three months later, Jefferson admitted to Adams that their ideas about how to deal with piracy continued to differ. Allowing that their "instructions" from Congress had "required us to proceed by way of negotiation to obtain peace," and that "Whatever might be our private opinions, they were to be suppressed," he acknowledged biting his tongue though he had followed his orders "honestly" and "zealously." "Though, it was therefore never material for us to consult together on the best plan of conduct toward these states," Jefferson continued to think "it would be best to effect a peace thro' the medium of war." He outlined his reasons systematically. These included ethical propositions, but no religious ones, and he assumed Adams's assent to the first four, though this compatriot thought "respect" from European powers would be won more easily by forging treaties, not waging war:

> 1. Justice is in favor of this opinion. 2. Honor favors it. 3. It will procure us respect in Europe, and respect is a safe-guard to interest. 4. It will arm the federal head with the safest of all the instruments of coercion over their delinquent members and prevent them from using what will be less safe. I think that so far you go with me.

Jefferson then outlined the "next steps," those "in which we shall differ":

> 5. I think it least expensive. 6. Equally effectual. I ask a fleet of 150. guns, the one half of which shall be in constant cruise. This fleet built, manned and victualled for 6. months will cost 450,000 £ sterling. It's annual expence is 300 £ sterl. a gun, including every thing: this will be 45,000 £ sterl. a year.[155]

After offering other financial calculations, Jefferson admitted that war carried risks, but he weighed these against "the greater uncertainty of the duration of a peace bought with money, from such a people, from a Dey 80. years old, and by a nation who, on the hypothesis of buying peace, is to have no power on the sea to enforce the observance of it."[156] It was not an unwarranted concern about the eighty-year-old ruler of Algiers, the end of whose life would likely not just end his rule but also abrogate his treaty arrangements.

Jefferson was optimistic that the United States would not bear "the whole weight of this war," for Naples would join them and possibly Portugal. He had an even more unusual hope: "that a Convention might be formed between Portugal, Naples and the U.S. by which the burthen of the war might be quotaed on them according to their prospective wealth, and the term of it should be when Algiers should subscribe to peace with all three on equal terms." He further envisioned that "sooner or later" the other powers of Europe (except France, England, Holland, and Spain) would "enter into the confederacy," increasing its efficacy and further distributing the costs.[157]

Knowing they were of very different minds on the matter, Jefferson was careful not to offend Adams, allowing that he shared his ideas to show that "a semblance of reason" had taken him thus far, "and not with the expectation of their changing your opinion." He even graciously admitted that because "The same facts impress us differently," this led him to humbly "suspect an error in my process of reasoning tho' I am not able to detect it."[158] But however polite, he was less than forthright about how far he had taken his plans for a naval force to oppose piracy.

Unbeknownst to Adams, sometime earlier in July 1786, Jefferson had started working behind the scenes in France to enlist international support for a multinational naval force to suppress piracy in the Mediterranean. The idea, forward-looking for the eighteenth century, had actually been first proposed by Benjamin Franklin, who informally observed that it was in the interest of the European powers to join forces against piracy.[159] There is evidence that Jefferson privately presented his plan for a naval confederation on July 4, 1786, to Del Pio, the Neapolitan minister to France. The only surviving copies of his Proposed Convention against the Barbary States are in French and Italian.[160]

Jefferson also discussed this plan with Lafayette, who on October 22, 1786, without mentioning Jefferson's role, proposed it to President George Washington,[161] as well as to John Jay, whom he urged to bring the idea before Congress. As Julian Boyd has concluded, Jefferson may have chosen to keep his authorship from Adams, knowing it "could only have accentuated the difference of opinion" between them and the legislature, thinking it would have "weakened the presentation of the plan to Congress."[162]

Jefferson's convention invited any willing nation to work "in concert" against the pirate states of North Africa, "beginning with the

Algerines." His object was nothing less than "to compel the pyratical states to perpetual peace, without price, and to guarantee that peace to each other."[163] This would be accomplished by the deterring effect of patrolling the Mediterranean, not by bombarding North African land targets. Once Algiers agreed to a perpetual peace, the attentions of the naval confederation would be directed to the less threatening pirate states. Though he never claimed public credit for the idea, Jefferson copied this proposal in his autobiography, but alas Secretary Jay and Congress were not convinced, "and so it fell through."[164]

THE PROBLEM OF HOSTAGES: JEFFERSON CONSIDERS CATHOLIC PRIESTS AS INTERMEDIARIES

On July 25, 1785, the schooner *Maria* of Boston was captured by Algerian pirates near Cape St. Vincent, off southern Portugal. Five days later, pirates of the same power took the *Dauphin* (or *Dolphin*) of Philadelphia off Lisbon.[165] The result was not simply the loss of both ships and cargoes, but the imprisonment of twenty-one American citizens.[166] That Adams and Jefferson were aware of this situation while negotiating the next year in London can have only exacerbated their frustration at not being empowered by Congress to offer ransom. Nevertheless, when the American agent John Lamb arrived in Algiers in March 1786, they instructed him to offer no more than two hundred dollars per man, a sum they thought they could answer for.[167] But the dey of Algiers was asking $59,486 for all twenty-one men, with $18,000 for the captains and much less for each of the ordinary sailors.[168]

The fate of the prisoners was still unresolved when Jefferson returned to Paris after the failed negotiations in London. It was then he turned to the Order of the Holy Trinity and Redemption of Captives, known as the Mathurins, for help.[169] The Catholic order had members throughout North Africa and a headquarters in Paris. Jefferson hoped that they might act as covert go-betweens to redeem the American prisoners in Algiers. This they agreed to do early in 1787, but Jefferson still awaited funds. While he did, he set about publicly affecting to have lost interest in the American prisoners, hoping thereby to reduce the price of their ransom.[170] But the posturing impressed no one but the prisoners themselves, who despaired. They wrote him with "the most afflicting reproaches."[171] It was not until Jefferson was about to return to the United States in August 1789 that the funds were finally secured from Holland. By then, however, the French Revolution had put an end to the Mathurin order, and with it American hopes for their intercession.[172] The group of twenty-one sailors seized by Algiers in 1785 would be held for eleven years. Two of them were released by private donations; almost half of them would die of disease waiting for their freedom.[173]

JEFFERSON, ADAMS, AND THE QUR'AN

As we have seen, Jefferson and Adams differed as to the best remedy for the piracy crisis. They also differed as to the role religion played in it. For while Jefferson took the pragmatic view that it was a matter of simple pecuniary opportunism, Adams was prepared to see an element of religious conflict, whatever he may have thought of Abd al-Rahman's Qur'anic justifications. It is interesting, then, to consider the efforts each man made to understand the religion of the nation's adversaries.

Jefferson bought his Qur'an eleven years before piracy became a practical diplomatic issue and his initialing of his copy bears scrutiny, offering tantalizing clues not only to his interest in consulting the holy book but also to the provenance of the copy that survives. In fact, his interview in London with the ambassador from Tripoli may explain why he placed his initials in his copy of Sale's translation precisely where he did, near verses that refer to warfare. There are different possible circumstances for his doing so.

First, presuming that Jefferson's Qur'an had survived the 1770 fire and remained behind in his Virginia library, he may have initialed the book sometime after his 1789 return to the United States, before becoming secretary of state in 1790. He may have then placed his initials beneath verses of the Qur'an's fourth chapter that detail the importance of fighting "in the path of God," and the wisdom that those who strive in this way are "preferred" by God for their industry (Qur'an 4:94–96). Equally, he may have been moved to mark these particular verses somewhat later, perhaps in 1801, when as president he faced the choice of whether or not to go to war against Tripoli.[174]

But if Jefferson had lost his two-volume Qur'an in the 1770 fire, he may have taken the opportunity while in London to purchase a replacement copy. There is no recorded evidence of this. What remains certain

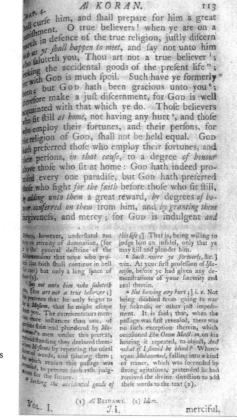

Page 113 of Jefferson's Qur'an with his initials inscribed at the bottom.

is that in volume 1, page 113, Jefferson inscribed his characteristic "T" and "I" at the bottom of the page (following the eighteenth-century practice of using the Latin "I" instead for the "J" in Jefferson).[175]

It is also possible, though less likely, that he randomly decided where to indicate his possession of the book when he first purchased it in 1765. He left no other notes in his copy.

John Adams, by contrast, for all his concern with religion, displayed only a belated if not decidedly lukewarm curiosity about the Qur'an. He would not buy a copy of the sacred text until 1806, five years after the end of his presidency, and twenty years after his negotiations with the ambassador from Tripoli. The text he ultimately purchased, now preserved in the Boston Public Library's collection of his books, was not Sale's English translation but the first American edition of the Islamic holy book, printed in 1806 in Springfield, Massachusetts, based on an earlier, flawed translation from Arabic via French undertaken in the mid-seventeenth century.[176] Well before the acquisition, in 1797 President Adams would sign the first U.S. peace treaty with Tripoli.

Jefferson may have been inspired to check Abd al-Rahman's Qur'anic references, to better understand his military opponents' ideology, but he never perceived the conflict with North African powers in primarily religious terms. Indeed, the one reference to "holy war" in his voluminous writings pertains to the only struggle Jefferson considered truly sacred: "for if ever there was a holy war, it was that which saved our liberties and gave us independence."[177] By the time he wrote these words in 1813, he had prosecuted a war against Tripoli during his first presidential term (1801–5) and signed a peace treaty with that power in 1806, at the beginning of his second. Perhaps it was because of what he gathered from the Qur'an that he initially understood the North African piracy crisis in terms economic, military, and diplomatic. Yet during his presidency, religion, both his own and that of the rulers of North African pirate powers, would appear as a factor in his diplomatic actions.

MUSLIMS ABROAD AND AT HOME IN DEBATES ABOUT THE CONSTITUTION, 1787

Not long after Jefferson and Adams's failure to negotiate an effective treaty with Tripoli in 1786, and as American captives continued to languish in North Africa, national debate assumed a new focus: the Constitution proposed in 1787. Thomas Bailey, a diplomatic historian, has asserted that the dey of Algiers might deserve "indirect" credit as one of the "Founding Fathers" of the United States because the plight of the imprisoned Americans did so much to prove the need for a new federal Constitution, with a system of taxation that could raise the funds to pay for their ransom.[178] A North Carolina Federalist, Hugh Williamson, made a similar point in 1788, asserting that without a navy the United States could not stave off the pirates from Algiers that one day might attack the coast of his state.[179]

While the new Constitution would meet the need for an effective response to actual threats from Muslims in North Africa, Federalists found themselves fending off anxieties about the charter's potential to create a threat from imaginary Muslims at home. Anti-Federalists worried that the proposed document opened the door to future Muslim citizens—and possibly even presidents. To accept the religious pluralism the Constitution envisioned, including the abolition of a religious test for federal office, was to risk not merely the exclusively Protestant character of the nation but even the possibility, however remote, that non-Protestants, once granted full political rights, might eventually exercise power over an American Protestant majority. It was precisely the sort of oppression that some Protestants had come to America to escape. And so Anti-Federalists instructed their delegates to state ratifying conventions to insist on an explicit guarantee of their own rights of conscience, which was absent from the document being debated.

Nowhere was the debate over religion and political rights more heated, or its record better preserved in detail, than at the Hillsborough, North Carolina, state convention. There, as the next chapter explores, the chief Federalist defenders of the Constitution became by extension the first and most ardent supporters of future Muslim citizens and their political equality.

5

Could a Muslim Be President?

Muslim Rights and the Ratification
of the Constitution, 1788

There is a door opened for Jews, Turks, and Heathens to enter into publick office, and be seated at the head of the government of the United
States.

> —Anonymous Anti-Federalist, Massachusetts,
> February 1788

But it is to be objected that the people of America may, perhaps, choose
representatives who have no religion at all, and that pagans and Mahometans may be admitted into offices. But how is it possible to exclude
any set of men, without taking away that principle of religious freedom
which we ourselves so warmly contend for?

> —James Iredell, Federalist, North Carolina,
> July 1788

IN A LETTER to Thomas Jefferson in Paris in October 1788, James
Madison in New York warned that "one of the objections in New
England was that the Constitution by prohibiting religious tests opened
a door for Jews Turks and infidels."[1] Madison clearly thought such fears
of non-Protestant officeholders were absurd, but they elicited no comment from Jefferson, who in 1776 had recorded in his notes Locke's support for the religious and civil rights of Muslims, along with Jews and
pagans.[2] He could not have forgotten that in 1779 opposition to his Bill
for Establishing Religious Freedom "dominated" the *Virginia Gazette*

and had elicited anxiety about the same issue Madison was inclined to dismiss.[3] By affirming "that all men shall be free to profess, and by argument to maintain, their opinions in matters of religion, and that the same shall in no wise diminish, enlarge, or affect their civil capacities,"[4] Jefferson's bill had indeed opened a door, at least theoretically, to a prospect of political equality many found unthinkable.

One of Jefferson's Virginia critics at the time, writing under the pseudonym a "Social Christian," admonished him about the need for laws to support a purely Protestant Christian America. He distinguished between toleration of non-Christians (freedom from persecution, not religious freedom), which he could endorse, and political equality, which he could not: "if there be a few who are Jews, Mahomedans, Atheists or Deists among us, though I would not wish to torture or persecute them on account of their opinions, yet to exclude such from our publick offices, is prudent and just."[5] To do so was necessary in order "to restrain them from publishing their singular opinions to the disturbance of society."[6] The access of non-Protestants to positions of government authority might one day result in their control over the Protestant majority, of which even the remotest possibility had to be avoided, argued Jefferson's opponents, at all costs. Accordingly, in November a petition was sent to the legislature from Amherst County, Virginia, demanding that no Catholic, "Jew, Turk, or Infidel" should "be allowed to hold a civil or military position" in the state.[7]

While Jefferson remained in Paris, attempting to forge treaties with North African and European powers, Madison helped draft and promote the new Constitution at home, where the ultimate fear of a Muslim becoming president entered national debates about the necessity of a religious test, nowhere more vociferously than in New England. In Massachusetts, an Anti-Federalist from Worcester in the western part of the Commonwealth wrote in February 1788, expressing fear that without a bill of rights, freedom of conscience would be imperiled. But the anonymous author only worried about religious freedom for Christians. Without a religious test in the Constitution, he wrote, "There is a door opened for Jews, Turks, and Heathens to enter into publick office, and be seated at the head of the government of the United States."[8] Meanwhile, in *Freeman's Oracle* that same month, an Anti-Federalist tract addressed to "the Inhabitants of New Hampshire" warned that "according to this" Constitution "we may have a Papist, a Mohomatan, a Deist, yea an Atheist at the helm of the Government."[9]

The same anxiety would echo throughout the New Hampshire ratification debate, during which at least one delegate to the state convention actually raised the specter of a Muslim president.[10] In a private letter to a friend in Massachusetts, John Sullivan of Durham, a supporter of the Constitution and former Revolutionary War general, reported the incident among various "specimens of New Hampshire ingenuity."[11] As president of the convention, Sullivan was in a position to observe all the arguments over the abolition of religious tests, which ran almost an entire day as Anti-Federalists struggled to limit government offices to Protestants.[12] Unfortunately, these exchanges were not preserved in their entirety.[13] Sullivan did, however, record with some irony the insistence of a fellow delegate that presidential candidates at least "ought to be compelled to submit" to the test, for otherwise "a Turk, a Jew, a Rom[an] Catholic, and what is worse than all, a Universal[ist], may be President of the United States."[14]

Universalism's doctrine of universal salvation was considered heretical by most Protestant denominations and as dangerous as Deism.[15] Coupling the Universalist with "a Turk," or Muslim, represented the height of Protestant invective, the ultimate sectarian slur, though the threat of a Universalist or Jewish or Catholic president was obviously considered marginally more imminent than that of a Muslim. Still, the fear was that members of all these religions were threats to American Protestant exclusivity in government control.[16]

Could a Muslim in fact become president of the United States? Only if at least nine of the thirteen states ratified the Constitution, including Article VI, section 3, which declared:

> The Senators and Representatives before mentioned, and the Members of the several State Legislatures, and all executive and judicial Officers, both of the United States and of the several States, shall be bound by Oath or Affirmation, to support this Constitution; but no religious Test shall ever be required as a Qualification to any Office or public Trust under the United States.

To swear to support the Constitution, a civic oath rather than a religious test of the sort then operative in all the states, seemed the unraveling of the Protestant order to some.[17] And although it was conceived mainly to eradicate "Protestant sectarian warfare"—the fear that one group would dominate and exclude others—unintended consequences nevertheless abounded in some delegates' imaginations.[18] Both Federalists and Anti-Federalists would refer to Muslims respectively to assuage fears or to stoke them about the fate of Protestant dominance.

It was quite inadvertently, then, that the abolition of a religious test heralded a new vision, one of a future that included Muslim citizens, as well as citizenship for minorities of Jews and Catholics already known to exist in the country. Previous studies of those groups in the early Republic have treated the presence of Muslims alongside them in this political rhetoric as accidental, derogatory, or unimportant. But the presence of all three in the North Carolina debate challenging religious tests defies prevailing scholarly assumptions that Muslims were deemed "totally behind the horizon of civility"[19] and "outlandish,"[20] and thus mentioned with other non-Protestants merely for rhetorical effect. In fact they played a more substantial role, particularly in North Carolina, where the record of debate concerning the question of a religious test is best preserved and most detailed.

On July 30, 1788, for the first time, Federalist delegates to North Carolina's ratification debate at Hillsborough defended a new American political ideal: the possibility that in the United States a Jew or a Catholic—or a Muslim—might become president. Analysis of their debate complicates our conceptions of Muslims in this context by introducing a momentous if momentary exception to this pivotal era's otherwise prevalent negative references to Muslims and Islam.

THE PREDOMINANCE OF TEST OATHS IN THE COLONIES PRIOR TO 1787

When the Constitution was first drafted in 1787 and presented for ratification, almost every one of the thirteen states promoted Christianity, and more specifically Protestantism, as the sole religion acceptable for political officeholders. Most state officials submitted to a religious test or otherwise affirmed their belief in God, along with particular aspects of some Protestant creed. And so to propose removing such a bar to non-Protestants was, at the federal level, truly new, provocative, and revolutionary, a precedent that would encourage a religiously plural future for the United States.[21]

Most states codified the superiority of Christianity, and particularly Protestantism. New York was the sole exception, with the thirty-eighth article of its 1777 state constitution extending religious liberty, implicitly at least, to its small Jewish community—and to whatever other non-Christians might one day appear, theoretically including Muslims:

> And whereas we are required by the benevolent principles of rational liberty, not only to expel civil tyranny, but also to guard against that spiritual oppression and intolerance, wherewith the bigotry and ambition of weak and wicked priests and princes have scourged mankind, this convention doth further, in the name and by the authority of the good people of the State, ordain, determine, and declare, that the free exercise and enjoyment of religious profession and worship, without discrimination or preference, shall forever hereafter be allowed, within this State to all mankind.[22]

Despite this promulgation of universal freedom of conscience, Catholics were excluded from holding state office under a clause that judged their religious beliefs "inconsistent with the peace and safety" of the state.[23] This exclusion, based on the prevailing fear that their political allegiance was to a foreign power, the pope, was the only one worth specifying, it seems, the prospects for non-Christians being so remote.

In Pennsylvania, Benjamin Franklin had opposed religious tests for state officeholders, but to no avail.[24] The 1776 state constitution extended religious freedom to all, affirming that "all men have a natural and inalienable right to worship Almighty God according to the dictates of their own consciences and understanding." But language that defended anyone "who acknowledges the being of a God" from being "deprived or abridged of any civil rights as a citizen, on account of his religious sentiments or peculiar mode of religious worship," was qualified by an oath for officeholders, inserted over Franklin's objections:[25]

> I do believe in one God, the creator and governor of the universe, the rewarder of the good and punisher of the wicked. And I do acknowledge the Scriptures of the Old and New Testament to be given by Divine inspiration.[26]

In contrast to New York, this requirement excluded Jews and Muslims, who would not accept the New Testament, but not Catholics. An earlier proposal that the oath affirm "merely belief in one God" met with opposition precisely because it would provide "Jews and Turks" access to political power.[27] An explicit provision against Jews and atheists taking seats in the legislature was enacted later in the year. But even this could not placate one Lutheran minister, who warned that Christians "were [to be] ruled by Jews, Turks, Spinozists, Deists [and] perverted naturalists."[28]

In Delaware, state officers were obliged to swear to the Trinity, the doctrine over which so many had died in Europe.[29] This provision excluded American Jews and any Muslims who might arrive. New Jersey allowed only Protestants to be elected.[30] Massachusetts in 1778 prohibited non-Protestants from public office, while the 1780 constitution more broadly allowed "Christians,"[31] though for Catholics a special oath "renouncing the superiority of papal authority" was required.[32] New Hampshire also prohibited non-Protestants, despite objections from William Plumer, later to be a senator but for now "a solitary voice."[33] Rhode Island and Connecticut both denied Jews political equality,[34] the former persisting in this arrangement until 1842.[35] In Maryland, Catholics, who had founded the colony, had political equality, but Jews did not.[36] Virginia was notably distinct, passing in 1786 Jefferson's first state law to mandate religious freedom and political equality for all faiths, including Catholics.[37]

Religious Tests in North Carolina Before the Constitution

North Carolina was geographically and politically positioned between Virginia, with its universal religious freedom and political equality, and South Carolina, which had Protestantism as the state's "established religion."[38] Farther south, Georgia similarly mandated that all representatives "shall be of the Protestant religion."[39] The 1776 state constitution of North Carolina ended the establishment of "any one religious church or denomination in the State, in preference to any other," but in Article 32 maintained that officeholders take an oath to affirm "the truth of the Protestant religion":

> That no person, who shall deny the being of God or the truth of the Protestant religion, or the divine authority either of the Old or New Testaments, or who shall hold religious principles incompatible with the freedom and safety of the State, shall be capable of holding any office or place of trust or profit in the civil department within the State.[40]

The insertion of this language was spearheaded by Reverend David Caldwell, a Presbyterian minister, who would later urge the inclusion of a religious test in the federal Constitution.[41] The state constitution also had more explicit language excluding Catholics for having religious principles "incompatible with the freedom and safety of the State," though Article 32 was deemed sufficient protection against Jews and, theoretically, Muslims.[42]

Samuel Johnston (1733–1816), who would preside over North Carolina's 1788 constitutional convention, had opposed a religious test for state officials since the 1776 state constitutional convention. As he wrote to his sister, Hannah, he had hoped to "get home in a few days, but unfortunately one of the members of the back country introduced a test, by which every person, before he should be admitted to a share in the Legislature, should swear that he believed in the Holy Trinity, and that the Scriptures of the old Testament was written by divine inspiration. This was carried after a very warm debate, and has blown up such a flame, that everything is in danger of being thrown into confusion."[43] The final version of Caldwell's Article 32 would leave out the oath to the Trinity, but inserted along with the Old Testament the affirmation that the New Testament was also of divine origin, to much the same effect.[44]

REFERENCES TO OTTOMAN DESPOTISM IN DEBATES ON THE CONSTITUTION

Although by 1788 the Ottoman Empire had long ceased to be a European military problem, its image as an oppressive regime remained central to British Whig rhetoric, which Americans then adopted in framing their Constitution. Islam came up sporadically during ratification debates throughout 1787 and 1788, with references to Ottoman despotism or the predations of the four pirate states of North Africa. It was ironically unknown to the delegates from the political parties in North Carolina, both of whose members owned slaves, that they themselves may have lived in proximity to real Muslims of West African origin, for whom they were the oppressors.[45] What they did know about Muslims had been filtered through a complex web of associations both foreign and frightening, as attested by their persistent allusions to Islam as a civilization of threat.

Robert J. Allison first noted that references to the Ottoman Empire as the source of eternal despotism worked for both Federalists and Anti-Federalists, who, despite their political differences, "agreed that Islam fostered religious and political oppression."[46] But the Anti-Federalist strategy of fearmongering in opposition to the Constitution found more use in invoking such images, particularly in Pennsylvania, New York, Virginia, and South Carolina.[47] The other side responded to these assertions but did not emphasize them in *The Federalist Papers,* the influential series of newspaper tracts written in support of the Constitution by James Madison, Alexander Hamilton, and John Jay.[48]

On May 22, 1788, the Anti-Federalist Patrick Dollard of South Carolina invoked the Ottoman infantry, the janissaries, to warn that similar forces of despotism threatened should the United States support a standing army under a central government.[49] It was an echo from the 1720s, when Radical Whig pamphlets, such as *Cato's Letters,* arrived in the colonies, portraying Ottoman tyranny as the very antithesis of a civil society with natural religious and political rights for individual men. In 1787, even Thomas Jefferson in Paris was not immune to this rhetorical tactic, writing James Madison about the constitutional feature, "I dislike, and greatly dislike: 'the abandonment in every instance of the necessity of rotation in office, and most particularly in the case of the President.'" In his litany of historical examples of hereditary power and its dangers, he included the Algerian ruler, known as the dey: "The Roman emperors, the popes, while they were of any importance, the German emperors till they became hereditary in practice, the kings of Poland, the Deys of the Ottoman dependencies." As Jefferson was learning, negotiating with these Islamic powers depended on the inclinations of one, usually disinclined, ruler.[50] In another letter to Madison, he would call Turkey a place where "the sole nod of the despot is death."[51]

In his forceful argument against the centralization of military power, the Anti-Federalist Dollard said that his constituents saw the new government as a breeding monster, "big with political mischiefs, and pregnant with a greater variety of impending woes to the good people of the southern states, especially South-Carolina, than all the plagues supposed to issue from the poisonous box of Pandora."[52] The people of South Carolina, he promised, would resist the standing army, believing it better left to "the meridian of despotic aristocracy" where "Turkish Janizaries enforcing despotic laws, must ram it down their throats with the point of Bayonets."[53]

His fears would be echoed on June 16, 1788, by another Anti-Federalist, Patrick Henry of Virginia, who in debate with James Madison at the Commonwealth's ratification convention invoked a more immediate image of military oppression: "Is the government to place us in the situation of the English?" The British army's abuses during the Revolutionary War were indeed fresh in the American memory, when Henry recalled how the redcoats had been billeted, even in times of peace, "in any manner—to tyrannize, oppress, and crush us."[54] But he too would eventually find his way to the Ottoman precedent:

> Who has enslaved France, Spain, Germany, Turkey, and other countries which groan under tyranny? They have been enslaved by the hands of their own people. If it will be so in America, it will be only as it has been every where else.[55]

Madison's reply to Henry, in defense of the Constitution, was that a national army "is to be employed for national purposes," and only "for executing its laws." He defied Henry to maintain the new nation without an armed force: "Would it be wise to say, that we should have no defence?" He added further, "There never was a Government without force," in the form of a national army.[56]

Writing nearly a year before Madison's response to Henry under the pen name "a Citizen of America," the Federalist Noah Webster of New Hampshire cited historical precedent to optimistically proclaim in October 1787 that the new Constitution contained "the wisdom of the ages" as well as the consensus of "the millions," who had formed "*an empire of reason.*"[57]

As if in anticipation of the Anti-Federalist arguments of the next year by Dollard and Henry, Webster attempted to assuage what he considered the groundless fears of a standing army, appropriating the Ottoman example for his own ends:

> It is said that there is no provision made in the new constitution against a standing army in time of peace. Why do not people object that no provision is made against the introduction of a body of Turkish Janizaries; or against making the Alcoran the rule of faith and practice, instead of the Bible? The answer to such objections is simply this—*no such provision is necessary.* The people in this country cannot forget their apprehensions from a British standing army, quartered in America; and they turn their

fears and jealousies against themselves. Why do not the people of most
of the states apprehend danger from standing armies from their own
legislatures?[58]

The danger from a standing army was, to Webster's way of thinking, no less absurd than the prospect that Americans would suddenly
embrace the Qur'an and jettison the Bible. So, concluded Webster,
since the presence of janissaries or a tyrannical janissary-like army was
impossible in the future, there was also no need to legislate against it.
Provisions against standing armies were as unnecessary analogously, he
argued, and the need to avoid janissaries being as fanciful as the need
"to prohibit the establishment of the Mahometan religion," an even-
tuality in this uniquely Protestant nation that he believed would never
come to pass.[59]

A New Positive Vision of Muslims in the United States, 1788

On one day of the North Carolina ratification convention, Federalist delegates challenged their opponents to consider whether American
liberty was consistent with a Protestant religious establishment. Should
the United States permit a form of religious tyranny that most North
Carolina delegates wrongly assumed existed only in the despotic Ottoman Empire? In pursuing this line of argument against a religious test—
and the injustice of including it—the Federalists would find themselves
forced to defend what to most Americans were then the three most
despised religious practitioners: Muslims, Jews, and Catholics.

Muslims in particular, with whom no one involved in the debates
had any direct acquaintance, had always been thought of collectively.
There had never been an attempt to consider the existence of the individual believer, nor any effort to hypothesize about a Muslim's potential
to be an American, and how this faith might determine status before
the law, as equal or not to any other American. But when the occasion
for just such a consideration occurred on July 30, 1788, it must have
seemed to most inconceivable that one could plausibly advance a case
for religious freedom and political rights, given the predominant transatlantic anti-Muslim bias.

The transcript of the North Carolina debate about religious tests
captures a moment when the multiple meanings of the word "Muslim"

collided, then shifted abruptly, from known threat to potential American citizen and even possible president. From the debate emerged a Federalist vision of Muslim rights at once hopeful and cynical: hopeful because it marked the first time American politicians accorded Muslims full rights, at least theoretically; but cynical, too, because the reluctant advocates of these rights assumed that they would never be exercised by actual people. Both Anti-Federalists and Federalists imagined the unimaginable: a population of free American Muslims. But while the Anti-Federalists envisioned, to their dread, a population in reality, the Federalists, for the sake of their principled argument, merely posited one in theory, assuming it would never exist. Racial bias occluded the awareness among all the delegates that actual Muslims might already live among them, and there were no visible, free Muslim inhabitants of the country, only negative stereotypes. Such stereotypes also prevailed in their understanding of Jews, and indeed, similar sentiments were expressed to argue against full citizenship for both groups. But in the debates about American citizenship, the Jews, however few and maligned, were real, the Muslims merely imaginary. Federalist and anti-Federalist alike had as their only recourse negative European precedents enshrined in Protestant imagination.[60] Still, it was the Federalists who charted new territory in their extension of American egalitarianism to the practitioners of Islam.

Debate on the Constitution's abolition of a religious test spanned one day, July 30, 1788. Speakers on that day included Anglicans, Presbyterians, and Baptists, among whom the notion of "true religion" remained a version of Protestantism. Nevertheless, some of these Protestants were able to discuss Muslims in a positive context even without setting aside the standard negative associations.

In all, Muslims were mentioned five times, with one additional reference to "the Great Turk," or Ottoman sultan.[61] Judaism and Jews ranked only slightly ahead, mentioned seven times.[62] But Catholicism inspired ten references, mostly to the pope and priests, an indication that this faith remained the source of the most immediate Protestant anxiety.[63] In various recorded speeches, Muslims were classed twice with pagans, once with Deists, once with pagans and Jews, once with Catholics, and once alone.[64] The possibility of a Muslim's election to governmental offices was raised three times, as was that of a Muslim president.[65] The connection between a Muslim and the presidency occurred twice as often as references involving either Jews or Catholics.

Anti-Federalists strategically linked Muslims to Jews and Catholics, in both cases to define them as minorities to be excluded from equal citizenship and access to power. To the contrary, Federalists invoked Muslims to argue for the equality and inclusion of Jews and Catholics in emerging American ideals of individual rights. For both sides, Muslims were the linchpin, whether the argument was for or against the status quo of Protestant majority rule, for or against the Constitution's abolition of a religious test, at a time when exclusionary religious tests prevailed in almost every state constitution.

ABBOT, THE ANTI-FEDERALIST, VERSUS IREDELL, THE FEDERALIST AND "THE ABLEST DEFENDER OF THE CONSTITUTION"—AND MUSLIMS

The North Carolina debate on religious tests began just after the third clause of the sixth article of the Constitution was read, the Anti-Federalists having forced Federalists to debate each clause separately.[66] Because James Iredell, the chief Federalist debater, paid a reporter to record the day's speeches, a fascinating series of exchanges has been preserved nearly verbatim.[67]

The relationship between religion and political power in the Constitution provoked a serious and heated disagreement. Anti-Federalists expressed worry about losing not only their Protestant control but their very rights of conscience, in the event non-Protestants should come to power, because the state religious test of 1776 had enshrined political officeholding as the exclusive prerogative of free white men who could swear to "the Truth of the Protestant Religion."[68]

The first Anti-Federalist to object to the Constitution was Henry Abbot (d. 1791), a Baptist minister. Born in London to an Anglican canon of St. Paul's Cathedral, as a teenager he ran off to America in the 1750s, settling in Camden County and teaching school.[69] He possessed three hundred acres of land and six slaves.[70] In 1758, he converted to the Baptist faith and was ordained by two elders. As an evangelist, Abbot made converts on both sides of Pasquotank River, from 1758 to 1764, when he was the pastor of the Shiloh Church, the first Baptist church in North Carolina. He supported American independence in 1776, joining several committees as a legislator, including the one that drafted a state constitution and bill of rights. He also introduced a bill to allow non-Anglicans to perform marriages, which became possible for

Baptists only after North Carolina's split from Great Britain.[71] Abbot is credited with authorship of the nineteenth article of the state declaration of rights, which affirms that "all men have natural and inalienable rights to worship almighty God according to the dictates of their own conscience."[72] Having suffered keenly for his own religious liberty, Abbot was not about to risk it by supporting a Constitution with no protection for Protestant rights of conscience.[73]

Abbot represented as rampant among his Protestant constituents the fear that "should the Constitution be received, they would be deprived of the privilege of worshipping God according to their consciences, which would be taking from them a benefit they enjoy under the present constitution."[74] He also expressed anxiety that a federal government's negotiation of treaties with foreign powers might cause Americans "to adopt the Roman Catholic religion in the United States, which would prevent the people from worshipping God according to their own consciences."[75] Abbot's fears of Catholic domination, a standard Protestant anxiety since the Reformation, were coupled with the assumption that one variety of Protestantism would "be established" as the state religion of the United States. He proclaimed, "I am, for my part, against any exclusive establishment; but if there were any, I would prefer the Episcopal."[76] Baptists, he knew, had no chance, and so Abbot presumably preferred the Anglican (or Episcopalian) faith he espoused prior to 1776, over another Protestant option. The rights of non–Protestants to worship freely were not his concern.

Abbot would be the first delegate to introduce the possibility of Muslims as officeholders if the Constitution were to be ratified. The elimination of a religious test, "by many thought dangerous and impolitic," presented the prospect that "pagans, deists, and Mahometans might obtain offices among us, and that the senators and representatives might all be pagans."[77] Abbot likely had no actual "pagans" in mind, making a classical allusion for rhetorical flourish; it would have seemed a witty remark to his listeners. The same absurdist humor inspired his mention of an oath sworn not on the truth of the Protestant religion but by the powers of "Jupiter, Juno, Minerva, Proserpine, or Pluto."[78]

Abbot's reference to Deists, however, was more serious. Members of this group existed in America among the Founders, Jefferson being perhaps the most noted for his belief in a remote God of reason and a disbelief in miracles. In fact, Abbot and other Protestant delegates would have regarded Deism as a far greater threat than atheism, since the latter commanded no public following in the period.[79]

Given a choice of pagans, Deists, and Mahometans, the latter at least represented no fanciful, long-extinct polytheism nor any population believed extant in the United States. Still, Muslims compared with Deists remained antithetical to Protestantism, as the Englishman Humphrey Prideaux's attacks in 1697 suggest. Both would continue to be condemned as inimical to emerging American religious ideals, however little Islam was actually understood.

Were Muslims really ever supposed to be present in America? Outside Abbot's mind and words, did the people he was referring to have any reality? No. Or none that Abbot's audience would have been aware of. Nevertheless, the impact of this first reference to Muslims in the ratification discourse was not only to invoke the widely perceived foreign threat, but also to introduce a strange, inconceivable new category into American political thought: the Muslim believer as citizen, even as potential officeholder. No matter how far-fetched, how incendiary this was meant to be, the very mention of Muslims throughout the day's debate endowed them with a reality Abbot's listeners had never before been forced to imagine. His initial reference, built on the traditional fears of Islamic foreign powers, insinuated Muslims into the national argument, obliging the delegates to consider new categories of belief and inclusion in the young Republic. (He had earlier taken the same approach with Catholics, making the usual charge of their connection to foreign powers, but Catholics had a reality that Muslims did not.) The image of Muslims as citizens, a projection toward the perimeter of possibility, thus revealed new strategic possibilities for opponents of the Constitution. But moving a threatening population from the edge to the center of the national debate would have more than the intended consequences.

Through his arguments against religious tests, the Federalist delegate James Iredell (1751–1799), dubbed "the ablest defender of the Constitution," became, by extension, the staunchest defender of the rights of Muslims.[80]

Born in Britain, he had found with the help of a relative a job as comptroller of customs for Port Roanoke in Edenton, North Carolina, a position he took after his father suffered a stroke.[81] He would go on to study law under Samuel Johnston, his eventual ally during the con-

James Iredell, Federalist of North
Carolina and "the ablest defender of
the Constitution."

vention, establishing a successful legal practice in the colonial era, and
being appointed a deputy king's attorney in 1774. With Blackstone as
his legal bible,[82] Iredell held fast to certain "governing axioms," understanding the law almost as a "science" and a "means to control politics."[83] Such temperate views informed political essays he published on
the eve of the Revolution, arguing against a break with Britain. Iredell
nevertheless finally chose the rebel cause, even though it cost him a siz-
able inheritance from an uncle.[84]

In 1776, Iredell drafted laws designing the state's judicial system.[85]
The next year, he was elected by the general assembly to the superior
court, serving as the state's attorney general from 1779 to 1781.[86] In
1787, the year before the ratification convention, Iredell was appointed
by the legislature to revise the state's laws, a task he wouldn't complete until 1791.[87] In the interim, in 1788, he responded to the Virginian George Mason's objections to the Constitution in a series of essays
under the pen name "Marcus,"[88] becoming the chief Federalist delegate
when reunited with Johnston.[89] The two men were more than political
allies; they were also kinsmen, Iredell having married Johnston's sister
Hannah in 1773.[90]

On July 30, Iredell attempted to calm Abbot's fears about religious
tests in a long-winded response that ultimately led back to the vexed
matter of Muslims as government representatives. He began with a series

of historical examples, knowing that in Britain, Baptists like Abbot had been denied their liberty of conscience and civil rights by the very means he now supported. While treating Abbot's anxieties with the utmost respect, Iredell nevertheless firmly argued that the new Constitution abolished the evil of intolerance and the mechanism for its enforcement.

That evil had recurred throughout history because, Iredell argued, "Those in power have generally considered all wisdom centred in themselves; that they alone had a right to dictate to the rest of mankind; and that all opposition to their tenets was profane and impious."[91] If the United States was to forestall wars of religious persecution, then potential citizens, Iredell argued, should be judged individually, not as part of an undifferentiated community. He used the term "toleration" to mean more than coexistence; it meant full equality before the law. This idea, enshrined in the Constitution, he asserted, set the United States apart from Europe and its failings. "America," he declaimed, had "set an example to mankind to think more modestly and reasonably—that a man may be of different religious sentiments from our own, without being a bad member of society."[92]

Iredell's ideals of toleration and universal rights were the very same as those in Locke's 1689 treatise. The argument over the Framers' intentions was already under way in America, and Iredell asserted that "the clause under consideration" was "one of the strongest proofs that could be adduced, that it was the intention of those who formed this system to establish a general religious liberty in America." But as that point was lost on some, he went on to remind his audience of how badly many of them had fared thanks to religious tests in England: "What is the consequence of such in England? In that country no man can be a member of the House of Commons, or hold any office under the crown, without taking the sacrament according to the rites of the Church." Though an Anglican himself, Iredell insisted that true religious belief was unintentionally undermined in this process, with the unscrupulous man assenting where the pious one refused: "It never was known that a man who had no principles of religion hesitated to perform any rite when it was convenient for his private interest." A religious test was in fact no guarantee of government by a "true believer." And so, Iredell would conclude, "the restriction on the power of Congress, in this particular, has my hearty approbation."[93]

Iredell's assertion "that a man may be of different religious sentiments from our own, without being a bad member of society" would normally have been understood as a call to toleration among Protestant denominations.[94] There was no strategic need to press his arguments further, and he could have ignored Abbot's initial reference to Muslims. But he deliberately focused on it, invoking their potential as elected officials. Locke's famous phrase cited by Jefferson in 1776, that "neither Pagan nor Mahamedan nor Jew ought to be excluded from the civil rights of the Commonwealth because of his religion,"[95] fairly echoes in Iredell's speech:

> But it is to be objected that the people of America may, perhaps, choose representatives who have no religion at all, and that pagans and Mahometans may be admitted into offices. But how is it possible to exclude any set of men, without taking away that principle of religious freedom which we ourselves so warmly contend for?[96]

With these two sentences, conflating Locke and Jefferson, Iredell overturns the standard American thinking about Muslims. In an instant, they become imaginable not as brigands or interlopers but as members and leaders of American society, deserving, irrespective of their religious convictions, equal representation under the Constitution. With no Muslims believed to exist then in America, Iredell could have made the point against religious tests without bringing them to the heart of constitutional debate. Abbot mentioned Muslims first, but his plan was to exclude them and provoke his listeners. Iredell, however, without immediate strategic necessity, defended the rights of Muslims in his principled, theoretical defense of all believers.

Iredell asserted that the exclusion of Muslim rights, if countenanced, would become emblematic of religious persecution, with the possible result that "the best men" of the country were kept from office while the truly unscrupulous, including "the worst part of the excluded sects," would affirm religious conviction they did not possess and find their way to power.[97]

Being a consummate politician, Iredell also found a way to appease his Anti-Federalist opponents by qualifying his principled calls for Muslim inclusion. "But it is never to be supposed," he assured his listeners, "that the people of America will trust their rights to persons who have no religion at all, or a religion materially different from their own."[98] Most would have been ready to believe as much, rendering

Iredell's plea for Muslims more a matter of high principle than practical politics.

Those on his own side would have seen it that way: Federalists may have supported political equality for all religions, but they too adhered to the limits of the Protestant status quo. And so it was perfectly plausible that Iredell should advocate equal rights for Muslims only to wave away Muslim equality in America as illusory. He could plausibly claim to be offering them no realistic place in the American polity, even as he seemed to include them within a new definition of American political equality.

Not unlike Jefferson, Iredell believed that religion was a private matter, one in which the federal government should not interfere. And like Locke, he saw no justification in divine authority for religious compulsion or persecution:

> It would be happy for mankind if religion was permitted to take its own course, and maintain itself by its own doctrines. The divine Author of our religion never wished for its support by worldly authority.[99]

Acceptance that Jesus's kingdom is not of this world, Iredell thought, was the best way to promote a bright future for Protestant Christianity in the United States—one without government interference.

ANTI-FEDERALIST FEARS OF THE POPE AS PRESIDENT DEBUNKED BY IREDELL

As Iredell began to observe, mention of Muslims also evoked similar fears of Catholics among the Anti-Federalists. In fact, Catholics were deemed the most menacing non-Protestant part of the population, their numbers estimated at twenty-five thousand, with most situated in Maryland.[100] Memories of "anti-Protestant plots," as well as England's conflicts with Catholic France and Spain, had fed anti-Catholic sentiment in America from the beginning, so that "by the 1700s every governor sent out to royal colonies . . . received instructions to allow Catholics no liberty of conscience, which literally meant that they were forbidden to express themselves as Catholics in those provinces."[101]

Later, even the one state founded by Catholics, Maryland, would order them disarmed "when war threatened[,] and denied them entry into the militia."[102] The question of potential Catholic access to political power, long denied them by pervasive religious oaths, provoked Protestant delegates in predictable ways in the North Carolina ratification debate. What those with pronounced anti-Catholic prejudice among the delegates could not predict was that James Iredell would find a novel and hilarious method to attack what he believed to be their groundless anxieties.

In defending the abolition of a religious test, Iredell had to address these sentiments toward an actual segment of the population, and he did so by means of an absurdist critique, ridiculing talk of a "Popish plot" to capture the office of president of the United States. Iredell described a pamphlet he claimed he had read that very morning "in which the author states, as a very serious danger, that the pope of Rome might be elected President."[103] At first he seemed in earnest: "I confess this never struck me before; and if the author had read all the qualifications of a President, perhaps his fears might have been quieted."[104] The Constitution's ablest defender then launched into a recital of the steps necessary for an American to assume the mantle of both pope and president:

> No man but a native, or one who has resided fourteen years in America, can be chosen President. I know not all the qualifications for pope, but I believe he must be taken from the college of cardinals; and probably there are many previous steps necessary before he arrives at this dignity. A native of America must have very singular good fortune, who, after residing fourteen years in his own country should go to Europe, enter into Romish orders, obtain the promotion of cardinal, afterwards that of pope, and at length be so much in the confidence of his own country as to be elected President.[105]

Then he delivered the coup de grâce. "It would be still more extraordinary if he should give up his popedom for our presidency," he mused, before finally allowing that "it is impossible to treat such idle fears with any degree of gravity." The danger of a pope as president was no more imminent than the election of "one of the kings of Europe."[106]

Earlier in debate with Abbot, Iredell had been obliged to rebut claims that were Catholics to become government officials they could make treaties with Catholic powers, resulting in the establishment of that religion. A little later he offered what would be the day's only favorable mention of Catholicism, observing, with respect to the growth of tolerance in Europe, "In the Roman Catholic countries, principles of moderation are adopted which would have been spurned at a century or two ago."[107] His words did not prevent other Anti-Federalist delegates from wishing that "the Constitution excluded Popish priests from offices."[108] Ultimately, Iredell could not dispel the single most horrific prospect, that of an eventual Catholic president.[109]

In Iredell's view, the real danger for the new Republic was not in the ascent of non-Protestants but in the rise of the sort of oppression the nation was founded to escape; for this reason, the omission of a religious test in the Constitution was "calculated to secure universal religious liberty, by putting all sects on a level—the only way to prevent persecution." It was of a piece with the other founding principles: "This country," Iredell argued, "has already had the honor of setting an example of civil freedom, and I trust it will likewise have the honor of teaching the rest of the world the way to religious freedom also." The lawyer and believer then pronounced his benediction: "God grant both may be perpetuated to the end of time!"[110]

Iredell went on to address other practical limitations of oaths based on religion, particularly in the case of Jews. They seemed less threatening to the Anti-Federalists, having, unlike Catholics and Muslims, no perceived claim on the help of a foreign power. And they were far fewer than Catholics, the Jewish population being estimated at no more than two thousand in 1776,[111] with most concentrated in the coastal towns of Charleston, South Carolina; Savannah, Georgia; New York City; Philadelphia; and Newport, Rhode Island.[112] But with religious oaths typically sworn on the New Testament, Jews were excluded from holding office. It was certainly so in Iredell's own state, though he chose not to emphasize that. Instead he noted that the practice had already presented a problem in British courts when it came to swearing in not only Jews but others he termed "heathens." In the case of the former, at least, a practical accommodation was made:

> It was long held that no oath could be administered but upon the New Testament, except to a Jew, who was allowed to swear upon the Old. According to this notion, none but Jews and Christians could take an oath; and heathens were altogether excluded.[113]

What was important to consider was the "form of an oath," which "according to the modern definition" was "a solemn appeal to the Supreme Being, for the truth of what is said." The essence of the oath's value was not merely the oath taker's belief in God, but also his expecta-tion of "a future state of rewards and punishments," designed "accord-ing to that form which will bind the conscience most." Warning against the consequences of "narrow notions," Iredell pled for those "many virtuous men in the world" who were neither Jews nor Christians, having "had not an opportunity of being instructed either in the Old or New Testament, who yet very sincerely believed in a Supreme Being, and in a future state of rewards and punishments." To whom might such a definition have referred? Muslims, at least theoretically, although he did not name them, instead merely reminding his listeners that "there are few people so grossly ignorant or barbarous as to have no religion at all. And if none but Christians or Jews could be examined upon oath, many innocent persons might suffer for want of the testimony of others. In regard to this form of an oath, that ought to be governed by the reli-gious person taking it."[114]

The lawyer's strategy bears remarking: The oaths of non-Protestants were often necessary to do justice in the law courts. If admissible there, how could they reasonably be excluded for other official purposes? They could not, and so having defended the rights of Muslims, Catho-lics, and Jews, Iredell went on to include the "heathen" among those capable of being sworn; the lawyer adduced a chancery court case from "forty years ago" involving "an East Indian," or Hindu, whose "answer upon oath to a bill filed against him was absolutely necessary":[115]

Not believing either in the Old or New Testament, he could not be sworn in the accustomed manner, but was sworn, according to the form of the Gentoo [Hindu] religion, which he professed by touching the foot of a priest. It appeared that, according to the tenets of his religion, its members believed in a Supreme Being, and in a future state of rewards and punishments. It was accordingly held by the judges, upon great consideration, that the oath ought to be received; they considering that it was probable those of that religion were equally bound in conscience by an oath according to their form of swearing, as they themselves were by one of theirs; and that it would be a reproach to the justice of the country, if a man, merely because he was of a different religion from their own, should be denied redress to an injury he had sustained.[116]

According to the *Laws of Manu,* the ancient code of law for Hindus still relevant under British rule, touching the foot was a common gesture in India, not in court cases but as a show of deference to elders, teachers, and those of higher castes.[117]

Iredell argued that since "this great case" involving a Hindu, "it has been universally considered that, in administering an oath, it is only necessary to inquire if the person who is to take it, believes in a Supreme Being, and in a future state of rewards and punishments." And so his proposed reliance on whatever "will bind his conscience most" had a legal precedent. He argued that there was no need for elected and appointed officials of the U.S. government to swear by whatever they believed about any one deity—or the next life—but only to uphold the Constitution.[118] The issues of religious belief and a future state of rewards or punishments were thus simultaneously stricken as incentives to tell the truth by government officials.

THE FEDERALIST SAMUEL JOHNSTON: HIS SUPPORT FOR IREDELL—AND MUSLIMS

Iredell's staunchest ally was also his brother-in-law, Samuel Johnston. An Anglican like Iredell, he had been elected governor in 1787, having moved to North Carolina from Scotland with his family when a relative of his had been appointed governor.[119] He studied at Yale, but left without earning a degree, returning to settle in Edenton, North Carolina, in 1753. An early subscriber of the Revolutionary cause, Johnston would help draft a state constitution in 1776.[120] Probably the richest man at the convention, he owned over eight thousand acres and ninety-six slaves.[121]

The Federalist Johnston was held in such high esteem in North Carolina that he was unanimously elected to be president of the state convention to ratify the Constitution, despite an overwhelming majority of Anti-Federalist delegates.[122] Johnston took up Iredell's arguments regarding Muslims, Catholics, and Jews. A less forceful orator than his brother-in-law, he concentrated on refining the limits of both tolerance and political equality. Like Iredell, Johnston attempted to remind his audience that "it would have been dangerous, if Congress could intermeddle with the subject of religion." He described "true religion" as "derived from a much higher source than human laws," a plea not unlike that made by Thomas Jefferson as well as Iredell for the separation of matters divine and political. Johnston warned, "When any attempt is made, by any government, to restrain men's consciences, no good consequence can possibly follow."[123]

Johnston extended the range of absurd presidential contenders proposed by Iredell beyond just the pope and European crowned heads: "It
might as well be said that . . . the Grand Turk, could be chosen to that
office. It would have been as good an argument."[124] Johnston's dismis-
sive twinning of the pope and the sultan harkened to nightmares of the
Reformation precisely in order to expose them as ludicrous and thereby
dispel them, together with the tyrannical associations of Islam. He also
sought to sunder the old associations of both Jews and Muslims with
pagans. The first two, he implicitly acknowledged, might be eligible
for elective office. At any rate, he wished to stress their common plight
as scorned religious groups, and a certain parallelism in their woes that
ought to be remedied in tandem: If Jews gained the right to elected
office, then so should Muslims.

Under the new Constitution, the office of the presidency would
indeed be open to Muslims in theory, but Federalists implied that they
would be excluded in practice. Thus, while admitting the possibility
of Jews and Muslims as officials—"It is apprehended that Jews, Mahometans, pagans &c., may be elected to high offices under the government of the United States"—Johnston nevertheless took pains to
assure the opposition that the presidency was safe from non-Christians:
"Those who are Mahometans, or any others who are not professors of
the Christian religion, can never be elected to the office of President, or
other high office, but in one of two cases."[125] These possible scenarios
were far-fetched enough to comfort his listeners:

> First, if the people of America lay aside the Christian religion alto-
> gether, it may happen. Should this unfortunately take place, the people
> will choose such men as think as they do themselves. Another case is, if
> any persons of such descriptions should, notwithstanding their religion,
> acquire the confidence and esteem of the people of America by their
> good conduct and practice of virtue, they may be chosen.[126]

It may seem quite plausible to us that civic virtue, "notwithstanding religion," could make a man electable. But no delegate at the time,
Johnston included, could have imagined a single factor of individual
qualification more compelling than religion. Their world of difference
and inclusion could not be defined without it, and therefore nor could
practical access to political power, whatever the Constitution might say.
Legal status in European and American societies had always been predi-

cated upon a faith-based hierarchy. Johnston's delineation of these two implausible exceptions to Protestant majority rule was intended to show precisely the status quo as immutable: "I leave it to gentlemen's candor to judge what probability there is of the people's choosing men of different sentiments from themselves."[127] And so a principle of inclusion would spare America the woes of Europe, but the normative impulse to exclude would safeguard the nation from untoward consequences.

Thus Johnston indicated how America could seem simultaneously both politically inclusive and exclusive, with respect to both Muslims and Jews. His brother-in-law's brave words, "if you admit the least difference, the door to persecution is opened," were only words after all, a flight of idealism alongside a more practical defense of toleration: "it is never to be supposed that the people of America will trust their dearest rights to persons who have no religion at all, or a religion materially different from their own."[128] Thus both Federalists championed the value of principles whose full practical application they would never have supported in practice. Ultimately, the rhetoric of these Federalists was fairly aligned with the prejudices of their opponents, like David Caldwell, who feared that Jews, most particularly, and others from "the eastern hemisphere" might migrate and overwhelm the electoral process of the United States. The Federalists' backsliding from stated ideals was calculated to advance the one goal they truly wished to realize: to win enough votes for a Constitution opposed by the majority of North Carolina delegates.

The Anti-Federalist David Caldwell Explains Why Jews Are a Threat

Although Jews represented the tiniest minority of non-Protestants in 1788, the Presbyterian minister David Caldwell (d. 1824) worried about the immigration of more of them to the United States. The Pennsylvania native had begun as a carpenter, before proposing to his three younger brothers that he would forgo his share in their parents' farm if they would help send him to college. Caldwell attended the College of New Jersey, now Princeton, graduating in 1761. Two years later he would be ordained, finally to begin his ministry in Guilford, North Carolina, in 1765.[129] He became pastor in 1768 of Alamance and Buffalo Church, a position he held for the next sixty years, living to nearly a hundred.[130]

Caldwell also established the "Log College," a school for the classical and theological education of young men, in 1767. He taught fifty to sixty students per year, among them future governors of several states, members of Congress, lawyers, physicians, and ministers. Ordering medical books from Philadelphia, he also became a self-taught physician.[131] As he could not raise his eight sons and one daughter on his minister's pay of two hundred dollars a year, he eventually relied on his 791 acres tended by eight slaves.[132]

Caldwell had been the delegate who insisted on a religious test to exclude both Jews and Catholics (and by extension, Muslims) from the North Carolina state constitution in 1776. The same determination would move him twelve years later to oppose the omission of a religious test in the Constitution. Holding forth on the threat of Jews to the nation, he was adamant that Christianity was essential to a virtuous citizenry:

> In the first place, he [Caldwell] said, there was an invitation for Jews and pagans of every kind to come among us. At some future period, said he, this might endanger the character of the United States. Moreover, even those who do not regard religion, acknowledge that the Christian religion is best calculated, of all religions, to make good members of society, on account of its morality. I think, then, added he, that, in a political view, those gentlemen who formed this Constitution should not have given this invitation to Jews and heathens.[133]

As a parting shot, Caldwell allowed, "All those who have any religion are against the emigration of people from the eastern hemisphere."[134] Johnston, the Federalist, agreed with him. While admitting the possibility of more Jews and other non-Christians entering the country, he assured his opponent that "in proportion to the emigration of Christians who should come from other countries; that, in all probability the children even of such people would be Christians; and that this, with the rapid population of the United States, their zeal for religion, and love of liberty, would, he trusted, add to the progress of the Christian religion among us."[135]

Clearly, neither the Anglican Johnston nor the Presbyterian Caldwell saw any value in debating which Protestant denomination deserved to prevail. It was enough that they agreed upon the impossibility that "the people of America lay aside the Christian religion altogether."[136]

The Certainty of a Catholic or Muslim President, Predicted by the Anti-Federalist William Lancaster

Could a Muslim be president of the United States? The assurance of the Federalists Iredell and Johnston that it was possible only in theory failed to persuade the Anti-Federalist William Lancaster, a Baptist minister, who believed, along with his constituents from Franklin County, that a religious test was the only certain way of keeping objectionable religious groups from the highest offices in the land.[137] He argued for upholding the state's current religious test, which made officeholding exclusively Protestant. He declared:

> As to a religious test, had the article which excludes it provided none but what had been in the states heretofore, I would not have objected to it. It would secure religion. Religious liberty ought to be provided for.[138]

Lancaster took Iredell's point about the pope: "For my part, in reviewing the qualifications necessary for a President, I did not suppose that the pope could occupy the President's chair." However, in a country without a religious test, where office was open to all free white men, he argued, anything short of papal usurpation might well happen, including a presidency occupied by a representative of either of the two faiths that had sown terror in the hearts of Protestants since the Reformation. Lancaster saw real and present danger in what Federalists would present as absurdities:

> But let us remember that we form a government for millions not yet in existence. I have not the art of divination. In the course of four or five hundred years, I do not know how it will work. This is most certain, that Papists may occupy that chair, and Mahometans may take it. I see nothing against it. There is a disqualification, I believe, in every state in the Union—it ought to be so in this system.[139]

While avoiding hyperbolic speculation about the pope or the Ottoman sultan, Lancaster focused on the somewhat more plausible future notion of an individual Catholic or Muslim. His vision of the world in four or five hundred years did not require a majority Catholic or Muslim population. Nor was it predicated on the emergence of Catholic or Muslim candidates so extraordinary that their countrymen would ignore religion and look only to excellence of character. Lancaster did not hang his fears on the two improbable scenarios that Johnston had described. It was enough for him that a non-Protestant president existed at the farthest edge of possibility; not feeling obliged to describe the unknowable future, he remained "most certain" that the presidency needed to be protected from the equal threats of a Catholic or a Muslim occupant. Thus the office became the focus of contestation between those determined to preserve Protestant hegemony and those who believed in an alternative of potential pluralism made possible by the elimination of religious tests for federal officeholders.

Catholicism and Judaism would have been better understood than Islam, but extant prejudices against adherents of the first two provided a serviceable enough template for characterizing those of the third, with whom the delegates had no direct acquaintance. Throughout the day's debate the three groups were linked together, with each stirring negative associations among the Protestant delegates. But if Muslims, Jews, and Catholics collectively embodied all that was alien and menacing to the American status quo, they also became simultaneously emblematic of the principles of universal religious freedom and political equality enshrined in the Constitution, principles that were uniquely American and that for many, Federalist and Anti-Federalist alike, had their own allure, irrespective of the chance of undesirable consequences. Assumed commonality would never be a basis for resident Jews and Catholics to make common cause; even after the ratification of the Constitution, they would remain enemies with similar problems.[140] And throughout the eighteenth century, whenever compared with Muslims, Jews would perceive an insult meant to cast them beyond the pale of full and equal rights.[141] Nevertheless, the three groups would continue united in the Protestant imagination, with arguments for and against their inclusion whenever definitions of rights and citizenship were discussed.

These three groups of non-Protestants were certainly considered outsiders. Each had a unique history and negative resonance for the Protestant delegates to the North Carolina constitutional convention. What these linkages provoked in their minds was precisely the challenge of a powerful, non-Protestant political category in which the most derided outsiders to the new country might one day become insiders. But the rights of Muslims, Jews, and Catholics to be insiders remained a primary fear for their Anti-Federalist opponents. Federalists defended political equality for Muslims, Jews, and Catholics even as they argued that the Protestant majority would most probably never elect them to any office. Arguments about the exclusion or inclusion of Muslims, Jews, and Catholics united them in eighteenth-century definitions of citizenship and rights.

Despite Iredell's eloquent attempts to win ratification and defend the rights of future American Muslim citizens, the Federalists had been outnumbered from the first. In the end, predictably, North Carolina's Anti-Federalist majority at this first convention would prevail by a landslide vote of 184 to 84.[142] Technically, the majority of the delegates "chose neither to ratify nor reject the Constitution," preferring instead to adopt a resolution in support of placing before Congress "a declaration of rights, asserting and securing from encroachment the great principles of civil and religious liberty, and the unalienable rights of the people." This included a desire to clarify other "ambiguous and exceptionable" parts of the document, presumably including the abolition of religious tests.[143] When Iredell attempted to circumvent this decision with a resolution for ratification with a request for amendments, his initiative was overwhelmingly defeated.[144] All those who spoke against the Constitution in the debate on religious tests also voted against ratification, with the outline roughly tracking religious affiliation and socioeconomic status. Iredell and Johnston, both lawyers and Anglicans, representatives of a privileged set, were staunch Federalists. The less affluent likes of the Baptist preachers Abbot and Lancaster, as well as the Presbyterian minister Caldwell, remained opposed.[145]

Iredell lamented the failure of his state to enter the Union in 1788, eventually writing a newspaper address to "The People of North Carolina" on September 15, 1788, in which he was blunt about the implications for the state's future:

> Eleven other states have a common united government: We have no share in it. If we can derive pride from the consideration, our independence is increased. We are now independent of all other nations in the world, but entirely independent of the other states. . . . We may form alliances at our pleasure with Great-Britain, France, Spain, Turkey, the Dey of Algiers, or Rhode Island.[146]

Only the state of Rhode Island was in the same predicament with regard to ratification of the Constitution.

Despite his local failure, Iredell's compelling arguments in support of the new Constitution and future American Muslim rights were read by congressmen throughout the new Union, especially in New York City. In this way, Iredell's foresight in having paid a secretary to record the proceedings paid off when they were published in 1789.[147] What Locke had only theorized and Jefferson had already concluded but had legislated only in Virginia, Iredell was thus first to champion in open, fractious debate about the Constitution.

Iredell's ardor impressed President George Washington, who appointed him to the Supreme Court in 1790, at the age of thirty-eight,[148] citing "the reputation he sustains for abilities, legal knowledge, and respectability of character."[149] Even Thomas Jefferson owned Iredell's 1790 revisions of the laws of North Carolina.[150] The new associate justice brought his family to Philadelphia, the nation's capital, in the 1790s, but he was also required to ride the southern judiciary circuit to adjudicate cases twice a year.[151] By the time of his Supreme Court appointment in 1790, Iredell owned forty-five hundred acres and eight slaves.[152]

The year before, Iredell's brother-in-law, Samuel Johnston, had left the governorship of North Carolina to become his state's first senator, but only after presiding over the ratification of the Constitution at a second convention, at Fayetteville in 1789. Returning to North Carolina after one term as senator, he would remain active in judicial matters until 1813, when he was seventy.[153] For his part, Iredell would not be so blessed, meeting an untimely death at forty-eight. The strain of riding circuit through rough terrain did him in only nine years after his appointment to the high court.[154]

IBRAHIMA ABD AL-RAHMAN AND OMAR IBN SAID: MUSLIM SLAVES IN AMERICA, 1788–1863

While Iredell argued for rights that would extend in theory to hypothetical future Muslim citizens, there were, unbeknownst to him, actual American Muslims in his state and throughout the new nation languishing in slavery, unable to exercise rights of any kind. Two coincidences, one chronological, the other geographical, invite us to consider them. The first, Ibrahima Abd al-Rahman (d. 1829), was transported against his will to the United States in 1788, the same year as North Carolina's debate.[155] The second, Omar ibn Said (d. 1863), arrived in the United States in chains at the age of thirty-seven in 1807, a year before the end of the slave trade. He ran away to Fayetteville, North Carolina, twenty-two years after the Constitution was adopted there at the second state convention in 1789. Neither of these men were the only Muslims in their vicinities, much less the United States, but both became famous in their time.[156]

Ibrahima and Omar had more than their faith and West African origin in common. I render their names as they traditionally appear in American sources, though in a more accurate transliteration from the Arabic they would be Ibrahim and Umar. It would perhaps have mattered to them, as both men knew Arabic, which skill they used to impress their white owners with their intelligence.[157] And both had studied the Qur'an in their West African homes. Despite appearing to profess Christianity in order to improve their conditions, there is evidence that neither truly abandoned Islam. In Ibrahima's case, his seeming conversion eventually allowed him to return to Africa and pay for the freedom of some of his children. Omar's two-page Arabic plea in 1819 for his release and repatriation, on the other hand, failed.[158] Neither man would ever be considered a free American citizen, or a voter, much less a potential candidate for political office.

Ibrahima Abd al-Rahman came from a town called Timbo in what is today Guinea.[159] According to his memoir, written by a secretary in English in 1828, this member of the Fulbe tribe spent a torturous six weeks in the Middle Passage before submitting to bondage in North America.[160] In what was presented as his words, Ibrahima tells us:

> They sold me directly, with fifty others, to an English ship. They took me to the Island of Dominica. After that I was taken to New Orleans. Then they took me to Natchez, and Colonel F[oster] bought me. I have lived with Colonel F. 40 years. Thirty years I laboured hard. The last ten years I have been indulged a good deal. I have left five children behind, and eight grand children. I feel sad, to think of leaving my children behind me. I desire to go back to my own country again; but when I think of my children, it hurts my feelings. If I go to my own country, I cannot feel happy, if my children are left. I hope, by God's assistance, to recover them.[161]

The characterization that he had been "indulged" was perhaps partly an effort to flatter his owner, who could have read the account.

Fac simile of the Moorish Prince's writing.

Ibrahima Abd al-Rahman, a Muslim slave who
became known as "the Moorish Prince." The
Arabic caption below the picture, in his own
hand, reads: "His name is 'Abd al-Rahman."
His Arabic literacy fascinated the public and
eventually secured his freedom.

Born in Timbuktu around 1762, Ibrahima had received a solid
Muslim education in the city that had been a famed center of Islamic
learning since medieval times.[162] His Arabic was learned in this context,
though it was not his native language. In fact, Ibrahima spoke three
African languages: Bambara, Mandingo, and Jallonke.[163]

His father having been a religious and military leader, Ibrahima
himself led men in local wars against enemy animist tribes, captives
from which were often sold to Europeans as slaves. Eventually he was
ambushed by these enemies and himself enslaved and sold to the British
in 1788.[164] His owner in Natchez, Mississippi, Colonel Foster, named
him "Prince" because "of his still proud ways" and Ibrahima's references

to his elite position in Africa.[165] He would manage Colonel Foster's plantation from 1800 to 1813, marrying a fellow slave who'd become a Baptist convert around 1794, with whom he had nine children.[166] As a Muslim man, Ibrahima was permitted to marry a Christian woman.

After nearly twenty years of slavery, Ibrahima met by chance a Dr. Cox, whom Ibrahima's father had saved when the white traveler was ill and lost in West Africa in the 1780s.[167] Cox recognized Ibrahima immediately. He, and later his sons, would attempt to buy Ibrahima's freedom. The effort would fail, but Cox's story made Ibrahima a celebrity. Local newspaper editors interviewed the slave in the 1820s.[168]

In 1826, the year Thomas Jefferson died, Ibrahima, at the suggestion of Andrew Marschalk, one of the local newspapermen, wrote a missive in Arabic, which was in fact a passage he remembered from the Qur'an.[169] Marschalk forwarded the letter to the senator from Mississippi, with an explanation wrongly identifying Ibrahima as a member of "the royal family of Morocco."[170] On Ibrahima's behalf, Marschalk pled for the slave known as Prince to be able to return to this homeland.[171] The ascription of Moroccan origin would have played into erroneous contemporary assumptions that African slaves necessarily differed from North Africans in color and faith. But since Ibrahima himself claimed an ethnic and religious superiority setting him apart from non-Muslim Africans, he would initially "not dispute" that he was "a Moor," and further claimed that he had "no 'negro' blood."[172]

In 1827, when Marschalk's letter reached the State Department, the U.S. government began to correspond with Morocco on the slave's behalf via the U.S. consul in Tangier. Sultan Abd al-Rahman II recognized that the author of the Arabic text was a Muslim, and volunteered to pay for his freedom and his passage home. Manumitting Ibrahima seemed a diplomatic windfall for the U.S. government, a way to improve relations with Morocco and secure the future return of any Americans shipwrecked on those North African shores. Secretary of State Henry Clay, a slaveholder himself, recommended the action, to which President John Quincy Adams assented.[173] Colonel Foster, Ibrahima's owner, agreed on two conditions: first, that he himself would pay nothing;[174] second, that his slave would "not remain free or at liberty in any part of the United States."[175] Only in Africa would Ibrahima find his freedom. When Colonel Foster finally permitted Ibrahima to leave for Washington, D.C., the slave refused to depart without his wife, who was still valuable as the plantation's midwife. Local whites raised the price of her freedom in a day.[176] But Ibrahima's children and grandchildren remained behind in Mississippi.

Colonel Foster described Ibrahima as "by birth and education a strict Mahometan," yet added that "he expresses the most reverential respect for the Christian religion, the moral precepts of which he appears to be well informed [about] and speaks of having read some of the Christian scripture of the Old Testament in his own country in the Arabic language," having even requested a copy of the Old Testament in Arabic.[177] Marschalk, the newspaperman, went so far as to imply that Ibrahima had renounced Islam for Christianity.[178] In this Ibrahima spied another opportunity. And so when the American Colonization Society, whose purpose was to return freed blacks back to Africa, volunteered to pay Ibrahima's passage to Liberia, their West African point of colonization, Ibrahima agreed to spread the Gospel and promote American trade in Africa. It was still hundreds of miles away from his former home and true destination, but it was closer than Morocco.[179]

One of Ibrahima's contemporary biographers stated that in 1828 he was "the most famous African in America." For the departure from the plantation, Marschalk bought Ibrahima a colorful costume he thought befitting only a Moroccan prince: "a white turban topped with a crescent, blue cloth coat with yellow buttons, white pantaloons gathered at the ankles, yellow boots—and, sometimes . . . a scimitar."[180] With much fanfare, Ibrahima embarked on a trip through many cities in the Northeast in the hope of raising enough money to free all his descendants and pay for their passage to Africa. His tour would take him up the Mississippi to Cincinnati, and then to Washington, Baltimore, Philadelphia, New York City, Boston, Worcester, Salem, and New Bedford, Massachusetts, as well as Providence, Rhode Island, and New Haven and Hartford, Connecticut.[181] He met with many dignitaries, including President John Quincy Adams, who earlier in his political career on his father's behalf had directed anti-Islamic invective against Thomas Jefferson.

Ibrahima was not the first Muslim Adams had met, having attended President Jefferson's dinner reception for the Tunisian ambassador in 1805. In his journal entry for May 15, 1828, the day of the meeting, he wrote, "Abdel Rahman is a Moor, otherwise called Prince or Ibrahim, who has been forty years a slave in this country. He wrote, two or three years since, a letter to the Emp of Morocco, in Arabic."[182] In that encounter, however, Ibrahima disabused Adams of the idea that he was originally from Morocco, and revealed his preference to go to Liberia, which was closer to his true native land.[183] The president, reported Secretary Clay, "thought it proper to yield to his inclination on this subject."[184] Ibrahima also asked the president to contribute to the emancipation fund for his enslaved children and grandchildren, but Adams declined.[185]

On his tour through the Northeast, whenever he was asked, Ibrahima never declined to demonstrate that he could write Arabic. Examples of his calligraphy still exist. Often he would claim that the specimen produced was the Lord's Prayer, but in fact he had written the *Fatiha,* the revered first chapter of the Qur'an, which has been called "the Lord's Prayer of the Muslims."[186] Of course, his American audience never knew the difference. His reliance on this one passage, no less than his actual calligraphy, suggests that after forty years of slavery Ibrahima's Arabic had become rusty.[187]

Ibrahima and his wife arrived in Monrovia, Liberia, on March 18, 1829.[188] As soon as the coast of Africa came into view, the former slave publicly resumed his Islamic prayers, proof that he had never truly embraced Christianity.[189] Ibrahima would never see his African family again or reach his homeland nearly three hundred miles away. Four months after his arrival, he would succumb to illness at age sixty-seven. His hope of raising money to bring his entire family back to Africa was only partially fulfilled. Eight of his children arrived in Liberia in 1830, a year after his death, and were reunited with their mother.[190] It is possible that seven other members of his family later migrated to Liberia in 1835,[191] but most of Ibrahima's progeny would remain in slavery in Mississippi, never to see him or his wife again.[192]

OMAR IBN SAID IN FAYETTEVILLE, NORTH CAROLINA

In 1789, Fayetteville, North Carolina, became the site for the state's second and final convention to consider ratification of the Constitution. Today, there is a mosque in that city, the Masjid Omar ibn Sayyid, which commemorates the Muslim slave Omar ibn Said.[193] Omar had fled to Fayetteville in 1811, after a month's journey from Charleston, South Carolina, to escape the harsh treatment of an owner he described as a "weak, small, evil man called Johnson, an infidel (*kafir*) who did not fear Allah at all."[194] Omar had been captured and taken in slavery from his home in Senegal.[195]

Omar ibn Said, another Muslim
slave from West Africa, wrote his
autobiography in Arabic, and likely
retained his faith until his death.

Although many American Muslim slaves distinguished themselves
by writing Arabic, Omar's proficiency allowed him to write an entire
autobiography of fifteen pages in that language in 1831.[196] Indeed, it was
his Arabic literacy that first brought him to the attention of his future
owners in North Carolina, the prominent and wealthy Owen family,
when Omar reportedly used coal to write Arabic on the walls of his
Fayetteville jail cell following his daring escape from South Carolina.[197]
In his autobiography, Omar praised the family with whom he would
live more than fifty years, before dying in his nineties.[198] In his Arabic
autobiography, he exclaimed:

> O, people of North Carolina; O, people of South Carolina; O, people
> of America, all of you: are there among you men as good as Jim Owen
> and John Owen? They are good men for whatever they eat, I eat; and
> whatever they wear they give me to wear.[199]

A decade before writing his life story Omar joined the Presbyterian
Church and was baptized.[200] David Caldwell, the Anti-Federalist delegate who expressed such fears about the "emigration of those people
from the eastern hemisphere" at the 1788 North Carolina ratification
debate, might have been shocked by Omar's presence at a church of

his Presbyterian denomination. In 1822, the convert was sent a copy of the Bible in Arabic by Francis Scott Key, who wrote the words to "The Star-Spangled Banner," and belonged to the American Colonization Society, the group that had helped Ibrahima and other freed slaves return to Africa.[201] Someone else would give Omar a Qur'an in English, though he would never own one in Arabic.[202] That nonetheless did not prevent his reproducing parts of it.

Omar begins his autobiography with the *bismillah*—"In the name of Allah"—followed by "the merciful, the compassionate" and "May God bless our Lord Mohammed."[203] He then re-creates from memory (despite a few errors) the sixty-seventh chapter of the Qur'an, known as *al-Mulk,* which can be translated as "the Sovereignty" but also as "the Dominion" or "the Ownership." Though the author does not identify or explain these verses, Omar's choice, as one scholar has suggested,[204] represents an implicit "resistance" to the earthly dominion of slavery, to ownership of him as a human being.[205] The chapter emphasizes Allah's role as the ultimate owner of "all things" and the Prophet Muhammad's role as "a warner."[206] The twelfth and thirteenth verses, which suggest that only God knows the nature of an individual's spiritual beliefs, may have had a special significance for Omar:

12 Lo! Those who fear their Lord in secret, theirs will be forgiveness and a great reward.

13 And keep your opinion secret or proclaim it, lo! He is Knower of all that is in the breasts (of men).[207]

Was this perhaps Omar's confession, even repudiation, of his outward conversion to Christianity?[208] In any case, most scholars of African Muslims in America believe that Omar, despite appearances, did not fully embrace Christianity.[209]

Omar does explicitly confess the faith into which he was born: "Before I came to the Christian country, my religion is the religion of Mohammad, the Prophet of Allah, may Allah bless him and grant him peace."[210] The sentence reads no less oddly in the original, with Omar deliberately using the Arabic present tense. Here is another potential indication of his religious ambivalence, or a refusal to put Islam in his past. He then describes essential Islamic rituals he no longer observed in North Carolina, including walking to the mosque, ablutions before prayer, and prayer several times a day. As a Muslim in Africa, he tells us, he gave *zakat,* or alms, one of the five pillars of the faith; fought in *jihad* against non-Muslim tribes; and even made the pilgrimage to Mecca.[211]

Omar may have outwardly embraced Presbyterianism in order to please his owners, or because he missed the fellowship of a community of believers of the sort he'd known in Africa. His church attendance may also reflect a Muslim reverence for Jesus as a prophet in Islam. But a few pages later, the tensions in Omar's religious commitment became more pronounced: "I am Omar," he declares, "I love to read the book, the Great Qur'an."[212] But literally the sentence could also be read, "I am Omar, he loves to read the book the Great Qur'an," because the verb is in the third-person masculine, not the first person. And this happens more than once.[213] All translators assume that Omar means the first person throughout his text, which is perfectly reasonable. Yet this remains an odd grammatical choice for an autobiography. In English translations, the repetition throughout of the first-person pronoun "I" evokes an immediacy and agency somewhat less palpable in the original. It may be another instance of his ambivalence, or simply that despite Omar's claims to have studied Islamic subjects for twenty-five years in Africa with various learned men, his Arabic-language skills had predictably eroded over time, reflecting the imperfect memory of a script that he could no longer accurately reproduce.[214]

While Omar tried to retain the memory of his past, his owner Jim Owen and his wife "used to read the Bible to me a lot." But rather than mention Jesus, Omar's account goes on simply to ask that his "heart" be "open to the Bible," and he concludes the thought with a Qur'anic form of praise for Allah, "Lord of the Worlds."[215] When he does mention Jesus on the following page, it is after Moses, described as the one to whom God gave the law. He does depict "Jesus the Messiah" as receiving "grace and truth,"[216] but then immediately states, "First, [following] Mohammed. To pray I said," after which he inserts the *Fatiha,* the first chapter of the Qur'an.[217] This sentence could also indicate his view of the superiority of the Prophet Muhammad in the prophetic continuum of the Qur'an.

Omar provides other clues that he never forsook belief in the Prophet Muhammad's singular importance. He did write out Christian prayers, and, unlike Ibrahima, when Omar claimed to have written out the Lord's Prayer or the twenty-third Psalm in Arabic, that is exactly what he wrote. He would never try to pass off verses from the Qur'an as

Christian scripture, his efforts no doubt facilitated by the Arabic Bible Scott Key gave him.[218] On the other hand, as late as 1855, eight years before his death, his Arabic transcription of the twenty-third Psalm is introduced by the *bismillah,* followed by this invocation of the Prophet: "May God have mercy on *our* Lord, the Prophet Muhammad."[219]

Omar died in 1863, two years before the passage of the Thirteenth Amendment to the Constitution, which would have finally granted his freedom. According to the Constitution under which he had lived, as a slave he remained only three-fifths of a person, a ratio accepted by the free, white male Protestant delegates to his state's 1788 ratification debate.[220]

The historian Michael Gomez has referred to both Omar and Ibrahima, among others, as "Founding Fathers of a Different Sort," a title both certainly deserve in the annals of American Muslim history.[221] These two lives remind us that while hypothetical Muslims inhabited the rhetoric of the Founders, in their midst there also lived flesh-and-blood Muslims who, as slaves, remained invisible and without rights. Only literacy in Arabic set both men apart from their coreligionists in the African slave population, and while that skill was enough to win Ibrahima a rare return journey from the Middle Passage, it would not save Omar, despite his protests, from languishing in the United States.

COULD A MUSLIM BE PRESIDENT? THE BIRTH OF AN EIGHTEENTH-CENTURY AMERICAN IDEAL OF POLITICAL EQUALITY

In constitutional history, Muslims are not traditionally associated with definitions of American citizenship, but for one day in 1788 the adherents of Islam came to symbolize the aspiration of political equality, irrespective of religion, in the new Republic. The lives of America's actual Muslim inhabitants, slaves from West Africa, like Ibrahima Abd al-Rahman and Omar ibn Said, could not have been more remote from the possibility that any Muslim could conceivably seek the presidency one day. And they remained invisible to the delegates, just as Omar's words written in Arabic after the vote, his plaintive plea, "O, People of North Carolina," would remain unread.

Nevertheless, it was in North Carolina's debate on religious tests that Muslims—albeit imaginary ones—stepped directly onto the American political stage for the first time. At a time when fearful visions of Islam as a fanatical religion and foreign threat prevailed, two Federalists in North Carolina promoted the simultaneous establishment of religious and political equality for Muslims as potential American citizens, meeting a predictable response from the majority of delegates, whose negative monolithic vision of Islam would persist and prevail. And yet a new vision of Muslims as individual believers, people who might yet enjoy a full membership in the new polity, was born. Iredell and Johnston created this possibility in debate, without believing or wishing that the rights they advocated in principle would ever come to be practically tested by real Muslims. Nevertheless, in the absence of a religious test, Federalists would be forced to concede the possibility of a Muslim president when they managed to win ratification for their Constitution in 1788. That they did so, however reluctantly, suggested that Americans might depart from inherited European prejudices in realizing their national ideals.

Thomas Jefferson was not in the United States during debates about the Constitution and Muslim rights, remaining in France until November 1789. The next month, he accepted the post of secretary of state and, returning to the United States, took up the problem of North African piracy once again. He did not expect that even on the domestic political scene references to Islam would figure in attempts to defame him.

6

Jefferson Wages War Against an Islamic Power;
Entertains the First Muslim Ambassador;
Decides Where to Place the Qur'an
in His Library; and Affirms His Support
for Muslim Rights, 1790–1823

The expressions, indeed, imply more; they seem, like the Arabian prophet, to call upon all true believers in the *Islam* of democracy, to draw their swords, and, in the fervour of their devotion, to compel their countrymen to cry out, "There is but one Goddess of Liberty, and Common Sense is her prophet."

—John Quincy Adams on
Thomas Jefferson, 1791

As the government of the United States of America is not in any sense founded on the Christian Religion,—as it has in itself no character of enmity against the laws, religion or tranquility of Mussulmen,—and as the said States never have entered into any war or act of hostility against any Mehomitan nation, it is declared by the parties that no pretext arising from religious opinions shall ever produce an interruption of the harmony existing between the two countries.

—Article 11, first U.S.
peace treaty with Tripoli, ratified 1797

IN 1790, Secretary of State Thomas Jefferson reported to President Washington and Congress that since the peace with the British in 1783, America's lucrative prewar trade in the Mediterranean had not "been resumed," owing to North African piracy.[1] It was something of an exaggeration. Despite the threat and lack of naval protection, American merchants did indeed continue to risk their ships, their freedom, and even their lives plying the waters of the Mediterranean. By 1785, Algiers had seized two American merchant vessels and twenty-one sailors.[2] By 1793, eleven more American merchant vessels and over a hundred sailors would be seized by the same power. Release for these captives in Algiers would not come until treaty and ransom negotiations succeeded in 1796–97.[3]

A solution to this crisis would elude Jefferson during his tenure as secretary of state, as vice president, and into his presidential term, until 1806.

In 1801, Jefferson would become the first executive of the United States to go to war with an Islamic nation. He would also be the first American holder of high office whose political opponents defamed him with accusations of being a Muslim. This experience notwithstanding, he would be the first president to entertain a Muslim ambassador in the nation's new capital, and in correspondence with Muslim rulers of

Portrait of Thomas Jefferson (1791) by
Charles Willson Peale.

North Africa he would repeatedly invoke a shared belief in one God. In the conduct of foreign relations, Jefferson had relied on his study of Islam, and when after leaving office he returned to his library at Monticello, he would choose a telling final place in his collection for the Qur'an that had informed his understanding of the Muslim faith. Let us now consider the arc of that understanding and its part in his political career.

JEFFERSON'S VIEW OF THE NORTH AFRICAN
PIRACY PROBLEM, 1790

In 1790, Jefferson reported to Congress that before the end of the Revolutionary War "about one-sixth of the wheat and flour exported from the United States and about one-fourth" of all "dried and pickled fish, and some rice, found their best markets in the Mediterranean ports."[4] These substantial exports, he estimated, required "eighty to one hundred ships annually, of twenty thousand tons, navigated by about twelve hundred seamen."[5] Jefferson emphasized the extent of the trade by way of rationalizing its continuation in treacherous circumstances, when it "was obvious to our merchants, that their adventures into that sea would be exposed to the depredations of the piratical States on the coast of Barbary." Temptation existed on both sides, and for the pirate states it was created by the Strait of Gibraltar, which Jefferson described as "only five leagues wide," and where enemy "cruisers, taking a safe and commanding position near the strait's mouth, may very effectually inspect whatever enters it. So safe a station, with certainty of receiving for their prisoners a good and stated price, may tempt their cupidity to seek our vessels particularly."[6] Greed, Jefferson took pains to imply, was a universal human motive, not particular to followers of any religion.

Having failed to ransom American captives during his time as ambassador to France, Jefferson was now to insist upon an earlier, more aggressive policy option: America should answer force with force.[7] As a feature of this policy, he proposed that captured North African pirates be held for ransom. He even had in mind a price schedule by nationality: North African rulers would, he rightly inferred, value prisoners of Turkish origin more than "Moors," or indigenous Muslims, because "their government is entirely in the hands of Turks, who are treated in every instance as a superior order of beings." Nevertheless, he knew the scheme was likely to be fruitless since the exchange of prisoners was not customary for the governments of Algiers, Tripoli, and Tunis.[8] Indeed the only Tripolitan pirates ever captured, in August 1804, would end up as spectacles on the New York stage in March of the next year; none were ever ransomed to free American captives.[9]

Something, however, had to be done for the sake of the American economy—and lives. As Jefferson told Congress, "The liberation of our citizens has an intimate connexion with the liberation of our commerce in the Mediterranean, now under the consideration of Congress. The distresses of both proceed from the same cause, and the measures which shall be adopted for the relief of one, may, very probably, involve the relief of the other."[10]

He recounted his and John Adams's efforts in 1786 to sue for peace with Tripoli, and how they had foundered on the fiscal "demands" of the ambassador Abd al-Rahman, which were "beyond the limits of Congress and of reason." Even if "purchasing" peace were financially feasible—he outlined how much it might cost—there remained the danger that an expensive peace might be abrogated by the untimely death of a North African ruler.[11]

Finally, he made his most direct case to "repel force for force," the option he had privately endorsed since 1784. To do this, a navy would be required, and it was only "prudent" that it be "a force equal to the whole of that" which "opposed" the Americans. Jefferson presented the options with a veneer of impartiality, concluding that "it rests with Congress to decide between war, tribute, and ransom."[12] But his own mind had long been made up, and as president he would choose war in 1801, without requesting the support of Congress.

Jefferson had disagreed with John Adams since 1786 about the best response to piracy, but five years later, their differences in this and other political matters would become more pronounced. When the rift became public, Islam became not only a subject for dispute but a means of personal and political insult.

ISLAM IN AMERICAN POLITICAL RHETORIC DIVIDES JEFFERSON AND ADAMS, 1791

Jefferson was first accused of being a Muslim as a result of words he wrote in 1791 in praise of his friend Thomas Paine's tract *The Rights of Man*. The context was innocent, a note to the father of Paine's American editor, wherein Jefferson referred to himself in the third person:

"He is extremely pleased to find it will be re-printed here, and that something is to be publicly said against the political heresies which have sprung up among us. He has no doubt our citizens will rally a second time round the standard of Common sense."[13]

Having assumed his words were private, Jefferson was soon chagrined to see them transposed into the first person and set in print as an introduction to the American edition. The expression "political heresies" particularly inflamed John Adams and his supporters, who took it as a damning reference to Adams's recently published ideas in support of aristocracy, an element of his opposition to the French Revolution.

As it happens, Adams had read Jefferson's words correctly, though Jefferson never intended for Adams to read them at all, which he privately admitted in a letter to George Washington. In the same letter, he nevertheless, made his reproach more explicit, insisting anew that the theories of government in Adams's *Discourses on Davila* represented "political heresies," referring as well to Adams's "apostacy to hereditary monarchy and nobility."[14] A day later, Jefferson wrote James Madison making the same confession. Having so assiduously avoided a public disagreement with Adams over his plan for a multinational force to fight piracy while both served as diplomats in Europe, he was appalled that his differences with his friend should now be in the open—appalled and worried, though not chastened, to judge by his letter to Madison:

> I thought no more of this and heard no more till the pamphlet appeared to my astonishment with my note at the head of it. . . . I had in view certainly the doctrines of Davila. I tell the writer freely that he is a heretic, but certainly never meant to step into a public newspaper with that in my mouth. I have just reason therefore to think he will be displeased.[15]

For his part, Madison staunchly supported Jefferson in a letter to him, concurring that Adams's political views warranted disparagement as attacks on "the Republican Constitutions of this Country," and "antirepublican discourses."[16]

Adams and Jefferson's divergent responses to Paine's latest work issued from another point of simmering disagreement between them: the French upheaval itself. Paine had written *The Rights of Man* in 1791 as a rebuttal to Edmund Burke's censorious *Reflections on the Revolution in France*. In *Discourses on Davila* the year before, Adams had couched his own disapproval of the Revolution in terms of British political tradi-

tions. But Jefferson, by contrast, heartily welcomed the events across
the Channel, the overthrow of an absolutist monarchy and the advent
of republicanism, in which he saw more affinities with the American
Revolution, where Adams saw destructive chaos.

By July, Jefferson realized that, awkward as it might be, he could
not publicly deny his endorsement of Paine's work: "I had written it: I
could not disavow my approbation of the pamphlet, because I was fully
in sentiment with it: and it would have been trifling to have disavowed
merely the publication of the note, approving at the same time of the
pamphlet." He "determined therefore to be utterly silent, except so
far as verbal explanations could be made."[17] As early as June, however,
he'd had reason to suspect that Adams had taken up the pen against
him under the pseudonym "Publicola."[18] Proxy newspaper duels ensued
between supporters of Jefferson and Adams, with some believing that
Jefferson had joined the fray personally under various classical pseu-
donyms.[19] In fact, he hadn't, and nor was Adams actually the one who
had taken up "the cudgels" to attack him and Paine as Publicola. That
author was in fact Adams's twenty-four-year-old son John Quincy, who
had commenced a series of letters in defense of his father on June 8 in
the Boston paper the *Columbian Centinel*.

In his first letter, John Quincy took immediate issue with Jefferson's phrase "political heresies," casting the words as an un-American
absurdity. He laced his counterattack with religious references linking
Jefferson's political views to the twin Protestant nightmares of Catholicism and Islam, imputing to Jefferson quasi-papal "infallibility" and
referring to Paine's book as canon law. As Publicola, he wrote:

> I confess, Sir, I am somewhat at a loss to determine, what this very
> respectable gentleman means by *political heresies*. Does he consider this
> pamphlet of Mr. Paine's as a canonical book of political scripture? As
> containing the true doctrine of popular infallibility, from which it
> would be heretical to depart in one single point?[20]

He went on to compare Jefferson's endorsement of Paine's political
philosophy to the violent incitements the younger Adams attributed to
the Prophet Muhammad:

> The expressions, indeed, imply more; they seem, like the Arabian
> prophet, to call upon all true believers in the *Islam* of democracy, to

draw their swords, and, in the fervour of their devotion, to compel their countrymen to cry out, "There is but one Goddess of Liberty, and Common Sense is her prophet."[21]

Negative caricatures of the Prophet had been circulating in America since the seventeenth century, and now the man who would become the sixth president was tarring the man who would soon be the third as the same sort of political rabble-rouser, an implication neatly distilled in John Quincy's parody of the *shahada,* the Islamic creedal statement ("There is no god but God, and Muhammad is His Prophet"). Jefferson's political assertions were derided as a new American religion—"the Islam of democracy"—whose prophet was Thomas Paine. And since both Jefferson and Paine were known to be Deists, the association with Islam would not have seemed strained, conforming to a hundred-year-old pattern of scurrilous political rhetoric in England.[22]

The younger Adams represented the very charge of "heresy" as an assault on the intellectual freedom of all Americans, reminding his readers that "the citizens of these States were possessed of a full and entire freedom of opinion upon all subjects, civil as well as religious; they have not yet established any infallible criterion of *orthodoxy,* either in church or state: their principles in theory, and their habits in practice, are equally averse to that slavery of the mind, which adopts, without examination, any sentiment that has the sanction of a venerable name."[23] By associating them with Islam, Publicola implied that Jefferson's beliefs were not only un-American but anti-American. Thus did he carry anti-Islamic rhetoric to a new level in American political discourse. It was the first but not the last time Jefferson's political opponents would so defame him.

When on July 17 Jefferson finally wrote to John Adams, explaining that he was "thunderstruck" to see his private note about Paine in print, he attributed the public furor not to his own words but to Publicola's answer:

> Soon after came hosts of other writers defending the pamphlet and attacking you by name as the writer of Publicola. Thus were our names thrown on the public stage as public antagonists. That you and I differ in our ideas of the best form of government is well known to us both: but we have differed as friends do, respecting the purity of each other's motives, and confining our difference of opinion to private conversation.[24]

He concluded with a confession that "nothing was further from my intention or expectation than to have had either my own or your name brought before the public on this occasion," adding that his explanation of the events was "required" because of the importance of the "friendship and confidence which has so long existed between us."[25]

Adams responded "with great pleasure" twelve days later, though he complained that his friend's words were "generally considered as a direct and open personal attack upon me, by countenancing the false interpretation of my Writings as favouring the Introduction of hereditary Monarchy and Aristocracy into this Country."[26] But he minced no words expressing injury: "The Question every where was, What Heresies are intended by the Secretary of State?" Adams described how papers in New York, Boston, and Philadelphia had picked up the story, with his local political enemies making much of the dispute. In Publicola's defense, Adams allowed the author had "thought [him] innocent" and "came forward," disingenuously attributing to the writer, whom he knew to be his own son, that he only "followed his own Judgment, Information and discretion, without any assistance from me."[27] By this time, Jefferson too had been informed of Publicola's true identity, a fact John Adams would never admit to his friend.

By the end of August, Jefferson would still take no responsibility for the trouble caused by his "political heresies" comment, insisting instead that "not a word on the subject would ever have been said had not a writer, under the name of Publicola, at length undertaken to attack Mr. Paine's principles," which Jefferson persisted in calling "the principles of the citizens of the U.S." (an indirect repetition of his original attack on Adams).[28] For his part, Adams had earlier discounted Publicola as the source of the controversy, noting that "an unprincipled Libeller in the New Haven Gazette" had attacked him—and these lies had been repeated in numerous northeastern newspapers.[29] But Jefferson wryly dismissed the "Libeller's" importance with his own reference to Islam: "You speak of the execrable paragraph in the Connecticut paper. This it is true appeared before Publicola. But it had no more relation to Paine's pamphlet and my note, than to the Alcoran. I am satisfied the writer of it had never seen either."[30]

It was an attempt to denigrate Adams's critic, but also perhaps a not-so-subtle dig at John Quincy Adams. One historian has suggested that Jefferson used the reference to the Islamic holy book merely as "an analogy for irrelevance" and a reflection of what was "alien to his experience."[31] But Jefferson knew the Qur'an well, having owned a copy of it for more than a quarter century, and it seems likelier his reference to it was simply meant to suggest the ignorance of Adams's critic.

With neither man much exerting himself to make amends, or even to tell the truth, serious and lasting damage was done to the friendship of Jefferson and Adams, and that damage is reflected in the vehemence of their later political battles.[32] With the appearance of references to Islam, the acrimony had escalated to a point of no return in character assassination. Ironically, Thomas Paine, whose writing had provoked the rift, held his own distorted view of Islam, one that both John Adams and John Quincy Adams might have endorsed, even as they condemned much else that the author wrote.

JOHN QUINCY ADAMS, JOHN ADAMS, AND THOMAS PAINE ON ISLAM, THE PROPHET, AND MUSLIM RIGHTS

Since Humphrey Prideaux's 1697 polemic had arrived from England, American readers had been primed for the sort of negative stereotypes of the Prophet that John Quincy Adams presented.[33] During the Revolutionary War, some might also have seen Voltaire's play tying Muhammad to religious fanaticism and violence.[34] Many others naturally considered him and Islamic regimes to be the antithesis of American religious and political liberties, as depicted in *Cato's Letters*.[35] John Quincy Adams would therefore have well understood the magnitude of his calumny, and the enmity behind it would not have been lost on Jefferson, despite his own views of Islam.

Did the elder Adams concur in his son's dark view of Islam? Not in 1776, when in *Thoughts on Government* he cast the faith in a considerably more positive light. In promoting "virtue" as the end of government, Adams listed a range of non-Christian exemplars, including the Prophet, whom he identified as one of the "sober inquirers after truth," all of whom, "ancient and modern, pagan and Christian, have declared that the happiness of man, as well as his dignity, consists in virtue. Confucius, Zoroaster, Socrates, Mahomet, not to mention authorities really sacred, have agreed in this."[36]

By 1790, however, the elder Adams was envisioning Muhammad as a violent impostor and Islam as a source of despotic governments, views he included in *Discourses on Davila*, the tract to which Jefferson had objected. There, he warned of "anarchy" and "fanaticism" as "the blessings" "of the first mad despot, who with the enthusiasm of another Mahomet, will endeavor to obtain them."[37] It was a view that would survive even this rupture with his friend: Long after their relations had been mended, in July 1816, John Adams wrote to Jefferson describing Napoleon as "a Military Fanatic like Achilles, Alexander, Caesar, Mahomet."[38]

Almost forty years after his attack on Jefferson, in the wake of his presidency (1825–29), John Quincy Adams would continue to deride Islam and the Prophet in an unsigned essay attributed to him.[39] In 1827–28, he described the ongoing conflict between the Ottoman Empire and Russia this way: "The precept of the Koran is, perpetual war against all who deny, that Mahomet is the prophet of God." Once again he depicted the Prophet as violent, resorting to the very same distortions with which he had disparaged Jefferson: "but the command to propagate the Moslem creed by the sword is always obligatory, when it *can* be made effective. The commands of the prophet may be performed alike, by fraud, or by force."[40] It is worth noting that John Quincy Adams also frequently denigrated American Jews as "aliens" and the purveyors of unique "tricks."[41]

Despite his own experience as the object of anti-Islamic slurs, Jefferson also believed and repeated the stereotype of a repressive religion, views his friend Thomas Paine also espoused in *Common Sense,* wherein he described the Prophet in relation to the evils of monarchy, founded on "some superstitious tale, conveniently timed, Mahomet like, to cram hereditary rights down the throats of the vulgar."[42] Such a view did not, however, prevent his endorsement in his *Rights of Man* of religious freedom for Muslims in the context of praising the 1789 French Constitution's "universal rights of conscience." Anything less was inadequate, as Paine deemed both "Toleration and Intolerance" to be "despotisms," whereby the state could interfere with the individual's religious freedom.[43]

Paine challenged his readers to respond to a bill he invented, entitled "AN ACT to tolerate or grant liberty to the Almighty to receive the worship of a Jew or a Turk," or "to prohibit the Almighty from receiving it." The point of this rhetorical coup was clear: "There would be an uproar" at such unthinkable "blasphemy." In proposing that these rights be granted to God, Paine sought to expose what he considered the preposterousness of Protestants determining control over the proper bounds of toleration for non-Christians. "The presumption of toleration in religious matters" he boldly charged, "would then present itself unmasked: worshipper and worshipped cannot be separated." When humans undertook to judge the beliefs of others, they did so heedless of the truth that "no earthly power can determine between you."[44] A few years later, declaring in *The Age of Reason* his Deist belief "in one God, and no more," Paine would simultaneously reject national establishments of Judaism, Catholicism, Greek Orthodoxy, Islam, and Protestantism as so many tyrannies.[45] For now, however, he was content to assert that human governments should have no say in matters of conscience.

ADAMS'S TREATY WITH TRIPOLI, 1797

On June 10, 1797, President John Adams fulfilled his long-held ambition of signing a treaty of peace and friendship with Tripoli, eleven years after he and Jefferson failed to make one with the ambassador Abd al-Rahman in London. The treaty's Article 11 unequivocally asserted that America's government was neither officially Christian nor inherently anti-Islamic:

> As the government of the United States of America is not in any sense founded on the Christian Religion,—as it has in itself no character of enmity against the laws, religion or tranquility of Mussulmen,—and as the said States never have entered into any war or act of hostility against any Mehomitan nation, it is declared by the parties that no pretext arising from religious opinions shall ever produce an interruption of the harmony existing between the two countries.[46]

Adams left no public comments on the treaty, nor did Jefferson as his vice president. And there is no debate preserved regarding its ratification. The final vote on June 7, 1797, was twenty-three out of thirty-five in the U.S. Senate in favor, but no votes against were registered.[47] Nevertheless, the assertion that the country had "no character of enmity against" Muslim beliefs was certainly a marked departure from prevailing anti-Islamic views. Article 11 attempted to excise officially any religious basis for conflict between the United States and Tripoli. To do this, both Christianity and Islam were overtly dismissed as grounds for war, a strategic move that distinguished the United States from the several Christian powers of Europe so long embroiled in what they described as a religious conflict with Islamic states.

Under the headline "Important State Papers," President Adams took full responsibility for the treaty on the front page of newspapers from Pennsylvania to Connecticut, Rhode Island, Massachusetts, New Hampshire, and New York.[48] His introductory note to the treaty text informed readers that he personally "had caused to be published and issued this Proclamation, commanding a strict observance of the following Treaty; regularly negotiated and ratified."[49]

All of these newspapers published the treaty without editorializing, with one exception. William Cobbett, Federalist editor of the *Porcupine Gazette* of Philadelphia, objected to the treaty's religious implications, in a paragraph appended to the text in the June 23, 1797, edition:

> The eleventh article of this treaty certainly wants some explanation. That "the government of the United States of America is in no sense founded on the Christian religion," is a declaration that one might have expected from Soliman Kaya, Hassan Bashaw, or the sansculotte Joel Barlow; but it sounds rather oddly from the President and the Senate. If it will admit of satisfactory explanation, it ought to receive it; for it certainly looks a little like trampling upon the cross.[50]

Cobbett, a Federalist, was in a political bind. He wished to criticize the basic premise that the U.S. government was "in no sense founded on the Christian religion" without criticizing the Federalist president who had negotiated the treaty and the Federalist senators who had already ratified it.[51] To him, the article seemed an attack on Christianity, and what he presumed to be the Christian character of his nation. And so he deflected the blame, speculating that Muslim officials in Tripoli or the American diplomat Joel Barlow were responsible for this article of the treaty.[52] John Adams had written that even by comparison to Thomas Paine, there "was not a more worthless fellow" than Joel Barlow.[53] The article was indeed consistent with Barlow's views on government and religion, and he likely was involved in crafting it. His ideas, however, were not unique but already well represented in the domestic politics of the United States.[54]

JOEL BARLOW'S PROBABLE AUTHORSHIP OF ARTICLE 11

Appointed U.S. consul to Algiers in February 1796, Joel Barlow was predictably on hand to sign and verify the final version of the Tripoli treaty in North Africa in January 1797.[55] After taking a degree from Yale in 1778, he served as a chaplain during the Revolutionary War. His views of religion changed, however, when he traveled to Europe, where he met Jefferson and Paine and, like them, came to embrace the French Revolution.[56]

Barlow's *Advice to the Privileged Orders in the Several States of Europe* (1792), reveals his aversion to religious violence and hints at his influence on Article 11.[57] He decries the millions of deaths in Europe resulting from "persecution of the Christian church,"[58] writing that "any mode of worship declared to be national" was antithetical to religious "liberty," a standard Deist claim.[59] He concludes with a declaration about Christianity and the United States that would seem to suggest his influence on Article 11:

> In the United States of America there is no church; and this is one of the principal circumstances which distinguish that government from all others that ever existed; it ensures the un-embarrassed exercise of religion, the continuation of public instruction in the science of liberty and happiness, and promises a representative government.[60]

Clearly, he meant that there was no established Christian faith in the United States, a fact in no way at odds with the free exercise of religion by the varied Protestant Christian majority. In fact, the assertion of the United States as "not in any sense founded on the Christian Religion" was already implicitly enshrined in the Constitution's First Amendment.[61]

And it had proponents other than Barlow. In 1803, in the midst of Jefferson's naval conflict with Tripoli, Secretary of State James Madison would also implicitly affirm the principle of Article 11 of the 1797 treaty, which he considered for the purposes of diplomacy with North African rulers a point in favor of the United States as compared with European Christian powers. He wrote the U.S. consul general at Algiers to remind him to press it:

> P.S. The universal toleration in matters of religion in most of our States, and the entire want of a power respecting them in the general Government, has as we understand induced the Barbary powers, to view us more favorably than other Christian Nations, who are exclusively so, and with whom these powers consider themselves in perpetual hostility,

suspended only at times, by temporary truces. It is recommended to you
to avail us of this fact & opinion, as far as it can be used to lessen the
unequal condition of the intercourse between us.[62]

But Madison was not merely being an opportunistic diplomat in
1803, his point being entirely consistent with his earlier attempts to end
the establishment of Christianity in Virginia in 1785, and his support
of Jefferson's Bill for Establishing Religious Freedom, which passed the
following year.

AMERICAN POLITICAL PRECEDENTS FROM THE FOUNDING FOR ARTICLE 11

Even before the U.S. Constitution affirmed that there would be no
religious test for federal officeholders and the First Amendment denied
any "establishment of religion," James Madison had promoted a religiously plural vision of the United States not unlike Jefferson's. While
the latter was in France, Madison had cleared the way for the passage of
his comrade's Bill for Establishing Religious Freedom. In 1785 his own
brilliant *A Memorial and Remonstrance against Religious Assessments* railed
against the proposal that Virginia tax proceeds be allocated to pay for
the propagation of Anglican Christianity, the state's established religion. In the third article of his tract Madison rejects an establishment of
any form of Christianity:

> Who does not see that the same authority which can establish Chris-
> tianity, in exclusion of all other Religions, may establish with the
> same ease any particular sect of Christians, in exclusion of all other
> Sects?[63]

And in the ninth article he argues for universal religious equality:

> Because the proposed establishment is a departure from the generous
> policy, which, offering an Asylum to the persecuted and oppressed of
> every Nation and Religion, promised a lustre to our country; and an
> accession to the number of its citizens. What a melancholy mark is the
> bill of sudden degeneracy? Instead of holding for an Asylum to the per-
> secuted, it is itself a signal of persecution.[64]

Such was Madison's appreciation of how inimical any established faith was to his conception of his nation.

Though Madison had been unable to persuade his neighbor George Washington to sign the *Memorial,* Washington would independently express his strenuous support of religious freedom for all, including Muslims:

> Altho' no mans Sentiments are more opposed to *any kind* of restraint
> upon religious principles than mine are; yet I must confess, that I am not
> amongst the number of those who are so much alarmed at the thoughts
> of making People pay toward the support of that which they profess, if of
> the denominations of Christians; or declare themselves Jews, Mahomi-
> tans, or otherwise, and thereby obtain proper relief.[65]

Washington knew that the hope of "relief" for non-Christians was small, because they would be forced to pay to support a religion they rejected, and so he wished that "the assessment had never been agitated" and would "die an easy death."[66] He would not, however, go so far as to oppose a probable majority in support of the measure.

But many others did express a wish for an end to a Christian religious establishment in Virginia. One group of Protestant petitioners from Chesterfield County wrote in support of Madison's *Memorial and Remonstrance* on November 14, 1785. In protesting the payment of teachers of Christianity with state taxes, they argued forcefully for a religiously plural Virginian society: "Let Jews, Mehomitans, and Christians of every Denomination enjoy religious liberty," and "thrust them not out by establishing the Christian religion lest thereby they become our own enemys and weaken this infant state."[67] Moreover, these Protestant petitioners reminded the Virginia House of Delegates that "it is mens labour in our manufactures, their services by sea and land that aggrandize our country and not their creed."[68] Civic contributions, not faith, were the proper standard of belonging for Jews and Muslims, not just Christians. Was this not an early domestic political statement compatible with Article 11 of the Tripoli treaty? Such sentiments had deep roots in European Protestantism, in which from the seventeenth century a significant minority had affirmed that religion was a private matter of conscience, between the believer and God. This relationship must always be exempt from any government control.

Barlow's contributions to the Tripoli treaty, however objection-able to the editor Cobbett, did not otherwise stir debate, either in the Senate or local newspapers. Having been circulating since Jefferson's Bill for Establishing Religious Freedom of 1779 and Madison's *Memorial and Remonstrance* of 1785, they were not unusual in eighteenth-century American thought.

Ironically, although Barlow attested to the accuracy of the treaty's text, because neither he nor any of his colleagues could read Arabic, he had to rely on European go-betweens to vet the agreement,[69] and he probably never knew that Article 11 never existed in an Arabic transla-tion.[70] The discrepancy would remain undiscovered until 1930, when a Dutch scholar was hired by the State Department to examine the Arabic document.[71] Nevertheless, similarly accepting language about Islam would appear in later treaties with North Africa—in both Arabic and English—endorsed by Thomas Jefferson, and later adopted by James Madison.

JEFFERSON "THE INFIDEL": ANTI-ISLAMIC RHETORIC, A CHRISTIAN AMERICA, AND THE PRESIDENCY, 1800–1801

President John Adams's campaign against the challenger Thomas Jef-ferson in the election of 1800 has been termed the first "smear cam-paign" in American electoral history—and it was the first, but not the last, in which a presidential candidate was accused of being a Muslim.[72] The Republican Jefferson's religious beliefs figured centrally in Feder-alist attacks, with Jefferson wrongly portrayed as an atheist and, more accurately, a Deist.[73] Sometimes he was also called an "infidel," a term suggesting not only one who has rejected Christianity but also "an adherent of a religion opposed to Christianity," specifically a Muslim.[74] It was a somewhat more subtle application of the tactic pioneered by John Quincy Adams in 1791, with the Federalists using slogans like "God and a religious president" or "Jefferson and no God."[75] The basis for the strategy was to play on the perception that America was a Chris-tian nation and that the danger of a non-Christian president was immi-nent in Jefferson.[76] It remained the worst fear of some Americans that a Muslim infidel might be elected, a possibility that the recently ratified Constitution, lacking a religious test for office, made theoretically possible. Mobilization of voters against Jefferson on grounds of religion was in effect an attempt to enforce such a test, a popular objective now plainly unconstitutional.[77]

Federalist clergymen were particularly keen to relitigate the religion question in the presidential contest. One Dutch Reformed minister asked, "Would Jews or Mahometans, consistently with their belief, elect a Christian?" Believing that he knew the answer, he insisted that Christians should be no "less zealous and active than they" in seeking to elect John Adams, a true Christian, as president.[78]

Jefferson's own words had rendered his Christianity suspect and him vulnerable to this attack. It was his now famous pluralist utterance published fifteen years earlier in *Notes on Virginia* that his adversaries repeatedly cited: "But it does me no injury for my neighbor to say there are twenty gods, or no god. It neither picks my pocket nor breaks my leg."[79] Historians have pointed out, with a latter-day irony missing in the eighteenth century, that "Jefferson's much vaunted toleration of all religion proved that he was no true Christian."[80] One irony lost at the time was that Jefferson himself had used the word "infidel" to similar calumnious effect in 1776 against George III. In his first draft of the Declaration of Independence, Jefferson decried the king's support for the slave trade, comparing it to the North African Muslim pirates' taking of captives: "This piratical warfare, the opprobrium of INFIDEL powers, is the warfare of the CHRISTIAN king of Great Britain."[81] Jefferson's words were excised in the final draft, as he explained in his autobiography, in deference to South Carolina and Georgia as well as "our northern brethren" who "had very few slaves themselves" but were "pretty considerable carriers of them to others."[82]

The term "infidel" as a synonym for Muslim remained one of the worst insults an American could hurl, whether against the British king or a fellow presidential candidate, from 1776 to 1800—and beyond. In an 1801 letter to a close friend a few months after his inauguration, Jefferson would lament the religious nature of these political slurs: "what an effort, my dear Sir, of bigotry in Politics & Religion have we gone through."[83] As president he would eschew this bigotry whether waging a naval action against Tripoli or making a peace treaty with the same North African nation.

JEFFERSON'S MILITARY ACTION AGAINST TRIPOLI, 1801–5

It would be the country's first conflict with a foreign power, the first, too, with an Islamic one, but Congress would never declare war. Having failed to reach terms for peace with Tripoli fifteen years earlier, Jefferson and his cabinet voted on May 15, 1801, to send a squadron of four vessels to the Mediterranean. They had received reports that Tripoli was demanding payment of tribute above the sums that America had been paying for peace under the treaty President Adams had signed in 1797.[84] What Jefferson did not know was that the day before, Yusuf Qaramanli, Tripoli's ruler, had ceremoniously declared war by cutting down the U.S. flag from his citadel.[85]

Although some American historians have presumed that the so-called First Barbary War was prompted by Jefferson's desire to end piracy for good, by 1801 Tripoli had in fact seized only two American vessels, far fewer than the more powerful Algiers.[86] And Pasha Yusuf Qaramanli had quickly released the American ships and their crews. It seems likelier that hostilities first arose on the other side, the first American peace treaty with Tripoli having sown the seeds of a military conflict that would stretch across Jefferson's first term.[87] American diplomats seem to have misread Tripoli's grievances, its annoyance at being perceived as subservient to Algiers and therefore not worthy of the same tribute. Tripoli also claimed that America was in arrears on payment required by treaty.

Like Jefferson, Qaramanli had ambitions of launching a strong navy; he expanded his fleet from nineteen armed ships in 1803 to twenty-four by the end of the conflict with the United States in 1805.[88] Each of Tripoli's vessels was commanded by a *ra'is,* or captain, and manned by a crew of twenty to thirty men. Captains were of Turkish, Berber, or Arab origin. Some, including, Murad Ra'is (the former Peter Leslie), admiral of the fleet, were European Christian renegades who had converted to Islam. Leslie had been a mutineer of Scottish origin, who avoided a British court-martial by joining Tripoli's navy in 1794. A year later, he was appointed admiral.[89]

For the next four years, American naval vessels attempted to blockade and bombard Tripoli, without decisive success.[90] In the first year, Jefferson was able to coordinate American naval forces with Sweden's, in just the sort of multilateral arrangement he'd proposed as a diplomat in France. Nevertheless, despite the capture of a Tripolitan ship early in 1801, the blockade failed, owing in part to the intervention of other North African states.[91] By 1802, Jefferson could still not secure a declaration of war from Congress, but he did win more official support for the military defense of American commerce.[92]

In 1803, a new force of seven American vessels began to patrol the Mediterranean.[93] It included the thirty-six-gun warship *Philadelphia,* which was seized with her crew of 307, having accidentally run aground on a reef in Tripoli harbor while chasing an enemy ship on October 31.[94] After a year of captivity, Jonathan Cowdery, the ship's doctor, reported that five men had died, while another few had "turned Turks"—adopted Islam to regain their freedom.[95] Rather than allow the pirates to use the captured American ship, on February 16, 1804, Lieutenant Stephen Decatur and a few of his men managed to burn the *Philadelphia,* a daring feat that would garner praise from no less august a seaman than Britain's Admiral Nelson.[96] But the *Philadelphia*'s demise did nothing to end the captivity of her languishing crew, much less the war with Tripoli.

Jefferson tried a new strategy when he appointed the diplomat William Eaton to begin negotiations with Ahmed—or as he was known then to Americans, "Hamet"—Qaramanli, Tripoli's deposed ruler and the brother of Pasha Yusuf.[97] From exile in Cairo, Hamet pledged to participate in the siege of Tripoli's port city of Derna, from which point would be launched the conquest of Tripoli and his return to power as a ruler friendly to U.S. interests. Thus had Thomas Jefferson ordered the first American covert attempt at a coup d'état against a foreign power.

Eaton directed the five-hundred-mile trek through the Libyan Desert from Alexandria, Egypt, to Derna, Libya. His forces included ten U.S. soldiers, who never actually made it "to the shores of Tripoli," as extolled by the Marine Corps anthem, as well as various mercenaries: three hundred Arabs, thirty-eight Greeks, and members of other nationalities.[98] On April 25, 1804, Eaton's force took Derna as it was also being bombarded by three U.S. ships.[99] But in the meantime, Yusuf Qaramanli had hastily made terms with the Americans, dashing Hamet's ambitions to rule once again and forcing Eaton to withdraw.

Jefferson was praised for prosecuting a successful war overall, but criticized vociferously by the Federalists, members of the navy, and his own envoy, Eaton, for failing to press the U.S. advantage with the capture of Tripoli, which might have put an end to tribute. By June 4, 1805, the United States would finally negotiate a $60,000 ransom for all prisoners, far less than the $3 million the pasha had initially demanded, with the understanding that there be no further payments.[100] If Jefferson did not end the practice of tribute for peace, he did at least prove that the United States would resist North African aggression militarily. The threat of piracy would not abate fully until after the U.S. Navy won a final battle with Algerian forces in June 1815, during the presidency of James Madison, but Jefferson's policy of armed resistance certainly marked the beginning of the end.[101]

Historians disagree on how many Americans were actually held prisoner in North Africa from 1784 to 1815, with estimates of between four and seven hundred men.[102] However, some argue that only slightly more than half of the 307 sailors captured when the American warship *Philadelphia* ran aground were native-born Americans, the rest being British.[103] Our best assessment is that almost 90 percent of Americans seized by North African pirates were eventually ransomed and returned home.[104]

JEFFERSON'S TREATY WITH TRIPOLI AND THE QUESTION OF ISLAM, 1806

Religion had never figured previously in Jefferson's diplomatic dealings with North African states, but the language of his treaty with Tripoli, compared with that of Adams's previous treaty, indicates that religion had entered into his thinking. Article 14 of Jefferson's Tripoli treaty, for instance, omits the clause Cobbett had complained about in Adams's earlier Article 11: "the government of the United States of America is not in any sense founded on the Christian Religion."[105] It is curious that Jefferson would have chosen to exclude mention of a principle of government that he had actively championed since 1776, but perhaps attacks upon his Christianity during the presidential election moved him toward reticence to avoid further conflict. He did, however, choose to retain and thus reaffirm Adams's end to anti-Islamic sentiments concerning America's official stance toward the beliefs of Muslims: "As the Government of the United States of America has in itself no character of enmity against the Laws, Religion or Tranquility of Musselmen."[106] Whatever Jefferson's calculations, the treaty was signed on June 4, 1805, in Tripoli and ratified by the U.S. Senate on April 17, 1806, by a vote of twenty-one to eight.[107] When it was published in various newspapers across the land, no outcry was heard, nor did Federalists renew their attack on Jefferson as being an infidel Muslim. He had after all only retained language that the unimpeachably Christian Adams had approved.

Unlike Adams's treaty, which contained no Arabic equivalent for this language about Islam and Muslims, Jefferson's Arabic version reflected these ideas accurately.[108] As a result of his naval action, however, Jefferson's treaty could no longer claim that the United States had never entered "into any war or act of hostility against any Mehomitan nation."[109] Language was therefore inserted to make military intervention seem less belligerent: "and as the said States never have entered into any voluntary war or act of hostility against any Mahometan Nation, except in the defence of their just rights to freely navigate the High Seas."[110] The United States might not have declared war on Tripoli, but it justified its use of force as a principled effort to reclaim the right to "freely navigate" the Mediterranean. To emphasize this point, Jefferson's version included, with minor variations, another clause from Adams's: "It is declared by the contracting parties that no pretext arising from Religious Opinions, shall ever produce an interruption of the Harmony existing between the two Nations."[111]

With these words, Article 11 of the first Tripoli treaty concluded, but Jefferson's Article 14 continued with new language about the freedom of religion, whose exercise was to be permitted the representatives of both nations—and their slaves: "And the Consuls and Agents of both Nations respectively, shall have liberty to exercise his Religion in his own house; all slaves of the same Religion shall not be impeded in going to said Consuls house at hours of Prayer."[112] This reciprocal guarantee was of course a constitutional, if not practical, reality in America. Nevertheless, both Jefferson and Madison, his secretary of state, believed it was important that the United States set itself apart from the European powers by espousing freedom of conscience. In the Islamic context, Christians already should have been able to practice their faith privately. In America, Jefferson's first chance to make good on this provision would come with the visit of a Muslim ambassador to Washington even before the treaty was approved by the Senate.

The treaty language defining Islam as a significant, relevant, and unthreatening faith in 1806 in fact confirmed an important new principle of American foreign policy. Navigation of the high seas might provoke disputes between the United States and Muslim states, but religious differences never would. Yet the fact remained that American treaties with European powers, whether Protestant or Catholic, did not even mention the Christian religion. Only Islam merited special mention in diplomatic documents, underscoring a central contradiction: Whatever the Constitution had accomplished regarding official neutrality in matters of religion, most Americans, Adams and Jefferson included, had little respect for Islam as a faith, making it necessary that these prejudices be formally overwritten, for the sake of peaceful relations with a more powerful nation. But unlike Adams, Jefferson, despite his negative views of Islam, would also demonstrate privately his diplomatic approbation of the faith and its North African practitioners.

James Madison would take a cue from Jefferson's precedent during his presidency in his later treaty with Algiers, the last of the pirate powers. President Madison's military action against the dey's dominion ended the threat of piracy once and for all in 1815. Article 15 of Madison's treaty channeled the spirit of Jefferson's Article 14, but without explicit mention of Islam, making instead a universalist statement: "As the Government of the United States of America has in itself no character of enmity against the laws, religion, or tranquility of any nation,"[113] despite its need for self-defense on the "high seas," "no pretext arising from religious opinions shall ever produce an interruption of Harmony between the two nations."[114] Interestingly, the Turkish version of Madison's treaty omitted this clause.[115] And American diplomats, once again, would unwittingly approve a treaty with an Islamic power whose foreign translation was faulty.

JEFFERSON RECEIVES THE FIRST MUSLIM AMBASSADOR IN WASHINGTON, 1805–6

In 1805, prior to the ratification of his treaty with Tripoli, President Jefferson welcomed a Tunisian envoy to his new capital, stirring great public fascination.[116] The presence of the North African diplomat would pose unusual challenges, but also an opportunity for Jefferson and Secretary Madison both to observe a Muslim ambassador up close and to demonstrate the genuineness of the American commitment to religious freedom with a show of awareness and sensitivity to Islamic ritual practice. Unfortunately, Jefferson's direct observations of the nearly year-long visit remain limited, with one key exception: a letter he composed, revised, and finally sent privately to Tunis with the returning envoy.

Sidi Suleyman Mellimelli arrived in Washington in November 1805 to negotiate the return of a Tunisian warship and two other vessels seized by the American navy.[117] (The Tunisian vessels had been caught attempting to aid Tripoli by running the American blockade of the harbor there.)[118] By now the Tunisian ruler also hoped to lift a naval blockade of his own harbor, which had come after an imprudent threat of war against the United States if his ships were not returned. In response, Commodore John Rodgers sailed into the harbor of Tunis with a force of "five frigates, two brigs, two schooners, one sloop, and eight gunboats," demanding that the bey decide within thirty-six hours whether he wanted war or peace.[119] The time ran out without a shot being fired by the United States, and it was now the Tunisian ruler who proposed to dispatch his representative to resolve the issue and arrange for the removal of the U.S. force from his harbor.[120] That end would be achieved thanks in no small part to a private correspondence that Jefferson had been conducting with the bey since a month after his inauguration in 1801.[121]

The visit would be Jefferson's second encounter with a Muslim ambassador and Madison's first. Senator William Plumer of New Hampshire recorded in his journal the most detailed observations of the Tunisian, along with some of his conversations about the visitor with President Jefferson. The senator was with Jefferson at the White House when cannon fire at Alexandria, Virginia, announced the ambassador's arrival. Though Plumer thought the visit a "mark of respect," Jefferson countered that the Tunisians undertook it "unwillingly,"[122] also telling Plumer that he would "Pay no tribute to Tunis."[123] It was a touchy point. Newspapers such as the *Hampshire Federalist* carried Jefferson's announcement of the visit, which he represented "as proof of friendship" that the Tunisian vessels would be "restored," which, he implied, was not tribute but rather reparations.[124]

Jefferson had rented Stelle's Hotel in Washington, D.C., to house the envoy and his eleven-person entourage, plus his Italian band.[125] He hoped to recoup these entertainment expenses by selling or putting out to stud the four horses brought by the ambassador as a gift.[126] What the president did not share with Senator Plumer, who found out anyway, was that Mellimelli had requested "one or more women" with whom to spend a portion of the night.[127] It was Secretary Madison who would procure for the ambassador one "Georgia a Greek," billing the Department of State with the droll notation, "Appropriations to foreign intercourse," as required by "very urgent and unforeseen occurrences."[128] He could not have done so without consulting the president, whose own private life, after all, still included the slave concubine Sally Hemings.[129]

Jefferson suffers by comparison with the Tunisian in Senator Plumer's review of the president's attire and the envoy's.[130] The senator writes that the president wore a "blue coat, red vest," and "white hose ragged slippers with his toes out—clean linen—but hair disheveled."[131] When the senator visited Mellimelli, he noted that "his military robes" shone in "fine scarlet," which was "inwrought with much gold" and complemented by "yellow shoes" and a "turban of fine white muslin," the entire aspect "elegant and rich" alongside Jefferson's shabbiness. Plumer further reports of the Muslim ambassador that "his complexion is about as dark as that of a Molatto [Mulatto]"[132] and that he described himself as "a Turk."[133] As for Mellimelli's retainers, they were all "large black men."[134]

Plumer was most impressed by the ambassador's "elegant" gold and diamond snuff box, from which his guest would later enjoy a snort with his host.[135] Like the ambassador from Tripoli, the ambassador from Tunis smoked a pipe that was "four feet long." For all this luxurious display, Plumer initially concluded of the Tunisian that he was "a man, between the Savage & civilized state." Despite these prejudices, he remained impressed to see that Mellimelli's "manners were easy & really graceful" and his "countenance is good—it bespeaks intelligence and integrity."[136]

When the secretary of the navy paid a call, he observed that because it was Ramadan, the Tunisian envoy was praying "on his hands & knees on a very fine skin that was spread on the carpet."[137] Actually, the ambassador's prayer times would have remained the same, even during the month-long holiday when all Muslims fast and abstain from liquids from dawn to dusk in remembrance of God's revelation of the Qur'an to the Prophet Muhammad.

Since the Tunisian explained to his visitor that "he could not eat this month until after sunset," the two met after sundown for coffee.[138] Mellimelli was, by his own account, "a very firm believer in the Alcoran—he reads and expounds a lesson from it every day to his household."[139]

Recognizing the importance of Ramadan, Jefferson too made accommodations for his guest, changing the time of the state dinner accordingly. The original invitation, probably issued December 6, had dinner scheduled for "half after three," when all Washington would have typically supped.[140] Jefferson moved it to "precisely at sunset," although this still did not allow the Muslim ambassador time enough to mark the end of daylight before breaking his fast.[141] Ironically, the most detailed account of this "Ramadan" dinner at the White House was recorded by John Quincy Adams, author of Publicola's anti-Islamic invective against Jefferson fourteen years earlier:

> I dined at the President's, in company with the Tunisian Ambassador and his two secretaries. By invitation, the dinner was to have been on the table precisely at sunset—it being in the midst of Ramadan, during which the Turks fast while the sun is above the horizon. He did not arrive until half an hour after sunset, and, immediately after greeting the President and the company, proposed to retire and smoke his pipe. The President requested him to smoke it there, which he accordingly did, taking at the same time snuff deeply scented with otto [attar] of roses. We then went to dinner, where he freely partook of the dishes on the table without enquiring into the cookery.[142]

During dinner, Mellimelli's two secretaries left and seized the opportunity "to take each a glass of wine." (They sipped surreptitiously, because alcohol was prohibited by their faith.) Adams added that their "manners are courteous," though an interpreter was needed, as usual, to facilitate communication in Italian.[143]

The Tunisian ambassador was in Washington at the same time as a delegation of Native Americans, also negotiating treaties with the United States. When they visited Mellimelli to pay their diplomatic respects, he asked them about their religion. Plumer recounts the exchange:

> The Minister asked them what God they worshipped. The Indians answered *The Great Spirit.* He then asked them if they believed in Mahomed, Abraham, or Jesus Christ? They answered neither. He then asked what prophet do you worship. They replied none. We worship the Great Spirit without an agent.[144]

The Tunisian immediately condemned them as "all vile Hereticks." Later, Plumer also reports an exchange between Jefferson and the Tunisian concerning Native American religion. Mellimelli asked Jefferson "how he could prove Indians were the descendants of Adam?" Jefferson answered both diplomatically and as a man who would never take scripture literally: "it was difficult."[145]

It wasn't until later in his stay that the Tunisian would reconsider the beliefs of the Native Americans. Attending the funeral oration of an Osage chief, Mellimelli heard an affirmation "that God was God, it was his work." This utterance Mellimelli understood as a declaration of the divine unity. It prompted him to allow these people into the monotheist fold, even to suggest that they were probably originally from Yemen.[146] Ultimately, Mellimelli would declare the Native Americans to be "descendants of Arabs" and "his brethren."[147] How he viewed Jefferson, Madison, Plumer, and other white Americans remains a mystery, though the president would express his own views of the Tunisian envoy in a letter of 1806.

MELLIMELLI'S JOURNEY HOME AND JEFFERSON'S LETTER TO THE RULER OF TUNIS, 1806

Secretary Madison had planned Mellimelli's departure for home from Boston after sojourns in various East Coast cities, among them Baltimore, Philadelphia, and New York. James Cathcart, a former prisoner in Algiers and a former U.S. consul, accompanied the ambassador on these travels.[148] In May 1806, Jefferson wrote Madison about his anxiety that the ambassador "should go away personally favorable to us," but his imminent departure left several problems unresolved.[149] For one, Jefferson had refused Mellimelli's persistent demands for tribute in exchange for a peace treaty. (The president was unmoved even by the envoy's claims that he feared for his life if he returned without substantial American monies.) Jefferson did, however, eventually send back with Mellimelli a U.S.-built ship as compensation for the one seized by the navy, together with a gift of $10,000 to cover the Tunisian ruler's losses.[150] In September 1806, the ambassador finally left Boston so laden with presents that they had to be shipped separately to Tunis by chartered vessel.[151] (Room on his personal transport was limited by the large quantity of commodities like coffee and sugar the envoy had acquired in the hope of turning a profit.)[152]

But the most diplomatically precious thing Mellimelli carried was a letter from Jefferson to Hammuda Bey, the Tunisian ruler, dated June 28, 1806.[153] Jefferson's correspondence with the ruler of Tunis, begun earlier in 1801, provides greater insight into his personal view of the relationship between the two countries. While emphasizing recognition and respect between the two powers, these exchanges also mark the culmination of Jefferson's references to spiritual common ground in pursuit of a lasting peace.[154] Jefferson was not the first president to mention God in his correspondence with Tunis. In 1800, President John Adams had written expressing hope that "Almighty God would cause to reign between our two nations, a peace firm and durable."[155] But Jefferson went further in his personal entreaties for a religiously based amity.

In April 1801, a month after the inauguration, the first letter from the bey arrived at the White House entreating Jefferson to send the presents agreed upon in the peace treaty the previous year, as well as renewing a request for the forty cannon also stipulated, as "real proof of friendship." In closing Hammuda Bey wrote, "I pray Almighty God to preserve you, and I assure you, Mr. President, of all the extent of my esteem and my most distinguished consideration."[156]

Doubtless, Jefferson would have noted the presumption of a shared God and God's presence blessing relations between the two men. The president duly responded in September, with regrets that the agreed presents had been delayed because of "distance," but with assurance that they would duly arrive, and a warning of his country's new problems with Tunis's neighbor Tripoli. In closing, Jefferson followed the bey's example in invoking the Almighty, expressing hope for the "continuance of your friendship in return for that which we sincerely bear to you; and pray to God that he may long preserve your life, and have you under the safeguard of his holy keeping."[157]

Jefferson had recapitulated the bey's formula, as well as adding his own prayer for "safeguard" of the Muslim ruler's life, which had a pious ring, but might also be considered in purely pragmatic terms: Anytime a North African ruler died, previous peace treaties were abrogated and needed to be renegotiated by the new Muslim sovereign. In wishing long life to Hammuda Bey, whose rule would run from 1777 to 1814, Jefferson was also praying that America would be spared further financial demands. His relationship with Hammuda and the bey's rule would endure through both of Jefferson's presidential terms.

On September 8, 1802, the Tunisian ruler responded to Jefferson with thanks for the receipt of "all the military and naval stores" and the "superb jewels" guaranteed by treaty. Hammuda Bey then praised the "harmony and alliance which, thank God, have been established and actually subsist between us." This did not keep the North African ruler from requesting "a good frigate of 36 guns" from the Americans. Nor would he refrain from aiding Tripoli in its war with the United States. Nevertheless, the bey concluded, "I pray Almighty God to have you in his holy keeping."[158] The bey had adopted a key part of Jefferson's formula for a personal benediction in his closing.

When, in the course of this correspondence with Tunis, Tripoli had declared war on the United States on May 14, 1801, Jefferson responded by ordering a U.S. naval squadron to the Mediterranean within a week. Even so, writing the Tripolitan ruler for the first time as president seven days after the declaration of war, Jefferson still expressed hope for "peace and friendship with all nations," signing his missive, "I pray God, very great and respected friend, to have you always in his holy keeping."[159] Jefferson the Deist's belief in a unitary God would be consonant with this assertion, even in the midst of his blockade of Tripoli's harbor. But invoking God's protection for an avowed enemy? It would appear that Jefferson was attempting to see whether the religious formula he had included in his response to the bey of Tunis might gain him anything in diplomacy with Tripoli. Jefferson's letters to the ruler of Tunis in 1803 and 1804, during the war with Tripoli, a period when Tunis offered military aid to that neighboring power, continued to invoke God in his final benedictions. These expressions had become a consistent part of the president's foreign policy.[160]

These letters must be understood in context. When Jefferson dispatched a letter in 1806 to the bey in the care of his ambassador, the American navy had already seized Tunisian vessels for assisting Tripoli. Despite conflict with Tunis, the need for conciliation with them was great, now that war against Tripoli was at last concluded, and the president's solicitous words reflect the fragility of the bilateral relationship, at a time when the United States was in no position of naval or diplomatic advantage. What is perhaps most interesting was that Jefferson, whatever his innermost intent, should express repeatedly a personal belief in God to a Muslim ruler at a time when many of his own countrymen considered their president an atheist, an infidel, or even a Muslim outright. These letters dare to assert that Jefferson, at least, agreed that North Africans and Americans worshipped the same deity, and that this common belief would enhance their diplomatic relations.

A sense of fellowship infuses the correspondence, with Jefferson addressing the Tunisian ruler as "Most Illustrious and Most Magnificent Prince, the Bey of Tunis," but also as "Great and Good Friend." To facilitate amicable understanding, Jefferson bluntly admonished his own naval commander Rodgers in the letter, describing his threat of war and a naval blockade in Tunis as "menaces" undertaken without the president's express "instructions" and carried out "in a manner not consisting with the respect due to your Excellency's character, nor with the friendship which I bear you." As proof that Rodgers had over-stepped the "spirit of conciliation" that Jefferson intended to foster between the two countries, the president assured the Tunisian ruler that the commander would be reprimanded on his return to the United States.[161]

Jefferson then broached the ambassador's visit, carefully balancing approbation with criticism of his conduct. He lauded Hammuda Bey for initiating the "special mission," as "proof of that desire for the main-tenance of peace between our two countries, which I have a pleasure of meeting and cherishing," and told of how he had received the ambas-sador "with all the cordiality and respect which a missionary from you so justly commands." Emphasizing a second time his desire "to preserve peace and good understanding," Jefferson underscored that "the inter-ests of both countries" could be "permanently established only by the practice of justice, equality, and mutual forbearance."[162]

At the same time, the president did not refrain from explaining his resistance to some of Mellimelli's demands, though softening his objections with a final complimentary flourish: "If the ambassador has pressed too strongly, and persevered too inflexibly in certain demands to which we cannot accede, I have ascribed it to a laudable zeal for the promotion of your service, and a desire to merit that favor with you, to which his talents and fidelity so justly entitle him." Jefferson expressed hope that returning to Tunis, Mellimelli would attest to the important differences between the United States and Europe:

> He will be able to inform you, on the evidence of his own observation, that the character, principles, and institutions of our Government, dis-tinguish us essentially from the Nations of Europe. Their practices can therefore be no rule for us.[163]

The president here refers implicitly to the fact that his country, unlike those in Europe, is not officially Christian, and therefore with-out any inherent antagonism toward Islam. It was of course true only officially, as his own political experience attested. But for Jefferson, the Constitution's Establishment Clause was not merely a measure to ward off sectarian strife, as it had been to many of the Framers. It was an affirmative American virtue, one that might well pay dividends in the conduct of foreign policy.

Jefferson's view of mutuality in foreign policy was as simple as this: "The law of our connection with other nations is to do justice and receive it, to ask and to yield nothing unequal." His understanding of maritime relations was already to be found in his treaty with Tripoli, drafted the previous year, but he reiterated it: "We hold particularly that nature having placed the ocean as a common highway for the intercourse of nations, all have equal right to use it, and in the maintenance of that right we calculate neither expence nor danger."[164] This was the basis for Jefferson's naval action against Tripoli and Tunis, and he assumed, with great optimism, that Hammuda Bey would approve "the correctness of these principles" because of his "known justice and high understanding."[165] In preparing the way for a new U.S. consul's arrival in Tunis, Jefferson also expressed hope that "our former Treaty will continue to be the law of our observance, that commerce between our two nations will be cherished, and that all our relations shall be founded on principles of equality and reciprocity."[166]

In the penultimate paragraph of his letter, Jefferson defended the seizure of the Tunisian ships that had been aiding America's enemy Tripoli: "A nation is surely authorized, by the common reason of mankind, to restrain all persons from passing the circumvallation by which it beleaguers its enemy, whether by land or sea, and to treat the individuals as transgressors who attempt it by fraud or force." However, he concluded by allowing that "our war with Tripoli being over, we can relax with safety its rigorous rights." As a new "proof of friendship," Jefferson not only "waived" the "right acquired to us by hostile act" to keep as prizes those Tunisian ships but also "substituted" a vessel "more worthy of your acceptance," a newer ship in place of the seized one that had suffered "unavoidable decay."[167]

Finally, thanking the Tunisian ruler for his "tokens of friendship," the gifts he had sent to Washington, Jefferson expressed his desire to reciprocate with presents "from our country." His last sentence appealed not just to common national interests, but to a mutual belief in the same divinity: "with these [gifts] my prayers that God will have you, great and good friend, in his holy keeping."[168] It was a startling benediction for an American president, to suggest that both men were equals before a shared God, but this formula was the same one Jefferson had included consistently since 1801. The president wrote this line again in 1806, not in haste but deliberately and twice in his own hand for the first draft and again in his final version of the letter.[169] These exact words also graced the more ornately scripted official copy dispatched with the ambassador, which remains to this day in the Tunisian National Archives.[170]

It must of course be remembered that the president never expected the sentiments in his private missives to Tunis or Tripoli to be made public. Indeed, at the time he "never allowed his private letters regarding religion to be published."[171] And it is likely that Jefferson had little hope that his appeal to ideals of "justice, equality, and mutual forbearance"[172] would result in actual diplomatic advantage. But if somehow, realpolitik notwithstanding, his words could nudge relations with Tunis closer toward "principles of equality and reciprocity," the status quo of American weakness and mercantile vulnerability might be marginally improved. At the same time, it is worth noting that Jefferson had long truly believed the principle first enunciated in Adams's treaty, that "the Government of the United States of America, has in itself no character of enmity against the Laws, Religion or Tranquility of Musselmen."[173] Indeed, since his first exposure in the 1760s to a British legal precedent about the toleration of Muslims, he rejected the idea that any "enmity" had ever existed between "Turks" and Englishmen due to a "difference between our religion and theirs."[174]

In pressing this point, Jefferson may have consulted his own copy of the Qur'an to support his religious assertions in North African diplomatic correspondence. A Qur'anic passage that commands Muslims not to argue with "People of the Scripture" (Jews and Christians) extols the very commonality that Jefferson invoked: "We believe in that which hath been revealed unto us and revealed unto you; our God and your God is One, and unto Him we surrender" (Qur'an 29:46).[175] There is certainly the distinct possibility that Jefferson would have used his knowledge of such verses to manipulate and cajole his adversaries to whatever extent he could. Nevertheless, it must at the same time be allowed that these inclinations are entirely compatible with Jefferson's own religious evolution, as reflected in other private letters of this time; his embrace of Deist and, finally, Unitarian ideas is in full harmony with the Muslim belief in a single, shared deity.

JEFFERSON THE UNITARIAN AND HIS CONTACT
WITH JOSEPH PRIESTLEY

In 1793, Jefferson bought *An History of the Corruptions of Christianity*, published nine years earlier by the British Unitarian Joseph Priestley (d. 1804); it would have a profound influence on his religious views.[176] Priestley's book, which denied the Trinity and emphasized the humanity of Jesus,[177] won the author disdain in Britain, and though he despised Islam, his enemies nevertheless taunted him in 1792 with a play on the Muslim creedal statement: "The real creed of the Unitarian is—There is one God and Priestley is his prophet."[178] The year before, Jefferson had been attacked in just the same way by John Quincy Adams for his support of the Deist Thomas Paine: "There is but one Goddess of Liberty, and Common Sense is her prophet."[179]

The Unitarian Priestley and the Deist Jefferson had, within a year of each other, been similarly condemned as Muslims. It was not the first time for Priestley. Two years before, he acknowledged, without irony, that "my opponents, who consider me already as half a Mahometan, will not suppose that I can have any objection to the society of persons of that religion."[180] As with Jefferson, a negative view of Islam on Priestley's part did not diminish his respect for its adherents, and Priestley would describe himself as the real acquaintance of members of the three non-Protestant faiths most despised by the British majority: Catholics, Jews, and Muslims.[181] As a legislator Jefferson had defended the rights of each, going so far as to meet with Muslims in person and to engage them in his private correspondence. But he would not be persecuted to the extent Priestley was.

Almost as objectionable in Britain as Priestley's Unitarianism was his support for the French Revolution. Together, these positions marked him as a traitor and precipitated a riot, which destroyed his house in Birmingham, including his library and laboratory.[182] Three years later he would leave Britain, at Jefferson's urging, settling with his family in Pennsylvania. There in 1797, Jefferson and Priestley met for the first time.[183] A friendship was born, and it flourished until Priestley died in 1804. Jefferson would aver that "Priestley's learned writings on" Unitarianism "are, or should be, in every hand."[184]

By 1801, the year Jefferson first wrote to Tunis, he had developed a serious interest in Unitarianism, entering into frequent and lengthy correspondence with Priestley's fellow Unitarian thinkers, an exchange that would continue to the end of the president's life.[185] In 1820, writing to Jared Sparks, he would link his belief in Jesus as a purely human moral exemplar to his vision of a unitary God. He affirmed these convictions as Unitarian but also ultimately universal. Indeed, they built upon his long-standing Deism, which extols Jesus as a human prophet, as Islam does. In fact, Jefferson declared, "The religion of Jesus is founded on the Unity of God."[186]

His private abandonment of the Trinity was of course a repudiation of the Anglican faith into which he'd been born, and not long before, if made public, it would have cost him dearly—though not as dearly as Servetus, who in sixteenth-century Geneva had been condemned to the pyre—but Jefferson could not have forgotten that in Virginia, before passage of his legislation establishing religious freedom in 1786, those who denied the Trinity suffered imprisonment.[187] In another letter in 1822, Jefferson described that persecution as the "hocus-pocus phantasm of a God . . . with one body and three heads," which "had its birth and growth in the blood of thousands and thousands of martyrs." In this same letter, Jefferson declared that true Christianity had been grounded in absolute monotheism at its inception: "No historical fact is better established, than that the doctrine of one God, pure and uncompounded, was that of the early ages of Christianity."[188]

This idea he derived from the seventeenth-century English forerunners of Unitarianism, the Socinians, who first espoused a return to what they deemed an original pristine Christianity,[189] considering all else, as Jefferson did, "corruptions of his religion." "Thinking men of all nations," Jefferson concluded, "rallied readily to the doctrine of one only god," a sentiment allowing for the beliefs of Muslims and Jews, as well as Christians.[190]

But Jefferson also allowed room for those who disagreed with his views on the Trinity:

> I write with freedom, because while I claim a right to believe in one God, if so my reason tells me, I yield as freely to others that believe in three. Both religions, I find, make honest men, and that is the only point society has any right to look to.[191]

His life's work would ultimately prove his interest in religion to be less theological than political and legal. His aim as a statesman was not the definition of transcendent truth but the foundation of a more civil, pluralist society at home and peaceful relations for America abroad. Still, his own ecumenism was not boundless.

Having, via Deist and then Unitarian reflection, come to believe in a unitary (rather than triune) God, Jefferson was able sincerely to claim a theological outlook with which the Muslim sovereign in Tunis could concur. He had certainly paid for this conviction, having been branded an infidel by his own countrymen, and his private letters to American and British Unitarians reflect a steadiness of innate belief whatever more expedient reasons he may also have had for expressing his spiritual sentiments to Hammuda Bey. Jefferson's impulse to share his beliefs with the bey of Tunis seems not unlike the wishes of seventeenth-century Unitarians in England to meet the Moroccan ambassador and affirm their shared view of God.[192] Against all other Protestant Christians at the time, these early Unitarians argued that "Islam was not a misshapen mirror image of Christianity, but an object of commendation."[193] It is quite possible, then, that Jefferson similarly found in the Tunisian ruler's religion at least one basic belief to commend. This of course did not negate the general disdain he had always felt for the faith of Islam—and every other organized religion, including Christianity.

JEFFERSON'S FINAL NEGATIVE VIEWS OF THE QUR'AN AND THE PROPHET, 1809–22

It would be wrong to suggest that personal belief in monotheism led Jefferson to anything like consistent admiration for the precepts of the Qur'an or the example of the Prophet. Indeed, not long after his letters to Tunis and his embrace of Unitarianism, from 1809 to 1822 he continued to write about the sacred book and the Prophet in quite disparaging terms.

In 1809, in an unsent draft of a letter to a Baptist minister, Jefferson describes the "bitter schisms of Nazarenes, Socinians, Arians, Athanasians in former times, and now of Trinitarians, Unitarians, Catholics, Lutherans, Calvinists, Methodists, Baptists, Quakers &c." He then adds a peculiar—and false—comparison to schisms in Islam: "Among the Mahometans we are told that thousands fell victims to the dispute whether the first or second toe of Mahomet was longest; and what blood, how many human lives have the words 'this do in remembrance of me' cost the Christian world!"[194] By way of this possibly fanciful analogy did Jefferson decry religious persecution as a universal problem.

The next year, in 1810, Jefferson refers to the Qur'an in a discussion of William Blackstone's *Commentaries,* the foundational British legal compendium published in 1765, the same year in which Jefferson had purchased his Qur'an.[195] While acknowledging the Qur'an as the source of Islamic law, Jefferson takes to task both American lawyers, whom he describes as "us," and "Mahometans," an implicit "them," for the same blinkered practice of relying on only one book as the fount of all law: "I have long lamented with you the depreciation of law science. The opinion seems to be that Blackstone is to us what the Alcoran is to Mahometans, that everything which is necessary is in him, and what is not in him is not necessary."[196] He might have asserted more parochially that "Blackstone is to us lawyers what the Bible is to Christians," but such a division between lawyer and Christian might have offended the letter's recipient, a judge who was certainly both.

Jefferson apparently did not recall George Sale's introduction to the Qur'an in which he mentions the four Sunni schools of Islamic law and the Muslim jurist al-Shafi'i, who had "reduced that science into a method."[197] Indeed he seems never to have been aware of the extrascriptural sources of Islamic law, including the Prophet's utterances and example, scholarly consensus, and human reason.[198] Likewise unbeknownst to Jefferson, by the eighteenth century, Muslims had been analyzing the Qur'an with the aid of a number of other sources for more than a millennium. But such historical particulars would have mattered less to Jefferson than the intellectual imperative to question all faiths, including Islam. What he objected to among Muslims he also faulted among both Jews and Christians: the dangers of a literal adherence to revealed truth.

Twenty-three years earlier, Jefferson had urged his nephew to make a logical examination of all assumed truths in religion: "Fix reason firmly in her seat, and call to her tribunal every fact, every opinion." This rational, even scientific approach he extended to the Bible, by which he meant the Hebrew Bible, or Old Testament, as well as the New. Jefferson believed that each book frequently failed his rationalist test. Of the Old Testament, he wrote:

> But those facts in the Bible which contradict the laws of nature, must be examined with more care, and under a variety of faces. Here you must recur to the pretensions of the writer to inspiration from God. Examine upon what evidence his pretensions are founded, and whether that evi-

dence is so strong, as that its falsehood would be more improbable than a change in the laws of nature, in the case he related.[199]

He could not believe, for example, that Joshua could make the sun stand still.[200]

Respecting the New Testament, Jefferson urged his nephew to consider "the opposite pretensions" of key Christian doctrines regarding Jesus's divinity, virgin birth, and whether he "ascended bodily into heaven." He also advised the lad not to fear if his analysis "ends in a belief that there is no God." Jefferson already lived by the words of his final exhortation: "Your own reason is the only oracle given you by heaven, and you are answerable, not for the rightness, but uprightness of the decision."[201] It was therefore necessary to read "all the histories of Christ," because even Christians should not simply rely on one sacred book. In requiring of a reasonable man such a skeptical outlook, then, the Qur'an was no different than the Hebrew Bible or the New Testament.

Jefferson's 1821 autobiography describes events witnessed at the outset of the French Revolution in 1789 by way of a final, negative analogy to Islam. On July 13, the day before the storming of the Bastille, Jefferson notes what amounted to a coup in the replacement of the king's key ministers. He blames the unscrupulous new advisors for the precipitation of violence that would provoke the Revolution. The weak king was now "completely in the hands" of men who, wrote Jefferson, "had been noted through their lives, for the Turkish despotism of their characters."[202] It was by now a rather timeworn image of political repression in the form of the Ottoman Empire that Jefferson used to condemn French royal officials he believed cared nothing for justice—or what his friend Lafayette had just proclaimed as "The Rights of Man."[203]

A similar stereotyping is evident in an 1822 letter to a professor of medicine at Harvard, wherein Jefferson offers a critique of Calvinism by way of Islam. He rejects as "demoralizing dogmas" five propositions he attributes to Calvin, of which the fourth is particularly relevant to his view of Islam: "4. That reason in religion is of unlawful use."[204] The suggestion that Calvin made reason "unlawful" to use in religion is the very same criticism of Islam he had derived from Voltaire. In the categories of "impious dogmatists" and "false shepherds," Jefferson places the Protestant reformer Calvin, together with the early father of the church Athanasius, comparing their distance from true Christianity to that of the Prophet: "They are mere usurpers of the Christian name, teaching a counter-religion made up of the *deliria* of crazy imaginations, as foreign from Christianity as is that of Mahomet."[205]

Here, Jefferson's views of Islam appear particularly derogatory; with no redeeming affinity with Unitarianism, it is reduced to something like a Christian heresy. What is perhaps more remarkable, however, is that even privately Jefferson should so freely compare something so "foreign" to the theology subscribed by most of his Protestant countrymen. In attributing the "*deliria* of crazy imaginations," to both Athanasius and Calvin, Jefferson implicitly invokes the standard charge of Christian theologians—and most Americans—that the Prophet was subject to fits of either epilepsy or madness. Yet his intent is to malign not the Prophet but the originators of faulty Christian dogma in a style of doctrinal denigration well established in earlier battles between Catholics and Protestants as among various forms of Protestantism.[206] For all Jefferson had suffered from scurrilous claims that he was a Muslim, he would, since the Virginia debates of the 1770s, never cease to find easy recourse to such rhetoric. However forward-looking he may have been about individual Muslim rights, and sympathetic to Islam's largest theological claim, in his general view of the faith, he remained rather tenaciously a man of his times. The final placement of his Qur'an in the library that he would term "a blueprint of his own mind" does, however, point the way, belatedly, to a more generous vision of Islam.[207]

THE ISLAMIC WORLD IN JEFFERSON'S LIBRARY, 1783–1823

In 1815, President Madison definitively ended North African piracy in the Mediterranean and Jefferson sold his treasured 6,700-volume library, then the country's largest private collection, to the U.S. government for $23,950. Jefferson had doubled the size of his holdings by frequenting London and Paris booksellers, where he purchased most of his volumes on the Middle East.[208] Among his books, which would become the nucleus of America's national library (what is now the Library of Congress), was his copy of the Qur'an.[209]

Inspired by categories drawn from the philosopher Francis Bacon, the unusual complexity of the catalog remained uniquely Jefferson's. He divided it into three sections: Memory, Philosophy, and Fine Arts.[210] Arabic, along with other languages, he placed under Fine Arts; history under Memory. Religion, the division in which he placed the Qur'an, he considered as a subcategory of Philosophy.

Jefferson purchased six volumes in the Arabic language, with a few in Farsi and Turkish, all of these texts including translations into Latin or some other European language. Kevin Hayes has suggested that Jefferson used these books to further his study of Arabic, but if that is true there is no evidence of any actual familiarity with the tongue.[211] It is clear, however, that in his earlier planning for the curriculum to be taught at his alma mater, the College of William and Mary, Jefferson did not include Arabic.[212] Among the languages he classified as "Oriental," he urged students to study Hebrew, Chaldean, and Syriac, all standard in the study of biblical exegesis, and all represented by grammars in his library.[213]

Jefferson's collection of Egyptian and Ottoman history[214] included a book about the revolt of Ali Bey in Egypt,[215] Rycaut's history of the Ottoman Empire, and a chronicle of the great Muslim conqueror Timur Lenk, or Tamerlane (d. 1405).[216] The histories of Syria, Arabia, and Iran are not represented, but he included European travelers' tales of these places as a division of Philosophy, under which he placed geography.[217] These travelers' accounts of the Islamic world ranged across three continental categories: Europe, Asia, and Africa.[218] There was, for example, Lady Mary Wortley Montagu's (d. 1762) report of her stay in Istanbul as a British diplomat's wife, wherein she challenges the then common erotically charged fantasies of European men concerning Muslim women, many of them written by male authors who, unlike Montagu, had never met a Turkish woman.[219]

Not surprisingly, eight volumes were of North African history, the largest concentration in Jefferson's collection on the Middle East. Half were general regional histories, written by European diplomats; the remaining four texts were more focused on piracy and the plight of European captives.[220] The single American account, written by William Ray and published in 1808, depicted the captivity of the U.S. frigate *Philadelphia*'s crew during Jefferson's undeclared war against Tripoli.[221] The president had received the book as a gift from the author, who sent it with fawning compliments, also soliciting a presidential donation of one hundred dollars. Jefferson refused, directing Secretary Madison to secure the author some remuneration.[222]

SALE'S QUR'AN IN JEFFERSON'S LIBRARY

Jefferson's ultimate placement of the Qur'an in his library exemplifies his understanding of Islam in relation to other world religions.[223] In the catalog's seventeenth chapter on Religion,[224] the Qur'an was the fourth book, after three on polytheism (Greek, Zoroastrian Iranian, and Roman deities), and just before several copies of the Old Testament.[225] These Old Testaments were followed by volumes containing both the Old and New Testaments and an even greater number containing versions of the New Testament alone.[226]

Jefferson described the order of his catalog as "sometimes analytical, sometimes chronological & sometimes a combination of both."[227] The placement of the Qur'an certainly defies chronology. According to Islamic tradition, the revelations it comprises occurred between 610 and 632 CE, while a single definitive, written Arabic version was not codified until the mid-seventh century. This means that the Qur'an dates historically to a time millennia after the polytheist deities of the ancient world, but also long after both the Old and New Testaments.[228]

One explanation of Jefferson's choice for his Qur'an's position suggests that Jefferson's Religion section was predicated on a notion of "progress"[229] and that in his view Islam was "an improvement over the pagan religions yet fell short of the belief system Christianity represented."[230] But could Jefferson plausibly have considered Islam "at a halfway point between paganism and Christianity"?[231] Certainly his express view of certain essential tenets of Christian orthodoxy would suggest otherwise.

Jefferson had a less than ideal view of both the New Testament and the Christian faith. That is why, beginning in 1804, while he was still president, and resuming in 1819–20, he privately undertook to create by excision his own version of the New Testament Gospels.[232] Omitting all miracles, the virgin birth of Jesus, his divinity, and his resurrection, this version would be known after his death as the Jefferson Bible.[233] It was his own private edition of the New Testament he endorsed, not those numerous other volumes on his shelves. Perhaps for this reason the version of the Gospels he created stayed among his private papers, never placed among his library collection.

A further complication in the theory of theological progress: In the midst of his numerous versions of the New Testament, one finds two volumes of Old Testament scripture, one of the prophet Isaiah and the other the Psalms of David, which at the very least represent an interruption in a supposed Christian teleology.[234] Then, following more New Testaments and their concordances, Jefferson placed a number of exclusively Christian works, focusing on matters ranging from martyrdom to heresy and theological schisms, and also includes a critique of Calvinism, an account of the Moravian sect, another on Anabaptism, a meditation on "toleration and religious liberty," and one on the subject of suicide.[235]

What seems to emerge in this section on Religion is less a chronological or thematic order than a degeneration of Christianity into faction and persecution, the opposite of what Jefferson considered religious or civil progress. If he had placed his Qur'an after the New Testaments in strict chronological order, he would have left his only Islamic work stranded between Christian scripture and a host of subsequent elaborations and studies.

Instead, placing the Qur'an next to numerous volumes of the Hebrew Bible, Jefferson appears to recognize an affinity between the Jewish and Muslim varieties of monotheism and that of the Deism and Unitarianism he would espouse, all these traditions similarly rejecting the Trinity of normative Christianity. Underscoring this linkage is the unassailable fact that he also continued to view both the Qur'an and the Old Testament as repositories of religious law, a category not applicable to the Gospels. Indeed in 1824 Jefferson wrote that "in my Catalogue, considering Ethics, as well as Religion, as supplements to law, in the government of man, I had placed them in that sequence."[236] It is important to recall that when Jefferson purchased his Qur'an in 1765, he was still a student of the law; Sale's description of the Prophet as the "lawgiver of the Arabians" in his introduction to the reader would surely have made an impression.[237]

JEFFERSONIAN PARADOXES: POSITIVE VIEWS OF ISLAM, PROBLEMS WITH PIRATES, AND THE FUTURE OF AMERICAN MUSLIM CITIZENS, 1821

With seven key exceptions, Jefferson never had a positive thing to say about Islam, either in public or in private. He twice publicly endorsed his government's tactful respect for "the Laws, Religion or Tranquility of Mussulmen," in the Tripoli treaties, once as vice president in 1797, and again as president in 1806. He privately affirmed a much more pointed approval of the faith in one letter to Tripoli and in four to Tunis, the last in 1806, wherein he assured his "great and good friend" of the mutuality of their beliefs in a single supreme being. Jefferson's kind words for Hammuda Bey's faith may have been purely an expression of diplomatic politesse, or even desperation, but considered alongside his final placement of the Qur'an, they suggest something more akin to respect for a monotheism that would have seemed to him theologically closer to the faith into which he had grown than the one into which he'd been born.

In contrast, his negative associations of Islam with fanaticism and tyranny, which continued throughout his life, may reflect his appropriation of a commonplace transatlantic political language, one that he also applied to gain his political ends. Jefferson's ambiguities in political thought about equality, race, and slavery have been noted by other historians.[238] These paradoxes blinded him to the possible presence of American Muslims in the United States. His perceptions of Islam in his political life remain, at the very least, ambiguous, even enigmatic. Only in the later evolution of his private religious beliefs does Jefferson's diplomatic appreciation for Islam's central tenet seem sincere.

In the autobiography written five years before his death in 1821, Jefferson, reviewing his conduct of foreign policy, still refused to indict Islam as the motivation behind the predations of those he called "the Barbary cruisers." And in this perspective too, he appears consistent. North African enemies remained, in his estimation, simply "lawless pirates," a generic designation for a universal problem.[239] Despite having gone to war against Tripoli, he would not inscribe "enmity" in his treaty of peace, preferring to reaffirm his nation's previous approbation of "the Laws, Religion or Tranquility" of Muslims. Insisting that not all the followers of Islam were enemies, he would never present their faith as a barrier to peaceful diplomatic relations.

Whatever his ambivalence about Islam, Jefferson's position on Muslim rights and potential for citizenship remained consistent from his days as a law student in the 1760s until the end of his life. Having first concurred with a seventeenth-century English legal case that had ruled as "groundless" the categorization of "Turks and Infidels" as "enemies for life," he held fast to the possibility of their eventual inclusion in the American experiment.[240] In fact, in his thinking about American citizenship, Jefferson subscribed an even more expansive and, at the time, unusual idea, borrowed from John Locke in 1776: "neither Pagan nor

Mahamedan nor Jew ought to be excluded from the civil rights of the Commonwealth because of his religion."[241]

The experience of engaging in military action against Tripoli might well have given Jefferson occasion to reconsider his lofty notions, and to ask whether all Muslims were not in fact foreign and potential enemies. But looking back in 1821 upon his efforts to advance his Virginia Bill for Establishing Religious Freedom in 1786, he would proudly recall how the omission of the words "Jesus Christ" from the legislation affirmed his lifelong intent "to comprehend, within the mantle of its protection, the Jew and the Gentile, the Christian and Mahometan, the Hindoo, and Infidel of every denomination."[242] These words affirm Jefferson's belief in the free exercise of religion in America, and the principle of American civic inclusion irrespective of faith.

Yet Jefferson's insistence on the universality of his bill's inclusive nature, confirmed by the excision of any reference to Christianity, had also been a cause taken up by numerous, often nameless Protestant dissenters in Virginia since the Revolution. There, Presbyterians and Baptists, who had suffered the most persecution under the state's Anglican establishment of religion, supported Jefferson and Madison with their "remarkably robust notion of religious liberty." This position, according to John A. Ragosta, also meant that these same Protestant dissenters "emphatically rejected the notion of a 'Christian nation' on both religious and political grounds."[243] Without the groundswell of this faith-based dissenting support, neither Jefferson nor Madison would have been able to realize their legislative goals in Virginia.[244]

But the dissenting Virginian ideal of a non-Christian nation that would also support religious pluralism for non-Protestants would meet with resistance throughout the country. In New England, state establishments of Congregational Protestantism persisted beyond the ratification of the Constitution and its First Amendment, leaving all other Protestants and all non-Protestants subject to state regulation of their faith and taxes. In 1785, Protestant dissenters in Virginia insisted that their government be separate from any interference in religious matters—and in this protection they included non-Protestants: "Let Jews, Mehomitans, and Christians of every Denomination find their advantage in living under your laws. Religion is of god to man the Civil Law is of you to your people."[245] This absolute separation of government from religion, in the interest of protecting any religion, including

Judaism and Islam, would be forcefully articulated by John Leland, one of Jefferson's and Madison's key Baptist allies in Virginia.

The evangelical minister Leland, arguably the most significant if unsung Baptist political activist of his generation, preached a new American gospel about the inalienable rights of conscience and political equality, not just for persecuted Baptists, but for all believers, including Muslims. In following Leland's remarkable ministry in the next chapter, from Virginia into New England through the mid-nineteenth century, we see combined the reverberations of key Jeffersonian precedents and the pleas of the earliest Baptists in England for the protection of all spiritual beliefs from government control.

7

Beyond Toleration

John Leland, Baptist Advocate for the Rights of Muslims, 1776–1841

The liberty I contend for is more than toleration. The very idea of toleration is despicable; it supposes that some have a pre-eminence above the rest, to grant indulgence; whereas, all should be equally free, Jews, Turks, Pagans and Christians. Test oaths and established creeds, should be avoided as the worst of evils.

—John Leland, "Virginia Chronicle," 1790

THE BAPTIST EVANGELICAL MINISTER John Leland (d. 1841) considered the "established creeds" of his native Massachusetts to be "the worst of evils" because they sanctioned religious and political inequality long after the ratification of the Constitution in 1788 and the passage of the First Amendment in 1791.[1] Leland would return to New England from Virginia, where he had first fought for religious liberty and political equality; now he would champion those rights in Connecticut and Massachusetts not just for his fellow Baptists but for all believers, including Muslims.[2] But Leland's principled insistence on citizenship for American Muslims was based, like Jefferson's, on an imagined rather than a real population.

Leland's dedication to the cause of Muslim rights echoed repeatedly in the sermons he preached and the editorials he published from 1790 until the end of his life. What he sought would not be fully realized until passage of the Fourteenth Amendment in 1868, which explicitly

John Leland, a Baptist minister and
a champion of religious freedom,
became one of Jefferson's staunchest
allies.

forbade any state to "abridge the privileges or immunities of citizens" or
"deny to any person within its jurisdiction the equal protection of the
laws," making good on what was already promised by the Constitution
and the First Amendment. But Leland did live long enough to witness
the end of Protestant Congregational religious establishments in Connecticut in 1818 and in Massachusetts in 1833. His writings and his election in 1811 to the Massachusetts legislature would contribute mightily
to those developments.[3]

Leland deemed toleration a "despicable" concept insofar as it com-
promised the "liberty," or complete political equality, he advocated
for Jews, Catholics, Baptists, Deists, and Muslims.[4] His Virginian ally
James Madison had already replaced the phrase "all men should enjoy
the fullest toleration in the exercise of religion" in the 1776 Virginia
Declaration of Rights with the more egalitarian "all men are equally
entitled to the free exercise of religion."[5] Madison too realized that,
unlike equality, "toleration" could be extended or withdrawn at whim,
depending on the degree of government tolerance.[6] He believed, as
Leland would write, that "religious liberty is a right and not a favor."[7]
It was not something the government could infringe or limit to select
believers.

Leland vocally championed the rights of Muslims as well as Catholics
and Jews at a time when such inclusiveness was unusual and unpopular.[8]
And unlike Jefferson and Madison, the two famed Virginian political

leaders whom he supported, Leland had himself suffered persecution because of his faith. Ultimately, he would surpass Jefferson in the absolutism of his insistence on the separation of church and state, and as an abolitionist, he would further develop his belief in the universality of civil rights to reach logical conclusions about slavery that Jefferson could never have approved.[9]

"The notion of a Christian commonwealth," Leland thundered, "should be exploded forever."[10] Emphasizing that the kingdom of Jesus had initially been "not of this world," Leland condemned "all state establishments of Christianity" as "ANTI-CHRISTOCRACIES," by which he meant regimes antithetical to true Christianity.[11] "The fondness of magistrates to foster Christianity," he argued, "has done it more harm than all the persecutions ever did." Unlike Thomas Jefferson, who wished to protect government from religion, Leland sought to preserve his cherished faith from state control, which he believed "corrupts Christianity and reduces it to a level with state policy."[12] Most of his fellow Baptists expressly limited their hope for the extension of civil rights to all Protestants, but not Leland. He thought they were naturally owed to all believers—among whom he consistently included Muslims.

POSSIBLE ROOTS OF LELAND'S THOUGHT ABOUT THE SEPARATION OF RELIGION FROM GOVERNMENT AND ABOUT MUSLIM RIGHTS

Where did Leland's universalism come from? Certainly not from the Congregational sermons he heard as a child. He recalled how "every Sunday afternoon," for nearly an hour, he'd listen to the minister repeat the same prayer: "Pity Mahomedan imposture—pagan idolatry—Jewish infidelity—papistry and superstition: bring the downfall of anti-Christian tyranny to a period." By the age of twelve, he had committed these prejudices to memory.[13]

There were only three books in his father's house: the Bible, Bunyan's Christian allegory *The Pilgrim's Progress,* and a volume of Protestant sermons.[14] With his father refusing support, Leland's formal education advanced no further than his local grammar school.[15] He seems, however, to have found his way eventually to certain other important influences from the seventeenth century.

Leland's ideas would echo those of John Smyth, an English Baptist, who in 1611 first asserted:

That the magistrate is not by virtue of his office to meddle with religion
or matters of conscience, to force or compel men to this or that form of
religion or doctrine, but to leave Christian religion free to every man's
conscience, and to handle only civil transgressions (Rom. xiii), inju-
ries, and wrongs of man against man, in murder, adultery, theft, etc.,
for Christ is the only king and lawgiver of the church and conscience
(James iv.12).[16]

Smyth enjoined the king from interfering in Christian practice. In
1612, Thomas Helwys carried this defense of the rights of conscience
beyond an exclusively Protestant application, boldly declaring that the
king retained no power over any believer: "Let them be heretikes,
Turcks, Jewes, or whatsoever it apperteynes not to the earthly power to
punish them in the least measure."[17] It was this more expansive vision of
Helwys's that Leland would ultimately follow to its marriage with the
Golden Rule, as enshrined in the Baptist confession of faith promulgated in London in 1660:

That it is the will and mind of God (in these gospel times) that all men
should have the free liberty of their own conscience in matters of religion,
or worship, without the least oppression or persecution, as simply upon
that account; and that for any in authority otherwise to act, we confi-
dently believe is expressly contrary to the mind of Christ, who requires
that whatsoever men would that others should do unto them, they should
even so do unto others. Matt. vii, 12, and that the tares and the wheat
should grow together in the field (which is the world), until the harvest
(which is the end of the world), Matt. xiii. 29, 30, 38, 39.[18]

Leland may have found further inspiration for his thoughts on the
separation of government from religion in the work of Roger Williams.
Although copies of Williams's seventeenth-century writings remained
scarce in eighteenth-century New England, Leland knew that Williams
had been banished from the Commonwealth of Massachusetts "because
he opposed the interference of law in matters of religion."[19] Doubtless,
Leland also read that Williams had briefly been a Baptist in Rhode
Island and continued to offer refuge in his Providence colony for his
former coreligionists at a time when they had faced whips and prison in
Massachusetts Bay.[20] Leland's advocacy for Muslims remained closer to
Williams's ideals than to any of his Baptist contemporaries.[21] Like the

earliest English Baptists, and now Leland, Williams believed that government could legitimately enforce only the second tablet of the Ten Commandments, which proscribed sins against others, such as murder and theft. In 1644, he had asked whether Muslims might be "peaceable and quiet *Subjects*, loving and helpful *neighbours*, faire and just *dealers*, true and loyall to the *civill government*?" Answering a resounding yes, he concluded that "Turkes" indeed might live harmoniously among Christians, based on "all *Reason* and *Experience* in many flourishing *Cities* and *Kingdomes* of the World."[22]

Admittedly, direct evidence of any connection between Leland and Williams is nonexistent. Suggestive, though by no means conclusive, is Leland's choice to refer to Muslims typically as "Turks," a term also preferred by all the English Baptists, as well as Williams, in the seventeenth century. He would refer to "Mahometans" only twice, once that term had become too dominant to avoid in eighteenth-century America.[23]

Lessons Leland Derived from Thomas Jefferson, James Madison, and John Locke, 1776–91

Leland, who underwent a personal conversion to the Baptist faith in 1774 in Massachusetts, resettled in Virginia, where he remained from 1776 to 1791, preaching and converting many during those pivotal fifteen years. There he also learned the art of active protest against the Anglican establishment. When he arrived in Virginia, Baptist ministers were often whipped, fined, and imprisoned.[24] Though spared such treatment, Leland was once accosted by a man wielding a sword, who attempted to stop him from preaching. Leland's daring wife, Sally, saved his life by locking the assailant's hands together in her iron grasp.[25]

However ambiguous his debt to seventeenth-century religious precedents, Leland found verifiable political inspiration in Virginia. Thomas Jefferson's Bill for Establishing Religious Freedom received early support among Baptists in 1779, despite failing to become law at the time. Leland closely studied Jefferson's proposed legislation as well as his later published observations about religion and government in *Notes on Virginia*. The Baptist preacher would later reproduce many of Jefferson's ideas nearly verbatim in his own writings in New England. Leland would not, however, make personal contact with the man he referred to as "my hero" until 1801.[26] In Virginia, he caught the notice of James

Madison, who continued the fight against the Anglican establishment of religion when Jefferson left for France in 1784. Leland and Madison may have met as early as the spring of 1785, during the campaign to garner support for Madison's *Memorial and Remonstrance against Religious Assessments,* which protested state taxes on non-Anglicans to support Anglican ministers and churches.[27] It was no surprise that Leland supported the measure; what is interesting is that some of its opponents nevertheless had doubts about the extent of religious liberty. Richard Henry Lee, for instance, despite believing fervently in religious taxes to "secure" what he termed "our morals," nevertheless wrote in a letter to Madison that "true freedom [of religion] embraces the Mahomitan and the Gentoo [Hindu] as well as the Christian religion."[28]

Leland studied Madison's *Memorial* as closely as he had Jefferson's legislation, and via the two Virginians he admired, he discovered the thought of John Locke, which would eventually find its way throughout his later writing. By then Leland would also be looking to Locke's work directly. In these years, the sparely educated preacher read extensively, impressing his contemporaries with his "retentive" memory and "the energetic vigor of his mind."[29]

By February 1788, James Madison would have renewed cause to take notice of Leland. While in New York, Madison learned by letter from Virginia that Leland, by now a powerful Baptist leader in Orange County, was "exceedingly averse to the adoption of the constitution."[30] His popularity among Baptists in Virginia had grown with his reputation as a compelling and humorous preacher,[31] who would baptize three hundred souls in the year 1788 alone, his lifetime tally eventually to exceed fourteen hundred.[32] In the letter to Madison, however, he was described as among those who "had much weight" with those people who "are opposed" to the state's ratification of the Constitution.[33] Indeed, the many Virginia Baptists under his influence seemed initially disinclined to support either the Constitution or Madison's quest to become a delegate to the state's convention. While supporting the new charter's abolition of a religious test, they worried that without an explicit protection of their rights of conscience, as affirmed in Virginia only in 1786 with the passage of Jefferson's Bill for Establishing Religious Freedom, they might once more be subject to religious and political oppression by the federal government. Without the Baptist vote, Madison could not be elected as a delegate, and without the formidable Madison, the chances for ratification in Virginia were bleak.

The same letter of February 1788 enclosed a transcription of Leland's point-by-point objections to the Constitution, which remain his earliest surviving statements on the subject of religious liberty. The first and the tenth go to the heart of his concerns:

> 1[st.] There is no Bill of Rights, whenever a Number of men enter into a state of Society, a Number of individual Rights must be given up to Society, but there should be a memorial of those not surrendered, otherwise every natural & domestic Right becomes alienable, which raises Tyranny at once, and this is as necessary in one Form of Government as in another. . . .
>
> 10[ly.] What is clearest of all—Religious Liberty, is not sufficiently secured, No Religious Test is Required as a qualification to fill any office under the United States, but if a Majority of Congress with the President favour one System more than another, they may oblige all others to pay for the support of their System as much as they please, and if Oppression does not ensue, it will be owing to the Mildness of Administration and not to any Constitutional defence, and if the Manners of People are so far Corrupted, that they cannot live by Republican principles, it is Very Dangerous leaving Religious Liberty at their mercy.[34]

Leland's first written political assertions demonstrate his understanding of Locke's notion of government as a compact among the governed, as well the philosopher's understanding of religious liberty as an inalienable right, not subject to surrender by way of entry into any compact. By this time, Leland had already served on two Baptist committees determined to lobby the Virginia General Assembly to disestablish the Anglican established creed; he would serve on one more before leaving the state.[35]

Scholars dispute whether Madison and Leland actually met in March, the following month, to discuss Baptist objections to the Constitution, though to this day a plaque in Virginia commemorates the event as a momentous historical certainty.[36] What is clear, however, is that Madison acknowledged the power of Baptist concerns because of the case Leland made, whether on paper or in person. Shortly after Virginia's ratification of the Constitution, Madison would have his father bring Leland a copy of *The Federalist Papers,* which contained the Framer's essays in defense of the nation's new charter.[37]

In exchange for Leland's Baptist support, Madison pledged to back an amendment to the Constitution protecting rights of conscience.[38] This would become the First Amendment, which affirms that "Congress shall make no law respecting an establishment of religion, or prohibiting the free exercise thereof." But these federal assurances did not apply at the state level. They would not end the Congregational establishment that had first driven Leland from his native New England, and against which he would launch a fight when he returned north.

Leland would never take credit for his influence, or that of his fellow Baptists, on Virginia's ratification of the Constitution, though he would later correspond for a brief time with Madison. In February 1789, he congratulated Madison on his election to Congress, taking the opportunity to affirm happily that he had cast his own vote in Madison's favor. Leland made one request: that Madison keep him informed about the details of legislative matters, in particular any concerning the "one thing" he needed to be warned about: "that if religious Liberty is anywise threatened, that I shall receive the earliest Intelligence." The letter also invites Madison to "pass by" and visit Leland in Virginia on his way to the first meeting of Congress in New York City.[39] If the two men had not met before ratification, they almost certainly did afterward.

A few months later, in 1789, Leland wrote to President George Washington on behalf of the united Baptist churches of Virginia. He reminded Washington of the state's persecution of his denomination, "when mobs, fines, bonds and prisons were our frequent repast." Pressing the newly elected Washington, Leland expressed hope that "the horrid evils that have been so pestiferous in Asia and Europe," namely "faction, ambition, war, perfidy, fraud, and persecution for conscience sake," might never approach "the borders of our happy nation" under the direction of "our beloved president."[40]

Washington reassured Leland that he remembered the Baptists, who "have been, throughout America, uniformly, and almost unanimously the firm friends to civil liberty, and persevering promoters of our glorious liberty." The president also reaffirmed his own defense of the universal free exercise of religion: "I have often expressed my sentiments, that any man, conducting himself as a good citizen, and being accountable to God alone for his religious opinions, ought to be protected in worshipping the Deity according to the Dictates of his own conscience."[41] As he had stated in 1784, Washington, like Leland, intended this protection not only for Baptists but all believers, including Muslims.[42] With support from the likes of Washington, Jefferson, Madison, and dissenting Protestants on the side of religious freedom, the disestablishment of Anglicanism in Virginia had been achieved.

Leland knew, however, that he could expect no such support from local political leaders when he began a similar effort in New England in 1791. The struggle against religious repression there would consume him into the nineteenth century.

LELAND RETURNS TO NEW ENGLAND TO END
CONGREGATIONAL ESTABLISHMENTS OF RELIGION, 1791

Leland, born in Grafton, Massachusetts, had begun his own spiritual quest in 1772 when, at the age of eighteen, he heard a voice from the skies telling him, "You are not about the work which you have got to do."[43] Two years later he became a Baptist and a "volunteer for Christ."[44] When he began his life's evangelical ministry in 1774, he heard that the eminent minister Isaac Backus, among other Baptists, had journeyed to Philadelphia to meet with John and Sam Adams, their representatives to the First Continental Congress. The delegation's aim was to protest not only their unjust taxation by George III, but that forced on them by the Bay State's Congregational establishment.[45] Baptists could avoid paying for the support of Congregational ministers and churches only by acquiring a certificate of spiritual dedication and economic contribution to their own faith, which document had to be sought annually from town authorities. The Baptists considered these requirements an infringement on their rights of conscience as well as a civil inequity.[46] Those who refused to pay taxes or produce the certificates were fined, imprisoned, and sometimes had their property confiscated.[47]

John Adams's recorded response to this Philadelphia meeting with Baptist and Quaker constituents in the same bind suggests a rather different outlook on religious persecution than that of Thomas Jefferson or James Madison during the 1770s: He privately notes that he was "somewhat indignant" at being "thus summoned before a self-created tribunal, which was neither legal nor constitutional,"[48] and he suspected the Baptists of treacherously wishing to "break up the [Continental] Congress" with their protests. Adams defended his state's maintenance of "the most mild and equitable establishment of religion that was ever known in the world, if indeed they could be called an establishment," and he concluded that he would "not deceive" the Baptists of his state "by insinuating the faintest hope" that the Congregational Protestant majority would ever end their ascendancy in Massachusetts.[49]

After visiting his family in New England in 1790, Leland resettled there the following year as minister of Cheshire, Massachusetts, a town founded by Baptists from Rhode Island a few years before the Revolution.[50] His duties in this small settlement in the western part of the state did not keep him from joining the public fight over religious and political equality elsewhere. Like other Baptists, he immediately objected to particularly onerous new certificate laws in neighboring Connecticut, which required applicants to get the signatures of two government officials or, if there were only one, that of the justice of the peace. These local officeholders, then, had complete discretion, without means for appeal, to decide whether non-Congregationalists would be granted exemption from being taxed to support an established religion from which they dissented.[51]

"I am not a citizen of Connecticut—the religious laws of the state do not oppress me, and I expect never will personally," Leland preached. "But a love of religious liberty in general induces me thus to speak."[52] In a powerful sermon, "The Rights of Conscience Inalienable and, therefore, Religious Opinions Not Cognizable by Law," first published in New London, Connecticut, in 1791, and later reprinted in Virginia and throughout New England, he outlined the historical evils of state-mandated religion.[53]

Leland might have protested as a Baptist, or solely in defense of other Protestants, but he elected to speak on behalf of non-Protestants as well. He argued that "heathens, deists, and Jews, are not indulged in the certificate law; all of them, as well as Turks, must therefore be taxed for the standing order" of the state's established Congregational faith.[54] In other words, the greatest unfairness was toward those not even acknowledged to be believers of a legitimate faith. There were no known Muslim residents, but there were minuscule Jewish and Catholic populations. If they had clergymen to support their claims of affiliation (and often there were none), those rabbis and priests had no standing in the eyes of state authorities, and thus "Jews, Turks, heathens, and deists, if such there are in Connecticut, are bound and have no redress."[55]

Leland had earlier argued that "forcing all to pay some preacher, amounts to an establishment," and such was an affront to the sanctity of religion by making the preacher beholden to civil authority:

That moment a minister is so fixed as to receive a stipend by legal force, that moment he ceases to be a gospel ambassador, and becomes a minister of state. This emolument is a temptation too great for avaricious men to withstand. This doctrine turns the gospel into merchandise, and sinks religion upon a level with other things.[56]

Notably, the plea he made on behalf of non-Protestants reveals a certain basic understanding of their traditions:

Is it the duty of a Jew to support the religion of Jesus Christ, when he really believes that he was an impostor? Must the Papists be forced to pay men for preaching down the supremacy of the pope, whom they are sure is the head of the church? Must a Turk maintain a religion opposed to the Alkoran, which he holds as the sacred oracle of heaven? These things want better confirmation. If we suppose that it is the duty of all these to support the Protestant Christian religion, as being the best religion in the world; yet how comes it to pass, that human legislatures have a right to force them so to do?[57]

Then Leland asked "for an instance, where Jesus Christ, the author of his religion, or the apostles, who were divinely inspired, ever gave orders to, or intimated, that the civil powers on earth, ought to force people to observe the rules and doctrines of the gospel." He proceeded, with recourse to a common notion, to appeal to the better nature of his Christian listeners: "Mahomet called in the use of the law and the sword, to convert people to his religion; but Jesus did not—does not."[58] George Sale, translator of Jefferson's Qur'an, had been among the earliest to refute the idea that conversion to Islam had been by force, but Leland's awareness did not extend that far. Unlike other contemporaries, however, he did propagate the misconception in defense of Islamic believers against a Christian regime.

In the same spirit he indicted all governments that presumed to dictate religion, from the first Christian emperor, Constantine, whom he charged with persecuting pagans and heretics; to the pope, who "exalts himself above all who are called gods (i.e., kings and rulers,) and where no Protestant heretic is allowed the liberty of a citizen"; to the Ottoman Empire, "where it is death to call in question the divinity of Mahomet, or the authenticity of the Alcoran."[59] Again, Leland's imperfect knowledge of Islam partially failed him: He did not understand that the Prophet's humanity is a tenet of the faith, though he was right about the consequence of a Muslim's questioning the divine authorship of the Qur'an.

Seeking to establish a historical foundation for rights of conscience, Leland explained that there were four forms of government on earth, one of which (the third) he distinguished for requiring "a religious test to qualify an officer of the state, proscribing all nonconformists from civil and religious liberty."[60] He then cited the Lockean notion of government as compact to describe the American system, asking "does a man, upon entering into a social compact, surrender his conscience to that society, to be controlled by laws thereof." Leland answered, "I judge not."[61]

The idea of inalienable rights Leland knew from both Madison and Jefferson's Virginia legislation. Jefferson's Bill for Establishing Religious Freedom in Virginia described any infringement on a citizen's "civil capacities" as interference with "the natural rights of mankind,"[62] while Madison's *Memorial and Remonstrance* of 1785 held:

> The Religion then of every man must be left to the conviction and conscience of every man; and it is the right of every man to exercise it as these may dictate. This right is in its nature an unalienable right. It is unalienable, because the opinions of men, depending only on the evidence contemplated by their own minds cannot follow the dictates of other men: It is unalienable also, because what is here a right towards men, is a duty toward the Creator.[63]

Leland would himself express the same sentiment this way:

> Every man must give an account of himself to God, and therefore every man ought to be at liberty to serve God in a way that he can best reconcile to his conscience. If government can answer for individuals at the judgment, let men be controlled by it in religious matters; otherwise, let men be free.[64]

Of course, Locke preceded all these Americans when he wrote a century earlier that "the care of souls does not belong to the magistrate."[65] Madison would render the idea somewhat more prosaically, denying that "the Civil Magistrate is a competent Judge of Religious Truth; or that he may employ Religion as an engine of Civil policy." Not unlike Leland, he believed that the Christian religion flourished "not only without the support of human laws, but in spite of every opposition from them."[66]

Jefferson had argued in his *Notes on Virginia* that any attempt to institute conformity in religion was the error of "fallible men" and their "coercion."[67] Leland mentioned those same "fallible men" in his tract on the rights of conscience to describe their coercive "tests of orthodoxy."[68] He also borrowed from his hero a reference to the legendary Greek robber Procrustes, who habitually chopped or stretched the limbs of his victims to fit the size of his bed. Jefferson argued, "Introduce the bed of Procrustes then, and as there is a danger that the large men may beat the small, make us all of a size, by lopping the former and stretching the latter." He concluded, "Difference of opinion is advantageous in religion."[69] Leland presses the image further, making the "iron bedstead" of his villain "Pocrustes" analogous to the state's coercive rack "to stretch and measure the consciences of all others by."[70] Jefferson reminded his readers, "Millions of innocent men, women, and children, since the introduction of Christianity, have been burnt, tortured, fined, imprisoned; yet we have not advanced one inch towards uniformity. What has been the effect of coercion? To make one half the world fools, and the other half hypocrites."[71]

Leland expresses the same idea this way: "Millions of men, women, and children, have been tortured to death to produce uniformity, and yet the world has not advanced one inch towards it." He writes, "Government has no more to do with the religious opinions of men than it has with the principles of mathematics,"[72] just as Jefferson had done earlier in his Virginia legislation, saying that "our civil rights have no dependence on our religious opinions, any more than our opinions in physics or geometry."[73] In fact, Leland would express more hyperbolically the very sentiment that had branded Jefferson an infidel. Following the latter's infamous and incendiary proclamation of 1784—"But it does me no injury for my neighbor to say there are twenty gods, or no God. It neither picks my pocket nor breaks my leg"[74]—Leland's tract of 1791 adds more faith options and explicitly sets monotheism on a par with the worshipping multiple gods or none: "Let every man speak freely without fear, maintain the principle that he believes, worship according to his own faith, either one God, three Gods, no God, or twenty Gods; and let government protect him in so doing."[75]

The same universal inclusion is evident when he argues that Christian, Islamic, and pagan forms of established religions are wrong: "The common objection 'that the ignorant part of the community are not capacitated to judge for themselves,' supports the Popish hierarchy, and all Protestant, as well as Turkish and Pagan establishments in idea."[76]

Leland was not above embarrassing the religious prejudices and provincialism of Connecticut authorities by pointing out that they discouraged foreign immigration. Demonstrating how certificates discouraged this, he even slipped in a cameo role for his hero Jefferson, referring to him simply as "an Episcopalian":

> How mortifying it must be to foreigners, and how far from conciliatory is it to citizens of the American states, that when they come into Connecticut to reside, they must either conform to the religion of Connecticut, or produce a certificate? Does this look like religious liberty or human friendship? Suppose that man, whose name need not be mentioned, but which fills every American heart with pleasure and awe, should remove to Connecticut for his health, or any other cause, what a scandal would it be to the state, to tax him . . . unless he produced a certificate, informing them that he was an Episcopalian.[77]

Such musings led Leland to conclude with praise for the federal Constitution's First Amendment and Article VI, paragraph 3, respectively, which forbids Congress ever to establish any kind of religion, or require any religious test to qualify any officer in any department of federal government. The beauty of his country's (as against Connecticut's) form of government, Leland argued, was its legal guarantee of universal inclusion: "Let a man be Pagan, Turk, Jew or Christian, he is eligible to any post in that government."[78]

Even when Connecticut's new certificate law was repealed after a six-month battle Leland waged alongside other dissenters, he would continue his advocacy for the rights of the state's Baptists, addressing a gathering of them on the steps of the state's assembly in 1794. As ever, he spoke in defense of the individual's right to worship without government interference.[79] But not until 1818 would Connecticut officially disestablish Congregational Protestantism, the referendum decided by a close vote of 13,918 to 12,361.[80] In Leland's native Massachusetts, once the heartland of the Puritans, his work would take considerably longer.

CONDEMNING THE PROTESTANT ESTABLISHMENT OF RELIGION IN MASSACHUSETTS, 1794

"What think you of the Constitution of Massachusetts?" Leland asked rhetorically three years later in his essay "The Yankee Spy."[81] His answer: "It is as good a performance as could be expected in a state where religious bigotry and enthusiasm have been so predominant."[82] Leland objected to several articles of the state's 1780 Bill of Rights on the grounds that they meddled in religion and discriminated against not just Baptists but also Deists, pagans, Muslims, Jews, and Catholics.[83]

Paraphrasing the second article of the Massachusetts constitution, he wrote that "it is the right and duty of all men publicly, and at stated seasons, to worship the Supreme Being" (adding, "This article would read much better in a catechism than in a state constitution, and sound more concordant in a pulpit than in a state-house").[84] He explained that the statute would coerce a pagan, who, "upon hearing that it is their *duty* to worship *one* Supreme Being only, must consequently renounce all other deities whom they have been taught to adore." He concluded that "here their consciences must be dispensed with, or the constitution broken." Leland made a similar case for the hardship inflicted upon a Deist, "who believes all religion to be a cheat," to either "act the hypocrite, or disregard the supreme law of the State." As a man of faith, he "heartily believed" that "it is the duty of men, and women too, to worship God publicly," but he no less heartily objected to the government's imposition of that duty, a stance he insisted was consistent with Christian precedent "until an instance can be given in the New Testament, that Jesus, or his apostles, gave orders therefore to the rulers of this world." And he supplemented biblical wisdom with that of Jefferson, paraphrasing his famous formulation once again: "If a man worships one God, three Gods, twenty Gods, or no God—if he pays adoration one day in a week, seven days, or no day—wherein does he injure the life, liberty or property of another?"[85]

Leland found the third article of the Massachusetts Bill of Rights no less an affront. It endowed the legislature "with power to authorize and require" taxes to maintain "Protestant preachers."[86] More than a decade before, Madison's *Memorial and Remonstrance* had successfully challenged the practice in Virginia of the state supporting Anglicanism. But supporting only Protestant clerics generally was still problematic state interference in religion for Leland. The evangelical Baptist took up the cause of all non-Protestant clergy:

> Pagans, Turks and Jews, must not only preach for nothing; but Papists, those marvelous Christians, cannot obtain a maintenance for their preachers by the laws of their commonwealth. Such preachers must either be supported voluntarily, support themselves, or starve. Is this good policy? Should one sect be pampered above others? Should not government protect all kinds of people, of every species of religion, without showing the least partiality?[87]

His familiar themes abounded: the pernicious preferment of one faith over another, with the familiar consequences—"Has not the world had enough proofs of the impolicy and cruelty of favoring a Jew more than a Pagan, Turk, or Christian; or a Christian more than either of them?" And finally, he added the wisdom of judging individuals not by spiritual beliefs but by civic virtues: "Why should a man be proscribed, or any wife disgraced, for being a Jew, a Turk, a Pagan, or a Christian of any denomination, when his talents and veracity as a civilian, entitles him to the confidence of the public."[88]

Another section of the third article was more inclusive, defining "every denomination of Christians" as "under the protection of the law." But this too provoked Leland, who demanded it be amended to read *"all men* instead of *every denomination of Christians."*[89] Nor could he help objecting that only self-professed Christians could be elected to office in his native state. His own revisionary constitutional language read this way:

> To prevent the evils that have heretofore been occasioned in the world by religious establishments, and to keep the proper distinction between religion and politics, no religious test shall ever be required as a qualification of any officer, in any department of government; neither shall the legislature, under this constitution, ever establish any religion by law, give one sect preference to another, or force any man in the commonwealth to part with his property for the support of religious worship, or the maintenance of ministers of the gospel.[90]

So determined, in fact, was Leland to change his state's constitution that he would eventually decide to run for office. But long before doing so, he would pay a visit to Thomas Jefferson, the man whose ideas had influenced him so profoundly.

LELAND DELIVERS TO JEFFERSON A "MAMMOTH CHEESE" AND A NOTE FROM THE BAPTISTS OF DANBURY, CONNECTICUT, 1802

John Leland and the Baptists of Cheshire, Massachusetts, demonstrated their devotion to the new president with an unusual gift. On New Year's Day 1802, Leland delivered to the White House what came to be popularly known as the "Mammoth Cheese." The 1,235-pound cheese had traveled there "by sled, boat, and wagon,"[91] creating "a sensation" much reported in the press.[92] The people of Cheshire even penned a lengthy poem, including a benediction encompassing themselves, their handiwork, and its esteemed recipient:

> God bless this Cheese—and kindly bless the makers,
> The givers—generous—good and sweet and fair,
> And the receiver—great beyond compare[93]

The letter Leland presented to Jefferson, signed by the "Committee of Cheshire," and dated December 30, 1801, also extolled the virtuous labor of "the freeborn farmers, with the voluntary and cheerful aid of their wives and daughters, without the assistance of a single slave."[94] (Cheesemaking was normally women's work in eighteenth-century America.)[95] Just as praiseworthy were the "beautiful features" of the national Constitution, among these "The prohibition of religious tests, to prevent all hierarchy." If Leland did not write these words, he surely assented to them and to the letter's description of Jefferson as God's preferred candidate: "But we believe the Supreme Ruler of the Universe, who raises up men to achieve great events, has raised up a *Jefferson* at this critical day, to defend *Republicanism,* and to baffle the arts of *Aristocracy*."[96]

By then Leland had already delivered to Jefferson another, more precious gift: the votes of all but one man in Cheshire.[97] (A story exists, confirmed by Leland's granddaughter, that the lone ballot cast for the native son and Federalist John Adams was thrown out because it was assumed to be a mistake.) Leland's sermons, published articles, and political activism had a profound effect within his flock and beyond. After the pivotal election in 1800, he galvanized his Baptist followers and, eventually, all of Berkshire County to embrace Jefferson and his party. This political support would endure for decades despite Federalist supremacy and anti-Jefferson sentiment in the rest of Massachusetts.[98]

In a private letter, on the first of January, the president noted that the cheese "is arrived" and calculated its precise weight and span. Jefferson well understood why the Baptists, as a persecuted minority, had supported him. He concluded astutely that the offering was "an ebullition of republicanism in a state where it has been under heavy oppression." Optimistically, he added that "there is a speedy prospect of seeing all the New England states come round to their ancient principles; always excepting the real Monarchists & Priests, who never lose sight of the natural alliance between the crown & mitre."[99]

On this same visit, Leland also delivered to Jefferson a letter from his coreligionists in Danbury, Connecticut.[100] It defined Baptist views on the separation of government from religion, in full conformity with the vision of the denomination's founders a century before and echoing positions Jefferson had long held, as Leland knew well from his days in Virginia. The Danbury Baptists declared, "Our Sentiments are uniformly on the side of Religious Liberty—That Religion is at all times and places a Matter between God and Individuals—That no man ought to suffer in Name, person or effects on account of his religious Opinions—That the legitimate Power of civil Government extends no further than to punish the man who *works ill to his neighbor.*"[101]

Describing the official inequity under which Baptists suffered in Connecticut, they explained that "what religious privileges we enjoy (as a minor part of the State) we enjoy as favors granted, and not as inalienable rights; and these favors we receive at the expense of such degrading acknowledgements, as are inconsistent with the rights of fre[e]men." They knew full well that "the national government cannot destroy the Laws of each State," but they hoped for relief by example nonetheless: "our hopes are strong that the sentiments of our beloved President, which have had such genial Effect already, like the radiant beams of the Sun, will shine & prevail through all these states and all the world till Hierarchy and tyranny be destroyed from the Earth."[102]

Jefferson's landmark response included the now famous words defining his sense of the First Amendment as "a wall of separation between

Church & State."[103] (The first draft had it as "a wall of *eternal* separation.")[104] Jefferson's reply provided the opportunity to vindicate his own enduring opposition to government interference in religion, a political creed the Baptists also embraced. It was an occasion meriting a grand restatement of what he had always thought true:

> Believing with you that religion is a matter which lies solely between Man & his God, that he owes account to none other for his faith or his worship, that the legitimate powers of government reach actions only, & not opinions, I contemplate with sovereign reverence that act of the whole American people which declared that *their* legislature should "make no law respecting an establishment of religion, or prohibiting the free exercise thereof," thus building a wall of separation between Church & State. [A]dhering to this expression of the supreme will of the nation in behalf of the rights of conscience, I shall see with sincere satisfaction the progress of those sentiments which tend to restore to man all his natural rights, convinced that he has no natural right in opposition to his social duties.[105]

Jefferson did Leland the honor of attending a sermon he preached to both houses of Congress on January 3, 1802. His words in his own hand do not survive, but we know he had chosen the biblical selection "And behold a greater than Solomon is here."[106] This obvious paean to Jefferson provoked the ire of the only eyewitness to write about the sermon, Representative Manasseh Cutler. A Massachusetts Federalist, Cutler was also a Congregational minister, who was offended by what he perceived as Leland's lack of restraint in the pulpit,[107] the way the Baptist "bawled with stunning voice, horrid tone, frightful grimaces, and extravagant gestures."[108] (Ironically, while still in Virginia, Leland had attempted to admonish his fellow Baptist preachers about the off-putting effects of just such displays, what he called "odd tones, disgusting whoops and awkward gestures"; he counseled them to make "their piety become more rational.")[109] But Cutler was even more scathing about the content than the style, the pandering to Jefferson, a presumed enemy of true Protestant religion:

> Shame or laughter appeared in every countenance. Such an outrage upon religion, the Sabbath, and common decency, was extremely painful to every sober, thinking person present. But it answered the much-

wished for purpose of the Democrats, to see religion exhibited in the most ridiculous manner.[110]

Jefferson recorded that Leland came to the White House one last time on the fourth of January, when the president paid the preacher two hundred dollars, because he could not ethically accept the cheese as a personal gift.[111] Jefferson and others would go on to consume the mammoth cheese, "with the occasional pruning of rotten bits, for at least two years."[112] The idea of a "wall of separation between Church & State" would, of course, last even longer, though Jefferson and Leland would continue to differ on the reason for its necessity.

Leland had spared no praise of Jefferson at the time of his election: "This exertion of the American genius, has brought forth the *Man of the People,* the Defender of the rights of man and the rights of conscience, to fill the chair of state; who, in his inaugural speech, cries out, 'America, be free, be happy, guard your own rights, and leave them not to the disposition of officers.' "[113] More than a decade later, Leland was still singing Jefferson's praises. On March 4, 1813, he addressed the Sons of Liberty in Cheshire, reminding them that "you assemble to commemorate the inauguration of the man who saved his country from the curse of despotism," the man who embodied "a mound of our liberties, who snatched the constitution from the talons of its enemies, and turned the government into its natural channel."[114] Leland's sentiments about his hero had not changed in the interim, but his expectations that Jefferson might deliver the Baptists of Massachusetts from their legal oppression had dimmed. Already by 1811, the evangelical activist had decided that to effect change he would have to seek office himself.

LELAND'S SPEECH AS AN ELECTED REPRESENTATIVE TO THE MASSACHUSETTS LEGISLATURE, 1811

John Leland won his seat in the Massachusetts legislature in 1811 as Baptists had new cause to fear that they were to be taxed to support Congregational ministers. The reason for alarm was an 1810 ruling by the state's chief justice declaring that "unincorporated societies," like the Baptists, were not led by legitimate religious authorities.[115] The ruling promised an end to the certificate dispensation: Baptist taxes would automatically be applied to the support of the established Congregational faith. Once in office, Leland took swift action to ensure this didn't happen. Within just a few months, he won passage of the "Religious Freedom Act" of June 1811, which allowed all nonincorporated Protestant denominations an exemption from paying taxes to the Congregationalists.[116] For the Baptists, one perennial frustration was ended.

Leland's speech to the legislature in 1811 boldly took aim at the state constitution specifically and government interference in matters of religion generally:

> From the face of the constitution, as well as from a knowledge of those times, there exists no doubt, that a decided majority believed that religious duties ought to be interwoven into the civil compact—that Protestant Christianity was the best religion in the world—and that all the inhabitants ought to be forced, by law, to support it with money, as a necessary institute for the good of the body politic, unless they did it voluntarily. While a respectable minority, equally firm in the belief of the divinity of Christianity, and still more Protestant in their views, conceived it to be a measure as presumptuous of the legislature, as in a Pope, to lord it over consciences, or interfere either in the mode or support of Christianity. This minority, Mr. Speaker, did *then,* and do still believe that religion is a matter between the individual and their God—a right inalienable—an article not within the cognizance of civil government, nor in any way under its control. . . . [A]ll such societies of Protestant Christians, properly demeaning themselves as peaceable citizens, shall not be forced by law to support the teachers or worship of any other society.[117]

Leland not only echoed founding Baptist values in support of the separation of government from matters of faith, but also tapped arguments Madison had made in his 1785 *Memorial* against Virginia's public support of the Anglican faith. His setting the legislature's majority on a par with the pope was a calculated insult to those Congregational members who had traditionally regarded him as the Antichrist. But Leland's complaint was not merely sectarian; he rejected outright government support for any clerics, down to those serving his fellow representatives:

> According to our best judgments, we cannot pay legal taxes for religious services, descending even to the grade of a chaplain for the legislature. It is disrobing Christianity of her virgin beauty—turning the churches of

Christ into creatures of state—and metamorphosing gospel ambassadors to state pensioners.[118]

It was a view some Baptists, including Isaac Backus, would not have agreed with. He and many others believed in a "sweet harmony" between religion and government, equating Protestant Christianity with beneficent rule.[119] Departing from that standard and even Jefferson's, Leland demanded a more absolute principle of separation, a wall impermeable to money as to everything else.[120] In this he was nearer to Locke and Madison, believing it was more beneficial for Christianity to take no support of any kind. Leland was as ever concerned foremost with the threat to religion from government, but the reverse danger was not lost on him: "Let Christianity stand upon its own basis, it is the greatest blessing that ever was among men; but incorporate it into the civil code and it becomes the mother of cruelties."[121]

Where beleaguered religious minorities typically pressed only for their own political equality and protection, Leland always pled for universal rights, envisioning a religiously plural society with full membership for all, including Muslims and Jews—a goal he had come to understand could be achieved only legislatively:

> Government should be so fixed, that Pagans, Turks, Jews and Christians, should be equally protected in their rights. The government of Massachusetts is, however, differently formed; under the existing constitution, it is not possible for the general court to place religion upon its proper footing; it can be done, however, much better than it is done. . . . I shall therefore take the liberty, at a proper time, to offer an amendment to the bill.[122]

Leland would propose that amendment, one separating religion from government and establishing political equality for all believers as a right and not a favor. But he would leave office without having won its passage. Reflecting on his two-year term, he remained convinced that matters of religion should be exempt from state interference, even his: "my conscience was not long enough for a legislator. I gained no evidence that the legislature of Massachusetts had inspiration sufficient to legislate about souls, conscience, or eternity."[123]

But Leland was far from defeated. In 1820, he proposed more changes to the state constitution, again imagining an ideal society of religiously diverse equals:

> Government is the formation of an association of individuals, by mutual agreement, for mutual defence and advantage; to be governed by specific rules. And when rightly formed, it embraces Pagans, Jews, Mahometans and Christians, within its fostering arms—proscribes no creed of faith for either of them—proscribes none of them for being heretics, promotes the man of talents and integrity, without inquiring after his religion—impartially protects all of them—punishes the man who works ill to his neighbor, let his faith and motives be what they may. Who, but tyrants knaves and devils, can object to such government?[124]

Again, too, we see his attachment to Locke's notion of government as compact, and to a civic arrangement that "promotes the man of talents and integrity, without inquiring after his religion." It had been a persuasive sentiment when expressed earlier by James Iredell and Samuel Johnston at North Carolina's ratification convention. Jefferson too had won many in Virginia to the idea that religion should cause no civil disabilities for any free white male citizen. Much to Leland's consternation, his home state was a harder case:

> In Massachusetts, however, the principle is not recognized. A religious test is required. The legislature is empowered to make laws to oblige the people to support Protestant teachers of piety, morality and religion. Papal Christian teachers cannot be provided for like Protestants. Pagans, Jews, Turks and Deists cannot be promoted to office, except they declare and subscribe a lie.[125]

In a later declaration against the "the kings-evil," a ruler's malevolence, or that of "priestcraft" (by which he means clerical interference in government), Leland makes a hypothetical case for his ideal plural society, which he believed already existed "in many parts of the world." He asks his fellow Christians to imagine themselves subject to a government whose official creed they despised:

> It is not only a supposable case, but a case that exists in fact, that in many parts of the world, Pagans, Jews, Turks and Christians, all have the bounds of their habitations fixed within the limits of one govern-

ment. These several sects unite and form one body politic; for mutual advantage alike for mutual defence. In such a case, what reason can be offered, why the last three should all be compelled to support the temple and worship Jupiter? or why the other sects should be forced to be circumcised and abstain from swine's flesh, etc.? or that all the rest should subscribe to the alcoran and worship the great prophet? Every Christian would say, "the demand is unreasonable and cruel."[126]

His ultimate plea, however, comes by way of admonishing Christians to conform their legal treatment of other faiths to the Golden Rule, which he believed condemned political injustice based on religious difference. In so doing he advances a defense of Deists, whom most ardent Christians of whatever denomination condemned as infidels:

In the United States, the above case has but small bearings, *where the number of Pagans, Jews, and Mahometans is so small;* but, there are thousands of Deists, who cannot be convinced of any revelation from God to man, except that of nature; and a thousand thousand who cannot conscientiously join with any religious society, from an honest conviction in their own judgments, that they themselves are not fit for Christian fellowship; or that the religious societies among whom they live, are not sound in faith.[127]

It was a remarkable gesture: a man who had devoted his life to preaching the divinity of Jesus and the existence of the Trinity now defending the consciences of those who denied both, not on account of having been born in a foreign culture but as a refusal of the faith of their fathers. Deists were far more numerous than any other non-Christian group, including imaginary Muslims, and as such were by far the greatest threat to Christian society in the eyes of most American Protestants. The defense of their rights attests to the purity of Leland's convictions, a purity limited only by lack of understanding.

Defending the Rights of Muslims While Misunderstanding and Condemning Islam and Other Faiths

Like his hero, Leland frequently misunderstood or condemned Islamic beliefs while championing equal rights for Muslims. We have seen how, in his tract on the rights of conscience, he criticizes the Prophet by contrast with a noncoercive, nonpolitical Jesus, accusing the former of spreading faith by force, a common Christian claim.[128] Leland also wrongly asserts a Muslim belief in the divinity of Muhammad. Unlike Jefferson, Leland never read the Qur'an. We cannot be sure of his sources, but he presents as "an article" of the holy book the strange notion "that the world stands upon a great ox—the ox stands upon a great stone—the stone rests upon the shoulders of an angel—and the angel stands upon God knows what."[129] We do know he shared Jefferson's reductive view of the sacred text as merely a book of law.[130]

Still, Leland correctly understood that all the verses of the Qur'an "by the Turks, have been considered as coming from God."[131] He also knew that the Islamic calendar began with "the flight of Mahomet," his *hijra* or emigration from Mecca to Medina in 622, marking the first Islamic year. And he rightly notes elsewhere that Muslims are not allowed to drink wine, though he attributes only to the Jews a prohibition against pork.[132]

As we have seen, in 1801, following the example of Thomas Helwys, his seventeenth-century coreligionist, Leland made the case for Muslims to be granted religious liberty based on the Golden Rule, which he expansively reformulated: "Do unto *all men* as you would they should do unto you." Indeed, he insisted they do so or "give up the name Christians." In return, he wished the same treatment be extended to Christians in the Ottoman Empire and North Africa:

> If Christians were in Turkey or Algiers, would they not wish to enjoy the liberty of their conscience without control? Would they not say, in their hearts at least, "We wish to be freed from paying the Turkish priests and supporting the Turkish religion, which is only an imposture, and that we might be respected according to our conduct, while we enjoy our religious opinions, as an inalienable right?"[133]

He did not know that in the Islamic world there already existed a form of toleration for Christians and Jews. But he rightly understood that non-Muslims were obliged to pay taxes in support of the Islamic faith.

Leland's disapproval was by no means limited to Islam. Like Jefferson, he held no high opinion of either Judaism or Catholicism, though he likewise defended the rights of their respective believers. During his time in Virginia, Leland had noted that neither group was numerous enough to establish a place of worship: "There are a few Jews, but they have no synagogue, nor is there any chapel for the Papists."[134] He may have met members of both minorities but provided no details of any such encounters.

We do know he considered Jews as deicides, a standard Christian calumny, believing that "the Jews contrived [Jesus's] death—slew him and hanged him on a tree; they meant it for an evil, but God meant it for good."[135] And that their villainy had precipitated the destruction of Jerusalem, because "they both killed the Lord Jesus and their own prophets—persecuted the apostles—pleased not God, and were contrary to all men. For their opposition to the truth, and malice prepense against the messengers of it ... *armies* ... *destroyed those murderers, and burnt up their city.*"[136] Leland's condemnation of the pope similarly followed a standard Protestant template, but where the defense of individual Catholics was concerned he was ready to part ways with his brethren.[137]

During the 1830s, rising Irish Catholic immigration to the United States stoked Protestant fears and eventually violence. In 1834, the Presbyterian minister Lyman Beecher incited a Boston mob to burn down the Ursuline Convent, a Catholic girls' school in neighboring Charlestown.

Leland would not remain silent. Acknowledging the truth that "Some men among us profess to be greatly alarmed at the spread of the Roman Catholicks," he went on to attack anti-Catholic fearmongering throughout the country: "They say that there are six hundred thousand [Catholics] within the limits of the United States; all busy at work, like a worm under the bark of a tree, to sap our free government, and set up papal hierarchy and all the horrors of the inquisition." To this conspiracy theory, Leland replied unequivocally that "no man who has the soul of an American, and the heart of affection for our democratic institutions, will either fear or wish to injure the papists." Reassuringly he allowed that even if the number of Catholics were a million, it was unlikely of ever being a match either "by births or emigration" for fourteen million Protestants. Leland insisted that Catholic "freedom of religion is guaranteed to them in our constitution of government, and no benevolent man can wish to have them oppressed as they are in Ireland." He also reminded American patriots, "The French Catholicks were great helpers to Americans in their struggles for independence, (Lafayette among the rest,) and now to deny them the hospitalities of good friends would be base ingratitude." He stressed that if Catholics "send their missionaries among those of a different religion to make proselytes, it is doing no more than Protestants do."[138] Unlike other Baptists, Leland didn't approve the rising popularity of missionary societies generally.[139] And unlike other Protestants, he concluded that if Catholics did somehow achieve a national majority, "they must of right have the rule; for no man who has the soul of an American will deny the maxim that 'the voice of a majority is the voice of the whole.'"[140]

No Christian Sabbath Should Be Mandated by the Government

"There is nothing in the starry heavens—in the atmosphere, or in the productions of the earth, that marks one day in seven to be more holy than another," pronounced Leland after a thorough examination of Old and New Testaments. For that reason, he, who had condemned government support for federal and state chaplains, also refused to accept the government's right to mandate Sunday as the Sabbath, or to make laws concerning worship, behavior, or the nondelivery of mail on that day:

> Let a Mahometan, a Jew and a Christian stand at any spot, and dispute about the holy day: the Mahometan says Friday—the Jew is for Saturday—the Christian pleads for Sunday: not agreeing in opinion, they part at variance. The Christian takes his course eastward and travels around the world, scrupulously keeping every Sunday for holy time. The Mahometan takes a western course, and, like the Christian circumambulates the earth, rigidly observing every Friday. The Jew remains stationary, keeping every Saturday in Mosaic style. In a lapse of time the travelers return to the spot where the Jew was residing, and to their astonishment find the holy day of all was the *same day*. The Christian traveling east had gained a day, and the Mahometan going west had lost a day.[141]

In showing that the Muslim, the Jew, and the Christian would inevitably end up at the same place at the same time, Leland hoped to demonstrate how their respective faiths might coexist despite differences. But the pluralist balance would not be achieved so long as the government endorsed one day of the week above another as holy:

Shall that sect, which is most numerous and ambitious, direct the scepter of government to interpose, and force all to submit to one standard, and fine, punish, and burn non-conformists? Let each sect enjoy their own rights and freedom, in respect of the God whom they wish to adore, the days on which they would pay that adoration, and the modes of performing it.[142]

The sanctification of time was for religions, not the state, to effect, and for the believer to observe, uncompelled by temporal authority.

Leland seemed uniquely able to see, imagine, and feel for others not of his faith—and he was no less well equipped to challenge those who were. He could turn the tables on Protestants: "Query: Are the Protestants in France as much abused by the Papists as the Papists are in Ireland by the Protestants?"[143] Or he could hold up a mirror to Christians generally—"Since Christianity became national, Christian nations have been equally cruel and bloodthirsty, and more unjust and perfidious than Turks or heathens"[144]—compelling them to see themselves as others saw them: "Accuse a Turk of any trick, he replies, 'What do you think that I will lie and cheat like a Christian?' "[145]

Leland's sense of justice was graced by a perfect symmetry: "The sybils of the heathens, the alcoran of the Turks, the tradition of the Jewish rabbis, the writings of the ancient fathers, the decrees of councils, the mandates of popes, religious creeds, and legislative acts to define and enforce religion, like broken china-ware, are worth what they will fetch."[146] He was equally impatient with all faiths interfering in government and of any government interfering in faith.

LELAND AGAINST SLAVERY

In Virginia in 1789, the Baptist General Committee passed a resolution that "slavery, is a violent deprivation of the rights of nature, and is inconsistent with a republican government; and we therefore recommend it to our brethren to make use of every legal measure, to extirpate the horrid evil from the land."[147] It was Leland's insistence that forced the approval of the resolution by his fellow Baptists, but by 1793 they would refuse to reaffirm it, deciding not to interfere in what they deemed a legislative matter.[148] Now, even Baptists in the southern states, who continued to convert African American slaves to their faith, refused, with the exception of Leland, to support the abolition of slavery. Leland wrote, "Though our skins are somewhat different in color, yet I hope to meet many of you in heaven; where your melodious voices that have often enchanted my ears and warmed my heart, will be incessantly employed in praise of our common Lord."[149]

Like his commitment to religious liberty, Leland's abolitionism was absolute; in this he surpassed his hero Jefferson, who attempted to end the slave trade but never freed all of his slaves. In Leland's eyes the treatment of African slaves, like that of Native Americans, was unequivocally and essentially unchristian:

> Because the nation of Israel had a divine right grant of the land of Canaan, and order to enslave the heathen, some suppose Christians have an equal right to take away the land of the Indians, and make slaves of the negroes. Wretched religion, that pleads for cruelty and injustice. . . . If Christian nations were nations of Christians, these things would not be so.[150]

In decrying the occupation of Native American lands he echoed Roger Williams's sentiments on the matter, unique in the seventeenth century.

Much as he considered slavery an institution "destructive of every humane and benevolent passion of the soul, and subversive to that liberty absolutely necessary to enoble the human mind," Leland, like Jefferson, could not imagine a viable alternative: a free African American citizenry. He admitted that he found it difficult to "form any plan, even in idea, for their manumission; and to expose evil, without pointing out the way of escape" was no solution.[151] In 1789, he also feared that any talk of freedom for slaves would only provoke masters to increase their abuse. He recorded an intense horror at the treatment of slaves he knew in Virginia.[152]

Toward the end of Leland's life, the question of slavery remained pressing. He would refuse to endorse contemporary plans supported by Protestant missionaries to ship freed slaves to Liberia to spread Christianity. A return to Africa, Leland argued, would destroy slave families, many of whom he knew were "descended from American parents more than ten generations."[153] Thus he anticipated precisely what had happened to the former slave, the Muslim Ibrahima Abd al-Rahman. Ibrahima, who had agreed to spread Christianity and American commerce on his return to Liberia, quickly reverted to Islam, leaving a fractured family stranded on both sides of the Atlantic. The best Leland could imagine was the creation of states for freed slaves "within the limits of other states."[154] A stunted, segregated future was the most this man of such remarkable moral imagination could conceive.

JOHN LELAND AND MUSLIM RIGHTS AS AN AMERICAN IDEAL

Leland, like Jefferson, composed his own epitaph: "Here lies the body of John Leland, who labored [sixty-seven years] to promote piety, and vindicate the civil and religious rights of all men."[155] The monument over his grave in Cheshire, Massachusetts, is framed majestically by the Berkshire Mountains but seldom visited. Ultimately, most of his fellow Baptists condemned Leland's most cherished convictions: the absolute wall of separation between government and religion; his anti-missionary and antisabbatarian stands; his abolitionism. These views his fellow Baptists denigrated as evidence of his "eccentricity."[156] But for his unwavering support of the equal rights of Muslims, Catholics, and Jews his own denomination labeled him an "embarrassment."[157]

In his repeated articulations of the ideal American government, Leland sought in principle and in practice "to vindicate the civil and religious rights of all men," not just of his fellow Protestants. That he never omitted to mention in his pleas for justice the rights of Muslims, who were not yet known to live in America, suggests the tenacity and absolutism of his principles. But it also reflects a certain fruition and ripening of ideas that had formed in extremely rarefied circles of sixteenth- and seventeenth-century European Christian thought, not to attain legal codification before coming to the United States. While Locke believed Muslims should be tolerated and Jefferson defended their civil rights, enshrining them in state law, it was in the person of John Leland that profound religious sentiment came to the defense of religious freedom for all Americans. An untutored but effective communicator in person and on paper, Leland, though never using the word, demanded what would later be termed secular government, precisely for the sake of his faith and individual freedom.[158]

To reach this conclusion, Leland drew upon his own persecution to articulate a compelling new form of American evangelical empathy that embraced the political equality of Muslims as well as Catholics and Jews at a time when all three groups were despised in the United States. Leland's devout Baptist evangelical faith supported uniquely American ideals of a religiously plural society long before this vision became a reality.

Why Can't a Muslim Be President?

Eighteenth-Century Ideals of the Muslim Citizen and Their Significance in the Twenty-First Century

All, too, will bear in mind this sacred principle, that though the will of the majority is in all cases to prevail, that will to be rightful must be reasonable; that the minority possess their equal rights, which equal law must protect, and to violate would be oppression. . . . And let us reflect that, having banished from our land that religious intolerance under which mankind so long bled and suffered, we have yet gained little if we countenance a political intolerance as despotic, as wicked, and capable of as bitter and bloody persecutions.

> —Jefferson's first inaugural address,
> March 4, 1801

And I should like to assure you, my Islamic friends, that under the American Constitution, under American tradition, and in American hearts, this Center, this place of worship, is just as welcome as could be a similar edifice of any other religion. Indeed, America would fight with her whole strength for your right to have here your own church and worship according to your own conscience.

The concept is indeed part of America, and without that concept we would be something else than what we are.

> —President Dwight Eisenhower's speech
> at the opening of the Islamic Center Mosque,
> Washington, D.C., June 28, 1957

To MANY of his political opponents, Thomas Jefferson may have been our first Muslim president. That a Muslim might legally have attained the office in the eighteenth century was not out of the question, insofar as the U.S. Constitution affirmed the possibility in theory. Jefferson was no practitioner, and his views of Islam, while mostly negative, remained mixed, based on his positive appreciation for the faith's central tenet of absolute monotheism. Nevertheless, he had been defamed and denigrated as a Muslim since 1791—especially during the vicious presidential campaign of 1800—as an infidel and atheist.

The accusation that Jefferson was a Muslim placed him, unknowingly, in the same category as his intellectual hero John Locke, who was charged with professing "the faith of a Turk,"[1] and even George Sale, the British translator of his Qur'an, derided as "half a Musulman."[2] These three (and others before them) became, as this book documents, victims of a long-standing tradition of anti-Islamic defamation perpetrated in the name of Christianity. The provocations were various. Sale had refused to sanction violence toward Muslims and had not vilified the Prophet Muhammad as thoroughly as his fellow Anglican Protestants would have wished. Political opponents condemned both Locke and Jefferson for advocating religious toleration, including civil rights for Muslims, as well as embracing Deism and Unitarianism.

The same charge made against Jefferson in the campaign of 1800 would be used in the twenty-first century against American citizens—some actually Muslim, some not—seeking national political office. In either case, the tactic is part of a strategy attempting to discredit legitimate candidates, whether for Congress or the presidency, by casting them as un-American and even anti-American. As in Jefferson's case, each candidate labeled a Muslim, whether accurately or not, would prevail when the votes were counted. Yet such defamations have persisted as political weapons. In fact, they have evolved into a broader campaign by a well-funded few to disenfranchise American Muslim citizens, denying them the civil rights granted them by the Founders.

This afterword briefly explores the practical life of Muslim civil rights as defended in theory by Jefferson and others—a defense that set the parameters of religious freedom and civic inclusion for all non-Protestants. Today, as in the eighteenth century, the civil rights of American Muslims symbolize the universality of religious pluralism in the United States. Thus challenges to Muslim civil rights continue to represent threats to the rights of all Americans. How the nation responds to these threats against this signal religious minority will determine whether or not founding ideals of inclusion will survive in practice or succumb to rank fear, prejudice, and discrimination.

————

In his first inaugural address of 1801, Jefferson attempted to unite the country after a polarizing presidential campaign. Characteristically, he argued for the rights of the minority in a democratic system, reminding his fellow Americans that "though the will of the majority is in all cases to prevail, that will to be rightful must be reasonable; that the minority possess their equal rights, which equal law must protect, and to violate would be oppression." While asserting that Americans had "banished from our land religious intolerance," the president knew that the legal and social reality remained well short of the constitutional ideal.[3]

In 1802, Jefferson was reminded by his ally the Baptist leader John Leland and his followers of the very real religious intolerance and political inequality they and all other non-Congregational Protestants continued to suffer in New England. Contemplating "a political intolerance as despotic, as wicked, and capable of as bitter and bloody persecutions,"[4] Jefferson had reason to fear that the bigotry he had fought his whole life to extirpate might never disappear from the nation. For if Protestants still faced intolerance from other Protestants, what hope for non-Protestants in America?

Three years after his election, fears of Jefferson's ungodly and possibly Islamic presidency persisted. In January 1803, a Walpole, New Hampshire, newspaper editor observed that "every candid friend of religion must . . . be convinced from Jefferson's own writings that he is an infidel."[5] It was the third time Jefferson's religious beliefs had been indicted by way of such an accusation. But he was adamant in his convictions, writing privately to a friend that same year, "I will never, by any word or act, bow to the shrine of intolerance, or admit a right of inquiry into the religious opinions of others."[6] That code he would maintain until the end of his days.

In 1834, eight years after Jefferson's death, his Baptist supporter John Leland recalled the dire predictions made in the wake of Jefferson's 1800 election but that never materialized:

When Mr. Jefferson was elected president, the pulpits rang with alarms, and all the presses groaned with predictions, that the Bibles would all be burned, meeting houses destroyed; the marriage bond dissolved, and anarchy, infidelity and licentiousness would fill the land. These clerical warnings and editorial prophecies all failed.[7]

By this time, Leland, who had also defended the rights of Muslims and all other believers, revealed that he too had been "advertised in the newspapers, through the states, as an infidel and outcast." In response to being thus condemned with the same epithet applied to both Locke and Jefferson, Leland replied humbly, "May the Lord increase my faith and make me more holy, which will be the best refutation of the libel."[8]

Although the ideal that citizenship would one day extend to American Muslims existed in the founding discourse, the eighteenth century remained a time when ignorance and fear about Islam predominated among Protestants. Because of racism and slavery, the earliest known American Muslims were never granted equal rights. It would not be until a century later, in the wake of the Civil War, that the Fourteenth Amendment, ratified in 1868, granted citizenship status to American-born former slaves of African descent, a population that still included practicing Muslims.[9] We do not know how many of the descendants of these first American Muslims, a scattered minority under pressure to conform to Protestantism prevalent among slaves, retained their faith into the twentieth century. Most could not create sustained communities of believers or pass down their religious beliefs over generations.[10]

But there were exceptions to this pattern.[11] In Georgia, for example, in the 1930s, the grandson of a former Muslim slave described aspects of Islamic prayer and ritual observance practiced in his family for two generations. His descendants continued to name their children Mahomet and Fatima.[12] By then, however, religion was no longer the chief impediment to the full rights of citizenship faced by Muslims in America.

The first American citizens to be legally defined as Muslims were not born in the United States; they were immigrants from the Middle East. Since 1790, they could not lawfully be denied citizenship based on their religion. But the Naturalization Act of that year, in addition to requiring "good moral character," limited citizenship among new arrivals to "free white persons."[13] Most Muslims, thought to be not white but either black or Asian, were excluded on that basis. In fact, the U.S. Census Bureau would classify Middle Easterners from Syria, Palestine, Armenia, and Turkey as non-white "Asiatics" as late as 1910.[14]

RACE, RELIGION, AND A PROTESTANT NATION: DISCRIMINATION AGAINST JEWS, CATHOLICS, AND MUSLIMS IN THE NINETEENTH AND TWENTIETH CENTURIES

An estimated sixty thousand Muslim immigrants arrived in the United States between 1890 and 1924.[15] Most hailed from what is today Syria, Lebanon, and Turkey, but a few others came from Eastern Europe and South Asia.[16] They were mostly young, uneducated male laborers, who sent money back to their dependents in their countries of origin.[17] By 1870, a new Naturalization Act had overridden the 1790 act's requirement that naturalized citizens be white, thus expanding the ranks of the qualified to include "aliens of African nativity and . . . persons of African descent."[18] This allowed for the immigration of Muslims from Africa in principle, but race and ethnicity would continue to be common reasons for denying citizenship to many of the first Muslim immigrants.

The arrival of these Muslims from abroad newly tested the limits of American national identity. As Kambiz GhaneaBassiri argues in his pathbreaking history of Islam in America, Muslim immigrants arrived in the nineteenth century to find a national ideal that was still very much white and Protestant.[19] And despite the influx during this same period of millions of immigrant Jews and Catholics, this ideal continued to be identified with the hope for national progress.[20] As their numbers increased, each non-Protestant group would be branded as foreign and a threat to the government of the United States. Eventually, Jews and Catholics would win acceptance, but Muslims would be the last to struggle for inclusion from among the founding triad of non-Protestant outsiders.

At the turn of the century, the stigma of being a Muslim immigrant in the United States prompted some aspirants to citizenship to change their names. For example, in 1903 Mohammed Asa Abu-Howah became A. Joseph Howar.[21] Many Jews did likewise, lest their names announce their religion.[22] Non-Protestant arrivals from Eastern and Southern Europe also changed their names for similar reasons. Muslims, however, faced discrimination based on race, not just religion.

The Civil Rights Act of 1964 began to end legalized "discrimination and segregation of any kind on the ground of race, color, religion or national origin,"[23] but before its passage, most Muslim immigrants, whether from Africa, Asia, or Europe, were at pains to insist that they were "white."[24] Most Americans would not have been prepared to see them that way, and religion certainly figured into their perceptions. In 1915, for instance, a federal judge would rule immigrants of Syrian origin to be officially "white," largely because most arrivals from Syria were Christian.[25] The ruling therefore offered no useful precedent for Muslims of other ethnicities. And Americans would continue to view Muslims as "not-quite-black, not-quite-white, not-quite American."[26]

Even when religion was not the explicit focus of immigration policy, Arab ethnicity remained problematic. In 1942, one judge denied citizenship to a Yemeni Arab immigrant because, he argued, "Arabs are not white persons within the meaning of the act." (The jurist here referred to the superseded 1790 Naturalization Act, deliberately ignoring the 1870 revision, which included persons of African descent.) Occasionally, the same label would not provoke condemnation: In 1944, for instance, a judge in Michigan granted an Arab from Arabia citizenship based on a quite accurate appreciation of the historical presence of Muslims in Europe and their contributions to Western civilization. That judge wrote, "The names of Avicenna and Averroes, the sciences of algebra and medicine, the population and the architecture of Spain and Sicily, the very words of the English language remind us as they would have reminded the Founding Fathers of the action and interaction of Arabic and non–Arabic element of our culture."[27] Such sentiments, however, were not representative of how most American Protestants saw Islamic history. Even Jefferson's expansive reading on the subject did not lead him to such conclusions, thanks to the distortions in most of his European sources.

Nativism would periodically flare with great intensity against Jews and Catholics, based on charges that would later be directed against Muslims. Beginning in the 1920s, extremist Protestant hate groups such as the Ku Klux Klan promoted violent resistance to the citizenship of immigrant Jews and Catholics, as well as African Americans. The Klan's slogan spoke to an ideal far from dead in America: "Native, white, Protestant supremacy."[28] In 1926, an imperial wizard of the KKK argued that Catholics were "incapable of American patriotism and democracy" because their church was "separatist, anti-democratic, and run by foreigners."[29] The charge that Catholics were eternal "aliens," who owed allegiance to a foreign power, was hardly changed from the eighteenth century, with slogans such as "Rome shall not rule America."[30] The difference now, however, was that the American Catholic population had expanded from twenty-five thousand at the time of the founding to twelve million by 1900, to become the largest religious denomination in the country.[31]

Also in 1926, the same KKK leader published the forged anti-Semitic libel *The Protocols of the Elders of Zion,* which stoked American Protestant fears of "a Jewish plot to take over the world."[32] This tract had been preceded by the arrival of two million Jewish immigrants by 1920, a massive increase from the original two thousand resident in 1776.[33] Resistance to the political equality of Catholics as well as Jews could also be found at the highest levels of American business and government. Henry Ford, the founder of the Ford Motor Company, despite eventually employing many immigrant Muslims, supported the *Protocols* and published a steady stream of anti-Semitic propaganda.[34] In 1942, President Roosevelt would confide to his sole Jewish cabinet member (only the second in U.S. history) and to a Catholic member of his government, "You know this is a Protestant country, and the Catholics and Jews are here under sufferance."[35] As Kevin Schultz documents, "discrimination in employment, housing, and social fraternization" against Jews and more generalized discrimination against Catholics in "civic and political affairs" persisted into the mid-twentieth century in the United States.[36] These prejudices have still not been eradicated, though the derogatory political discourse they fed had mostly disappeared from the mainstream by the 1970s.

In order to refute the national ideal of Protestant supremacy, groups of Protestants, Jews, and Catholics came together in the 1920s. As Schultz's important history reveals, organizations such as the National Conference of Christians and Jews promoted a religiously plural ideal of a "tri-faith America," in which Catholics and Jews would be equal to Protestants.[37] From this egalitarian vision issued the new phrase "Judeo-Christian,"[38] which, although it can be dated to 1899, did not enter usage in the United States until the 1930s, becoming a commonplace of popular expression in the 1950s.[39] It remains a common but largely unexamined characterization of the nation's religious identity.[40]

As a practical matter, the "Judeo-Christian" rubric excluded Muslims despite their explicit mention in the eighteenth-century founding

. discourse, though in 1953 only one member of the National Conference of Christians and Jews recognized this inconsistency: "And so American popular prejudice against the peoples of the Middle East, among others, based as it largely is on false concepts of their religious beliefs and institutions, is now a serious factor in American foreign policy, as anti-Catholicism was a generation ago."[41] Nor did all Americans embrace the phraseology. For one thing, it was not historical, insofar as no eighteenth-century Founder, including supporters of the most expansive religious pluralism like Jefferson and Washington, had ever used it. Others found it misleading for other reasons. In 1971, Arthur Cohen rejected the term as "myth": "We can learn much from the history of Jewish-Christian relations, but one thing we cannot make of it is a discourse of community, fellowship, and understanding."[42] Preferring perhaps not to dwell on past divisions, in the 1980s American Muslim scholar and activist Isma'il Raji al-Faruqi suggested the country be described as "Judeo-Christian-Islamic," a nod to unifying features of the three Abrahamic faiths.[43] More recently, the historian Richard W. Bulliet renewed an objection to papering over Jewish/Gentile animosities: "No one with the least knowledge of the past two thousand years of relations between Christians and Jews can possibly miss the irony of linking in a single term two faith communities that decidedly did not get along during most of that period." In fact, he has advanced a new "case" for what he calls an "Islamo-Christian civilization," arguing that far from a "clash," the encounter of these two civilizations has been one of important convergences.[44]

The "Judeo-Christian" rubric embraced by Protestant Americans as a counter to discrimination against Jews and Catholics in the twentieth century inadvertently became the basis for discrimination against Muslims in the twenty-first century, overwriting the founding "Protestant promise" of universal religious and political equality.[45] In part, this happened because the American Muslim population before World War II was relatively small, with a few Arab arrivals in New York and Chicago during the 1930s and 1940s, the majority settling in Dearborn and Detroit, Michigan, and finding jobs on the Ford automotive assembly line.[46] Still, the immigration quota system of the 1920s ensured that Middle Eastern immigration was minimal.

Not until the passage of the Immigration and Nationality Act in 1965 would preferences for arrivals from Europe be lifted, allowing significant numbers of Muslims from the Middle East and South Asia to enter the country and seek citizenship.[47] In contrast to the earliest Muslim immigrants, these new arrivals were often professionals or students, who chose the United States as an alternative to repressive political and economic conditions in their countries of origin. The American Muslim population has grown rapidly ever since, through the last forty years of the twentieth century and into the twenty-first, helping to create what Diana Eck, a scholar of religious pluralism, describes as "the world's most religiously diverse nation." Also included in the new wave of immigrants have been Hindus, Buddhists, Sikhs, Jains, and Zoroastrians, none of whom fit under the Judeo-Christian rubric.[48]

How many American Muslim citizens now reside in the United States? Scholars and pollsters disagree, with estimates ranging from two to eight million.[49] A Pew Research poll of August 2011 put the total at just under three million out of a total U.S. population of just over three hundred million.[50] (Since the U.S. Census cannot ask Americans about their religion, claims about the number of American Muslims remain unverifiable.) What is clear, despite these divergent estimates, is that no American Muslim monolith exists: American Muslims represent the most ethnically, racially, and theologically diverse Islamic community in the world. American Muslim citizens hail from seventy-seven countries of origin.[51] Sixty-three percent were born abroad, with 37 percent indigenous to the United States. For those in the former category, the Middle East and North Africa were originally home to 26 percent, with Pakistan, India, Bangladesh, and Afghanistan accounting for another 26 percent of the population. The remaining 11 percent among the foreign-born come from sub-Saharan Africa, Europe, and other places.[52]

Of the 37 percent indigenous American Muslims, the largest group, 40 percent, are African Americans whose families at some point "reverted" to what they perceived as their original African faith. Many opted for Islam in response to the racism and slavery associated with the Christian past.[53] But the ranks of American Muslim converts are racially diverse: 18 percent are white, 10 percent are Asian, 10 percent are Hispanic, and 21 percent claim to be of mixed racial origin.[54] Hispanic converts, like African Americans, also identify Islam as their ancestral faith in Spain prior to the fifteenth century.[55] As to varieties of Islam, 65 percent of American Muslims identify as Sunnis, with 11 percent professing Shi'ism, and another 24 percent refusing classification as either. Many American Muslims also embrace the mystical strain of Sufism, which may explain a certain degree of nonsectarianism.[56] In any case, Islam is the fastest-growing religion in the country.[57] Among the high number of foreign-born Muslims, 81 percent have won U.S. citizenship.[58]

AMERICAN MUSLIM CITIZENS AND CIVIL RIGHTS BEFORE AND AFTER 9/11

Resistance to the founding ideal of citizenship for Muslims is not new, but Muslim citizenship is no longer merely a theoretical concept. Consequently, the nature of resistance to it has evolved. Anti-Muslim hate groups, members of major and fringe political parties, and certain extreme conservative elements among Protestants and Jews have all been party to defaming American Muslims and denying their religious and political equality. Many of these movements were galvanized by the events of September 11, 2001, when nineteen foreign extremists rationalized their violence in the name of Islam and perpetrated deadly terrorist attacks against the United States. On that day, some Americans expressed a willingness to indict all American Muslims en masse as potential co-conspirators in terrorism. For their part, American Muslims refused to equate their faith with acts of terrorism against their own country.

A coalition of American Muslim organizations issued a joint statement immediately after 9/11:

> American Muslims utterly condemn what are vicious and cowardly acts of terrorism against innocent civilians. We join all Americans in calling for the swift apprehension and punishment of the perpetrators. No political cause could ever be assisted by such immoral acts.[59]

The Muslim Students' Association's national headquarters, representing seven hundred organizations on campuses across the United States, issued press releases about their "grief and support for the larger American community."[60] But these statements were largely ignored, a response since described as "selective deafness."[61] As a result, American Muslims continue to be criticized for their supposed failure to denounce terrorism.[62]

Sixty American Muslims perished in the World Trade Center on September 11, 2001, but this fact was not remembered by most non-

Muslim Americans. American Muslims were in fact victimized twice by the attacks: once by the criminals who profaned their faith by their violent actions, and a second time by many of their fellow citizens who suspected their loyalty.[63] The case of Talat Hamdani is striking: As a New York City police cadet and emergency technician trainee, the Pakistani-born Hamdani, a U.S. citizen since 1990, had raced into the World Trade Center to render aid. With his disappearance at the site of the attack, accusations against him as a potential terrorist persisted until his body was recovered in 2002 under the North Tower—in thirty-four pieces.[64] Only then was his name cleared. The New York City police commissioner "called him a hero." But his mother's bitterness about the slander of her son remains: "My anger comes from his own country casting suspicion on him." She concluded of all those killed on 9/11, "They died for one reason. Not because they were Muslims or from Pakistan or anywhere else. They died because they were Americans."[65]

It is notable how much the anti-Islamic invective inflamed by 9/11 resembles the denigration of Islam in America as far back as the seventeenth century. The evangelical Protestant minister Franklin Graham's assertion that Islam is "a very evil and wicked religion"[66] could have equally been uttered by any number of Protestant leaders over the centuries. Perhaps this is because while there have been few encounters with the Islamic world since the founding, the limited experience of the twentieth century tended only to reinforce negative impressions.

Lack of knowledge about Islam and the Middle East ensured that twentieth-century media coverage of major news events involving U.S. interests in the region portrayed the Muslim world as the inevitable adversary of the West. These include the 1973 oil embargo; the 1979–80 Iranian Revolution and seizure of American hostages; the 1983 car bombing of the U.S. embassy in Beirut with the death of hundreds of marines; the hijacking of a TWA flight to Beirut; the murder of Leon Klinghoffer during the seizure of the *Achille Lauro* cruise ship; and the First Gulf War of 1990–91.[67] Adding to this steady stream of images of anti-American violence in the news, according to Jack Shaheen, were hundreds of American movies depicting Arabs negatively, mostly as terrorists.[68] As Shaheen asserts, Hollywood has "indicted all Arabs as Public Enemy #1—brutal, heartless, uncivilized, religious fanatics and money-mad cultural 'others' bent on terrorizing civilized Westerners, especially Christians and Jews."[69] Television also promoted the story line of American Muslims as enemies within.

This negative imaging did not begin with 9/11.[70] After the 1993 bombing of the World Trade Center in New York City, one poll found that 43 percent of Americans defined their fellow Muslim citizens as "religious fanatics" and associated them with violence.[71] It is therefore not surprising that in 1995 most Americans assumed the bombing of the federal building in Oklahoma that killed 168 must be the work of foreign Muslims. The devastation was, of course, perpetrated by two white, homegrown American terrorists. One, Timothy McVeigh, was associated with the white supremacist "radical Christian Identity Movement," but there was no backlash against Protestant Christians as a result of his violent acts.[72] In contrast, after 9/11 American Muslims "immediately feared for their lives."[73] Not without cause.

Days after the 9/11 attacks, three murders prompted by hatred for Muslims occurred. On September 15, 2001, an American Sikh, who wore a turban as a sign of his faith, was wrongly identified as a Muslim and shot dead in Mesa, Arizona. On the same day, an American Muslim citizen of Pakistani descent was gunned down in his own store in Dallas by a white supremacist. Incidents of physical and verbal violence against other American Muslims mounted in the days that followed.[74] On September 17, President George W. Bush spoke to the nation, declaring that "Islam is peace" and attempting to end the violence by affirming that "America counts millions of Muslims amongst our citizens, and Muslims make an incredibly valuable contribution to our country."[75] But his words did not stem the tide of intimidation felt by American Muslims throughout the country.

Two days after President Bush's speech, an American Muslim of Yemeni descent fleeing an attacker in Lincoln Park, Michigan, was shot in the back. In early October 2001, the Indian American owner of a gas station was shot in Mesquite, Texas, by the same white supremacist who had a month earlier murdered an American Muslim in the Lone Star State.[76] In 2001, anti-Islamic hate crimes reported to the FBI numbered 546, a huge spike from the previous year's thirty-three.[77] Between 2001 and 2006, the Department of Justice's Civil Rights Division investigated seven hundred cases of crimes motivated by religious bigotry against Muslims, Sikhs, Arabs, and South Asians. Federal courts tried twenty-seven cases, while local law enforcement pursued 150.[78]

Beginning in the fall of 2001, the FBI and other law enforcement authorities held "voluntary" interviews with almost eight thousand young Muslim men with student or visitor visas throughout the country. Faced with the unannounced interrogations, none dared refuse to answer questions focused on their religious and political views. None of those interviewed would be accused of any tie to terrorism. Seven hundred immigrant Muslim men were arrested while trying to register under the new National Security Entry-Exit Registration System. There followed detentions without cause, and for those with visa infractions, deportations. In addition, three American Muslim citizens, including one captain in the U.S. Army, were "arrested, held in solitary confinement for weeks, and labeled 'terrorists.' "[79] Eventually, all three would be exonerated, but the American Muslim community at large would grow suspicious of their own government.

The 342-page USA PATRIOT Act (H.R. 3162), hastily passed by Congress and signed into law by the president on October 26, 2001, provided the government unprecedented powers to monitor all American citizens. Intended to "deter and punish terrorist acts in the United States and around the world, to enhance law enforcement investigatory tools, and for other purposes," the law actually targeted the American Muslim community directly, despite its disclaimer that "Arab Americans, Muslim Americans, and Americans from South Asia play a vital role in our Nation and are entitled to nothing less than the full rights of every American."[80] What most security-conscious Americans have failed to appreciate, however, is that these laws also may be used against non-Muslim citizens as part of any investigation in which the possibility of terrorism is alleged. In this way, too, the civil rights of American Muslims serve to test those of all Americans.

The PATRIOT Act's Section 213, for example, eliminates previous legal requirements that a warrant be provided to the owner of any home or business at the time of a search. Instead, legal authorities can "sneak and peek" without informing the subject until weeks or months later.[81] Although the Supreme Court has ruled that such secret searches violate the Fourth Amendment's protection against "unreasonable searches and seizures," the act "has discarded this interpretation of the Fourth Amendment."[82] Section 215 allows the government, all without probable cause, the right to seize any document or record of any individual suspect being investigated for criminal activity. These materials include e-mails, computer records, and medical and education documents, as well as credit and bank statements.[83] Legal experts have noted that the provisions are particularly damaging to the rights of Muslim immigrants with legal visas and green cards. Section 412 states that these would-be citizens may be indefinitely detained, jailed, or deported, whether or not charges of terrorism are ultimately substantiated.[84] As the sociologist Lori Peek asserts, the PATRIOT Act's provisions have led to the "systematic erosion of civil rights for all Americans but have been especially devastating to Arab and Muslim communities."[85]

In addition, American Muslim citizens have been subject to religious profiling at airports. (Enterprising young Muslims created T-shirts that read "FLYING WHILE MUSLIM—IT'S NOT A CRIME.")[86] Special surveillance of mosques continues, and not until recently has the FBI's infiltration of Muslim Student Associations in New York and New England colleges in 2005–6 been made public.[87] Such policies have resulted in no convictions but have very effectively emboldened those inclined to suspect their fellow citizens who happen to be Muslim, as well as fortifying the stereotype of a religious minority as an enemy within.[88]

Some American Muslims have responded by redoubling their efforts at public education and forging closer ties with Jewish and Christian organizations.[89] Young American Muslims have undertaken campus outreach, including comedy tours attempting to neutralize bigotry with humor.[90] There have been those among the young for whom 9/11 permanently confirmed a sense of alienation and exclusion, as was the case of one young man interviewed in 2003: "I look different from them. I believe different things. I think that is when I figured out that to be American was to be Christian and Jewish. To be Muslim and brown was to be not American."[91]

Still, despite experiencing prejudice, many American Muslims have seized the opportunity for greater civic engagement at the local and national levels, including running for public office. Such political involvement has been identified as an important alternative path for the frustrations that might have led to domestic terrorism.[92] Yet Muslims remain underrepresented in American politics, even as they are called upon to run in order to "defend" the community's civil rights and to "consolidate the sense of ownership and belonging of this vulnerable minority."[93] But those who answer the call often face an intensified version of the hostilities directed against the community. The election of the first American Muslim congressman, while cause for communal celebration, also resulted in an unprecedented demonstration of anti-Islamic bigotry.

THE FIRST AMERICAN MUSLIM CONGRESSMAN

Thomas Jefferson's Qur'an made headlines in the twenty-first century resting beneath the hand of the Democrat Keith Ellison, the first Muslim elected to Congress. Ellison's election in 2006 and his decision to use Jefferson's Qur'an in his private swearing-in ceremony in January 2007 stirred a controversy in which American ideals about universal civil rights clashed with long-held anxieties about American Muslim citizens as the "distrusted Other."[94]

Ellison's election was answered with "hostile phone calls and e-mail," along with "some death threats."[95] Republican congressman Virgil Goode Jr. wrote a letter to constituents in Virginia warning that Americans must "wake up"; otherwise, there might "likely be many more Muslims elected to office and demanding the use of the Koran."[96] The Virginia congressman failed to remind those he represented that Ellison's use of the Qur'an had followed a formal pledge of allegiance to the Constitution, the only form of oath he was obliged to take. For Ellison, the Qur'an was optional and private, but also personal.[97] Why, after all, should he swear upon a religious text in which he did not believe? Ironically, Representative Goode's district included Thomas Jefferson's Monticello home, the site near where, in 1776, this Founder first quoted John Locke: "[He] sais 'neither Pagan nor Mahamedan nor

Congressman Keith Ellison taking the oath on Jefferson's Qur'an in 2007.

Jew ought to be excluded from the civil rights of the Commonwealth because of his religion.' "[98]

Goode's alarmism failed to consider that Ellison's election had been the result of a democratic process in which the candidate's civic virtues mattered more than his creed, a possibility first predicted by the Federalist Samuel Johnston of North Carolina in 1788: "Another case is, if any persons of such descriptions should, notwithstanding their religion, acquire the confidence and esteem of the people of America by their good conduct and practice of virtue, they may be chosen."[99]

Another faulty assumption on Goode's part was that Ellison as a Muslim must be "foreign," as betrayed in his warning, "I fear that in the next century we will have many more Muslims in the United States if we do not adopt the strict immigration policies that I believe are necessary to preserve the values and beliefs traditional to the United States of America." Ellison, an African American convert to Islam, explained that his ancestors had resided in North America since 1742.[100] Indeed, his conversion may well have been a reversion to the Muslim beliefs of his West African ancestors. Ellison was also Minnesota's first African American congressman, but it was his religion, not his race, that his critics seized upon.

Dennis Prager, the conservative columnist, talk show host, and President George W. Bush's appointee to the Holocaust Museum Board, insisted that Ellison's swearing-in on the Qur'an should not be tolerated "because the act undermines American civilization."[101] He asserted, "The centrality of the Bible as a repository of our values is the main issue," arguing that "if you are incapable of taking an oath on that book [the Bible], don't serve in Congress."[102] His assumption contradicted recent American political practice. Democratic congresswoman Debbie Wasserman Schultz had sworn her private oath of office upon a Tanakh, the Hebrew Bible, termed by Christians the Old Testament. As a Jew, she found the New Testament represented no repository of sacred truth. Why, as the Baptist evangelical John Leland had once asked in the eighteenth century, should anyone of any faith be forced by their government to swear upon a text whose truth they rejected? Such would amount not only to coercion, but also to hypocrisy. Indeed, considering that the Constitution explicitly forbade a religious test, why should an individual be condemned for using or not using any sacred text?

Prager further speculated that Ellison's election would somehow "embolden Islamic extremists and make new ones, as Islamists, rightly or wrongly, see the first sign of the realization of their greatest goal—the Islamicization of America."[103] He did not elaborate upon how this implicitly democratic end would be achieved. Would Islamic extremists from abroad arrive in the United States covertly, wait years to gain citizenship, and then *all* run for elected office—*and win*? Who, after all, would vote for Muslim candidates if their allegedly subversive political goals were unmasked by people like Prager? But if Americans did endorse a slate of American Muslim candidates, would that not simply be an affirmation of the Republic's democratic health? The suggestion in Prager's speech of Muslim conspiratorial intentions would not be successfully countered in any media venue, but would fester among select Muslim hate groups, seeping unremarked into mainstream national media and politics.

Immediately after Ellison's election, Glenn Beck, then with CNN's Headline News (HLN), congratulated the new congressman but refused to define him as fully American, suggesting rather that he must be in league with the nation's foreign adversaries. Beck asked, "Sir, prove to me that you are not working with our enemies."[104] Congressman-elect Ellison had been indicted as un-American and possibly anti-American, based solely on the commentator's prejudices about Islam. Beck qualified his insistence that the congressman prove his loyalty to the country by adding, "I'm not accusing you of being an enemy, but that's the way I feel, and I think a lot of Americans feel that way."[105]

There was no public outcry in response to Beck's remarks. Ellison's brief answer was to affirm his "deep love and affection for my country." He concluded, "There's no one who is more patriotic than I am. And so, you know, I don't need to—need to prove my patriotic stripes."[106] He also wrote an editorial in which he declared, "I was elected to articulate a new politics in which no one is cut out of the American dream, not immigrants, not gays, not poor people, not even a Muslim committed to serve his nation."[107]

In spite of opposition, many Americans, Muslims in particular, took heart. The editor of the *Arab American News* in Dearborn, Michigan, observed, "It's a step forward: it gives Muslims a little bit of a sense of belonging. It is also a signal to the rest of the world that America has nothing against Muslims."[108] Indicating this might be the case, a second Muslim, Democrat André Carson of Indiana, was elected to Congress in 2008, winning reelection in 2010. Carson's religion would not attract the sort of notice that Ellison's had. And Ellison would be reelected repeatedly by his predominantly non-Muslim constituents in Minneapolis. Still, the tactics used to undermine him, far from being retired, would be brought to bear, as early as 2004, against a bigger target, a potential candidate in the 2008 presidential election.

Could a Muslim Be President? No—and Yes

False reports that Senator Barack Obama was a "secret" Muslim began to circulate just after his impressive keynote speech at the Democratic National Convention in 2004, long before a real Muslim, Keith Ellison, became a candidate for Congress.[109] The initial anonymous e-mail, created by a fringe Republican political operative describing himself as "independent," promoted a range of lies: that Obama concealed "the fact that he is a Muslim"; that his stepfather "introduced his stepson to Islam"; that he was enrolled in a Muslim school in Indonesia where he learned "radical teaching that is followed by the Muslim terrorists"; and that his Christianity was only "politically expedient," a cover for his true faith. The e-mail's author also deliberately referred to Obama as "Osama."[110] The allegations would circulate more widely on the Web in 2006, as Obama actively considered a presidential bid. By 2007, "CNN and others" had "thoroughly debunked the smear," but as Chris Hayes reported, "the original false accusation has clearly sunk into people's consciousness."[111] The idea would not die during the presidential campaign. Indeed, the confusion over Obama's religion remains for some.

As when Jefferson was branded an "infidel," attacks on Obama's Christian self-identification were intended to undermine his appeal among the Christian majority. In both cases, the association with Islam was intended to depict the candidate as decidedly un-American. That Jefferson and Obama would both be elected nevertheless did not prevent enemies from continuing the attack well into the first term of each.

Still, there are key differences in the two smear campaigns. First, unlike Jefferson, Barack Hussein Obama does have an actual Islamic heritage: his father, a Kenyan, and his stepfather, an Indonesian, were both Muslim. Even the name Barack Hussein is Muslim in origin: Barack, *baraka* in Arabic, means "blessing," and Hussein is the name of the Prophet Muhammad's grandson. Obama's stepfather would list the boy's religion as "Islam" on a school form in Indonesia, but as Obama explained, he practiced no religion until he joined the United Church of Christ in Chicago,[112] his family being, by his own account, not "folks who went to church every week." Obama relates that he chose Christianity in part because of the centrality of the Golden Rule:

> So I came to my Christian faith later in life, and it was because the precepts of Jesus spoke to me in terms of the kind of life that I would want to lead—being my brothers' and sisters' keeper, treating others as they would treat me.[113]

Apart from but not unconnected to claims about Obama's faith were those made about his place of birth. The evolution of what has come to be called "birtherism," or the conspiracy theory denying that Obama was a Hawaii-born American citizen, fed the same fears of foreign infiltration as claims he was Muslim.[114] Indeed, books propagating these myths would proliferate during and after the presidential campaign of 2008 and even into the following election cycle, despite the failure of any proof to materialize after nearly four years of the Obama presidency.[115]

Another difference between the smearing of Jefferson and that of Obama was that in the former case there were no ramifications for actual American Muslims, whereas the treatment of Obama insulted and alienated millions of American Muslim citizens. (It was also designed to instill fear in American Jews, because for some the specter of a Muslim president cast doubt on their country's future support for the state of Israel.) Among a substantial group of voters, the falsehood that Obama was a Muslim had assumed a frightening truth in the campaign. A month before the 2008 election, a Pew Forum poll recorded that 12 percent of Americans believed it, despite repeated media corrections to the contrary.[116] It is not particularly surprising that this number correlated to those who overwhelmingly disapproved of him.

"I can't trust Obama," said one woman at the Minnesota rally for Obama's Republican opponent John McCain, on October 10, 2008. Holding the microphone the candidate had given her to ask a question, she continued, "I have read about him and he's not, he's not uh—he's an Arab. He's not—" At which point McCain reclaimed the microphone, contradicting her: "No ma'am. He's a decent family man [and] citizen that I just happen to have disagreements with on fundamental issues and that's what this campaign is about. He's not [an Arab]." In response, McCain's own supporters booed him as a "liar" and "terrorist."[117] It was a confusing moment, one in which McCain, attempting to defend his opponent, inadvertently seemed to say that being an Arab (or Muslim) was somehow at odds with being "a decent family man" or a "citizen."[118]

The inflammatory accusation that Obama was a Muslim (and that all Muslims were terrorists) also changed the Democratic candidate's campaign strategy and self-representation. Muslims across the nation had hoped that Obama would be "a long-awaited champion of civil liberties, religious tolerance and diplomacy in foreign affairs." But while he accepted offers to speak to Christian and Jewish organizations, Obama "ignored" invitations from American Muslim voters to address them. He even asked Congressman Ellison not to speak on his behalf at one of the nation's oldest mosques in Cedar Rapids, Iowa, "because it might stir controversy." In June 2008, volunteers for Obama told two American Muslim women in headscarves to move off camera, away from where they were standing behind the candidate as he spoke in Detroit. Obama later telephoned the two to apologize: "I take deepest offense and will continue to fight against discrimination against people of any religious group or background." While some Muslims understood Obama's avoidance of their community, others felt "betrayed." That the candidate's Web site referred to claims about his religion as a "smear," seemed implicitly to affirm the idea that American Muslims were un- or anti-American, even while noting that such "rumors were offensive to American Muslims because they played into 'fearmongering.'"[119] Nowhere had Obama defended the idea that to be a Muslim presented no impediment to being an American citizen.

Even after the election, anti-Islamic tactics would continue to affect how President Obama spoke to his Muslim constituents in public. His earliest official speeches in recognition of the American Muslim community were presented to Islamic audiences abroad, in Egypt, not directly to his own constituency in the United States. Not until 2009, after a year as president, would Obama declare in Cairo, "I also know that Islam has always been a part of America's story." Only while speaking to his Egyptian university audience would he allow that "since our founding American Muslims have enriched the United States."[120]

Three days after the incident at the McCain rally, the reporter Campbell Brown, then of CNN, proposed a response that finally reflected American ideals of religious pluralism and political equality. In her commentary, she answered the key question: "So What If Obama Were a Muslim or an Arab?" Brown succinctly described Obama as "an American" and "a Christian," but then asked reproachfully, "So what if John McCain was Arab or Muslim? Would it matter? When did this become a disqualifier for higher office in our country? When did Arab or Muslim become dirty words? The equivalent of dishonorable or radical?"[121]

Brown admitted that "the media is complicit here, too," pointedly identifying the problem: "We've all been too quick to accept the idea that calling someone Muslim is a slur."[122] (This was the response Congressman Ellison had hoped Obama himself might offer in the face of these accusations.)[123] She recognized that millions of American Arab and Muslim citizens were "being maligned here," and then insisted, "We can't tolerate this ignorance—not in the media, not on the campaign trail." Brown concluded, "Of course, he's not an Arab. Of course, he's not a Muslim. But honestly, it shouldn't matter."[124]

Almost a week later in October 2008, General Colin Powell, former secretary of state under President George W. Bush, endorsed Barack Obama for president. Troubled by the accusation that Obama was a Muslim, Powell focused on the death of Kareem R. Khan, an American Muslim soldier killed in Iraq and buried in Arlington National Cemetery, to rebuke those in his party who defamed citizens because of their Islamic faith. Civic virtue in rendering the ultimate sacrifice of one's life for one's country, Powell reminded Americans, should be considered a testament to loyalty and citizenship, regardless of religion. On the television show *Meet the Press*, Powell echoed Brown's withering question about then presidential candidate Obama: "The really right answer is, what if he is? Is there something wrong with being Muslim in this country? No, that's not America."[125]

Since the eighteenth century, many Americans have feared the possibility of a Muslim or Catholic or Jewish president, echoing the dread expressed by the Federalist William Lancaster in 1788 at what the Constitution had made possible: "But let us remember that we form a government for millions not yet in existence. I have not the art of divination. In the course of four or five hundred years, I do not know how it will work. This is most certain, that Papists may occupy that chair, and Mahometans may take it."[126]

Lancaster's fears of a Catholic president were realized in less than his predicted four or five hundred years, when John F. Kennedy won the office in 1960. That the nation did not then succumb to some "Papist plot" should perhaps have given those errant patriots terrified by Obama's election some cause for comfort, but there is no indication that these anxieties have abated.

Why not? Why did polls four years into Obama's presidency indicate that 31 to 46 percent of Republicans still thought he was a Muslim?[127] Scholars of conspiracy theory in American politics point out false claims are spread rather than debunked by repetition.[128] Another view suggests that those polled did not actually believe Obama to be a Muslim, but told the pollsters they did in order to register ideological opposition.[129] In this way, the reality of whether or not Obama is a Muslim has become equivalent to what the idea of a Muslim president has come to signify. Could a Muslim become president? Not a few of Obama's detractors may still be convinced that one already has. As to whether an actual, self-described Muslim could ascend to the office, that seems far more problematic until a much larger proportion of the electorate becomes Muslim and/or more non-Muslim Americans take to heart what Jefferson proclaimed in his Bill for Establishing Religious Freedom:

> [T]hat our civil rights have no dependance on our religious opinions . . . that therefore the proscribing any citizen as unworthy the public confidence by laying upon him an incapacity of being called to offices of trust and emolument, unless he profess or renounce this or that religious opinion, is depriving him injuriously of those privileges and advantages to which, in common with his fellow citizens, he has a natural right.[130]

In the meantime, democracy may impose its own de facto religious test, where the Constitution and the several states abolished one. No successful U.S. presidential candidate need swear on anything but the Constitution, but during campaigns for the highest office, religion remains, for some, a powerful factor.

Efforts to malign candidates through imputed associations with Islam would seem, as in the cases of Ellison and Obama, to focus exclusively on Democratic contenders for office. But that impression could not be further from the truth. Both parties have in fact been targeted, including two Republican governors who have dared to support their Muslim constituents as citizens and believers.[131] Governor Rick Perry of Texas has been attacked for maintaining a productive friendship since 2000 with the Aga Khan, the progressive leader of one Ismaili Shi'i Muslim sect. Numbering twenty million worldwide, this group includes many U.S. citizens. The Aga Khan's relationship with Governor Perry has resulted in his funding the "Muslim Histories and Cultures Project," which has trained Texas high school teachers at the University of Texas at Austin to implement new nonsectarian methods for teaching their students about the Islamic world.[132]

Another arrangement, in 2009, between the Aga Khan and Governor Perry provided for more and better cooperation in the "fields of education, health sciences, natural disaster preparedness and recovery, culture and environment."[133] In addition, Governor Perry has been credited with supporting the passage in 2003 of the Texas Halal Law (HB-470), which regulates the accurate labeling of ritually slaughtered meat for Muslim consumers. (In practice, it does what regulated kosher designations of meat and other products already accomplish for the nation's Jewish religious minority.) Right-wing Web sites labeled the governor of Texas "a Muslim enabler" and a supporter of Sharia, or Islamic, law.[134] Both accusations would likely have made the Republican vulnerable to the conservative extreme of his own base had he not suspended his run for the 2012 Republican presidential nomination.

Republican governor Chris Christie of New Jersey also found himself the object of serious criticism from within his own party when he nominated the American Muslim lawyer Sohail Mohammed to the state supreme court in the spring of 2011. While in practice, Christie's appointee had represented Muslims "detained by the FBI" after 9/11. Christie defended Mohammed's work, saying that he had "played an integral role" in "creating trust between the Islamic community and law enforcement." After he was sworn in to the office on July 26, 2011, the Muslim jurist was falsely accused of links to terrorism and of supporting Sharia law rather than state or federal statutes. Governor Christie responded bluntly, "This Shariah law business is crap. It's just crazy and I'm tired of dealing with the crazies."[135]

In contrast, other Republicans, including Michele Bachmann and Newt Gingrich during their bids for the 2012 presidential nomination, have supported the notion that Islamic law is the new great threat to the nation.[136] Indeed, Gingrich declared that only an American Muslim candidate who "denounced" Sharia law could ever win his support for the presidency.[137] In taking this stand, these politicians expressed little understanding of Islamic law, having been briefed by the same small cadre of interconnected anti-Muslim groups.[138] But even some who support the anti-Sharia cause allow that "for all its fervor, the movement is arguably directed at a problem more imagined than real. Even its leaders concede that American Muslims are not coalescing en masse to advance Islamic law."[139]

ANTI-SHARIA AND ANTI-MOSQUE INITIATIVES AS ATTEMPTS TO DENY ALL AMERICAN MUSLIMS THEIR CIVIL RIGHTS

When anti-Islamic attacks against Congressman Ellison and President Obama failed, key components of the conspiracy theory directed against them were expanded to sow fear and undermine the civil rights and citizenship of all American Muslims. Those committed to resisting Sharia law espouse a view of American identity that, contrary to the founding discourse, is exclusively Judeo-Christian or even exclusively Christian, denying the legitimacy of American Muslim citizenship and political rights. According to Islamic legal expert Anver Emon, "more than any particular Muslim man or woman," for these anti-Muslim activists Sharia "represents the enemy within, the terror threat."[140]

Those American Muslims who might follow aspects of Sharia law— and these applications vary widely among believers—do so in their daily prayers, precepts for marriage, divorce, wills, and international commercial transactions. But these commitments do not remotely amount to a collective effort to seize political power in the United States and impose Sharia law on all its citizens. Nevertheless, in seventeen states, laws or amendments to state constitutions now target Sharia law and/ or "foreign law" as illegal.[141] As reporters have discovered, this "movement" did not begin as a spontaneous, grassroots political priority; it was manufactured and dispersed by a handful of activists.[142]

In 2006, anti-Muslim activist David Yerushalmi created the Society of Americans for National Existence (SANE), a nonprofit that denounces Sharia law. His "expertise" in Islamic law is not based on any formal academic training. In fact, Yerushalmi has been denounced by the Jewish civil rights organization the Anti-Defamation League as well as by the U.S. Catholic bishops for his bigoted views of Muslims and African Americans.[143] He is the author of the model for many of these anti-Sharia bills, which in some instances repeat the wording of his legislative template exactly.[144] In 2009, with the help of Frank J. Gaffney Jr., president of the conservative Center for Security Policy, Yerushalmi funneled many of his anti-Sharia ideas through the Tea Party movement. Not surprisingly, Gaffney had once promoted the idea that President Obama "might secretly be Muslim." The Gaffney-Yerushalmi connection helps explain how Republican legislatures and primary candidates were briefed to adopt a position on a subject about which they knew nothing of substance. For this service, Yerushalmi received $153,000 in consulting fees from the Center for Security Policy.[145]

Yerushalmi also served as legal counsel for the 2010 report *Shariah: The Threat to America,* a manifesto promoted by Gaffney's right-wing Center for Security Policy.[146] Running to over two hundred pages, the report was produced by a team headed by two retired generals, William G. "Jerry" Boykin and Harry Edward Soyster. After 9/11, Boykin, then a senior Pentagon official, "described the fight against terrorism as a Christian battle against Satan." President George W. Bush publicly rebuked Boykin for that statement, affirming that the United States was not at war "with Islam but with violent fanatics." After Boykin's retirement in 2007, he became a speaker popular among extreme conservative Christians. Even before helping to author the report on Sharia, he stated that Islam "should not be protected under the First Amendment." In 2012, Boykin's anti-Muslim views resulted in West Point's withdrawal of an invitation for him to address cadets at a prayer breakfast. Speaking anonymously, one cadet noted that the invitation had at first been extended to Boykin despite his anti-Islamic remarks: "I know Muslim cadets here, and they are great, outstanding citizens, and this ex-general is saying they shouldn't enjoy the same rights."[147]

The Center for Security Policy report describes Sharia as "a serious threat" to the United States, while simultaneously admitting that "there may not be a single 'true' Islam" practiced by over one billion Muslims worldwide.[148] Neither does the manifesto deny the claims of "hopeful pundits" who may be "correct in claiming that shariah adherent Islam is not the preponderant Muslim ideology" in the United States.[149] It does, however, propose that all Muslims are liars,[150] an assertion based on the deliberate misinterpretation of the term *taqiyya,* which the authors translate as "lying," but which is better known in Islamic history as "dissimulation," or concealment of one's religious convictions, when threatened with "danger or death." In very few instances have members of the Sunni Muslim majority employed this tactic, though dissimulation has historically served the Shi'i minority, as well as Sufi mystics threatened with persecution by fellow believers. It was in any case never conceived as a way to mislead non-Muslims, nor to have Muslims apply it as such.[151] Both Gaffney and Yerushalmi, the latter the center's self-styled Islamic legal expert, have been designated as members of "the anti-Muslim inner circle" identified in 2011 by the Southern Poverty Law Center.[152]

That all American Muslim citizens who adhere to Sharia are necessarily disloyal and threatening to the U.S. government and its Constitution is a claim carefully weighed and dismissed by scholars of Islamic law, such as Andrew March. In his 2009 book *Islam and Liberal Citizenship: The Search for an Overlapping Consensus,* he asserts that a Muslim "who accepts the security of a non-Muslim state finds himself with a very strict set of duties toward that state, duties that can be argued to fulfill liberal demands of civic loyalty, including a duty to avoid harming or betraying (even during a legitimate war against that state)."[153] As the scholar of law and ethics Martha Nussbaum has pointed out, Muslims are not the only group in America routinely thought treacherous because of the legalism of their faith: "Muslims, like Jews, are always accused of having a double loyalty, and both are seen to submit themselves to a double set of legal requirements—religious law somehow making them bad subjects of civil law."[154] The legitimate question is not whether Islam or Sharia is compatible with democracy, but whether American democratic institutions truly support the religious and legal equality of Muslim citizens, as they claim to do.[155]

The grounds upon which the U.S. Court of Appeals for the Tenth Circuit struck down the legality of Oklahoma's "Save Our State" anti-Sharia constitutional amendment in January 2012 remain instructive. As approved by a majority of voters, the amendment read, in part, that "the courts shall not consider international law or Sharia law." The suit brought by a single American Muslim from Oklahoma was joined by representatives of Islamic, Jewish, Baptist, and secular interest groups such as the Association of the Bar of the City of New York, the Islamic Law Committee, the American Jewish Committee, Americans United for Separation of Church and State, the Anti-Defamation League, the Baptist Joint Committee for Religious Liberty, the Center for Islamic Pluralism, Interfaith Alliance, and the Union for Reform Judaism.[156]

The claimant argued that the law had the effect of "stigmatizing him and others who practice the Islamic faith, inhibiting the practice of Islam, disabling a court from probating his last will and testament (which contains references to Sharia law), limiting the relief Muslims can obtain from Oklahoma state courts, and fostering excessive entanglements between government and religion." Ultimately, the court of

appeals found that the amendment was illegal for "singling out his religion for negative treatment" in violation of "both the Establishment
and Free Exercise Clause of the First Amendment" of the Constitution.[157] In response to this precedent, many state legislative attempts to
ban Sharia have been altered to regulate only "foreign law," though the
objection to Islamic law remains implicit.[158]

Dovetailing with the anti-Sharia movement was a slew of attempts
to attack, threaten, deface, oppose, or even ban the building of mosques
at thirty sites throughout the country in 2010. There have been more
since.[159] Such opposition is also not new in the United States.[160] But
in 2010 sentiments coalesced to resist the Park 51 project in New York
City, later known as the Cordoba House Initiative, which had been
planned, according to Imam Feisal Abdul Rauf, as a "multifaith worship
space, including a dedicated Islamic prayer space (a mosque), in a building that architecturally would be thoroughly American."[161] Opponents
of Cordoba House dubbed the project, inaccurately, "the Ground Zero
mosque," even though the structure is two and a half blocks away from
the site of the 9/11 attacks and not visible from there.[162]

The reference to Cordoba, while intended to recall a time when
Muslims, Christians, and Jews peacefully coexisted in eighth-century
Spain, unfortunately also provided grist for critics who pointed out that
this was a period of Islamic rule, when Christians and Jews, though
allowed to worship freely, did not enjoy equality. Opponents of the
mosque thus charged it with Islamic triumphalism, reminiscent of the
appropriation of Spanish churches for Muslim worship. In fact, under
the medieval Muslim rule only half of the original cathedral was taken
over and turned into a mosque, "leaving the other half free for Christian use—an unmistakable symbol of confessional tolerance."[163] Eventually, the Muslims purchased the land under the structure that came to
be known as La Mezquita from the Christians resident there. But in any
case, the custom of taking over houses of worship was not particular to
Muslims; Christian conquerors commonly built their churches on the
ruins of pagan or Jewish sites, the latter an especially common practice
in Christian Spain. It is important to remember that the space for the
proposed mosque in New York City was already the property of an
American Muslim businessman—and that the two extant local mosques
were unable to accommodate all worshippers.[164]

Nonetheless, this planned mosque in Manhattan inflamed for many
the painful memory of 9/11, a wound on the national psyche that had

not healed a decade later and remains associated with Islam, despite ample evidence dissociating terrorism from the faith. Loss and fear remain powerful emotions for all Americans who witnessed the attacks. Ironically, those who planned the mosque intended the building to bring Americans of different faiths together, not to divide them. But divide Americans it did.[165]

Anti-Muslim activists like Pamela Geller and Robert Spencer joined the fray insisting that the mosque represented an attempt by Muslims to take over the country, finishing what they claimed 9/11 had left half done. The two are the cofounders of Stop Islamization of America (SIOA), which is defined as a hate group by the Southern Poverty Law Center. In 2011, their film *The Ground Zero Mosque: Second Wave of the 9/11 Attacks* was presented at the Conservative Political Action Conference.[166] (Not surprisingly, Geller believes President Obama to be a Muslim.)[167]

New York City's mayor, Michael Bloomberg, defended the right of American Muslims to build the mosque complex in lower Manhattan in 2010, citing clear constitutional principle in the midst of overwrought emotions: "Whatever you may think of the proposed mosque and community center, lost in the heat of the debate has been a basic question: Should government attempt to deny private citizens the right to build a house of worship on private property based on their particular religion? That may happen in other countries, but we should never allow it to happen here."[168]

Bloomberg even cited the Flushing Remonstrance of 1657 as a precedent for contemporary freedom of religion. If he had been informed that the religious freedom of Muslims as well as Jews and all sects of Christians had been included in this extraordinary protest by Dutch settlers, his point might have been even more powerful. The Remonstrance clearly espouses a universal religious freedom in the seventeenth century, a time when to do so was to risk jail and banishment, as two members of the community eventually suffered. Still, the signatories insisted:

The law of love peace and libertie in the states extending to *Jewes Turkes* and *Egiptians* as they are Considered the sonnes of Adam which is the glory of the outward State of *Holland,* soe love peace and libertie, extending to all in Christ Jesus Condemns hatred, warre and bondage; . . . our desire is not to offend one of his little ones in what soever forme name or title hee appears in whether presbyterian independent Baptist or Quaker, but shall bee glad to see anything of god in any of them: desireing to doe unto all men as wee desire all men shoulde doe unto us which is the true law both of Church and State.[169]

In 1957, President Dwight D. Eisenhower made his own case for the construction of the Islamic Center Mosque in the nation's capital. Visiting the site in June of that year, he offered a definition of American principles that might seem entirely un-American to the anti-Muslim opponents of mosques throughout the United States. Eisenhower saw no difference between the new Muslim "church" in Washington, D.C., and "a similar edifice of any other religion." His message to American Muslims was simple and direct:

> Meeting with you now, in front of one of the newest and most beautiful buildings in Washington, it is fitting that we re-dedicate ourselves to the peaceful progress of all men under one God.
>
> And I should like to assure you, my Islamic friends, that under the American Constitution, under American tradition, and in American hearts, this Center, this place of worship, is just as welcome as could be a similar edifice of any other religion. Indeed, America would fight with her whole strength for your right to have here your own church and worship according to your own conscience.
>
> The concept is indeed part of America, and without that concept we would be something else than what we are.[170]

In the same spirit, Eisenhower would authorize the military to identify Muslim servicemen on their dog tags.[171]

Would a majority of Americans still affirm that "America would fight with her whole strength for your right to have here your own church and worship according to your conscience"? It bears mentioning that Eisenhower embraced Muslims as fellow believers "under one God," at a time when the gravest threat to the United States was thought to be "godless" Communists, both at home and abroad.[172] Events in the Middle East that would darken the image of Islam in the latter twentieth century had yet to occur. Nevertheless, it is difficult to deny that acceptance of Muslims into the American fold has deteriorated considerably in the past half century.

Remembering Thomas Jefferson's Qur'an: A Dispute over the Past and the Future

Although many editorials celebrated the existence of Jefferson's Qur'an as a novelty in the midst of Congressman Keith Ellison's swearing-in controversy in 2007, those wedded to fears of Islam were at pains to deny what Ellison had affirmed about Jefferson, that he was "a visionary" who "believed that wisdom could be gleaned from many sources."[173] The Boykin- and Soyster-directed anti-Sharia screed of 2010 argued that Jefferson had purchased the Qur'an in order to better know his enemies: "When confronted with an Islamic threat, they took the effort to consult primary sources and to conduct competent analysis of that threat."[174] According to Boykin and Soyster, the book was merely a remnant of his diplomatic encounter with the Muslim ambassador from Tripoli in London in 1786.[175]

Such assertions ignore the fact that Jefferson actually bought his Qur'an in 1765, twenty-one years before the diplomatic effort in question, and eleven years before he wrote the Declaration of Independence. Although Jefferson doubtless did check the Qur'anic basis for Islamic piracy sometime after his 1786 meeting with the Muslim ambassador in London, he had much earlier documented his interest in the sacred text unrelated to foreign policy. Those who claim otherwise similarly ignore Jefferson's pointed refusal to consider Muslims as either perpetual foreign or domestic enemies and his defense of their future, and that of all non-Christians, as potential citizens.

In March 2011, Bryan Fischer, director of issues analysis for the socially conservative American Family Association, a group with two million members headquartered in Tupelo, Mississippi, denied that Muslims and other non-Christians enjoyed the full protection of the First Amendment. To justify this assertion, he appears to repeat the analysis of Thomas Jefferson's Qur'an found in the 2010 Boykin and Soyster anti-Sharia manifesto, defining Islam not as a religion but as a "totalitarian ideology dedicated to the destruction of the United States." Fischer writes, "The First Amendment was written by the Founders to protect the free exercise of Christianity. They were making no effort to give special protections to Islam." As to Thomas Jefferson's Qur'an, Fischer explains that too in a way that follows the Boykin-Soyster treatise:

> We actually at the time were dealing with our first encounters with jihad in the form of the Barbary pirates, which is why Jefferson bought a copy of the Koran. He was told by the Bey of Tripoli that Islam requires Muslims to rob, kill and pillage infidel Christians where they find them. Jefferson naturally found that hard to believe, so he bought a copy of the Koran to read it for himself. Sure enough, it's right in there.[176]

In fact, Jefferson had not met the ruler of Tripoli, but only his ambassador, who told him that the Qur'an provided the rationale for North African piracy. (Jefferson was also told, as chapter 4 of this book attests, that the devil had enabled those successful forays.) Of course, Fischer evinces no awareness that the treaty concluded with Tripoli states at the very outset that "the government of the United States of America is not in any sense founded on the Christian Religion."[177] Nor, one expects, would Fischer be interested in the inconvenient historical truth that Jefferson as president addressed the Islamic rulers of both Tripoli and Tunis with an emphasis on their shared deity: "I pray God, very great and respected friend, to have you always in his holy keeping."[178] Possessing a serviceable knowledge of its basic tenets, Jefferson clearly thought Islam was a religion.

Jefferson did not hate Muslims, nor did he allow fear to inform his views of their future in the United States. In direct opposition to the stated goals of Jefferson's most cherished legislation, Fischer's excision of the civil rights of American Muslims also forecloses those of all non-Christian citizens:

> Islam has no fundamental First Amendment claims, for the simple reason that it was not written to protect the religion of Islam. Islam is entitled only to the religious liberty we extend it out of courtesy. While there certainly ought to be a presumption of religious liberty for non-Christian religious traditions in America, the Founders were not writing a suicide pact when they wrote the First Amendment.[179]

Nowhere is it more explicit that those who overtly deny the civil rights of Muslims often hold the rights of all non-Christians in equal contempt. And so the ultimate strength of those guarantees that in the eighteenth century deliberately included Muslims are now being tested, together with the seriousness of our national commitment to the cherished ideals of religious freedom, political equality, and pluralism. We remain in the midst of this struggle over the definition of national identity and citizenship.

JEFFERSON, THE GOLDEN RULE, AND THE CIVIL RIGHTS OF MUSLIMS

A year before his death, Thomas Jefferson wrote to a friend's son. The young man's father had urged him to do so in order to "have a favorable influence." Contemplating his own mortality, "as one from the dead," Jefferson advised, "Love your neighbor as yourself, and your country more than yourself."[180] His final reference to the Golden Rule is as clear a signal as we have of its irreducible importance and universal application in his personal ethics, as well as its centrality to his conception of patriotism.

On the very day of his swearing-in upon Jefferson's Qur'an in 2007, Representative Ellison also invoked the Golden Rule as a pointed admonition to fellow citizens. In the editorial he wrote entitled, "Choose Generosity, Not Exclusion," Ellison argued that the Christian majority had a pivotal decision to make about religious pluralism, based on their understanding of the New Testament. Was the Golden Rule applicable only to Christians—or all Americans, no matter their religion?

> Will the preacher tell our young couple, "God loves you—but only you and people like you"? Or will the preacher say "God loves you and you must love your neighbors of all colors, cultures, or faiths as yourselves"? One message will lead to a stinginess of spirit, an exclusion of the "undeserving," and the other will lead to a generosity of spirit and inclusion of all.[181]

Even Ellison's opponents might agree that this was now an unavoidable question for the nation, however differently they might phrase it. What cannot be denied is how Jefferson and other important Founders answered.

Invoking the Golden Rule in this way, as a commandment to embrace humanity without qualification, linked Jefferson to a select fraternity of men who had suffered for the sake of this seemingly simple belief. When those who first espoused it in Europe refused to accept violence or coercion in religion's name, they laid the foundation for the crucial question that Jefferson would pose in 1776, answering it with universal legislation: "Why persecute for difference in religious opinion?"[182] In his own answer, the Italian miller Menocchio invoked his love for all who were his neighbors—whether Muslim, Christian heretic, or Jew—before his death on the Inquisition's pyre in 1601. Just over a decade later, the Baptist Thomas Helwys echoed him from the London prison in which he would die, still proclaiming, "Let them be heretikes, Turcks, Jewes, or whatsoever it apperteynes not to the earthly power to punish them in the least measure."[183] After a little more than thirty years, this same belief in the separation of religion from government and the individual's absolute right to "soul liberty" would be expressed for the first time in North America by Roger Williams, who asserted:

> And I aske whether or no such as may hold forth other *Worships* or *Religions* (*Jews, Turkes,* or *Antichristians*) may not be peaceable and quiet *Subjects,* loving and helpfull *neighbours,* faire and just *dealers,* true and loyall to the *civill government*? It is cleare they may from all *Reason* and *Experience* in many flourishing *Cities* and *Kingdomes* of the World.[184]

Aspects of Christian thought, often articulated as dissent by those the ruling majority decreed heretical, contained the roots of an end to religious persecution and the seeds of pluralism. These same inclusive precedents for the practice of the Golden Rule existed also in the Hebrew Bible.

Now, as in the eighteenth century, American Muslims symbolize the universality of religious inclusion and equality promised at the nation's founding by Jefferson, Washington, Madison, Leland, and others, an ideal still in the course of being fully realized more than two centuries later. Any attack upon the rights of Muslim citizens should be recognized for what it remains: an assault upon the universal ideal of civil rights promised all believers at the country's founding. No group, based on religion, should be excluded from these rights. To do so now would betray both our hard-won national legacy and the genius of those who conceived it.

Notes

PREFACE AND ACKNOWLEDGMENTS

1. For the early Ottoman and European trade in this luxury, which actually began in the sixteenth century, see Ariel Salzmann, "The Age of Tulips: Confluence and Conflict in Early Modern Consumer Culture (1550–1730)," in *Consumption Studies and the History of the Ottoman Empire, 1550–1922,* ed. Donald Quataert (Albany: State University of New York Press, 2000), 84, 87, 89; Mike Dash, *Tulipomania: The Story of the World's Most Coveted Flower and the Extraordinary Passions It Aroused* (New York: Crown, 1999), 34, 224. Although tulips were propagated in England as early as 1582 and may have crossed into their North American colonies in the seventeenth century, the flowers also became transatlantic at the same time with the arrival of the Pennsylvania Dutch, who counted the three petals of the tulip as symbols of the Trinity. The Ottomans also imbued the tulip with powerful but very different Islamic religious symbolism.

2. Edwin M. Betts and Hazelhurst Bolton Perkins, *Thomas Jefferson's Flower Garden at Monticello,* revised by Peter J. Hatch, 3rd ed. (Monticello, VA: Jefferson Memorial Foundation, 2000), 25–26.

3. Damien Cave and Anne Barnard, "Minister Wavers on Plans to Burn Koran," *New York Times,* September 9, 2010, http://www.nytimes.com/2010/09/10/us/10obama.html?pagewanted=all; Enayat Najafizada and Rod Nordland, "Afghans Avenge Florida Koran Burning, Killing 12," *New York Times,* April 1, 2011, http://www.nytimes.com/2011/04/02/world/asia/02afghanistan.html?...all. It is worth noting that the Southern Poverty Law Center has designated the minister Terry Jones and his Dove World Outreach Center based in Florida as an anti-Muslim hate group; see Robert Steinback, "The Anti-Muslim Inner Circle," *Intelligence Report,* no. 142 (Summer 2011), Southern Poverty Law Center.

INTRODUCTION:
IMAGINING THE MUSLIM AS CITIZEN
AT THE FOUNDING OF THE UNITED STATES

1. For a study that finds that American magazines included a range of attitudes toward Muslims, including "naïve curiosity, obsessive exoticism, geopolitical calculation, gentle condescension, and unabashed bigotry," see Robert Battistini, "Glimpses

of the Other Before Orientalism: The Muslim World in Early American Periodicals, 1785–1800," *Early American Studies* 8, no. 2 (Spring 2010): 446–74, quote on 447.

2. The first person to connect Jefferson with Locke's interest in Muslim civil rights is the distinguished historian and head of the Manuscript Division of the Library of Congress, James H. Hutson, "The Founding Fathers and Islam," *Library of Congress Information Bulletin* 61, no. 5 (2002): 1, http://www.loc.gov/loc/lcib/0205/tolerance .html. The first analysis of Jefferson's focus on the Qur'an as an extension of his interest in history and religion, without reference to Locke, may be found in the pathbreaking article and subsequent book by Kevin J. Hayes, "How Thomas Jefferson Read the Qur'an," *Early American Literature* 39, no. 2 (2004): 247–61; and Kevin J. Hayes, *The Road to Monticello: The Life and Mind of Thomas Jefferson* (New York: Oxford University Press, 2008), 9, 130, 201, 258, 259, 316.

3. Naomi Cohen describes Jews and Muslims as "linked" with "other perceived deviants whose enjoyment of political rights made a mockery of the dominant religion"; see Naomi Cohen, *Jews in Christian America: The Pursuit of Religious Equality* (New York: Oxford University Press, 1992), 13, 16–17, 24–26, quote on 24; Gerard V. Bradley, "The No Religious Test Clause and the Constitution of Religious Liberty: 'A Machine That Has Gone of Itself,'" *Case Western Reserve Law Review* 37 (1986–87): 702; Arthur Hertzberg, *The Jews in America: Four Centuries of an Uneasy Encounter* (New York: Simon and Schuster, 1989), 15.

4. Bret E. Carroll, *Routledge Historical Atlas of Religion in America* (New York: Routledge, 2000), 90–95; Francis Newton Thorpe, ed., *The Federal and State Constitutions, Colonial Charters, and Other Organic Laws of the States, Territories, and Colonies Now or Heretofore Forming the United States of America*, 7 vols. (Washington, DC: U.S. Government Printing Office, 1909), 5:2637; Morton Borden, *Jews, Turks, and Infidels* (Chapel Hill: University of North Carolina Press, 1984), 13.

5. Carroll, *Routledge Historical Atlas of Religion*, 90–95.

6. "George Washington to the Members of the Volunteer Association and Other Inhabitants of the Kingdom of Ireland Who Have Lately Arrived in the City of New York," December 2, 1783, in *The Writings of George Washington from the Original Manuscript Sources, 1745–1799*, ed. John C. Fitzpatrick, 39 vols. (Washington, DC: U.S. Government Printing Office, 1938), 27:254.

7. In 1790, Washington wrote to Jewish congregations in Savannah, Newport, Philadelphia, New York, Charleston, and Richmond; see Paul F. Boller Jr., *George Washington and Religion* (Dallas: Southern Methodist University Press, 1963), 152–62; for the actual missives, see 184–88; Carroll, *Routledge Historical Atlas of Religion*, 52.

8. "George Washington to Tench Tilghman," March 24, 1784, in *Writings of George Washington*, 27:367. (I have corrected Washington's original spelling of "Athiests.")

9. For a study of American views of the Islamic world as "a remarkably useful rhetorical device," see the important analysis of Robert J. Allison, *The Crescent Obscured: The United States and the Muslim World, 1776–1815* (Chicago: University of Chicago Press, 2000), 35–59, quote on 59. A specialized form of American "Orientalism" is defined by Timothy Marr, *The Cultural Roots of American Islamicism* (New York: Cambridge University Press, 2006), 1–114. Edward Said first recognized "the late eighteenth century as a very roughly defined starting point" for his study of European views of the Middle East, even though America's foreign policy there at that time did not conform to the model of emerging European military superiority, which Said describes as "the ineradicable distinction between Western superiority and Oriental inferiority." America in the eighteenth century inherited key European ideas about Islam and the Middle East that could be termed Orientalist, but the United States was not yet in a position of political or scholarly dominance in defining the area. Instead, the United States remained less militarily powerful than the Islamic world but still vulnerable to negative European precedents about the area; see Edward Said, *Orientalism* (New York: Vintage, 1979), quotes on 3, 42. Others who have nodded to Said's powerful precedent include

Thomas S. Kidd, "'Is It Worse to Follow Mahomet Than the Devil?' Early American Uses of Islam," *Church History* 72, no. 4 (December 2003): 767–78; Thomas S. Kidd, *American Christians and Islam: Evangelical Culture and Muslims from the Colonial Period to the Age of Terrorism* (Princeton: Princeton University Press, 2009), 12. Scholars of American literature and culture have repeatedly drawn upon Said's precedent, but with caveats; for example, see Malini Johar Schueller, *U.S. Orientalisms: Race, Nation, and Gender in Literature, 1790–1890* (Ann Arbor: University of Michigan Press, 1998), 3; Battistini, "Glimpses of the Other before Orientalism," 447, 468–69; Fuad Shaban, *Islam and Arabs in Early American Thought* (Durham, NC: Acorn Press, 1991), 199–205; Marwan M. Obeidat, *American Literature and Orientalism* (Berlin: K. Schwarz, 1998); Jennifer Costello Brezina, "A Nation in Chains: Barbary Captives and American Identity," in *Captivating Subjects: Writing, Confinement, Citizenship, and Nationhood in the Nineteenth Century,* ed. Jason Haslam and Julia M. Wright (Toronto: University of Toronto Press, 2005), 201–19.

10. Thomas S. Kidd, *God of Liberty: A Religious History of the American Revolution* (New York: Basic Books, 2010), 16–20; Jon Butler, *Awash in a Sea of Faith: Christianizing the American People* (Cambridge, MA: Harvard University Press, 1999), 52, 198.

11. There is evidence of similar ideas of toleration even earlier, in the late fifteenth century; see chapter 2 in Stuart B. Schwartz, *All Can Be Saved: Religious Tolerance and Salvation in the Iberian Atlantic World* (New Haven: Yale University Press, 2008), 53.

12. Mary V. Thompson, "Mount Vernon," in *Encyclopedia of Muslim-American History,* ed. Edward E. Curtis IV, 2 vols. (New York: Facts on File, 2010), 2:392.

13. Michael A. Gomez, *Black Crescent: The Experience and Legacy of African Muslims in the Americas* (New York: Cambridge University Press, 2005), 166; Michael A. Gomez, *Exchanging Our Country Marks: The Transformation of African Identities in the Colonial and Antebellum South* (Chapel Hill: University of North Carolina Press, 1998), 66.

14. The only historical reference to "six" Muslims who served in the American Revolutionary War may be found on a Web site that includes several chronological errors about Muslims in the eighteenth century. It provides only five names. One such was the slave Peter Salem, who was freed for his participation in the battle of Bunker Hill in Boston. He is assumed to be Muslim based on his surname, which might not reflect Islamic heritage even though *salam* is the word in Arabic for peace. "Salem" as a surname might instead refer to Salem, Massachusetts, an important seacoast town north of Boston. This speculation has not been found in other academic treatments; see "Collections of Stories of American Muslims: Presenting America's Islamic Heritage, the 1700s," http://www.muslimsinamerica.org. For the unverifiable assertion that Crispus Attucks, shot by the British in 1770 during the Boston Massacre, had Native American, black, and Muslim roots, see Jerald F. Dirks, *Muslims in American History: A Forgotten Legacy* (Beltsville, MD: Amana Publications, 2006), 206.

15. Gomez, *Black Crescent,* 3–184. For the earliest compendium of these encounters, see Allan D. Austin, *African Muslims in Antebellum America: A Sourcebook* (New York: Garland, 1984). In Spanish New World territories, Muslims outwardly professing to be Christians and known as Moriscos were present earlier than the seventeenth century; see Karoline P. Cook, "Forbidden Crossings: Morisco Emigration to Spanish America, 1492–1650" (PhD diss., Princeton University, 2008).

16. Quoted in Marilyn C. Baseler, *"Asylum for Mankind": America, 1607–1800* (Ithaca: Cornell University Press, 1998), 330–31, quote on 331; Kambiz GhaneaBassiri, *A History of Islam in America* (New York: Cambridge University Press, 2010), 152.

17. A contemporary observer, Senator William Plumer of New Hampshire, after meeting with the Tunisian ambassador wrote that he described himself as "a Turk," and observed of this man that "his complexion is about as dark as that of a Molatto [mulatto]," whereas others in the ambassador's entourage were "large black men"; see *William Plumer's Memorandum of Proceedings in the United States, 1803–1807,* ed. Everett Somerville Brown (New York: Macmillan, 1923), quotes on 358–59.

18. This is emphasized as a general American perspective by Allison, *Crescent Obscured*, 35–60. The idea that Jefferson's view of the North African pirates was directly linked to his negative view of Islam, an argument more reflective of John Adams's opinion, is asserted by Michael Oren, *Power, Faith, and Fantasy: America in the Middle East 1776 to Present* (New York: W. W. Norton, 2007), 17–70. Jefferson did not focus on the religion of Islam as the main North African foreign policy problem, which is a position correctly asserted but not documented in a brief article by Sebastian R. Prange, "Thomas Jefferson's Qur'an," *Saudi Aramco World* 62, no. 4 (July/August 2011): 7.

19. Quoted in Benedict Anderson, *Imagined Communities: Reflections on the Origin and Spread of Nationalism*, rev. ed. (London: Verso, 1991), 6.

20. John Esposito, *What Everyone Needs to Know About Islam* (New York: Oxford University Press, 2002), 228, 172 (quote).

21. For a breakthrough survey of the experience of American Muslims, see Jane Smith, *Islam in America* (New York: Columbia University Press, 1999). A second edition of this work appeared in 2009. The most expansive history of Muslims in America and their agency, with a focus on "living Muslims in colonial and antebellum America," is by GhaneaBassiri, *A History of Islam in America*, quote on 13. A recent attempt to analyze the concept of citizenship in Western political theory and Islamic law may be found in Andrew F. March, *Islam and Liberal Citizenship: The Search for an Overlapping Consensus* (New York: Oxford University Press, 2009). March offers a cogent analysis of the issue that does not include American historical precedents. For a very different view of Islamic law and the place of the Qur'an in recent American political discourse, see Kathleen M. Moore, *The Unfamiliar Abode: Islamic Law in the United States and Britain* (New York: Oxford University Press, 2010), 81–101.

22. Important works that find evidence for this assertion include Allison, *Crescent Obscured*, xv–xviii, 35–59, 61–106; Marr, *Cultural Roots*, 1–114; Kidd, "Is It Worse to Follow Mahomet Than the Devil?," 766–90, and more recently, Kidd, *American Christians and Islam*, 11–36; Shaban, *Islam and the Arabs in Early American Thought*, 1–81; Obeidat, *American Literature and Orientalism*, 3–40. Slightly more mixed views of Muslims in literary sources about North Africa are presented by Johar Schueller, *U.S. Orientalisms*; Paul Baepler, introduction to *White Slaves, African Masters: An Anthology of American Barbary Captivity Narratives* (Chicago: University of Chicago Press, 1999), 1–51; Costello Brezina, "A Nation in Chains," 201–19; Jacob Rama Berman, "The Barbarous Voice of Democracy: American Captivity in Barbary and the Multicultural Specter," *American Literature* 79 (March 2007): 1–27; James Lewis, "Savages of the Seas: Barbary Captivity Tales and Images of Muslims in the Early Republic," *Journal of American Culture* 13 (Summer 1990): 75–84; Battistini, "Glimpses of the Other before Orientalism," 446–74. New work on European and American captives may be found in Lawrence A. Peskin, *Captives and Countrymen: Barbary Slavery and the American Public, 1785–1816* (Baltimore: Johns Hopkins University Press, 2009), 137–214; and Ann Thompson, *Barbary and Enlightenment: European Attitudes toward the Maghreb in the 18th Century* (Leiden: E. J. Brill, 1987), 11–92. Counterevidence for entirely negative and/or oppositional sets of cultural premises about Islam is offered in sobering economic terms by Frank Lambert, *The Barbary Wars: American Independence in the Atlantic World* (New York: Hill and Wang, 2005), 3–13. For more complicated British views of Islam and Muslims before 1750, see Linda Colley, *Captives: Britain, Empire and the World, 1600–1850* (London: Jonathan Cape, 2002), 99–113.

23. Allison, *Crescent Obscured*, xvii, 3–106; Marr, *Cultural Roots*, 1–81. For echoes of both Allison and Marr's definition of American views of North Africa as "a kind of inverse mirror of their own democracy, probity, and enlightenment," see Michael Oren, *Power, Faith, and Fantasy*, quote on 32.

24. For a survey of cultural views of Islam, American domestic political rhetoric and, most in depth, an analysis of the Barbary Wars and their "legacy," see Allison, *Crescent Obscured*, xiii–59; Marr, *Cultural Roots*, 1–114. A focus on inter-Protestant uses of Islam and early American sermons in provided by Kidd, "Is It Worse to Follow Mahomet Than the Devil?," and Kidd, *American Christians and Islam*, 10–11, 18.

25. Quoted in Esposito, *What Everyone Needs to Know*, 1st ed., 172.

26. James Hutson wrote a two-page argument in 2002 that Jefferson and other Founders intended to include Muslims "in their vision of the future republic"; see "The Founding Fathers and Islam." Jefferson, Washington, and Madison are identified as supporting pluralism, which is attributed to "their ethnic backgrounds" by Akbar Ahmed, *Journey into America: The Challenge of Islam* (Washington, DC: Brookings Institution Press, 2010), 58–61.

27. Those who study Jews and Catholics in founding discourse sometimes refer to Muslims in relation to sources that link the three groups, but either dismiss these references without historical context or see Muslims as ways of making Jews and Catholics even farther from normative Protestants. Arthur Hertzberg casts references to Muslims in relations to Jews as "outlandish"; see Hertzberg, *The Jews in America*, 15. Morton Borden makes multiple references to Muslims in his important study of Jews, but never explains them; see Borden, *Jews, Turks, and Infidels*, 14, 16, 33. Naomi W. Cohen, like Hertzberg, sees Muslims as markers that place Jews beyond Christian norms; see Cohen, *Jews in Christian America*, 24–25. Gerard V. Bradley refers to Muslims as "totally behind the horizon of civility"; see Bradley, "The No Religious Test Clause," 702. References to Muslims appear in works on the relationship of religion to the state in the founding era but without explanation in Leonard Levy, *The Establishment Clause: Religion and the First Amendment* (Chapel Hill: University of North Carolina Press, 1994), 10, 47, 55, 59, 68, and Michael McConnell, "The Origins and Historical Understanding of the Free Exercise of Religion," *Harvard Law Review* 103 (1990): 1473 n. 323.

28. For the best history of this twentieth-century struggle for both Jews and Catholics, see Kevin M. Schultz, *Tri-Faith America: How Catholics and Jews Held Postwar America to Its Protestant Promise* (New York: Oxford University Press, 2011).

29. Perhaps the first to note the continued exclusion of Muslims from "a tripartite pluralism" of "Protestants, Catholics, and Jews" in the twentieth century was the historian William G. McLoughlin, *Soul Liberty: The Baptists' Struggle in New England, 1630–1833* (Hanover, NH: Brown University Press/University Press of New England, 1991), xi. For a study of the concept of Muslims as "not fully American," see Yvonne Yazbeck Haddad, *Not Quite American? The Shaping of Arab and Muslim Identity in the United States* (Waco, TX: Baylor University Press, 2004).

30. Some scholars, myself included, have used Edward Said's model of Orientalism to characterize Muslims as quintessential Others in eighteenth-century American thought, part of an unending binary of "Them" and "Us" that Said would have recognized in the American context. But my intent in this study is not to define or indicate new or old forms of Orientalism in America, but rather to document the more elusive opposition to these negative visions. For earlier work with an emphasis on Orientalism, see D. A. Spellberg, "Islam on the Eighteenth-Century Stage: Voltaire's *Mahomet* Crosses the Atlantic," in *Views from the Edge: Essays in Honor of Richard W. Bulliet*, ed. Neguin Yavari, Lawrence G. Potter, and Jean-Marc Ran Oppenheim (New York: Columbia University Press for the Middle East Institute, 2004), 245–60, and Denise A. Spellberg, "Islam in America: Adventures in Neo-Orientalism," *Review of Middle East Studies* 43, no. 1 (Summer 2009): 25–35. Neither Said nor American specialists have ever documented what might be termed an anti-Orientalist pattern. A unique attempt to argue a form of philo-Islamic belief for England with a brief suggestion of its transfer to the early American Republic may be found in Humberto Garcia, *Islam and the English Enlightenment, 1670–1840* (Baltimore: Johns Hopkins University Press, 2012), 1–29, 243 n. 28. Until now, historians of early America have not focused on correcting or explaining the distorted images of anti-Islamic materials. The result has been unquestioning acceptance of anti-Islamic references without attention to concocted distortions, errors, and caricatures. Emphasis on this negative data has inadvertently resulted in the accep-

tance of these distortions as normative. This type of analysis does not provide insight into what Muslims actually believed or why these misrepresentations became particularly problematic for Americans. Most important, historians of Islam in early America have not focused on exceptions to the predominant anti-Islamic rule of completely negative representations.

I. THE EUROPEAN CHRISTIAN ORIGINS OF NEGATIVE BUT SOMETIMES ACCURATE AMERICAN IDEAS ABOUT ISLAM AND MUSLIMS, 1529–1797

1. Quoted in John Leland, "Extracts from Number Two, A Little Sermon Sixteen Minutes Long," in *The Writings of the Elder John Leland*, ed. L. F. Greene (New York: G. W. Wood, 1845), 410.

2. This is not a new idea. Anti-Islamic representations predominate in most historical works. For example, see Robert J. Allison, *The Crescent Obscured: The United States and the Muslim World, 1776–1815* (Chicago: University of Chicago Press, 2000), 35–59; Thomas S. Kidd, *American Christians and Islam: Evangelical Culture and Muslims from the Colonial Period to the Age of Terrorism* (Princeton: Princeton University Press, 2009), xii–xiii; Timothy Marr, *The Cultural Roots of American Islamicism* (New York: Cambridge University Press, 2006), 5–9. One exception to this pattern is David S. Reynolds, *Faith in Fiction: The Emergence of Religious Literature in America* (Cambridge, MA: Harvard University Press, 1981), 15–20. Most recently, Edward E. Curtis IV, "Stereotypes," in *Encyclopedia of Muslim-American History*, ed. Edward E. Curtis IV, 2 vols. (New York: Facts on File, 2010), 2:529–30.

3. Kidd, *American Christians and Islam*, 11–12, 15–17.

4. Allison, *Crescent Obscured*, 35, 57–59.

5. The historian who first noted, "There was a Christian picture in which the details (even under the pressure of facts) were abandoned as little as possible, and in which the general outline was never abandoned. . . . There were shades of difference, but only within a common framework," is Norman Daniel, *Islam and the West: The Making of an Image* (Edinburgh: Edinburgh University Press, 1966), quote on 260. See also R. W. Southern, *Western Views of Islam in the Middle Ages* (Cambridge, MA: Harvard University Press, 1962), 91–92, 108–9; Edward Said, *Orientalism* (New York: Vintage, 1994), 61–73; Daniel J. Sahas, *John of Damascus on the "Heresy of the Ishmaelites"* (Leiden: E. J. Brill, 1972), 127–59; John Tolan, *Saracens: Islam in the Medieval European Imagination* (New York: Columbia University Press, 2002), 40–67.

6. Daniel, *Islam and the West*, 184–88. The idea that, with the exception of John of Damascus in the eighth century, Islam was perceived until the twelfth century as a form of idolatry or paganism has been documented by Daniel, *Islam and the West*, 70, 105–34; Sahas, *Heresy of the Ishmaelites*, 93–95, 131–37; Alberto Ferreiro, *Simon Magus in Patristic, Medieval, and Early Modern Traditions* (Leiden: E. J. Brill, 2005), 221; Frederick Quinn, *The Sum of All Heresies: The Image of Islam in Western Thought* (New York: Oxford University Press, 2008), 24–43, 221. The idea of the heretical Christian monk was described first as an Arian by John of Damascus; Daniel, *Islam and the West*, 4–5. The same monk later was referred to as a heretical Nestorian Christian. Later, his name was revealed as Sergius (or in Islamic texts Bahira); see Susan R. Boettcher, "Insiders and Outsiders," in *Reformation Christianity*, ed. Peter Matheson (Minneapolis: Fortress Press, 2007), 239.

7. Robert Fuller, *Naming the Antichrist: The History of an American Obsession* (New York: Oxford University Press, 1995), 3, 33, 157.

8. Quoted in George W. Forrell, "Luther and the War Against the Turks," *Church History* 14, no. 4 (December 1945): 264.

9. R. W. Scribner, *For the Sake of the Simple Folk: Popular Propaganda for the German Reformation* (Oxford: Clarendon Press, 1994), 182–83, plates 150–52. My thanks go to Caroline Castiglione for this reference.

10. Daniel, *Islam and the West,* 184–85.

11. Nabil Matar, *Islam in Britain, 1558–1685* (New York: Cambridge University Press, 1998), 110.

12. Forrell, "Luther and the War Against the Turks," 260.

13. Quinn, *Sum of All Heresies,* 44.

14. Forrell, "Luther and the War Against the Turks," 259, 263 (quote); Adams S. Francisco, *Martin Luther and Islam: A Study in Sixteenth-Century Polemics and Apologetics* (Leiden: E. J. Brill, 2007), 4–5, 45–69, 75–121, 174–237; Sean Foley, "Muslims and Social Change in the Atlantic Basin," *Journal of World History* 20, no. 3 (2009): 380–85; Egil Grislis, "Luther and the Turks," *Muslim World* 64, no. 3 (July 1974): 180.

15. Quoted in Tolan, *Saracens,* 275.

16. Quinn, *Sum of All Heresies,* 44; Tolan, *Saracens,* 275.

17. Margaret Meserve, *Empires of Islam in Renaissance Historical Thought* (Cambridge, MA: Harvard University Press, 2008), 14; Elizabeth L. Eisenstein, *The Printing Press as an Agent of Change* (Cambridge: Cambridge University Press, 1979), 3.

18. Quoted in Jan Slomp, "Calvin and the Turks," in *Christian-Muslim Encounters,* ed. Yvonne Yazbeck Haddad and Wadi Z. Haddad (Gainesville: University Press of Florida, 1995), 134.

19. Quoted in J. Gregory Miller, "Holy War and Holy Terror: Views of Islam in German Pamphlet Literature, 1520–1545" (PhD diss., University of Michigan, 1994), 146.

20. Quoted in Albert Hourani, *Europe and the Middle East* (Berkeley: University of California Press, 1980), 26.

21. Thomas S. Kidd, " 'Is It Worse to Follow Mahomet Than the Devil?' Early American Uses of Islam," *Church History* 72, no. 4 (December 2003): 767, 774, 776, 787; Kidd, *American Christians and Islam,* 1–2.

22. Thomas S. Freeman, "Foxe, John (1516/17–1587)," *Oxford Dictionary of National Biography,* 58 vols. (New York: Oxford University Press, 2004), 20:165–209.

23. John Foxe, *The Acts and Monuments of John Foxe, with a Life and Defence of the Martyrologist by the Late Rev. George Townsend, D.D.* (London: George Seeley, 1870), 4:80, 39–41, quotations on 4:80.

24. Muhammad M. Pickthall, trans., *The Meaning of the Glorious Qur'an: Text and Explanatory Translation* (New York: Muslim World League, 1977), 40; Yohanan Friedmann, *Tolerance and Coercion in Islam: Interfaith Relations in Muslim Tradition* (Cambridge: Cambridge University Press, 2003), 87–120.

25. Friedmann, *Tolerance,* 6–7.

26. In Turkish, *yeni çeri.*

27. Foxe, *Acts,* 4:36.

28. Ibid., 4:122.

29. Susan Juster, "What's 'Sacred' about Violence in Early America? Killing and Dying in the Name of God in the New World," *Commonplace* 6, no. 1 (October 2005): 6–7.

30. Humphrey Prideaux, *The True Nature of Imposture Fully Display'd in the Life of Mahomet. With a Discourse Annex'd for the Vindicating of Christianity from this Charge, Offered to the Consideration of the Deists of the Present Age* (London: E. Curll, J. Hooke, and T. Caldecott, 1716), 16–20. Stress on the Prophet as "impostor" has been defined as an "Oriental category" opposite to Jesus; see Edward Said, *Orientalism,* 72; Allison, *Crescent Obscured,* 37–39, 41.

31. Prideaux, *True Nature of Imposture,* 141–44.

32. Quoted in Richard H. Popkin, "The Deist Challenge," in *From Persecution to Toleration: The Glorious Revolution in England,* ed. Ole Peter Grell, Jonathan I. Israel, and Nicholas Tyacke (Oxford: Clarendon Press, 1991), 195.

33. Kerry Walters, *Revolutionary Deists: Early America's Rational Infidels* (Amherst, NY: Prometheus Books, 2011), 8.

34. Popkin, "Deist Challenge," 20.

35. Ernest Campbell Mossner, "Deism," in *Encyclopedia of Philosophy,* ed. Donald M. Borchert (Detroit: Macmillan Reference USA, 2006) 2:680–93.

36. Kidd, *American Christians and Islam,* 17; Humberto Garcia, *Islam and the English Enlightenment, 1670–1840* (Baltimore: Johns Hopkins University Press, 2012), 5, 10–11, 47–48, 134.

37. G. J. Toomer, *Eastern Wisedome and Learning: The Study of Arabic in Seventeenth-Century England* (Oxford: Clarendon Press, 1996), 289–92.

38. James R. Jacob, *Henry Stubbe, Radical Protestantism and the Early Enlightenment* (Cambridge: Cambridge University Press, 1983), 114; Marwan M. Obeidat, *American Literature and Orientalism* (Berlin: K. Schwarz, 1998), 18.

39. P. M. Holt, "The Treatment of Arab History by Prideaux, Ockley, and Sale," in *Historians of the Middle East,* ed. Bernard Lewis and P. M. Holt (London: Oxford University Press, 1962), 293–94; Toomer, *Eastern Wisedome,* 292. Also noting Prideaux's distortions is Kevin J. Hayes, "How Thomas Jefferson Read the Qur'an," *Early American Literature* 39, no. 2 (2004): 249–50.

40. Humberto Garcia believes that Prideaux was responding directly to Henry Stubbe; see Garcia, *Islam and the English Enlightenment,* 51.

41. Jacob, *Stubbe,* 115.

42. Henry Stubbe, *An Account of the Rise and Progress of Mahometanism: with the Life of Mahomet and a Vindication of Him and His Religion from the Calumnies of the Christians,* ed. Hafiz Mahmud Khan Shairani (Lahore: Oxford and Cambridge Press, 1911; repr. 1975).

43. P. M. Holt, *A Seventeenth-Century Defender of Islam: Henry Stubbe (1632–1676) and His Book* (London: Dr. Williams's Trust, 1972), 9; Toomer, *Eastern Wisedome,* 291. Toomer says three editions of Prideaux were published in England the first year, as opposed to Holt's two. For the assertion of a far greater circulation of Stubbe's manuscript, see Garcia, *Islam and the English Enlightenment,* 30–59.

44. Allison, *Crescent Obscured,* 41; Kidd, *American Christians and Islam,* 9.

45. Quoted in David A. Pailin, *Attitudes to Other Religions: Comparative Religion in Seventeenth- and Eighteenth-Century Britain* (Manchester: Manchester University Press, 1984), 103.

46. Quinn, *Sum of All Heresies,* 43–47.

47. Marr, *Cultural Roots,* 29, 97, 102–3; Kidd, *American Christians and Islam,* 8; Quinn, *Sum of All Heresies,* 24, 30, 38, 43.

48. Kidd, *American Christians and Islam,* 8.

49. Cotton Mather, *The Christian Philosopher,* ed. Winton U. Solberg (Urbana: University of Illinois Press, 1994), 111; Allison, *Crescent Obscured,* 47.

50. Solberg, introduction to Mather, *Christian Philosopher,* lxxiii.

51. Mather, *Christian Philosopher,* 11–12.

52. The point that these slurs were launched by Protestants against one another is made by Kidd, *American Christians and Islam,* 14; Kidd, "Is It Worse to Follow Mahomet Than the Devil?," 767, 774, 776, 787. This point was made earlier for British authors on Islam; Pailin, *Attitudes to Other Religions,* 104.

53. Roger Williams, *George Fox Digg'd out of His Burrowes,* ed. Rev. J. Lewis Diman, in *The Complete Writings of Roger Williams,* 7 vols. (New York: Russell and Russell, 1963), 5:125.

54. Daniel, *Islam and the West,* 283, also 13, 32, 39, 41, 231, 234–35, 240, 287, 341, 382.

55. Williams, *George Fox,* 5:125, in the margin.

56. Marr, *Cultural Roots,* 89; Kidd, *American Christians and Islam,* 13–17.

57. Quoted in Boyd Stanley Schlenther, "Whitefield, George (1714–1771)," *Oxford Dictionary of National Biography,* 58:643; Kidd, *American Christians and Islam,* 13–14.

58. Quoted in Schlenther, "Whitefield," 58:646.

59. Benjamin Franklin, *Autobiography and Other Writings,* ed. Russell B. Nye (Cambridge, MA: Riverside Press, 1958), 97.

60. A similar point about Catholics and Jews as the objects of Great Awakening opprobrium was first made by H. W. Brands, *The First American: The Life and Times of Benjamin Franklin* (New York: Anchor, 2002), 149.

61. Bernard Bailyn, *The Ideological Origins of the American Revolution,* enlarged ed. (Cambridge, MA: Belknap Press of Harvard University Press, 1992), 63.

62. Ibid., 35–52; Pauline Maier, *From Resistance to Revolution: Colonial Radicals and the Development of American Opposition to Britain, 1765–1776* (New York: Vintage, 1974), 27–48.

63. The first to note this as a transatlantic phenomenon that impacted the American colonies was Bailyn, *Ideological Origins,* 63–64 n. 8. See also Allison, *Crescent Obscured,* 47, 52–53, 56; Kidd, *American Christians and Islam,* 18; Marr, *Cultural Roots,* 23–26.

64. Allison, *Crescent Obscured,* 35, 57–59.

65. Bailyn, *Ideological Origins,* 36.

66. Ibid., 63–64 n. 8; Allison, *Crescent Obscured,* 47, 52–53, 56.

67. John Trenchard and Thomas Gordon, *Cato's Letters, or Essays on Liberty, Civil and Religious, and Other Important Subjects,* ed. Ronald Hamowy, 2 vols. (Indianapolis: Liberty Fund, 1995), 2:526.

68. Ibid., 1:183.

69. Marking 1750 as a turning point in British maritime control of the Mediterranean, see Linda Colley, *Captives: Britain, Empire and the World, 1600–1850* (London: Jonathan Cape, 2002), 103.

70. Trenchard and Gordon, *Cato's Letters,* 1:461.

71. Caroline Finkel, *Osman's Dream: The Story of the Ottoman Empire, 1300–1923* (New York: Basic Books, 2005), 200–201, 325, 329.

72. Trenchard and Gordon, *Cato's Letters,* 1:462, 470–71.

73. Ibid., 1:224, 333, 350–76, 381–82, 394, 403, 2:941.

74. Ibid., 2:907.

75. Bailyn, *Ideological Origins,* 35–36, 44–52; Allison, *Crescent Obscured,* 47, 52–53.

76. Samuel West, "On the Right to Rebel Against Governors," in *American Political Writing During the Founding Era, 1760–1805,* ed. Charles S. Hyneman and Donald S. Lutz, 2 vols. (Indianapolis: Liberty Fund, 1983), 1:438.

77. Curtis, "Stereotypes," in *Encyclopedia of Muslim-American History,* 2:530.

78. C. A. Patrides, "'The Bloody and Cruell Turke': The Background of a Renaissance Commonplace," *Studies in the Renaissance* 10 (1963): 126–35; Kevin M. McCarthy, "The Derisive Use of Turk and Turkey," *American Speech* 45, no. 1–2 (Spring–Summer 1970): 157–59.

79. "Mahometan," *Oxford English Dictionary,* 13 vols. (Oxford: Clarendon Press, 1970), 6:38.

80. Robert Battistini, "Glimpses of the Other Before Orientalism: The Muslim World in Early American Periodicals, 1785–1800," *Early American Studies* 8, no. 2 (Spring 2010): 474.

81. Marr, *Cultural Roots,* 6.

82. Battistini, "Glimpses of the Other," 473–74.

83. "Moor," *Oxford English Dictionary,* 6:645.

84. Ahmad Gunny, *Images of Islam in Eighteenth-Century Writings* (London: Grey Seal, 1996), 156; "Alcoran," *Oxford English Dictionary,* 5:260.

85. The earliest identification of the importance of Voltaire's play in circulation in Britain, Dublin, and New York, but not Baltimore, was found by Allison, *Crescent Obscured,* 43–46.

86. Allison, *Crescent Obscured,* 43–46. In opposition, Voltaire's play is cast as "atypical" by Garcia, *Islam and the English Enlightenment,* 5.

87. Jack B. Moore, introduction to Royall Tyler, *The Algerine Captive (1797),* ed.

Jack B. Moore, 2 vols. in 1 (Gainesville, FL: Scholars Facsimiles and Reprints, 1967), 1:viii. English captivity accounts began in the sixteenth century, but the genre as nonfiction and fiction survived into the eighteenth. See Nabil Matar, *Turks, Moors and Englishmen in the Age of Discovery* (New York: Columbia University Press, 1999), 169–83; Colley, *Captives*, chapter 2, "The Crescent and the Sea," and chapter 4, "Confronting Islam."

88. Malini Johar Schueller, *U.S. Orientalisms: Race, Nation, and Gender in Literature, 1790–1890* (Ann Arbor: University of Michigan Press, 1998), 49–58.

89. Allison, *Crescent Obscured*, 35–59, 94; Marr, *Cultural Roots*, 7–8; Johar Schueller, *U.S. Orientalisms*, 4, 8–10; Battistini, "Glimpses of the Other," 446, 472–73.

90. Allison, *Crescent Obscured*, 43–46, 57–59, 94; Marr, *Cultural Roots*, 7–8; Kidd, *American Christians and Islam*, xii; Johar Schueller, *U.S. Orientalisms*, viii–ix, 4, 10; Battistini, "Glimpses of the Other," 446.

91. Daniel, *Islam and the West*, 101, 144–45, 242, 267; Tolan, *Saracens*, 54.

92. Daniel, *Islam and the West*, 96–102.

93. One historically extant Islamic name chosen by Voltaire might be Seide, or Zayd, who was the Prophet's foster son. See Gunny, *Images of Islam*, 136.

94. Jonathan A. C. Brown, *Muhammad: A Very Short Introduction* (New York: Oxford University Press, 2011), 54.

95. Voltaire, *Mahomet the Prophet or Fanaticism: A Tragedy in Five Acts*, trans. Robert L. Myers (New York: Frederick Ungar, 1964), 57.

96. Voltaire, *Le Fanatisme, ou Mahomet le Prophète, tragédie*, in *Les oeuvres complètes de Voltaire*, ed. Christopher Todd (Oxford: Voltaire Foundation, 2002), 20B:207–8. In Voltaire's original French, "Le glaive et l'Alcoran dans mes sanglantes mains, / Imposerait silence au reste des humains."

97. For Voltaire's description of the character "Mahomet" and "sa physionomie de singe," see Magdy Badir, *Voltaire et l'Islam*, in *Studies on Voltaire and the Eighteenth Century*, vol. 125 (Banbury, UK: Voltaire Foundation, 1974), 23; Robert Edward Mitchell, "The Genesis, Sources, Composition, and Reception of Voltaire's *Mahomet*" (PhD diss., Ohio State University, 1961), 75; Gunny, *Images of Islam*, 137–38; Allison, *Crescent Obscured*, 43.

98. Gunny, *Images of Islam*, 134, 136, 141; Ziad Elmarsafy, *The Enlightenment Qur'an: The Politics of Translation and the Construction of Islam* (Oxford: Oneworld Press, 2009), 81, 84.

99. Badir, *Voltaire*, 96–97.

100. Fatima Müge Göçek, *East Encounters West: France and the Ottoman Empire in the Eighteenth Century* (New York: Oxford University Press), 80.

101. "La présence de l'ambassadeur turc risquait de provoquer un incident." For the quotation, see Jeroom Verycruysse, *Les Voltairiens* (Nendeln: KTO Press, 1978), 1:x; Marvin Carlson, *Voltaire and the Theatre in the Eighteenth Century* (Westport, CT: Greenwood Press, 1998), 55.

102. Where Voltaire describes the pope as "al capo della vera religione," and the Prophet as "il fondatore d'una falsa e barbara seta," see François-Marie Arouet de Voltaire, *Le Fanatisme, ou Mahomet le Prophète* (Paris: Garnier Frères, 1938), 222–23.

103. Harold Lawton Bruce, "Voltaire on the English Stage," *University of California Publications in Modern Philology* 8 (1918): 57.

104. Quoted in Arthur H. Scouten, ed., *The London Stage, 1600–1800: A Calendar of Plays, Part 3: 1729–1747* (Carbondale: Southern Illinois University Press, 1961), 1104.

105. Quoted in Allison, *Crescent Obscured*, 234 n. 14.

106. Quoted in Ronald Hamowy, introduction to Trenchard and Gordon, *Cato's Letters*, 1:xxiv; Bailyn, *Ideological Origins*, 37; Pauline Maier, *From Resistance to Revolution* (New York: Vintage, 1972), 27, 30.

107. Hamowy, introduction to Trenchard and Gordon, *Cato's Letters*, 1:xxiv; Garcia, *Islam and the English Enlightenment*, 56.

108. John Hoadly, prologue to James Miller, *Mahomet the Impostor* (London, 1744), Humanities Research Center, University of Texas at Austin.

109. James Miller, *Mahomet the Impostor,* in *Bell's British Theatre* (London, 1776); James Miller, *Mahomet the Impostor* (London, 1777), Houghton Library, Harvard University. A very similar "portrait" exists on a fresco in the Supreme Court in Washington, D.C. The image, designed in the 1930s, became the object of American Muslim protest in 1997, when sixteen Islamic organizations requested that the Supreme Court remove it because Sunni Islamic tradition rejects any visual rendering of the Prophet, but also because the message sent to viewers was that Muhammad spread his faith by violence. Chief Justice William Rehnquist refused to remove the image of the Prophet, adding that to have the image was a sign of honor and the sword "a general symbol of justice"; see Marr, *Cultural Roots,* 1–2.

110. Bruce, "Voltaire on the English Stage," 147–48. The play was reprinted in 1776, 1777, 1782, 1786, 1795, and 1796.

111. Allison, *Crescent Obscured,* 45.

112. *Rivington's Royal Gazette,* New York City, November 11, 1780.

113. Ibid.

114. Without reference to the prologue, the soldiers "may have felt under siege by passionate zealots who were rousing the innocent colonists to kill their symbolic father, George III," and they doubtless did see in the play "a vindication of their role as protectors of the established order," from those rebels who might destroy "empire." For these observations, see Allison, *Crescent Obscured,* 45.

115. The play was performed in the United States later in 1795 and 1796 as a critical response to the violence of the French Revolution; see Allison, *Crescent Obscured,* 45.

116. Quoted in J. Thomas Scharf, *The Chronicles of Baltimore* (Baltimore: Turnbull Brothers, 1874), 203–5. My thanks to Marilyn Baseler for this reference. See also *Maryland Journal and Baltimore Advertiser,* September 3, 1782, which states that "about 500 French troops remain in and near the town under the command of General La Valette."

117. Theatrical Playbill Collection, MS 2415, Maryland Historical Society, Baltimore; *Maryland Journal and Baltimore Advertiser,* June 28, 1782.

118. "At the Theatre in Baltimore on Tuesday Evening the 1st of October, 1782, will be presented the Tragedy of Mahomet, the Impostor," Broadside, New-York Historical Society, #Y1782. The broadside for October 15, 1782, is also at the New-York Historical Society.

119. Allison, *Crescent Obscured,* 45.

120. Battistini, "Glimpses of the Other," 447. There were 130 American captives by 1793; see Richard B. Parker, *Uncle Sam in Barbary: A Diplomatic History* (Gainesville: University Press of Florida, 2004), 208.

121. Bubonic and pneumonic plague outbreaks were common in eighteenth-century North Africa; see H. G. Barnby, *The Prisoners of Algiers: An Account of the Forgotten American-Algerian War, 1785–1787* (New York: Oxford University Press, 1966), 86.

122. G. Thomas Tanselle, *Royall Tyler* (Cambridge, MA: Harvard University Press, 1967), 141.

123. Hunter Miller, ed., *Treaties and Other International Acts of the United States of America,* 8 vols. (Washington, DC: U.S. Government Printing Office, 1931), 2:185–227, 275–317, 329–425.

124. Tanselle, *Royall Tyler,* 10–12.

125. Tyler, *Algerine Captive,* 1:166. The novel has been carefully read as a reflection of American ideals regarding slavery by Allison, *Crescent Obscured,* 94–95, and as depiction of a despotic Islam and a liberty-loving United States by Marr, *Cultural Roots,* 55–58. Race is more emphasized by Johar Schueller, *U.S. Orientalisms,* 50–58; see also Reynolds, *Faith in Fiction,* 15–20.

126. Tyler, *Algerine Captive,* 1:184, 186 (quote).

127. Ibid., 1:187.

128. Ibid., 1:185; Marr, *Cultural Roots*, 55.

129. Tyler, *Algerine Captive*, 2:27.

130. Ibid., 2:6; Johar Schueller, *U.S. Orientalisms*, 56; Marr, *Cultural Roots*, 56.

131. Tanselle, *Royall*, 168–69.

132. Tyler, *Algerine Captive*, 2:19, 20–21 (quote).

133. Ibid., 2:24–27, 28–30.

134. Ray W. Irwin, *The Diplomatic Relations of the United States with the Barbary Powers, 1776–1816* (New York: Russell and Russell, 1931), 204.

135. Tyler, *Algerine Captive*, 2:33.

136. Ibid., 2:38–39.

137. Ibid., 2:42; Allison, *Crescent Obscured*, 94; Jill Lepore, "Prior Convictions: Did the Founders Want Us to Be Faithful to Their Faith?" *New Yorker*, April 14, 2008, 71. Thanks to Neil Kamil for this reference.

138. Tyler, *Algerine Captive*, 2:42–43.

139. Ibid., 2:43. The assertion about the Bible as other than divine in origin seems to reflect a Deist position.

140. Ibid., 2:44.

141. Ibid., 2:46.

142. Ibid., 2:46–49.

143. Ibid., 1:8.

144. Ibid., 2:50; Allison, *Crescent Obscured*, 50.

145. Tyler, *Algerine Captive*, 2:50.

146. Ibid., 2:52.

147. Ibid., 2:143.

148. Ibid., 2:53.

149. Ibid.

150. Ibid., 2:56.

151. Tanselle, *Royall*, 6.

152. Tyler, *Algerine Captive*, 2:70, 72.

153. Ibid., 2:132–33; Tanselle, *Royall*, 172–73.

154. Tyler, *Algerine Captive*, 2:167.

155. Ibid., 2:168.

156. Ibid., 2:177–88.

157. Ibid., 2:187, 216–21.

158. Ibid., 2:221–23.

159. Ibid., 2:120–30.

160. Ibid., 2:129.

161. Tanselle, *Royall*, 172; Allison, *Crescent Obscured*, 94; Marr, *Cultural Roots*, 58; Reynolds, *Faith in Fiction*, 16; Lepore, "Prior Convictions," 74.

162. Quoted in Tanselle, *Royall*, 268 n. 29.

163. "Infidel," *Oxford English Dictionary*, 5:260.

164. Reynolds, *Faith in Fiction*, 17.

165. Quoted ibid.

166. Ibid., 17–18; Allison, *Crescent Obscured*, 94–96.

167. Tyler, *Algerine Captive*, 2:145.

2. POSITIVE EUROPEAN PRECEDENTS FOR THE TOLERATION OF MUSLIMS, AND THEIR PRESENCE IN COLONIAL AMERICA, 1554–1706

1. Quoted in Carlo Ginzburg, *The Cheese and the Worms: The Cosmos of a Sixteenth-Century Miller*, trans. John and Anne C. Tedeschi (Baltimore: Johns Hopkins University Press, 1992), 9–10.

2. Ginzburg first observed this religious equality; see ibid., 92.

3. Quoted ibid., 92–93. For a study of Spain, Portugal, and their transatlantic empires as sites for the Inquisition's charge of the heresy of Origen, as inspired by Carlo Ginzburg, see Stuart B. Schwartz, *All Can Be Saved: Religious Tolerance and Salvation in the Iberian Atlantic World* (New Haven: Yale University Press, 2008), 1–13. Origen believed "that the Jews were a wicked nation of deicides who deserved to suffer"; see Marvin Perry and Frederick M. Schweitzer, eds., *Antisemitic Myths: A Historical and Contemporary Anthology* (Bloomington: University of Indiana Press, 2008), quote on 5.

4. Ginzburg, *Cheese*, 92–95.

5. Many general histories of European religious toleration include sporadic references to Muslims (or Turks), but no single history of these ideas exists. This chapter is an initial but not a fully inclusive attempt to survey the varied roots of these ideas. See, for disparate examples: Henry Kamen, *The Rise of Toleration* (London: Weidenfeld and Nicolson, 1967), 65, 74, 78, 100, 116, 126–27, 133, 178, 201; Perez Zagorin, *How the Idea of Religious Toleration Came to the West* (Princeton: Princeton University Press, 2003), 2, 7–8, 265, 279, 287; and the classic Joseph Lecler, *Toleration and the Reformation*, trans. T. L. Westow, 2 vols. (New York: Association Press, 1960) 1:74–78, 87, 107–8, 111, 137, 161, 175, 220, 239, 420; 2:38–39, 53, 72–76, 104, 109, 182, 198, 369, 401, 458, 463. I do not treat, for example, John Goodwin (1594–1665), an Englishman who supported "full liberty of conscience to all sects, even Turks, Jews, Papists," in 1644, the same year as Roger Williams; see Kamen, *Toleration*, 178; Lecler, *Toleration*, 2:458. John Marshall devotes two chapters to the importance of toleration discourse about Muslims and Jews; see John Marshall, *John Locke, Toleration and Early Enlightenment Culture: Religious Intolerance and Arguments for Religious Toleration in Early Modern and "Early Enlightenment" Europe* (Cambridge: Cambridge University Press, 2006), 371–95, 593–617. For a study of "sympathetic" views of early Islamic history as a discourse in support of religious toleration for Christian dissenters and in opposition to the English government that he terms "Islamic Republicanism," see Humberto Garcia, *Islam and the English Enlightenment, 1670–1840* (Baltimore: Johns Hopkins University Press, 2012), xi–59. However, much support for the toleration of Muslims does not conform at all to the pattern of "Islamic Republicanism." Many who embraced Deism and Unitarianism, such as John Locke and Joseph Priestley, would be castigated as Muslims. John Locke's borrowing of a key precedent for the toleration of Muslims from Edward Bagshaw may be found in Nabil Matar, "John Locke and the 'Turbanned Nations,'" *Journal of Islamic Studies* 2, no. 1 (1991): 68, 71.

6. Norman Daniel, *Islam and the West: The Making of an Image* (Edinburgh: Edinburgh University Press, 1966), 18–192; Zachary Lockman, *Contending Visions of the Middle East: The History and Politics of Orientalism* (New York: Cambridge University Press, 2004), 36–37.

7. Quoted in Benjamin J. Kaplan, *Divided by Faith: Religious Conflict and the Practice of Toleration in Early Modern Europe* (Cambridge: Belknap Press of Harvard University, 2007), 296, 294–330; Susan R. Boettcher, "Insiders and Outsiders," in *Reformation Christianity*, ed. Peter Matheson (Minneapolis: Fortress Press, 2007), 242.

8. Kaplan, *Divided by Faith*, 296. For a discussion of the term "infidel" for Muslims, see "Infidel," *Oxford English Dictionary*, 13 vols. (Oxford: Clarendon Press, 1970), 5:260; Zagorin, *Toleration*, 5–6.

9. David Nirenberg, *Communities of Violence: Persecution of Minorities in the Middle Ages* (Princeton: Princeton University Press, 1996), 14–15, 200–49; Perry and Schweitzer, *Antisemitic Myths*, 2–3.

10. Quoted in Kaplan, *Divided by Faith*, 296.

11. One of the first to combine tolerationist views toward Muslims and Jews in his work is Marshall, *John Locke, Toleration and Early Enlightenment Culture;* see chapters 12 and 19.

12. I would like to thank my colleague Neil Kamil for his initial suggestion that I read Ginzburg's history of Domenico Scandella in conjunction with his own important

observations about this text; see Neil Kamil, *Fortress of the Soul: Violence, Metaphysics, and Material Life in the Huguenots' New World, 1517–1751* (Baltimore: Johns Hopkins University Press, 2005), 192–202, 219, 889–92; Ginzburg, *Cheese*, 51, 152; Stuart Schwartz, *All Can Be Saved*, 1, 8.

13. Ginzburg, *Cheese*, 112–13, quote on 113.

14. Caroline Finkel, *Osman's Dream: The Story of the Ottoman Empire, 1300–1923* (New York: Basic Books, 2005), 127–28.

15. Menocchio admitted that he had read the tale in the *Decameron* ("Cento novella") by Giovanni Boccaccio. It appears there as the third story of the first day, which was "prohibited" by the church by the miller's time, but had circulated in a "a late thirteenth-century collection of short stories"; see Ginzburg, *Cheese*, 49–50; Schwartz, *All Can Be Saved*, 41.

16. Quoted in Ginzburg, *Cheese*, 49.

17. Ibid.

18. Quoted ibid., 49–50.

19. Ibid., 51.

20. The reference is to the miller nicknamed *Pighino*, or "the Fat"; see ibid., 124–25.

21. Samuel P. Scott, trans., "*Siete Partidas*," in *Medieval Iberia: Readings from Christian, Muslim, and Jewish Sources*, ed. Olivia Remie Constable (Philadelphia: University of Pennsylvania Press, 1977), 271–73.

22. Quoted in Schwartz, *All Can Be Saved*, 53.

23. Ibid., 43–118.

24. Quoted ibid., 66.

25. Ibid., 2, 138.

26. Ginzburg, *Cheese*, 28–30, 41–51.

27. Ibid., 43.

28. Quoted ibid., 43, 101.

29. Quoted ibid., 102.

30. Ibid., 30.

31. Quoted ibid., 101.

32. Kaplan, *Divided by Faith*, 304–5. By 1621, two decades after Menocchio's death, the Venetians built the Fondaco dei Turchi on the banks of the Grand Canal as their official residence. The ornate building contained the capacity for the storage of goods and Islamic worship, based on the plan of an Islamic *funduq*, or merchant hostel, a structure common throughout the Middle East.

33. Ginzburg, *Cheese*, 110–12.

34. Ibid., 111. The Italian term for the torture device is *strappado*.

35. Ibid., 128.

36. Ibid., 18–19. Earl Morse Wilbur, *A History of Unitarianism: Socinianism and Its Antecedents*, 2 vols. (Cambridge, MA: Harvard University Press, 1945–52), 1:76–96.

37. Quoted in Adam S. Francisco, *Martin Luther and Islam: A Study in Sixteenth-Century Polemics and Apologetics* (Leiden: E. J. Brill, 2007), 46–47; Robert H. Schwoebel, "Coexistence, Conversion, and the Crusade against the Turks," *Studies in the Renaissance* 12 (1965): 175. Earlier instances of religious universalism that included Islam may be found in Robert H. Schwoebel, *The Shadow of the Crescent: The Renaissance Image of the Turks, 1453–1577* (Nieukoop: B. Degraaf, 1967), 219–20.

38. Wilbur, *History of Unitarianism*, 1:84–85.

39. Zagorin, *Toleration*, 97; Sebastian Castellio, *Concerning Heretics: Whether They Are to Be Persecuted and How They Are to Be Treated: A Collection of the Opinions of Learned Men Both Ancient and Modern*, trans. Roland H. Bainton (New York: Columbia University Press, 1935), 3, 217; Ginzburg, *Cheese*, 122.

40. Quoted in Daniel, *Islam and the West*, 187; John Tolan, *Saracens: Islam in the Medieval European Imagination* (New York: Columbia University Press, 2002), 135–69.

Important research on real Muslims in France and England during the premodern period continues, see Bernard Vincent and Jocelyne Dakhlia, eds., *Les Musulmans dans l'Histoire de l'Europe* (Paris: Albin Michel, 2011).

41. The date of Servetus's death is provided as October 27 in Zagorin, *Toleration*, 93. In contrast, the event occurred on October 23 according to Roland Bainton in Castellio, *Concerning Heretics*, 3. See also Roland Bainton, *Hunted Heretic: The Life and Death of Michael Servetus* (Boston: Beacon, 1960), 219.

42. Bainton, *Hunted Heretic*, 67; Zagorin, *Toleration*, 93–94.

43. Bainton, *Hunted Heretic*, 207.

44. Castellio, *Concerning Heretics*, 3.

45. Wilbur, *History of Unitarianism*, 1:62–63.

46. The number of Jews expelled is estimated between 150,000 and 400,000 by Henry Kamen, "The Mediterranean and the Expulsion of Spanish Jews in 1492," *Past and Present* 119 (May 1988): 30.

47. Bainton, *Hunted Heretic*, 5–16.

48. Ibid., 16; Wilbur, *History of Unitarianism*, 1:61.

49. Wilbur, *History of Unitarianism*, 1:52; Garcia, *Islam and the English Enlightenment*, 161, 278 n. 9.

50. Wilbur, *History of Unitarianism*, 1:71; Garcia, *Islam and the English Enlightenment*, 161.

51. Zagorin, *Toleration*, 99; Castellio, *Concerning Heretics*, 9–10.

52. Quoted in Roland Bainton, *The Travail of Religious Liberty* (New York: Harper, 1958), 120.

53. Castellio, *Concerning Heretics*, 126.

54. Ibid., 123.

55. Ibid., 132.

56. Ibid.

57. Ibid., 132–34.

58. Ibid., 133.

59. Tolan, *Saracens*, 214–74. Peter the Venerable had advocated this position since the twelfth century; see Schwoebel, "Coexistence," 174.

60. Castellio, *Concerning Heretics*, 150–51.

61. Lecler, *Toleration*, 1:161.

62. Perry and Schweitzer, *Antisemitic Myths*, 43, 47.

63. Castellio, *Concerning Heretics*, 71; Jan Slomp, "Calvin and the Turks," in *Christian-Muslim Encounters*, ed. Yvonne Yazbeck Haddad and Wadi Zaidan Haddad (Gainesville: University Press of Florida, 1995), 131.

64. Castellio, *Concerning Heretics*, 203.

65. Ibid. For discussions of "Saracen," see Daniel, *Islam and the West*, 14, 79; Tolan, *Saracens*, 105–34. The term existed as early as the ninth century in Middle English to mean nomadic Arab peoples. For the best discussions of the "obscure" etymology, see Katharine Scarfe Beckett, *Anglo-Saxon Perceptions of the Islamic World* (Cambridge: Cambridge University Press, 2003), 93–104. See also the multiple pre-sixteenth-century English usages of "Saracen," *Oxford English Dictionary*, 9:106.

66. Robert White, "Castellio against Calvin: The Turk in the Toleration Controversy of the Sixteenth Century," *Bibliothèque d'Humanisme et Renaissance* 46 (1984): 573–74.

67. Ibid., 573–86.

68. Ibid., 575.

69. Castellio, *Concerning Heretics*, 101.

70. Wilbur, *History of Unitarianism*, 1:37.

71. Ibid.; Castellio, *Concerning Heretics*, 93–94.

72. Castellio, *Concerning Heretics*, 94.

73. Zagorin, *Toleration*, 86.

74. Castellio, *Concerning Heretics,* 95.

75. Ibid., 97–98.

76. Schwoebel, "Coexistence," 180; Castellio, *Concerning Heretics,* 96; Franco Cardini, *Europe and Islam,* trans. Caroline Beamish (London: Blackwell, 1999), 147–49.

77. Steven Ozment, *Mysticism and Dissent: Religious Ideology and Social Protest in the Sixteenth Century* (New Haven: Yale University Press, 1973), 141.

78. Franck quoted in Castellio, *Concerning Heretics,* 96; in the Qur'an, see 2:256. Franck also observed, "At Constantinople there are Turks, there are Christians, and there are also Jews, three peoples widely differing from one another in religion. Nevertheless they live together in peace, which certainly they could not do if there were persecution."

79. The French scholar Jean Bodin (d. 1596) saw the burning of Servetus in Geneva; see Clarence Dana Rouillard, *The Turk in French History, Thought, and Literature (1520–1660)* (Paris: Boivin, 1941), 390–91; Marshall, *John Locke, Toleration and Early Enlightenment Culture,* 593.

80. This tendency among Protestants would continue into the seventeenth century; see Ahmad Gunny, "Protestant Reactions to Islam in Late Seventeenth-Century French Thought," *French Studies* 40 (April 1986): 131–34. Not only radical English Protestants in the seventeenth century embraced the Ottoman example of religious toleration. Catholics and Protestants applied this comparative tactic, beginning in the sixteenth century. For the English precedent, see Garcia, *Islam and the English Enlightenment,* 1–59.

81. Castellio, *Concerning Heretics,* 97.

82. Franck quoted ibid., 101–2.

83. Ibid., 97; Nabil Matar, *Islam in Britain, 1558–1685* (New York: Cambridge University Press, 1998), 137.

84. Castellio, *Concerning Heretics,* 3–4, 107–11.

85. Ginzburg, *Cheese,* 51, suggests this.

86. Castellio, *Concerning Heretics,* 113–17.

87. H. Wheeler Robinson, introduction to Thomas Helwys, *The Mistery of Iniquity* (London: Kingsgate Press, 1935), viii.

88. Ibid., viii–x.

89. Ibid., 69. As the "first in England to demand universal liberty," see Robinson's introduction, xiii; Marshall, *John Locke, Toleration and Early Enlightenment Culture,* 150.

90. Robinson, introduction to Helwys, *Mistery,* vii–viii, x.

91. Ibid., xiv.

92. Helwys, *Mistery,* 69.

93. Nabil Matar, *Turks, Moors, and Englishmen in the Age of Discovery* (New York: Columbia University Press, 1999), ix–42.

94. Cecil Roth, "England," in *Encyclopaedia Judaica,* ed. Michael Berenbaum and Fred Skolnik, 16 vols. (Detroit: Macmillan Reference USA, 2007), 6:412–13.

95. Robinson, introduction to Helwys, *Mistery,* xiv.

96. Ibid., ix.

97. Helwys, *Mistery,* 212.

98. Robinson, introduction to Helwys, *Mistery,* x.

99. Helwys, *Mistery,* 42.

100. Robinson, introduction to Helwys, *Mistery,* xiii; William R. Estep, *Revolution within the Revolution: The First Amendment in Historical Context, 1612–1789* (Grand Rapids, MI: William B. Eerdmans, 1990), 50–58.

101. L. H. Butterfield, "Elder John Leland, Jeffersonian Itinerant," *Proceedings of the American Antiquarian Society* 62 (October 1952): 164.

102. Smyth quoted ibid.

103. Helwys, *Mistery,* 69.

104. I take this definition from David Hackett Fischer, *Albion's Seed: Four British Folkways in America* (New York: Oxford University Press, 1991), 293.

105. Edwin S. Gaustad, *Roger Williams* (New York: Oxford University Press, 2005), 96.

106. Zagorin, *Toleration,* 198–99.

107. Gaustad, *Roger Williams,* 19–20.

108. Zagorin, *Toleration,* 198.

109. Gaustad, *Roger Williams,* 22.

110. Zagorin, *Toleration,* 199.

111. Roger Williams, *The Bloudy Tenent of Persecution,* ed. Samuel L. Caldwell, vol. 3 of *The Complete Writings of Roger Williams* (New York: Russell and Russell, 1963), 3:52; Zagorin, *Toleration,* 200. My thanks to Holly Snyder for first suggesting I investigate Roger Williams. For a thoughtful discussion of Williams's impact on liberty of conscience that includes his references to Muslims, see Martha Nussbaum, *Liberty of Conscience: In Defense of America's Tradition of Religious Equality* (New York: Basic Books, 2010), 34, 37, 50, 66. The idea that Williams included Islam as a potential American religion is mentioned by Akbar Ahmed, *Journey into America: The Challenge of Islam* (Washington, DC: Brookings Institution Press, 2010), 46–50.

112. Gaustad, *Roger Williams,* 107.

113. Roger Williams, *George Fox Digg'd out of His Burrowes,* ed. Rev. J. Lewis Diman, vol. 5 of *The Complete Writings of Roger Williams* (New York: Russell and Russell, 1963), 125.

114. Nussbaum, *Liberty of Conscience,* 37, 68.

115. Gaustad, *Roger Williams,* 95–96.

116. Ibid., 115; "soul liberty" discussed in William G. McLoughlin, *Soul Liberty: The Baptists' Struggle in New England, 1630–1833* (Hanover, NH: Brown University Press/University Press of New England, 1991), 19–20; definition of Williams quoted in Kamen, *Toleration,* 187; Zagorin, *Toleration,* 196–208.

117. Williams, *George Fox,* 5:125, 240; Thomas S. Kidd, " 'Is It Worse to Follow Mahomet Than the Devil?' Early American Uses of Islam," *Church History* 72, no. 4 (December 2003): 777–78; Thomas S. Kidd, *American Christians and Islam: Evangelical Culture and Muslims from the Colonial Period to the Age of Terrorism* (Princeton: Princeton University Press, 2009), 10–11.

118. Gaustad, *Roger Williams,* 66, 75.

119. Ibid., 100.

120. Ibid., 93–94; Williams, *Bloudy Tenent,* 3:3.

121. Williams, *Bloudy Tenent,* 3:3.

122. Ibid., 3:3–4.

123. Quoted in Naomi W. Cohen, *Jews in Christian America: The Pursuit of Religious Equality* (New York: Oxford University Press, 1992), 17. Another view of the usage of "Turkes" with pagans suggests that Muslims linked to Jews "were not on the same plane with Christianity"; see Maxwell H. Morris, "Roger Williams and the Jews," *American Jewish Archives* 3 (January 1951): 27.

124. Williams, *Bloudy Tenent,* 3:11.

125. Marshall, *John Locke, Toleration and Early Enlightenment Culture,* 327.

126. Williams, *Bloudy Tenent,* 3:142. The importance of Williams's views of Muslims as tolerated beings is ably made by Marshall, *John Locke, Toleration and Early Enlightenment Culture,* 327.

127. Kamen, *Toleration,* 181.

128. Gaustad, *Roger Williams,* 16–20.

129. John Cotton, "A Discourse about Civil Government," in *The Sacred Rights of Conscience: Selected Readings on Religious Liberty and Church-State Relations in the American Founding,* ed. Daniel L. Dreisbach and Mark David Hall (Indianapolis: Liberty Fund, 2009), 133.

130. Ibid., 145.

131. Williams, *Bloudy Tenent,* 3:43. The New Testament verses Williams referred

to were these: "Let them both grow together until the harvest: and in the time of the harvest I will say to the reapers, Gather ye together first the tares, and bind them in bundles to burn them: but gather the wheat into my barn" (Matthew 13:30), and "The field is the world; the good seed are the children of the kingdom; but the tares are the children of the wicked one" (Matthew 13:38), King James Bible.

132. Williams, *Bloudy Tenent*, 3:43; Zagorin, *Toleration*, 202.

133. Gaustad, *Roger Williams*, 100; quote on 102.

134. Williams, *Bloudy Tenent*, 3:10.

135. Lecler, *Toleration*, 2:467; Gaustad, *Roger Williams*, 52. The two disagree on whether 1639 or 1638 was the year in which Williams briefly joined the Baptist faith.

136. Gaustad, *Roger Williams*, 52–53.

137. James Hutson, *Church and State: The First Two Centuries* (New York: Cambridge University Press, 2008), 24; Gaustad, *Roger Williams*, 53, 107–8.

138. The status of Catholics in Williams's Rhode Island, however, is debated. For the idea of Catholics as the one exception to his otherwise universal support for religious freedom, see Hutson, *Church and State*, 24. In contrast, the idea that Williams's charter "made no exceptions . . . nor denied any civil privileges to Roman Catholics" is promoted by McLoughlin, *Soul Liberty*, 261; Nussbaum, *Liberty of Conscience*, 50, 66.

139. Gaustad, *Roger Williams*, 106–7.

140. Roger Williams, "To the Town of Providence," in *The Letters of Roger Williams*, ed. John Russell Bartlett, *The Complete Writings of Roger Williams* (New York: Russell and Russell, 1963), 6:278–79; Nussbaum, *Liberty of Conscience*, 50.

141. Ahmed, *Journey*, 46–50.

142. Jacob R. Marcus, *The Colonial American Jew*, 3 vols. (Detroit: Wayne State University Press, 1970), 1:314–15.

143. For the assumption that Williams did not include Muslims or Jews in office-holding, despite their "freedom of worship and equality before the courts," see Morris, "Roger Williams and the Jews," 27.

144. I follow Kaplan in his helpful discussion of the practical division of public and private worship and religious dissent in Holland; see Kaplan, *Divided by Faith*, 177–78.

145. Kamil, *Fortress of the Soul*, 869.

146. Quoted ibid.

147. Kaplan, *Divided by Faith*, 178, defines the word.

148. Kamil, *Fortress of the Soul*, 871.

149. Ibid., 875.

150. I have quoted Kamil's term "inclusiveness" in describing the Flushing Remonstrance; ibid.

151. "Flushing Remonstrance, 1657," in *The Sacred Rights of Conscience: Selected Readings on Religious Liberty and Church-State Relations in the American Founding*, ed. Daniel L. Dreisbach and Mark David Hall (Indianapolis: Liberty Fund, 2009), 108–9.

152. Ibid.

153. Ibid.

154. Kamil, *Fortress of the Soul*, 872; Martin Marty, *Pilgrims in Their Own Land* (New York: Penguin, 1984), 71.

155. Quoted in Gaustad, *Roger Williams*, 113.

156. Quoted ibid.

157. Quoted ibid., 114. Similar universal protections for religious freedom appeared in the Quaker William Penn's 1682 laws for the government of Pennsylvania, but Penn made no explicit mention of Muslims in his treatise on the rights of conscience; see Hutson, *Church and State*, 37; Matar, "Turbanned Nations," 77.

158. Gaustad, *Roger Williams*, 100.

159. See Perry Miller, *Roger Williams: His Contribution to the American Tradition* (Indianapolis: Bobbs-Merrill, 1953); Leroy Moore, "Religious Liberty: Roger Williams and the Revolutionary Era," *Church History* 34 (1965): 68.

160. Moore, "Religious Liberty," 68.

161. Gaustad, *Roger Williams*, 117; Moore, "Religious Liberty," 65–66; Martha Nussbaum, *Liberty of Conscience*, 66–69.

162. Gaustad asserts that neither Thomas Jefferson nor James Madison borrowed from Williams, but insists that Locke did. See Gaustad, *Roger Williams*, 117; Edwin S. Gaustad, *Sworn on the Altar of God: A Religious Biography of Thomas Jefferson* (Grand Rapids, MI: William B. Eerdmans, 1996), 72.

163. John Marshall, *John Locke: Resistance, Religion, and Responsibility* (New York: Cambridge University Press, 1994), 60–61. Hereafter cited as *John Locke*.

164. For the best comparison of the differences between Williams and Locke, see Nussbaum, *Liberty of Conscience*, 67–68.

165. Moore, "Religious Liberty," 66. For the Christian underpinnings of Locke's theory, see Jeremy Waldron, *God, Locke, and Equality: Christian Foundations of John Locke's Political Thought* (New York: Cambridge University Press, 2002), 12–20.

166. Marshall, *John Locke*, 367. This idea of a Christian duty is Marshall's idea.

167. I am indebted to the pathbreaking work on Locke and Islam by G. A. Russell, "Introduction: The Seventeenth Century: The Age of 'Arabick,'" 1–19, and "The Impact of *The Philosophus Autodidactus*: Pocockes, John Locke, and the Society of Friends," 236–53, both in *The "Arabick" Interest of the Natural Philosophers in Seventeenth-Century England*, ed. G. A. Russell (Leiden: E. J. Brill, 1994); Matar, "Turbanned Nations," 1–19, 67–77; G. J. Toomer, *Eastern Wisedome and Learning: The Study of Arabic in Seventeenth-Century England* (Oxford: Clarendon Press, 1996), 113 n. 36, 221, 265–68; Marshall, *John Locke, Toleration and Early Enlightenment Culture*, 388–95, 593–617.

168. Russell, "*Philosophus*," 237.

169. Ibid., 8.

170. Matar, *Islam in Britain*, 1–20, 21–49.

171. While Russell believes this to be the case ("*Philosophus*," 236–38), Toomer, *Eastern Wisedome*, 267 n. 258, disputes this, pointing out that Locke never took exams in Arabic, but instead focused on Latin and Hebrew at Westminster.

172. Russell, "*Philosophus*," 239; Toomer, *Eastern Wisedome*, 113 n. 36.

173. Marshall, *John Locke, Toleration and Early Enlightenment Culture*, 389–90.

174. Quoted in Russell, "*Philosophus*," 242.

175. Matar, *Islam in Britain*, 98–102.

176. Russell, "*Philosophus*," 225–26, 229–31. See Lenn Evan Goodman, trans., *Ibn Tufayl's Hayy Ibn Yaqzan: A Philosophical Tale* (New York: Twayne, 1972). In this process of intellectual and spiritual self-realization, the protagonist evolves into autodidactic omniscience, which explains the English for the Latin title "The Self-Taught Philosopher." For a study of how the text diffused throughout Europe and how it impacted Locke via Pococke, see Avner Ben-Zaken, *Reading Hayy Ibn-Yaqzan: A Cross-Cultural History of Autodidacticism* (Baltimore: Johns Hopkins University Press, 2011), 5, 9–10, 102–3, 119–24, 137–39, 161–70, 181.

177. Samar Attar, *The Vital Roots of the European Enlightenment: Ibn Tufayl's Influence on Modern Western Thought* (New York: Lexington Books, 2007), 49–60; Garcia, *Islam and the English Enlightenment*, 133–34.

178. Attar, *Vital Roots*, 19–31.

179. Cotton Mather, *The Christian Philosopher*, ed. Winton U. Solberg (Urbana: University of Illinois Press, 1994), 11–12.

180. Russell, "*Philosophus*," 224–65.

181. Ibid.; J. R. Milton, "Locke, John (1632–1704)," *Oxford Dictionary of National Biography*, 58 vols. (New York: Oxford University Press, 2004), 34:216–28.

182. Attar, *Vital Roots*, 49–50.

183. Marshall, *John Locke*, 6–7, 11, 14, 59–60.

184. John Locke, *Epistola de Tolerantia: A Letter on Toleration*, ed. Raymond Klibansky, trans. J. W. Gough (Oxford: Clarendon Press, 1968), 3–4. For the seventeenth-

century English translation, I also use John Locke, *A Letter Concerning Toleration (1689)*, ed. James H. Tully (Indianapolis: Hackett, 2010). I refer to the Latin version hereafter as Locke, *Epistola,* and the English as Locke, *Letter Concerning Toleration (1689)*; P. M. Holt, *A Seventeenth-Century Defender of Islam: Henry Stubbe (1632–1676) and His Book* (London: Dr. Williams's Trust, 1972), 11.

185. E. S. De Beer, ed., *The Correspondence of John Locke,* 2 vols. (Oxford: Clarendon Press, 1976), 1:109–12.

186. Tully, introduction to Locke, *Letter Concerning Toleration (1689),* 3–4.

187. De Beer, *Correspondence,* 1:111.

188. For the most in-depth study of Stubbe's impact in England, but without reference to Locke, see Garcia, *Islam and the English Enlightenment,* 30–59.

189. P. M. Holt, "The Treatment of Arab History by Prideaux, Ockley, and Sale," in *Historians of the Middle East,* ed. Bernard Lewis and P. M. Holt (London: Oxford University Press, 1962), 293–94; P. M. Holt, *Defender of Islam,* 19; Garcia, *Islam and the English Enlightenment,* 30–59.

190. Henry Stubbe, *An Account of the Rise and Progress of Mahometanism: with the Life of Mahomet and a Vindication of Him and His Religion from the Calumnies of the Christians,* ed. Hafiz Mahmud Khan Shairani (Lahore: Oxford and Cambridge Press, 1911; repr. 1975), 72.

191. Ibid., 2, 1.

192. Ibid., 74–75; Holt, *Defender of Islam,* 20.

193. Stubbe, *Mahometanism,* 89.

194. Ibid., 141–42.

195. Ibid., 145–46.

196. James R. Jacob, *Henry Stubbe, Radical Protestantism and the Early Enlightenment* (Cambridge: Cambridge University Press, 1983), 71–72; Garcia, *Islam and the English Enlightenment,* 1–59.

197. Stubbe, *Mahometanism,* 180.

198. Ibid., 181.

199. Ibid., 181–84.

200. László Kontler, "The Idea of Toleration and the Image of Islam in Early Enlightenment English Thought," in *Sous le signe des lumières: Articles rédigés à l'occasion du VIIe Congrès International de Lumières,* ed. Eva Balazs (Budapest: n.p., 1987), 6–26. Humberto Garcia rightly argues that Stubbe's references to "Islamic toleration" were used "as a beating stick against English toleration—the entitlement to freedom of conscience that in practice excluded many nonconformists for citizenship." See Garcia, *Islam and the English Enlightenment,* 5–6.

201. Stubbe, *Mahometanism,* 188.

202. Ibid., 71.

203. Marshall, *John Locke,* 6–7, 11, 14, 59–60.

204. Locke, *Epistola,* 81; Garcia, *Islam and the English Enlightenment,* 58–59; Matar, "Turbanned Nations," 71–72. Matar stresses not the Ottoman precedent but instead the importance of the English dissenter Edward Bagshaw's work on toleration.

205. Jacob, *Stubbe,* 147, 154, 161; Holt, *Defender of Islam,* 10.

206. See John Toland, *Nazarenus or Jewish, Gentile, and Mahometan Christianity* (London, 1718), 14–16; J. A. I. Champion, *The Pillars of Priestcraft Shaken: The Church of England and Its Enemies, 1660–1730* (Cambridge: Cambridge University Press, 1992), 126. For this connection between Deists, Unitarians, and Islam, see also Kidd, "Is It Worse to Follow Mahomet Than the Devil?," 785–86; Marshall, *John Locke, Toleration and Early Enlightenment Culture,* 391–92; Garcia, *Islam and the English Enlightenment,* 30–59.

207. Garcia, *Islam and the English Enlightenment,* 51. The first use of the term "Unitarian" in English print dates to 1672, according to Earl Morse Wilbur, *A History of*

Unitarianism in Transylvania, England, and America, 2 vols. (Cambridge, MA: Harvard University Press, 1952), 1:199.

208. Jacob, *Stubbe*, 155; David A. Pailin, *Attitudes to Other Religions: Comparative Religion in Seventeenth- and Eighteenth-Century Britain* (Manchester: Manchester University Press, 1984), 129–32.

209. Marshall, *John Locke, Toleration and Early Enlightenment Culture*, 393.

210. Holt, "Arab History," 292.

211. Champion, *Pillars*, 99–132. This "Islamophilia" was a limited English religious and political construction, which embraced toleration, following the impact of Stubbe and Toland, but had its most decided impact on English literature rather than actual political change regarding Muslims on either side of the Atlantic. See Srinivas Aravamudan, *Enlightenment Orientalism: Resisting the Rise of the Novel* (Chicago: University of Chicago Press, 2012), 3. These ideas are most fully explored as they move into the eighteenth-century by Garcia, *Islam and the English Enlightenment*, 1–59. For a revisionist view of early Islamic history as comprised of a collective of monotheist "believers" that included Jews and Christians as well as Muslims that Socinian/Unitarians might have hailed as their own, see Fred M. Donner, *Muhammad and the Believers: At the Origins of Islam* (Cambridge, MA: Belknap Press of Harvard University, 2010).

212. Jacob, *Stubbe*, 155; Champion, *Pillars*, 110–11; Marshall, *John Locke, Toleration and Early Enlightenment Culture*, 391–92.

213. Matar, "Turbanned Nations," 72.

214. Garcia, *Islam and the English Enlightenment*, 1–7.

215. A response to Prideaux titled *Mahomet No Impostor, or A Defence of Mahomet*, allegedly authored by a Muslim fictively named Abdullah Mahumed Omar, is found in Daniel, *Islam and the West*, 288; Robert J. Allison, *The Crescent Obscured: The United States and the Muslim World, 1776–1815* (Chicago: University of Chicago Press, 2000), 35–42.

216. Russell, "*Philosophus*," 258 n. 63.

217. Holt, *Defender of Islam*, 10. For a detailed account of the first Muslims to publish this treatise and its ramifications, see Garcia, *Islam and the English Enlightenment*, 225–31.

218. Garcia, *Islam and the English Enlightenment*, 30–59, 159–68, 243 n. 28.

219. Russell, "*Philosophus*," 258 n. 63.

220. Milton, "Locke," suggests that Locke was not directly involved with Shaftesbury's plan to foment rebellion or the assassination plot against the king, but the scholar James H. Tully disagrees; see Tully, introduction to Locke, *Letter Concerning Toleration (1689)*, 9–11.

221. Tully, introduction to Locke, *Letter Concerning Toleration (1689)*, 9–11.

222. Matar, "Turbanned Nations," 76.

223. Kamen, *Toleration*, 231.

224. J. W. Gough, introduction to Locke, *Epistola*, 4–7; Marshall, *John Locke*, 12, 14, 17–18, 20–21; Marshall, *John Locke, Toleration and Early Enlightenment Culture*, 597–98.

225. Matar, "Turbanned Nations," 68–69; Kamen, *Toleration*, 224.

226. See Robin R. Mundill, *England's Jewish Solution: Experiment and Expulsion, 1262–1290* (New York: Cambridge University Press, 1998); David S. Katz, *Philo-Semitism and the Readmission of the Jews to England, 1603–1665* (New York: Oxford University Press, 1982); David S. Katz, *The Jews in the History of England, 1485–1850* (New York: Oxford University Press, 1994).

227. Matar, "Turbanned Nations," 68–69. For an in-depth study of the presence of Christian converts to Islam in Britain as well as diplomatic and commercial relations with Islamic nations during this period, see Matar, *Islam in Britain*, 1–50, and also Nabil Matar, *Britain and Barbary, 1589–1689* (Gainesville: University Press of Florida, 2005).

228. Zagorin, *Toleration*, 248. Locke did not know that Samuel Richardson, a Baptist, had advanced the same argument about Muslims much earlier in 1646 in debate with Presbyterians; see Estep, *Revolution*, 67.

229. Matar, "Turbanned Nations," 68; John Locke, *Two Tracts on Government*, ed. and trans. Philip Abrams (Cambridge: Cambridge University Press, 1967), 127. Bagshaw may have been implicitly referring to a legal precedent promulgated under King Charles I (r. 1625–49) that warned that it "would be a sin in us to hurt their Persons," referring to "Turks and Infidels," meaning Muslims and, presumably, Jews; see William Salkeld, *Reports of Cases Adjudg'd in the Court of King's Bench* (London: E. Nutt and R. Gosling, 1717), 1:46.

230. For the best account of Locke's change of attitude about toleration, see Marshall, *John Locke*, 62–83; Zagorin, *Toleration*, 250.

231. Quoted in Matar, "Turbanned Nations," 69.

232. Marshall, *John Locke*, 62–89.

233. Zagorin, *Toleration*, 251–52; Marshall, *John Locke*, 62–89.

234. Zagorin, *Toleration*, 251–52, 255.

235. Locke, *A Letter Concerning Toleration (1689)*, x.

236. Zagorin, *Toleration*, 259. Locke met Philip von Limborch (d. 1712), a follower of Arminius (d. 1609), and member of a group known in Holland as the Remonstrants. They embraced the idea of universal grace, avoided the persecution of all others, and felt it their duty to follow their own consciences "and to leave others to the judgment of God." Russell, "Philosophus," 249. In Rotterdam, Locke lived for two years in the house of Benjamin Furly (d. 1714), an English Quaker, who had worked with Henry Stubbe.

237. Marshall, *John Locke*, 357.

238. Zagorin, *Toleration*, 245.

239. Quoted in Marshall, *John Locke, Toleration and Early Enlightenment Culture*, 593.

240. Matar, "Turbanned Nations," 71–73, 75.

241. Marilyn C. Baseler, *"Asylum for Mankind": America, 1607–1800* (Ithaca: Cornell University Press, 1998), 326.

242. Salkeld, *Reports of Cases*, 1:46.

243. Ibid.; Baseler, *"Asylum for Mankind,"* 242, 326, 330.

244. Matar, "Turbanned Nations," 75–76; Baseler, *"Asylum for Mankind,"* 330.

245. Locke, *Letter Concerning Toleration (1689)*, 50. For the difference between English citizens and denizens, see Baseler, *"Asylum for Mankind,"* 329–30.

246. Locke, *Epistola*, 135. That this mistaken precedent came from John Greaves's text on the Ottoman Empire, see Matar, "Turbanned Nations," 76. On the connection between the mufti and the pope, see Waldron, *God, Locke, and Equality*, 220–21; Marshall, *John Locke, Toleration and Early Enlightenment Culture*, 593–617, 597 (quote).

247. Locke, *Letter Concerning Toleration (1689)*, 50.

248. R. C. Repp, "Shaykh al-Islam," in *Encyclopaedia of Islam*, 11 vols. (Leiden: E. J. Brill, 1960), 9:399–402; Matar, "Turbanned Nations," 75–76.

249. This point was first made by Matar, "Turbanned Nations."

250. Richard L. Smith, *Ahmad al-Mansur, Islamic Visionary* (New York: Pearson Longman, 2006), 58–61, 138–40.

251. Khaled Abou El Fadl, "Islamic Law and Muslim Minorities: The Juristic Discourse on Muslim Minorities from the Second/Eighth to the Eleventh/Seventeenth Centuries," *Islamic Law and Society* 1 (1994): 141–87.

252. Nabil Matar, introduction to *In the Lands of the Christians: Arabic Travel Writing in the Seventeenth Century*, ed. and trans. Nabil Matar (New York: Routledge, 2003), xxv. The dispute between the Hanafi, which would become the dominant Ottoman Sunni school of law, and the Maliki or North African precedents in the premodern period are noteworthy; see Abou El Fadl, "Islamic Law," 147, 149.

253. Abou El Fadl, "Islamic Law," 152. On legal precedents for Muslim concepts of

"religious freedom" in non-Muslim lands, see Andrew F. March, *Islam and Liberal Citizenship: The Search for an Overlapping Consensus* (New York: Oxford University Press, 2009), 165–79.

254. Abou El Fadl, "Islamic Law," 171–73.

255. Ibid., 175; March, *Islam and Liberal Citizenship*, 183–89, 261–63.

256. Quoted in Abou El Fadl, "Islamic Law," 175.

257. Locke, *Letter Concerning Toleration (1689)*, 54.

258. Waldron, *God, Locke, and Equality*, 220–21.

259. Waldron makes this point for Muslims and Catholics, ibid., 220–22.

260. Tully, "Note on the Text," in *Letter Concerning Toleration (1689)*, 19. Locke's Latin original had listed Christian groups found in Holland: "Remonstrants, Antiremonstrants, Lutherans, Anabaptists, or Socinians."

261. Marshall, *John Locke*, 369–70.

262. Locke, *Letter Concerning Toleration (1689)*, 54. This is a facsimile of the first edition of the anonymous publication of the Latin *Epistola de Tolerantia* in English by William Popple.

263. John Dunn, "The Claim to Freedom of Conscience: Freedom of Speech, Freedom of Thought, Freedom of Worship?" in *From Persecution to Toleration: The Glorious Revolution and Religion in England*, ed. Ole Peter Grell, Jonathan I. Israel, and Nicholas Tyacke (Oxford: Clarendon Press, 1991), 180.

264. Locke, *Letter Concerning Toleration (1689)*, 54. Locke, *Epistola*, 144–45.

265. The key phrase is "ne ethicus quidem vel Mahumedanus vel Judaeus religionis causa a repulica arcendus": see Locke, *Epistola*, 144 (Latin), 145 (English). I would like to thank Elizabeth Dickenson for confirming for me that the verb *arcendus* means "to exclude," but that words equivalent to *ius civile*, or "civil rights," are nowhere mentioned in Locke's original Latin.

266. Locke, *Letter Concerning Toleration (1689)*, 54. Locke, *Epistola*, 144–45. Locke approved Popple's English translation, which "is not a literal translation"; see J. W. Gough, "William Popple's Translation," in Locke, *Epistola*, 43–50.

267. Quoted in Matar, "Turbanned Nations," 77.

268. Locke, *Letter Concerning Toleration (1689)*, 54.

269. Jack Turner, "John Locke, Christian Mission, and Colonial America," *Modern Intellectual History* 8 (2011): 291–92.

270. Matar, *Islam in Britain*, 21–49.

271. Locke, *Letter Concerning Toleration (1689)*, 56. If checked against the Latin original, Gough's English translation from the Latin is faithful to the original word *Maumetanus*, or "Mahometan," rather than the English translation's "Turk," and, more important, Locke's key use of *Islamismum*, or "Islam," rather than the English translation's "Mahumetanism"; see Locke, *Epistola*, 148–49. Locke also uses *Alcoranum* for Qur'an in signifying the holy scripture in which Muslims believe; see Locke, *Epistola*.

272. Matar, "Turbanned Nations," 74; Marshall, *John Locke, Toleration and Early Enlightenment Culture*, 614–15.

273. Marshall, *John Locke*, 370–76.

274. J. W. Gough, introduction to Locke, *Epistola*, 32.

275. John Locke, *A Second Letter Concerning Toleration: To the Author of the Argument of the Letter concerning Toleration, briefly considered and answered*, in *Four Letters on Toleration by John Locke* (London: Ward, Lock and Tyler, 1876), 40.

276. Ibid.

277. Locke, *A Third Letter Concerning Toleration*, in *Four Letters on Toleration by John Locke*, 154.

278. Ibid., 157.

279. Ibid., 198.

280. Ibid., 203. Locke's "sociological relativism" is referred to by Matar, "Turbanned Nations," 73.

281. Matar, "Turbanned Nations," 74; Marshall, *John Locke, Toleration and Early Enlightenment Culture,* 615.

282. Locke, *A Third Letter Concerning Toleration,* 203.

283. Marshall, *John Locke, Toleration and Early Enlightenment Culture,* 595, 617.

284. Locke, *A Third Letter Concerning Toleration,* 204.

285. Locke, *A Fourth Letter Concerning Toleration,* in *Four Letters on Toleration by John Locke,* 387.

286. Ibid., 389.

287. Garcia, *Islam and the English Enlightenment,* 58–59.

288. Matar, "Turbanned Nations," 74.

289. Champion, *Pillars,* 111. Richard H. Popkin, "The Deist Challenge," in *From Persecution to Toleration,* ed. Grell, Israel, and Tyacke, 209.

290. Marshall, *John Locke,* 320, 415, 419.

291. Ibid., 413–15.

292. Ibid., 460.

293. For accounts of this controversy, see ibid., 441–51; Marshall, *John Locke, Toleration and Early Enlightenment Culture,* 391–95.

294. Quoted in Champion, *Pillars,* 111; Marshall, *John Locke, Toleration and Early Enlightenment Culture,* 391.

295. Quoted in Champion, *Pillars,* 112; Marshall, *John Locke, Toleration and Early Enlightenment Culture,* 391.

296. Matar, "Turbanned Nations," 69; Ziad Elmarsafy, *The Enlightenment Qur'an: The Politics of Translation and the Construction of Islam* (Oxford: Oneworld Press, 2009), 8–9.

3. WHAT JEFFERSON LEARNED—AND DIDN'T— FROM HIS QUR'AN: HIS NEGATIVE VIEWS OF ISLAM, AND THEIR POLITICAL USES, CONTRASTED WITH HIS SUPPORT FOR MUSLIM CIVIL RIGHTS, 1765–86

1. Paul P. Hoffman, ed., *Virginia Gazette Daybooks, 1750–1752 and 1764–1766,* (Charlottesville: University of Virginia Library Microfilm Publications, 1967), Segment 2, folio 202. The text is described as "Sali's [*sic*] Koran" that was "interspersed among his purchases of law books in 1764 and 1765" by Frank L. Dewey, *Thomas Jefferson, Lawyer* (Charlottesville: University Press of Virginia, 1986), 14. See also James Gilreath and Douglas L. Wilson, eds., *Thomas Jefferson's Library: A Catalog with the Entries in His Own Order* (Washington, DC: Library of Congress, 1989), 58; Kevin J. Hayes, "How Thomas Jefferson Read the Qur'an," *Early American Literature* 39, no. 2 (2004): 247; Kevin J. Hayes, *The Road to Monticello: The Life and Mind of Thomas Jefferson* (New York: Oxford University Press, 2008), 9, 130, 201, 258–59, 316; E. Millicent Sowerby, ed., *Catalogue of the Library of Thomas Jefferson,* 5 vols. (Washington, DC: Library of Congress, 1952–53) 2:90, catalog #1457.

2. The original *Gazette* entry has after his name the word "Note," which appears but indicates no further information.

3. George Sale, trans., *The Koran, commonly called the Alcoran of Mohammed, Translated into English from the Original Arabic; with Explanatory Notes, taken from the Most Approved Commentators, to which is prefixed a Preliminary Discourse,* 2 vols. (London: L. Hawes, W. Clarke, R. Collins, and T. Wilcox, 1764), Rare Books and Special Collections Division, Library of Congress. I will refer to Jefferson's first volume of the Qur'an through xvi as Sale, "To the Reader," or "Preliminary Discourse," or "To the Right Honourable John Lord Carteret (Dedication)," *Koran (1764).* All other references to "To the Reader" or "Preliminary Discourse" refer to the 1734 first-edition facsimile of a Harvard manuscript in one volume, George Sale, trans., *The Koran* (New York: Garland, 1984), cited hereafter as Sale, "To the Reader," or "Preliminary Discourse,"

Koran (1734). There are no substantial differences between the two editions, except that Jefferson's version is in two volumes rather than the initial one.

4. Arnoud Vrolijk, "Sale, George (b. in or after 1696–d. 1736)," in *Oxford Dictionary of National Biography,* 58 vols. (New York: Oxford University Press, 2004), 48:685–87. Vrolijk asserts that 1746 was the second edition in opposition to 1764, as stated by Sebastian R. Prange, "Thomas Jefferson's Qur'an," *Saudi Aramco World* 62, no. 4 (July/August 2011): 5. Four editions are mentioned, without dates, by Hartmut Bobzin, "Translations of the Qur'an," in *Encyclopaedia of the Qur'an,* ed. Jane D. McAuliffe, 6 vols. (Leiden: E. J. Brill, 2006), 5:348.

5. My thanks for this important reference belong to two University of Texas at Austin graduate students: Sharon Silzell, whose own research interest in the Qur'an alerted me to the importance of this reference, which she heard about from her graduate colleague Ben Breen. He located the citation while researching for Professors James Sidbury of Rice University and Cassandra Pybus of the University of Sydney. I am grateful to the latter two historians for allowing me to cite this document, headed "Property Taken from Dr. James Bryden by the British Troops, '81," Library of Virginia, among a box of uncataloged documents referred to as "the British Depredations" of Goochland County, Virginia, 1782, call number BC 114 7038.

6. Thomas Jefferson, "Letter to John Page," February 21, 1770, in *The Papers of Thomas Jefferson,* ed. Julian P. Boyd et al., 40 vols. (Princeton: Princeton University Press, 1950–), 1:548. Hereafter cited as *Papers of Thomas Jefferson*.

7. Dewey, *Thomas Jefferson,* 154 n. 25.

8. *Papers of Thomas Jefferson,* 1:35.

9. Dewey, *Thomas Jefferson,* 154 n. 2; *Papers of Thomas Jefferson,* 1:35.

10. Although Jefferson may have lost between three hundred and five hundred volumes, this letter to Page may have been "an exaggeration," according to Hayes, *Road to Monticello,* 2–3, 8; quote on 2–3.

11. Hoffman, *Virginia Gazette Daybooks,* Segment 2, folios 7, 11, 12, 13, 28, 159, 175.

12. Prange, "Thomas Jefferson's Qur'an," 4. Jefferson's study of religion and law are paramount in the explanation for his interest in the Qur'an; see Hayes, "How Thomas Jefferson Read the Qur'an," 247, 252; Hayes, *Road to Monticello,* 9.

13. An emphasis on Jefferson's interest in Islamic law is offered by Azizah Y. al-Hibri, "Islamic and American Constitutional Law: Borrowing Possibilities or a History of Borrowing?" *University of Pennsylvania Journal of Constitutional Law* 1, no. 3 (1999): 499–500.

14. Jefferson initialed volume 1, page 113, of the Qur'an, Rare Books and Special Collections Division, Library of Congress, with a "T" and "I" rather than a "T" and "J." On the commonality of Jefferson's use of his initials in his books, see Hayes, *Road to Monticello,* 6–8.

15. The first person to assert that "most likely Jefferson owned two copies of the Qur'an" because of the Shadwell fire was al-Hibri, "Islamic and American Constitutional Law," 498 n. 30.

16. Hayes, "How Thomas Jefferson Read the Qur'an," 251, 257–58.

17. Edwin S. Gaustad, *Sworn on the Altar of God: A Religious Biography of Thomas Jefferson* (Grand Rapids, MI: William B. Eerdmans, 1996), 18–19. I would like to commend the generosity of the late Shearer Davis (Dave) Bowman, a historian and colleague who recommended this work when he kindly shared his brief overview of Jefferson's views of Christianity with me.

18. Sale, "Preliminary Discourse," *Koran (1764),* 1:A; Hayes, "How Thomas Jefferson Read the Qur'an," 247–48, 251–52; Hayes, *Road to Monticello,* 9.

19. Ziad Elmarsafy, *The Enlightenment Qur'an: The Politics of Translation and the Construction of Islam* (Oxford: Oneworld Press, 2009), 1–2. For a more in-depth assessment of medieval translations of the Qur'an, see Thomas E. Burman, *Reading the Qur'an in Latin Christendom, 1140–1560* (Philadelphia: University of Pennsylvania Press, 2007).

20. For the best account of translation as a "political act," see Elmarsafy, *Enlightenment Qur'an,* ix–xii, 1–80; Bobzin, "Translations of the Qur'an," 5:340, 344–49.

21. Elmarsafy, *Enlightenment Qur'an,* 1–2; Bobzin, "Translations of the Qur'an," 5:344–45; Norman Daniel, *Islam and the West: The Making of an Image* (Edinburgh: Edinburgh University Press, 1966), 19, 22, 24–25, 37, 75. Sale's translation is described "as best expressing in English the meaning traditionally understood in Islam" by Daniel, *Islam and the West,* 14.

22. Elmarsafy, *Enlightenment Qur'an,* 1.

23. Ibid., 22 (quote).

24. Ibid.

25. Thomas S. Kidd, " 'Is It Worse to Follow Mahomet Than the Devil?' Early American Uses of Islam," *Church History* 72, no. 4 (December 2003): 767.

26. Sale, "To the Reader," *Koran (1764),* 1:vii.

27. Ibid.

28. Bobzin, "Translations of the Qur'an," 5:345; Elmarsafy, *Enlightenment Qur'an,* 10–14, 37–63.

29. Elmarsafy, *Enlightenment Qur'an,* 74–75; Sale, "To the Reader," *Koran (1764),* 1:vii.

30. Elmarsafy, *Enlightenment Qur'an,* 8–9; Bobzin, "Translations of the Qur'an," 5:346–47.

31. Nabil Matar, *Islam in Britain, 1558–1685* (New York: Cambridge University Press, 1998), 8, 76–82; Bobzin "Translations of the Qur'an," 5:347; Elmarsafy, *Enlightenment Qur'an,* 8.

32. Quoted in Matar, *Islam in Britain,* 79.

33. Elmarsafy, *Enlightenment Qur'an,* 9. The translation by Alexander Ross is considered by Nabil Matar, "Alexander Ross and the First English Translation of the Qur'an," *Muslim World* 88 (January 1998): 81–92. See also Matar, *Islam in Britain,* 76, 81.

34. Hayes, "How Thomas Jefferson Read the Qur'an," 251; Elmarsafy, *Enlightenment Qur'an,* 22–23.

35. Sale, "To the Reader," *Koran (1764),* vi.

36. Sale, "Preliminary Discourse," *Koran (1734),* 46. This observation appears in a marginal comment about the inhabitants of Medina.

37. Anthony Grafton, *The Footnote: A Curious History* (Cambridge, MA: Harvard University Press, 1997), 191; Elmarsafy, *Enlightenment Qur'an,* 28.

38. Sale, "To the Reader," *Koran (1764),* vii; Matar, *Islam in Britain,* 82; P. M. Holt, "The Background to Arabic Studies in Seventeenth-Century England," in *Historians of the Middle East,* ed. Bernard Lewis and P. M. Holt (London: Oxford University Press, 1962), 21–25, 27; G. A. Russell, "The Impact of *The Philosophus Autodidactus*: Pocockes, John Locke, and the Society of Friends," in *The "Arabick" Interest of the Natural Philosophers in Seventeenth-Century England,* ed. G. A. Russell (Leiden: E. J. Brill, 1994), 226–27, 232, 239–46; Samar Attar, *The Vital Roots of European Enlightenment: Ibn Tufayl's Influence on Modern Western Thought* (New York: Lexington Books, 2007), 1, 7.

39. Elmarsafy, *Enlightenment Qur'an,* 35–36; Bobzin, "Translations of the Qur'an," 5:348.

40. Bobzin, "Translations of the Qur'an," 5:348; Hayes, "How Thomas Jefferson Read the Qur'an," 257–59.

41. Voltaire, *Essai sur les moeurs et l'esprit des nations et sur les principaux faits de l'histoire depuis Charlemagne jusqu'à Louis XIII,* 2 vols. (Paris: Editions Garnier Frères, 1963), 1:255.

42. Elmarsafy, *Enlightenment Qur'an,* 22–23.

43. Sale, "To the Reader," *Koran (1764),* 1:viii.

44. Sale, *Koran (1734),* 31 note a.

45. Sale, "To the Reader," *Koran (1764),* 1:viii.

46. Ibid., 1:ix.

47. Ibid. Claims that Sale's translation was "pro-Unitarian," are made by J. A. I. Champion, *The Pillars of Priestcraft Shaken: The Church of England and Its Enemies, 1660–1730* (Cambridge: Cambridge University Press, 1992), 105 n. 16. This position is also endorsed by Elmarsafy, *Enlightenment Qur'an*, 18, 21, 25–28, 30. However, Sale would contradict this position in his own words to the reader.

48. Sale, "To the Reader," *Koran (1764)*, 1:vii–viii; Elmarsafy, *Enlightenment Qur'an*, 18, 21, 25–28, 30.

49. Sale, "To the Reader," *Koran (1764)*, 1:vii.

50. Elmarsafy, *Enlightenment Qur'an*, 24–35.

51. Sale, "To the Reader," *Koran (1734)*, v.

52. Elmarsafy, *Enlightenment Qur'an*, 24–26; Humberto Garcia, *Islam and the English Enlightenment, 1670–1840* (Baltimore: Johns Hopkins University Press, 2012), 106–8, 136, 149–50.

53. Sale, "To the Right Honourable John Lord Carteret (Dedication)," *Koran (1764)*, 1:A3; Elmarsafy, *Enlightenment Qur'an*, 30–31; Garcia, *Islam and the English Enlightenment*, 106–7.

54. Champion, *Pillars*, 120–23, 186, 188–90; Elmarsafy, *Enlightenment Qur'an*, 30. Numa Pompilius (715–673 BCE) had also figured centrally in the works of seventeenth-century English authors, who argued that Muhammad, like Numa, had introduced a religion that promoted civic virtues.

55. Elmarsafy, *Enlightenment Qur'an*, 24–25; Robert J. Allison, *The Crescent Obscured: The United States and the Muslim World, 1776–1815* (Chicago: University of Chicago Press, 2000), 27–43. Regarding Prideaux's work, see Sale, "To the Reader," *Koran (1734)*, iii. For disputes with Prideaux about the birth order of the Prophet's father and the story of the first mosque in Medina, see Sale, "Preliminary Discourse," *Koran (1734)*, 38, 51, respectively.

56. Sale, "Preliminary Discourse," *Koran (1734)*, 64.

57. Sale, "To the Right Honourable John Lord Carteret (Dedication)," *Koran (1764)*, 1:A3; al-Hibri, "Islamic and American Constitutional Law," 499–500; Hayes, "How Thomas Jefferson Read the Qur'an," 255.

58. The presumption that Sale read Stubbe may be found in Elmarsafy, *Enlightenment Qur'an*, 25–27. This premise is also supported by Garcia, *Islam and the English Enlightenment*, 106. But neither author can prove this definitively.

59. Sale, "To the Reader," *Koran (1764)*, 1:ix.

60. Ibid., 1:ix–x; Champion, *Pillars*, 101.

61. Sale, "To the Reader," *Koran (1764)*, 1:x.

62. Sale, "Preliminary Discourse," *Koran (1734)*, 41.

63. Garcia, *Islam and the English Enlightenment*, 106.

64. Sale, "To the Reader," *Koran (1764)*, 1:vii.

65. Sale, "Preliminary Discourse," *Koran (1734)*, 142.

66. Ibid.

67. Ibid., 143.

68. Ibid., 63; Elmarsafy, *Enlightenment Qur'an*, 64–80.

69. Elmarsafy, *Enlightenment Qur'an*, 21, 23–24; Champion, *Pillars*, 120–32.

70. The Qur'an explicitly notes twenty-four prophets who preceded Muhammad, with references that suggest there may have been others who remain unnamed.

71. Sale, "Preliminary Discourse," *Koran (1734)*, 76.

72. Ibid., 33–34; Elmarsafy, *Enlightenment Qur'an*, 34.

73. Sale, "Preliminary Discourse," *Koran (1734)*, 35.

74. Ibid., 35, 71.

75. This Qur'anic verse begins with the injunction to People of the Book (Jews and Christians) to reject the divinity of Jesus and the Trinity and to embrace the divine unity of God. The pivotal sentence in this verse: "So believe in Allah and His messengers, and say not 'Three'—Cease! (it is) better for you! Allah is only One God. Far

is it removed from His transcendent majesty that He should have a son. His is all that is in the heavens and all that is in the earth. And Allah is sufficient as Defender." See Muhammad M. Pickthall, trans., *The Meaning of the Glorious Qur'an: Text and Explanatory Translation* (New York: Muslim World League, 1977), 98. See also Neal Robinson, *Christ in Islam and Christianity* (Albany: State University of New York Press, 1991), 26–30.

76. Robinson, *Christ in Islam,* 5–7.

77. The translator's erudition regarding the four "perfect" women in Islam may be found in Sale, "Preliminary Discourse," *Koran (1734)*, 102, 251, chapter 66, 458 note d.

78. Ibid., 102.

79. Sale, *Koran (1734),* 458. The original is found in Abu Ja'far Muhammad ibn Jarir al-Tabari, *Jami' al-bayan 'an ta'wil ay al-Qur'an,* ed. M. Shakir and A. Shakir, 16 vols. (Cairo: Dar al-Ma'arif, 1955–69), 6:397–98. For a discussion of the importance of these women in early Islamic history, see D. A. Spellberg, *Politics, Gender, and the Islamic Past: The Legacy of 'A'isha bint Abi Bakr* (New York: Columbia University Press, 1994), 167–70.

80. Sale, "Preliminary Discourse," *Koran (1734)*, 71.

81. Ibid., 114–22.

82. Ibid., 122–24, 135, 139–40.

83. Matar, *Islam in Britain,* 110–15. See also Ralph S. Hattox, *Coffee and Coffee Houses: The Origins of a Social Beverage in the Medieval Near East* (Seattle: University of Washington Press, 1985).

84. Sale, "Preliminary Discourse," *Koran (1734)*, A2.

85. Ibid., 152–54.

86. Ibid., 156.

87. Ibid., 132–38.

88. Ibid., 178; Elmarsafy, *Enlightenment Qur'an,* 31.

89. Hayes, "How Thomas Jefferson Read the Qur'an," 248; al-Hibri, "Islamic and Constitutional Law," 498, 501.

90. Sale, "To the Right Honourable John Lord Carteret (Dedication)," *Koran (1764)*, 1:A4.

91. Thomas Jefferson, *Notes on Virginia,* in *The Life and Selected Writings of Thomas Jefferson,* ed. Adrienne Koch and William Peden (New York: Modern Library, 1998), 246.

92. Jefferson actually compiled two separate collections of extracts from the New Testament, the first in 1804, the second in 1819–20. See Thomas Jefferson, *The Jefferson Bible: The Life and Morals of Jesus of Nazareth* (Boston: Beacon, 1989).

93. Peter K. Conkin, "The Religious Pilgrimage of Thomas Jefferson," in *Jeffersonian Legacies,* ed. Peter Onuf (Charlottesville: University Press of Virginia, 1993), 30.

94. Vrolijk, "Sale, George," 48:685–87.

95. Edward Gibbon, *The History of the Decline and Fall of the Roman Empire,* ed. J. B. Bury (London: Methuen, 1911; rprt. 1974), 5:356 n. 68; Vrolijk, "Sale, George," 48:685–87.

96. Quoted in G. Thomas Tanselle, *Royall Tyler* (Cambridge, MA: Harvard University Press, 1967), 268 n. 29.

97. Thomas Jefferson, *Jefferson's Literary Commonplace Book,* ed. Douglas Wilson (Princeton: Princeton University Press, 1989), 214; Hayes, "How Thomas Jefferson Read the Qur'an," 250.

98. Thomas Jefferson, *The Commonplace Book of Thomas Jefferson: A Repertory of His Ideas on Government,* ed. Gilbert Chinard (Baltimore: Johns Hopkins University Press, 1926), 76.

99. William Salkeld, *Reports of Cases Adjudg'd in the Court of King's Bench* (London: E. Nutt and R. Gosling, 1717), 1:46.

100. Ibid.

101. Jefferson, *Jefferson's Literary Commonplace Book,* 155–56.

102. Ibid., 156; Gaustad, *Sworn on the Altar of God,* 22–23.

103. Quoted in Wilson, introduction to *Jefferson's Literary Commonplace Book,* 156 n. 5; H. T. Dickinson, *Bolingbroke* (London: Constable, 1970), 298.

104. Wilson, introduction to *Jefferson's Literary Commonplace Book,* 156.

105. Ibid., 42–43.

106. Ibid., 45–46.

107. Jefferson, *Notes on Virginia* in *Life and Selected Writings,* 255.

108. Jefferson, *Jefferson's Literary Commonplace Book,* 25.

109. Edward Dumbauld, *Thomas Jefferson and the Law* (Norman: University of Oklahoma Press, 1978), 4–5.

110. Dewey, *Thomas Jefferson,* 59.

111. Ibid., 63.

112. Ibid., 65–66; Hayes, "How Thomas Jefferson Read the Qur'an," 247–48.

113. Dewey, *Thomas Jefferson,* 57.

114. Ibid., 70–72.

115. Ibid., 70; Hayes, "How Thomas Jefferson Read the Qur'an," 247–48, 252.

116. Von Pufendorf's legal reference is borne out for its inaccuracy in *Redhouse Yeni Türkçe-Ingilizce Sözlük/New Redhouse Turkish-English Dictionary* (Istanbul: Redhouse Press, 1974), 573.

117. I am grateful to Leslie Peirce, an Ottoman expert on gender and the law, for setting me straight on the nuances of the term *kabin*'s application in the Ottoman Empire. E-mail communication, August 11, 2011. Without her intervention, I would have continued to assume that Von Pufendorf was completely rather than only partly wrong in his definition.

118. W. Heffening, "Mut'a," *Encyclopaedia of Islam,* 11 vols. (Leiden: E. J. Brill, 1960), 757–59; Noel Coulson, *A History of Islamic Law* (Edinburgh: University Press, 1964), 31–32.

119. *Redhouse Yeni Türkçe-Ingilizce Sözlük,* 573.

120. S. A. Skilliter, "Khurrem," *Encyclopaedia of Islam,* 5:66–67. See also Leslie P. Peirce, *The Imperial Harem: Women and Sovereignty in the Ottoman Empire* (New York: Oxford University Press, 1993), 58–65, especially 59 n. 3.

121. Sale, "Preliminary Discourse," *Koran (1734),* 134.

122. Jefferson, *Commonplace Book,* 10.

123. Voltaire, *Essai,* 1:255–76.

124. The French, as recorded by Jefferson and Voltaire, is included for interested readers in the notes below.

125. Voltaire, *Essai,* 1:255–61.

126. Ibid., 1:255. Voltaire's note on Sale was signaled with an asterisk.

127. Jefferson took note: "Whilst Omar, the second of the successors of Mohamed was extending his conquests over Syria, Phoenicia, Palestine, etc., his lieutenants s'avançaient en Perse. . . . Alors tomba cette ancienne religion des mages." See Jefferson, *Commonplace Book,* 334.

128. Jefferson's notes on Voltaire's view of Zoroastrians continue: "Ils ne purent abandonner une religion consacrée par tant de siècles.—La plupart se retirèrent aux extrémités de la Perse, et de l'Inde . . ." Jefferson noted Voltaire's comparison of Zoroastrians to Jews: "mais ignorans, méprisés, et, à leur pauvreté près, semblables aux Juifs si longtems [*sic*] dispersés sans s'allier aux autres nations." Ibid., 334–35.

129. "Tandis qu'un lieutenant d'Omar subjugue la Perse, un autre enlève l'Egypte entière aux Romains, et une grande partie de la Lybie. C'est dans cette conquête qu'est brûlée la fameuse bibliothèque d'Alexandrie, monument des connoissances et des erreurs des hommes, commencée par Ptolémée." Ibid., 335.

130. The myth of the Islamic destruction of the ancient library at Alexandria persists in the work of the classicist Luciano Canfora, whose *The Vanished Library* (London: Hutchinson Radius, 1989) attempts to refute several sound arguments made by the

classicist and Arabist Alfred Joshua Butler in *The Arab Conquest of Egypt and the Last Thirty Years of the Roman Dominion*, ed. P. M. Fraser (Oxford: Clarendon Press, 1978), 407–26. My thanks to Richard Bulliet for this reference. The best, final refutation of the myth of the Muslim destruction of the library may be found in the analysis of both the classical and Arabic sources by Mostafa El-Abbadi, *Life and Fate of the Ancient Library of Alexandria* (Paris: UNESCO, 1990), 167–79. El-Abbadi explains that the problematic five-century-long silence of Arabic sources about Umar's command to destroy the Alexandria library may actually reflect the era of the Crusades, during which Christian plunderers sought out Islamic libraries in the Middle East to take back to Europe. During this period, the Sunni warrior Salah al-Din (Saladin), in taking control of Egypt from the Shi'i Fatimid dynasty, seized their famed library in Cairo and sold their books. Saladin also used books to pay his followers, as he did in dismantling a million books in a Syrian library. Saladin's treatment of these great libraries, according to El-Abbadi, created within the Islamic world "the widespread feeling of resentment and discontent at the loss of such a priceless legacy of learning"; see El-Abbadi, *Life and Fate*, 179. El-Abbadi concludes that the reason the anecdote about Umar's destruction of the Alexandrian library in the seventh century emerged only in the twelfth century in Arabic accounts is explained by the author Ibn al-Qifti's debt to his employer, Saladin. He argues that this was his attempt to ameliorate Saladin's real destruction of libraries by comparison to Umar's invented, earlier conflagration. Much about the details of the anecdote in the Arabic versions extant seems absurd.

131. Butler, *Arab Conquest*, 401–2.

132. Jefferson recorded from Voltaire the falsehood that Muslims wanted no science. He copied, "Alors les Sarrazins ne vouloient de science que l'Alcoran; mais ils faisaient déjà à voir que leur génie pouvait s'étendre à tout." Jefferson, *Commonplace Book*, 335.

133. Voltaire admits more Islamic precedents in medicine and algebra; see Voltaire, *Essai*, 1:268. For more on Western borrowing, see Richard W. Bulliet, *The Case for Islamo-Christian Civilization* (New York: Columbia University Press, 2004), 31. On the diffusion of new Islamic hybrids to Europe in the medieval era, see Andrew M. Watson, *Agricultural Innovation in the Early Islamic World: The Diffusion of Crops and Farming Techniques, 700–1100* (Cambridge: Cambridge University Press, 1983), 42–51 (citrus); 20–24 (sugar); 24–31 (cotton); 15–20 (rice).

134. Voltaire says, "La chimie et la médecine étaient cultivées par les Arabes. La chimie, perfectionée aujourd'hui par nous, ne nous fut connue que par eux." Here he admits Islamic scientific advances, but these were not recorded by Jefferson. See Voltaire, *Essai*, 1:267–68.

135. "Letter to Rev. Madison," Paris, July 19, 1788, in Thomas Jefferson, *Thomas Jefferson: Writings*, ed. Merrill D. Peterson (New York: Library of America, 1984), 926.

136. Jefferson, *Commonplace Book*, 341.

137. "Letter to John Page," August 20, 1785, in *Papers of Thomas Jefferson*, 8:418.

138. Jefferson, *Commonplace Book*, 335; Voltaire, *Essai*, 1:263.

139. For an explanation of the slow stages of conversion to Islam in the Middle East, see Richard W. Bulliet, *Conversion to Islam in the Medieval Period: An Essay in Quantitative History* (Cambridge, MA: Harvard University Press, 1979).

140. *Papers of Thomas Jefferson*, 1:530, 532, 535–36.

141. Gaustad, *Sworn on the Altar of God*, 13–16.

142. *Papers of Thomas Jefferson*, 1:526.

143. Ibid., 1:527.

144. "Memorial of the Presbytery of Hanover (October 24, 1776)," in *The Sacred Rights of Conscience: Selected Readings on Religious Liberty and Church-State Relations in the American Founding*, ed. Daniel L. Dreisbach and Mark David Hall (Indianapolis: Liberty Fund, 2009), 269.

145. Jefferson, "Autobiography," in *Life and Selected Writings*, 40.

146. "Memorial of the Presbytery of Hanover," 269.

147. John A. Ragosta, *Wellspring of Liberty: How Virginia's Religious Dissenters Helped Win the American Revolution and Secured Religious Liberty* (New York: Oxford University Press, 2010), 142–44.

148. Differences in the spelling of "Muhammad" and "Qur'an" abound in these sources. "Mahomed" and "Alchoran" are used in *Papers of Thomas Jefferson,* 1:526. Instead, "Mahommed" and "Al-Coran" appear in "Memorial of the Presbytery of Hanover," 269.

149. The meaning of this document is read quite differently by Thomas S. Kidd, *God of Liberty: A Religious History of the American Revolution* (New York: Basic Books, 2010), 182–83.

150. *Virginia Gazette Daybooks,* Segment 2, fol. 18; Gilreath, *Thomas Jefferson's Library,* 54. See also "Alcoran," in *Oxford English Dictionary,* 13 vols. (Oxford: Clarendon Press, 1970), 1:210.

151. *Papers of Thomas Jefferson,* 1:530–39.

152. Jefferson, "Autobiography," in *Life and Selected Writings,* 24.

153. *Papers of Thomas Jefferson,* 1:547.

154. Jefferson, "Autobiography," in *Life and Selected Writings,* 40.

155. S. Gerald Sandler, "Lockean Ideas in Thomas Jefferson's *Bill for Establishing Religious Freedom,*" *Journal of the History of Ideas* 21 (1960): 113.

156. J. G. A. Pocock, "Religious Freedom and the Desacralization of Politics: From the English Civil Wars to the Virginia Statute," in *The Virginia Statute for Religious Freedom: Its Evolution and Consequences in American History,* ed. Merrill D. Peterson and Robert C. Vaughan (New York: Cambridge University Press, 1988), 61.

157. Gaustad, *Sworn on the Altar of God,* 13–16.

158. Champion, *Pillars,* 111–32; P. M. Holt, "The Treatment of Arab History by Prideaux, Ockley, and Sale," in *Historians of the Middle East,* ed. Bernard Lewis and P. M. Holt (London: Oxford University Press, 1962), 292; Kidd, "Is It Worse to Follow Mahomet Than the Devil?," 767.

159. *Papers of Thomas Jefferson,* 1:529. The phrase is Boyd's.

160. Ibid., 1:539.

161. Ibid., 1:535.

162. "Jefferson's Outline of Argument in Support of His Resolutions," in *Papers of Thomas Jefferson,* 1:535–39.

163. Thomas E. Buckley, S.J., "The Political Theology of Thomas Jefferson," in *Virginia Statute for Religious Freedom,* 89.

164. *Papers of Thomas Jefferson,* 1:536. The second line inside brackets is the author's translation.

165. Jefferson, *Notes on Virginia,* in *Life and Selected Writings,* 255.

166. *Papers of Thomas Jefferson,* 1:536. The second line in brackets is author's translation.

167. Ibid., 1:537.

168. Ibid., 1:538.

169. Ibid. Jefferson made reference to the pivotal impact of the Reformation: "Had not free inquiry been indulged at the era of the Reformation, the corruptions of Christianity could not have been purged away." Clearly, Jefferson believed that Islam had had no such turning point in its religious history. See Jefferson, *Notes on Virginia,* in *Life and Selected Writings,* 255.

170. *Papers of Thomas Jefferson,* 1:538.

171. Alberto A. Martínez, *Science Secrets: The Truth About Darwin's Finches, Einstein's Wife, and Other Myths* (Pittsburgh: University of Pittsburgh Press, 2011), 36–37, 39–41, 43–45; Jefferson, *Notes on Virginia,* in *Life and Selected Writings,* 255.

172. Al-Hibri, "Islamic and American Constitutional Law," 501 n. 50.

173. This assumption was first made by Hayes, but not regarding Jefferson's legisla-

tion; Hayes, "How Thomas Jefferson Read the Qur'an," 250; Sowerby, *Catalogue*, 3:133, catalog #2738. Jefferson also owned *Gordon's Independent Whig*, subtitled *or a defense of primitive Christianity, and of our ecclesiastical establishment, against the exorbitant claims and encroachments of fanatical and disaffected clergymen*, Sowerby, *Catalogue*, 3:133, catalog #2739.

174. Bernard Bailyn, *The Ideological Origins of the American Revolution*, enlarged ed. (Cambridge, MA: Belknap Press of Harvard University; repr. 1992); 35–36, 44–52; Allison, *Crescent Obscured*, 47, 52–53.

175. Hayes, "How Thomas Jefferson Read the Qur'an," 250.

176. Bailyn, *Ideological Origins*, 63–64 n. 8; Allison, *Crescent Obscured*, 47.

177. John Trenchard and Thomas Gordon, "Cato's Letters: Letter 66, Arbitrary Government proved incompatible with true Religion, whether Natural or Revealed," in *Sacred Rights*, 59.

178. Allison, *Crescent Obscured*, 47, 52–53, 56.

179. For the idea that Jefferson surpassed Locke, but without regard to Muslims, see John Marshall, *John Locke, Toleration and Early Enlightenment Culture: Religious Intolerance and Arguments for Religious Toleration in Early Modern and "Early Enlightenment" Europe* (Cambridge: Cambridge University Press, 2006), 697.

180. Dumas Malone, *Jefferson the Virginian*, vol. 1 of *Jefferson and His Time* (Boston: Little, Brown, 1948), 274–84.

181. Nabil Matar, "John Locke and the 'Turbanned Nations,'" *Journal of Islamic Studies* 2, no. 1 (1991): 72.

182. *Papers of Thomas Jefferson*, 1:544; Thomas Jefferson, *The Writings of Thomas Jefferson*, ed. Paul Leicester Ford (New York: G. P. Putnam's Sons, 1893), 2:92 n. 1, says that this phrase about the date is inscribed in Jefferson's own hand, but *Papers of Thomas Jefferson*, 1:528, contradicts this.

183. *Papers of Thomas Jefferson*, 1:548.

184. James Hutson first made this connection between Jefferson and Locke in "The Founding Fathers and Islam," *Library of Congress Information Bulletin* 61, no. 5 (2002): 1, http://www.loc.gov/loc/lcib/0205/tolerance.html.

185. *Papers of Thomas Jefferson*, 1:550, below note N. The editor, Julian P. Boyd, states that Jefferson was using volume 2 of a 1714 edition of Locke's *Works* published in London, but that volume does not exist in Jefferson's library. See Sowerby, *Catalogue*, 2:44, catalog #1338. Sowerby states that a 1791 edition of Locke's work on toleration did not make it into the Library of Congress because it "was either not delivered or disappeared at an early date."

186. John Locke, *A Letter Concerning Toleration (1689)*, ed. James H. Tully (Indianapolis: Hackett, 1983), 54. Hereafter, Locke, *Letter Concerning Toleration (1689)*. Curiously, Jefferson's spelling of the word for Muslim was not the original English 1689 "Mahumetan." Instead, Jefferson's version has been rendered by three American editors of his papers in three different ways: "Mahomedan," "Mahometan," and in the official collection, "Mahamedan." These discrepancies arise in part from the difficulty of deciphering the original handwriting, which certainly includes a final "d," but presents the more difficult challenge of deciphering the last three vowels. I think it more likely that Jefferson intended to follow Popple's original 1689 spelling "Mahumetan," and rendered it as "Mahumedan," but this remains conjecture, a fourth variant spelling at a time when precision in orthography for the term was not consistent. There is no doubt, however, that the word he transcribed from Locke, whatever the spelling, continued to mean "Muslim" in eighteenth-century usage.

187. Locke, *Letter Concerning Toleration (1689)*, 54.

188. *Papers of Thomas Jefferson*, 1:548.

189. Locke, *Letter Concerning Toleration (1689)*, 54.

190. Jack Turner, "John Locke, Christian Mission, and Colonial America," *Modern Intellectual History* 8 (2011): 267–71.

191. Ibid., 270, 291–92. The odd reference to "a faith in Mahomet, Foe, or any

other except Christ" caused the editor Boyd, *Papers of Thomas Jefferson*, 1:550, 551 n. 5, to consider the reference "enigmatic." The word "Foe" is also found in Bolingbroke but not in Locke: "the Mahometans and worshippers of Foe," in Jefferson, *Jefferson's Literary Commonplace Book*, 25.

192. *Papers of Thomas Jefferson*, 1:559.

193. Ibid., 1:559 note. The importance of this legislation for non-Protestants is noted by Buckley, "The Political Theology of Thomas Jefferson," in *Virginia Statute for Religious Freedom*, 91.

194. *Papers of Thomas Jefferson*, 1:558.

195. Ibid., 1:599 note, second column, second paragraph.

196. Locke, *Letter Concerning Toleration (1689)*, 52.

197. *Papers of Thomas Jefferson*, 1:558–59.

198. Robert M. Healey, "Jefferson on Judaism and the Jews: 'Divided We Stand, United We Fall,'" *American Jewish History* 73 (1984): 360.

199. *Papers of Thomas Jefferson*, 1:558–59.

200. Ibid., 1:558.

201. Bret E. Carroll, *The Routledge Historical Atlas of Religion in America* (New York: Routledge, 2000), 52; Morton Borden, *Jews, Turks, and Infidels* (Chapel Hill: University of North Carolina Press, 1984), 6; Jacob R. Marcus, *The Colonial American Jew, 1492–1776*, 3 vols. (Detroit: Wayne State University Press, 1970), 1:330–42, who emphasizes that although a few Jews passed through Virginia on business, "no established community would rise in Richmond until the 1780s." John Leland, a Baptist evangelical preacher, observed that by 1790 there was "no synagogue" for Jews in Virginia; see John Leland, *The Writings of the late Elder John Leland: Including Some Events in His Life*, ed. L. F. Greene (New York: G. W. Wood, 1845), 121. Naomi W. Cohen, *Jews in Christian America: The Pursuit of Religious Equality* (New York: Oxford University Press, 1992), 26. Cohen believes that for Jefferson and his contemporaries the word "Jew" signified neither neighbor nor acquaintance but, "like Turk, Mohammedan, atheist, or Deist, a genus distinct from the familiar Christian American." It is true that Jefferson's inclusive assertion did not refer to Jews—or Muslims—that he knew.

202. Healey, "Jefferson on Judaism," 363, 365.

203. "Letter to William Short," August 4, 1820, in *Memoir Correspondence, and Miscellanies, from the Papers of Thomas Jefferson*, ed. Thomas Jefferson Randolph (Boston: Gray and Bowen, 1830), 4:327.

204. Healey, "Jefferson on Judaism," 360–61 n. 11.

205. Quoted ibid., 361.

206. *Papers of Thomas Jefferson*, 1:548.

207. Locke, *Letter Concerning Toleration (1689)*, 51.

208. John Marshall, *John Locke, Toleration and Early Enlightenment Culture*, 697.

209. *Papers of Thomas Jefferson*, 1:551 n. 2.

210. Ibid. Jefferson considered the crime a misdemeanor, not treason.

211. *Papers of Thomas Jefferson*, 2:589.

212. Jefferson, *Notes on Virginia*, in *Life and Selected Writings*, 254.

213. Frank Lambert, *The Founding Fathers and the Place of Religion in America* (Princeton: Princeton University Press, 2003), 280–87; Hayes, *Road to Monticello*, 259.

214. *Papers of Thomas Jefferson*, 1:548.

215. Ibid., 1:551 n. 2.

216. Sebastian Castellio, *Concerning Heretics: Whether They Are to Be Persecuted and How They Are to Be Treated: A Collection of the Opinions of Learned Men Both Ancient and Modern*, trans. Roland H. Bainton (New York: Columbia University Press, 1935), 9.

217. Sowerby, *Catalogue*, 2:101, catalog #1485, the Latin New Testament; 2:89, catalog #1454, Châteillon's collection of pagan oracles, including those of Apollo and Zoroaster; and 2:130, catalog #1547, *Castaliones dialogi sacri*, Bible stories for the young.

218. Jefferson, *Commonplace Book*, 339.

219. "Thomas Jefferson to John Adams," April 11, 1823, in *Life and Selected Writings*, 644.

220. Thomas Jefferson, "Letter to Dr. Benjamin Rush," January 16, 1811, ibid., 558.

221. Gaustad, *Sworn on the Altar of God*, 2–22.

222. *Papers of Thomas Jefferson*, 1:547.

223. Ibid., 2:545.

224. Jefferson, *Notes on Virginia*, in *Life and Selected Writings*, 255–56.

225. Ibid., 256.

226. Locke, *Letter Concerning Toleration (1689)*, 54.

227. Locke, *Epistola de Tolerantia: A Letter on Toleration*, ed. Raymond Klibansky, trans. J. W. Gough (Oxford: Clarendon Press, 1968), 145.

228. *Papers of Thomas Jefferson*, 1:548.

229. Jefferson, *Notes on Virginia*, in *Life and Selected Writings*, 255.

230. *Papers of Thomas Jefferson*, 2:545–47; Rhys Isaac, *The Transformation of Virginia, 1740–1790* (Chapel Hill: University of North Carolina Press, 1982), 282–95; "Thomas Jefferson, epitaph, no date," in *The Thomas Jefferson Papers Series 1. General Correspondence, 1651–1827*, Library of Congress, image 1135, http://hdl.loc.gov/loc.mss/mtj .mtjbib024905.

231. For the succinct outline of these ideas, see Merrill D. Peterson and Robert C. Vaughan, introduction to *Virginia Statute*, vii.

232. *Papers of Thomas Jefferson*, 1:545.

233. Locke, *Letter Concerning Toleration (1689)*, 37.

234. *Papers of Thomas Jefferson*, 1:547.

235. Ibid., 2:545.

236. Peterson, introduction to *Virginia Statute*, vii.

237. Sandler, "Lockean Ideas," 114; Locke, *Letter Concerning Toleration (1689)*, 31.

238. Sandler, "Lockean Ideas," 114; *Papers of Thomas Jefferson*, 2:545–46.

239. The first to suggest that Jefferson had Muslims "in mind" when he first proposed his Bill for Establishing Religious Freedom was Hayes, "How Thomas Jefferson Read the Qur'an," 258–59.

240. Merrill D. Peterson, *Thomas Jefferson and the New Nation: A Biography* (New York: Oxford University Press, 1990), 141.

241. Thomas E. Buckley, S.J., *Church and State in Revolutionary Virginia* (Charlottesville: University Press of Virginia, 1977), 157–58.

242. Jefferson, "Autobiography," in *Life and Selected Writings*, 45.

243. Ibid., 45–46. In Jefferson's hand, "words Jesus Christ."

244. Sandler, "Lockean Ideas," 111–12.

245. *Papers of Thomas Jefferson*, 1:544; Sandler, "Lockean Ideas," 112.

246. *Papers of Thomas Jefferson*, 2:545.

247. Jefferson, "Autobiography," in *Life and Selected Writings*, 46; I differ in my reading of Locke and Jefferson from the thoughtful work of Garry Willis, *Head and Heart: American Christianities* (New York: Penguin, 2007), 175–97.

248. This connection in Jefferson's thought was first observed by James H. Hutson, "The Founding Fathers and Islam," *Library of Congress Information Bulletin* 61, no. 5 (2002): 1; Hayes, "How Thomas Jefferson Read the Qur'an," 259; Ragosta, *Wellspring of Liberty*, 145–46; Jon Meacham, *Thomas Jefferson: The Art of Power* (New York: Random House, 2012), 123–24. Dismissing the bill as pertaining only to "religious freedom" is Allison, *Crescent Obscured*, 5–7.

249. Quoted in Buckley, *Church and State*, 157–58 n. 45. Buckley provides the most detailed account of the context of this amendment. However, in direct opposition to Jefferson and Madison, Buckley states that "it is not readily apparent how, in fact, the inclusion of these words [Jesus Christ] would have in any way affected the latitude of

the enabling clause." Wills, *Head and Heart*, 196, misses Madison's support for the excision of "Jesus Christ."

250. *Papers of Thomas Jefferson*, 2:546–47.

251. Jeremy Waldron, *God, Locke, and Equality: Christian Foundations of John Locke's Political Thought* (New York: Cambridge University Press, 2002), 201; Turner, "John Locke, Christian Mission, and Colonial America," 279–80.

252. Michael A. Gomez, *Black Crescent: The Experience and Legacy of African Muslims in the Americas* (New York: Cambridge University Press, 2005), 143–200; Kambiz GhaneaBassiri, *A History of Islam in America* (New York: Cambridge University Press, 2010), 1–94.

253. Carroll, *Routledge Historical Atlas*, 52, 102.

254. Gomez, *Black Crescent*, 166.

255. Ibid.; Michael A. Gomez, *Exchanging Our Country Marks: The Transformation of African Identities in the Colonial and Antebellum South* (Chapel Hill: University of North Carolina Press, 1998), 66.

256. Sylviane A. Diouf, *Servants of Allah: African Muslims Enslaved in the Americas* (New York: New York University Press, 1998), 48.

257. Gomez, *Exchanging Our Country Marks*, 21.

258. Thomas Jefferson, *Thomas Jefferson's Farm Book, with Commentary and Relevant Extracts from Other Writings*, ed. Edwin Morris Betts (Princeton: Princeton University Press, 1953), 5.

259. Jefferson, "Autobiography," in *Life and Selected Writings*, 26.

260. Jefferson, *Farm Book*, 5–31, 39, 42–43, 49–60, 114, 128–31, 134–37, 139–40, 142–52, 154–56, 158–62, 164–69, 172, 174–76. He lists his hogs on 173, between his lists of slaves on 172 and 174–75.

261. Mary V. Thompson, "Mount Vernon," *Encyclopedia of Muslim-American History*, ed. Edward E. Curtis IV, 2 vols. (New York: Facts on File, 2010) 2:392–93.

262. Gomez, *Black Crescent*, 149, 152–53, 155, 159.

263. Thompson, "Mount Vernon," 2:392–93.

264. Gomez, *Black Crescent*, 146–48.

265. Thompson, "Mount Vernon," 2:392–93.

266. "George Washington to Tench Tilghman," March 24, 1784, in *Writings of George Washington from the Original Manuscript Sources, 1745–1799*, ed. John C. Fitzpatrick, 39 vols. (Washington, DC: U.S. Government Printing Office, 1938), 27:367.

267. Henry Wiencek, *Master of the Mountain: Thomas Jefferson and His Slaves* (New York: Farrar, Straus and Giroux, 2012), 274–75, quote on 275, where Wiencek opines the choice of Jefferson as "the moral standard of the Founders' era, not Washington." Thompson, "Mount Vernon," 2:393, notes that Washington freed 123 of his slaves, with others who had belonged to Martha Washington's first husband remaining enslaved. For an earlier critique of Jefferson's view of slavery and treatment of slaves, see Paul Finkelman, *Slavery and the Founders: Race and Liberty in the Age of Jefferson*, 2nd ed. (Armonk, NY: M. E. Sharpe, 2001), 153–54, 189, who notes that all of those slaves freed were Hemingses, part of Jefferson's family.

268. The possible presence of Muslims on Jefferson's plantation was first noted by al-Hibri, "Islamic and American Constitutional Law," 502.

269. See Annette Gordon-Reed, *The Hemingses of Monticello: An American Family* (New York: W. W. Norton, 2008), 272; Wiencek, *Master of the Mountain*, 191, refers to six childbirths only.

270. Elizabeth Hemings (d. 1807) was the daughter of a "full-blooded African" woman whose name remains unknown. Elizabeth was the mother of Sarah (Sally) Hemings (d. 1835). Their great-grandmother's African religion and ethnicity remain a mystery, according to Annette Gordon-Reed, *Hemingses of Monticello*, 47–52.

271. Wiencek, *Master of the Mountain*, 228; Finkelman, *Slavery and the Founders*, 154.

Jefferson never freed Sally, although those slaves freed on his death were Hemingses, their children.

4. JEFFERSON VERSUS JOHN ADAMS: THE PROBLEM OF NORTH AFRICAN PIRACY AND THEIR NEGOTIATIONS WITH A MUSLIM AMBASSADOR IN LONDON, 1784–88

1. "John Adams to Thomas Jefferson," February 21, 1786, in *The Adams-Jefferson Letters: The Complete Correspondence Between Thomas Jefferson and Abigail and John Adams,* ed. Lester J. Cappon, 2 vols. (Chapel Hill: University of North Carolina Press, 1959), 1:123. I have regularized capitalization in all of these exchanges. Hereafter cited as *Adams-Jefferson Letters.*

2. Thomas A. Bailey, *A Diplomatic History of the American People* (New York: Meredith Corporation, 1969), 64–65.

3. Robert C. Davis, *Holy War and Human Bondage: Tales of Christian-Muslim Slavery in the Early Modern Mediterranean* (Santa Barbara, CA: Praeger, 2009), vii–36.

4. The classic treatment is by Ray W. Irwin, *The Diplomatic Relations of the United States with the Barbary Powers, 1776–1816* (New York: Russell and Russell, 1931). A more recent, thorough reading is provided by Michael L. S. Kitzen, *Tripoli and the United States at War: A History of American Relations with the Barbary States* (Jefferson, NC: McFarland and Co., 1993). A historically problematic reading regarding "terror" and piracy is offered by Joseph Wheelan, *America's First War: Jefferson's War on Terror, 1801–1805* (New York: Carroll and Graf, 2003). Whelan's assumption is countered thoughtfully and thoroughly by Richard B. Parker, *Uncle Sam in Barbary: A Diplomatic History* (Gainesville: University Press of Florida, 2004), and Frank Lambert, *The Barbary Wars: American Independence in the Atlantic World* (New York: Hill and Wang, 2005). See also the popular history by A. B. C. Whipple, *To the Shores of Tripoli: The Birth of the U.S. Navy and Marines* (New York: William Morrow and Company, 1991). For a cultural analysis, focused in part on American views of Islam, see Robert J. Allison, *The Crescent Obscured: The United States and the Muslim World, 1776–1815* (Chicago: University of Chicago Press, 2000). The issue of captivity in North Africa has received renewed attention of late. A helpful introduction to the cultural construction of the British encounter with Barbary may be found in Linda Colley, *Captives: Britain, Empire and the World, 1600–1850* (London: Jonathan Cape, 2002), 99–113. Accounts of American captivity narratives in North Africa may be found in Paul Baepler, ed., *White Slaves, African Masters: An Anthology of Barbary Captivity Narratives* (Chicago: University of Chicago Press, 1999); see also Timothy Marr, *The Cultural Roots of American Islamicism* (New York: Cambridge University Press, 2006), 26–68; Lawrence A. Peskin, *Captives and Countrymen: Barbary Slavery and the American Public, 1785–1816* (Baltimore: Johns Hopkins University Press, 2009); Thomas S. Kidd, *American Christians and Islam: Evangelical Culture and Muslims from the Colonial Period to the Age of Terrorism* (Princeton: Princeton University Press, 2009), 19–36.

5. Sebastian R. Prange, "Thomas Jefferson's Qur'an," *Saudi Aramco World* 62, no. 4 (July/August 2011): 7.

6. For a comparison of Jefferson and Adams on religion, see Lambert, *Barbary Wars,* 8, 113, 117–18.

7. I paraphrase Lambert here, with whom I concur based on Jefferson's writing, that U.S. conflicts with North Africa "were primarily about trade, not theology, and that rather than being holy wars, they were extensions of America's War of Independence"; see Lambert, *Barbary Wars,* 8. Offering a more religion-centered explanation of the conflict is Michael B. Oren, *Power, Faith, and Fantasy: America in the Middle East, 1776 to Present* (New York: W. W. Norton, 2007), 20–42.

8. Lambert, *Barbary Wars,* 8–9.

9. Baepler, introduction to *White Slaves, African Masters*, 8–58.

10. "Adams to Jefferson," July 3, 1786, *Adams-Jefferson Letters*, 1:139.

11. Davis, *Holy War*, 15.

12. Allison, *Crescent Obscured*, 125. For Qur'anic verses about captives as differentiated from slaves, see Jonathan E. Brockopp, "Captives," *Encyclopaedia of the Qur'an*, ed. Jane D. McAuliffe, 6 vols. (Leiden: E. J. Brill, 2001), 1:289–90, and Jonathan E. Brockopp, "Slaves," *Encyclopaedia of the Qur'an*, 5:56–60. The humanity of the slaves and their kind treatment and manumission are regarded as a way to expiate sins (Qur'an 4:36, 5:89, 58:3).

13. Quoted in Nabil Matar, *Britain and Barbary, 1589–1689* (Gainesville: University Press of Florida, 2005), 114–15.

14. Adrian Tinniswood, *Pirates of Barbary: Corsairs, Conquests, and Captivity in the Seventeenth-Century Mediterranean* (New York: Riverhead, 2010), 172.

15. James Leander Cathcart, "The Captives: Eleven Years a Prisoner in Algiers," in Baepler, *White Slaves, African Masters*, 103–46; see also Jacob Rama Berman, *American Arabesque: Arabs, Islam, and the 19th-Century Imaginary* (New York: New York University Press, 2012), 31–69.

16. Tinniswood, *Pirates of Barbary*, 172; Cathcart, "Captives," in *White Slaves, African Masters*, 136–39.

17. Allison, *Crescent Obscured*, 24, 263, 168–69.

18. Ibid., 16, 96–97.

19. The connection between American captivity in North Africa and abolitionist thought in the United States was first documented by Allison, *Crescent Obscured*, 121–26, 223–25.

20. Henry Wiencek, *Master of the Mountain: Thomas Jefferson and His Slaves* (New York: Farrar, Straus and Giroux, 2012), 76–83, 245–51, 273–75.

21. Allison, *Crescent Obscured*, 103; Kidd, *American Christians and Islam*, 19–27.

22. Quoted in Paul Finkelman, *Slavery and the Founders: Race and Liberty in the Age of Jefferson*, 2nd ed. (Armonk, NY: M. E. Sharpe, 2001), 161.

23. "From Martha Jefferson to Thomas Jefferson," May 3, 1787, Paris, in Julian P. Boyd et al., eds., *The Papers of Thomas Jefferson*, 40 vols. (Princeton: Princeton University Press, 1950–), 11:334. Hereafter *Papers of Thomas Jefferson*. Allison, *Crescent Obscured*, 89–90.

24. *Papers of Thomas Jefferson*, 11:334; Allison, *Crescent Obscured*, 89–90.

25. Allison, *Crescent Obscured*, 89.

26. *Papers of Thomas Jefferson*, 11:334; Allison, *Crescent Obscured*, 89–90.

27. "We cannot know what her father thought, since he never mentioned this episode, or Martha's comments on it, when he wrote back to her. Nor did he mention it to anyone else," as noted by Allison, *Crescent Obscured*, 90.

28. Annette Gordon-Reed, *The Hemingses of Monticello: An American Family* (New York: W. W. Norton, 2008), 163–90; Oren, *Power, Faith, and Fantasy*, 24.

29. Wiencek, *Master of the Mountain*, 190, who states that they never hired a lawyer to investigate proceedings that would have freed them under French law.

30. "The Marquis de Lafayette to John Adams," February 22, 1786, in John Adams, *The Works of John Adams, Second President of the United States*, ed. Charles Francis Adams, 10 vols. (Boston: Little, Brown, 1850–56), 8:376–77.

31. "Adams to Granville Sharp," March 8, 1786, ibid., 8:387.

32. Ibid., 8:388.

33. Ibid.

34. Irwin, *Diplomatic Relations*, 17; Phillip Chiviges Naylor, *North Africa: A History from Antiquity to Present* (Austin: University of Texas Press, 2009), 121.

35. Quoted in Irwin, *Diplomatic Relations*, 24–25; Kitzen, *Tripoli*, 9; Magali Morsy, *North Africa, 1800–1900: A Survey from the Nile Valley to the Atlantic* (London: Longman, 1984), 73; Naylor, *North Africa*, 123.

36. Quoted in Irwin, *Diplomatic Relations*, 17 n. 68.

37. Dumas Malone, *Jefferson and the Rights of Man*, vol. 2 of *Jefferson and His Time* (Boston: Little, Brown, 1951), 27; Irwin, *Diplomatic Relations*, 17 n. 70. This same quotation was attributed to others, including the French king Louis XIV; see Louis B. Wright and Julia H. Macleod, *The First Americans in North Africa: William Eaton's Struggle for a Vigorous Policy Against the Barbary Pirates, 1799–1805* (Princeton: Princeton University Press, 1945), 14–15.

38. "John Adams to Secretary Jay," February 17, 1786, Adams, *Works*, 8:372.

39. Matar, *Britain and Barbary*, 113.

40. Irwin, *Diplomatic Relations*, 204.

41. Matar, *Britain and Barbary*, 113.

42. Quoted in Karoline P. Cook, "Forbidden Crossings: Morisco Emigration to Spanish America, 1492–1650" (PhD diss., Princeton University, 2008), 96.

43. Wright and Macleod, *First Americans*, 14.

44. Matar, *Britain and Barbary*, 113.

45. Lambert, *Barbary Wars*, 31.

46. Tinniswood, *Pirates of Barbary*, 29–30.

47. Ibid., 31–103.

48. Ibid., 28–29.

49. Lambert, *Barbary Wars*, 30.

50. Naylor, *North Africa*, 123.

51. Matar, *Britain and Barbary*, 116–32.

52. Davis, *Holy War*, vii.

53. Janice E. Thomson, *Mercenaries, Pirates, and Sovereigns* (Princeton: Princeton University Press, 1994), quote on 23.

54. Tinniswood, *Pirates of Barbary*, quote on 30.

55. Naylor, *North Africa*, 131.

56. Allison, *Crescent Obscured*, 4–8.

57. "Thomas Jefferson to John Page," Paris, August 20, 1785, *Papers of Thomas Jefferson*, 8:418.

58. Gary Edward Wilson, "American Prisoners in the Barbary Nations, 1784–1816" (PhD diss., North Texas State University, 1979), 314.

59. *Papers of Thomas Jefferson*, 10:426.

60. Ibid., 8:418.

61. Ibid., 8:419.

62. Thomas Jefferson, "Autobiography," in *The Life and Selected Writings of Thomas Jefferson*, ed. Adrienne Koch and William Peden (New York: Modern Library, 1998), 59; Merrill D. Peterson, *Jefferson and the New Nation* (New York: Oxford University Press, 1970), 292.

63. *Papers of Thomas Jefferson*, 8:347–48.

64. Ibid., 8:348, 353.

65. Claimed sightings of North African vessels were recorded for the West Indies in the *Massachusetts Centinel*, April 29, 1786, and the presence of malevolent Algerians in the United States was featured in the *Pennsylvania Gazette*, April 5, 1786; the *Connecticut Gazette*, April 7, 1786; and the *Maryland Gazette*, April 13, 1786; see Wilson, "American Prisoners," 72.

66. Allison, *Crescent Obscured*, 3–7.

67. "Moor," *Oxford English Dictionary*, 13 vols. (Oxford: Clarendon Press, 1970), 6:645.

68. Kitzen, *Tripoli*, 1; Baepler, introduction to *White Slaves, African Masters*, 2–3.

69. Hans Wehr, ed., *A Dictionary of Modern Written Arabic*, trans. Milton Cowan (Urbana, IL: Spoken Language Services, 1994), 62.

70. "Barbary," *Oxford English Dictionary*, 1:665.

71. Thomas Jefferson, "Fourth Annual Message," November 8, 1804, in *The Writings of Thomas Jefferson, 1801–1806,* ed. Paul Leicester Ford, 10 vols. (New York: G. P. Putnam's Sons, 1897), 8:328.

72. Jefferson described the Greek and Ottoman Turkish conflict this way: "This is only to substitute one set of Barbarians for another." *Papers of Thomas Jefferson,* 8:418.

73. Ibid., 8:352.

74. "Treaty with Morocco, 1786," *Papers of Thomas Jefferson,* 10:425.

75. "Adams to Jefferson," February 21, 1786, *Adams-Jefferson Letters,* 1:123.

76. "Adams to Jefferson," June 6, 1786, Adams, *Works,* 8:400.

77. "Thomas Jefferson to James Monroe," November 11, 1784, Paris, *Papers of Thomas Jefferson,* 7:512; Bernard Bailyn, *To Begin the World Anew: The Genius and Ambiguities of the American Founders* (New York: Knopf, 2003), 40.

78. *Papers of Thomas Jefferson,* 7:511.

79. Ibid., 7:511–12.

80. Ibid., 2:437–40.

81. "Adams to Jefferson," February 17, 1786, London, *Adams-Jefferson Letters,* 1:121.

82. "Adams to John Jay," February 17, 1786, Adams, *Works,* 8:372.

83. "Adams to Jefferson," *Adams-Jefferson Letters,* 1:122.

84. Ibid., 1:121.

85. Jefferson, "Autobiography," in *Life and Selected Writings,* 62.

86. "Adams to Jefferson," *Adams-Jefferson Letters,* 1:121.

87. Ibid.

88. John Foss, "A Journal of the Captivity and Sufferings of John Foss," in Baepler, *White Slaves, African Masters,* 89.

89. "Adams to Jefferson," *Adams-Jefferson Letters,* 1:121.

90. Ibid.; Adams, *Works,* 8:373.

91. "To Samuel Henley with a List of Books," March 3, 1785, *Papers of Thomas Jefferson,* 8:14 n. 1; Kevin J. Hayes, "How Thomas Jefferson Read the Qur'an," *Early American Literature* 39, no. 2 (2004): 258; E. Millicent Sowerby, ed., *Catalogue of the Library of Thomas Jefferson,* 5 vols. (Washington, DC: Library of Congress, 1952–53), 5:44.

92. *Papers of Thomas Jefferson,* 8:11–13; Sowerby, *Catalogue,* 5:44.

93. "Adams to Jefferson," *Adams-Jefferson Letters,* 1:121; Irwin, *Diplomatic Relations,* 17.

94. "Adams to Jefferson," *Adams-Jefferson Letters,* 1:121.

95. Ibid. The interview is also detailed in Hayes, "How Thomas Jefferson Read the Qur'an," 257; Kevin J. Hayes, *The Road to Monticello: The Life and Mind of Thomas Jefferson* (New York: Oxford University Press, 2008), 309.

96. "Adams to Jefferson," *Adams-Jefferson Letters,* 1:121.

97. Ibid.; Hayes, *Road to Monticello,* 309–17.

98. "Adams to Jefferson," *Adams-Jefferson Letters,* 1:121.

99. Ibid., 1:121–22.

100. Adams, *Works,* 8:373. While Tunis was omitted in Adams's letter to Jefferson, it was present in his other communication to the secretary of state, along with Morocco.

101. "Adams to Jefferson," *Adams-Jefferson Letters,* 1:122.

102. Ibid.

103. Ibid., 1:123.

104. Ibid., 1:122.

105. Adams, *Works,* 8:373. For a darker version of the first meeting with the ambassador from Tripoli, mistakenly dated 1785 instead of 1786, which presumes that Adams "was outraged by the impertinence that 'Abd al-Rahman, the agent of a powerful but primitive kingdom, displayed toward the enlightened United States" despite Adams's

multiple positive observations to the contrary about the ambassador's credentials and personality, see Oren, *Power, Faith, and Fantasy*, 26.

106. "John Adams to Secretary Jay," February 20, 1786, *Works*, 8:374.

107. Ibid., 8:377.

108. For more on the presence of Jews in Tripoli, see Harvey E. Goldberg, *Jewish Life in Muslim Libya* (Chicago: University of Chicago Press, 1990).

109. Wright and Macleod, *First Americans*, 32, 42–43.

110. "Adams to Jefferson," June 6, 1786, London, *Adams-Jefferson Letters*, 1:134.

111. Adams, *Works*, 8:374.

112. Ibid., 8:377.

113. Ibid., 8:374.

114. Ibid., 8:375.

115. Ibid.

116. Ibid.

117. Ibid., 8:376.

118. Ibid.

119. Ibid.

120. Ibid., 8:377.

121. Ibid., 8:378.

122. Ibid., 8:379.

123. "Thomas Jefferson to John Jay," March 12, 1786, in *The Diplomatic Correspondence of the United States of America* (Washington, DC: Blair and Rives, 1837), 3:4–5.

124. Parker, *Uncle Sam*, 41–42; Irwin, *Diplomatic Relations*, 40–42.

125. "American Commissioners to John Jay," March 28, 1786, London, *Papers of Thomas Jefferson*, 9:357.

126. Ibid., 9:358.

127. Ibid.; Malone, *Jefferson and the Rights of Man*, 27–32, 51–52.

128. The exchange rates then and now are provided by Parker, *Uncle Sam*, 42.

129. *Papers of Thomas Jefferson*, 9:358.

130. Ibid.

131. This interaction is interpreted differently by Hayes, "How Thomas Jefferson Read the Qur'an," 256–57; Hayes, *Road to Monticello*, 315–16.

132. Majid Khadduri, *War and Peace in the Law of Islam* (Baltimore: Johns Hopkins University Press, 1955), 100–101.

133. Ella Landau-Tasseroin, "Jihad," *Encyclopaedia of the Qur'an*, 3:41.

134. Ibid., 3:36.

135. Patricia Crone, "War," *Encyclopaedia of the Qur'an*, 5:456. Other verses about being wronged include Qur'an 22:39 and punishing wrongdoers, Qur'an 9:13–14. All translations are from Muhammad M. Pickthall, trans., *The Meaning of the Glorious Qur'an: Text and Explanatory Translation* (New York: Muslim World League, 1977), 526.

136. "Richard O'Brien to Thomas Jefferson," June 8, 1786, in *Naval Documents Related to the United States Wars with the Barbary Powers: Naval Operations Including Diplomatic Background from 1785 Through 1801*, 3 vols. (Washington, DC: U.S. Government Printing Office, 1939), 1:3.

137. Pickthall, trans., *Qur'an*, 29.

138. Ibid., 33.

139. Ibid., 29.

140. Ibid., 176. Earl Waugh, *Peace as Seen in the Qur'an* (Jerusalem: Franciscan Printing Press, 1986), 12, 42.

141. Pickthall, trans., *Qur'an*, 87.

142. Ibid., 272.

143. Khadduri, *War and Peace*, 217–18.

144. Crone, "War," *Encyclopaedia of the Qur'an*, 5:455.

145. *Papers of Thomas Jefferson,* 9:359.

146. *Naval Documents,* 1:3; Lambert, *Barbary Wars,* 118; Kitzen, *Tripoli,* 13.

147. *Papers of Thomas Jefferson,* 9:358.

148. Khadduri, *War and Peace,* 119.

149. Andrew Rippin, "Devil," *Encyclopedia of the Qur'an,* 1:526.

150. *Papers of Thomas Jefferson,* 9:358.

151. Ibid., 9:359.

152. For the assumption that Jefferson viewed North Africa as "the repository of despotism, depravity, and backwardness," which the Founder never articulated this way, see Oren, *Power, Faith, and Fantasy,* 26–27, 32.

153. Quoted in Lambert, *Barbary Wars,* 118.

154. Parker, *Uncle Sam,* 42.

155. "Jefferson to Adams," July 11, 1785, *Adams-Jefferson Letters,* 1:142.

156. Ibid.

157. Ibid., 1:143.

158. Ibid.

159. Irwin, *Diplomatic Relations,* 48.

160. "Jefferson's Proposed Concert of Powers against the Barbary States: Editorial Note," *Papers of Thomas Jefferson,* 10:560–61.

161. Ibid., 10:562–63.

162. Ibid., 10:564.

163. Jefferson, "Proposed Convention against the Barbary States," before July 4, 1786, *Papers of Thomas Jefferson,* 10:567.

164. Jefferson, "Autobiography," in *Life and Selected Writings,* 63–67.

165. Kitzen, *Tripoli,* 11.

166. Wilson, "American Prisoners," 320.

167. Irwin, *Diplomatic Relations,* 27–28.

168. Ibid., 38 n. 2.

169. Ibid., 11.

170. Ibid., 45.

171. Quoted ibid., 45 n. 41.

172. Ibid., 44; Kitzen, *Tripoli,* 13.

173. Bubonic and pneumonic plague outbreaks were common in eighteenth-century North Africa; see H. G. Barnby, *The Prisoners of Algiers: An Account of the Forgotten American-Algerian War, 1785–1787* (New York: Oxford University Press, 1966), 86.

174. Some contemporary writers insist that Jefferson bought his Qur'an in response to the issue of North African piracy. This seems unlikely given that this diplomatic problem for Jefferson dates from eleven years *after* his 1765 purchase of the book, not his 1786 interview with the ambassador from Tripoli. For an example of this assumption, see Samuel Blumenfeld, "Thomas Jefferson's Qur'an," *New American,* September 1, 2010, and Christopher Hitchens, "Jefferson's Qur'an," *Slate,* January 9, 2007.

175. George Sale, trans., *The Koran, commonly called the Alcoran of Mohammed, Translated into English from the Original Arabic; with Explanatory Notes, taken from the Most Approved Commentators, to which is prefixed a Preliminary Discourse,* 2 vols. (London: L. Hawes, W. Clarke, R. Collins, and T. Wilcox, 1764), Rare Books and Special Collections Division, Library of Congress, 1:113; Hayes, *Road to Monticello,* 6–7.

176. *The Qur'an: Commonly Called the Alcoran of Mahomet* (Springfield, MA: Henry Brewer for Isaiah Thomas, 1806), John Adams Library, Boston Public Library.

177. "Thomas Jefferson to John Wayles Eppes," November 6, 1813, in Ford, *Writings of Thomas Jefferson,* 9:416.

178. Quoted in Bailey, *Diplomatic History,* 65.

179. Marshall Smelser, *The Congress Founds the Navy, 1787–1798* (Notre Dame: University of Notre Dame Press, 1959), 9, 20 n. 15.

5. COULD A MUSLIM BE PRESIDENT?
MUSLIM RIGHTS AND THE RATIFICATION
OF THE CONSTITUTION, 1788

1. "Madison to Jefferson," October 17, 1788, in James Morton Smith, ed., *The Republic of Letters: The Correspondence between Thomas Jefferson and James Madison, 1776–1826*, 3 vols. (New York: W. W. Norton, 1995), 1:564.

2. Julian P. Boyd et al., eds., *The Papers of Thomas Jefferson*, 40 vols. (Princeton: Princeton University Press, 1950–), 1:548. Hereafter cited as *Papers of Thomas Jefferson*.

3. Quoted in Thomas E. Buckley, *Church and State in Revolutionary Virginia, 1776–1787* (Charlottesville: University Press of Virginia, 1977), 49.

4. *Papers of Thomas Jefferson*, 2:546.

5. *Virginia Gazette*, September 18, 1779.

6. Ibid.; Buckley, *Church and State*, 50.

7. Quoted in Buckley, *Church and State*, 51.

8. "Address by a Watchman, No. 1," *Worcester Magazine*, February 8, 1788, in Herbert J. Storing, ed., *The Complete Anti-Federalist*, 7 vols. (Chicago: University of Chicago Press, 1981), 4:232.

9. "A Friend to the Rights of the People," in *Complete Anti-Federalist*, 4:242.

10. A similar objection to "Christians, Pagans, Mahometans, or Jews" may be found in the Anti-Federalist tract "The Federal Farmer," January 12, 1788, in *Complete Anti-Federalist*, 2:295.

11. "Letter of John Sullivan to Jeremy Belknap," February 26, 1788, in *Collections of the Massachusetts Historical Society*, 6th ser., 9 vols. (Boston: Massachusetts Historical Society, 1891), 4:394. See also Jere R. Daniell, "Ideology and Hardball: Ratification of the Federal Constitution in New Hampshire," in *New Hampshire: The State That Made Us a Nation: A Celebration of the Bicentennial of the United States Constitution*, ed. William M. Gardner, Frank C. Mevers, and Richard F. Upton (Portsmouth, NH: Peter E. Randall, 1989), 8.

12. Daniell, "Ideology and Hardball," 12.

13. Jonathan Elliot, ed., *The Debates in the Several State Conventions on the Adoption of the Federal Constitution, as Recommended by the General Convention at Philadelphia, in 1787*, 5 vols. (Philadelphia: J. B. Lippincott, 1888), 2:203–4.

14. "Letter of John Sullivan," *Collections of the Massachusetts Historical Society*, 4:394.

15. William G. McLoughlin, *New England Dissent, 1680–1883*, 2 vols. (Cambridge, MA: Harvard University Press, 1971), 2:717–20.

16. This tendency among Protestants to assert their superiority over other denominations of Protestants as well as Catholics, Deists, and Unitarians was first noted in Thomas S. Kidd, " 'Is It Worse to Follow Mahomet Than the Devil?' Early American Uses of Islam," *Church History* 72, no. 4 (December 2003): 767, 774, 776, 787; Thomas S. Kidd, *American Christians and Islam: Evangelical Culture and Muslims from the Colonial Period to the Age of Terrorism* (Princeton: Princeton University Press, 2009), 8–9.

17. This Anti-Federalist rhetoric of fear against non-Protestants, including Muslims, was observed by Gerard V. Bradley, "The No Religious Test Clause and the Constitution of Religious Liberty: 'A Machine That Has Gone of Itself,' " *Case Western Reserve Law Review* 37 (1986–87): 710. The absence of a religious test "ran well ahead of contemporary Anglo-American practice," asserts Akhil Reed Amar, *America's Constitution: A Biography* (New York: Random House, 2005), 166.

18. Quoted in Bradley, "No Religious Test," 711.

19. Quoted ibid., 702.

20. Quoted in Arthur Hertzberg, *The Jews in America: Four Centuries of an Uneasy Encounter* (New York: Simon and Schuster, 1989), 15. This attitude about rhetorical references to Muslims and Jews has also been adopted more recently by Naomi W. Cohen,

Jews in Christian America: The Pursuit of Equality (New York: Oxford University Press, 1992), 13, 24, 25–26.

21. The crucial nature of this precedent was first noted by Morton Borden, *Jews, Turks, and Infidels* (Chapel Hill: University of North Carolina Press, 1984), 10.

22. Francis Newton Thorpe, ed., *The Federal and State Constitutions, Colonial Charters, and Other Organic Laws of the States, Territories, and Colonies Now or Heretofore Forming the United States of America*, 7 vols. (Washington, DC: U.S. Government Printing Office, 1909), 5:2636; Cohen, *Jews in Christian America*, 25.

23. Thorpe, *Federal and State Constitutions*, 5:2637; Borden, *Jews, Turks, and Infidels*, 13.

24. Borden, *Jews, Turks, and Infidels*, 11.

25. Thorpe, *Federal and State Constitutions*, 5:3082.

26. Ibid., 5:3085.

27. Quoted in Cohen, *Jews in Christian America*, 24.

28. Quoted in Borden, *Jews, Turks, and Infidels*, 11.

29. Thorpe, *Federal and State Constitutions*, 1:566.

30. Ibid., 5:2597.

31. Ibid., 3:1890.

32. Quoted in Borden, *Jew, Turks, and Infidels*, 12.

33. Thorpe, *Federal and State Constitutions*, 4:2454, 2460–62; Borden, *Jews, Turks, and Infidels*, 13 (quote).

34. Thorpe, *Federal and State Constitutions*, 5:537, 544–45; Borden, *Jews, Turks, and Infidels*, 13.

35. Thorpe, *Federal and State Constitutions*, 6:3222–23; Borden, *Jews, Turks, and Infidels*, 13.

36. Thorpe, *Federal and State Constitutions*, 3:1700; Borden, *Jews, Turks, and Infidels*, 13.

37. Thomas Jefferson, "Autobiography," in *The Life and Selected Writings of Thomas Jefferson*, ed. Adrienne Koch and William Peden (New York: Modern Library, 1998), 46; Cohen, *Jews in Christian America*, 26.

38. Thorpe, *Federal and State Constitutions*, 5:3256.

39. Ibid., 2:779.

40. Ibid., 5:2793.

41. Griffith J. McRee, ed., *Life and Correspondence of James Iredell: One of the Associate Justices of the Supreme Court of the United States*, 2 vols. (New York: Peter Smith, 1949), 1:339 note.

42. Thorpe, *Federal and State Constitutions*, 5:2793.

43. McRee, *Life and Correspondence*, 1:339.

44. John Locke's contribution to the Carolinas' statutes for religious freedom of the seventeenth century acknowledged "that Jews, heathens, and other dissenters from the purity of Christian religion" might practice their beliefs in the colony. Locke advocated the toleration of Jews and other non–Christian, indigenous peoples, with an eye to their eventual conversion "by good usage and persuasion," in the hope that they could "be won over to embrace and unfeignedly receive the truth"; see Thorpe, *Federal and State Constitutions*, 5:2783–84. In the meantime, Locke pragmatically planned that "civil peace may be maintained amidst diversity of [religious] opinions."

45. Members of both parties owned slaves; Bernard Bailyn, ed., *The Debate on the Constitution: Federalist and Antifederalist Speeches, Articles, and Letters During the Struggle for Ratification*, 2 vols. (New York: Library of America, 1993). James Iredell, Federalist, owned eight slaves (2:982); Samuel Johnston, Federalist, owned ninety-six slaves (2:986); David Caldwell, Anti-Federalist, owned eight slaves (2:971); Henry Abbot, Anti-Federalist, owned six slaves (2:967).

46. Quoted in Robert J. Allison, *The Crescent Obscured: The United States and the*

Muslim World, 1776–1815 (Chicago: University of Chicago Press, 2000), 57–59; quote on 35.

47. Storing, *Complete Anti-Federalist,* 2:159, written in Philadelphia, 1787; 2:410, written in New York, 1788; 3:119, written in Philadelphia, 1787; 5:227, written in Virginia, 1788.

48. Historical precedents, from ancient to modern, remained European, not Islamic; see Alexander Hamilton, James Madison, and John Jay, *The Federalist Papers,* ed. J. R. Pole (Indianapolis: Hackett, 2005), xxi.

49. "Patrick Dollard Fears a Corrupt, Despotic Aristocracy," May 22, 1788, in *Debate on the Constitution,* 2:593–94; Allison, *Crescent Obscured,* 57–59.

50. "Thomas Jefferson Replies to Madison," December 20, 1787, in *Debate on the Constitution,* 1:211.

51. "Thomas Jefferson Replies to James Madison," December 20, 1787, in *The Writings of Thomas Jefferson,* ed. Saul K. Padover (Lunenburg, VT: Stinehour Press, 1967), 314.

52. "Patrick Dollard Fears a Corrupt, Despotic Aristocracy," May 22, 1788, in *Debate on the Constitution,* 2:593; Allison, *Crescent Obscured,* 57–58.

53. "Patrick Dollard Fears a Corrupt, Despotic Aristocracy," May 22, 1788, in *Debate on the Constitution,* 2:593–94.

54. "Patrick Henry's Objections to a National Army and James Madison's Reply," June 16, 1788, in *Debate on the Constitution,* 2:695.

55. Ibid., 2:695–96.

56. Ibid., 2:697–99.

57. "'A Citizen of America' [Noah Webster]," in *Debate on the Constitution,* 1:129.

58. Ibid., 1:150–51.

59. Ibid., 1:151.

60. Allison, *Crescent Obscured,* 35–59; Timothy Marr, *The Cultural Roots of American Islamicism* (New York: Cambridge University Press, 2006), 1–65; Kidd, "Is it Worse to Follow Mahomet Than the Devil?," 767–89.

61. Elliot, *Debates,* 4:192, 194, 198 (three times on this page, including reference to "the Grand Turk"), 215; Bradley, "No Religious Test," 691, 697, 702, 710.

62. Elliot, *Debates,* 4:197 (Jews referenced twice and Jewish religion once), 198, 199 (Jews mentioned twice), 200.

63. Ibid., 4:192 (Catholic religion), 193 (Catholic countries), 195 (pope), 196 (pope twice and priest once), 198 (pope), 212 (priests), 215 (pope and "Papists").

64. Ibid., 4:192 (pagans and Deists), 194 (pagans), 198 (pagans, Jews, and alone), 215 (with "Papists").

65. Ibid., 4:194, 197, 198; for president: 4:198 (twice), 215 (once).

66. Ibid., 4:191.

67. The speeches will be recorded here, with a few minor thematic exceptions, exactly in the order in which they occurred in the eighteenth century. See Willis P. Whichard, *Justice James Iredell* (Durham, NC: Carolina Academic Press, 2000), 81. The Federalist partisanship of the hired secretary, Thomas Lloyd, probably did not affect the Anti-Federalist but may have enhanced the Federalist speeches; see M. E. Bradford, *Original Intentions: On the Making and Ratification of the United States Constitution* (Athens: University of Georgia Press, 1993), 73.

68. John V. Orth, *The North Carolina State Constitution: A Reference Guide* (Westport, CT: Greenwood Press, 1993) 4.

69. Jerry W. Cotten, "Henry Abbot," in *Dictionary of North Carolina Biography,* ed. William Steven Powell, 6 vols. (Chapel Hill: University of North Carolina Press, 1979), 1:1; Bernard Bailyn, "Biographical Notes: Speakers, Writers, and Letter Recipients," in *Debate on the Constitution,* 2:981–82.

70. Bailyn, "Biographical Notes" in *Debate on the Constitution,* 2:967.

71. Cotten, "Henry Abbot," 1:1–2.

72. Bailyn, "Biographical Notes," in *Debate on the Constitution,* 2:967.

73. Cotten, "Henry Abbot," 1:1.

74. Elliot, *Debates,* 4:191.

75. Ibid., 4:192. Abbot may have remembered "an agreement between King Charles II of England and Louis XIV of France, the Sun King—that memory, and a network of old fears and resentments coming down from the Reformation," according to Bradford, *Original Intentions,* 82.

76. Elliot, *Debates,* 4:192; Bradford, *Original Intentions,* 82.

77. Elliot, *Debates,* 4:192; Pauline Maier, *Ratification: The People Debate the Constitution* (New York: Simon and Schuster, 2010), 420.

78. Elliot, *Debates,* 4:192.

79. Bradley, "No Religious Test," 698.

80. Louise Irby Trenholme, *Ratification of the Federal Constitution in North Carolina* (New York: Columbia University Press, 1932), 120; Whichard, *Iredell,* 45.

81. Don Higginbotham, "James Iredell, Sr.," in *Dictionary of North Carolina Biography,* 3:253.

82. Whichard, *Iredell,* 43–86.

83. Ibid., 56; quoted in McRee, *Life and Correspondence,* 2:225–39.

84. Higginbotham, "Iredell," 3:254.

85. Bailyn, "Biographical Notes," in *Debate on the Constitution,* 2:982.

86. Higginbotham, "Iredell," 3:254.

87. Bailyn, "Biographical Notes," in *Debate on the Constitution,* 2:982.

88. "Answers to Mason's 'Objections': 'Marcus' [James Iredell] I–V," in *Debate on the Constitution,* 1:363–98.

89. Whichard, *Iredell,* 56.

90. McRee, *Life and Correspondence,* 1:174; Higginbotham, "Iredell," 3:253.

91. Elliot, *Debates,* 4:192–93.

92. Ibid., 4:193.

93. Ibid., 4:193–94.

94. Ibid., 4:193.

95. *Papers of Thomas Jefferson,* 1:548.

96. Elliot, *Debates,* 4:194; Maier, *Ratification,* 420.

97. Elliot, *Debates,* 4:194.

98. Ibid.

99. Ibid.

100. Bret E. Carroll, *Routledge Historical Atlas of Religion in America* (New York: Routledge, 2000), 90–95.

101. Quoted in Jacob R. Marcus, *The Colonial American Jew, 1492–1776,* 3 vols. (Detroit: Wayne State University Press, 1970), 1:502.

102. Marcus, *Colonial American Jew,* 1:503.

103. Elliot, *Debates,* 4:195.

104. Ibid., 4:195–96.

105. Ibid., 4:196.

106. Ibid.

107. Ibid., 4:193.

108. Ibid., 4:212.

109. Ibid., 4:215.

110. Ibid., 4:196.

111. Borden, *Jews, Turks, and Infidels,* 6.

112. Cohen, *Jews in Christian America,* 13.

113. Elliot, *Debates,* 4:196–97.

114. Ibid., 4:196.

115. Ibid.

116. Ibid., 4:197–98.

117. This gesture of respect has a precedent in Hindu law under British rule; see Georg Bühler, trans., *The Laws of Manu*, vol. 25 of *The Sacred Books of the East* (1886; repr., Delhi: Motilal Benarsidass, 1964), 42–43, 54–55. I am grateful to Xinru Liu for this reference.

118. Elliot, *Debates*, 4:198.

119. Bailyn, "Biographical Notes," in *Debate on the Constitution*, 2:986.

120. Anna Withers Bair, "Samuel Johnston," *Dictionary of North Carolina Biography*, 3:306–7.

121. Bailyn, "Biographical Notes," in *Debate on the Constitution*, 2:986.

122. Bair, "Samuel Johnston," 3:307–8.

123. Elliot, *Debates*, 4:198.

124. Ibid.

125. Ibid.

126. Ibid., 4:198–99.

127. Ibid., 4:199.

128. Ibid., 4:194.

129. Blackwell F. Robinson, "David Caldwell," in *Dictionary of North Carolina Biography*, 1:300.

130. Ibid., 1:301; Bailyn, "Biographical Notes," in *Debate on the Constitution*, 2:971.

131. Robinson, "David Caldwell," 1:301.

132. Bailyn, "Biographical Notes," in *Debate on the Constitution*, 2:971. The number of acres owned is disputed at 550 by Robinson, "David Caldwell," 1:301.

133. Elliot, *Debates*, 4:199.

134. Ibid.; Thomas S. Kidd, *God of Liberty: A Religious History of the American Revolution* (New York: Basic Books, 2010).

135. Elliot, *Debates*, 4:200.

136. Ibid., 4:199.

137. Trenholme, *Ratification*, 108. Unfortunately, less is known about Lancaster than other delegates.

138. Elliot, *Debates*, 4:215.

139. Ibid.

140. Borden, *Jews, Turks, and Infidels*, 54–58.

141. Ibid., 25.

142. Whichard, *Iredell*, 74.

143. Quoted in Trenholme, *Ratification*, 183.

144. Whichard, *Iredell*, 74.

145. Trenholme, *Ratification*, 152–55.

146. James Iredell, "To the People of North Carolina," August 18, 1788, in *The Papers of James Iredell*, ed. Donna Kelly and Lang Baradell, 3 vols. (Raleigh, NC: Division of Archives and History, Department of Cultural Resources, 2003), 3:418.

147. Whichard, *Iredell*, 81; McRee, *Life and Correspondence*, 2:235.

148. Bailyn, "Biographical Notes," in *Debate on the Constitution*, 2:982.

149. Quoted in Higginbotham, "Iredell," 3:254.

150. E. Millicent Sowerby, ed., *Catalogue of the Library of Thomas Jefferson*, 5 vols. (Washington, DC: Library of Congress, 1952–53), 2:388.

151. Whichard, *Iredell*, 90–91; Bailyn, "Biographical Notes," in *Debate on the Constitution*, 2:982.

152. Bailyn, "Biographical Notes," in *Debate on the Constitution*, 2:982.

153. Bair, "Samuel Johnston," 3:307.

154. Bailyn, "Biographical Notes," in *Debate on the Constitution*, 2:982.

155. The classic biography of Ibrahima is by Terry L. Alford, *Prince Among Slaves* (New York: Harcourt Brace Jovanovich, 1977), xvi; see also Michael A. Gomez, *Black Crescent: The Experience and Legacy of African Muslims in the Americas* (New York: Cambridge University Press, 2005), 168.

156. The study of specific Muslim slaves in North America includes at least seventy-five men before the Civil War, including both Ibrahima Abd al-Rahman and Omar ibn Said; see Allan D. Austin, *African Muslims in Antebellum America: Transatlantic Stories and Spiritual Struggles* (New York: Routledge, 1997), 30, 54–83, 128–56. In his earlier volume, he includes primary sources: Allan D. Austin, *Africans in Antebellum America: A Sourcebook* (New York: Garland, 1984), 121–263, 445–523. Hereafter cited as *Sourcebook*. There is also a PBS documentary of Ibrahima, based on Terry Alford's biography, *Prince Among Slaves,* directed by Andrea Kalin (n.p.: National Black Programming Consortium and Unity Productions, 2008), DVD. For Omar ibn Said, the earliest Arabic autobiography with the translation of Isaac Bird (d. 1876), a Christian missionary to Syria, with the revision of Dr. F. M. Moussa, secretary of the Egyptian legation in Washington, is presented by J. F. Jameson, "Autobiography of Omar ibn Said, Slave in North Carolina, 1831," *American Historical Review* 30, no. 4 (1925): 787–95. A reprint of this exact translation may be found in Muhammad A. al-Ahari, *Five Classic Muslim Slave Narratives* (Chicago: Maghribine Press, 2006), 187–200. A new translation, featuring Arabic-English facing pages of the original manuscript is provided by Ala A. Alryyes, trans., "The Life of Omar Ibn Said, Written by Himself," in *The Multilingual Anthology of American Literature,* ed. Marc Shell and Werner Sollors (New York: New York University Press, 2000), 58–93 (Arabic-English), 712–14. The newest, stand-alone translation, also with original Arabic text and English translation, may be found in Ala Alryyes, ed. and trans., *A Muslim American Slave: The Life of Omar ibn Said* (Madison: University of Wisconsin Press, 2011), 48–79. My references to the Arabic and English are to this edition, cited hereafter as *Life*. See also Gomez, *Black Crescent,* 169–72, 176–79, 181–82 (Ibrahima Abd al-Rahman), and 168, 172, 176–79 (Umar [Omar] ibn Said). For a recent, brief overview of Omar, see Jonathan Curiel, "The Life of Omar ibn Said," *Saudi Aramco World* 61, no. 2 (March/April 2010): 34–39.

157. For the racial implications for Ibrahima and Omar of their Arabic literacy, see Jill Lepore, *A Is for American: Letters and Other Characters in the Newly United States* (New York: Knopf, 2002), 111–35.

158. For the best linguistic and historical analysis of Omar's Arabic, see John Hunwick, "'I Wish to Be Seen in Our Land Called Afrika': Umar B. Sayyid's Appeal to Be Released from Slavery (1819)," *Journal of Arabic Studies* 5 (2003–2004): 62–77; see also John Hunwick, "West Africa and the Arabic Language," *Sudanic Africa* 15 (2004): 133–44.

159. Austin, *African Muslims,* 80; Austin, *Sourcebook,* 224; Gomez, *Black Crescent,* 169.

160. Austin, *African Muslims,* 70.

161. Quoted ibid., 81.

162. Ibid., 69.

163. Ibid., 70.

164. Ibid.

165. Quoted ibid., 71.

166. Ibid., 71–72.

167. Austin, *Sourcebook,* 127, says that the meeting took place around 1807.

168. Ibid., 128.

169. Austin, *African Muslims,* 72.

170. Quoted in Alford, *Prince,* 78.

171. Ibid., 98.

172. Quoted in Gomez, *Black Crescent,* 181–82.

173. Alford, *Prince,* 99–101.

174. Ibid., 101.

175. Quoted ibid., 102.

176. Austin, *Sourcebook,* 128.

177. Quoted in Alford, *Prince,* 103.

178. Ibid., 104.

179. Austin, *African Muslims*, 73.

180. Quoted ibid., 66.

181. Ibid.

182. Quoted in Alford, *Prince*, 119–20.

183. Ibid., 120.

184. Quoted ibid.

185. Ibid., 120, 129.

186. Gomez, *Black Crescent*, 172; Austin, *African Muslims*, 74–75, figures 11 and 12. The comment about the *Fatiha* is found in Muhammad M. Pickthall, trans., *The Meaning of the Glorious Qur'an: Text and Explanatory Translation* (New York: Muslim World League, 1977), 1.

187. Austin, *African Muslims*, 76.

188. Ibid., 65.

189. Alford, *Prince*, 183.

190. Ibid., 185.

191. Austin, *African Muslims*, 77.

192. Alford, *Prince*, 185–87.

193. Austin, *African Muslims*, 129.

194. Alryyes, *Life*, 62–63, his translation; Austin, *Sourcebook*, 465, has a slightly different translation.

195. Austin, *African Muslims*, 133–34.

196. Alryyes, *Life*, 48–79.

197. Jameson, "Autobiography of Omar ibn Said," 790.

198. Alryyes, *Life*, xii.

199. Ibid., 66–67. On page 66 of the Arabic original, at the end of the first line, beginning of the second, Omar writes, for "America," *mrk,* for which vowels would render the word "Amrika." He addressed the "people of America" not as "all of you" but as "all of them."

200. Austin, *African Muslims*, 135.

201. Austin, *Sourcebook*, 450.

202. Jameson, "Autobiography of Omar ibn Said," 790.

203. Alryyes, *Life*, 50–51.

204. Austin, *African Muslims*, 73.

205. This is the interpretation quoted in Alryyes, *Life*, 22–27; for the Qur'anic verses, 51–57.

206. Qur'an 67:1, 3, 9; Alryyes, *Life*, 22–27.

207. Pickthall, trans., *Qur'an*, 640.

208. Alryyes, *Life*, 23. For the idea that Omar's church attendance signaled his eventual conversion to Christianity, see Jameson, "Autobiography of Omar ibn Said," 790.

209. Alryyes, *Life*, 25–26; Gomez, *Black Crescent*, 176–77; Austin, *Sourcebook*, 452.

210. Alryyes, *Life*, 66 (Arabic), 67 (English). Alryyes translates "my religion was/is the religion of Mohammed." But the Arabic is unequivocally in the present tense: "*dini din Muhammad.*" Elsewhere, Omar chose to use the verb *kana,* which would indicate the past tense, on 74, line 2.

211. Ibid., 66–67.

212. Alryyes, *Life*, 72–73, transfers the third-person masculine singular to the first person and does not translate the first line *al-awwal,* meaning "first" or "before."

213. Omar's use of the third-person masculine singular in place of the first person was first noted in his autobiography and his earlier 1819 plea for freedom by Hunwick, "I Wish to Be Seen in Our Land Called Afrika," 67 n. 10.

214. Alryyes, *Life*, 60–61. Omar frequently wrote an "f" (*fa'*) in Arabic for a "q" (*qaf*), the visual difference between the former and the latter being one rather than two

dots, respectively. My thanks to Margaret Larkin for sharing her insightful observations about what Omar's errors in Arabic might mean in the telling of his life story.

215. Ibid., 72–73.

216. Ibid., 74–75.

217. Ibid. This sentence could be read as, "First, Muhammad, he prays, he said: 'Praise be . . .'" Again, Omar is not using the first person but the verb in the third-person masculine singular.

218. Austin, *African Muslims,* 135–36.

219. Austin, *Sourcebook,* 476–77. The Arabic translation given by Austin from Professor R. D. Wilson of Princeton Theological Seminary omits the "our Lord" from "our Lord Muhammad," 476.

220. Constitution, Article I, section 2, third paragraph, struck down by the Fourteenth Amendment, section 2, which was ratified on July 9, 1868. For discussion of this passage of the Constitution in North Carolina on July 30, 1788, see Elliot, *Debates,* 4:205.

221. Mine is a variation of Gomez's original title, "Founding Mothers and Fathers of a Different Sort," *Black Crescent,* 143–84.

6. JEFFERSON WAGES WAR AGAINST AN ISLAMIC POWER; ENTERTAINS THE FIRST MUSLIM AMBASSADOR; DECIDES WHERE TO PLACE THE QUR'AN IN HIS LIBRARY; AND AFFIRMS HIS SUPPORT FOR MUSLIM RIGHTS, 1790–1823

1. Thomas Jefferson, "Report of the Secretary of State to the Congress of the United States: Mediterranean Trade," December 28, 1790, in *Naval Documents Related to the United States Wars with the Barbary Powers: Naval Operations Including Diplomatic Background from 1785 through 1801,* 3 vols. (Washington, DC: U.S. Government Printing Office, 1939), 1:23. Hereafter cited as "Mediterranean Trade, 1790."

2. Gary Edward Wilson, "American Prisoners in the Barbary Nations, 1784–1816" (PhD diss., North Texas State University, 1979), 320.

3. Richard B. Parker, *Uncle Sam in Barbary: A Diplomatic History* (Gainesville: University Press of Florida, 2004), xxiv.

4. Jefferson, "Mediterranean Trade, 1790," 1:22; Ray W. Irwin, *The Diplomatic Relations of the United States with the Barbary Powers, 1776–1816* (New York: Russell and Russell, 1931), 17–18.

5. Jefferson, "Mediterranean Trade, 1790," 1:22; Michael L. S. Kitzen, *Tripoli and the United States at War: A History of American Relations with the Barbary States* (Jefferson, NC: McFarland and Co., 1993), 10.

6. Jefferson, "Mediterranean Trade, 1790," 1:22–23.

7. Kitzen, *Tripoli,* 14.

8. Thomas Jefferson, "Report of the Secretary of State on the subject of citizens of the United States in captivity in Algiers . . . ," December 30, 1790, in *Naval Documents,* 1:21–22. Hereafter cited as Jefferson, "Report, citizens . . . in Algiers."

9. Timothy Marr, *The Cultural Roots of American Islamicism* (New York: Cambridge University Press, 2006), 67; Robert J. Allison, *The Crescent Obscured: The United States and the Muslim World, 1776–1815* (Chicago: University of Chicago Press, 2000), 33.

10. Jefferson, "Report, citizens . . . in Algiers," in *Naval Documents,* 1:22.

11. Jefferson, "Mediterranean Trade, 1790," ibid., 1:23–24.

12. Ibid., 1:26.

13. "Thomas Jefferson to Jonathan B. Smith," April 26, 1791, in *The Papers of Thomas Jefferson,* ed. Julian P. Boyd et al., 40 vols. (Princeton: Princeton University Press, 1950–), 20:290. Hereafter cited as *Papers of Thomas Jefferson.* Allison, *Crescent Obscured,* 40.

14. "Thomas Jefferson to George Washington," May 8, 1791, in *Papers of Thomas Jefferson*, 20:291; John Ferling, *Adams vs. Jefferson: The Tumultuous Election of 1800* (New York: Oxford University Press, 2012), 50–51. My thanks to Neil Kamil for this reference.

15. "Thomas Jefferson to James Madison," May 9, 1791, in *Papers of Thomas Jefferson*, 20:293.

16. "James Madison to Thomas Jefferson," May 12, 1791, ibid., 20:284; Kevin J. Hayes, *The Road to Monticello: The Life and Mind of Thomas Jefferson* (New York: Oxford University Press, 2008), 400–401.

17. "Thomas Jefferson to Thomas Mann Randolph, Jr.," July 3, 1791, in *Papers of Thomas Jefferson*, 20:296.

18. John Quincy Adams, *Writings of John Quincy Adams*, ed. Worthington Ford, 7 vols. (Boston: Macmillan, 1913), 1:65. This fractious incident has been covered by Julian P. Boyd, *Papers of Thomas Jefferson*, 20:277–90; Merrill D. Peterson, *Adams and Jefferson: A Revolutionary Dialogue* (Athens: University of Georgia Press, 1976), 55–61; Allison, *Crescent Obscured*, 39–40.

19. *Papers of Thomas Jefferson*, 20:283.

20. John Quincy Adams, *Writings*, 1:67–68.

21. Ibid.

22. Craig Nelson, *Thomas Paine: Enlightenment, Revolution, and the Birth of Modern Nations* (New York: Penguin, 2007), 261–62; Humberto Garcia, *Islam and the English Enlightenment, 1670–1840* (Baltimore: Johns Hopkins University Press, 2012), 152–53.

23. John Quincy Adams, *Writings*, 1:68.

24. Lester J. Cappon, *The Adams-Jefferson Letters: The Complete Correspondence Between Thomas Jefferson and Abigail and John Adams*, 2 vols. (Chapel Hill: University of North Carolina Press, 1959), 1:246. Hereafter cited as *Adams-Jefferson Letters*.

25. Ibid., 1:246.

26. Ibid., 1:247.

27. Ibid., 1:248.

28. Ibid., 1:250.

29. Ibid., 1:248.

30. Ibid., 1:251.

31. Kevin J. Hayes, "How Thomas Jefferson Read the Qur'an," *Early American Literature* 39, no. 2 (2004): 259.

32. Ferling, *Adams vs. Jefferson*, 51, declares that the friendship "perished that spring."

33. Allison, *Crescent Obscured*, 39–40; Thomas S. Kidd, *American Christians and Islam: Evangelical Culture and Muslims from the Colonial Period to the Age of Terrorism* (Princeton: Princeton University Press, 2009), 6–10.

34. Allison, *Crescent Obscured*, 43–45.

35. Ibid., 47, 52–53, 56.

36. John Adams, "Thoughts on Government, 1776," in *American Political Writing During the Founding Era, 1750–1805*, ed. Charles S. Hyneman and Donald S. Lutz, 2 vols. (Indianapolis: Liberty Fund, 1983), 1:402.

37. John Adams, *The Works of John Adams, Second President of the United States*, ed. Charles Francis Adams, 10 vols. (Boston: Little, Brown, 1850–56), 6:275.

38. *Adams-Jefferson Letters*, 2:434–35.

39. Although disputed, this unsigned essay, which expresses anti-Islamic sentiments similar to those directed earlier against Thomas Jefferson, is attributed to Adams as part of his bibliography by Lynn H. Parsons, *John Quincy Adams: A Bibliography* (Westport, CT: Greenwood Press, 1993), 41.

40. *The American Annual Register; for the Years 1827–8–9* (New York: E. & G. W. Blunt, 1830), 274.

41. Quoted in Morton Borden, *Jews, Turks, and Infidels* (Chapel Hill: University of North Carolina Press, 1984), 25. See also George A. Lipsky, *John Quincy Adams: His Theory and Ideas* (New York: Crowell, 1950), 122.

42. Thomas Paine, *Thomas Paine: "Rights of Man," "Common Sense" and Other Political Writings,* ed. Mark Philip (New York: Oxford University Press, 1998), 16; Kidd, *American Christians and Islam,* 19.

43. Paine, *Rights of Man,* 137.

44. Ibid.

45. Thomas Paine, *The Age of Reason: Being an Investigation of True and Fabulous Theology, Part I (1794)* (Cutchogue, NY: Buccaneer Books, 1976), 5–7; Kerry Walters, *Revolutionary Deists: Early America's Rational Infidels* (Amherst, NY: Prometheus Books, 2011), 121–22; Nelson, *Thomas Paine,* 262.

46. *The Debates and Proceedings of the Congress of the United States with an Appendix, containing Important State Papers and Public Documents, and All the Laws of a Public Nature, with a Copious Index; Fifth Congress, Comprising the Period from May 15, 1797, to March 3, 1799, inclusive* (Washington, DC: Gales and Seaton, 1851), 3:3094–95. For the treaty with the Arabic version, see "Tripoli: November 4, 1796, and January 3, 1797," in *Treaties and Other International Acts of the United States of America,* ed. Hunter Miller, 8 vols. (Washington, DC: U.S. Government Printing Office, 1931), 2:365 (English), 2:360 (presumed Arabic equivalent). Variations in capitalization and punctuation exist between the two sources, with the quotation from the treaty taken from Miller, *Treaties,* 2:365.

47. "Journal of the executive proceedings of the Senate of the United States of America, 1789–1805: Wednesday, June 7, 1797," http://memory.loc.gov/ll/llej/001/0200/02510244.gif.

48. Newspapers that published the treaty with Tripoli include: *Philadelphia Gazette,* June, 17, 1797; *American Mercury* (Hartford, CT), June 26, 1797; *Boston Gazette,* June 26, 1797; *Boston Price-Current and Marine Intelligencer,* June 26, 1797; *Hudson Gazette* (Hudson, NY), June 27, 1797; *Newport Mercury* (Newport, RI), June 27, 1797; *Impartial Herald* (Newburyport, MA), June 27, 1797; *Connecticut Gazette* (New London, CT), June 28, 1797; *Courier of New Hampshire* (Concord, NH), July 25, 1797.

49. Adams's promulgation appeared on the front page of the *Boston-Price Current and Marine Intelligencer,* Monday, June 26, 1797. See also Jon Meacham, *American Gospel: God, the Founding Fathers, and the Making of a Nation* (New York: Random House, 2006), 262, where Article 11 is reprinted with the assertion that it "was widely discussed and published."

50. William Cobbett, *Porcupine Gazette,* June 23, 1797.

51. For the first to note Cobbett's criticism, see Frank Lambert, *The Founding Fathers and the Place of Religion in America* (Princeton: Princeton University Press, 2003), 238–41.

52. For the idea of Barlow as the author of Article 11, see Borden, *Jews, Turks, and Infidels,* 77–78.

53. Quoted ibid., 77.

54. Although some have attempted to attribute Article 11 to George Washington because negotiations for it occurred during his presidency, this connection has no basis in fact; see Paul F. Boller, *George Washington and Religion* (Dallas: Southern Methodist University Press, 1963), 87–88.

55. "Appointment of Joel Barlow, as U.S. Agent, Algiers," February 10, 1796, in *Naval Documents,* 1:133.

56. Arthur L. Ford, *Joel Barlow* (New York: Twayne, 1971), 18–19, 27.

57. Sam Haselby, "The Enigma of America's Secular Roots: Joel Barlow's Disavowal of Christianity as the Basis for US Government in the 1797 Treaty of Tripoli Is a Mystery," *Guardian,* January 3, 2011. Haselby refers to Barlow's *Advice to Privileged*

Orders. My thanks to Bernard Bailyn for this reference. See also Robert Boston, "Joel Barlow and the Treaty with Tripoli," http://www.stephenjaygould.org/ctrl/archive/boston_tripoli.html.

58. Joel Barlow, *Advice to the Privileged Orders in the Several States of Europe, resulting from the Necessity and propriety of a general revolution in the principles of government,* Part I (London: Childs and Swaine, 1792), 39.

59. Ibid., 53; Marr, *Cultural Roots,* 58.

60. Barlow, *Advice,* 53.

61. Lambert, *Founding Fathers,* 240.

62. "To Tobias Lear, appointed U.S. Consul General, Algiers, from Secretary of State, [James Madison]," July 14, 1803, in *Naval Documents,* 2:485; Frank Lambert, *The Barbary Wars: American Independence in the Atlantic World* (New York: Hill and Wang, 2005), 118.

63. James Madison, *A Memorial and Remonstrance against Religious Assessments,* in *The Sacred Rights of Conscience: Selected Readings on Religious Liberty and Church-State Relations in the American Founding,* ed. Daniel L. Dreisbach and Mark David Hall (Indianapolis: Liberty Fund, 2009), 311.

64. Ibid., 312.

65. Robert A. Rutland, ed., *The Papers of George Mason,* 3 vols. (Chapel Hill: University of North Carolina Press, 1970), 2:832; also cited in Thomas E. Buckley, *Church and State in Revolutionary Virginia, 1776–1787* (Charlottesville: University Press of Virginia, 1977), 136.

66. *Papers of James Mason,* 2:832; Buckley, *Church and State,* 136.

67. "Chesterfield Assembly Petition (Virginia), November 14, 1785," *Religious Petitions Virginia,* Library of Congress, http://memory.loc.gov/ndlpcoop/relpet.215. I would like to thank James Hutson for this reference; see also James H. Hutson, "The Founding Fathers and Islam," *The Library of Congress Information Bulletin* 61, no. 5 (2002): 1, http://www.loc.gov/loc/lcib/0205/tolerance.html.

68. "Chesterfield Assembly, 1785"; for the importance of Virginia's dissenters in this movement to end an establishment of the Christian religion, see John A. Ragosta, *Wellspring of Liberty: How Virginia's Religious Dissenters Helped Win the American Revolution and Secured Religious Liberty* (New York: Oxford University Press, 2010), 12, 144–45.

69. American diplomats relied upon the consul from Spain, Gerardo de Souza, to verify the Arabic seals; see "Tripoli: November 4, 1796, and January 3, 1797," in Miller, *Treaties,* 2:378–79.

70. Even James Cathcart, a prisoner in Algiers eleven years before taking up his post as consul at Tripoli, "did not read Arabic, although he seems to have been familiar with Turkish and Italian"; see ibid., quote on 2:382.

71. See "The Annotated Translation of 1930," by Dr. C. Snouck Hurgronje, of Leiden, in Miller, *Treaties,* 2:368–79.

72. Charles O. Lerche Jr., "Jefferson and the Election of 1800: A Case Study in the Political Smear," *William and Mary Quarterly,* 3rd ser., 5, no. 4 (October 1948): 467–91; Azizah Y. al-Hibri, "Islamic and American Constitutional Law: Borrowing Possibilities or a History of Borrowing?" *University of Pennsylvania Journal of Constitutional Law* 1, no. 3 (1999): 501. For a chapter dedicated to Jefferson as "The Pious Infidel," without any connection to Islam, see Steven Waldman, *Founding Faith: Providence, Politics, and the Birth of Religious Freedom in America* (New York: Random House, 2008), 72–84.

73. Lerche, "Jefferson and the Election of 1800," 470, 472, 473; Ferling, *Adams vs. Jefferson,* 154; Thomas S. Kidd, *God of Liberty: A Religious History of the American Revolution* (New York: Basic Books, 2010), 234–43.

74. "Infidel," *Oxford English Dictionary,* 13 vols. (Oxford: Clarendon Press, 1970), 5:260; al-Hibri, "Islamic and American Constitutional Law," 501, who cites this term as a politically viable one, albeit without specific reference to the presidential campaign of 1800.

75. Quoted in Lambert, *Founding Fathers*, 276–77; Lerche, "Jefferson and the Election of 1800," 473; Ferling, *Adams vs. Jefferson*, 154.

76. Lambert, *Founding Fathers*, 266.

77. Ibid., 265–68, 276–77.

78. Quoted ibid., 265.

79. Thomas Jefferson, *Notes on Virginia*, in *The Life and Selected Writings of Thomas Jefferson*, ed. Adrienne Koch and William Peden (New York: Modern Library, 1998), 254.

80. Quoted in Lambert, *Founding Fathers*, 278. This assertion was earlier made by Lerche, "Jefferson and the Election of 1800," 273.

81. Jefferson, "A Declaration by the Representatives of the United States of America, in General Congress Assembled," a part of "Autobiography," in *Life and Selected Writings*, 26.

82. Jefferson, "Autobiography," in *Life and Selected Writings*, 23.

83. "Jefferson to Joseph Priestley," March 21, 1801, in *The Papers of Thomas Jefferson*, ed. Barbara Oberg (Princeton: Princeton University Press, 2006), 33:393.

84. Irwin, *Diplomatic Relations*, 103, gives the date of the meeting as May 10; Kitzen, *Tripoli*, 46, gives May 10; Irving Brant, *James Madison: Secretary of State, 1800–1809*, 6 vols. (Indianapolis: Bobbs-Merrill, 1953), 4:60, where the date for the vote is May 15.

85. Irwin, *Diplomatic Relations*, 106.

86. For disagreement about the exact number of ships and American captives, compare Allison, *Crescent Obscured*, 230 n. 37, with Wilson, "American Prisoners," 320–21.

87. Kola Folayan, *Tripoli During the Reign of Yusuf Pasha Qaramanli* (Ife, Nigeria: University of Ife Press, 1979), 31.

88. Ibid., 27.

89. Ibid., 28.

90. For disagreement on the success of these measures, see Allison, *Crescent Obscured*, 27; Folayan, *Tripoli*, 35.

91. Irwin, *Diplomatic Relations*, 122–23, 110. The captured Tripolitan ship was allowed to return to her port, with her armaments thrown overboard; Allison, *Crescent Obscured*, 26–27.

92. Allison, *Crescent Obscured*, 27.

93. Irwin, *Diplomatic Relations*, 130.

94. Folayan, *Tripoli*, 36; Allison, *Crescent Obscured*, 28, says "300 sailors."

95. Irwin, *Diplomatic Relations*, 134; Jonathan Cowdery, "American Captives in Tripoli," in Paul Baepler, ed., *White Slaves, African Masters: An Anthology of American Barbary Captivity Narratives* (Chicago: University of Chicago Press, 1999), 167, 171, 180.

96. Irwin, *Diplomatic Relations*, 135; Allison, *Crescent Obscured*, 190–95.

97. Irwin, *Diplomatic Relations*, 143.

98. Lambert, *Barbary Wars*, 151; the ten Americans included "eight marines and two navy midshipmen."

99. Parker, *Uncle Sam*, xxvii; Irwin, *Diplomatic Relations*, 147–48, offers a slightly different date.

100. Parker, *Uncle Sam*, xxvii; Irwin, *Diplomatic Relations*, 135.

101. Dumas Malone, *Jefferson the President: First Term, 1801–1805*, vol. 4 of *Jefferson and His Time* (Boston: Little, Brown, 1970), 97–99; Allison, *Crescent Obscured*, 25–33; Parker, *Uncle Sam*, xxviii.

102. "Over four hundred and fifty citizens" are estimated by Irwin, *Diplomatic Relations*, 204. Presumably Irwin includes the three hundred souls of the frigate *Philadelphia*. See, in contrast, for a total count of seven hundred American prisoners, Wilson, "American Prisoners," 321.

103. "A large number of British deserters" on the captured U.S. vessel *Philadelphia*

were encouraged to petition for their freedom as British naval officers, which 140 did; see Wilson, "American Prisoners," 197. By contrast, it is estimated that only twenty of that crew were considered native-born Americans by their captain; see Parker, *Uncle Sam*, 62.

104. For the most thorough list of American captives from 1784 to 1816, see Wilson, "American Prisoners," 321; Irwin, *Diplomatic Relations*, 204

105. "Tripoli: November 4, 1796, and January 3, 1797," in Miller, *Treaties*, 2:365.

106. "Tripoli: June 4, 1805," ibid., 2:532.

107. Irwin, *Diplomatic Relations*, 154; "Tripoli: June 4, 1805," in Miller, *Treaties*, 2:529.

108. "Tripoli: 1805," in Miller, *Treaties*, 2:541 (Arabic). The Arabic version uses *madhab*, meaning school of law for laws, and also *shar‘*, for the revelation of the Qur'an and its laws, as well as *din* for religion.

109. "Tripoli: November 4, 1796, and January 3, 1797," ibid., 2:365.

110. "Tripoli: 1805," ibid., 2:532.

111. "Tripoli: November 4, 1796, and January 3, 1797," ibid., 2:365; "Tripoli: 1805," ibid., 2:532. The variations are slight, with new capitals in the 1806 version and the addition of "contracting" to parties and the substitution in the last of "nations" instead of the original "countries."

112. "Tripoli: 1805," ibid., 2:532.

113. "Algiers: June 30 and July 3, 1815," ibid., 2:588–89; "Algiers: December 22 and 23, 1816," ibid., 2:620.

114. "Algiers, June 30 and July 3, 1815," ibid., 2:589.

115. "Algiers: December 22 and 23, 1816," ibid., 2:632, 2:639.

116. Marr, *Cultural Roots*, 65–66; Allison, *Crescent Obscured*, 183–84. For the impact on early national identity, see Robert Battistini, "Glimpses of the Other before Orientalism: The Muslim World in Early American Periodicals, 1785–1800," *Early American Studies: An Interdisciplinary Journal* 8, no. 2 (Spring 2010): 469; Jennifer Costello Brezina, "A Nation in Chains: Barbary Captives and American Identity," in *Captivating Subjects: Writing, Confinement, Citizenship and Nationhood in the Nineteenth Century*, ed. Jason Haslam and Julia M. Wright (Toronto: University of Toronto Press, 2005): 202–5. See also Jacob Rama Berman, "The Barbarous Voice of Democracy: American Captivity in Barbary and the Multicultural Specter," *American Literature* 79 (March 2007): 1–27; James Lewis, "Savages of the Seas: Barbary Captivity Tales and Images of Muslims in the Early Republic," *Journal of American Culture* 13 (Summer 1990): 75–84.

117. Irwin, *Diplomatic Relations*, 164–66, refers to him as Mellimelni; Marr, *Cultural Roots*, 66–67; Allison, *Crescent Obscured*, 183–84; L. B. Wright and J. H. Macleod, "Mellimelli," *Virginia Quarterly Review* 20 (1944): 556–65; a uniquely detailed account of the incident that sparked the visit—and Jefferson's involvement—is recounted by Parker, *Uncle Sam*, 151–55.

118. Irwin, *Diplomatic Relations*, 161.

119. Parker, *Uncle Sam*, 152–53.

120. Wright and Macleod, "Mellimelli," 556.

121. "From Hammuda Bey to Jefferson," April 15, 1801, in *Papers of Thomas Jefferson*, 33:591.

122. William Plumer, *William Plumer's Memorandum of Proceedings in the United States Senate, 1803–1807*, ed. Everett Somerville Brown (New York: Macmillan, 1923), 334.

123. Ibid., 335.

124. *Hampshire Federalist*, May 29, 1806.

125. Plumer, *Memorandum*, 333–34. Accounts may also be found in James Morton Smith, ed., *The Republic of Letters: The Correspondence Between Thomas Jefferson and James Madison, 1776–1826*, 3 vols. (New York: W. W. Norton, 1995), 3:1411, where Morton refers to the visit as "an Arabian Nights' tale"; Dumas Malone, *Jefferson the President:*

Second Term, 1805–1809, vol. 5 of *Jefferson and His Time* (Boston: Little, Brown, 1974), 43–44; Brant, *James Madison,* 4:305–10; Annette Gordon-Reed, *Thomas Jefferson and Sally Hemings: An American Controversy* (Charlottesville: University Press of Virginia, 1997), 231–32.

126. Plumer, *Memorandum,* 334.

127. Ibid., 359.

128. Quoted in Brant, *James Madison,* 4:306; Gordon-Reed, *Thomas Jefferson and Sally Hemings,* 232.

129. Gordon-Reed, *Thomas Jefferson and Sally Hemings,* 232.

130. Brant, *James Madison,* 4:305.

131. Plumer, *Memorandum,* 333.

132. Ibid., 358.

133. Ibid., 344.

134. Ibid., 359.

135. Wright and Macleod, "Mellimelli," 557.

136. Plumer, *Memorandum,* 358.

137. Ibid., 343.

138. Ibid., 344.

139. Ibid., 359.

140. Dr. Samuel L. Mitchill received an invitation from Jefferson for the December 9 dinner, which he noted as received on December 6, listing the dinnertime as "precisely at sunset." Although it has not been published, Anna Berkes, research librarian at Monticello, kindly provided me with the transcript of the invitation in a personal communication from the editors of *The Papers of Thomas Jefferson* at Princeton University Press on September 1, 2010.

141. Gaye Wilson, "Dealing with Mellimelli, Colorful Envoy from Tunis," *Monticello Newsletter* 14, no. 2 (Winter 2003): 3. This event was first documented by Richard Schrodermier, "An Invitation to Dinner with Thomas Jefferson," *Manuscripts* 51, no. 4 (1999): 313–16.

142. John Quincy Adams, *Memoirs,* ed. Charles Francis Adams, 12 vols. (Philadelphia: J. B. Lippincott and Co., 1874), 1:378.

143. Ibid.

144. Plumer, *Memorandum,* 349.

145. Ibid.

146. Brant, *James Madison,* 4:307.

147. Plumer, *Memorandum,* 366.

148. Allison, *Crescent Obscured,* 183–84.

149. "Jefferson to Madison," May 19, 1806, in Smith, *Republic of Letters,* 3:1421.

150. "Madison to Jefferson," June 14, 1805, ibid., 3:1426 n. 21; Irwin, *Diplomatic Relations,* 164–66.

151. "Madison to Jefferson," June 14, 1805, in Smith, *Republic of Letters,* 3:1426–27; Brant, *James Madison,* 4:308.

152. Parker, *Uncle Sam,* 155.

153. The letter and a draft in Jefferson's hand exist in the Library of Congress: "Thomas Jefferson to Bey of Tunis," June 28, 1806, in *The Thomas Jefferson Papers Series 1. General Correspondence. 1651–1827,* Library of Congress, http://hdl.loc.gov/loc.mss/mtj.mtjbib016251. Images 302–3 are the final draft, while images 304–5 are the first draft. The final version exists in the National Archives of Tunisia in a scribe's hand, signed by both Thomas Jefferson and, for the first time, James Madison as secretary of state. The Tunisian version is reproduced in Parker, *Uncle Sam,* appendix 13, 239–41. References to Thomas Jefferson's original hereafter "Thomas Jefferson to Bey of Tunis" and image number, with additional references to the final version as "Thomas Jefferson to Bey of Tunis," Tunisian Archives, 1–3. I am deeply grateful to my colleague Anver

Emon, who kindly contacted one of his colleagues, Laryssa Chomiak, in Tunis. She generously sent me a scanned copy of the Jefferson letter from the Tunisian National Archives. Personal e-mail, February 14, 2012.

154. "Thomas Jefferson to Bey of Tunis," *Thomas Jefferson Papers*, Library of Congress, 302.

155. "To the Bey of Tunis from President John Adams," January 15, 1800, in *Naval Documents*, 1:344.

156. "From Hammuda Bey to Jefferson," April 15, 1801, Barbara Oberg, ed., *Papers of Thomas Jefferson*, 33:591.

157. "Thomas Jefferson to Hammuda Bey," September 9, 1801, *Papers of Thomas Jefferson*, 35:241.

158. "To President Thomas Jefferson from the Bey of Tunis," September 8, 1802, *Naval Documents*, 2:269.

159. "Thomas Jefferson to Bashaw of Tripoli," May 21, 1801, ibid., 1:470.

160. "Thomas Jefferson to Bey of Tunis, April 14, 1803," in *The Thomas Jefferson Papers Series 1. General Correspondence. 1651–1827*, Library of Congress, http://hdl.loc .gov/loc.mss/mtj.mtjbib012313, image 131; "Thomas Jefferson to Bey of Tunis, January 24, 1804," ibid., Library of Congress, http://hdl.loc.gov/loc.mss/mtj.mtjbib013116, images 967–68.

161. "Thomas Jefferson to Bey of Tunis," June 28, 1806, *Thomas Jefferson Papers*, Library of Congress, 302.

162. Ibid.

163. Ibid.

164. Ibid.; Miller, "Tripoli: 1805," *Treaties*, 2:532.

165. "Thomas Jefferson to Bey of Tunis," June 28, 1806, *Thomas Jefferson Papers*, Library of Congress, 303.

166. Ibid.

167. Ibid.

168. Ibid.

169. "Thomas Jefferson to Bey of Tunis, June 28, 1806," *Thomas Jefferson Papers Series 1. General Correspondence, 1651–1827*, Library of Congress, http://hdl.loc.gov/loc .mss/mtj.mtjbib016251, image 303 (final), image 305 (draft).

170. Parker, *Uncle Sam*, 239–41.

171. Quoted in Edwin Gaustad, *Sworn on the Altar of God: A Religious Biography of Thomas Jefferson* (Grand Rapids, MI: William B. Eerdmans, 1996), 207.

172. "Thomas Jefferson to Bey of Tunis," June 28, 1806, *Thomas Jefferson Papers*, Library of Congress, 302.

173. Miller, "Tripoli: 1805," *Treaties*, 2:532.

174. William Salkeld, *Reports of Cases Adjudg'd in the Court of King's Bench* (London: E. Nutt and R. Gosling, 1717), 1:46. The precedent dates from the mid-seventeenth century.

175. Muhammad M. Pickthall, trans., *The Meaning of the Glorious Qur'an: Text and Explanatory Translation* (New York: Muslim World League, 1977), 419. The line is similarly translated by Yusuf Ali, trans., *The Qur'an Translation* (Elmhurst, NY: Tahrike Tarsile Qur'an, 2005), 262, as "our God (Allah) and your God (Allah) is One."

176. Gaustad, *Sworn on the Altar of God*, 112. For a broader discussion of Priestley's Unitarian beliefs, his anti-Islamic views, and attacks against him as a Muslim, see Garcia, *Islam and the English Enlightenment*, 165–68.

177. Gaustad, *Sworn on the Altar of God*, 112–13.

178. Alexander Pirie, *An attempt to expose the weakness, fallacy and absurdity of the Unitarian or Socinian arguments against the divinity of the Son of God* (Perth: R. Morrison Junior, 1792), 32; Garcia, *Islam and the English Enlightenment*, 168.

179. John Quincy Adams, *Writings*, 1:67–68.

180. Joseph Priestley, *Letters to the Rev. Edward Burn, of St. Mary's Chapel Birmingham* (Birmingham: J. Thompson, 1790), v–vi; Garcia, *Islam and the English Enlightenment,* 168.

181. Priestley, *Letters,* v–vi, where he states that he had met in London with "an eminent popish priest," while he recalled, "I have since enriched my acquaintance with that of some very intelligent Jews."

182. Robert E. Schofield, "Priestley, Joseph (1733–1804)," *Oxford Dictionary of National Biography,* 58 vols. (New York: Oxford University Press, 2004), 45:351–59.

183. Gaustad, *Sworn on the Altar of God,* 112.

184. "Thomas Jefferson to James Smith," December 8, 1822, in *Life and Selected Writings,* 642.

185. Gaustad, *Sworn on the Altar of God,* 205–7.

186. "Thomas Jefferson to Jared Sparks," November 4, 1820, *Thomas Jefferson Papers,* Library of Congress, http://hdl.loc.gov/loc.mss/mtj.mtjbib023929, image 346.

187. Gaustad, *Sworn on the Altar of God,* 51.

188. "Thomas Jefferson to James Smith," December 8, 1822, in *Life and Selected Writings,* 642.

189. J. A. I. Champion, *The Pillars of Priestcraft Shaken: The Church of England and Its Enemies, 1660–1730* (Cambridge: Cambridge University Press, 1992), 101; Gaustad, *Sworn on the Altar of God,* 24–25; Walters, *Revolutionary Deists,* 30–33.

190. "Thomas Jefferson to Jared Sparks," *Thomas Jefferson Papers,* Library of Congress.

191. "Thomas Jefferson to James Smith," December 8, 1822, in *Life and Selected Writings,* 642–43.

192. James R. Jacob, *Henry Stubbe: Radical Protestantism and the Early Enlightenment* (Cambridge: Cambridge University Press, 1983), 155; Champion, *Pillars,* 110–11; John Marshall, *John Locke, Toleration and Early Enlightenment Culture: Religious Intolerance and Arguments for Religious Toleration in Early Modern and "Early Enlightenment" Europe* (Cambridge: Cambridge University Press, 2006), 391–92.

193. Quoted in Champion, *Pillars,* 108.

194. "Thomas Jefferson to James Fishback," September 27, 1809, in *Jefferson's Extracts from the Gospels: "The Philosophy of Jesus" and "The Life and Morals of Jesus,"* ed. Dickinson W. Adams (Princeton: Princeton University Press, 1983), 344 n. 1.

195. The earliest, somewhat different reading of this reference may be found in Hayes, "How Thomas Jefferson Read the Qur'an," 255–56; Hayes, *Road to Monticello,* 315–16.

196. "Thomas Jefferson to John Tyler," May 26, 1810, in *Thomas Jefferson: Writings,* ed. Merrill D. Peterson (New York: Library of America, 1984), 1227.

197. George Sale, trans., *The Koran (1734)* (New York: Garland, 1984), 156.

198. Hayes, "How Thomas Jefferson Read the Qur'an," 256; Azizah al-Hibri, "Islamic and American Constitutional Law," 505–6.

199. "Thomas Jefferson to Peter Carr," August 10, 1787, in *Life and Selected Writings,* 399.

200. Ibid.; al-Hibri, "Islamic and American Constitutional Law," 501.

201. "Thomas Jefferson to Peter Carr," in *Life and Selected Writings,* 400.

202. Jefferson, "Autobiography," in *Life and Selected Writings,* 92.

203. Ibid., 91.

204. "Thomas Jefferson to Benjamin Waterhouse," June 26, 1822, in *The Writings of Thomas Jefferson,* ed. Saul K. Padover (Lunenburg, VT: Stinehour Press, 1967), 359.

205. Ibid., 359–60.

206. Thomas S. Kidd, " 'Is It Worse to Follow Mahomet Than the Devil?' Early American Uses of Islam," *Church History* 72, no. 4 (December 2003): 767, 774.

207. Quoted in James Gilreath and Douglas L. Wilson, eds., *Thomas Jefferson's Library: A Catalog with the Entries in His Own Order* (Washington, DC: Library of Con-

gress, 1989), 3 n. 3; Dumas Malone, *The Sage of Monticello,* vol. 6 of *Jefferson and His Time* (Boston: Little, Brown, 1981), 167–99.

208. Gilreath and Wilson, *Thomas Jefferson's Library,* 1.

209. Ibid. The British had burned the nascent national library in Washington, D.C., the year before.

210. Ibid., v–vi.

211. E. Millicent Sowerby, ed., *Catalogue of the Library of Thomas Jefferson,* 5 vols. (Washington, DC: Library of Congress 1952–53), 5:59; Hayes, "How Thomas Jefferson Read the Qur'an," 256–58. Jefferson's library included many books that contained Arabic and sometimes Persian; for example, see Sowerby, *Catalogue,* 5:65–67. These works included the four-volume *Specimina Arabica et Persica à Vieyra* (#4743). Another tome contained a sixteenth-century Arabic translation of Euclid's *Elements,* with commentary by the thirteenth-century mathematician Nasir al-Din al-Tusi: *Euclidis elementorum libris XXII Arabice* (#1594). Jefferson also owned an apocryphal Gospel in Arabic and Latin (#4744), as well as a book on the rudiments of the Arabic language (#4746) and the eight-volume *Simplification des langues arabe, persanne et turque* by his friend Constantin Volney (#4747). The library also contained William Jones's *Poesesos Asiaticae commentaria* (#4709), an eight-volume collection of poetry in Arabic, Persian, Greek, and Hebrew. The books from his friend Samuel Henley did not arrive in Virginia from Britain until 1785, when Jefferson was away in Paris; see *Papers of Thomas Jefferson,* 8:11–14. For assertions that the volumes arrived much earlier, see Hayes, "How Thomas Jefferson Read the Qur'an," 258.

212. Arabic was not part of Jefferson's plan for the future curriculum, despite the assertion by Hayes in "How Thomas Jefferson Read the Qur'an," 258. See *Papers of Thomas Jefferson,* 2:540–45.

213. Sowerby, *Catalogue,* 5:67, for Chaldean and Syriac grammars (#1651). Multiple Hebrew grammars also existed in the library.

214. Ibid., 1:vi.

215. Hayes, "How Thomas Jefferson Read the Qur'an," 257; Sowerby, *Catalogue,* 1:133, for *The Revolt of Ali Bey* by S. L. Kosmpolitos (#314).

216. Hayes, "How Thomas Jefferson Read the Qur'an," 257.

217. Sowerby, *Catalogue,* 4:138–42, where four tomes recounted journeys in the Levant, Persia, and Egypt. For additional works on Egypt and North Africa, see ibid., 5:152–55.

218. Under European geography, Jefferson placed four travelogues about Turkey; see ibid., 4:135–36.

219. Ibid., 4:135. For the prurient interest of Americans in "the seraglio," see Allison, *Crescent Obscured,* 61–85. A more thorough contextualization of European women's travels in the East is provided by Billie Melman, *Women's Orients: English Women and the Middle East, 1718–1918* (Ann Arbor: University of Michigan Press, 1992), 75–98.

220. Sowerby, *Catalogue,* 1:134–37.

221. Ibid., 1:136–37; "Tripoli: November 4, 1796, and January 3, 1797," in Miller, *Treaties,* 2:371.

222. "Tripoli: 1796–1797," in Miller, *Treaties,* 2:371.

223. First to explore this issue was Hayes, "How Thomas Jefferson Read the Qur'an," 252.

224. Ibid., 250–54, 259; Gilreath and Wilson, *Thomas Jefferson's Library,* 58; Sowerby, *Catalogue,* 2:90.

225. Gilreath and Wilson, *Thomas Jefferson's Library,* 58.

226. Sowerby, *Catalogue,* 2:89–102. The first Old Testament is in Greek and Hebrew, with subsequent copies of the Old and New Testament in Greek, Latin, and English. Many works contained both the Old and New Testaments.

227. Quoted in Gilreath and Wilson, *Thomas Jefferson's Library,* 3.

228. Hayes, "How Thomas Jefferson Read the Qur'an," 253–54.

229. Ibid., 254 (quote); Hayes, *Road to Monticello*, 259.

230. Gilreath and Wilson, *Thomas Jefferson's Library*, 58–59; Hayes, "How Thomas Jefferson Read the Qur'an," 254 (quote); Hayes, *Road to Monticello*, 258–59.

231. Hayes, "How Thomas Jefferson Read the Qur'an," 259.

232. Walters, *Revolutionary Deists*, 258–60.

233. Ibid., 159. See also Adams, *Jefferson's Extracts from the Gospels.*

234. Gilreath and Wilson, *Thomas Jefferson's Library*, 59.

235. Ibid., 60–62.

236. "Thomas Jefferson to Augustus B. Woodward," March 24, 1824, quoted in Sowerby, *Catalogue*, 2:1; Hayes, *Road to Monticello*, 258.

237. Sale, trans., *Koran*, iii; earlier in his dedication, Sale also refers to the Prophet as the "legislator of the Arabs," A; Hayes, "How Thomas Jefferson Read the Qur'an," 248, 251.

238. Bernard Bailyn, *To Begin the World Anew: The Genius and Ambiguities of the American Founders* (New York: Knopf, 2003), 42, 45–46, 52.

239. Jefferson, "Autobiography," in *Life and Selected Writings*, 63.

240. Thomas Jefferson, *The Commonplace Book of Thomas Jefferson: A Repository of His Ideas on Government*, ed. Gilbert Chinard (Baltimore: Johns Hopkins University Press, 1926), 76.

241. *Papers of Thomas Jefferson*, 1:548.

242. Jefferson, "Autobiography," in *Life and Selected Writings*, 46.

243. Quoted in Ragosta, *Wellspring of Liberty*, 12.

244. Ibid., 142–60.

245. "Chesterfield Assembly, 1785," *Religious Petitions Virginia*, Library of Congress.

7. BEYOND TOLERATION: JOHN LELAND, BAPTIST ADVOCATE FOR THE RIGHTS OF MUSLIMS, 1776–1841

1. The chapter epigraph is drawn from John Leland, "Virginia Chronicle," 1790, in *The Writings of the Late Elder John Leland, Including Some Events in His Life, Written by Himself*, ed. L. F. Greene (New York: G. W. Wood, 1845), 118. John Leland's works in this edition have recently been republished in an exact reproduction in the public domain; see John Leland, *The Writings of the Late Elder John Leland, Including Some Events in His Life, Written by Himself*, ed. L. F. Greene (LaVergne, TN: Nabu Public Domain Reprints, 2011). Hereafter cited as *Writings*. The most thorough view of John Leland's life remains L. H. Butterfield, "Elder John Leland, Jeffersonian Itinerant," *Proceedings of the American Antiquarian Society* 62, no. 2 (1952): 155–242. This has been republished as a separate volume: L. H. Butterfield, *Elder John Leland: Jeffersonian Itinerant* (New York: Arno, 1980). My references to Butterfield's article are as Butterfield, "John Leland."

Leland has figured lately in popular histories of church-state relations, with special appearances in the presentation of a huge cheese to Jefferson in Washington, D.C.; see Steven Waldman, *Founding Faith: Providence, Politics, and the Birth of Religious Freedom in America* (New York: Random House, 2008), ix–x, 125–26, 134, 171–73. The alliance between Leland and Jefferson is emphasized by Thomas S. Kidd, *God of Liberty: A Religious History of the Revolution* (New York: Basic Books, 2010), 4–6, 8. However, this chapter clearly refutes Kidd's assertion that the evangelical Baptist John Leland "united around public religious principles . . . to articulate the basis of American rights"; see Kidd, *God of Liberty*, 253–54. Kidd's views of Leland in relation to Islam in his earlier work advance only the Baptist's condemnation of the Prophet, without mentioning a single instance of his insistence on religious pluralism, specifically his advocacy for the rights of Muslims in his vision of the new nation; see Thomas S. Kidd, "'Is It Worse to Follow Mahomet Than the Devil?' Early American Uses of Islam," *Church History* 72, no. 4 (December 2003): 787, and Thomas S. Kidd, *American Christians and Islam:*

Evangelical Culture and Muslims from the Colonial Period to the Age of Terrorism (Princeton: Princeton University Press, 2009), 18.

Debates about Leland's standing among Baptists continue; see Richard Curry Huff, "How High the 'Wall'? A Comparison of the Church-State Separation Positions of Thomas Jefferson and John Leland" (PhD diss., Westminster Theological Seminary, 2003), 320–22, 412–24. Huff criticizes Leland as a theological problem for Baptists because of his absolute separation of all religion from government—in contrast to what he perceives as Jefferson's more "godly" vision of the country. In contrast, some contemporary Baptists laud Leland's insistence on absolute separation of religion from the state as a definitive Baptist principle; see William R. Estep, *Revolution Within the Revolution: The First Amendment in Historical Context, 1612–1789* (Grand Rapids, MI: William B. Eerdmans, 1990), xi, xvii, 159–75. The local impact of John Leland in Virginia and his absorption of church-state separation there has been studied by Andrew M. Manis, "Regionalism and Baptist Perspectives on Separation of Church and State," *American Baptist Quarterly* 2, no. 3 (1983): 218. Parallels with Jefferson and Madison's political thought have been considered by Martha Eleam Boland, "Render unto Caesar: The Political Thought of John Leland" (PhD diss., New Orleans Baptist Seminary, 1998), 86, 139–47.

2. Butterfield, "John Leland," 157.

3. Ibid.; Huff, "How High the 'Wall'?," 274–394; Boland, "Render unto Caesar," 84–148.

4. Butterfield, "John Leland," 157; William G. McLoughlin, *New England Dissent, 1630–1883: The Baptists and the Separation of Church and State*, 2 vols. (Cambridge, MA: Harvard University Press, 1971), 2:933.

5. Quoted in Thomas E. Buckley, *Church and State in Revolutionary Virginia, 1776–1787* (Charlottesville: University Press of Virginia, 1977), 18.

6. The point is made by Butterfield, "John Leland," 174, and Buckley, *Church and State*, 18.

7. Leland, *Writings*, 188.

8. McLoughlin, *New England Dissent*, 2:933.

9. Huff, "How High the 'Wall'?," 5, 389–415.

10. Leland, *Writings*, 107; McLoughlin, *New England Dissent*, 931. Leland's quotation clearly undermines any support by him for "religion in public life"; see Kidd, *God of Liberty*, 254. John A. Ragosta, *Wellspring of Liberty: How Virginia's Religious Dissenters Helped Win the American Revolution and Secured Religious Liberty* (New York: Oxford University Press, 2010), 12, 137–38, 150, places Leland directly within the movement of Virginia dissenters who wished not for a Christian nation but for absolute separation of religion from government.

11. Leland, *Writings*, 279.

12. Ibid., 278.

13. Ibid., 410. He wrote about this in 1810.

14. Butterfield, "John Leland," 160. The sermons were by Philip Doddridge, *Rise and Progress of the Soul*, a sixth edition published in Boston in 1749.

15. Leland, *Writings*, 10. Leland recalled that his local minister told his father to send him to college to become a minister, while the doctor "was equally solicitous to make me a physician," and his own inclination was "to be a lawyer." However, his father refused all these possibilities because, Leland said, he "designed me to live with him, to support his declining years."

16. Quoted in Butterfield, "John Leland," 164.

17. Thomas Helwys, *The Mistery of Iniquity* (London: Kingsgate Press, 1935), 69; Estep, *Revolution*, 50–53.

18. Quoted from "A Brief Confession or Declaration of Faith" (London, 1660), in Edward Bean Underhill, ed., *Confessions of Faith, and other Public Documents Illustrative of*

the History of the Baptist Churches of England in the Seventeenth Century (London: Haddon Brothers, 1854), 118.

19. Leland, *Writings*, 241; Huff, "How High the 'Wall'?," 259. Leland doubtless read his contemporary Isaac Backus's *History of the Baptists in New England,* which described Roger Williams's travails, but Backus stopped short of repeating Williams's universal claims for the religious freedom and civil protection of Muslims and Jews in his ideal state.

20. Leland, *Writings,* 241.

21. McLoughlin, *New England Dissent,* 2:929.

22. Roger Williams, *The Bloudy Tenent of Persecution for Cause of Conscience,* ed. Samuel L. Caldwell, vol. 3 of *The Complete Writings of Roger Williams* (New York: Russell and Russell, 1963), 142.

23. In two instances, Leland did refer to "Mahometans," but the majority of his references are to "Turks."

24. Butterfield, "John Leland," 172–73; Buckley, *Church and State,* 12–16. For the role of Baptists in pre-Revolutionary Virginia, see Rhys Isaac, *The Transformation of Virginia, 1740–1790* (Chapel Hill: University of North Carolina Press, 1982), 161–80.

25. Leland, *Writings,* 27; Ragosta, *Wellspring of Liberty,* 29.

26. Leland, *Writings,* 255; Kidd, *God of Liberty,* 157.

27. James Madison, *The Papers of James Madison,* ed. Robert A. Rutland and William M. E. Rachal et al., 17 vols. (Chicago: University of Chicago Press, 1973), 8:298–304. Hereafter cited as *Papers of James Madison.*

28. "From Richard Henry Lee to James Madison," November 26, 1784, *Papers of James Madison,* 8:149; Buckley, *Church and State,* 101–2, 116, 174.

29. Butterfield, "John Leland," 181; Robert B. Semple, *A History of the Rise and Progress of Baptists in Virginia* (Philadelphia: American Baptist Society, 1894), 207.

30. "James Gordon, Jr., to James Madison," February 17, 1788, *Papers of James Madison,* 8:516.

31. Butterfield, "John Leland," 169.

32. Leland, *Writings,* 27, 38; Huff, "How High the 'Wall'?," 237–73.

33. *Papers of James Madison,* 8:516.

34. "Joseph Spencer to James Madison," February 28, 1788, *Papers of James Madison,* 2:541. Leland's comments, and an enclosure to Madison, are reprinted in *Documentary History of the Constitution and the United States, 1786–1870,* 5 vols. (Washington, DC: Department of State, 1905), 4:526–29. The relationship between Leland and Madison, with a focus on Leland "*as a Baptist preacher,* not just a private citizen," is recounted in detail by Mark S. Scarberry, "John Leland and James Madison: Religious Influence on the Ratification of the Constitution and on the Proposal of the Bill of Rights," *Penn State Law Review* 113, no. 3 (April 2009): 733–800, quote on 797.

35. Robert M. Calhoon, "John Leland," in *American National Biography,* ed. John Garraty and Mark Carnes (New York: Oxford University Press, 1999), 13:466.

36. Butterfield, "John Leland," 188–92. Scarberry is more positive about the meeting than Butterfield: "John Leland and James Madison," 769–75; Kidd, *God of Liberty,* 222–24. The plaque is near Orange, Virginia, at the intersection of Highway 20 and Clifton Road (County Route 628) in Leland-Madison Monumental Park. The inscription reads, "Courageous leader of the Baptist Doctrine. Ardent advocate of the principles of democracy. Vindicator of separation of church and state." http://www.hmdb.org/marker.asp?MarkerID=4697.

37. "To James Madison, Sr., from James Madison," July 1, 1788, *Papers of James Madison,* 11:185.

38. "Madison's Election to the First Federal Congress, Editorial Note," October 1788–February 1789, *Papers of James Madison,* 11:302–4; Kidd, *God of Liberty,* 221–23; Ragosta, *Wellspring of Liberty,* 167–68.

39. "John Leland to James Madison," February 15, 1789, *Papers of James Madison,* 11:442–43.

40. Leland, *Writings,* 53.

41. George Washington, *Writings of George Washington,* ed. Jared Sparks (Boston: Ferdinand Andrews, 1840), 12:155.

42. "George Washington to Tench Tilghman," March, 24, 1784, in George Washington, *The Writings of George Washington from the Original Manuscript Sources, 1745–1799,* ed. John C. Fitzpatrick, 39 vols. (Washington, DC: U.S. Government Printing Office, 1938), 27:367.

43. Leland, *Writings,* 10. For a profile of the Baptists of Leland's native Worcester County, see John L. Brooke, *The Heart of the Commonwealth: Society and Political Culture in Worcester County, Massachusetts, 1713–1861* (New York: Cambridge University Press, 1989), 61, 158–72.

44. Ibid., 18.

45. John Adams, *The Works of John Adams, Second President of the United States,* ed. Charles Francis Adams, 10 vols. (Boston: Little, Brown, 1850–56), 2:397–400; Butterfield, "John Leland," 165–67.

46. Butterfield, "John Leland," 165.

47. Ibid., 165–67; McLoughlin, *New England Dissent,* 1:512–30.

48. Adams, *Works,* 2:398.

49. Ibid., 2:399.

50. Butterfield, "John Leland," 202–3.

51. M. Louise Greene, *The Development of Religious Liberty in Connecticut* (Cambridge, MA: Houghton Mifflin, 1905), 372–74; Huff, "How High the 'Wall'?," 331–56.

52. Leland, *Writings,* 190.

53. Ibid., 177–92; Ellis Sandoz, ed., *Political Sermons of the American Founding Era, 1730–1805* (Indianapolis: Liberty Fund, 1991), 1080; Greene, *Religious Liberty,* 374–77.

54. Leland, *Writings,* 187.

55. Ibid., 189.

56. Ibid., 118.

57. Ibid., 187.

58. Ibid.; Kidd, "Is It Worse to Follow Mahomet Than the Devil?," 787; Kidd, *American Christians and Islam,* 18.

59. Leland, *Writings,* 179.

60. Ibid.

61. Ibid., 181.

62. Julian P. Boyd et al., eds., *The Papers of Thomas Jefferson,* 40 vols. (Princeton: Princeton University Press, 1950–), 2:546–47. Hereafter cited as *Papers of Thomas Jefferson.*

63. *Papers of James Madison,* 8:299.

64. Leland, *Writings,* 181.

65. John Locke, *Epistola de Tolerantia: A Letter on Toleration,* ed. Raymond Klibansky, trans. J. W. Gough (Oxford: Clarendon Press, 1968), 91.

66. *Papers of James Madison,* 8:301.

67. Thomas Jefferson, *Notes on Virginia,* in *The Life and Selected Writings of Thomas Jefferson,* ed. Adrienne Koch and William Peden (New York: Modern Library, 1998), 255.

68. Leland, *Writings,* 182.

69. Jefferson, *Notes on Virginia,* in *Life and Selected Writings,* 255.

70. Leland, *Writings,* 182.

71. Jefferson, *Notes on Virginia,* in *Life and Selected Writings,* 255–56.

72. Leland, *Writings,* 184.

73. *Papers of Thomas Jefferson,* 2:545–46.

74. Jefferson, *Notes on Virginia,* in *Life and Selected Writings,* 254.

75. Leland, *Writings*, 184. Leland is accused of "plagiarism" by Edwin Gaustad, *Sworn on the Altar of God: A Religious Biography of Thomas Jefferson* (Grand Rapids, MI: William B. Eerdmans, 1996), 202–3: In contrast, "When Jefferson, quoting from John Leland . . ." Actually, the reverse is true; see Frank Lambert, *The Founding Fathers and the Place of Religion in America* (Princeton: Princeton University Press, 2003), 281; Kidd, *God of Liberty,* 176–77; Ragosta, *Wellspring of Liberty,* 146.

76. Leland, *Writings,* 185.

77. Ibid., 191.

78. Ibid.; Ragosta, *Wellspring of Liberty,* 144.

79. Greene, *Religious Liberty,* 287–88. Leland later published several notable political statements attacking the Connecticut state constitution, including "A Blow at the Root, a fashionable Fast-Day Sermon," and in 1803, "Van Tromp lowering his Peak with a Broadside"; see Leland, *Writings,* 423, 329.

80. Greene, *Religious Liberty,* 376; Lambert, *Founding Fathers,* 285.

81. Leland, "The Yankee Spy," in *Writings,* 213.

82. Leland, *Writings,* 229; Huff, "How High the 'Wall'?," 357–94.

83. Brooke, *Heart of the Commonwealth,* 172–88; see also Charles P. Hanson, *Necessary Virtue: The Pragmatic Origins of Religious Liberty in New England* (Charlottesville: University Press of Virginia, 1998), 205–6.

84. Leland, *Writings,* 220. Article II, in the original, read, "It is the right as well as the duty of all men in society, publicly, and at stated seasons, to worship the SUPREME BEING, the great Creator and Preserver of the universe. And no subject shall be hurt, molested, or restrained, in his person, liberty or estate, for worshipping God in the manner and season most agreeable to the dictates of his own conscience; or for his religious profession of sentiments; provided he doth not disturb the public peace, or obstruct others in religious worship"; in Francis Newton Thorpe, ed., *The Federal and State Constitutions, Colonial Charters, and Other Organic Laws of the States, Territories, and Colonies Now or Heretofore Forming the United States of America,* 7 vols. (Washington, DC: U.S. Government Printing Office, 1909), 3:1889.

85. Leland, *Writings,* 220–21.

86. Ibid., 221, 223. The Declaration of Rights, Article III, read, in part, "Therefore, to promote their happiness, and to secure the good order and preservation of their government, the people of this commonwealth have a right to invest their legislature with power to authorize and require, and the legislature shall, from time to time, authorize and require the several towns, parishes, precincts, and other bodies politic, or religious societies, to make suitable provision, at their own expense, for the institution of the public worship of God, and for the support and maintenance of public Protestant teachers of piety, religion, and morality in all cases where such provision shall not be made voluntarily"; in Thorpe, *Federal and State Constitutions,* 3:1889–90.

87. Leland, *Writings,* 223–24.

88. Ibid., 224.

89. Ibid., 226.

90. Ibid., 229.

91. Quoted in Jeffrey L. Pasley, "The Cheese and the Words: Popular Political Culture and Participatory Democracy in the Early American Republic," in *Beyond the Founders: New Approaches to the Political History of the Early American Republic,* ed. Jeffrey L. Pasley, Andrew W. Robertson, and David Waldstreicher (Chapel Hill: University of North Carolina Press, 2004), 34. The episode was first described by Butterfield, "Elder John Leland," 154–56, 214–29. A more up-to-date overview is given by Barbara B. Oberg, ed., "Editorial Note," in *The Papers of Thomas Jefferson* (Princeton: Princeton University Press, 2009), 36:246–49; and Daniel L. Dreisbach, "Mr. Jefferson, a Mammoth Cheese, and the 'Wall of Separation between Church and State': A Bicentennial Commemoration," *Journal of Church and State* 43 (2001): 725–45. Recent

historians who offer an account of this event include Steven Waldman, *Founding Faith,* ix–x, 171–73; Kidd, *God of Liberty,* 4–5; and Kevin J. Hayes, *The Road to Monticello: The Life and Mind of Thomas Jefferson* (New York: Oxford University Press, 2008), 474–76.

92. Pasley, "Cheese," 34, describes the "sensation" in the eighteenth-century newspapers.

93. Butterfield, "John Leland," 154; *Papers of Thomas Jefferson,* 36:406.

94. "From the Committee of Cheshire, Massachusetts," December 30, 1801, *Papers of Thomas Jefferson,* 36:249.

95. Pasley, "Cheese," 47.

96. "From the Committee of Cheshire, Massachusetts," December 30, 1801, *Papers of Thomas Jefferson,* 36:249.

97. Pasley, "Cheese," 45; Dreisbach, "Mr. Jefferson," 743–45; Oberg, "Editorial Note," *Papers of Thomas Jefferson,* 36:246–49.

98. Butterfield, "John Leland," 214–18.

99. "Thomas Jefferson to John Wayles Eppes," January 1, 1802, *Papers of Thomas Jefferson,* 36:261. Jefferson weighed the cheese at 1,230 pounds. Butterfield, "Leland," 220, quotes a newspaper source that asserts the weight was 1,238 pounds.

100. Pasley, "Cheese," 36; Oberg, "Editorial Note," *Papers of Thomas Jefferson,* 36:253.

101. "Letter from Danbury Baptist Association to Thomas Jefferson," October 7, 1801, in *The Sacred Rights of Conscience: Selected Readings on Church-State Relations in the American Founding,* ed. Daniel L. Dreisbach and Mark David Hall (Indianapolis: Liberty Fund, 2009), 526.

102. Ibid.; Lambert, *Founding Fathers,* 284–85.

103. Pasley, "Cheese," 36, emphasizes the day's importance.

104. "Draft Reply to the Danbury Baptist Association," on or before December 31, 1801, *Papers of Thomas Jefferson,* 36:255 n. 2. Italics are mine.

105. "To the Danbury Baptist Association," January 1, 1802, *Papers of Thomas Jefferson,* 36:258.

106. Butterfield, "John Leland," 226.

107. Ibid., 226–27.

108. Quoted ibid., 226.

109. Quoted ibid., 170–71.

110. Quoted ibid., 226–27.

111. Ibid., 227.

112. Pasley, "Cheese," 80.

113. Leland, *Writings,* 255.

114. Ibid., 373.

115. Butterfield, "John Leland," 212–13.

116. Leland, *Writings,* 213.

117. Ibid., 353–54.

118. Ibid., 355–56.

119. The phrase and source of contrast is that of William G. McLoughlin, *Soul Liberty: The Baptists' Struggle in New England, 1630–1833* (Hanover, NH: Brown University Press/University Press of New England, 1991), 195.

120. McLoughlin distinguishes Leland from Isaac Backus and most other Baptists, stating that Leland, "regarding separation of church and state . . . like Roger Williams, favored total separation, not sweet harmony [with Christianity] like Backus"; see McLouglin, *New England Dissent,* 2:292; Edwin S. Gaustad, "The Backus-Leland Tradition," *Foundations* 22 (October 1959): 131–52. Philip Hamburger, however, who dubs Leland "Jefferson's friend and ally," disagrees directly but incorrectly with McLoughlin on Leland's church-state separation position. Hamburger asserts, "Even Leland, however, did not clearly wish to separate church and state. Although, in attacking the existing connection between church and state, he used language that may, in retrospect,

seem to come close to a demand for separation, he did not unequivocally go so far, and indeed, he typically demanded a religious liberty that remained unmistakably within Baptist and other evangelical dissenting traditions." See Philip Hamburger, *Separation of Church and State* (Cambridge, MA: Harvard University Press, 2002), quotations on 165 and 169, respectively. In fact, Leland's evangelical Baptist vision of an absolute separation of church and state connected him directly to seventeenth-century founding English Baptist precedents, such as those professed by Thomas Helwys. Leland's church-state stance, while not representative of the majority of his coreligionists, did represent an important historical current in Baptist history. As Richard Curry Huff demonstrates, in challenging Hamburger's position, Leland ultimately chose a "Church-State position that *exceeds* that of Thomas Jefferson's, erecting such a high wall of separation that it ignores religion's and especially Christianity's vital role in the preservation of America's liberties." See Huff, "How High the 'Wall'?," 5. Huff designates Leland's position an error. I contend that it was Leland's absolute separation, following Jefferson, that allowed him to envision a religiously plural and politically equal citizenship for Muslims, Jews, and Catholics as well as all other non-Protestants.

121. Leland, *Writings,* 356.
122. Ibid., 358.
123. Quoted in Butterfield, "John Leland," 213 n. 32.
124. Leland, *Writings,* 476.
125. Ibid., 477.
126. Ibid., 490.
127. Ibid. Italics mine.
128. Ibid., 187.
129. Ibid., 498.
130. Ibid., 187.
131. Ibid., 198.
132. Ibid., 295.
133. Ibid., 251.
134. Ibid., 121.
135. Ibid., 310.
136. Ibid., 404.
137. Ibid., 179; on Leland's views of Catholics, see Hanson, *Necessary Virtue,* 218.
138. Leland, *Writings,* 671.
139. Butterfield, "John Leland," 233.
140. Leland, *Writings,* 672.
141. Ibid., 691.
142. Ibid., 428.
143. Ibid., 724.
144. Ibid., 459.
145. Ibid., 503.
146. Ibid., 735.
147. Ibid., 96–97.
148. Butterfield, "John Leland," 182–83.
149. Leland, *Writings,* 175.
150. Ibid., 118.
151. Ibid., 173.
152. Ibid., 174.
153. Ibid., 612.
154. Ibid.; Boland, "Render unto Caesar," 148–49. Jefferson spoke about the emancipation of slaves, but feared violence or "convulsions, which will probably never end but in the extermination of the one or the other race"; see Jefferson, *Notes on Virginia,* in *Life and Selected Writings,* 238.
155. Butterfield, "John Leland," 241.

156. Quoted in McLoughlin, *New England Dissent,* 2:929. Leland's position was so extreme that it "bordered upon solipsism," according to Huff, "How High the 'Wall'?," 415.

157. Quoted in McLoughlin, *New England Dissent,* 2:929.

158. "In American religion, Leland, not Jefferson, represented the wave of the future," argues Thomas S. Kidd, but he does not recognize Leland's consistent insistence on exploding forever a Christian state, political equality for non-Christians, and religious pluralism in this prediction; see Kidd, *God of Liberty,* 208.

AFTERWORD:
WHY CAN'T A MUSLIM BE PRESIDENT?
EIGHTEENTH-CENTURY IDEALS OF THE MUSLIM CITIZEN
AND THEIR SIGNIFICANCE IN THE TWENTY-FIRST CENTURY

1. Quoted in J. A. I. Champion, *The Pillars of Priestcraft Shaken: The Church of England and Its Enemies, 1660–1770* (New York: Cambridge University Press, 1992), 111.

2. Edward Gibbon, *The History of the Decline and Fall of the Roman Empire,* ed. J. B. Bury (London: Methuen, 1911; repr. 1974), 5:356 n. 68.

3. Thomas Jefferson, "First Inaugural Address, March 4, 1801," in *Thomas Jefferson: Writings,* ed. Merrill D. Peterson (New York: Literary Classics of the United States, 1984), 492–93.

4. Ibid.

5. *Farmer's Museum or Literary Gazette* (Walpole, NH), January 4, 1803, 4.

6. Thomas Jefferson, *The Writings of Thomas Jefferson,* ed. Andrew A. Lipscomb and Albert E. Bergh, 20 vols. (Washington, DC: Thomas Jefferson Memorial Association of the United States, 1903–7), 10:378.

7. John Leland, *The Writings of the Late Elder John Leland: Including Some Events of His Life, Written by Himself,* ed. L. F. Greene (New York: G. W. Wood, 1845; repr. La Vergne, TN: Nabu Public Domain Reprints, 2011), 652.

8. Ibid., 38.

9. Kathleen M. Moore, *Al-Mughtaribun: American Law and the Transformation of Muslim Life in the United States* (Albany: State University of New York Press, 1995), 23.

10. For the argument that there may be "at least one uninterrupted chain of transmission of Islamic influence from the eighteenth century to the twentieth," see Michael A. Gomez, *Black Crescent: The Experience and Legacy of African Muslims in the Americas* (New York: Cambridge University Press, 2005), 185–200; quote on 186.

11. Ibid., 185–200.

12. Ibid., 154.

13. Quoted in Marilyn C. Baseler, *"Asylum for Mankind": America, 1607–1800* (Ithaca: Cornell University Press, 1998), 330–31.

14. Anny Bakalian and Mehdi Bozorgmehr, *Backlash 9/11: Middle Eastern and Muslim Americans Respond* (Berkeley: University of California Press, 2009), 78.

15. Kambiz GhaneaBassiri, *A History of Islam in America* (New York: Cambridge University Press, 2010), 96.

16. Ibid., 96, 136.

17. Ibid., 293; see Jacob Rama Berman, *American Arabesque: Arabs, Islam, and the 19th-Century Imaginary* (New York: New York University Press, 2012), 179–210.

18. GhaneaBassiri, *History of Islam in America,* 152; quoted in Moore, *Al-Mughtaribun,* 45.

19. GhaneaBassiri, *History of Islam in America,* 135–64.

20. Ibid., 96.

21. Ibid., 141. For other name changes, see Yvonne Yazbeck Haddad, *Not Quite American: The Shaping of Arab and Muslim Identity in the United States* (Waco, TX: Baylor University Press, 2004), 4.

22. Kevin M. Schultz, *Tri-Faith America: How Catholics and Jews Held Postwar America to Its Protestant Promise* (New York: Oxford University Press, 2011), 23.

23. "Transcript of Civil Rights Act (1964)," Section 202, http://www.our documents.gov/doc.php?doc=97.

24. GhaneaBassiri, *History of Islam in America*, 153.

25. Ibid., 158.

26. The idea is GhaneaBassiri's, *History of Islam in America*, 29–30, 380. For the most nuanced consideration of race as a challenging category for American Muslims, see Sherman A. Jackson, "Muslims, Islam(s), Race and American Islamophobia," in *Islamophobia: The Challenge of Pluralism in the 21st Century*, ed. John L. Esposito and Ibrahim Kalin (New York: Oxford University Press, 2011), 93–108.

27. Quoted in GhaneaBassiri, *History of Islam in America*, 159.

28. Quoted in Schultz, *Tri-Faith America*, 20–21.

29. Quoted ibid., 18–19; quote on 19.

30. Quoted ibid., 20.

31. Bret E. Carroll, *The Routledge Historical Atlas of Religion in America* (New York: Routledge, 2000), 91.

32. Quoted in Schultz, *Tri-Faith America*, 22.

33. Carroll, *Routledge Historical Atlas*, 94. The Jewish population was 150,000 by 1860.

34. Richard W. Bulliet, *The Case for Islamo-Christian Civilization* (New York: Columbia University Press, 2004), 5.

35. Quoted in Michael Beschloss, "FDR's Auschwitz Secret," *Daily Beast*, October 13, 2002, http://www.thedailybeast.com/newsweek/2002/10/13/fdr-s-auschwitz -secret.html.

36. Quoted in Schultz, *Tri-Faith America*, 23.

37. Ibid., 1–42.

38. Ibid., 28, 42.

39. Ibid., 57–58; Bulliet, *Case for Islamo-Christian Civilization*, 6, emphasizes the acceptance of the term by the 1950s.

40. Bulliet, *Case for Islamo-Christian Civilization*, 6.

41. Quoted in Schultz, *Tri-Faith America*, 35.

42. Arthur A. Cohen, *The Myth of the Judeo-Christian Tradition and Other Dissenting Essays* (New York: Schocken, 1971), xiii; Bulliet, *Case for Islamo-Christian Civilization*, 8–9.

43. Moore, *Al-Mughtaribun*, 2–3.

44. Bulliet, *Case for Islamo-Christian Civilization*, 8–9.

45. This idea of a founding "Protestant promise" is Schultz's premise; *Tri-Faith America*, 3–12.

46. Carroll, *Routledge Historical Atlas of Religion*, 102.

47. GhaneaBassiri, *History of Islam in America*, 292–93.

48. The phrase comprises part of a book title by Diana Eck, *A New Religious America: How a "Christian" Country Became the World's Most Religiously Diverse Nation*, 2nd ed. (New York: HarperCollins E-book, 2007). Eck carefully surveys these non-Judeo-Christian American religious groups.

49. "Muslim Americans: Middle Class and Mostly Mainstream," Pew Research Center, May 22, 2007, http://pewresearch.org/files/old-assets/pdf/muslim-americans; GhaneaBassiri, *History of Islam in America*, 2 n. 1, based on the Pew findings estimates around three million; Eck, *New Religious America*, 2–3, suggests six million; John Esposito, *What Everyone Needs to Know About Islam*, 2nd ed. (New York: Oxford University Press, 2011), 221, offers the estimate of five to seven million. Oddly, Bret E. Carroll, *Routledge Historical Atlas*, 103, more than a decade ago estimated eight million.

50. "Muslim Americans: No Signs of Growth in Alienation or Support for Extremism. Section 1: A Demographic Portrait of Muslim Americans," Pew Research Center,

August 30, 2011, http://www.people-press.org/2011/08/30/section-1-a-demographic
-portrait-of-muslim-americans/, 6, puts the total Muslim population at 2.92 million.

51. Sixty-eight countries of origin are mentioned by Esposito, *What Everyone Needs to Know About Islam,* 221.

52. "Muslim Americans," Pew Research Center, August 30, 2011, 2.

53. Jane I. Smith, *Islam in America,* 2nd ed. (New York: Columbia University Press, 2009), 78–103. These indigenous African American movements included what most Muslims perceive as heterodox Islamic variants, including the Moorish Science Temple, the Nation of Islam, and, more recently the Five Percenters.

54. "Muslim Americans," Pew Research Center, August 30, 2011, 2.

55. Smith, *Islam in America,* 2nd ed., 68–70.

56. Ibid., 70–75.

57. Lori Peek, *Behind the Backlash: Muslim Americans after 9/11* (Philadelphia: Temple University Press, 2011), 10.

58. "Muslim Americans," Pew Research Center, August 30, 2011, 2.

59. Quoted in Peek, *Behind the Backlash,* 24–25.

60. Quoted ibid., 25.

61. Quoted in Bakalian and Bozorgmehr, *Backlash 9/11,* 186.

62. See Riad Z. Abdelkarima and Jason Erb, "How American Muslims Really Responded to the Events of September 11," *CounterPunch,* September 7, 2002, www .CounterPunch.org/riad0907.html.

63. This "double pain" is recorded in an interview with an American Muslim; see Bakalian and Bozorgmehr, *Backlash 9/11,* 171.

64. Rick Hampson, "For Families of Muslim 9/11 Victims, a New Pain," *USA Today,* September 2, 2010.

65. Quoted ibid.

66. Quoted in Peek, *Behind the Backlash,* 5.

67. I have re-created the list offered in Bakalian and Bozorgmehr, *Backlash 9/11,* 40. A similar list of violent events in the twentieth century is included in Peter Gottschalk and Gabriel Greenberg, *Islamophobia: Making Muslims the Enemy* (Lanham, MD: Rowman and Littlefield, 2008), 111. Earlier, twentieth-century precedents are also found in GhaneaBassiri, *History of Islam in America,* 329–44.

68. Bakalian and Bozorgmehr, *Backlash 9/11,* 40.

69. Quoted in Jack G. Shaheen, *Reel Bad Arabs: How Hollywood Vilifies a People* (New York: Olive Branch Press, 2001), 4.

70. GhaneaBassiri, *History of Islam in America,* 329; Peek, *Behind the Backlash,* 23.

71. Moore, *Al-Mughtaribun,* xi.

72. Quoted in Peek, *Behind the Backlash,* 24.

73. Quoted in Bakalian and Bozorgmehr, *Backlash 9/11,* 40.

74. Ibid., 2–4.

75. "'Islam Is Peace' Says President: Remarks by the President at the Islamic Center of Washington, D.C., September 17, 2001," georgewbush-whitehouse.archives .gov.

76. Bakalian and Bozorgmehr, *Backlash 9/11,* 3.

77. Ibid., 130.

78. Ibid., 131.

79. This description is based on Peek, *Behind the Backlash,* 34.

80. Sec. 102, "Sense of Congress Condemning Discrimination against Arab and Muslim Americans," U.S. Congress, "Uniting and Strengthening America by Providing Appropriate Tools Required to Intercept and Obstruct Terrorism (USA PATRIOT ACT) Act of 2001, H.R. 3162 (Washington, DC: U.S. Government Printing Office, 2001), 1, 8–10. The best analysis of this contradictory governmental policy is provided by Wendy Brown, *Regulating Aversion: Tolerance in the Age of Identity and Empire* (Prince-

ton: Princeton University Press, 2006), 84. Brown offers this pertinent observation of the U.S. government: "Yet at the same time that the state represents itself as securing social equality and rhetorically enjoins the citizenry from prejudice and persecution, the state engages in extralegal persecutorial actions toward the very group that it calls upon the citizenry to be tolerant toward."

81. Herbert N. Foerstel, *The Patriot Act: A Documentary and Reference Guide* (Westport, CT: Greenwood, 2008), 58–60; Smith, *Islam in America*, 2nd ed., 186–89.

82. Quoted in Foerstel, *Patriot Act*, 60.

83. Ibid., 61–63.

84. Ibid., 66.

85. Quoted in Peek, *Behind the Backlash*, 32; GhaneaBassiri, *History of Islam in America*, 328.

86. Quoted in Bakalian and Bozorgmehr, *Backlash 9/11*, 197.

87. Ibid., 139; Peek, *Behind the Backlash*, 31; "NYPD Monitored Muslim Students All over Northeast," *Huffington Post*, February 18, 2012, http://www.huffingtonpost .com/2012/02/18/nypd-monitored-muslim-stu__O_n_1286647.htm.

88. This is not a new observation; precedents for it may be found in GhaneaBassiri, *History of Islam in America*, 327, and Bakalian and Bozorgmehr, *Backlash 9/11*, 141.

89. GhaneaBassiri, *History of Islam in America*, 362–63.

90. Bakalian and Bozorgmehr, *Backlash 9/11*, 197; GhaneaBassiri, *History of Islam in America*, 365–77. Comedic pioneers include *The Axis of Evil Comedy Tour*, starring Maz Jobrani, Aron Kader, Ahmed Ahmed, and Dean Obeidallah, which aired April 3, 2007 (Chatsworth, CA: Levity Productions, 2007), DVD, and, more recently, Negin Farsad and Dean Obeidallah's hilarious film critique of American Islamophobia, *The Muslims Are Coming!*, which premiered in Austin, Texas, in October 2012.

91. Quoted in Peek, *Behind the Backlash*, 39. For a thoughtful analysis of youthful American Muslim responses to citizenship options, see Sunaina Maira, "Islamophobia and the War on Terror: Youth, Citizenship, and Dissent," in *Islamophobia*, ed. Esposito and Kalin, 113–22.

92. These are the partial findings of a study funded by the U.S. Department of Justice and authored by David Schanzer, Charles Kurzman, and Ebrahim Moosa, "Anti-Terror Lessons of Muslim-Americans," January 6, 2010, http://www.sanford.duke .edu/news/Schanzer_Kurzman_Moosa_Anti-Terror_Lessons.pdf.

93. Quoted in Abdulkader H. Sinno, "Muslim Underrepresentation in American Politics," in *Muslims in Western Politics*, ed. Abdulkader H. Sinno (Bloomington: Indiana University Press, 2009), 80–90.

94. I have borrowed this phrase from Peter Gottschalk and Gabriel Greenberg, *Islamophobia*, 111.

95. Ibid.; GhaneaBassiri, *History of Islam in America*, 347; Sinno, "Muslim Underrepresentation in American Politics," 80–90.

96. Quoted in Rachel L. Swarns, "Congressman Criticizes Election of Muslim," *New York Times*, December 21, 2006, http://www.nytimes.com/2006/12/21/us/ 21koran.html.

97. For the most detailed reading of Ellison's election, with a different conclusion about the issue of Jefferson's Qur'an and religious tests, see Kathleeen M. Moore, *The Unfamiliar Abode: Islamic Law in the United States and Britain* (New York: Oxford University Press, 2010), 82–101.

98. Julian P. Boyd et al., eds., *The Papers of Thomas Jefferson*, 40 vols. (Princeton: Princeton University Press, 1950–), 1:548. Hereafter cited as *Papers of Thomas Jefferson*.

99. Jonathan Elliot, *The Debates in the Several State Conventions on the Adoption of the Federal Constitution, as Recommended by the General Convention at Philadelphia, in 1787*, 5 vols. (Philadelphia: J. B. Lippincott, 1888), 4:198–99. For one editorial that referenced the eighteenth-century North Carolina debate, see Sam

Fleischacker, "Muslim in Congress? Framers of Constitution Would Approve," *Philadelphia Inquirer,* January 1, 2007, http://articles.philly.com/2007-01-01/news/25221193_1_constitution-strict-immigration-policies-muslims.

100. Quoted in Swarns, "Congressman Criticizes Election of Muslim."

101. Quoted in Jacqueline Trescott, "Ed Koch Calls for Ouster of 'Bigot' on Holocaust Board," *Washington Post,* December 14, 2006, http://www.washingtonpost.com/wp-dyn/content/article/2006/12/13/AR2006121302260.html.

102. Quoted in Omar Sacirbey, "Conservatives Attack Use of Koran for Oath," *Washington Post,* December 9, 2006, http://www.washingtonpost.com/wp-dyn/content/article/2006/12/08/AR2006120801482.html.

103. Quoted in Swarns, "Congressman Criticizes Election of Muslim."

104. Quoted in "CNN's Beck to First-Ever Muslim Congressman: '[W]hat I Feel Like Saying Is, "Sir, Prove to Me That You Are Not Working with Our Enemies,"'" *Media Matters for America,* November 15, 2006, http://www.mediamatters.org/video/2006/11/15/cnns-beck-to-first-ever-congressman-what-137311; Gottschalk and Greenberg, *Islamophobia,* 144.

105. Quoted in "CNN's Beck."

106. Quoted ibid.

107. Quoted in Keith Ellison, "Choose Generosity, Not Exclusion," *Newsweek, Washington Post,* January 4, 2007, http://newsweek.washingtonpost.com/onfaith/guest voices/2007/01/04/.

108. Quoted in Neil MacFarquhar, "Muslim's Election Is Celebrated Here and in Mideast," *New York Times,* November 10, 2006, http://www.nytimes.com/2006/11/10/us/politics/10muslims.html.

109. Christopher Hayes, "The New Right-Wing Smear Machine," *Nation,* November 12, 2007, http://www.thenation.com/article/new-right-wing-smear-machine.

110. Quoted ibid. Hayes first noted the importance of this supposed typo.

111. Ibid.

112. Charles Babington and Darlene Superville, "Obama 'Christian by Choice': President Responds to Questioner," *Huffington Post,* September 29, 2010, http://www.huffingtonpost.com/2010/09/28/obama-christian-by-choice_n_742124.html.

113. Quoted ibid.

114. David Weigel, "Birtherism Is Dead. Long Live Birtherism: The History of a National Embarrassment, and Why It's Not Over Yet," *Slate,* April 27, 2011, http://www.slate.com/articles/news_and_politics/2011/04/birtherism_is_dead_long_live_birtherism.html.

115. For documentation of attacks on Obama's loyalty and citizenship, see Bill Press, *The Obama Hate Machine: The Lies, Distortions, and Personal Attacks on the President and Who Is Behind Them* (New York: St. Martin's, 2012), 75–76, 137–71. For an example of this Islamic conspiracy, see B. J. Armstrong, *Is Barack Hussein Obama "Claiming America" for Islam? Obama's Ancestry vs. America & Christianity* (2011).

116. This report includes data beginning in 2008; "Growing Number of Americans Say Obama Is a Muslim," Pew Research Center, August 18, 2010, http://www.pewforum.org/Politics-and-Elections/Growing-Number-of-Americans-Say-Obama-is-a-Muslim.aspx.

117. Quoted in Jonathan Marin and Amie Parnes, "McCain: Obama Not an Arab, Crowd Boos," *Politico,* October 10, 2008, http://politico.com/news/stories/1008/14479.html.

118. This incident has been analyzed by Sherman A. Jackson, "Muslims, Islam(s), Race and American Islamophobia"; Juan Cole, "Islamophobia in American Foreign Policy Rhetoric"; and Mohamed Nimer, "Islamophobia and Anti-Americanism: Measurements, Dynamics, and Consequences," all in *Islamophobia,* ed. Esposito and Kalin, 103–4, 135–38.

119. Andrea Elliott, "Muslim Voters Detect a Snub from Obama," *New York Times,* June 24, 2008, www.nytimes.com/2008/06/24/us/politics/24muslim.html.

120. President Barack Obama, "Remarks by the President on a New Beginning," Cairo, Egypt, June 4, 2009, www.whitehouse.gov/blog/NewBeginnings/transcripts.

121. Campbell Brown, "Commentary: So What If Obama Were a Muslim or an Arab?" *CNN Politics,* October 13, 2008, www.cnn.com/2008/POLITICS/10/13/campbell.brown.obama/.

122. Ibid.

123. Elliott, "Muslim Voters Detect a Snub from Obama."

124. Brown, "So What If Obama Were a Muslim or an Arab?"

125. Quoted in Robert Mackey, "More on the Soldier Kareem R. Khan," *The Lede* blog, *New York Times,* October 19, 2008.

126. Elliot, *Debates,* 4:215.

127. Josh Gerstein, "Poll: 46% of GOP Thinks Obama's Muslim," *Politico,* August 19, 2010, http://www.politico.com/blogs/joshgerstein/0810/Poll_46_of_GOP_thinks_Obamas_Muslim.html.

128. The two scholars are Brendan Nyhan and Jason Reifler, as cited by David A. Graham, "The Problem with Polls about Whether Obama Is a Muslim," *Atlantic,* March 2012, http://www.theatlantic.com/politics/archive/2012/03/the-problem-with-polls-about-whether-obama-is-a-muslim/254380/.

129. The scholar is Julian Sanchez, cited ibid.

130. *Papers of Thomas Jefferson,* 2:545–46.

131. Nimer, "Islamophobia and Anti-Americanism," in *Islamophobia,* ed. Esposito and Kalin, 82–84.

132. David Weigel, "Perry Dodges the Sharia Bullet," *Slate,* August 19, 2011, http://www.slate.com/blogs/weigel/2011/08/19/perry_dodges_the_sharia_bullet.html.

133. Quoted ibid.

134. Quoted in Justin Elliott, "Rick Perry: The Pro-Shariah Candidate?" *Salon,* August 10, 2011, http://www.salon.com/2011/08/10/rick_perry_muslims/; Weigel, "Perry Dodges the Sharia Bullet"; Glen Rose, "Is Rick Perry Upholding Shariah Law in Texas? Halal Food Law HB 470-2003," *Salon,* August 20, 2011, http://salon.glenrose.net?view=plink&id=14147.

135. Quoted in Terrence Dopp, "Christie Defends Muslim Pick for New Jersey Judge, Calls Critics 'Crazies,'" *Bloomberg,* August 5, 2011, http://www.bloomberg.com/news/2011-08-05/christie-defends-muslim-pick-for-new-jersey-judge-calls-critics-crazies-.html.

136. Amanda Terkel, "Newt Gingrich: I'd Support a Muslim Running for President Only If They'd Commit to 'Give Up Sharia,'" *Huffington Post,* January 17, 2012; http://www.huffingtonpost.com/2012/01/17/newt-gingrich-muslim-president-sharia_n_; "Michele Bachmann: Sharia Law Would 'Usurp' the U.S. Constitution," *Huffington Post,* November 3, 2011, http://www.huffingtonpost.com/2011/11/03/michele-bachmann-sharia-law-constitution-_n_1074009.html.

137. "Gingrich: I'd Support a Muslim Only If."

138. Andrea Elliott, "The Man Behind the Anti-Shariah Movement," *New York Times,* July 30, 2011, http://www.nytimes.com/2011/07/31/us/31shariah.html?pagewanted=all.

139. Quoting the assertion of reporter Andrea Elliott, ibid.

140. Anver Emon, "Banning Shari'a," *The Immanent Frame,* September 9, 2011, Social Science Research Council, http://blogs.ssrc.org/tif/2011/09/06/banning-shari'a/.

141. Ibid.

142. Elliott, "The Man Behind the Anti-Shariah Movement."

143. Ibid.

144. Emon, "Banning Shari'a."

145. Elliott, "The Man Behind the Anti-Shariah Movement."

146. William G. "Jerry" Boykin and Harry Edward Soyster et al., *Shariah: The Threat to America,* Center for Security Policy, September 13, 2010, http://www .shariahthethreat.org/wp-content/uploads/2011/04/Shariah-The-Threat-to-America -Team-B-Report-Web-09292010.pdf.

147. Quoted in Erik Eckholm, "General Withdraws from West Point Talk," *New York Times,* January 30, 2012.

148. Boykin and Soyster, *Shariah,* 4.

149. Ibid., 5.

150. Ibid., 50.

151. Muhammad Ali Amir-Moezzi, "Dissimulation," in *Encyclopaedia of the Qur'an,* ed. Jane D. McAuliffe, 6 vols. (Leiden: E. J. Brill, 2001), 1:540-42.

152. Robert Steinback, "The Anti-Muslim Inner Circle," *Intelligence Report,* no. 142 (Summer 2011), Southern Poverty Law Center.

153. Andrew F. March, *Islam and Liberal Citizenship: The Search for an Overlapping Consensus* (New York: Oxford University Press, 2009), 262.

154. Martha Nussbaum, *The New Religious Intolerance* (Cambridge, MA: Belknap Press of Harvard University, 2012), 148.

155. John Esposito also raises this point in *What Everyone Needs to Know About Islam,* 162.

156. *Muneer Awad v. Paul Ziriax et al.* (112 KB) No. 10-6273 (10th Cir. January 10, 2012) (unpublished) (available at http://www.ca10.uscourts.gov/opinions/10/10-6273 .pdf).

157. Ibid.

158. Emon, "Banning Shari'a"; Nussbaum, *New Religious Intolerance,* 11–12. For insightful historical perspective on the practical role of Sharia law in the United States, see Sadakat Kadri, *Heaven on Earth: A Journey Through Shari'a Law from the Deserts of Ancient Arabia to the Streets of the Modern Muslim World* (New York: Farrar, Straus and Giroux, 2012), 279–81.

159. "Map—Nationwide Anti-Mosque Activity," American Civil Liberties Union, http://www.aclu.org/maps/map-nationwide-anti-mosque-activity.

160. Moore, *Al-Mughtaribun,* 117–34.

161. Imam Feisal Abdul Rauf, *Moving the Mountain: Beyond Ground Zero to a New Vision of Islam in America* (New York: Free Press, 2012), 18.

162. Nussbaum, *New Religious Intolerance,* 188–202.

163. Quoted in Robert Hillenbrand, "'The Ornament of the World': Medieval Cordoba as a Cultural Center," in *The Legacy of Islamic Spain,* ed. Salma Khadra Jayyusi, 2 vols. (Leiden: E. J. Brill, 1994), 1:114, says the origin of this Islamic precedent in Cordoba was in Umayyad Damascus.

164. Nussbaum, *New Religious Intolerance,* 189.

165. Ibid., 237.

166. Robert Steinback, "The Anti-Muslim Inner Circle."

167. Nussbaum, *New Religious Intolerance,* 195.

168. Quoted in Adam Lisberg, "Mayor Bloomberg Stands Up for Mosque," *New York Daily News,* August 3, 2010, http://www.nydailynews.com/blogs/dailypolitics/ 2010/08/bloomberg-stands-up-for-mosque.html.

169. "Flushing Remonstrance, 1657," in *The Sacred Rights of Conscience: Selected Readings on Religious Liberty and Church-State Relations in the American Founding,* ed. Daniel L. Dreisbach and Mark David Hall (Indianapolis: Liberty Fund, 2009), 109.

170. "Eisenhower's 1957 Speech at Islamic Center of Washington," available at: iipdigital.usembassy.gov/st/english/texttrans/2007/06/20070626154822lnkaiso.6946985 .html#axzz2NjGVfXDB. The speech appears in a somewhat redacted form in Ghanea-Bassiri, *History of Islam in America,* 255–57.

171. Jane Smith, *Islam in America* (New York: Columbia University Press, 1999), 168.

172. For the best analysis of the Cold War and changing American views of Muslims, see Mahmood Mamdani, *Good Muslim, Bad Muslim: America, the Cold War, and the Roots of Terror* (New York: Doubleday, 2004).

173. Quoted in Frederic J. Frommer, "Ellison Uses Thomas Jefferson's Quran," *Washington Post* (Associated Press), January 4, 2007, http://www.washingtonpost.com/wp-dyn/content/article/2007/01/04/AR2007010401188.html.

174. Boykin and Soyster, *Shariah*, 223–24. Frank J. Gaffney Jr. and David Yerushalmi, both listed by the Southern Poverty Law Center as belonging to anti-Islamic hate groups, also contributed to this report; see Steinback, "The Anti-Muslim Inner Circle."

175. Boykin and Soyster, *Shariah*, 223–24.

176. Bryan Fischer, "Islam and the First Amendment: Privileges but Not Rights," *Rightly Concerned* blog, American Family Association, March 23, 2011, http://www.afa.net/Blogs/BlogPost.aspx?id=2147504696. I would like to thank my colleague Kamran Aghaie for drawing my attention to this statement.

177. "Treaty of Peace and Friendship, signed at Tripoli . . . ratified by the U.S. June 10, 1797," in *Treaties and Other International Acts of the United States of America,* ed. Hunter Miller (Washington, DC: U.S. Government Printing Office, 1931), 2:365.

178. "To the Bashaw of Tripoli from President Thomas Jefferson," May 21, 1801, in *Naval Documents Related to the United States Wars with the Barbary Powers: Naval Operations Including Diplomatic Background from 1785 Through 1801,* 3 vols. (Washington, DC: U.S. Government Printing Office, 1939), 1:470; "Thomas Jefferson to Bey of Tunis," June 28, 1806, in *The Thomas Jefferson Papers Series 1. General Correspondence. 1651–1827,* Library of Congress, http://hdl.loc.gov/loc.mss/mtj.mtjbib016251, image 303.

179. Fischer, "Islam and the First Amendment."

180. "To Thomas Jefferson Smith from Thomas Jefferson," February 21, 1825, in *The Life and Selected Writings of Thomas Jefferson,* ed. Adrienne Koch and William Peden (New York: Modern Library, 1998), 655.

181. Ellison, "Choose Generosity, Not Exclusion." In June 2012 Congressman Ellison's loyalties were attacked by Republican congresswoman Michele Bachmann and four congressional colleagues from the Republican Party, who baselessly claimed that the American Muslim congressman was somehow in league with the country's enemies, specifically the Muslim Brotherhood; see Tomer Ovadia, "Rep. Keith Ellison: Michele Bachmann 'Wanted Attention,'" *Politico,* July 20, 2012, http://www.politico.com/news/stories/0712/78784.html.

182. *Papers of Thomas Jefferson,* 1:544.

183. Thomas Helwys, *The Mistery of Iniquity* (London: Kingsgate Press, 1935), 69.

184. Roger Williams, *The Bloudy Tenent of Persecution,* ed. Samuel L. Caldwell, vol. 3 of *The Complete Writings of Roger Williams* (New York: Russell and Russell, 1963), 142.

Index

Abbot, Henry, 169–71, 185
Abd Allah, Muhammad ibn, Moroccan
    sultan, 133
Abd al-Rahman. *See* Tripolitan ambassador
Abd al-Rahman, Ibrahima, Muslim slave, 10,
    186, 187–91, 349n156
Abdul Rauf, Feisal, 296
abolitionism, 268
Account of the Rise and Progress of Mahometanism
    (Stubbe), 67–70, 322n200
Act of Toleration (1689), 75
Adams, John
    on Baptist protests against taxes for
        Congregational churches, 248–9
    and Britain's stand on North African
        pirates, 131
    and election of 1800, 212–13
    and Islam, 205–6
    and Jefferson, 124, 151–3, 201–4, 205
    and Jews, 142–3
    letter to Tunisian ruler, 223
    and North African pirates, 126–7, 135–6,
        200
    and Qur'an, 154–6
    on slavery, 129–30
    and Tripolitan ambassador, 124, 125,
        138–40, 140–6
    Tripoli treaty, 207–12, 354nn69–70
Adams, John Quincy
    and Ibrahima, 189, 190–1
    on Islam, 205–6
    and Jefferson's support of Paine, 228
    as "Publicola," 202–5
    on Ramadan dinner at the White House,
        221
*Advice to the Privileged Orders in the Several
    States of Europe* (Barlow), 209
Aga Khan, 291–2
"Age of Arabick" (G. A. Russell), 65–6

'A'isha, wife of the Prophet, 90
Alcoran, 26. *See also* Qur'an
Alexandria, Egypt, burning of library at, 98,
    331n130
Al-Faruqi, Isma'il Raji, 277
Algerine Captive, The (Tyler), 27–8, 34–9, 40,
    92, 313n125
Algiers, 34, 132, 134, 143, 151–2. *See also*
    Barbary States; North African
    pirates
Algiers treaty, 218
Allison, Robert J., 164–5
Al-Tabari, 90
America
    and European negative views of Muslims,
        6, 14, 15–18, 20, 22–7, 304n9
    and European positive views of Muslims,
        42–8, 49–55, 66–70, 323n211
    Mahomet the Impostor as critique of British
        tyranny, 32–3
    and Ottoman Empire, 22–5
    Williams's "soul liberty" experiment, 56,
        57–8, 64, 302
    See also United States
American Colonization Society, 190
American Jews. *See* Jewish Americans
American Muslims. *See* Muslim Americans
American Revolution, 31–2, 265–6
Anabaptists, 47
Anglicanism
    and divorce, 96
    and Jefferson, 84, 100–4, 229
    and Muhammad, 87–8, 89
    resistance to Anglican establishment in
        Virginia, 100–2
    Society for Promoting Christian
        Knowledge, 84–5, 92
    tax proceeds for propagation of, 113–14,
        210–11

Anglicans
  Edwards, 79–80
  Hoadly, 30
  Jefferson as, 6–7, 229, 253
  Miller, 30
  Prideaux, 18–19, 24, 69–70, 87, 310*n*43
  Proast, 77
  Sale, 84
  Williams, 56
  See also Iredell, James; Johnston, Samuel;
    Locke, John
Antichrist, 15, 16–18, 20–2
Anti-Federalists
  Abbot, 169–71, 185
  Caldwell, 164, 181–2, 185
  Dollard, 165
  fearmongering in opposition to
    Constitution, 165–7, 170
  fears of pope as president, 175–8
  Henry, 166
  Lancaster, 183–5
  and Muslim "civil rights," 168–9
  and Protestant character of the nation,
    156–7, 159, 160–1
  and religious test for public office, 169–71
anti-Islamic polemic
  by Calvin, 16–17
  claim that Islam spread by violence, 19, 29,
    30, 88, 99, 206, 250
  by Foxe, 17–18
  by Luther, 15–16
  and Orientalism, 307*n*30
  by Prideaux, 18–19, 24, 69–70, 87, 310*n*43
  propagation by the sword, 19, 29, 30, 88,
    99, 206, 250
  and separation of church and government,
    8–9, 101–4
  Stubbe's challenge to, 19, 67–70, 322*n*200
  by Trenchard and Gordon, 23–5
  by Voltaire, 27, 28–33, 97–9
anti-Semitism, 276
anti-Sharia movement, 292–3, 295–6, 299
Arab American News, 286
Arabic language
  and American slaves, 187, 188, 190
  and Hebrew Bible, 65
  and Jefferson's library, 234, 360*n*211
  and Locke, 65
  and meetings with Arabs, 139–40
  Pococke's translation of *Hayy ibn Yaqzan,*
    65–6
  and Sale, 86
  slaves writing in, 194–5
  and Tripoli treaty, 212, 354*nn*69–70
Arabigo, Joseph, 45
Arabs, 26. *See also* Islam; Muslims; North
    African pirates; Saracens
"Arbitrary Government proved incompatible
    with true Religion" (Trenchard and
    Gordon), 24, 105

Aristotle, 98–9
army, national, 165–7
Arouet, François-Marie "Voltaire," 27,
    28–33
Article 11 of the Tripoli Treaty, 207–12,
    354*n*69
atheists and atheism
  Edwards on, 80
  exclusion from Act of Toleration of 1689, 75
  exclusion from public office, 159–60, 163
  Iredell on, 174–5
  Jefferson accused of, 212, 224, 271
  Jefferson on, 106, 111, 113
  Locke on, 111
  Washington on, 5
"Autobiography" (Jefferson)
  on Bill for Establishing Religious Freedom,
    101, 102, 119
  on French Revolution, 232
  on king's support for slave trade, 213
  on North African pirates' motives, 237

Bachmann, Michele, 292, 375*n*181
Backus, Isaac, 248, 363*n*19
Bagshaw, Edward, 71, 72, 76, 324*n*229
Bailey, Thomas, 156
Bailyn, Bernard, xi–xii, 136
Baptists
  Abbot, 169–71, 185
  and Anglicans, 101, 102, 238
  corporal punishment in Virginia, 244
  English Baptists, 52, 53–6, 242–3
  fleeing England to Holland, 52
  Helwys, 53–5, 243
  and Jefferson, 256–7
  Lancaster, 183–6
  and Leland, 269
  on slavery, 267
  and tax supporting Protestants, 248–9
  Williams as, 60–1
  See also Leland, John
Barbary, meaning of, 134–5
Barbary States
  Adams on need for treaties, 136
  Algiers, 34, 132, 134, 143, 151–2, 218
  Algiers treaty, 218
  defined as, 126
  Jefferson on need for war with, 125, 136–7,
    151–3
  naval conflict of U.S. with Tripoli, 214–17,
    237
  and Ottoman Empire, 73
  overview, 134–5
  piracy and religion, 126–7
  Spanish military incursions, 131–2
  U.S. negotiations with, 8, 34, 124–6,
    133–6, 138–50
  See also Moroccans and Morocco; North
    African pirates; Tripolitans and Tripoli;
    Tunisians and Tunis

Barbary Wars, 8, 34, 130–1, 137, 198–200, 214–17, 238

Barlow, Joel, 208–10, 212

Bayle, Pierre, 72

Beck, Glenn, 286

Beecher, Lyman, 265

Bellius, Martin, known as "Castellio" or "Sébastien Châteillon," 48–51, 52–3

Benamor, Mr., 142–3

Benedict XIV, Pope, 29–30

Betsey (American merchant ship), 133

Bill for Establishing Religious Freedom (Jefferson)
  Baptist support for, 244
  inalienable rights outlined in, 251
  and Muslim as president, 291
  omitting Jesus Christ from, 118–20, 238, 336*n*249
  overview, 106, 115–20
  and support for Muslim rights, 117–20, 236–8
  on taxation to support Anglican Church, 113–14
  Virginia Gazette coverage, 158–9

Bill for the Naturalization of Persons, 108–10

Bill of Rights of Massachusetts, 254–6

Bill Prescribing the Oath of Fidelity and the Oaths of Certain Public Officers (Jefferson), 111–12

Bill to Prevent Losses by Pirates, Enemies, and Others on the High Seas (Jefferson), 137–8

Bjorck, Erick Tobias, 20

Blackstone, William, 231

Blair, James, 96–7

Bloody Tenent Yet More Bloody, The (Williams), 60

Bloomberg, Michael, 297–8

Bloudy Tenent, of Persecution for Cause of Conscience, The (Williams), 57–9, 64, 319*n*131

Bloudy Tenent, Washed and Made White in the Bloud of the Lamb, The (Cotton), 60

Blount, Charles, 69

Bolingbroke, Henry St. John, Viscount, 94–5

Bowne, John, 63

Boyd, Julian, 109

Boykin, William G. "Jerry," 294, 299

Brown, Campbell, 289–90

Brown, Wendy, 370–1*n*80

Bryden, James, 82

Buckley, Thomas E., 336*n*249

Bulliet, Richard W., 277

Bush, George W., 281

Caldwell, David, 164, 181–2, 185

Calvin, John, 16–17, 48, 50–1, 113

Calvinism, Jefferson on, 232–3

Canfora, Luciano, 331*n*130

Carson, André, 286

Castellio, Sebastian, 48–51, 52–3, 113

Castilian legal codes, 45

catalog system, Jefferson's, 233–6

Cathcart, James, 127, 222, 354*n*70

Catholic Inquisition, 42, 47–8, 104

Catholicism
  as Antichrist, 15, 20
  Anti-Federalists' concerns about, 175–8
  as antithetical to American liberty, 6, 67
  comparing Luther and Turks, 17
  comparing or equating to Turks/Islam, 22, 24, 30, 36
  conversion to, 45, 48, 84–5
  the Crusades, 84, 88, 331–2*n*130
  Islam linked to, in Sale's *Koran,* 84–5
  and Jefferson, 104, 109
  Leland on, 265–6
  pope as U.S. president, 176, 180, 183
  Protestants' fear of Catholic domination, 101, 168, 170, 175, 260, 265
  sanctification of Mary, 89
  as tyranny, 24
  and Voltaire's play *Mahomet,* 27, 29–31
  See also Inquisition

Catholics
  and Act of Toleration of 1689, 75
  discrimination against, 162, 164, 175–6
  double loyalty issue, 67, 74–5, 111, 162, 163, 275–6
  exclusion from public office, 162–3
  immigration to the U.S., 5, 265–6, 274, 275–6
  Iredell's defense of, 176–9
  Jefferson on, 111
  Jews, Muslims, and, 5, 168–9, 184–5, 304*n*3, 307*n*27
  Leland's fight for rights of, 241–2, 265–6
  Locke on, 111
  Mathurins, 153
  on Muslims and Protestants, 17
  overview, 10–11
  plot to blow up Parliament, 54–5
  prejudice against Muslims, 14, 15
  as President of the United States, 176, 177–8, 183–6
  religious intolerance of, 28–31
  and religious test for public office, 162, 183
  and slavery, 132
  and Williams, 61, 320*n*138

Cato's Letters (Trenchard and Gordon), 23–5, 30, 105–6

Cato the Younger, 23

Center for Security Policy, 293–5

Charles II, King of England, 63

Chaucer, Geoffrey, 101–2

Cheese and the Worms, The (Ginzburg), 42

Cheshire, Massachusetts, 249, 256–7, 259

"Choose Generosity, Not Exclusion" (Ellison), 301, 375*n*181

Christianity
and Adams's treaty with Tripoli, 207–12, 354nn69–70
The Algerine Captive on, 35–8
Calvinism, 16–17, 48, 50–1, 113, 232–3
church building in conquered nations, 296
Day of Judgment, 60
duty to tolerate others, 64, 65–6
history of schism, persecution, and torture, 94–5, 114
inclusiveness plea in Flushing Remonstrance, 62–3, 297–8
intolerance of, 88
Islam as antithesis of, 18–19, 171
Jefferson on, in letter to Hammuda Bey, 225–6
Jesus Christ, references to, 118–20, 250, 336n249
Leland's condemnation of state establishments, 242, 262–3
and piracy, 126–7, 131–3
prejudice against Muslims, 14–15, 16–17, 18
and religious freedom in the U.S., 101, 182
and Sabbath, 266–7
superiority codified by colonies, 161
superiority over Islam and Judaism, 49–50, 53, 56–7
weakness in seventh-century Middle East, 89
See also Anglicanism; Baptists; Catholicism; conversion to Christianity; Golden Rule; New Testament; Old Testament; Protestantism; Trinity doctrine; Unitarians and Unitarianism
Christian Philosopher, The (Mather), 20
Christians
boys seized by Turks, 18
Jews and Muslims compared to, 14, 49, 58–9
Muslims compared to, 78
as People of the Book, 14, 49, 142, 146–7, 227, 329n75
Christie, Chris, 292
Church and State in Revolutionary Virginia (Buckley), 336n249
Church of England. *See* Anglicanism; Anglicans; Episcopalians
Civil Rights Act (1964), 275
civil servants. *See* Constitution of the United States, No Religious Test Clause
Cobbett, William, 208
coffee, 91, 140
Cohen, Arthur, 277
colonies. *See* states or colonies
Commentaries (Blackstone), 231
Common Sense (Paine), 206
Concerning Heretics (Castellio as Martin Bellius), 48–51, 52–3, 113
conformity in religion, 252–3

Congregational Protestantism in New England, 14, 238, 247, 253–6
Connecticut, 163, 249–54, 365n79
Constitution of Massachusetts, 254–6, 260–3, 365n86
Constitution of the United States
and captives of North African pirates, 156–7
and centralization of military power, 165–7
debates referring to Ottoman despotism, 164–7
Fourteenth Amendment, 240–1, 273
Fourth Amendment, 282
Leland's opposition to, 245–6, 247
and religious freedom, 184–5
religious intolerance as evil to be subverted by, 173
Thirteenth Amendment, 195
See also First Amendment of the Constitution of the United States
Constitution of the United States, No Religious Test Clause
and Jews, 158–64, 167–9, 177–8, 180, 181–2, 184
Lancaster's argument for religious tests, 183–6
and Muslims (cited in eighteenth century as Mahometans, Turks), 158–63, 167–71, 174, 180
North Carolina debate in favor of, 169–71, 172–5, 177–83
North Carolina debate on, 167–9
North Carolina's failure to ratify due to, 167–9, 185–6
North Carolina's ratification, 161
Protestant opposition to, 158–61
See also religious freedom
conversion by Inquisition, 36
conversion to Catholicism, 45, 48, 84–5
conversion to Christianity
Locke opposes moderate force and other penalties, 77
overview, 40, 45, 71
peaceful approaches, 53–4, 58, 77
as reason to tolerate Muslims or Jews, 42, 49–50, 77–9, 345n44
as road to salvation, 78
Sale's views of, 86–7
salvation of Muslims and Jews without conversion vs., 42–3, 58
of slaves, 267–8
violent tactics, 57, 58, 72, 94–5, 113–15
conversion to Islam
in *The Algerine Captive,* 35–8
for captives of North African pirates, 76, 127
toleration for converts, 76–7
violent tactics, 18
Cordoba House Initiative, New York, 296–8
Cotton, John, 59–60

court cases
  on citizenship for Muslim immigrants, 275
  on illegal searches, 282–3
  on oaths of non-Protestants, 178–9
  on Oklahoma's anti-Sharia constitutional
    amendment, 295–6
  *Reports on Cases Adjudg'd in the Court of the
    King's Bench* (Salkeld), 93
cover artwork for *Mahomet the Impostor*, 31,
  313n109
Crusades, the, 84, 88, 331–2n130
cultural neutrality, 108
Cutler, Manasseh, 258–9

Danbury, Connecticut, 257
Dauphin or *Dolphin* (schooner), 153
Decline and Fall of the Roman Empire, The
  (Gibbon), 92
Deists and Deism
  Barlow, 208–10
  exclusion from public office, 159–60
  Islam compared to, 89
  Jews equated to, 110
  Leland on, 263
  Paine, 200–7
  Prideaux's attack on, 18–19
  Protestants' fear of, 170–1
  unitary God and God of Islam
    connection, 69
  See also Jefferson, Thomas
Delaware's oath for public officeholders, 163
Discourse About Civil Government, A (Cotton),
  59–60
Discourses on Davila (Adams), 201–2
dissimulation, 294
divorce case, 95–7
Dollard, Patrick, 165

Eaton, William, 215
Eck, Diana, 278–9
Edict of Expulsion, Jews from England, 54, 71
Edwards, John, 79–80
Edwards, Jonathan, 21
Egyptian history, Jefferson's collection of, 234
Egypt, Obama speaking in, 289
Eisenhower, Dwight D., 298
El-Abbadi, Mostafa, 331–2n130
Ellison, Keith, x, 284–7, 375n181
Emon, Anver, 293
England. *See* Great Britain
English Baptists, 52, 53–6, 243–4
Episcopalians. *See* Anglicanism; Anglicans
Errors of the Trinity, The (Servetus), 47–8
Esposito, John, 9
Essai sur les moeurs et l'esprit des nations
  (Voltaire), 97–9
Essay Concerning Toleration, An (Locke), 72
Essay in Defence of the Good Old Cause, An
  (Stubbe), 66
Essay on Human Understanding (Locke), 66

*Essay on the Universal History, Manners, and
  Spirit of Nations, An* (Voltaire), 97–9
Europe and Ottoman Empire, 15–16, 44
European views of Muslims
  fictional representations, 27, 28–33
  Menocchio's argument for salvation of
    Muslims and Jews, 42–7
  negative influence on early Americans, 6,
    14, 15–18, 20, 22–7, 304n9
  positive influence on early Americans,
    42–8, 49–55, 66–70, 323n211
  terminology distortions, 25–6
Eustace, Kitty, 96–7

Fanatisme, ou Mahomet le Prophète, Le
  (Voltaire), 27, 28–33
Fatiha, first chapter of the Qur'an, 191, 194
Fatima, daughter of the Prophet, 7, 90, 121
"Fatimer," or Fatima, as Muslim slave name,
  7, 121, 273
Feake, Tobias, 63
fearmongering
  of Anti-Federalists, in opposition to
    Constitution, 165–7, 170
  anti-Sharia campaign as, 292–3, 295–6, 299
  counter to, 289–90
  Federalists, in election of 1800, 212–13
  Jefferson accused of being Muslim, 9,
    200–1, 212, 228, 271, 287–9
  and non-Protestants in public office, 161,
    169, 176–7, 184, 290–1
  Obama accused of being Muslim, 287–9,
    291, 293–4
  politics of Islamic fearmongering, 271,
    287–8
  and Protestants' fear of Catholics, 101, 170,
    265–6
  and Protestants' fear of Deism, 170–1
Federalist Papers, The (Madison, Hamilton, and
  Jay), 165, 245
Federalists
  Cobbett, 208
  fearmongering in presidential election of
    1800, 212–13
  and Muslim "civil rights," 168–9, 180–1,
    184–5, 195–6
  and Ottoman Empire as despotic, 164–5
  on religious freedom, 161, 167, 181
  Webster, 166–7
  See also Iredell, James; Johnston, Samuel;
    Madison, James
Ferdinand and Isabella, King and Queen of
  Spain, 45, 131, 132
Finkelman, Paul, 128
First Amendment of the Constitution of the
  United States
  Boykin on, 294
  and court ruling on Oklahoma's anti-
    Sharia law, 295–6
  Jefferson on "wall of separation," 257–8

First Amendment of the Constitution of the United States *(continued)*
and Leland, 246–7, 253
and Muslim "civil rights," 299, 300–1
New England's Congregational Protestantism after passage of, 238, 241
and religious freedom, 209
and Tripolitan treaty, 210–11
Fischer, Bryan, 299–300
Flushing Remonstrance, 62–3, 297–8
Fondaco dei Turchi, Venice, 316n32
Ford, Henry, 276
Foss, John, 139
Foster, Mr. (slave owner in Mississippi), 187, 188–9
Fox, George, 21
Foxe, John, 17–18
France
Le Fanatisme, ou Mahomet le Prophète in, 27, 28–30
French Revolution, 201–2, 228, 232
Huguenots in, 72
rights of conscience in Constitution, 206
Franck, Sebastian, 51–3, 318n78
Franklin, Benjamin, 21, 22, 130, 152, 162
Franks, David S., 110
freedom of religion. *See* religious freedom; religious tolerance
Freeman's Oracle, 158–9
French Revolution, 201–2, 228, 232

Gaffney, Frank J., Jr., 293–5
Garcia, Humberto, 70, 322n200
Geller, Pamela, 297
George III, King of England, 32, 313n114
Georgia, 163, 273
GhaneaBassiri, Kambiz, 274
Gibbon, Edward, 92
Gingrich, Newt, 292–3
Ginzburg, Carlo, 42
Golden Rule
Castellio on, 49–50
Ellison on, 301
Flushing Remonstrance on, 63
Jefferson on, xv, 301–2
Leland on, 243, 263, 265
Menocchio on, 42–5
Obama on, 288
Williams on, 59
Goode, Virgil, Jr., 284–5
Gordon, Thomas, 23–5
government
centralization of military power, 165–7
established Puritan religion, 59–60
Helwys's proposed degree of toleration, 53–4
imagined Muslim political community in U.S., 8–9, 10, 168, 174–5, 195, 240
and national army provision in Constitution, 165–7

Protestant Founders of U.S., 4
and religious tolerance, 6–7
tyranny identified with Muslims, 14, 22, 23–4
Williams's ideal society, 61
See also politics; public officeholders; separation of church and state
Graham, Franklin, 280
Great Awakening, the, 21
Great Britain
accommodations for swearing in of Jews, 177
and American ships and crew, 137–8
expulsion of Jews, 54, 71, 317n46
Jefferson studying legal precedents of, 93–5
Mahomet the Impostor in, 30–1
and North African pirates, 130–1
and Ottoman Empire, 22–5
Prize Act (1708), 133
religious tests in, 173
and Williams's Bloudy Tenent, 57–8
Ground Zero Mosque (film), 297

Halal Law of Texas (2003), 292
Hamburger, Philip, 366n120
Hamdani, Talat, 280
Hammuda Bey, 222–7, 237
Hayes, Chris, 287
Hayy ibn Yaqzan (Ibn Tufayl), 65–6, 321n176
Hebrew Bible. *See* Old Testament
Helwys, Thomas, 53–5, 243
Hemings, Elizabeth, 337n270
Hemings, Sara "Sally," 122, 129, 337n270
Henry, Patrick, 166
heresy
Deism and Unitarianism as, 69
Locke accused of, 79–80
Origen's heresy, 42, 52
of Pelagius, 45
religious tolerance as, 40, 42, 45, 51, 52
of Servetus, 48
of seventh-century Christians, 89
universalist doctrine as, 160
heretics
Concerning Heretics (Castellio), 48–51, 52–3, 113
Helwys on acceptance of, 53
Muslims and Jews excluded from by Locke, 76–7
royal religious authority over, 71–2
tolerance for, as dissenters, 70, 71, 72
Hindus and Hinduism, 178–9
History of the Corruptions of Christianity, An (Priestley), 228
Hoadly, Benjamin, 30
Hoadly, John, 30–1
Holland
freedom of conscience in 1579, 62
as refuge for Whigs from England, 70

religious tolerance in, 52, 59, 60, 63
Remonstrants, 324*n*236
Huff, Richard Curry, 366–7*n*120
Huguenots (French Protestants), 72
Humanity in Algiers (anon.), 40
Hume, David, 102
Hutchinson, Anne, 20
Hutson, James, 307*n*26

Ibn al-Khattab, Umar, 97, 98
Ibn Rushd "Averroes," 99
Ibn Said, Omar, 10, 186–7, 191–5, 349*n*156
Ibn Tufayl, Muhammad ibn 'Abd al-Malik,
20, 65–6, 321*n*176
Ibrahima Abd al-Rahman, Muslim slave, 10,
186, 187–91, 349*n*156
immigration
Irish Catholic immigrants, 5, 265–6
Jefferson's Virginia Bill for Naturalization
of Immigrants, 108–10
Muslims, 274–5, 277–9
name changes, 274
post–Immigration and Nationality Act of
1965, 278–9
Immigration and Nationality Act (1965),
277–9
inalienable natural rights theory, 64, 251–2
Independent Whig (weekly), 23
infidels
and Constitution of the United States,
158–9, 212–13
Deists as, 263
Jefferson branded as, 120, 212, 230, 271,
272–3
Jefferson on, 119–20, 238
and Origen's heresy, 42
overview, 39
as political slur, 213, 224
as preferable to heretic, 76
Qur'an on, 88
as religious slur, 21, 37
Inquisition
Catholic Inquisition, 42, 47–8, 104
conversion by, 36
and Galileo, 104
and Menocchio, 42–7, 302, 316*n*15
and Servetus, 47–8
Spanish Inquisition, 45, 48, 54
Institutes of the Christian Religion (Calvin),
50–1
International Seminar on the History of the
Atlantic World, xi
Iredell, James, 196
as associate justice, 186
on Catholic threat, 176–7
on Hindus and oaths, 178–9
and Johnston, 172, 179–81
and Muslim "civil rights," 10, 196
and North Carolina's failure to ratify the
Constitution, 185–6

on religious test for public office, 169,
171–5
on swearing of oaths, 177–9
Irish Catholic immigrants, 5, 265–6
Islam
Adams on, 205–6
afterlife and women, 90
The Algerine Captive on, 35–8
as Antichrist, 15, 16–18, 20–2
anti-Sharia movement, 292–3, 295–6,
299
as antithesis of true Christianity, 18–19,
171
bismillah, 193, 195
Christian superiority, 49–50, 53, 56–7
conversion to, 18, 35–8, 76–7, 127, 278–9
and Deist or Unitarian viewpoints, 69
dissimulation, 294
on divorce, 96–7
and First Amendment, 299, 300–1
five pillars, 90, 194
and French Revolution, 232
Jefferson's negative views of, 4, 8, 84,
230–3
Jefferson's positive views of, 93, 97–100,
103–4, 227, 230, 236–8
in Jefferson's Tripoli treaty, 216, 217–18
Jefferson's use of, to critique other
religions, 102–4, 105–6, 230–3, 237
Leland's erroneous beliefs, 250–1, 263–4
Mandeville on, 46
Mather's selective approach, 20
Muhammad, 31, 67, 87–8, 89, 313*n*109
Paine on, 206–7
place in Jefferson's library, 233–6
and political rhetoric of Jefferson and
Adams, 200–5
prohibitions, 91
pro-Islamic materials by Stubbe, 19
and Ramadan, 90, 220–1, 357*n*140
scientific discoveries, 98, 99
Sharia compatible with American
citizenship, 295
Sharia compatible with English
citizenship, 74
Sharia law, 292, 293–6
Stubbe on, 67–70, 322*n*200
terminology distortions, 25–6, 334*n*186
treatment of slaves, 127–8, 339*n*12
as tyranny, 22–4
as weapon for vilifying fellow Christians,
16–17, 18–19, 20–1
See also anti-Islamic polemic; conversion to
Islam; Muhammad; Muslim Americans;
Muslims; Qur'an
Islam and Liberal Citizenship (March), 295
Islamic legal schools, 91
Islamo-Christian civilization, 277
"Islamophilia," 323*n*211
Ismail, Sultan of Morocco, 23

janissaries, 18, 22, 23–4, 165–7
Jefferson, Martha, 128–9
Jefferson, Thomas
  accusations of being a Muslim, 9, 200–1,
    212, 228, 271, 287–9
  and Anglicanism, 84, 100–4
  as Deist, 170–1, 230
  divorce case, 95–7
  on Golden Rule, 301–2
  and Islam, x, 3–10, 93–100, 102–4, 200,
    202–3, 207, 216–18, 226–7, 230–3,
    236–8
  and Jews, 109–10, 335n201
  and Leland, 244, 251, 256–9
  Leland on, 257–8, 259
  letters to Tunisian ruler, 222–7, 237
  letter to Tripolitan ruler, 224
  library catalog system, 233–6
  library of, 83–4, 140, 233–4, 360n211
  and Locke, 106–8, 111–17
  losses from house fire, 83
  and "Mammoth Cheese" from
    Massachusetts, 256, 257, 259
  and Muslim rights, 106–10, 117–20, 122–3,
    236–8
  Muslim slaves of, 7–8, 120–3
  Obama compared to, 287–8
  and Qur'an, ix–xi, 81–4, 91–2, 105, 154–5,
    199, 227, 235–6
  and racial differences, 128
  and Ramadan, 220–1, 357n140
  on reception at Court of St. James's, 138–9
  religion of, 8, 224, 227, 228–30, 229
  religious tolerance of, 6–7, 92, 93–4,
    106–13, 213
  on rotation of public officeholders, 165
  as secretary of state, 196, 197–205
  slaves of, 121–3, 128
  studying British legal precedents, 93–5,
    106–8
  and Voltaire's view of Islam, 97–9
  See also "Autobiography" (Jefferson); Bill
    for Establishing Religious Freedom
    (Jefferson); Deists and Deism; *Notes on
    Virginia* (Jefferson)
Jefferson, Thomas, as president
  first inaugural address, 272
  military action against Tripoli/North
    African pirates, 34, 136–8, 151–3,
    214–17, 237, 238, 306n18, 355n91
  predictions of doom resulting from his
    presidency, 272–3
  Tripoli treaty, 216–18, 237
  Tunisian ambassador Mellimelli's visit to
    D.C., 218–22
Jefferson Bible, 91–2, 235
Jefferson's Qur'an
  acquisition of, 3, 81–2, 83–4, 154, 343n174
  Ellison's oath on, 284
  importance of, 91–3

at Library of Congress, ix
  overview, 299–301
  place in Jefferson's library, 235–6
Jesus Christ
  Leland's references to, 250
  Locke's references to, 118
  omitting from Bill for Establishing
    Religious Freedom, 118–20, 336n249
Jewish Americans
  Adams, J. Q., on, 206
  on anti-Muslim activist Yerushalmi, 293
  and Flushing Remonstrance, 62–3, 297–8
  and Jefferson's Virginia Bill for
    Naturalization of Immigrants, 108–10,
    335n201
  negative stereotypes, 38–9, 143, 168
  and Obama accused of being Muslim, 288
  and religious test for public office, 177,
    182
  See also Judaism
Jews
  and Adams, 142
  The Algerine Captive on, 38–9
  and Barbary ambassadors, 142
  double loyalty issue, 295
  Edict of Expulsion from England, 54, 71,
    317n46
  exclusion from Act of Toleration of
    1689, 75
  exclusion from public office, 159–60,
    162–3
  immigration to the U.S., 274, 275, 276–7
  and Jefferson, 3, 5–6, 96–8, 106–10
  Leland's fight for rights of, 241–2
  Locke on, 3, 75–7, 79, 106–7
  Menocchio's argument for salvation of
    Muslims and, 42–7, 302
  Muslims and Christians compared to, 14,
    49, 58–9
  Muslims, Catholics, and, 5, 168–9, 184–5,
    304n3, 307n27
  and Muslims, equated, 94, 106–8, 180
  overview, 10–11
  as People of the Book, 14, 49, 142, 146–7,
    227, 329n75
  and presence in North Africa, 142–3
  and religious liberty in New York, 161–2
  and religious test for public office, 164
  as threat to Christian society, 43, 275–77
  toleration of, 5
  Zoroastrians compared to, 98
  See also Judaism
jihad, 147, 300
Johnson, Samuel, 94
Johnston, Samuel
  on civic virtues vs. creed, 180, 285
  and North Carolina constitutional
    ratification debates, 10, 164, 171–2,
    179–81, 182, 186, 196
Jones, Terry, ix–x, 304n3

Judaism
  Christian superiority, 49–50, 53, 56–7
  Jefferson on, 92, 110
  Leland on, 264–5
  and polygamy, 88
  See also Jews; Old Testament
Judeo-Christian-Islamic religious identity,
  277
Judeo-Christian religious identity, 276–7

Kamil, Neil, xii, 62
Ketton, Robert, 84
Kidd, Thomas S., 361*n*1
Koran, 26. *See also* Qur'an
Koran (Sale)
  and *The Algerine Captive,* 39
  on God, Jesus, and the Trinity in the
    Qur'an, 89–91
  introduction, 84, 91, 231
  Jefferson's negative views of the Qur'an,
    230–3
  Jefferson's neglect of, 105–6
  Jefferson's positive views of the Qur'an,
    227, 230, 235–6
  Jefferson's purchase of, 81–2, 83–4
  place in Jefferson's library, 235–6
  "Preliminary Discourse," 86–8
  translation issues, 84–6
  use of Koran vs. Qur'an, 26
  and Voltaire, 29

Lafayette, Marquis de, 129–30, 152
Lambert, Frank, 126, 132, 150
Lancaster, William, 183–4
Lee, Richard Henry, 245
Legal Commonplace Book, 97
legal decisions. *See* court cases
Legend of the Three Rings, The (folklore), 44
Leland, John
  beyond religious tolerance, 241–2
  biography, 10, 14, 239, 240, 241, 242, 244,
    248, 267, 362*n*15
  on conformity in religion, 252–3
  and Connecticut's tax to support
    Congregational Protestantism, 249–54,
    365*n*79
  and Helwys, 243
  on Islam, 250–1
  and Jefferson, 244, 256–9
  on Jefferson, 253, 257–8, 259
  Kidd on, 361*n*1
  as legislator in Massachusetts, 259–63
  and Leland's erroneous understanding of
    Islam, 264
  and Locke, 245
  and Madison, 244–7, 363*n*36
  and Massachusetts's tax to support
    Congregational Protestantism, 254–6
  and Muslim rights, 240–2, 249–50, 253,
    255, 261–3, 269

  opposition to Constitution, 245–6, 247
  on religious freedom, 240–1, 361*n*1, 365*n*84
  on separation of church and state, 242,
    260–1, 266–7, 362*n*10, 366*n*120
  on slavery, 267–9
  and Smyth, 242–3
  and Washington, 247–8
  and Williams, 243–4
Leslie, Peter, 214
Letter Concerning Toleration, A (Locke), 64, 72,
  75–7, 106–8, 109, 116–17
Liberia, 191
liberty of conscience principle, Williams's,
  62–3, 64
library at Alexandria, Egypt, burning of, 98,
  331*n*130
Library of Congress, 233–6
Life and Fate of the Ancient Library of Alexandria
  (El-Abbadi), 331–2*n*130
Lingua Franca, 139
Literary Commonplace Book (Jefferson), 94
Locke, John
  accusations of being a Muslim, 271
  and "Age of Arabick" (G. A. Russell),
    65–6, 321*n*171
  attacked as Muslim, Socinian, or Deist,
    79–80
  and Bagshaw, 71, 72, 76
  and Carolinas' statutes for religious
    freedom, 345*n*44
  on Christianity, 114–15
  defense of Unitarians and Muslims, 69
  in Holland, 72, 324*n*236, 325*n*260
  on inalienable rights, 251
  and Jefferson, 106–8, 111–17
  and Leland, 245
  on Muslim "civil rights," 3, 64, 71–9, 109,
    174
  references to Jesus Christ, 118
  religious tolerance of, 64, 65–7, 69–72,
    76–9, 108, 111, 315*n*5
  and Shaftesbury, 70, 323*n*220
  and Stubbe, 68
  and Unitarianism, 79–80
Louis XIV, King of France, 72
Luther, Martin, 15, 16, 17, 50

Madison, James
  Algiers treaty, 218
  and Article 11 of the Tripoli treaty, 209–10
  beyond religious tolerance, 241
  and Bill for Establishing Religious
    Freedom, 117, 120
  on inalienable rights, 251
  Jefferson's letter on Adams dispute, 201
  and Leland, 244–7, 251, 363*n*36
  and Muslim rights, 7
  on national army, 166
  on national army provision in
    Constitution, 165

Madison, James *(continued)*
  on prohibiting religious tests for public
    office, 158
"Mahomet: A Dream," 39
Mahometans, and other premodern
    variations of Muslims (Mahamadens,
    Mahomedans, Mahumetans,
    Mehomitans, Musselmen, Mussulmans),
    3, 13–14, 20, 39–40, 41–2, 92, 95, 104,
    106–7, 197, 207, 211, 216–17, 227–28,
    231, 236, 238, 242, 245, 249, 263, 266,
    284
  Locke's usage, 73, 75–6, 77–9
  and North Carolina debate on religious
    test, 158–9, 167, 170–1, 174, 180, 183,
    190
  term defined, 25–6, 335*n*186
  See also Muslims; Saracens; Turks
Mahomet the Impostor (Voltaire), 30–3
"Mammoth Cheese" from Massachusetts, 256,
    257, 259
Mandeville, Sir John, 46
Maracci, Ludovico, 85
Maria (schooner), 153
Marschalk, Andrew, 189
Marshall, John, 73
Marx, Joseph, 110
Maryland, 163, 175
Massachusetts/Massachusetts Bay Colony
  ban on religious tolerance, 37
  Constitution of Massachusetts, 254–6,
    260–3, 365*n*86
  Leland as legislator, 259–63
  Leland on, 240
  Leland's fight against tax to support
    Congregational Protestantism, 254–6
  and religious test for public office, 163,
    262–3
  Williams's exile from, 52–3, 59–60
Matar, Nabil, 71, 131, 322*n*204
Mather, Cotton, 20, 66
McCain, John, 288–9
McLoughlin, William G., 366*n*120
McVeigh, Timothy, 281
media coverage of Muslim world, 280
Medina, Tomé de, 45
Mediterranean and U.S. trade
  forces against peace, 130–1
  and Mediterranean markets, 126, 136, 145,
    197–8
  paying off pirates, 136, 144–5, 147
  post–Revolutionary War risks, 197–8
  and start of U.S. naval power, 137, 152–3
  and Tripolitan ambassador, 125, 141
  and U.S. naval action against Tripoli,
    214–17
  See also Barbary States; North African
    pirates
Meet the Press (TV program), 290
Mellimelli, Sidi Suleyman, 218–22, 225–6

*Memorial and Remonstrance against Religious
    Assessments, A* (Madison), 210–11, 245,
    251
"Memorial of the Presbytery of Hanover," 101
Menocchio "Domenico Scandella," 42–7,
    302, 316*n*15
Middle Eastern immigrants, 274, 277–9
military action against Tripoli/North African
    pirates, 34, 136–8, 151–3, 214–17, 237,
    238, 306*n*18, 355*n*91
military power, centralization of, 165–7
Miller, James, 30
Mistery of Iniquity, The (Helwys), 53–5
Mitchill, Samuel L., 357*n*140
Mohammed, Sohail, 292
Moors, 26, 45, 134, 189–90, 199. *See also*
    Muslims
Moroccans and Morocco
  and England, 73
  Ibrahima, 10, 186, 187–91, 349*n*156
  overview, 25–6
  seizure of the *Betsey*, 133
  Sultan Ismail, 23
  U.S. peace treaty with, 34, 139, 141, 144
  See also Barbary States; North African
    pirates
mosques, bans on building of, 296–8
movies with negative depictions of Arabs,
    280
Muhammad
  as final Prophet, 89
  images of, 31, 313*n*109
  Sale on, 87–8
  Stubbe on, 67
Muntzer, Thomas, 47
Muslim Americans
  and 9/11, 279–83, 296–7
  acceptance of, 289–90
  and anti-Muslim bigotry, ix–x, 9, 275,
    280–97
  and Deists, 170–1
  demographics, 278–9
  FBI interviews, 281–2
  first citizens defined as Muslims, 273
  and Flushing Remonstrance, 62–3, 297–8
  forging ties with Jewish and Christian
    organizations, 283
  and Fourteenth Amendment, 273
  historical views, 10–11
  Jefferson accused of being Muslim, 9,
    200–1, 212, 228, 271, 287–9
  and Judeo-Christian rubric, 277
  Leland's fight for rights of, 241–2
  Locke accused of being Muslim, 79–80, 271
  mosque-building bans, 296–8
  and North Carolina debate on religious
    freedom, 167–9
  Obama accused of being Muslim, 287–9,
    291, 293–4
  overview, 11, 302

as President of the United States, 159–60, 168, 183–6
as public officeholders, 283, 284–7
and religious test for public office, 158–61, 160–3, 164, 182
rights of, 9
violence against, 281
Muslim "civil rights"
American Founders' support for, 6–9, 10, 307*n*26
in England, 72–3
and Federalists, 168–9
Federalist vision of, 168–9
and First Amendment, 299, 300–1
Helwys on, 53–4, 56
Iredell's defense of, 171–5
Jefferson on, 3, 5–7, 106–8, 118–20, 237–8
Jefferson's vision of, 106–10, 117–20, 272
Leland's fight for, 240–2, 263–4, 269
Locke on, 3, 64, 71–9, 109, 174
overview, 4–5, 271–2
and PATRIOT Act, 282–3, 370–1*n*80
slaves excluded from, 121–3
utilizing to encompass all non-Protestants, 161, 168, 170–1
Muslim Histories and Cultures Project, Texas, 292
Muslims
and boundaries of toleration, 3–5
Christians compared to, 78
double loyalty issue, 295
exclusion from Act of Toleration of 1689, 75
exclusion from public office, 159–60
as imagined U.S. constituency, 5–6, 8–9, 10, 168, 174–5, 195, 240
immigration to the U.S., 274–5, 277–9
Jefferson's attitude toward, 92–3, 198–9
Jews and Christians compared to, 14, 49, 58–9
Jews, Catholics, and, 5, 168–9, 184–5, 304*n*3, 307*n*27
and Jews, equated, 94, 106–8, 180
links with Deists and Unitarians, 69
living outside Muslim lands, 73–4
in London, 72–3
Menocchio's argument for salvation of Jews and, 42–7, 302
Shi'i, 278, 291–2, 294, 331–2*n*130
as slaves in America, 7–8, 10, 35, 76, 120–3, 186–91, 349*n*156
See also European views of Muslims; Muslim Americans; Ottoman Empire; Sunni Muslims
Muslim Students' Association, 279

national army, 165–7
National Conference of Christians and Jews, 276
Native Americans, 221, 222, 268

nativism, 275–6
Naturalization Act (1790), 273–4
Naturalization Act (1870), 274
naval force for the United States, 152–3
Netherlands. *See* Holland
New England, 159–60, 238. *See also specific states*
New Hampshire's religious test for public office, 163
New Jersey's religious test for public office, 163
New Testament
Arabic translation, 86
and Golden Rule, 301
Jefferson on, 232, 235–6
Leland quoting from, 258
oaths sworn on, 177–9
and religious test for public office, 164
New York
Cordoba House Initiative, 296–8
religious liberty in, 161–2
New York Magazine, 39
9/11 terrorist attacks, 279–83, 296–7
non-Protestants
Jefferson's acceptance of, 4, 6, 106, 108–11, 118–20
Protestant opposition to non-Protestants as public officeholders, 158–61, 170–1, 180
See also Catholics; Deists and Deism; Jews; Muslims; taxes for supporting churches
North Africa
Jefferson's collection of books on, 234
Muslims to reside only in Islamic lands, 74
U.S. peace treaties with, 34
vilification of Islam and, 23
See also Algiers; Barbary States; Moroccans and Morocco; Tripolitans and Tripoli; Tunisians and Tunis
North African pirates
Adams on, 135
American captives of, 124–5, 127–8, 143, 153–4, 216, 339*n*12
and Arabic language, 65
cost of safe passage, 126
economic motives, 126, 132, 146
guarding Strait of Gibraltar, 199
Jefferson's military response to, 34, 136–8, 151–3, 214–17, 237, 238, 306*n*18, 338*n*7
Jefferson's view of, 199–200
overview, 8, 124–5, 131–3, 306*n*18
Qur'anic justification for, 146–50
ransom for captured pirates, 199–200
religious vs. political motives, 126–7
response to Spanish incursions, 131–3
seizure of the *Betsey,* 133
sighting in West Indies, 340*n*65
"A Treaty of Amity and Commerce" (Jefferson draft, 1785), 134–5
U.S. captives of, 34, 311–12*n*87, 313*n*121

North African pirates *(continued)*
  U.S. negotiations with, 126–7, 133–6, 138–50, 200
  See also Barbary States; Moroccans and Morocco; Tripolitans and Tripoli; Tunisians and Tunis
North Carolina
  Constitution ratification debates, 161
  debate on religious freedom, 167–71, 172–5
  failure to ratify Constitution, 185–6
  and Iredell, 158, 171–9, 185–6
  and Johnston, 164, 179–81
  overview, 195–6
  and religious test for public office, 163–4, 168
  second convention to ratify the Constitution, 191–5
Notes on Virginia (Jefferson)
  on coercion, 114
  on conformity in religion, 252
  on history, 91
  Leland's use of, 244
  on reason and free inquiry, 103–4
  on religious freedom, 112
  on religious tolerance, 213
  on religious uniformity, 95
Nussbaum, Martha, 295

oath of toleration, 112
oaths for citizenship, 109, 111–12
oaths for public office
  Bill Prescribing the Oath of Fidelity and the Oaths of Certain Public Officers, 111–12
  Constitution of the United States on, 160–1
  Ellison's oath on Jefferson's Qur'an, x, 284
  in Pennsylvania, 162
  swearing on New Testament, 177–9
  swearing on Old Testament, 285
  test oaths, 161–4
  See also public officeholders
Obama, Barack, 287–93
O'Brien, Richard, 127–8, 130, 149
Of the Law of Nature and Nations (von Pufendorf), 96
Oklahoma City bombing, 281
Oklahoma's "Save Our State" anti-Sharia amendment, 295–6
Old Testament (Hebrew Bible)
  and Arabic language, 65
  and Golden Rule, ix, 50, 264, 302
  Jefferson on, 110, 231–2, 235–6
  and Jefferson's library catalog system, 236
  oaths sworn on, 285
  polygamy in, 35
  and religious test for public office, 164
Omar Ibn Said, 10, 186–7, 191–5, 349n156
"On the Right to Rebel against Governors" (West), 25

Oracles of Reason (Blount), 69
Order of the Holy Trinity and Redemption of Captives "Mathurins," 153–4
Orientalism, 307n30
Origen's heresy, 42, 52
Ottoman Empire
  as Antichrist, 15
  British and American depictions of, 22–5
  Calvin's beliefs, 16–17
  as cause of French Revolution, 232
  chief mufti of Istanbul, 73
  despotism alleged in constitutional ratification debates, 164–7
  divorce or alimony in, 96
  and English businesses, 65
  Fondaco dei Turchi, Venice, 316n32
  Foxe's view of, 17–18
  janissaries, 18, 22, 23–4, 165–7
  Jefferson's collection of books on, 234
  local uprising and assassination of sultans, 23–4
  Luther's beliefs, 16
  threat to Western Europe, 15–16, 44
Ottoman Turkish language, 139
Owen, Jim (slave owner in North Carolina), 192, 194
Oxford University, 65

Paine, Thomas
  on Islam, 206–7
  and *The Rights of Man,* 200–5
PATRIOT Act (2001), 282–3, 370–1n80
Peek, Lori, 283
Penn, William, 320n157
Pennsylvania, 162
People of the Book, 14, 49, 142, 146–7, 227, 329n75
Pérez, Juana, 45
perpetui inimici (enemies for life), 93–4
Perry, Rick, 291–2
Peterson, Merrill D., 116
Philadelphia, Pennsylvania, 21–2
Philadelphia (warship), 215–16, 234, 355n103
Philosophical Works (Bolingbroke), 94–5
piracy in the seventeenth century, 132. *See also* North African pirates
Plumer, William, 163, 219, 220, 221–2, 305n17
Pococke, Edward, 65–6
political officeholders. *See* public officeholders
politics
  anti-Sharia movement, 292–3, 295–6, 299
  and Article 11 of the Tripoli Treaty, 210–12, 354n69
  and early American hatred of Catholics and Turks, 22–5
  of fearmongering about Muslims, 9, 200–1, 212–28, 271, 291, 293–4
  Jefferson's interest in religion as, 229–30, 237
  Muslims in, x

and Muslims in office, 9
See also fearmongering; government; Whig
    ideology
polygamy, 88
Pompilius, Numa, 329*n*54
Popple, William, 75, 107
Porcupine Gazette, 208
Powell, Colin, 290
Prager, Dennis, 285–6
"Prayer against the Turks, A" (Foxe), 18
"Preliminary Discourse" (Sale), 86
Presbyterians and Presbyterianism
    and Anglicans, 101, 238
    Beecher, 265
    Caldwell, 164, 181–2, 185
    Ibn Said as, 192–3
    and Jefferson, 7, 100–2
    and Jews, 181–2
    Locke on, 75, 78
    Omar ibn Said, 192–5
    slave's possible conversion to, 194
President of the United States
    Catholic as, 176, 177–8, 183–6, 290–1
    election of 1800, 212–13, 256–7
    Johnston's reassurances about non-
        Christians not attaining office, 180
    Muslim as, 159–60, 168, 183–6, 287–91
    pope as, 176, 183
    religion factor, 291–2
    universalism and Muslim president issue,
        160
    See also Constitution of the United States,
        No Religious Test Clause
Prideaux, Humphrey, 18–19, 24, 69–70, 87,
    310*n*43
Priestley, Joseph, 228
Prize Act (1708), 133
Proast, Jonas, 77
Procrustes, and "Pocrustes" of Leland, 252
Prophet, the. *See* Muhammad
Protestantism
    Congregational Protestantism in New En-
        gland, 238, 241
    and Constitution of the United States,
        156–7
    and Deism, 170–1
    the Great Awakening, 21
    and Jefferson's argument for freedom of
        religion, 102–3
    and religious test for public office, 159–63
    and religious tolerance, 6–7, 52, 100,
        318*n*80
    sectarian warfare, 160–1
    See also Anglicanism; Baptists
Protestants
    America's Founders as, 4–5
    Calvin, 16–17, 48, 50–1, 113
    fear of Catholic domination, 101, 168, 170,
        175, 260, 265
    Luther, 15, 16, 17, 50

in New England, 238
See also Baptists; Presbyterians and
    Presbyterianism
Providence, Rhode Island, 20–1, 56–7, 60–1,
    63–4, 243
public officeholders
    civic virtue vs. religion, 180–1
    and debate on religious test for public
        office, 168
    Muslims as, 283, 284–7
    Protestant opposition to non-Protestants as,
        158–61, 170–1
    See also Constitution of the United States,
        No Religious Test Clause; government;
        oaths for public office; President of the
        United States
"Publicola" (pseudonym of J. Q. Adams),
    202–5
Puritans, 20. *See also* Massachusetts/
    Massachusetts Bay Colony; Williams,
    Roger

Qaramanli, Ahmed "Hamet," 215
Qaramanli, Yusuf, 214–15
Quakers
    Bowne arrest by Stuyvesant, 63
    Locke on, 75, 78
    and religious freedom, 320*n*157
    and tax supporting Protestants, 248–9
    Williams's condemnation of, 20–1
    Williams's offer of refuge to, 60–1
Qur'an
    Abd al-Rahman's use of, to justify piracy,
        125, 146–50, 300
    Christians' awareness of, 101–2
    on compulsion in religion, 17–18, 86
    Fatiha, first chapter, 191, 194
    Jefferson's negative views of, 230–3
    Jefferson's positive views of, 227, 236–7
    on Jesus, 40, 89–90
    Luther on, 16
    People of the Book, 14, 49, 142, 146–7,
        227, 329*n*75
    religious tolerance as principle of, 37–8,
        52, 68, 77
    on slavery vs. captivity, 127
    "the Sovereignty" (*al-Mulk*) chapter, 193
    translation issues, 84–6
    on unity of God, 89
    See also Islam; Jefferson's Qur'an; *Koran*
        (Sale)

racial discrimination, 128
Ragosta, John A., 238
Ra'is, Murad (formerly Peter Leslie), 214
Ramadan, 90, 220–1, 357*n*140
Reformation, Jefferson on, 104, 333*n*169
religion
    importance to colonists, 180–1
    and piracy, 126–7

religion (*continued*)
  slavery defined by, 132–3
  "true" religion and tyrannical
    governments, 24
  Zoroastrians and Zoroastrianism, 97–8
  See also Christianity; Deists and Deism;
    Islam; Judaism
religious freedom
  Carolinas' statutes for, 345*n*44
  and Christianity in the U.S., 101, 182
  conformity in religion vs., 252–3
  and Constitution of the United States,
    184–5
  debate on, in North Carolina, 167–9
  English treatises on, 22
  Federalists on, 161, 167, 181
  and immigration, 108–10
  Jefferson on, 102–3, 106–8, 112, 115–20
  in Jefferson's Tripoli treaty, 217–18
  Leland on, 240–1, 361*n*1, 365*n*84
  Locke on, 71–9
  in New York, 161–2
  North Carolina debate on, 167–71, 172–5
  in Pennsylvania, 162
  Presbyterians quest for, 100–2
  and Quakers, 320*n*157
  religious equality compared to, 101
  and swearing an oath, 177–9
  tyranny vs., 24
  in Virginia, 100, 163, 238–9
  Virginia Declaration of Rights, 100, 241
  Washington on, 247–8
  Williams's charter for Providence, 63–4
  See also Bill for Establishing Religious
    Freedom; Constitution of the United
    States, No Religious Test Clause; First
    Amendment of the Constitution of the
    United States; Muslim "civil rights";
    rights of conscience; taxes for supporting
    churches
Religious Freedom Act (Massachusetts, 1811),
    260
religious test. *See* Constitution of the United
    States, No Religious Test Clause
religious tolerance
  The Algerine Captive on, 35–9
  of Castellio, 49–51, 52–3
  Christian inclusiveness, 62–3
  in Flushing Remonstrance, 62–3, 297–8
  of Franck, 51–3
  of Franklin, 21, 22
  as full equality under the law, 173
  Helwys on, 53–5
  as heresy, 40, 42, 45, 51, 52
  of Jefferson, 6–7, 92, 93–4, 106–13, 213
  Leland's disgust for, 241
  of Locke, 64, 65–7, 69–72, 76–9, 108, 111,
    315*n*5
  in medieval European peasant lore, 43–4
  of Menocchio, 42–7, 302

  for Muslims, 3–5, 41–7, 49–50, 52–4, 58–9,
    61–3, 71–2, 75–9, 106–8, 119–20, 197,
    207, 209, 216, 218, 237–8
  overview, 6, 315*n*5
  political equality vs., 159
  and Protestantism, 6–7, 52, 100, 318*n*80
  in Qur'an, 37–8, 52, 68, 77
  of Servetus, 47–8
  of Smyth, 55
  of Stubbe, 66–70, 322*n*200
  of Williams, 56–7, 58–9
  See also Muslim "civil rights"
Remonstrants, 324*n*236
*Reports on Cases Adjudg'd in the Court of the
  King's Bench* (Salkeld), 93
Revolutionary War
  British army's abuses, 166
  and Iredell, 172
  Muslims serving in, 7–8, 305*n*14
  performance of *Mahomet the Impostor*
    during, 31–3
Rhode Island, and religious test for public
  office, 163
rights of conscience
  and Constitution, 245
  in French Constitution, 206
  Helwys on, 243
  Jefferson on, 112, 258–9
  Leland's fight for, 239, 249–54, 263–4
  Protestant concerns about losing, 169–71,
    245–7
  "soul liberty" experiment, 56, 57–8, 64,
    302
  See also taxes for supporting churches
"Rights of Conscience Inalienable and
  therefore, Religious Opinions Not
  Cognizable by Law, The" (Leland),
  249–52
Rights of Man, The (Paine), 200–5, 206
Rodgers, John, 219, 225
Roosevelt, Franklin D., 276
Ross, Alexander, 85

Said, Edward, 304*n*9, 307*n*30
Saladin (Salah al-Din), 331–2*n*130
Sale, George, 26, 92, 271. *See also Koran*
  (Sale)
Salem, Peter, 305*n*14
Salkeld, William, 93
Saracens, 18, 50, 84, 98, 105
Scandella, Domenico "Menocchio," 42–7,
  302, 316*n*15
Schultz, Debbie Wasserman, 285–6
Schultz, Kevin, 276
Schwartz, Stuart, 45
Second Letter on Toleration (Locke), 77
separation of church and state
  anti-Islamic polemic on, 8–9, 102–4
  Christianity and Sabbath, 266–7
  Jefferson on, 100–4, 105–6, 108

in Jefferson's Bill for Establishing Religious
Freedom, 115–17
Johnston on, 179
Leland's desire to protect church from state
influence, 242, 260–1, 266–7, 362n10,
366n120
overview, 4, 55–6, 57, 59–60
See also First Amendment of the
Constitution of the United States
September 11, 2001, terrorist attacks, 279–83,
296–7
Servetus, Michael, 47–8, 113, 317n41
Shaftesbury, Lord, 70, 323n220
Shaheen, Jack, 280
Shariah: The Threat to America (Boykin,
Soyster, and Yerushalmi), 294–5
Sharia law, 292, 293–6
Sheffield, Lord, 130
Shi'i Muslims, 278, 291–2, 294, 331–2n130
slavery
Adams on, 129–30
The Algerine Captive on, 34–5, 37–8,
313n121
captivity in Islam vs., 127
Islam and Catholicism compared to, 24
Jefferson and his slaves, 8, 120–3, 128–9
Leland on, 267–9
Muslims as slaves in America, 7–8, 10, 35,
76, 120–3, 186–91, 349n156
returning slaves to Africa, 268–9
Washington freeing his slaves, 122, 337n267
West African and North African slavery
compared, 128
Smyth, John, 53, 55, 242–3
Society for Promoting Christian Knowledge,
84–5, 92
Society of Americans for National Existence
(SANE), 293
Socinians, 18–19, 75, 79–80, 229. *See also*
Unitarians and Unitarianism
"soul liberty" experiment, 56, 57–8, 64, 302
Southern Poverty Law Center, 294–5
Souza, Gerardo de, 354n69
Soyster, Harry Edward, 294, 299
Spain, 131–2, 147
Spanish Inquisition, 45, 48, 54
Sparks, Jared, 229
Spencer, Robert, 297
states or colonies
New England's Congregational
Protestantism establishment, 238
oaths sworn on New Testament, 177–9
and religious freedom, 247
and religious test for public office, 161–3
See also specific states
Stop Islamization of America (SIOA), 297
Stubbe, Henry, 19, 66–70, 322n200
Stuyvesant, Peter, 62–3
Sufi Muslims, 279
Sullivan, John, 160

Sunni Muslims
al-Tabari, 90
and dissimulation, 294
on duration of treaties, 148
on images of the Prophet, 313n109
as majority of Muslims, 278
on Muslims living outside Muslim lands, 74
Saladin as, 331–2n130
schools of law, 91, 147, 231
Syrian immigrants, 275

taxes for supporting churches
Anglicanism, 113–14, 210–11
certificate to exempt Baptists but not other
religions, 248, 249, 253
Congregational Protestantism, 248–9, 253,
254–5, 259–60
Tea Party movement, 293–4
terminology, 25–6, 334n186
Third Letter (Locke), 77–8
Thoughts on Government (Adams), 205
tobacco, 91, 140
Toleration Act (1689), 112. *See also* religious
tolerance
toleration, exceptions to, 112. *See also*
religious tolerance
Travels (Mandeville), 46
treaties in Qur'an, 148
"Treaty of Amity and Commerce, A"
(Jefferson), 134–5
Trenchard, John, 23–5
Trinity doctrine
Deist and Socinian rejection of, 19, 69, 75
The Errors of the Trinity (Servetus), 47–8
and Islam, 69, 89–90
Jefferson's abandonment of, 229, 230
Locke's rejection of, 79–80
Priestley's denial of, 228
and religious test for public office, 163,
164
Sale on, 87
Stubbe on, 67–8
tulips as symbol of, 303n1
Tripolitan ambassador
Adams's and Jefferson's letters about,
138–40
Adams's and Jefferson's negotiations with,
133–6, 145–50
Adams's negotiations with, 124, 126–7,
138–45, 341n105
justifying naval attacks with Qur'an, 125,
300
notifying Adams of war with U.S., 140–1
Qur'anic defense of piracy, 146–50, 155–6
Tripolitans and Tripoli
Jefferson's letter to, 224, 300
Jefferson's military action against, 34,
136–8, 151–3, 214–17, 237, 238, 306n18,
355n91
and Ottoman Empire, 73, 131–2

Tripolitans and Tripoli *(continued)*
 overview, 26
 U.S. treaty with, 34, 207–12, 354nn69–70
 See also Barbary States; North African
  pirates
Tripoli treaty, Adams's, 207–12, 354n69
Tripoli treaty, Jefferson's, 216–18, 237
True Nature of Imposture (Prideaux), 18–19
tulips, ix, 304n1
Tunisians and Tunis
 ambassadors, 8, 218–22, 305n17
 Jefferson's letters to ruler of, 222–7, 237
 overview, 26
 ships of, seized by United States, 219, 226
 See also Barbary States; North African
  pirates
Turkish ambassadors, 8, 305n17
Turks, 13, 15–18, 24–5, 41–4, 46, 49, 50, 51–3,
  93, 96, 140, 143, 158–60, 162, 168, 180,
  199, 220–1, 227, 244
 in Leland, 240, 244, 249, 250, 253, 255,
  261–2, 267
 in Locke, 71–2, 78, 80
 in Williams, 58–9, 61, 63, 302
 See also Mahometans; Muslims
Two Tracts on Government (Locke), 71
Tyler, Royall, 27–8, 34–9, 40, 92, 313n125
tyranny, Ottoman Empire as, 22–5

Umar Ibn al-Khattab, 97, 98
Unitarians and Unitarianism
 Deists and Muslims linked to, 69
 Islam compared to, 89
 Jefferson's acceptance of, 227, 228–30
 and Locke, 79–80
 Priestley, 228
 Sale's criticism of, 87
 as Socinians, 18–19, 75, 79–80, 229
United States
 bans on building mosques, 296–8
 citizenship requirements, 109, 111–12,
  273–4, 275
 importance of religion, 180–1
 Judeo-Christian rubric, 276–7
 PATRIOT Act, 282–3, 370–1n80
 peace treaties with North Africa, 34
 See also America; President of the United
  States
universalism
 of Iredell, 173
 of Jefferson, 106, 114–15, 117, 228–9
 of Leland, 242–4
 and Muslim President issue, 160
 in Spanish and Portuguese dominions, 45
 of Tyler, 39
 See also Leland, John
universal theism, 51–3

Vanished Library, The (Canfora), 331n130
Venice and Venetians, 46, 316n32

Virginia
 Bill for the Naturalization of Persons,
  108–10
 Bill Prescribing the Oath of Fidelity and
  the Oaths of Certain Public Officers,
  111–12
 Declaration of Rights, 100, 241
 religious freedom and political equality for
  all, 100, 163, 238–9
 tax proceeds supporting Anglicanism,
  210–11
 See also Bill for Establishing Religious
  Freedom; Jefferson, Thomas; Madison,
  James
Virginia Gazette, 81–2, 158–9
Voltaire, 27, 28–33, 32, 86, 97–9
Von Limborch, Philip, 324n236
Von Pufendorf, Freiherr, 96

war, Qur'an on, 149–50
Washington, George, 5
 freeing his slaves, 122, 337n267
 and Iredell, 186
 and Leland, 247–8
 and Muslim rights, 7–8
 Muslim slaves of, 121–2
 on religious freedom, 211
Webster, Noah, 166–7
West, Samuel, 25
Whig ideology
 Cato's Letters, 23–5, 30, 105–6
 and *Mahomet the Impostor,* 30–3
 and Ottoman Empire, 164
 overview, 22–4, 70
 and Shaftesbury, 70, 323n220
Whitefield, George, 21
Williamson, Hugh, 156
Williams, Roger
 on boundaries of "Christian liberty," 55–6
 and Catholics, 320n138
 condemnation of Quakers, 20–1
 exile from Massachusetts Bay Colony,
  52–3, 59–60
 failure of message, 63–4
 and Leland, 243–4, 363n19
 and Muslims (Turks), 57–61
 and Providence, Rhode Island, 20–1, 56–7,
  60–1, 63–4, 243
 religious tolerance with Christian
  superiority, 56–7
 "soul liberty" experiment, 56, 57–8, 64,
  302
Wilson, Douglas L., 94
World Trade Center bombing (1993), 280

"Yankee Spy, The" (Leland), 254
Yemeni Arab immigrant, 275
Yerushalmi, David, 293–5

Zoroastrians and Zoroastrianism, 97–8

ILLUSTRATION CREDITS

33 Broadside of Voltaire's play *Mahomet,* English version by Miller performed for American and French troops. "At the Theatre in Baltimore on Tuesday Evening, the 1st of October 1782, will be presented the Tragedy of Mahomet, the Impostor." Broadside #Y1782. Courtesy of the Collection of the New-York Historical Society.

82 Excerpted record of Thomas Jefferson's purchase of Sale's Koran from October 1765. In *Virginia Gazette Daybooks,* edited by Paul Hoffman (Charlottesville: University of Virginia Microfilm Publications, 1967), segment 2, folio 202. Courtesy of Special Collections, University of Virginia Library.

82 First page of Thomas Jefferson's Qur'an, Sale translator, 1764 edition. Courtesy, Rare Books and Special Collections Division, Library of Congress.

107 Jefferson's handwritten quotation of Locke, c. 1776. Courtesy, Jefferson Papers, Library of Congress.

119 Jefferson's "Autobiography," 1821, describing the span of believers he intended to cover in his 1786 Bill for Establishing Religious Freedom. Courtesy, Jefferson Papers, Library of Congress.

155 Jefferson's initials in his Qur'an, in volume 1, at bottom of p. 113, as "T" and "I." Courtesy, Rare Books and Special Collections Division, Library of Congress.

172 Engraving of James Iredell (d. 1799), Federalist supporter of the Constitution and Supreme Court justice, etched by Albert Rosenthal, Philadelphia, 1889. Courtesy of the North Carolina Collection, University of North Carolina at Chapel Hill.

188 Portrait of Ibrahima Abd al-Rahman (d. 1829), a Muslim slave, who wrote in Arabic, described as a "Moorish Prince," April 1833. Courtesy of New York Public Library.

192 Portrait of Omar ibn Said (d. 1863), a Muslim slave from North Carolina, who wrote his autobiography in Arabic. Courtesy of E. H. Little Library, Davidson College.

198 Thomas Jefferson by Charles Willson Peale, from life, 1791–92. Courtesy of Independence National Historical Park.

241 John Leland (d. 1841), evangelical Baptist ally of James Madison and Thomas Jefferson. Engraved portrait by T. Doney, painted by A. B. Moore, 1845.

284 Congressman Keith Ellison swears his private oath of office on Thomas Jefferson's Qur'an, pictured as Sale's Koran in 2 volumes, January 4, 2007. Photograph by Win McNamee, Courtesy of Getty Images.

A NOTE ABOUT THE AUTHOR

DENISE A. SPELLBERG is an associate professor of history and
Middle Eastern studies at the University of Texas at Austin,
where she teaches courses on Islamic civilization and Islam in
Europe and America. She won a prestigious Carnegie Scholarship in support of this book project.

A NOTE ON THE TYPE

The text of this book was set in Bembo, a facsimile of a type-face cut by Francesco Griffo for Aldus Manutius, the celebrated Venetian printer, in 1495. The present-day version of Bembo was introduced by the Monotype Corporation of London in 1929. Bembo is a face of rare beauty and great legibility.

Composed by North Market Street Graphics,
Lancaster, Pennsylvania

Printed and bound by Berryville Graphics,
Berryville, Virginia

Designed by Cassandra J. Pappas